THIRD BOOK

Latin

FOR AMERICANS

Latin
FOR AMERICANS

B. L. Ullman
Albert I. Suskin

Mc Graw Hill **Glencoe McGraw-Hill**

New York, New York   Columbus, Ohio   Woodland Hills, California   Peoria, Illinois

Front cover:

Gaspar Adriaens van Wittel, *The Tiber Island in Rome,* 1685,
Kunsthistorisches Museum, Vienna, Austria. Photobusiness—ARTOTHEK

The city of Rome has fascinated both its citizens and tourists for centuries.
The city itself, spread out on seven hills, with its ancient and modern bridges,
churches, palaces, and public buildings, has been the subject of painters for
well over five hundred years. One of the most popular subjects is the Tiber,
which flows through the most ancient part of the city.

The painting on the cover shows a part of the river that passes near the
Isola Tiberiana (Tiber Island—left side of the cover), on which was built the
Temple of Aesculapius, the Roman god of medicine. On this site now stands
the medieval church of St. Bartholomew, the Christian patron of medicine.
In the background is one of the oldest bridges in Rome, the Ponte Cestio, and
beyond that a view of the Renaissance city with the Basilica of St. Peter. The
painting evokes fifteen hundred years of Roman history and memories, and
shows how the combination of "ancient" and "modern" which is seen
throughout the city still continues to inspire visitors to Rome.

Title page:

PHOTRI/J. A. Cash

The Roman Forum with the Sacred Way running through the middle. The
Sacred Way was the main processional street in the Forum. It ran from the Arch
of Titus through the Forum and up to the Temple of Jupiter on the Capitoline
Hill. The main building in the photo is the Temple of Antoninus and Faustina
reconstructed as a church on the Via Sacra. In the upper left of the photo is
the Basilica Aemilia. In the foreground is the garden of the Vestal Virgins.

Glencoe/McGraw-Hill

*A Division of The **McGraw·Hill** Companies*

Send all inquiries to:
Glencoe/McGraw-Hill
21600 Oxnard Street
Woodland Hills, CA 91367

ISBN 0-02-640914-3 (Student Text)

Printed in the United States of America

4 5 6 7 8 9 10   027   02 01 00 99

Contents

Unit III—Cicero Against Catiline

Unit IV—Sallust's Catiline (Selections)

Unit V—Cicero for Archias (Entire)

Unit IX—Two Thousand Years of Latin

Introduction

This book combines two approaches to the Latin course in the third year. One approach continues to make Cicero the core of the third-year curriculum; the other approach presents a wide range of Latin literature. Some teachers prefer the one, some the other, and still other teachers would like to see the two approaches reconciled. The present book makes this possible.

As a result, the book contains much more reading matter than can be completed in one year. Teachers will have to select what is most useful for a particular class. A survey of the contents unit by unit will be helpful for this purpose.

Unit I continues the lesson form of the *Second Book* in this series and is a review of second-year grammar and vocabulary. The stories are taken from Pliny because that author's simple style is familiar from the numerous selections in the *Second Book* and because his letters are interesting.

Unit II presents simple and interesting stories from Aulus Gellius. These may be omitted in whole or in part.

Unit III contains Cicero's orations against Catiline. The first and third orations are given in complete form, the second and fourth in selections. The material is presented in lessons, with vocabulary drills and English sentences for translation into Latin. Paragraphs on Cicero's style help in the mastery of his periodic sentence structure. Most teachers will wish to teach this entire unit.

Unit IV gives selections from Sallust's *Catiline* to supplement Cicero's version. The lesson form is kept. Some teachers may prefer to omit part of this unit.

Unit V consists of Cicero's speech for Archias. This is a universal favorite because of its praise of literature, and most teachers will wish to read it. But some chapters dealing with the technical matters of citizenship may well be omitted.

Unit VI, containing selections from the speeches against Verres, with which Cicero had his first great success, and Antony, the last of his orations, is optional. Parts may be read at sight.

Unit VII presents some of Cicero's letters. These may be read at sight. It is urged, however, that they not be omitted entirely; they are interesting and valuable for the light they throw on Cicero's personality.

Unit VIII contains selections from Cicero's philosophical works and, like Unit VI, is optional.

Unit IX in its "Two Thousand Years of Latin" continues the popular unit of a similar name in the *Second Book,* but gives a different selection from twenty-four authors. Rapid reading at sight is suggested for part of this unit.

Unit X has six stories from Ovid's *Metamorphoses* and is particularly useful in schools which do not offer a fourth year of Latin.

English sentences for translation into Latin are given in Units I–IV. This fact may cause teachers to decide to teach those units.

An attempt has been made to key the numerous illustrations to the text. They supplement the reading matter in giving a broad idea of the Roman civilization. Two special visual sections are in the text. One deals with the Forum Romanum, with photos and captions on surviving monuments that follow a path from the Arch of Titus up and onto the Capitoline Hill. The other section deals with photos of various manuscripts that show how Roman and Greek works were transmitted through the centuries up to the invention of printing. A list of these photos is found at the end of the Contents (p. ix).

Words translated in the footnotes do not appear in the end vocabulary.

Tapes to Accompany Latin for Americans, Second Book, include some readings from the selections in the present *Third Book.*

Unit I

Pliny's Letters

In the Church of St. Mary in Cosmedin, not far from the Roman Forum and the Cloāca Maxima, is the Mouth of Truth, an ancient marble mask with a human face. Legend has it that anyone who put his hand in the mouth and swore falsely would be unable to pull his hand out.

Pliny's Life

You may have read some of Pliny's letters in *Latin for Americans, Second Book*. You may even remember those about the eruption of Mt. Vesuvius. Pliny was born at Como, north of Milan, in A.D. 62. He was a successful lawyer and officeholder. After serving in various preliminary offices, he became consul in A.D. 100, during the reign of Nerva. He was later appointed governor of Bithynia, in Asia Minor. Among the following readings are some interesting letters he wrote to the emperor Trajan from Bithynia.

April Showers Bring Verse Flowers

[1] *crop* (literally, *coming forth*)
[2] *public places*
[3] *from time to time*
[4] *by Hercules*
[5] *they say*
[6] *all the idlest*
[7] *I have failed no one* (i.e., he attended everyone's readings)

Magnum prōventum[1] poētārum annus hic attulit. Tōtō mēnse Aprīlī nūllus ferē diēs quō nōn recitāret aliquis. Iuvat mē quod vigent studia, prōferunt sē ingenia hominum et ostentant, tametsī ad audiendum pigrē coitur.[1] Plērīque in statiōnibus[2] sedent tempusque audiendī fābulīs con-
5 terunt ac subinde[3] sibi nūntiārī iubent an iam recitātor intrāverit, an dīxerit praefātiōnem, an ex magnā parte ēvolverit librum. Tunc dēmum, ac tunc quoque lentē cūnctanterque veniunt; nec tamen permanent, sed ante fīnem recēdunt, aliī dissimulanter et fūrtim, aliī simpliciter et līberē. At hercule[4] memoriā parentum Claudium Caesarem[2] ferunt,[5] cum in Palātiō spatiārētur
10 audīssetque clāmōrem, causam requīsīsse, cumque dictum esset recitāre Nōniānum, subitum recitantī vēnisse. Nunc ōtiōsissimus quisque,[6] multō ante rogātus et identidem admonitus, aut nōn venit aut, sī venit, queritur sē diem, quia nōn perdiderit, perdidisse. Sed tantō magis laudandī probandīque sunt quōs ā scrībendī recitandīque studiō haec audītōrum vel dēsidia vel
15 superbia nōn retardat. Equidem prope nēminī dēfuī.[7] Erant sānē plērīque amīcī; neque enim est ferē quisquam quī studia, ut nōn simul et nōs amet.[3] Hīs ex causīs longius quam dēstināveram tempus in urbe cōnsūmpsī.[4] Possum iam repetere sēcessum et scrībere aliquid quod nōn recitem, nē videar, quōrum[5] recitātiōnibus adfuī, nōn audītor fuisse sed crēditor. Nam ut in cēterīs
20 rēbus, ita in audiendī officiō perit grātia sī reposcātur. Valē.   (I, 13)

---

[1] People do not want to go but feel they have to.
[2] Emperor Claudius, who ruled A.D. 41–54
[3] Supply **amet** with the **quī** clause.
[4] He went to his country home later than usual.
[5] The antecedent **eōrum** is understood.

1. What happened in the month of April?
2. What did Pliny do during his vacations?
3. What does one have to do to get people to attend a reading?
4. Why does Pliny criticize those who attend readings of poetry?

Grammar

Form Review

1. Review **ferō,** including principal parts and meanings. Pay particular attention to the present tense, active and passive.
2. Review **eō,** including principal parts and meanings. Pay particular attention to the present and future tenses.
3. Review the formation and translation of deponent verbs. Remember that deponent verbs are passive in form but active in meaning.

Syntax Review

1. Review impersonal verbs, including **decet** (it becomes, benefits), **libet** (it pleases), **licet** (it is permitted; one may), **oportet** (it is fitting, necessary; ought), **piget** (it grieves), **pudet** (it makes ashamed), and **taedet** (it causes weariness, boredom). Remember that impersonal verbs are used only in the third person singular and the infinitive.
2. Review indirect questions. Remember that an indirect question is introduced by a main verb of asking, knowing, telling, or perceiving and includes an interrogative word such as who, what, or where. The subordinate verb is in the subjunctive.
3. Review descriptive relative clauses. Remember that a relative clause with the subjunctive may be used to describe an indefinite antecedent. This construction is especially common after **ūnus, sōlus, sunt quī** (there are those who), and **nēmō est quī** (there is no one who).
4. Review the gerund and gerundive. Remember that the gerund is a verbal noun and the gerundive is a verbal adjective. The gerundive is used to express obligation (what *must be* done) with a form of **sum.** The person who must do the obligation is in the dative. The gerundive may also simply modify a noun or pronoun. Finally, the gerund and gerundive may be used with **ad** + accusative or **causā** or **grātiā** + genitive to express purpose.

1. Ask him to what city he is going.
2. I shall complain because no one is bringing my books.
3. Those who come for the sake of hearing recitations should be praised.
4. People come (*use impersonal construction*) quickly for the sake of talking with friends.

Vocabulary

ingenium	aliquis	afferō	equidem
mēnsis	plērīque	dēsum	ferē
		eō	fūrtim
		ferō	identidem
		iuvō	simul
		perdō	tunc
		queror	
		requīrō	
		sedeō	
		volvō	

Word Studies

From what Latin words are the following derived: **coeō, ostentō, prōventus, retardō, sēcessus, spatior, statiō?**

Explain *dissimulate, evolution, furtive, querulous, secession.*

A Perfect Wife

Cum sīs pietātis exemplum frātremque optimum et amantissimum tuī[1]
parī cāritāte dīlēxerīs fīliamque eius ut tuam dīligās nec tantum amitae[1] eī
affectum vērum etiam patris āmissī repraesentēs, nōn dubitō maximō tibi
gaudiō fore, cum cognōveris dignam patre,[2] dignam tē, dignam avō ēvādere.[2]
Summum est acūmen, summa frūgālitās; amat mē. Accēdit hīs studium lit- 5
terārum, quod ex meī[1] cāritāte concēpit. Meōs libellōs[3] habet, lēctitat,
ēdiscit etiam. Quā illa sollicitūdine, cum videor āctūrus,[4] quantō, cum ēgī,
gaudiō afficitur! Dispōnit[5] quī nūntient sibi quem assēnsum, quōs clāmōrēs
excitārim, quem ēventum iūdicī tulerim. Eadem, sī quandō recitō, in proximō discrēta vēlō sedet laudēsque nostrās avidissimīs auribus excipit. 10
Versūs quidem meōs cantat etiam fōrmatque[3] citharā, nōn artifice aliquō
docente sed amōre, quī magister est optimus.

Hīs ex causīs in spem certissimam addūcor perpetuam nōbīs maiōremque
in diēs futūram esse concordiam. Nōn enim aetātem meam aut corpus,
quae paulātim occidunt ac senēscunt, sed glōriam dīligit. Nec aliud decet 15
tuīs manibus ēducātam, tuīs praeceptīs īnstitūtam, quae nihil in contuberniō
tuō vīderit nisi sānctum honestumque, quae dēnique amāre mē ex tuā praedi-
cātiōne cōnsuēverit. Nam cum mātrem meam parentis locō verērēris, mē ā
pueritiā statim fōrmāre, laudāre, tālemque quālis nunc uxōrī meae videor
ōminārī solēbās. Certātim ergō tibi grātiās agimus, ego quod illam mihi, 20
illa quod mē sibi dederīs, quasi in vīcem[4] ēlēgerīs. Valē.   (IV, 19)

QUESTIONS

1. What did Calpurnia do with Pliny's verses?
2. How did Calpurnia find out what success Pliny had had in court?
3. How does Pliny account for his wife's admirable qualities?
4. How did Calpurnia find out what sort of reception Pliny's readings had?

---

[1] *aunt*
[2] *worthy of her father*
[3] *sets to music and accompanies*
[4] *for each other*

---

[1] pronoun, not adjective
[2] Supply **eam** as subject.
[3] his speeches in court
[4] Supply **causam:** *plead a case.*
[5] Supply a word such as **hominēs.**

Grammar

Form Review

Review personal pronouns including: **ego, nōs; tū, vōs;** and **is, ea, id.**
Remember that with the ablative of accompaniment, the **cum** attaches
directly to the ablative form (**mēcum,** etc.).

Syntax Review

1. Review the datives of reference and purpose. Remember that the dative
   is sometimes used to express purpose (dative of purpose) or to show
   the person concerned or referred to (dative of reference). These two
   constructions are often used together as a double dative.
2. Review relative purpose clauses. Remember that **quī** may replace **ut** in
   a purpose clause if the antecedent is clear and definite.
3. Review **cum** clauses. Recall that in secondary sequence, **cum** translated
   as *when* is used only with the imperfect and pluperfect subjunctive.
   When **cum** means *since* or *although,* the verb in the subordinate clause
   can be in any tense of the subjunctive.

TRANSLATION

1. She sends slaves to find out what I have said.
2. I must thank you because your words caused Calpurnia to love me.
3. Calpurnia sang Pliny's verses, although she never had a singing teacher.
4. It is an honor to you and to me that she likes my speeches and verses.

Vocabulary

auris	**avidus**	**accēdō**	**paulātim**
avus	**dignus**	**concipiō**	**statim**
cāritās	**perpetuus**	**cōnsuēscō**	
clāmor		**dubitō**	
ēventus		**īnstituō**	
gaudium		**occidō**	
iūdicium		**soleō**	
		vereor	

Word Studies

Review intensive prefixes in the Appendix. Give an example from the
reading. Give an English derivative of **amita, cāritās, decet, dispōnō.**

Oratorical Twins

Librum tuum lēgī et, quam dīligentissimē potuī, adnotāvī quae commū-
tanda, quae eximenda arbitrārer. Nam et ego vērum dīcere assuēvī et tū
libenter audīre. Neque enim ūllī patientius reprehenduntur quam quī
maximē laudārī merentur. Nunc ā tē librum meum cum adnotātiōnibus tuīs
exspectō. Ō iūcundās, ō pulchrās vicēs! Quam[1] mē dēlectat quod, sī qua 5
posterīs cūra nostrī,[1] usquequāque nārrābitur quā concordiā, simplicitāte,
fidē vīxerīmus! Erit rārum et īnsigne duōs hominēs aetāte, dignitāte propemodum aequālēs, nōn nūllīus in litterīs nōminis (cōgor enim dē tē quoque
parcius dīcere, quia dē mē simul dīcō), alterum alterius studia fōvisse.

Equidem adulēscentulus, cum iam tū fāmā glōriāque flōrērēs, tē sequī 10
"longō sed proximus intervāllō" et esse et habērī concupīscēbam. Et erant
multa clārissima ingenia; sed tū mihi (ita similitūdō nātūrae ferēbat)
maximē imitābilis, maximē imitandus vidēbāris. Quō magis gaudeō quod,
sī quis dē studiīs sermō, ūnā nōmināmur, quod dē tē loquentibus statim
occurrō. Nec dēsunt quī utrīque nostrum praeferantur. Sed nōs, nihil inter- 15
est meā[2] quō locō, iungimur: nam mihi prīmus quī ā tē proximus. Quīn
etiam in testāmentīs dēbēs adnotāsse: nisi quis forte alterutrī nostrum amīcissimus, eadem lēgāta et quidem pariter accipimus.

Quae omnia hūc spectant, ut in vicem ardentius dīligāmus, cum tot vinculīs nōs studia, mōrēs, fāma, suprēma dēnique hominum iūdicia cōnstringant. 20
Valē.   (VII, 20)

[1] *how*
[2] *it makes no difference to me*
(the feminine ablative adjective
is used with **interest**)

QUESTIONS

1. What had Pliny done for Tacitus?
2. What four things link Tacitus and Pliny?
3. What is Pliny expecting to get from Tacitus?

---

[1] genitive plural of the pronoun

Grammar

Form Review

Review the comparison of adjectives and adverbs. Remember that most superlatives are formed by adding **–issimus, –a, –um** to the base; but that some add **–rimus, –a, –um**; others **–limus, –a, –um**; and some are quite irregular. There is a list of the irregular comparatives and superlatives in the Appendix.

Syntax Review

1. Review the genitive of description. Remember that the descriptive genitive requires that an adjective be used. Generally, it is used to describe permanent qualities.
2. Review the ablative of respect. Remember that the ablative of respect tells in what respect a certain condition applies. There is no preposition.

 **TRANSLATION**

1. Pliny's friend was a man of great reputation.
2. Pliny was not inferior in oratory, but Tacitus also wrote histories.
3. A man who heard Pliny talk about his writings asked him whether he was Pliny or Tacitus.

Vocabulary

aetās	īnsignis	arbitror	iam
fidēs	iūcundus	flōreō	libenter
sermō	proximus	foveō	quīn etiam
	tot	gaudeō	
quis	ūllus	legō	
	uterque	loquor	
		sequor	

Word Studies

Review the diminutive suffix **–lus** and find an example in the reading.

Give an English derivative of each: **adnotō, cōnstringō, eximō, posterī, praeferō.**

Scala/Art Resource, NY

*This aerial view of the Roman Forum is taken from the **Tabulārium**, or Record Office. The three columns are the remains of the Temple of Castor and Pollux. The large area in front of that temple was the Basilica Julia. To the left of the three columns of Castor and Pollux is the small, round Temple of Vesta. The road leading toward the Temple of Vesta and passing by the single Column of Phocas is part of the Via Sacra. The Palatine Hill with its mansions serves as the backdrop to it all. In the distance is the Arch of Titus.*

Working Hours in Vacation

1 *in my Tuscan* (*villa*)
2 *terrace*
3 *covered walk*
4 *concentration*
5 *nap*
6 *musician* (nominative)
7 *however long*
8 *sometimes* (literally, *not never*)
9 (*a thing*) *which*
10 *tenant farmers*
11 *literary activity*

Quaeris quem ad modum in Tuscīs[1] diem aestāte dispōnam. Ēvigilō cum libuit, plērumque circā hōram prīmam,₁ saepe ante, tardius rārō: clausae fenestrae manent. Mīrē enim silentiō et tenebrīs ab iīs₂ quae āvocant abductus et līber et mihi relīctus, nōn oculōs animō sed animum oculīs
5 sequor, quī eadem quae mēns vident, quotiēns nōn vident alia. Cōgitō scrībentī ēmendantīque similis. Notārium vocō et, diē admissō, quae fōrmāveram dictō; abit rūrsusque revocātur rūrsusque dīmittitur. Ubi₃ hōra quārta vel quīnta (neque enim certum dīmēnsumque tempus), ut diēs suāsit, in xystum[2] mē vel cryptoporticum[3] cōnferō, reliqua meditor et
10 dictō. Vehiculum ascendō. Ibi quoque idem₄ quod ambulāns aut iacēns.₄ Dūrat intentiō[4] mūtātiōne ipsā refecta. Paulum redormiō,[5] deinde ambulō, mox ōrātiōnem Graecam Latīnamve clārē et intentē, nōn tam vōcis causā quam stomachī, legō; pariter tamen et₅ illa firmātur. Iterum ambulō, ungor, exerceor,₆ lavor.₆ Cēnantī mihi, sī cum uxōre vel paucīs, liber legitur; post
15 cēnam comoedus aut lyristēs.[6] Mox cum meīs₇ ambulō, quōrum in numerō sunt ērudītī. Ita variīs sermōnibus vespera extenditur, et quamquam[7] longissimus diēs citō conditur. Nōn numquam[8] ex hōc ōrdine aliqua mūtantur. Nam sī diū iacuī vel ambulāvī, post somnum dēmum lēctiōnemque nōn vehiculō sed (quod[9] brevius, quia vēlōcius) equō gestor. Interveniunt amīcī
20 ex proximīs oppidīs partemque diēī ad sē trahunt interdumque lassō mihi opportūnā interpellātiōne subveniunt. Vēnor aliquandō, sed nōn sine pugillāribus, ut, quamvīs nihil cēperim,₈ nōn nihil referam. Datur et colōnīs,[10] ut vidētur ipsīs, nōn satis temporis, quōrum mihi agrestēs querēlae litterās[11] nostrās et haec urbāna opera commendant.₉ Valē.   (IX, 36)

QUESTIONS

1. When does Pliny usually wake up?
2. What is the first thing he does?
3. What kind of exercise does Pliny take?
4. What does Pliny do before going to bed?

₁ i.e., after daybreak
₂ neuter antecedent of **quae**
₃ Supply **est.**
₄ Supply **faciō** in both places.
₅ for **etiam**
₆ used reflexively; the usage is called "middle voice"
₇ i.e., **amīcīs**
₈ **Quamvis** is used with the subjunctive.
₉ i.e., make them seem relatively more pleasant

Grammar

Form Review

Review demonstrative pronouns. Remember that **hic** is translated as *this* or *the latter;* **ille** as *that* or *the former.* **Is** can be translated as *this, that,* or *he (she, it).* The demonstrative **idem** is best translated as *the same, also, likewise,* and the emphatics **ipse** by *–self, very* and **iste** by *that (of yours), such, this.* Pay particular attention to the irregular forms.

Syntax Review

1. Review the ablative absolute. Remember that the ablative absolute must be grammatically unconnected to the rest of the sentence. It exists in three combinations: noun + noun, noun + adjective, noun + participle.
2. Review the genitive of the whole. Also called the partitive genitive, it represents the whole to which a part belongs. The genitive of the whole is often used after such words as **nihil, satis,** and **quid**; the English word "of" is omitted.

 **TRANSLATION**

1. He decided to walk in the garden with his friends.
2. When the windows were opened, Pliny began to dictate.
3. He complained that too much time had to be given to his tenants.
4. Pliny lived in the mountains in the summer for the purpose of writing books.

Vocabulary

causa	**ambulō**	**citō**
ōrdō	**claudō**	**iterum**
	cōgitō	**plērumque**
reliquus	**mē cōnferō**	**mox**
	dormiō	**quem ad modum**
	iaceō	**quotiēns**
	quaerō	**rūrsus**
	suādeō	**tamen**
	trahō	

Word Studies

Review prefixes **dis–** and **ex–,** and explain the meaning of words in the reading that contains them.

Define *defenestration, quotient, ambulatory, mutation, dormitory.*

Fame

Frequenter agentī[1] mihi ēvēnit ut centumvirī,[2] cum diū sē intrā iūdicum auctōritātem gravitātemque tenuissent, omnēs repente quasi victī coāctīque cōnsurgerent laudārentque; frequenter ē senātū fāmam, quālem maximē optāveram, rettulī. Numquam tamen maiōrem cēpī voluptātem quam nūper
5 ex sermōne Cornēlī Tacitī. Nārrābat sēdisse sēcum Circēnsibus proximīs[1] equitem Rōmānum; hunc post variōs ērudītōsque sermōnēs requīsisse: "Ītalicus es an prōvinciālis?", sē respondisse: "nostī mē, et quidem ex studiīs." Ad hoc illum,[3] "Tacitus es an Plīnius?" Exprimere nōn possum quam sit iūcundum mihi quod nōmina nostra, quasi litterārum propria,[2] nōn hominum,
10 litterīs redduntur, quod uterque nostrum hīs etiam ex studiīs nōtus quibus aliter ignōtus est.

Accidit aliud ante pauculōs diēs simile. Recumbēbat[4] mēcum vir ēgregius, Fadius Rūfīnus, super[3] eum mūniceps ipsīus, quī illō diē prīmum vēnerat in urbem; cui Rūfīnus, dēmōnstrāns mē, "vidēs hunc?" Multa deinde dē studiīs
15 nostrīs. Et ille[5] "Plīnius est" inquit.

Vērum fatēbor, cupiō magnum labōris meī frūctum. An, sī Dēmosthenēs iūre laetātus est quod illum anus Attica ita nōscitāvit, ego celebritāte nōminis meī gaudēre nōn dēbeō? Ego vērō et gaudeō et gaudēre mē dīcō. Neque enim vereor nē iactantior videar, cum dē mē aliōrum iūdicium, nōn
20 meum prōferō, praesertim apud tē, quī nec ūllīus invidēs laudibus et favēs nostrīs. Valē.   (IX, 23)

[1] *the last Circus games*
[2] *the private property*
[3] *beyond*

QUESTIONS

1. What is the point of this letter?
2. What honor was shown Pliny in court?
3. What did Tacitus and the stranger talk about?

Grammar

Form Review

Review **volō, nolō,** and **malō,** while paying particular attention to the present indicative and subjunctive.

---

[1] Supply **causās.**
[2] a kind of supreme court, consisting originally of 100 men
[3] Supply **quaesīsse.**
[4] at the dinner table
[5] i.e., the man from out of town

Syntax Review

1. Review the dative with special verbs. Remember that the dative is used with a few special verbs, including **cōnfīdō, crēdō, dēsum, faveō, ignōscō, imperō, invideō, minitor, noceō, parcō, pāreō, persuādeō, placeō, praestō, resistō, serviō,** and **studeō.** Some of these verbs become impersonal in the passive and the dative is retained.

2. Review noun clauses of result. Remember that after **accido** (to happen) and **efficio** (to cause or effect) you use **ut** (or **ut nōn**) plus the subjunctive to express a result clause.

3. Review the subjunctive after verbs of fearing. Remember that a verb of fearing is following by a clause in the subjunctive introduced by **nē** if it is positive and **ut** if it is negative.

 **TRANSLATION**

1. Do you think that Pliny envied Tacitus?
2. Pliny feared that he might not be recognized.
3. Pliny persuaded Tacitus to tell what the Roman knight had said.
4. It happened that all praised Pliny when he finished his speech.

Vocabulary

frūctus	ēveniō	diū	apud
gravitās	faveō	frequenter	intrā
voluptās	invideō	numquam	
	nārrō	praesertim	
proprius	reddō	quasi	
quidem	respondeō	repente	
	surgō		

Word Studies

Give an English derivative of each of the following: **ērudītus, exprimō, faveō, invideō, recumbō.**

Review the prefixes **ad–, con–, in–, re–** in the Appendix and find three examples of each in the readings you have encountered thus far. Note the assimilated forms of each.

Pliny's Kindness to a Servant

[1] *you treat your (servants)*
[2] *therefore* (literally, *by which the more frankly*)
[3] *this (phrase of) ours*
[4] *all the more* (literally, *by so much by which*)
[5] *his occupation* (literally, *his label, so to speak*)
[6] *put too much strain on*
[7] *a slight cough*
[8] *i.e., servants*
[9] *at his expense*

Videō quam molliter tuōs habeās;[1] quō[2] simplicius tibi cōnfitēbor quā indulgentiā meōs trāctem. Est mihi semper in animō hoc nostrum[3] "pater familiae." Quod sī essem nātūrā asperior et dūrior, frangeret mē tamen īnfirmitās lībertī meī Zōsimī, cui tantō[4] maior hūmanitās exhibenda est, 5 quantō[4] nunc illā magis eget. Homō probus, officiōsus, litterātus; et ars quidem eius et quasi īnscrīptiō[5] comoedus, in quā plūrimum facit. Nam prōnūntiat ācriter, sapienter, aptē, decenter etiam. Īdem tam commodē ōrātiōnēs et historiās et carmina legit ut hoc sōlum didicisse videātur.

Haec tibi sēdulō exposuī quō magis scīrēs quam multa ūnus mihi et 10 quam iūcunda ministeria praestāret. Accēdit longa iam cāritās hominis, quam ipsa perīcula auxērunt. Ante aliquot annōs, dum intentē īnstanterque prōnūntiat, sanguinem reiēcit,[1] atque ob hoc in Aegyptum missus ā mē, post longum peregrīnātiōnem cōnfirmātus rediit nūper. Deinde dum per continuōs diēs nimis imperat[6] vōcī, veteris īnfirmitātis tussiculā[7] admoni-15 tus, rūrsus sanguinem reddidit. Quā ex causā dēstināvī eum mittere in praedia tua quae Forō Iūlī possidēs. Audīvī enim tē saepe referentem esse ibi et āera salūbrem et lac eius modī cūrātiōnibus accommodātissimum. Rogō ergō scrībās[2] tuīs[8] ut illī vīlla, ut domus pateat, offerant[3] etiam sūmptibus[9] eius sī quid opus erit; erit autem opus modicō. Est enim tam 20 parcus et continēns ut nōn sōlum dēliciās vērum etiam necessitātēs valētūdinis frūgālitāte restringat. Ego proficīscentī[4] tantum viāticī dabō quantum sufficiat euntī in tua. Valē.   (V, 19)

QUESTIONS

1. About whom is Pliny writing?
2. What does he ask his friend to do?
3. What duties does Zosimus perform in Pliny's home?
4. To what country had Pliny previously sent Zosimus? Why?

---

[1] He had tuberculosis.
[2] **ut** is generally used
[3] Supply the subject from **tuīs**; the object is the **sī** clause (*whatever*; literally, *if anything*).
[4] modifies **eī**, to be supplied

Built in A.D. 81, the Arch of Titus is a fairly simple triumphal arch with just a single archway. It was erected after his death to commemorate the conquest of Jerusalem. The inside contains two well-preserved and well-known reliefs, one of the emperor on his triumphal chariot and the other a procession of Roman soldiers carrying away the sacred furnishings of the Temple of Jerusalem during the siege of Jerusalem in A.D. 70.

Grammar

Form Review

Review irregular adjectives and numerals. Remember that **alius, alter, ūllus, nūllus, sōlus, tōtus, neuter,** and **uterque** are declined like **ūnus.** The plurals are regular. **Ambō** is declined like **duo.**

Syntax Review

1. Review the ablative of degree of difference. Remember that the ablative without a preposition is used to express the degree or measure of difference.
2. Review purpose clauses with **quō.** Remember that if the purpose clause contains an adjective or adverb in the comparative degree, **quō** generally replaces **ut.**

TRANSLATION

1. My friend is a foot taller than I.
2. Pliny gave him as much money as sufficed for the journey.
3. I fear that the man is very ill and may not be well again.
4. He walked to the top of the hill so that he might see better.

Vocabulary

carmen	admoneō	aptē
hūmānitās	augeō	nimis
lībertus	discō	semper
valētūdō	expōnō	
	pateō	
asper	praestō	
dūrus	proficīscor	
parcus	redeō	
vetus	sciō	

Word Studies

Give English derivatives of the following: **asper, comoedus, discō, lac, mollis, possideō, probus, salūbris, sanguis, sēdulus.**

In the reading, find one word with suffix **–tia,** five words with suffix **–tās,** and three words with suffix **–tiō.**

Three Strikes and Out for Regulus

Assem parā[1] et accipe auream fābulam, fābulās immō. Verānia, Pīsōnis uxor, graviter iacēbat,[2] huius dīcō Pīsōnis quem Galba adoptāvit. Ad hanc Rēgulus vēnit. Prīmum impudentiam hominis quī vēnerit ad aegram, cuius marītō inimīcissimus, ipsī invīsissimus fuerat! Estō,[3] sī vēnit tantum;[4] at ille etiam proximus torō sēdit, quō diē, quā hōrā nāta esset interrogāvit.₁   5 Ubi audiit, compōnit vultum,[5] intendit oculōs, movet labra, agitat digitōs,₈ computat; nihil. Ut diū miseram exspectātiōne suspendit, "habēs," inquit, "clīmactēricum[6] tempus, sed ēvādēs. Quod ut tibi magis liqueat,[7] haruspicem cōnsulam quem sum frequenter expertus." Nec mora; sacrificium facit, affirmat exta[8] cum sīderum significātiōne congruere. Illa, ut in 10 perīculō crēdula, poscit₍ codicillōs, lēgātum Rēgulō scrībit. Mox ingravēscit, clāmat moriēns hominem nēquam,[9] perfidum, ac plūs etiam quam periūrum, quī sibi per salūtem fīliī peierāsset. Facit hoc Rēgulus nōn minus scelerātē quam frequenter, quod īram deōrum, quōs ipse cotīdiē fallit, in caput īnfēlīcis puerī dētestātur.   15

Velleius Blaesus, ille locuplēs cōnsulāris, novissimā[10] valētūdine cōnflīctābātur; cupiēbat mutāre testāmentum. Rēgulus, quī spērāret aliquid ex novīs tabulīs, quia nūper captāre₂ eum coeperat, medicōs hortārī, rogāre quōquō modō spīritum hominī prōrogārent. Postquam signātum est testāmentum, mūtat persōnam, vertit allocūtiōnem, īsdem medicīs,₃ "quō usque miserum 20 cruciātis?" Moritur Blaesus, et tamquam omnia audīsset, Rēgulō nē tantulum[11] quidem.

Sufficiunt duae fābulae, an scholasticā lēge tertiam poscis? Est unde fīat. Aurēlia, ōrnāta fēmina, signātūra testāmentum sūmpserat pulcherrimās tunicās. Rēgulus cum vēnisset ad signandum, "rogō," inquit, "hās mihi 25 lēgēs." Aurēlia lūdere hominem putābat, ille sēriō īnstābat. Nē multa,[12] coēgit mulierem aperīre tabulās ac sibi tunicās lēgāre. Observāvit scrībentem, īnspexit an scrīpsisset. Et Aurēlia quidem vīvit, ille tamen istud tamquam moritūram coēgit.   (II, 20, 1–11)

[1] get your penny ready
[2] lay seriously (ill)
[3] so be it, okay
[4] merely
[5] put on a (thoughtful) expression
[6] dangerous
[7] be clear
[8] entrails
[9] worthless (indeclinable)
[10] last illness
[11] a tiny bit
[12] not (to say) much, to cut the story short

₁ for the purpose of making her horoscope
₂ i.e., he was "buttering him up" to get something out of him
₃ Supply **inquit.**

QUESTIONS

1. How did Aurelia outwit Regulus?
2. Why was Verania angry with Regulus?
3. What did Velleius leave Regulus in his will?
4. What sort of questions did Regulus ask Verania?

Grammar

Form Review

1. Review the conjugation of **fiō,** paying particular attention to the present tense.
2. Review defective verbs and contracted verb forms. Remember that **coepī** is used only in the perfect tenses; likewise, **meminī** and **ōdī,** although they have a present meaning. The verbs **inquam** and **aiō** are lacking several persons. Verbs whose perfect stems end in **–āv–, –ēv–,** or **–īv–** may be contracted, depending on the consonant that follows.

Syntax Review

1. Review the use of the reflexive pronoun. Remember that reflexive pronouns have no nominative. Personal pronouns are used for the first and second persons; **suī** for the third person.
2. Review indirect command. Remember that an indirect command is introduced by a verb such as **hortor, imperō, moneō, persuādeō, petō,** and **rogō,** plus **ut** (or **ne**) and the subjunctive.

 TRANSLATION

1. Will Regulus become the heir of many Romans?
2. Regulus asked that the tunics be given to him.
3. Aurelia began to ask herself why Regulus wished the will to be opened.
4. Sacrifice is being made by Regulus in order to find out what the gods desire.

Vocabulary

diēs	aperiō	nūper
mora	coepī	tamquam
	cōgō	
aeger	experior	quia
aureus	hortor	
īnfēlīx	īnstō	
	morior	
	mūtō	
	nāscor	
	poscō	
	sūmō	
	vertō	

Word Studies

Give English derivatives of the following words: **computō, congruō, digitus, oculus, sīdus, suspendō.**

A Home by the Seaside

Mīrāris cūr mē Laurentīnum[1] meum tantō opere dēlectet; dēsinēs mīrārī, cum cognōveris grātiam vīllae, opportūnitātem locī, lītoris spatium.

Decem septem mīlibus passuum ab urbe sēcessit, ut, perāctīs[2] quae agenda fuerint, salvō iam et compositō diē,[3] possīs ibi manēre. Aditur nōn ūnā viā; nam et Laurentīna et Ōstiēnsis eōdem ferunt, sed Laurentīna ā quārtō decimō lapide,[1] Ōstiēnsis ab ūndecimō relinquenda est. Utrimque excipit iter aliquā ex parte arēnōsum, iūnctīs[4] paulō gravius et longius, equō breve et molle. Varia hinc atque inde faciēs; nam modo occurrentibus silvīs via coartātur, modo lātissimīs prātīs diffunditur et patēscit; multī gregēs ovium, multa ibi equōrum, boum armenta, quae montibus hieme dēpulsa herbīs et tepōre vernō nitēscunt. Vīlla ūsibus capāx,[2] nōn sūmptuōsā tutēlā.[3] Cuius in prīmā parte ātrium frūgī[4] nec tamen sordidum, deinde porticūs in D litterae similitūdinem circumāctae, quibus parvula sed fēstīva ārea inclūditur. Ēgregium hae adversus tempestātēs receptāculum:

5

10

[1] *milestone*
[2] *big (enough) for one's needs*
[3] *upkeep not expensive*
[4] *modest (indeclinable adjective)*

---

[1] villa at Laurentum
[2] Supply the subject of the ablative absolute from **quae.**
[3] i.e., at the end of the business day
[4] i.e., a carriage with a team of horses; **equō** refers to riding on horseback

⁵ = **ātrium**
⁶ *African* (*wind*)
⁷ *the last* (i.e., *ends*) *of the waves*
⁸ *curve, apse,* i.e., *a bay window*
⁹ *cold baths*
¹⁰ *massage room and furnace*
¹¹ *swimming pool*
¹² *ball ground*

15 nam speculāribus ac multō magis imminentibus tēctīs mūniuntur. Est contrā mediās cavaedium⁵ hilare, mox trīclīnium satis pulchrum, quod in lītus excurrit, ac sī quandō Āfricō⁶ mare impulsum est, frāctīs iam et novissimīs⁷ flūctibus leviter adluitur. Undique valvās aut fenestrās nōn minōrēs valvīs habet, atque ita ā lateribus, ā fronte quasi tria maria prōspectat.

20 Annectitur angulō cubiculum in apsida⁸ curvātum, quod ambitum sōlis fenestrīs omnibus sequitur. Parietī eius in bibliothēcae speciem armārium īnsertum est, quod nōn legendōs librōs sed lēctitandōs capit. Adhaeret dormītōrium membrum, trānsitū interiacente, quī suspēnsus₅ et tubulātus conceptum vapōrem salūbrī temperāmentō hūc illūc dīgerit et ministrat.

25 Inde balneī cella frīgidāria spatiōsa et effūsa, cuius in contrāriīs parietibus duo baptistēria⁹ abundē capācia, sī mare in proximō cōgitēs. Adiacet ūnctōrium,¹⁰ hypocauston;¹⁰ cohaeret calida piscīna¹¹ mīrifica, ex quā natantēs mare aspiciunt. Nec procul sphaeristērium,¹² quod calidissimō sōlī, inclinātō iam diē, occurrit.

30 Iustīsne dē causīs iam tibi videor incolere, inhabitāre, dīligere sēcessum, quem tū nimis urbānus es nisi concupīscis? Atque utinam concupīscās! Ut tot tantīsque dōtibus vīllulae nostrae maxima commendātiō ex tuō contuberniō accēdat. Valē.   (II, 17, 1–5, 8–9, 11–12, 29)

QUESTIONS

1. How far was Pliny's country place from Rome?
2. In what direction did one get a view of the sea?
3. What provisions were made for getting exercise?
4. Name three things that make it seem like a modern house.

Grammar

Form Review

Review **possum,** paying particular attention to the present tense and the use of **–s** or **–t** in the stem.

₅ i.e., it had a double floor with pipes distributing heat

Syntax Review

Review the ablative of comparison. Remember that you must omit
quam if you use the ablative after the comparative.

 TRANSLATION

1. The facilities for swimming were excellent.
2. The chances of seeing friends were numerous.
3. In order to be able to reach Rome quickly, we had to go on horse(back).
4. After leaving Rome Pliny proceeded on a road narrower than the
   Appian Way to reach his villa.

Vocabulary

bōs	calidus	adhaereō	hūc
faciēs	ēgregius	cognōscō	
flūctus	lātus	frangō	
hiems		iungō	
lītus		mīror	
passus		mūniō	
tēctum		occurrō	
tempestās		pellō	

Word Studies

Review suffixes **–āx, –ium, –lus, –ōsus, –tūdō** and find examples of
their use in the reading.

Give an English derivative of each of the following words and show its
connection in meaning with the Latin word: **bōs, capāx, flūctus, grex,
hilaris, lītus, sordidus, tutēla, valva, vernus.**

Over Sea and Over Land

Sīcut salūberrimam nāvigātiōnem, domine,[1] usque Ephesum expertus, ita inde, postquam vehiculīs iter facere coepī, gravissimīs aestibus atque etiam febriculīs vexātus Pergamī substitī. Rūrsus, cum trānsīssem in ōrāriās nāviculās, contrāriīs ventīs retentus aliquantō tardius quam spērāveram, id 5 est XV Kal. Octōbrēs,[1] Bithyniam intrāvī. Nōn possum tamen dē morā querī, cum mihi contigerit, quod erat auspicātissimum, nātālem tuum in prōvinciā celebrāre.

Nunc reī pūblicae Prūsēnsium impendia, reditūs, dēbitōrēs excutiō; quod ex ipsō trāctātū magis ac magis necessārium intellegō.[2] Multae enim 10 pecūniae variīs ex causīs ā prīvātīs dētinentur; praetereā quaedam minimē lēgitimīs sūmptibus ērogantur.[2] Haec tibi, domine, in ipsō ingressū meō scrīpsī.

Dispice, domine an necessārium putēs mittere hūc mēnsōrem.[3] Videntur enim nōn mediocrēs pecūniae posse revocārī ā cūrātōribus operum, sī 15 mēnsūrae fidēliter agantur.[4] Ita certē prōspiciō ex ratiōne Prūsēnsium, quam cum maximē[5] trāctō. (X, 17)

Cuperem[6] sine querēlā corpusculī tuī et tuōrum pervenīre in Bithyniam potuissēs ac simile tibi iter ab Ephesō ut[7] nāvigātiōnī fuisset, quam expertus usque illō[8] erās. Quō autem diē pervēnissēs in Bithyniam cognōvī, 20 Secunde[3] cārissime, litterīs tuīs. Prōvinciālēs, crēdō, prōspectum[4] sibi ā mē intellegent. Nam et tū dabis operam[9] ut manifēstum sit illīs[5] ēlēctum tē esse quī ad eōsdem meī locō mitterēris. Ratiōnēs autem in prīmīs tibi rērum pūblicārum excutiendae sunt; nam et esse eās vexātās satis cōnstat.

Mēnsōrēs vix etiam iīs operibus quae aut Rōmae aut in proximō fīunt 25 sufficientēs habeō; sed in omnī prōvinciā inveniuntur quibus crēdī possit, et ideō nōn deerunt tibi, modo[10] velīs dīligenter excutere. (X,18)

1. About when was Trajan's birthday?
2. What made the land journey in Asia difficult?
3. What request did Trajan turn down?
4. What was the first job that Pliny undertook in the province of Bithynia?

---

[1] *Master, Sir,* i.e., Trajan
[2] *are being paid out*
[3] *architect*
[4] *if they should be made*
[5] **cum maximē = nunc**
[6] *I could wish . . . that you might have been able*
[7] *as*
[8] *there* (adverb)
[9] *see to it*
[10] *provided that*

[1] September 17
[2] He is doing an audit of the books of the city of Prusa.
[3] Pliny's cognomen
[4] Supply **esse**: *that I have looked out for them.*
[5] with **manifēstum**

The Basilica of Maxentius is also called the Basilica of Constantine. It was begun by the former but completed by the latter. Immense in size, it is one of the last monuments built in the memory and style of ancient Rome during the early 4th century. Its enormous vaults and arches set it apart from most other monuments. After Diocletian split the empire into two, Maxentius ruled in the west, but he was ultimately defeated by Constantine, the first Christian emperor. It is said that the Basilica of Maxentius served as the inspiration for the new St. Peter's Basilica in Rome, built in the 16th century.

Grammar

Form Review

Review indefinite pronouns. Remember that the pronoun forms are **aliquis, –quid**, whereas the adjective is **aliquī, –qua, –quod**; similarly the pronoun is **quīdam, quaedam, quiddam** and the adjective has **quoddam** for **quiddam**; the pronoun **quisque, quidque** has as an adjective **quisque, quaeque, quodque**.

Syntax Review

Review the locative case. Remember that the locative is used with the names of cities, towns, small islands, **domus, humus,** and **rūs.** Otherwise, use the ablative of *place where*.

Conditions

A condition consists of two clauses: a subordinate clause (the condition) introduced by **si, nisi,** or **si nōn,** and a principal clause (the conclusion). There are three main types of conditions.

A *simple* condition, or condition of fact, can have any combination of tenses, as in English.

Sī loquitur, audiō.	*If he speaks, I listen.*

A *contrary to fact* condition can have three different tense sequences.

Sī loquerētur, audīrem.	*If he were speaking (but he isn't), I should listen.*
Sī locūtus esset, audīvissem.	*If he had spoken (but he didn't), I should have listened (then).*
Sī locūtus esset, audīrem.	*If he had spoken (but he didn't), I should listen.*

Note that in the first example, the *present* condition, the imperfect subjunctive is used in both clauses. In the second example, a *past* condition, the pluperfect subjunctive is used in both clauses. In the third example, the *mixed* condition, the condition is past but the conclusion is present.

A *future less vivid* (should/would) condition uses the present subjunctive in both clauses.

> **Sī loquātur, audiam.**   *If he should speak, I would listen.*

⟨⟩ TRANSLATION ⟨⟩

1. He stopped at Pergamum on account of the heat.
2. Trajan sent Pliny to Bithynia to examine the accounts of the cities.
3. The people of Prusa had paid too much money for their buildings.
4. If they had been more careful they should now have more money.

Vocabulary

aestus	contrārius	cōnstat	dīligenter
opus	gravis	contingō	inde
ratiō	mediocris	cupiō	praetereā
vehiculum	varius	dētineō	sīcut
		intrō	usque
		trānseō	
		vexō	

Word Studies

From what Latin words are the following derived: **contingō, contrārius, cūrātor, lēgitimus, mediocris, nāvicula, reditus**?

More Carelessness and Waste in Building

[1] with **centiēns:** *more than ten million sesterces;* literally, *one hundred times (100,000) sesterces*
[2] *cracks*
[3] *rotten*
[4] *supports*
[5] *here and there*
[6] *promises*
[7] *larger*
[8] *irregular and sprawling*
[9] *to see*
[10] *about, with reference to*

Theātrum, domine, Nicaeae maximā iam parte cōnstrūctum, imperfectum tamen, sēstertium,[1] ut audiō (neque enim ratiō excussa est), amplius centiēns[1] hausit; vereor nē frūstrā. Ingentibus enim rīmīs[2] dēsēdit et hiat, sīve in causā solum[1] ūmidum et molle, sīve lapis ipse gracilis et putris.[3]
5 Dignum est certē dēlīberātiōne sitne faciendum an sit relinquendum an etiam dēstruendum. Nam fultūrae[4] ac substrūctiōnēs quibus subinde[5] suscipitur nōn tam firmae mihi quam sūmptuōsae videntur.

Huic theātrō ex prīvātōrum pollicitātiōnibus[6] multa dēbentur, ut basilicae circā, ut porticūs suprā caveam. Quae nunc omnia differuntur, cessante
10 eō quod ante peragendum est.

Iīdem Nicaeēnsēs gymnasium incendiō āmissum ante adventum meum restituere coepērunt, longē numerōsius[7] laxiusque quam fuerat, et iam aliquantum[2] ērogāvērunt; perīculum est nē parum ūtiliter; incompositum[8] enim et sparsum est. Praetereā architectus, sānē aemulus eius ā quō opus
15 inchoātum est, affirmat parietēs, quamquam vīgintī et duōs pedēs lātōs, imposita onera sustinēre nōn posse. Cōgor petere ā tē mittās architectum dispectūrum[9] utrum sit ūtilius post sūmptum quī factus est quōquō modō cōnsummāre opus.   (X, 39, 1–4, 6)

Quid oporteat fierī circā[10] theātrum quod inchoātum apud Nicaeēnsēs
20 est in rē praesentī optimē dēlīberābis et cōnstituēs. Mihi sufficiet indicārī cui sententiae accesserīs. Tunc autem ā prīvātīs exigī opera tibi cūrae sit cum theātrum, propter quod illa prōmissa sunt, factum erit.

Gymnasiīs indulgent Graeculī;[3] ideō forsitan Nicaeēnsēs maiōre animō cōnstrūctiōnem eius aggressī sunt. Sed oportet illōs eō contentōs esse quod
25 possit illīs sufficere. Architectī tibi dēesse nōn possunt. Nūlla prōvincia est quae nōn perītōs et ingeniōsōs hominēs habeat.   (X, 40)

QUESTIONS

1. What was the matter with the unfinished theater at Nicaea?
2. What was the matter with the gymnasium that had been begun?
3. What did Pliny want Trajan to do about these two projects?
4. What did Trajan tell Pliny to do about the projects at Nicaea?

---

[1] noun
[2] Supply **pecūniae.**
[3] The diminutive is contemptuous.

Grammar

Form Review

Review infinitives. Remember that most verbs have six infinitives: present, perfect, and future, active and passive.

Syntax Review

1. Review the accusative of extent. Remember that extent of time or space is expressed by the accusative without a preposition.
2. Review the ablative with **dignus**. Remember that both **dignus** *(worthy)* and **indignus** *(unworthy)* are followed by the ablative.

Vocabulary

adventus	**aggredior**	**enim**
incendium	**differō**	**frūstrā**
lapis	**exigō**	
onus	**hauriō**	**sīve**
	oportet	
ingēns	**restituō**	
mollis	**spargō**	
perītus	**sufficiō**	
	suscipiō	
	sustineō	

Word Studies

From what Latin words are the following derived: **cessō, imperfectus, restituō, suscipiō**?

Give English derivatives of the following: **aemulus, cōnsummō, dēstruō, frūstrā, hauriō, hiō, incendium, inchoō, spargō.**

Excutiō literally means *to shake out.* So *discuss* means *to shake apart* the arguments. A *concussion* is a *shaking up. Percussion* instruments are played by being *shaken thoroughly,* or *struck.* What is *repercussion?*

Hunting with a Notebook

Verba Ūtilia: contemnō, genus, licet, omnīnō, quiēs, rīdeō

Rīdēbis, et licet rīdeās. Ego ille quem nōstī[1] aprōs trēs et quidem pulcherrimōs cēpī. "Ipse?"[2] inquis. Ipse;[2] nōn tamen ut[3] omnīnō ab inertiā meā et quiēte discēderem. Ad rētia sedēbam: erat in proximō nōn vēnābulum[4] aut lancea, sed stilus et pugillārēs; meditābar[5] aliquid ēnotābamque, ut, sī manūs vacuās, plēnās tamen cērās[6] reportārem. Nōn est quod[7] contemnās hoc studiendī genus. Mīrum est ut[8] animus agitātiōne mōtūque corporis excitētur. Iam undique silvae et sōlitūdō ipsumque illud silentium quod vēnātiōnī datur magna cōgitātiōnis incitāmenta sunt. Proinde cum vēnābere, licēbit, auctōre[9] mē, ut[10] pānārium[11] et lagunculam,[11] sīc[10] etiam pugillārēs ferās. Experiēris nōn Diānam magis montibus quam Minervam inerrāre. Valē. (I, 6)

Buying a Home in the Country

Verba Ūtilia: dēlecto, emō, magis, pretium, sollicitō

Tranquillus,[1] contubernālis meus, vult emere agellum quem vēnditāre amīcus tuus dīcitur. Rogō cūrēs quantī[2] aequum est emat:[1] ita enim dēlectābit ēmisse. Nam mala ēmptiō[3] semper ingrāta, eō maximē, quod exprobrāre stultitiam dominō vidētur. In hōc autem agellō, sī modo adrīserit pretium, Tranquillī meī stomachum[4] multa sollicitant, vīcīnitās urbis, opportūnitās viae, mediocritās vīllae, modus rūris,[5] quī āvocet magis quam distringat. Scholasticīs porrō dominīs, ut hic est, sufficit abundē tantum solī ut relevāre caput, reficere oculōs, rēptāre per līmitem ūnamque sēmitam terere omnīsque vīticulās suās nōsse et numerāre arbusculās possint.

Haec tibi exposuī quō magis scīrēs quantum esset ille mihi, ego tibi dēbitūrus, sī praediolum istud, quod commendātur hīs dōtibus, tam salūbriter[6] ēmerit ut paenitentiae locum nōn relinquat. Valē. (I, 24)

---

[1] **ut** is omitted

Many old Roman temples were changed or converted into churches or basilicas as
Christianity spread. In Rome, the old church of Saints Cosmas and Damian was established
in 527 in the older Temple of Romulus. The vestibule rises over the round Temple of Romulus
and still has the bronze door with the original lock that was used in the temple.

What Shall We Do About the Christians?

Verba Ūtilia: cōnsulō, fallō, interim, intersum, negō, nesciō, prōsum, pūniō, saeculum, scelus, speciēs, vetō

Sollemne est mihi, domine, omnia dē quibus dubitō ad tē referre. Quis enim potest melius vel cūnctātiōnem meam regere vel ignōrantiam īnstruere?

Cognitiōnibus dē Chrīstiānīs interfuī numquam; ideō nesciō quid et quātenus[1] aut pūnīrī soleat aut quaerī. Nec mediocriter haesitāvī sitne
5 aliquod discrīmen aetātum an quamlibet[2] tenerī nihil ā rōbustiōribus different, dētur paenitentiae venia an eī quī omnīnō Chrīstiānus fuit dēsīsse nōn prōsit,[1] nōmen[3] ipsum sī flāgitiīs careat, an flāgitia cohaerentia nōminī pūniantur.

Interim iīs quī ad mē tamquam Chrīstiānī dēferēbantur hunc sum
10 secūtus modum. Interrogāvī ipsōs an essent Chrīstiānī. Cōnfitentēs iterum ac tertiō interrogāvī, supplicium minātus; persevērantēs dūcī[2] iussī. Neque enim dubitābam, quālecumque esset[4] quod fatērentur, pertināciam certē et īnflexibilem obstinātiōnem dēbēre pūnīrī. Fuērunt aliī similis āmentiae quōs, quia cīvēs Rōmānī erant, adnotāvī in urbem remittendōs. Mox ipsō
15 trāctātū,[5] ut fierī solet, diffundente sē crīmine, plūrēs speciēs incidērunt.[6]

Prōpositus est libellus sine auctōre[3] multōrum nōmina continēns. Quī negābant esse sē Chrīstiānōs aut fuisse, cum, praeeunte mē,[7] deōs appellārent et imāginī tuae, quam propter hoc iusseram cum simulācrīs nūminum afferrī, tūre ac vīnō supplicārent, praetereā maledīcerent[8][4]
20 Chrīstō, quōrum nihil posse cōgī dīcuntur[9] quī sunt rē vērā Chrīstiānī, dīmittendōs[5] esse putāvī.

Aliī ab indice nōminātī esse sē Chrīstiānōs dīxērunt et mox negāvērunt: fuisse quidem, sed dēsīsse, quīdam ante triennium, quīdam ante plūrēs annōs, nōn nēmō[10] etiam ante vīgintī. Hī quoque omnēs et imāginem tuam
25 deōrumque simulācra venerātī sunt et Chrīstō maledīxērunt.

---

[1] *to what extent*
[2] *the very young* (with **tenerī**)
[3] *the name* (*Christian*). Should a man be punished for being a confessed Christian or only for any crimes he might commit in the name of Christianity?
[4] *whatever it was*
[5] *by the handling* (*in the trials*). The more Pliny looked into the matter the more complex it became.
[6] *more types turned up*
[7] *with me speaking* (*the words of the oath*) *first*
[8] *reviled*
[9] *none of which things, it is said, they can be compelled* (*to do*) (literally, *they are said not to be able to be,* etc.)
[10] *not none = some*

---

[1] The subject is **dēsīsse** (from **dēsinō**).
[2] i.e., to prison and death
[3] i.e., anonymous
[4] What was patriotism to the Romans was idolatry to the Christians.
[5] modifies the antecedent (not expressed) of **quī**

Affirmābant autem hanc fuisse summam vel culpae suae vel errōris, quod essent solitī statō diē[5] ante lūcem convenīre carmenque Chrīstō quasi deō dīcere sēcum in vicem,[11] sēque sacrāmentō nōn in scelus aliquod obstingere, sed nē fūrta, nē latrōcinia, nē adulteria committerent,[6] nē fidem fallerent, nē dēpositum appellātī[12] abnegārent; quibus perāctīs, mōrem sibi 30 discēdendī fuisse, rūrsusque coeundī ad capiendum cibum,[7] prōmiscuum tamen et innoxium;[13] quod ipsum facere dēsīsse post ēdictum meum, quō secundum mandāta tua hetaeriās[14] esse vetueram. Quō magis necessārium crēdidī ex duābus ancillīs quae ministrae[8] dīcēbantur, quid esset vērī et[15] per tormenta quaerere. Nihil aliud invēnī quam superstitiōnem prāvam, 35 immodicam.

Ideō, dīlātā cognitiōne, ad cōnsulendum tē dēcurrī. Vīsa est enim mihi rēs digna cōnsultātiōne, maximē propter perīclitantium numerum. Multī enim omnis aetātis, omnis ōrdinis, utrīusque sexūs etiam, vocantur in perīculum et vocābuntur. Neque cīvitātēs tantum sed vīcōs etiam atque 40 agrōs superstitiōnis istīus contāgiō pervagāta est; quae vidētur sistī et cor-rigī posse. Certē satis cōnstat prope iam dēsōlāta templa coepisse celebrārī et sacra sollemnia diū intermissa repetī pāstumque venīre[16] victimārum, cuius adhūc rārissimus ēmptor inveniēbātur. Ex quō facile est opīnārī quae turba hominum ēmendārī possit, sī sit paenitentiae locus.   (X, 96)   45

———————

Āctum quem dēbuistī, mī Secunde, in excutiendīs causīs eōrum quī Chrīstiānī ad tē dēlātī fuerant secūtus es. Neque enim in ūniversum[17] aliq-uid quod quasi certam fōrmam habeat cōnstituī potest. Conquīrendī nōn sunt; sī dēferantur et arguantur, pūniendī sunt, ita tamen ut quī negāverit sē Chrīstiānum esse idque rē ipsā manifēstum fēcerit, id est supplicandō dīs 50 nostrīs, quamvīs suspectus in praeteritum,[18] veniam ex paenitentiā impe-tret. Sine auctōre vērō prōpositī libellī in nūllō crīmine locum habēre dēbent. Nam et pessimī exemplī[19] nec nostrī saeculī est.   (X, 97)

[11] *responsively*
[12] *when requested*
[13] *ordinary and harmless* (not the flesh of human beings, as was charged, probably through misunderstanding of Communion)
[14] *political clubs*
[15] *even*
[16] *is being sold* (from **vēneo**)
[17] *in general*
[18] *in the past*
[19] *both (a matter) of bad precedent and not*

———————

[5] Sunday
[6] The clause is object of **obstringere**.
[7] the "love feast" of the early Christians
[8] Pliny so translates the Greek word (**diakonissai**), from which comes our word "deaconess." The language of Bithynia was Greek.

Unit II

Short Selections from Aulus Gellius

*This Flemish tapestry depicts
two great generals and their armies,
Scīpiō Āfricanus and Hannibal Barca.
The Romans and Carthaginians fought
three long wars that spanned over 120
years. The second Punic War was the
most important and one of the most
decisive wars in history. Hannibal,
who at the age of 9 was taken to Spain
where he was forced to swear lifelong
hostility against Rome, crossed the Alps
with a train of elephants. Harassed
and frustrated by the delaying tactics
of the general Fabius Maximus, he was
finally broken down. Meanwhile, the
Roman general Scīpiō entered Spain
and succeeded in driving out the
remaining Carthaginian forces. Scīpiō
then continued into Africa where he
finally defeated Hannibal at Zama
in 201 B.C.*

Aulus Gellius

Aulus Gellius, a Roman writer of the second century (born about A.D. 130), has preserved in his only extant work, *Attic Nights* (**Noctēs Atticae**), an extremely miscellaneous but often valuable and interesting collection of literary material from earlier times.

Written during winter nights in Attica, this huge scrapbook (twenty books) contains anecdotes, bits of history and poetry, and essays on various phases of philosophy, geometry, and grammar. Of particular interest are quotations from Greek and Latin authors whose works are now wholly or in great part lost.

A Filibuster in the Senate

[1] *at times . . . at other times*
[2] = **eīs**
[3] *it seemed (best)*
[4] *(the rule) was kept*
[5] *than*
[6] *was under deliberation*
[7] *to the best interests of*
[8] *prolonging*
[9] *messenger,* though more like a sergeant-at-arms
[10] *let go*

Ante lēgem quae nunc dē senātū habendō observātur, ōrdō rogandī sententiās varius fuit. Aliās[1] prīmus rogābātur quī prīnceps ā cēnsōribus in senātum lēctus fuerat, aliās[1] quī dēsignātī cōnsulēs erant; quīdam ā cōnsulibus studiō aut necessitūdine aliquā adductī, quem īs[2] vīsum[3] erat,
5 honōris grātiā extrā ōrdinem sententiam prīmum rogābant. Observātum[4] tamen est, cum extrā ōrdinem fieret, nē quis quemquam ex aliō quam[5] ex cōnsulārī locō sententiam prīmum rogāret. C. Caesar in cōnsulātū quem cum M. Bibulō gessit, quattuor sōlōs extrā ōrdinem rogāsse sententiam dīcitur. Ex hīs quattuor prīncipem rogābat M. Crassum; sed postquam
10 fīliam Cn. Pompeiō dēsponderat, prīmum coeperat Pompeium rogāre.

Eius reī ratiōnem reddidisse eum₁ senātuī Tīrō Tullius, M. Cicerōnis lībertus, refert itaque sē ex patrōnō suō audīsse scrībit. Id ipsum Capitō Ateius in librō quem dē officiō senātōriō composuit scrīptum relīquit.

In eōdem librō Capitōnis id quoque scrīptum est: "C. Caesar cōnsul M.
15 Catōnem sententiam₂ rogāvit. Catō rem quae cōnsulēbātur,[6] quoniam nōn ē[7] rē pūblicā vidēbātur, perficī nōlēbat. Eius reī dūcendae[8] grātiā longā ōrātiōne ūtēbātur eximēbatque dīcendō diem. Erat enim iūs senātōrī, ut sententiam rogātus dīceret ante quicquid vellet aliae₃ reī et quoad vellet. Caesar cōnsul viātōrem[9] vocāvit eumque, cum fīnem nōn faceret, prēndī loquentem et in
20 carcerem dūcī iussit. Senātus cōnsurrēxit et prōsequēbātur Catōnem in carcerem. Hāc invidiā factā, Caesar dēstitit et mittī[10] Catōnem iussit." (IV, 10)

₁ Caesar
₂ Two accusatives are used with verbs of asking.
₃ for the more usual **alterius; alīus** was avoided.

1. Who was Caesar's colleague as consul?
2. What was the relationship of Caesar and Pompey?
3. What was the reaction of the senate to Caesar's arrest of Cato?
4. What was the order of calling upon senators for their opinions?

Grammar

The Subjunctive by Attraction

When a verb is in a clause that is dependent on a verb in the subjunctive or infinitive, the dependent clause verb is frequently "attracted" to the subjunctive. This most often happens in a dependent clause within an indirect statement (infinitive) or indirect command or question (subjunctive).

Plīnius dicit Traiānum, quī imperātor sit, mēnsōrem mittere debēre.	*Pliny says that Trajan, who is emperor, ought to send an architect.*
Caesar petīvit ut copiae quās sociī pollicitī essent missae sint.	*Caesar demanded that the troops that the allies had promised be sent.*

 TRANSLATION

1. It did not seem best to Caesar to ask Crassus.
2. He did not think that Cato should talk so much.
3. Cato was present for the sake of giving his opinion.
4. He was not ready, however, to give his opinion immediately.

Vocabulary

cōnsul	**dēspondeō**	**quoad**
lēx	**nōlō**	
prīnceps	**observō**	
senātus	**rogō**	
studium		

Scīpiō, a Man Beyond Reproach

[1] *the Elder;* subject of **praestiterit**
   and **fuerit**
[2] *highminded*
[3] *recall* (with **memoriā**)
[4] *glorious*
[5] *we should not be*
[6] *toward* (preposition)
[7] *rascal,* i.e., Naevius
[8] *to congratulate*

Scīpiō Āfricānus antīquior[1] quantā virtūtum glōriā praestiterit et quam fuerit altus animī[2] atque magnificus, plūrimīs rēbus quae dīxit quaeque fēcit dēclārātum est. Ex quibus sunt haec duo exempla eius fīdūciae atque exsuperantiae ingentis:

5   Cum M. Naevius, tribūnus plēbis, accūsāret eum ad populum dīceretque accēpisse ā rēge Antiochō pecūniam ut condiciōnibus grātiōsīs et mollibus pāx cum eō populī Rōmānī nōmine fieret, et quaedam item alia crīminī[1] daret indigna tālī virō, tum Scīpiō pauca praefātus quae dignitās vītae suae atque glōria postulābat: "memoriā," inquit, "Quirītēs, repetō[3] diem esse
10 hodiernum quō Hannibalem Poenum imperiō vestrō inimīcissimum magnō proeliō vīcī in terrā Āfricā pācemque et victōriam vōbīs peperī[2] īnspectābilem.[4] Nōn igitur sīmus[5] adversum[6] deōs ingrātī et, cēnseō, relinquāmus nebulōnem[7] hunc, eāmus hinc prōtinus Iovī optimō maximō grātulātum."[8] Id cum dīxisset, āvertit et īre ad Capitōlium coepit. Tum cōntiō ūniversa,
15 quae ad sententiam dē Scīpiōne ferendam convēnerat, relīctō tribūnō, Scīpiōnem in Capitōlium comitāta atque inde ad aedēs eius cum laetitiā et grātulātiōne solemnī prōsecūta est.   (IV, 18)

QUESTIONS

1. What did Naevius, the tribune, accuse Scīpiō of?
2. Whom did Scīpiō conquer?
3. What did Scīpiō do after he spoke?
4. How did the assembly (**cōntiō**) react to Scīpiō's statement?

Grammar

Review the hortatory and jussive subjunctives. Remember that they are essentially a command (or suggestion) in the first or third person and are generally translated using *Let*. For the negative, use **nē**.

TRANSLATION

1. Everybody asked what Scīpiō had done.
2. Let us not believe that Scīpiō ever did such things.
3. When Scīpiō heard the charges, he decided to go away.
4. Do you believe that the charges were worthy of so great a man?

---

[1] dative of purpose
[2] from **pariō**

Vocabulary

condiciō	hodiernus	āvertō
contiō	sollemnis	cēnseō
crīmen	ūniversus	pariō
dignitās		postulō
fīdūcia		prōsequor
laetitia		relinquō

Word Studies

Explain *exemption, fiduciary, incarcerate, incriminate, indignity, ingrate, mollify, preface.*

Explain the force of the prefix in **āvertō, exsuperantia, indignus, inimīcus, praestō, repetō.**

A Promise Must Be Kept

Iūs iūrandum apud Rōmānōs inviolātē sānctēque habitum servātumque est. Id et mōribus lēgibusque multīs ostenditur, et hoc quod dīcēmus eī reī nōn tenue argumentum esse potest. Post proelium Cannēnse[1] Hannibal, Carthāginiēnsium imperātor, ex captīvīs nostrīs ēlēctōs decem Rōmam mīsit mandāvitque eīs pactusque est, ut, sī populō Rōmānō vidērētur,[2] permūtātiō fieret captīvōrum. Hoc, priusquam proficīscerentur, iūs iūrandum₁ eōs adēgit reditūrōs esse in castra Poenica, sī Rōmānī captīvōs nōn permūtārent.

Veniunt Rōmam decem captīvī. Mandātum Poenī imperātōris in senātū expōnunt. Permūtātiō senātuī nōn placita.[3] Parentēs, cognātī, affīnēsque captīvōrum amplexī eōs, dīcēbant statum eōrum integrum incolumemque esse ac nē ad hostes redīre vellent ōrābant. Tum octō ex hīs iūstum nōn esse respondērunt, quoniam dēiūriō[4] vīnctī forent,[5] statimque, utī iūrātī erant,₂ ad Hannibalem profectī sunt. Duo reliquī Rōmae mānsērunt solūtōsque esse sē ac līberātōs religiōne₃ dīcēbant, quoniam, cum ēgressī castra hostium fuissent, commentīciō[6] cōnsiliō regressī eōdem,₄ tanquam sī ob aliquam fortuitam causam, īssent atque ita, iūre iūrandō satisfactō, rūrsus iniūrātī abīssent. Haec eōrum fraudulenta calliditās tam esse turpis exīstimāta est ut contemptī vulgō sint, cēnsōrēsque eōs posteā et damnīs et ignōminiīs affēcerint, quoniam quod factūrōs dēierāverant nōn fēcissent. (VI, 18, 1–10)

[1] *the battle of Cannae*
[2] *it seemed best*
[3] *did not please* (deponent)
[4] *by an oath*
[5] = **essent**
[6] *pretended, tricky*

₁ subject of **adēgit**
₂ deponent
₃ i.e., the oath
₄ adverb

1. What was the Roman attitude toward an oath?
2. What oath did Hannibal compel the prisoners to take?
3. How did the Romans react to the two prisoners who broke their word?

Grammar

Anticipatory Clauses

An anticipatory clause in the subjunctive occurs after **dum** (until), **antequam** (before), and **priusquam** (before) to express an action that is anticipated. To express an actual fact, the indicative is used.

Exspectābat dum cōnsul loquerētur.	*He waited until the consul spoke.*
Priusquam loquerētur, occupātus est.	*Before he could speak, he was seized.*
Antequam locūtus est, rīsit.	*Before he spoke, he laughed.*

Causal Clauses

A causal *(because, since)* clause introduced by **quod, proptereā quod,** or **quoniam** is in the indicative when it expresses the reason of the writer or speaker and in the subjunctive when the reason is someone else's.

Quod tardē erās, excēdere nōn poteram.	*Because you were late, I was unable to leave.*
Dixērunt sē irā movēre quod tardē esses.	*They said they were angry because you were late.*

TRANSLATION

1. We begged them not to return to Carthage.
2. Because we believe you, you will be permitted to go to Rome.
3. Before they could go to Rome, they had to swear that they would return.
4. The enemy said that they would not trust the Romans because they never told the truth.

The Temple of Antoninus and Faustina is one of the best-preserved in the Roman Forum.
Faustina was the beloved daughter of Emperor Antoninus Pius. She married Marcus Aurelius,
who was the adopted son of Antoninus, and who became emperor upon his father's death.
The Antonines were fairly traditional builders, but when Faustina died, the emperor deified
her and erected a magnificent temple in her honor. Later the temple was converted into a
Christian church which, in turn, was renovated in the 16th century.

Vocabulary

affīnis	amplector	priusquam
cognātus	iūrō	quoniam
ignōminia	ōrō	sānctē
iūs iūrandum	ostendō	
	permūtō	
incolumis	vinciō	
turpis		

Word Studies

Note the many words related to **iūs** in the selection above: **iūs iūrandum, iūstus, dēiūrium, iūrō, iniūrātus, dēierō.**

Cognātus (**co-gnātus**, *born together*) is a blood relative. **Affīnis** (**ad-fīnis**, *neighboring to*) is a relative by marriage.

Crow Eats Man

Dē Maximō Valeriō, quī Corvīnus appellātus est ob auxilium prōpugnātiōnemque corvī[1] ālitis, haud quisquam est nōbilium scrīptōrum quī secus[2] dīxerit. Ea rēs prōrsus mīranda sīc profectō est in librīs annālibus memorāta: Adulēscēns tālī genere ēditus,[3] L. Fūriō, Claudiō Appiō 5 cōnsulibus,[4] fit tribūnus mīlitāris. Atque in eō tempore cōpiae Gallōrum ingentēs agrum Pomptīnum īnsēderant. Dux intereā Gallōrum vāstā et arduā prōcēritāte armīsque aurō praefulgentibus grandia ingrediēns[5] et manū tēlum reciprocāns[6] incēdēbat perque contemptum et superbiam circumspiciēns dēspiciēnsque omnia₁ venīre iubet et congredī, sī quis 10 pugnāre sēcum ex omnī Rōmānō exercitū audēret. Tum Valerius tribūnus, cēterīs inter metum pudōremque ambiguīs,[7] impetrātō₂ prius ā cōnsulibus ut in Gallum tam arrogantem pugnāre sēsē permitterent, prōgreditur intrepidē modestēque obviam. Et congrediuntur et cōnsistunt, et cōnserēbantur iam manūs.[8] Atque ibi vīs quaedam dīvīna fit: corvus repente imprōvīsus 15 advolat et super galeam tribūnī īnsistit atque inde in adversārī ōs atque oculōs pugnāre incipit; īnsilībat, obturbābat, et unguibus manum laniābat et prōspectum ālīs arcēbat atque, ubi satis saevierat, revolābat in galeam

[1] *crow*
[2] *otherwise, differently*
[3] *sprung from such a family,* i.e., that of the Valerii
[4] *during the consulship of L. Furius and Appius Claudius*
[5] *taking big steps* (literally, *walking big*)
[6] *brandishing*
[7] *hesitating*
[8] *they were fighting hand to hand* (literally, *hands were being joined*)

₁ for **omnēs**; the neuter is more inclusive and contemptuous.
₂ The **ut** clause is the subject of the ablative absolute.

tribūnī. Sīc tribūnus, spectante utrōque exercitū, et suā virtūte nīxus[9] et operā ālitis prōpugnātus, ducem hostium ferōcissimum vīcit interfēcitque atque ob hanc causam cognōmen habuit "Corvīnus." Id factum est annīs 20 quadringentīs quīnque post Rōmam conditam.[10]

Statuam Corvīnō istī dīvus[11] Augustus in forō suō statuendam cūrāvit.[12] In eius statuae capite corvī simulācrum est, reī pugnaeque quam dīximus monumentum.   (IX, 11)

[9] *relying on* (with ablative)
[10] *after the founding of Rome*
[11] *deified*
[12] *caused to be set up*

QUESTIONS

1. What does the word "annals" mean?
2. How did Augustus honor Corvinus?
3. How did Valerius get his cognomen, Corvinus?
4. What was the attitude of the leader of the Gauls toward the Romans?

Grammar

Ablative of Origin

The ablative case with or without a preposition (**ab, ex, dē**) is used to express origin.

Ampliō genere natus est.	*He was born of a distinguished family.*

Ablative of Description

The ablative, without a preposition but with an accompanying adjective, is used to describe a person or thing. It is generally used to describe temporary qualities, such as appearance.

Erat equus magnā amplitūdine.	*He was a horse of great size.*

TRANSLATION

1. Was there anyone who fought more bravely for freedom?
2. There is no one who has done greater things for his country.
3. Maximus, a young man of no great height, was born of a noble family.
4. A crow that fought so fiercely deserves to be rewarded with a monument.

Vocabulary

adulēscēns	ferōx	intereā
metus		obviam
oculus	arceō	prōfectō
ōs	condō	
pudor	impetrō	
superbia	statuō	

quisquam

Word Studies

Explain *ingress, congress, progress; circumspect, despise, spectator.*
Give the literal meaning of **imprōvīsus, prōpugnātiō.**

Reconciliation, a Sign of Greatness

P. Āfricānus superior et Tiberius Gracchus, Tiberiī et C. Gracchōrum
pater, rērum gestārum magnitūdine et honōrum atque vītae dignitāte illus-
trēs virī, dissēnsērunt saepe dē rē pūblicā et eā[1] sīve quā aliā rē nōn amīcī
fuērunt. Ea simultās cum diū mānsisset et sollemnī diē epulum Iovī
5 lībārētur atque ob id sacrificium senātus in Capitōliō epulārētur, fors fuit
ut apud eandem mēnsam duo illī iūnctim locārentur. Tum quasi diīs
immortālibus arbitrīs in convīviō Iovis optimī maximī dextrās eōrum
condūcentibus,[2] repente amīcissimī factī. Neque sōlum amīcitia incepta,
sed affīnitās simul īnstitūta; nam P. Scīpiō fīliam virginem habēns iam virō
10 mātūram[3] ibi tunc eōdem in locō dēspondit eam Tiberiō Gracchō.

Aemilius quoque Lepidus et Fulvius Flaccus nōbilī genere amplis-
simīsque honōribus ac summō locō in cīvitāte praeditī, odiō inter sēsē
gravī et simultāte diūtinā cōnflīctātī sunt. Posteā populus eōs simul
cēnsōrēs facit. Atque illī, ubi vōce praecōnis renūntiātī sunt, ibīdem in
15 campō statim, nōndum dīmissā cōntiōne, ultrō uterque[4] et parī voluntāte
coniūnctī complexīque sunt, exque eō diē et in ipsā cēnsūrā et posteā iūgī[5]
concordiā fīdissimē amīcissimēque vīxērunt.   (XII, 8)

[1] *because of this or some other thing*
[2] *joining* (ablative absolute with **diīs**)
[3] *old enough for a husband*
[4] *they, both of them* (with **illī**)
[5] from **iūgis,** *everlasting*

1. How were the enemies Africanus and Tiberius Gracchus reconciled?
2. Who was the father of Tiberius and Gaius Gracchus?
3. What office did the enemies Aemilius Lepidus and Fulvius Flaccus hold?
4. After the election, what did these two men do?

Grammar

Two Accusatives

Certain verbs, including verbs of *asking, demanding,* and *teaching,* take two accusatives, one of the person, the other of the thing. Verbs of *making, naming, choosing, showing* may take two accusatives of the *same* person or thing.

Magister eōs scientiam docuit.	*The teacher taught them science.*
Populus Marcum ducem dēlēgit.	*The people chose Marcus leader.*

TRANSLATION

1. The people made them censors and they became firm friends.
2. When their enmity had lasted a long time, they met at a dinner.
3. Because they disagreed about public affairs they had become enemies.
4. It so happened that Scīpiō had a daughter whom he betrothed to Tiberius Gracchus.

Vocabulary

convīvium	**illūstris**	**posteā**
fors	**praeditus**	**ultrō**
odium		
simultās	**coniungō**	
	dissentiō	

Word Studies

Explain *arbitrate, convivial, dexterity, dissension, voluntary.* What does *ibid.* stand for and what does it mean?

How to Give a Dinner Party

[1] *Menippean,* after the Greek philosopher Menippus
[2] *parts*
[3] diminutive of **homō,** here used affectionately: *nice people*
[4] *the bench,* i.e., *the courtroom*
[5] *at that time*
[6] *of that kind*
[7] *the host*
[8] *luxurious*
[9] *stinginess*
[10] **biōphelē,** *helpful to life*

Lepidissimus liber est M. Varrōnis ex satirīs Menippēīs[1] quī īnscrībitur: "Nescis quid vesper sērus vehat," in quō disserit dē aptō convīvārum numerō dēque ipsīus convīviī habitū cultūque. Dīcit autem convīvārum numerum incipere oportēre ā Grātiārum numerō et prōgredī ad Mūsārum,[1]
5 id est, proficīscī ā tribus et cōnsistere in novem, ut, cum paucissimī convīvae sunt, nōn pauciōrēs sint quam trēs, cum plūrimī, nōn plūrēs quam novem. "Nam multōs," inquit, "esse nōn convenit, quod turba plērumque est turbulenta. Ipsum deinde convīvium cōnstat ex rēbus quattuor et tum dēnique omnibus suīs numerīs[2] absolūtum est sī bellī[2] homunculī[3] collēctī
10 sunt, sī ēlēctus locus, sī tempus lēctum, sī apparātus nōn neglēctus. Nec loquācēs autem convīvās nec mūtōs legere oportet, quia ēloquentia in forō et apud subsellia,[4] silentium vērō nōn in convīviō, sed in cubiculō esse dēbet." Sermōnēs igitur id temporis[5] habendōs cēnset nōn super rēbus ānxiīs, sed iūcundōs et cum quādam voluptāte ūtilēs, ex quibus ingenium
15 nostrum venustius fīat et amoenius. "Quod prōfectō," inquit, "ēveniet, sī dē id genus[6] rēbus ad commūnem vītae ūsum pertinentibus cōnfābulēmur, dē quibus in forō atque in negōtiīs agendī nōn est ōtium. Dominum[7] autem convīviī esse oportet nōn tam lautum[8] quam sine sordibus.[9] In convīviō legī nōn omnia dēbent, sed ea potissimum quae simul sint βιωφελῆ[10] et
20 dēlectent." (XIII, 11, 1–5)

QUESTIONS

1. How many guests should there be at a dinner party?
2. What sort of conversation should there be at dinner?
3. What was the title of Varro's book of satires? What was the title of the particular book here referred to?

Grammar

Review conditions on page 307. Remember that simple conditions are in the indicative, whereas contrary-to-fact and future-less-vivid conditions require the subjunctive.

---

[1] Supply **numerum.**
[2] adjective

C. M. Dixon

Located near the Temple of Vesta is the House of the Vestal Virgins. You can still see many statues and inscriptions there, including the names of some of the Vestals. One name has been erased, leaving only the letter C. It is possible that it is a reference to Claudia, who converted to Christianity in the 4th century.

1. I prefer a dinner which is good but not luxurious.
2. If the dinner should not be good, would you tell the host?
3. If there were only four guests, it would be difficult to find places for them.

Vocabulary

ēloquentia	**amoenus**	**cōnsistō**	**dēnique**
habitus	**aptus**	**conveniō**	**potissimum**
vesper	**lepidus**	**dēlectō**	
	paucus	**incipiō**	
		īnscrībō	
		neglegō	

Word Studies

Explain *amenities, delectable, loquacious, negligent, sordid, turbulence, vespers.*

What does *biology* deal with?

Which Is Right?

[1] *study*
[2] *of no slight reputation* (with **grammaticōs**)
[3] *nominative;* literally, *upright*

Dēfessus ego quondam diūtinā commentātiōne,[1] laxandī levandīque animī grātiā in Agrippae campō deambulābam. Atque ibi duōs forte grammaticōs cōnspicātus nōn parvī in urbe Rōmā nōminis[2] certātiōnī[1] eōrum ācerrimae adfuī, cum alter in cāsū vocātīvō "vir ēgregī" dīcendum contenderet, alter "vir ēgregie."

5 Ratiō autem eius quī "ēgregī" oportēre dīcī cēnsēbat huiusce[2] modī fuit: "Quaecumque," inquit, "nōmina seu vocābula rēctō[3] cāsū numerō singulārī 'us' syllabā fīniuntur, in quibus ante ultimam syllabam posita est 'i' littera, ea omnia cāsū vocātīvō 'i' littera terminantur, ut 'Caelius Caelī,' 'modius modī,' 10 'tertius tertī,' 'Accius Accī,' 'Titius Titī,' et similia omnia; sīc igitur 'ēgregius,' quoniam 'us' syllabā in cāsū nōminandī fīnītur eamque syllabam praecēdit 'i' littera, habēre dēbēbit in cāsū vocandī 'i' litteram extrēmam, et idcircō 'ēgregī,' nōn 'ēgregie,' rēctius dīcētur."

[1] with **adfuī**
[2] emphatic form of **huius**

Hoc ubi ille alter audīvit: "ō," inquit, "ēgregie grammatice vel, sī id māvīs, ēgregissime, dīc, ōrō tē, 'īnscius' et 'impius' et 'sōbrius' et 'ēbrius' et 'proprius' 15 et 'propitius' et 'ānxius' et 'contrārius,' quae 'us' syllabā fīniuntur, in quibus ante ultimam syllabam 'i' littera est, quem cāsum vocandī habent? Mē enim pudor et verēcundia tenent[4] prōnūntiāre ea secundum[5] tuam dēfīnītiōnem." Sed cum ille paulisper oppositū[6] hōrum vocābulōrum commōtus reticuisset et mox tamen sē collēgisset[7] eandemque illam quam dēfīnierat rēgulam[8] 20 retinēret et prōpugnāret, eaque inter eōs contentiō longius dūcerētur, nōn arbitrātus ego operae pretium[9] esse eadem istaec diūtius audīre, clāmantēs compugnantēsque illōs relīquī.   (XIV, 5)

[4] *keep me from*
[5] *according to* (preposition)
[6] *by the opposition*
[7] *had collected his wits*
[8] *rule*
[9] *worthwhile; literally, the price of the effort*

QUESTIONS

1. Where was Gellius walking?
2. Why had he gone there?
3. What were the grammarians discussing?
4. What was Gellius' evident opinion of the grammarians' discussion?
5. What were the grammarians doing as Gellius left them?

 TRANSLATION

1. Tell me why you prefer to say "ēgregī."
2. Give me a good reason why you prefer "ēgregie."
3. First I was wearied by my work, then I was wearied by the grammarians.

Vocabulary

cāsus	dēfessus	cōnspicor	forte
fīnis	extrēmus	contendō	
	ultimus	levō	
	verēcundus		

Newfangled Education
Not Wanted

[1] = cōnsulibus
[2] *as*
[3] *to the best interests of, in accordance with*
[4] = īre

C. Fanniō Strabōne, M. Valeriō Messālā cōss.,[1] senātūs cōnsultum dē philosophīs et dē rhētoribus Latīnīs factum est: "M. Pompōnius praetor senātum cōnsuluit. Quod verba facta sunt dē philosophīs et dē rhētoribus, dē eā rē ita cēnsuērunt, ut M. Pompōnius praetor animadverteret cūrāretque,
5 utī[2] eī ē[3] rē pūblicā fidēque suā vidērētur, utī Rōmae nē essent."

Aliquot deinde annīs post id senātūs cōnsultum Cn. Domitius Ahēnobarbus et L. Licinius Crassus cēnsōrēs dē coercendīs rhētoribus Latīnīs ita ēdīxērunt: "Renūntiātum est nōbīs esse hominēs quī novum genus disciplīnae īnstituērunt, ad quōs iuventūs in lūdum conveniat; eōs sibi nōmen
10 imposuisse Latīnōs rhētoras;[1] ibi hominēs adulēscentulōs diēs tōtōs dēsidēre. Maiōrēs nostrī quae līberōs suōs discere et quōs in lūdōs itāre[4] vellent īnstituērunt. Haec nova, quae praeter cōnsuētūdinem ac mōrem maiōrum fīunt, neque placent neque rēcta videntur."

Neque illīs sōlum temporibus nimis rudibus necdum Graecā disciplīnā
15 expolītīs philosophī ex urbe Rōmā pulsī sunt, vērum etiam, Domitiānō imperante, senātūs cōnsultō ēiectī atque urbe et Ītaliā interdictī sunt. Quā tempestāte Epictētus quoque philosophus propter id senātūs cōnsultum Nīcopolim Rōmā dēcessit.   (XV, 11)

QUESTIONS

1. Why did Epictetus withdraw from Rome?
2. What was the decree of the Roman senate against the philosophers?
3. Who in ancient Roman times determined the education of the young?

---

[1] a Greek form of the masculine accusative

Grammar

1. Review the ablative of separation. Remember that most verbs use a preposition, but that **abstineō, careō, dēiciō, desistō, excēdō,** and **līberō** do not; separation from people, however, generally requires a preposition (**ab, ex, dē**).
2. Review the ablative of *place from which.* Remember that the prepositions **ab, ex,** and **dē** are used to express *place from which,* except with **domus** and the names of towns and cities, where the preposition is often omitted.

TRANSLATION

1. They departed from Rome before they could be seized.
2. At Rome in the time of Domitian the philosophers were driven out of Rome.
3. Freed from the dangers of the new ideas (*things*), they were able to learn the right (*things*).

Vocabulary

cēnsor	**aliquot**	**animadvertō**
cōnsuētūdō		**coerceō**
iuventūs		**cūrō**
praetor		**ēiciō**
		placeō

Word Studies

The abbreviation **cōss.** for **cōnsulēs** indicates that in the word **cōnsul** the *n* was nasalized, as in French, and not fully pronounced. The *ss* shows that in abbreviations the last consonant of the abbreviation was doubled to indicate the plural, as in English *pp.* for *pages.*

Haec ubi ōrdine quō dīxī prōposita atque, singulīs sorte ductīs, disputāta
20 explānātaque sunt, librīs corōnīsque omnēs dōnātī sumus nisi ob ūnam
quaestiōnem, quae fuit dē verbō "vērant." Nēmō enim tum commeminerat
dictum esse ā Q. Enniō id verbum in tertiō decimō annālium. Corōna igitur
huius quaestiōnis deō fēriārum istārum Sāturnō data est.   (XVIII, 2, 1–5,
9–10, 12, 15–16)

QUESTIONS

1. Who used the rare word **vērant?**
2. What was the prize offered at the dinner?
3. How were the guests selected for the problems?
4. What sort of problem was presented to the guests?

✦✦✦ TRANSLATION ✦✦✦

1. We came to dinner not only to eat but also to win prizes.
2. Many had heard the same teachers and read the same books.
3. The questions were difficult, and we did not know what the correct
   answers were.

Vocabulary

cornū	**singulī**	**colō**
corōna	**totidem**	**mentior**
nēmō		**solvō**
pactum		
sors		

The Temple of Vesta was one of the most sacred temples in Rome. According to tradition, the round temple was built by Numa, the second king of Rome, to safeguard the image of Minerva and other sacred objects that were carried from Troy by Aeneas. It was here that the six Vestal Virgins tended the sacred fire and kept it burning.

Boys, Young Men, and Old Men

Verba Ūtilia: cēnsus, idōneus, senex, suprā

Tuberō in historiārum prīmō scrīpsit Servium Tullium, rēgem populī Rōmānī, cum illās quīnque classēs seniōrum et iūniōrum cēnsūs faciendī grātiā īnstitueret, puerōs esse exīstimāsse quī minōrēs essent annīs septem decem, atque inde ab annō septimō decimō, quō[1] idōneōs iam esse reī pūblicae arbitrārētur, mīlitēs scrīpsisse,[1] eōsque ad annum quadrāgēsimum sextum "iūniōrēs" suprāque eum annum "seniōrēs" appellāsse.

Eam rem proptereā notāvī, ut discrīmina quae fuerint iūdiciō mōribusque maiōrum pueritiae,[2] iuventae, senectae, ex istā cēnsiōne Servī Tullī, prūdentissimī rēgis, nōscerentur.   (X, 28)

[1] enrolled as
*[2] those (i.e., **discrīmina**) of boyhood*

---

[1] The antecedent is **annō.**

The Etiquette of Swearing

Verba Ūtilia: asseverō, dēiūrō, nusquam, vetus

In veteribus scrīptīs neque mulierēs Rōmānae per Herculem dēiūrant neque virī per Castorem. Sed cūr illae nōn iūrāverint Herculem,[1] nōn obscūrum est, nam Herculāneō[1] sacrificiō abstinent. Cūr autem virī Castorem iūrantēs nōn appellāverint, nōn facile dictū[2] est. Nusquam igitur scrīptum invenīre est[3] apud idōneōs quidem scrīptōrēs aut "mehercle" fēminam dīcere aut "mēcastor" virum; "edepol" autem, quod iūs iūrandum per Pollūcem est, et virō et fēminae commūne est. Sed M. Varrō assevērat antīquissimōs virōs neque per Castorem neque per Pollūcem dēiūrāre solitōs, sed id iūs iūrandum fuisse tantum fēminārum; paulātim tamen īnscitiā antīquitātis virōs dīcere "edepol" coepisse factumque esse ita dīcendī mōrem, sed "mēcastor" ā virō dīcī in nūllō vetere scrīptō invenīrī. (XI, 6)

[1] to Hercules
[2] to say
[3] is it (possible) to find it written

---

[1] Supply **per.**

How to Write Plays

Verba Ūtilia: eximiē, gignō, proinde, sapiēns, sapiō

Eximiē hoc atque vērissimē Āfrānius poēta dē gignendā comparandāque Sapientiā opīnātus est, quod eam fīliam esse Ūsūs et Memoriae dīxit. Eō namque argūmentō dēmōnstrat, quī sapiēns rērum[1] esse hūmānārum velit, nōn librīs sōlīs neque disciplīnīs rhētoricīs dialecticīsque opus esse, sed oportēre eum versārī quoque exercērīque in rēbus comminus[1] nōscendīs 5 eaque omnia ācta et ēventa firmiter meminisse et proinde sapere atque cōnsulere ex hīs quae perīcula[2] ipsa rērum docuerint, nōn quae librī tantum aut magistrī tamquam in mīmō[3] aut in somniō dēlīrāverint. Versūs Āfrānī sunt in togātā cui Sellae nōmen est:

> Ūsus mē genuit, māter peperit Memoria,   10
> Sophiam vocant mē Grāī, vōs Sapientiam.
>
> (XIII, 8)

[1] *at first hand* (adverb)
[2] *experience*
[3] *mime, play*

---

[1] genitive with **sapiēns**

Can You Speak Twenty-Five Languages?

Verba Ūtilia: diciō, haud, loquor

Quīntus Ennius tria corda habēre sēsē dīcēbat, quod loquī Graecē et Oscē[1] et Latīnē scīret. Mithridātēs autem, Pontī atque Bithyniae rēx inclutus, quī ā Cn. Pompeiō bellō superātus est, quīnque et vīgintī gentium quās sub diciōne habuit linguās percalluit[1] eārumque omnium gentium virīs haud umquam per interpretem collocūtus est, sed ut[2] quemque ab eō 5 appellārī ūsus[3] fuit, proinde linguā et ōrātiōne ipsīus nōn minus scītē quam sī gentīlis[4] eius esset locūtus est. (XVII, 17)

[1] *knew well*
[2] *when*
[3] *need*
[4] *fellow countryman*

---

[1] Oscan, spoken in southern Italy, was related to Latin.

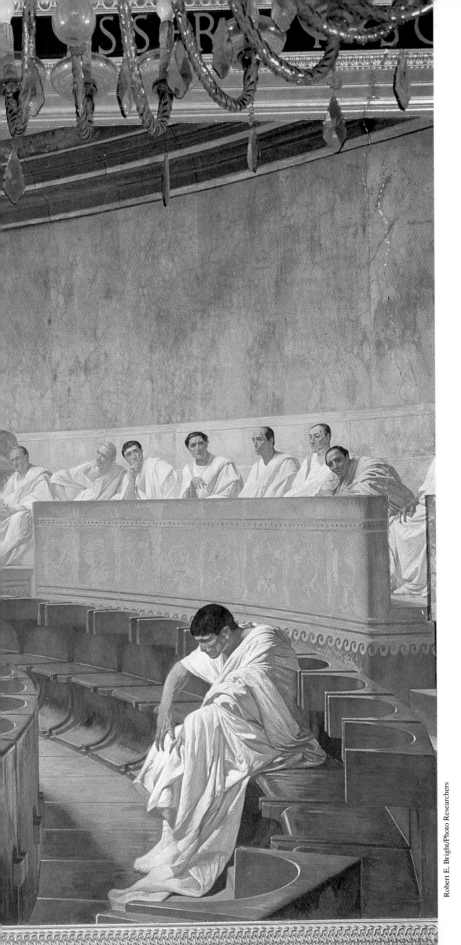

Unit III

Cicero Against Catiline

Cicero denounced Catiline in a series of speeches to the Roman Senate that left Catiline with no options but to run and try to hide. Frustrated by his inability to secure the consulship in 65 B.C., Catiline and his followers conspired to murder the two consuls who were elected. Unsuccessful, they plotted anew and were caught when Cicero intercepted correspondence between the conspirators and immediately convened a meeting of the Senate. Cicero's role in suppressing the conspiracy earned him the title **pater patriae**.

Cicero's Life

Marcus Tullius Cicero was intimately connected with every movement of history in the fateful period in which he lived. But although a great political figure, he is an incomparably greater literary figure, representing the combination of Greek learning and Latin culture and its practical application in Roman thought and institutions that characterized the whole of Roman literature.

Cicero was born near Arpinum (about sixty miles southeast of Rome) on January 3, 106 B.C. On December 7, 43 B.C., the year following Caesar's assassination, he was put to death. Cicero was of a well-to-do equestrian family, not of the nobility. He was sent to Rome for his education, where he studied literature, rhetoric, oratory, and philosophy under the best teachers available. In his study of law he attended the courts to hear the famous orators. He was also trained in acting to contribute to his stage presence in the making of speeches. In the Social War, Cicero completed his military service, which was a prerequisite to a public career.

Cicero made his first appearance in the courts in 81 B.C. in behalf of Publius Quinctius, who was involved in a suit for debt. The following year, in a courageous speech, he defended an anti-Sullan, Sextus Roscius, on a murder charge. After this, at the age of 26, Cicero traveled in the East (Athens, Rhodes) to pursue his studies further, particularly in philosophy and rhetoric. He returned to Rome after two years abroad and married Terentia, a wealthy woman, by whom he had two children, Tullia and Marcus.

The order of advancement in public offices, known as the "cursus honorum," was fixed by law and by custom. When Cicero had reached the age at which Romans were permitted to enter upon the cursus honorum, he began his official career with his election to the quaestorship (75 B.C.), in which he served with distinction in Sicily. Because of his ability and fairness, the Sicilians retained him as their counsel against their ex-governor, Verres, brought to trial for his shameless record of high-handed tyranny and rapacity. As a result of Cicero's brilliant advocacy of the Sicilian cause, Verres went into exile and Cicero supplanted Hortensius, who had defended Verres, as the leading orator of his day.

Cicero became aedile in 69 B.C. and praetor in 66, the momentous year in which he supported Pompey for an extraordinary command in the East against Mithridates, King of Pontus.

Cicero's election to the consulship in 63 B.C. resulted from a split in the opposition and from Pompey's support. Cicero, although a **novus homō,** that is, the first of his family to hold a curule office, won the election because he was considered politically safe. During his term as consul,

Cicero was confronted with the conspiracy of Catiline, crushed this attempt at revolution, and as a result was called father of his country (**pater patriae**), the first Roman to receive this title.

The five years following Cicero's consulship marked a change in political alignments. The first triumvirate, formed in 60 B.C., consisted of Pompey, Crassus, and Caesar, who was elected consul for the year 59 B.C. This three-man consolidation of political power made various overtures to Cicero, who in his patriotism refused them all; he could not reconcile himself to what he considered the unconstitutional attitude of Caesar. In the year 58 Cicero was forced into exile on the charge, brought by Clodius, whom Cicero had offended, of having put to death Roman citizens—the conspirators associated with Catiline—without a proper trial. Cicero lived in exile from April 58 until August 57, when he was recalled with the consent of Caesar. The exile was a crushing blow to Cicero, but on his return he was enthusiastically welcomed by the people, re-entered political life, and began again to make speeches.

In 53 B.C. Cicero was elected to the College of Augurs, a religious position, and in 51 went to Cilicia in Asia Minor as governor, where he served honestly and well. On his return to Rome in 50, Cicero found Rome on the brink of the Civil War between Pompey and Caesar, which actually began in January 49. Cicero tried to effect a reconciliation between the two opponents, but he was unsuccessful. He finally left the city after Caesar crossed the Rubicon River and occupied Italy proper. Pompey fled from Italy to the Balkans, but Cicero did not follow him out of Italy. Caesar, however, pursued Pompey and defeated him at the battle of Pharsalus in 48 B.C. Subsequently Cicero was reconciled with Caesar and allowed to return to Rome, but he did not engage in political activity for some time.

In the year 46 Cicero divorced his wife Terentia and married a younger woman, Publilia, who had been his ward. In 45 Tullia, his beloved daughter, died, and he was overwhelmed with grief. It was at this time that Cicero devoted himself to writing on philosophic and literary subjects.

Cicero returned to political life after the death of Caesar (44 B.C.) because he thought he saw a chance for the restoration of the commonwealth and envisaged his duty as a fight against Antony, who was trying to seize control of the government. He wrote fourteen speeches against Antony, called the *Philippics*.

When the second triumvirate, consisting of Octavian, Antony, and Lepidus, was formed in 43 B.C., Cicero was proscribed (Octavian had reluctantly agreed) and killed by agents of Antony on December 7 of the same year.

Cicero's prose writings include speeches (over fifty still remain), treatises on political science, rhetoric, and philosophy, and approximately 800 letters. His letters, not written for publication, form one of the most interesting and valuable documents of Roman times. Cicero also wrote poetry which, although not of the highest quality, was always technically competent.

Cicero was the greatest orator of Rome, one of its most important statesmen, and its greatest known prose writer. His influence has been incalculable, justifying Macaulay's statement, "Cicero taught Europe how to write."

Cicero's Style

Greece had long been the home of famous orators, and, in the time of Cicero especially, the Romans studied and imitated the Greek masters. Roman orators generally adopted one of three styles of Greek oratory—the Attic, which was simple, the Asiatic, characterized by ornateness, or the middle style. Cicero, who as Rome's greatest orator is often compared with Demosthenes, adopted a combination of Attic and Asiatic.

In his zeal to become a first-rate orator, Cicero studied rhetoric—the principles and rules for speaking and writing effectively—and related subjects in both Rome and Athens. His fine training, plus a natural talent and firmness of purpose, paid rich literary dividends. For generations, the perfection of Cicero's style has been an object of admiration and imitation.

What do we mean when we speak of a literary style? Style may be defined as those characteristics of a writer that exhibit his or her individuality, and distinguish him or her from other writers. Cicero's style, for example, is characterized by both terse sentences and the resounding period style, which you will study on p. 90. His style is also graceful, flowing, balanced, witty, informal, charming, and many other things, depending on the circumstances under which he was composing.

Another characteristic of Cicero's style is his frequent use of figures of speech, modes of expression that help embellish thoughts. While reading Cicero, you will meet these figures of speech, many of which are still used by writers today. These patterns, as well as other aspects of Cicero's style, will be pointed out and discussed as they occur.

Try to put yourself in the midst of Cicero's style, so that you begin to absorb it, as if by osmosis, and to feel at ease with it. From time to time the text will give you some help in this. Here are a few suggestions to get you started:

As you prepare your lesson, always read a part of the assignment *aloud in Latin,* pausing at the end of *thought groups,* often indicated by punctuation. After you have read (once or more) a paragraph or sentence, see if the notes are of any help in giving the meaning. Then attempt to translate *before* you look up any of the meanings in the vocabulary (the word list should be a last and not a first resort), guessing at some of the meanings. If you should find the first sentence too difficult, go on to the second sentence, which may throw light on the first.

Catiline's Conspiracy

The revolution that resulted in the establishment of the Empire under Augustus had early origins at Rome in inequalities of representation, economic unrest, and lack of harmony among the three orders of citizens (**nōbilēs, equitēs, plēbs**). It is often said to have begun with the Gracchi brothers' attempt at reform (133–121 B.C.). In the early part of the first century B.C. there was civil war at Rome between forces led by Sulla, an autocratic dictator, and those led by Marius, a dictator supported by the people. Lucius Sergius Catilīna was an active supporter of Sulla, the winner in this civil war.

Catiline was born of an old patrician family in 108 B.C. In the reaction against conservatism following the regime of Sulla (who died in 79), Catiline joined the liberals. He went through the steps of the cursus honorum and was governor of Africa for two years. He returned to Rome in 66 B.C. and became a candidate for the consulship but was prevented from running by a charge, brought by the conservatives, of maladministration in Africa.

Catiline formed a conspiracy to murder the consuls of 65, but the plot was exposed and Catiline acquitted. He again ran for consul in 64 but was defeated by Cicero. Once more Catiline formed a plot to seize the government by force. Cicero learned of the secret plans of the conspirators and had enacted by the senate a **senātūs cōnsultum ultimum** that gave authority to the consuls to suppress the conspiracy. Catiline made plans to have Cicero killed on the morning of November 8, but Cicero knew about this plot immediately after the meeting at which Catiline's plans were made. On the same day Cicero called a meeting of the senate in the Temple of Jupiter Stator and made the first speech against Catiline, who was present to listen to the charges against him.

First Oration
Against Catiline

Catiline's Audacity

Verba Ūtilia: audācia, caedēs, coniūrātiō, furor, iam prīdem, ignōrō, immō vērō, orbis terrae, patientia, praesidium, praetereō, studeō, timor, vigilia, vultus

[1] *How long, tell me*
[2] *still*
[3] *that madness of yours* (**iste** is contemptuous)
[4] *expressions on the faces*
[5] *to death, you, Catiline*

I, 1. Quō usque tandem[1] abūtēre,[1] Catilīna, patientiā[2] nostrā? Quam diū etiam[2] furor iste[3] tuus nōs ēlūdet? Quem ad fīnem sēsē effrēnāta iactābit audācia? Nihilne tē[3] nocturnum praesidium Palātī, nihil urbis vigiliae, nihil timor populī, nihil concursus bonōrum[4] omnium, nihil hic mūnītissimus habendī senātūs locus, nihil hōrum ōra vultūsque[4] mōvērunt? Patēre tua cōnsilia nōn sentīs, cōnstrictam iam hōrum omnium scientiā tenērī coniūrātiōnem tuam nōn vidēs? Quid[5] proxima,[6] quid superiōre nocte ēgerīs, ubi fuerīs, quōs convocāverīs, quid cōnsilī[7] cēperīs, quem nostrum[8] ignōrāre arbitrāris?

2. Ō tempora, ō mōrēs![9] Senātus haec intellegit, cōnsul videt; hic tamen vīvit. Vīvit? Immō vērō etiam in senātum[10] venit, fit pūblicī cōnsilī particeps, notat et dēsignat oculīs ad caedem ūnum quemque nostrum.[8] Nōs autem, fortēs virī,[11] satis facere reī pūblicae vidēmur, sī istīus furōrem ac tēla vītāmus. Ad mortem[5] tē, Catilīna, dūcī[12] iussū cōnsulis iam prīdem oportēbat, in tē cōnferrī pestem quam tū in nōs omnīs iam diū māchināris.

[1] future second person singular
[2] with **abūtēre**
[3] object of **mōvērunt**
[4] The "good" people were those who supported the government.
[5] The indirect questions depend on **ignōrāre**.
[6] November 7
[7] genitive of the whole
[8] from **nōs,** not **noster**
[9] accusative of exclamation
[10] Cicero does not mean that Catiline had no right to attend a meeting of the senate (he was a member) but that he dared to after his plans were exposed.
[11] ironical
[12] The tense is indicated by **oportēbat;** in English, we show it by the translation of **dūcī:** *you ought to have been led.*

3. An vērō vir amplissimus, P. Scīpiō, pontifex maximus, Ti. Gracchum mediocriter labefactantem statum reī pūblicae prīvātus interfēcit: Catilīnam orbem terrae caede atque incendiīs vāstāre cupientem nōs cōnsulēs perferēmus? Nam illa nimis antīqua praetereō, quod[6] C. Servīlius Ahāla Sp. Maelium[13] *the fact that* (explains **illa**) novīs rēbus studentem manū suā occīdit. Fuit, fuit ista quondam in hāc rē 20 pūblicā virtūs ut virī fortēs ācriōribus suppliciīs cīvem perniciōsum quam acerbissimum hostem coercērent. Habēmus senātūs cōnsultum[14] in tē, Catilīna, vehemēns et grave, nōn deest reī pūblicae cōnsilium neque auctōritās huius ōrdinis: nōs, nōs, dīcō apertē, cōnsulēs dēsumus.

Literary Style: Anaphora and Praeteritiō

One of Cicero's favorite figures of speech is anaphora, the repetition of a word at the beginning of successive phrases and clauses without the use of a connective such as **et**. A splendid example occurs at the beginning of the preceding chapter: **nihil** is used six times, and the clauses are divided into three pairs: the guards, the people, the senate.

Cicero is fond of saying that he will not talk about some point and in doing so will reveal the whole thing. This is called **praeteritiō**, from **praetereō**, *I pass over,* the word often used (see line 19) in saying a great deal while pretending to say nothing.

 TRANSLATION

1. We know what you did last night.
2. I pass over the fact that Scipio killed Gracchus.
3. Catiline thought that he could kill Cicero and seize the government.
4. He ought (*imperfect*) to have been killed (*present*) before he could destroy the government.

Word Studies

The word *palace* almost tells the story of the city of Rome. It is derived from Palatium, the hill named after Pales, the goddess of the shepherds who used to roam over that hill before Rome was founded. Because it was so convenient to the Forum, it became the most desirable district in Rome for the rich senators and other officials. Cicero owned a house on it, as did Caesar and Augustus. Gradually the emperors covered the entire hill with their buildings, and so it was that Palatium became *palace.*

---

[13] Maelius distributed grain to the poor during a famine (439 B.C.).
[14] The senate passed a resolution (called the **senātūs cōnsultum ultimum**) on October 21 delegating full powers to the consuls. It was something like a declaration of martial law today.

Why Not Put Catiline to Death?

Verba Ūtilia: audeō, clēmēns, condemnō, cōnfestim, crēscō, crūdēlis, dēcernō, improbus, inclūdō, maiōrēs, moenia, mōlior, nēquitia, patior, perditus

II, 4. Dēcrēvit quondam senātus utī L. Opīmius cōnsul vidēret[1] nē quid[2] rēs pūblica dētrīmentī[1] caperet: nox nūlla intercessit: interfectus est propter quāsdam sēditiōnum suspīciōnēs C. Gracchus,[2] clārissimō patre, avō, maiōribus, occīsus est cum līberīs M. Fulvius cōnsulāris. Similī
5 senātūs cōnsultō C. Mariō et L. Valeriō cōnsulibus est permissa rēs pūblica: num ūnum diem posteā L. Sāturnīnum tribūnum plēbis et C. Servīlium praetōrem mors[3] ac reī pūblicae poena[3] remorāta est? At vērō nōs vīcēsimum[3] iam diem patimur hebēscere aciem hōrum auctōritātis. Habēmus enim eius modī senātūs cōnsultum, vērum inclūsum in tabulīs, tamquam in vāgīnā
10 reconditum, quō ex[4] senātūs cōnsultō cōnfestim tē interfectum esse,[4] Catilīna, convēnit.[4] Vīvis, et vīvis nōn ad dēpōnendam sed ad cōnfirmandam audāciam. Cupiō, patrēs cōnscrīptī,[5] mē esse clēmentem, cupiō[5] in tantīs reī pūblicae perīculīs nōn dissolūtum vidērī, sed iam mē ipse inertiae[6] nēquitiaeque condemnō. **5.** Castra sunt in Italiā contrā populum Rōmānum
15 in Etrūriae faucibus[7] collocāta, crēscit in diēs singulōs[8] hostium numerus; eōrum autem castrōrum imperātōrem ducemque hostium intrā moenia atque adeō in senātū vidētis intestīnam aliquam cotīdiē perniciem reī pūblicae mōlientem. Sī tē iam,[9] Catilīna, comprehendī, sī interficī iusserō, crēdō,[6] erit verendum mihi nē nōn hoc potius omnēs bonī sērius ā mē
20 quam quisquam crūdēlius factum esse dīcat.[10] Vērum ego hoc quod iam prīdem factum esse oportuit certā[11] dē causā nōndum addūcor ut faciam. Tum dēnique interficiēre cum iam nēmō[12] tam improbus, tam perditus, tam tuī similis invenīrī poterit quī id nōn iūre factum esse fateātur.[7] **6.** Quam diū quisquam erit quī tē dēfendere audeat, vīvēs, et vīvēs ita ut nunc vīvis,
25 multīs meīs et firmīs praesidiīs obsessus nē commovēre tē contrā rem pūblicam possīs. Multōrum tē etiam oculī et aurēs nōn sentientem,[13] sīcut adhūc fēcērunt, speculābuntur atque custōdient.

---

[1] should see to it
[2] any
[3] penalty of death
[4] in accordance with
[5] senators
[6] for inaction
[7] the mountain passes
[8] day by day (**singulōs** is not really needed)
[9] right now
[10] I suppose I shall have to fear, not that all good citizens may say that this was done too late by me, but rather that some one person may say that it was done too cruelly.
[11] specific, definite
[12] no one any longer (with **iam**)
[13] though you do not realize it (with **tē**)

---

[1] genitive of the whole with **quid**
[2] younger brother of Tiberius
[3] a round number; it was actually the eighteenth day
[4] Both infinitive and main verb are in the perfect for emphasis.
[5] Emphasis is gained by position and repetition.
[6] ironical; therefore the meaning is the opposite of what is stated
[7] result clause

The Temple of Julius Caesar was begun in 42 B.C. by Octavian to honor his uncle. After Caesar's assassination, his body was brought to this site and honored with a funeral pyre. Built on the spot where he was cremated, the temple and its altar were finally consecrated 13 years later in 29 B.C. You can see the remains of this Temple at the far left on page 9.

Literary Style: Irony and Chiasmus

Irony consists of saying one thing but meaning the opposite. In Cicero it serves to produce a laugh at Catiline's expense. Usually an ironical statement is introduced by **crēdō,** I *suppose,* as in this reading, **scīlicet** or **vidēlicet,** *of course.*

As a rule, series of words are arranged in parallel order, as in lines 6-7 on p. 70:

$$\overset{a}{\text{L. Sāturnīnum}} \ \overset{b}{\text{tribūnum plēbis}} \ \text{et} \ \overset{a}{\text{C. Servīlium}} \ \overset{b}{\text{praetōrem.}}$$

But Cicero at times uses a cross order with striking effect, as in line 16:

$$\overset{a}{\text{castrōrum}} \ \overset{b}{\text{imperātōrem}} \ \overset{b}{\text{ducemque}} \ \overset{a}{\text{hostium.}}$$

This is called chiasmus, from the Greek letter **chī,** formed like an *X,* from two crossed lines.

⟨⟨⟨ TRANSLATION ⟩⟩⟩

1. There will be no one who will dare speak for Catiline.
2. If any harm is done to the state, the fault will be Catiline's.
3. It is our good fortune that few men like Catiline live in Rome.
4. The senate decreed that Catiline should not be allowed to be present.

We Know Your Plans, Catiline

Verba Ūtilia: amplus, atrōx, coetus, cōnfīdō, domus, etenim, īnfitior, lūx, nefārius, nocturnus, oblīvīscor, pariēs, plānē, sentiō, undique

III. Etenim quid est, Catilīna, quod iam amplius exspectēs, sī neque nox tenebrīs obscūrāre coetūs nefāriōs nec prīvāta domus parietibus continēre vōcēs coniūrātiōnis tuae potest, sī illūstrantur, sī ērumpunt omnia? Mūtā iam istam mentem, mihi crēde, oblīvīscere caedis atque incendiōrum.
5 Tenēris undique; lūce sunt clāriōra nōbīs tua cōnsilia omnia, quae iam mēcum licet recognōscās.[1] 7. Meministīne mē ante diem XII Kalendās Novembrīs[1] dīcere[2] in senātū fore[3] in armīs certō diē, quī diēs futūrus esset[2] ante diem VI Kal. Novembrīs, C. Mānlium, audāciae satellitem atque administrum tuae?[4] Num mē fefellit, Catilīna, nōn modo rēs tanta, tam atrōx
10 tamque incrēdibilis, vērum, id quod multō magis est admīrandum, diēs? Dīxī ego īdem[3] in senātū caedem tē optimātium[4] contulisse in[5] ante diem V

[1] *you may review* (literally, *it is permitted that you review*)
[2] *which was going to be*
[3] *likewise* (literally, *the same I*)
[4] *the optimates,* (the conservative party in power)

---

[1] October 21
[2] **Meministī** is a perfect form, though we translate it with a present.
[3] =**futūrum esse**; the subject, **Mānlium,** follows
[4] an interesting type of chiasmus; **tuae audāciae** belongs with both of the nouns
[5] The entire following phrase is the object of **in.**

Kalendās Novembrīs, tum cum multī prīncipēs cīvitātis Rōmā nōn tam suī cōnservandī[5] quam tuōrum cōnsiliōrum reprimendōrum causā profūgērunt. Num īnfitiārī potes tē illō ipsō diē meīs praesidiīs, meā dīligentiā circum- clūsum commovēre tē contrā rem pūblicam nōn potuisse, cum tū discessū 15 cēterōrum, nostrā tamen quī remānsissēmus caede contentum tē esse dīcēbās?[6] **8.** Quid?[7] Cum tē Praeneste Kalendīs ipsīs Novembribus occupātūrum noc- turnō impetū esse cōnfīderēs, sēnsistīn[8] illam colōniam meō iussū meīs praesidiīs, custōdiīs, vigiliīs esse mūnītam? Nihil agis, nihil mōlīris, nihil cōgitās quod nōn ego nōn modo audiam sed etiam videam plānēque sentiam. 20

[5] *for the sake of saving themselves* (an illogical singular modifying **suī**, which actually is plural)
[6] *when on the departure of the others you said you were satisfied with the murder of (those of) us who remained*
[7] *Listen!*
[8] = **sēnsistīne**

Literary Style: Correlatives

All authors make some use of correlatives, that is, of conjunctions and adverbs used in pairs, to form balanced clauses. But Cicero is particularly fond of this stylistic device. Among the correlatives he uses are: **et... et, neque (nec)... neque (nec), aut... aut, vel... vel.** These should be well known to you from your previous reading. Others are:

cum (etsī)... tamen	*although . . . nevertheless*
cum(tum)... tum	*not only . . . but also*
nōn modo (sōlum)... sed (vērum)	*not only . . . but also*
sīve... sīve	*if . . . or if*
tam... quam	*so . . . as*
tot... quot	*so many . . . as*

Find three examples of correlatives in the preceding passage; also two examples of anaphora.

 **TRANSLATION**

1. Catiline did nothing which Cicero did not know.
2. I shall never forget the murders which you were planning.
3. Not only Catiline but also many others were plotting against the state.
4. Although you plan to kill us all, nevertheless we will be able to defend ourselves.

Word Studies

Explain *atrocity, fallacious, illustrious, incendiarism, mutation, pari- etal, satellite.*

tium, interitus, obscūrus, paulum,
...tus, taceō, tandem, vigilō, vulnerō

[1] *I ask you*
[2] *soon* (as always with the ...)
[3] *last night*
[4] *Scythemaker's Street* (such ... names used to be common ... *Barbieri* (*Barbers*), *Falegn...* (*Carpenters*), etc., in mod... Rome)
[5] *Why?*
[6] *where in the world*
[7] *of all of us*
[8] *scarcely, almost before*
[9] *to greet* (important people had many callers early in the morning)
[10] *at that time* (adverbial)

...ctem illam superiōrem; iam[2] intel-
...m quam tē ad perniciem reī pūbli-
...falcāriōs[4]—nōn agam obscūrē—in
...m₂ complūrīs eiusdem āmentiae
...Quid[5] tacēs? Convincam, sī negās.
...ī quī tēcum ūnā₃ fuērunt. **9.** Ō dī
...Quam rem pūblicam habēmus? In
...numerō, patrēs cōnscrīptī, in hōc
orbis terrae sānctissimō gravissimōque cōnsiliō, quī dē nostrō omnium[7]
10 interitū, quī dē huius urbis atque adeō dē orbis terrārum exitiō cōgitent.
Hōs ego videō cōnsul et dē rē pūblicā sententiam rogō, et quōs ferrō
trucīdārī oportēbat, eōs nōndum vōce vulnerō! Fuistī₄ igitur apud Laecam
illā nocte, Catilīna, distribuistī partīs Italiae, statuistī quō quemque proficīscī
placēret, dēlēgistī quōs Rōmae relinquerēs,₅ quōs tēcum ēdūcerēs, dīscrīp-
15 sistī urbis partīs ad incendia, cōnfirmāstī tē ipsum iam esse exitūrum, dīxistī paulum tibi esse etiam nunc morae₆ quod ego vīverem. Repertī sunt
duo equitēs Rōmānī quī tē istā cūrā līberārent₅ et sē illā ipsā nocte paulō
ante lūcem mē in meō lectō interfectūrōs esse pollicērentur. **10.** Haec ego
omnia, vixdum[8] etiam coetū vestrō dīmissō, comperī;₇ domum meam
20 maiōribus praesidiīs mūnīvī atque firmāvī, exclūsī eōs quōs tū ad mē
salūtātum[9] māne mīserās, cum illī ipsī vēnissent quōs₈ ego iam multīs ac
summīs virīs ad mē id temporis[10] ventūrōs esse praedīxeram.

Literary Style: Two's and Three's

Cicero often uses words, phrases, and clauses in groups of two and three. For example, there are three questions in lines 7-8 of the preceding chapter. Next is a series of pairs: **hīc, hīc; in numerō, in cōnsiliō; sānctissimō, gravissimō; quī dē interitū, quī dē exitiō; urbis, orbis**

₁ When **domus** has an adjective or genitive modifier, **in** or **ad** may be used.
₂ adverb
₃ adverb
₄ Cicero suddenly turns to Catiline, and rapidly fires seven bullets, so to speak, at him: the seven verbs at the beginning of their clauses all end in –**stī**.
₅ purpose
₆ with **paulum**
₇ through Fulvia, who got the information from Curius, one of Catiline's men
₈ subject of **ventūrōs esse**

terrārum. Then we find three clauses with the verbs **videō, rogō, vulnerō.** As often occurs, the last clause is longer and more complicated. Finally come the seven verbs mentioned in footnote 4. The first verb is introductory, setting the stage for the other six, that is, giving the meeting place of the conspirators. The others tell what was done. The first two verbs go together; they tell about dividing up Italy and assigning persons to various regions. The next pair of verbs assigns men to Rome and divides up the city for burning. Within this pair of verbs is another kind of pair, the two **quōs** clauses. The last pair indicates that Catiline is leaving Rome but is being delayed by the fact that Cicero is still alive.

TRANSLATION

1. Where in the world were you last night?
2. There are men in this city who are preparing to burn it.
3. Catiline sent men to various parts of Italy to occupy all the cities.
4. We believe that Catiline brings too much danger and Cicero brings little protection.

Get Out of Rome, Catiline

Verba Ūtilia: aliquandō, calamitās, comes, concitō, cōnor, dīligentia, ēgredior, exsilium, īnfestus, mūrus, pergō, sinō, tumultus, ūtilis, versō

V. Quae cum ita sint,[1] Catilīna, perge quō coepistī: ēgredere aliquandō ex urbe; patent portae; proficīscere. Nimium diū tē imperātōrem tua[1] illa Mānliāna castra dēsīderant. Ēdūc tēcum etiam omnīs tuōs, sī minus,[2] quam plūrimōs; purgā urbem. Magnō mē metū līberāveris, modo[3] inter mē atque tē mūrus intersit. Nōbīscum versārī iam diūtius nōn potes; nōn feram, nōn 5 patiar, nōn sinam.[2] **11.** Magna[3] dīs immortālibus habenda est atque[4] huic ipsī Iovī Statōrī,[4] antīquissimō custōdī huius urbis, grātia, quod hanc tam taetram, tam horribilem tamque īnfestam reī pūblicae pestem totiēns iam effūgimus. Nōn est saepius[5] in ūnō homine summa salūs perīclitanda reī pūblicae. Quam diū mihi cōnsulī dēsignātō, Catilīna, īnsidiātus es, nōn 10 pūblicō mē praesidiō, sed prīvātā dīligentiā dēfendī. Cum proximīs comitiīs[6] cōnsulāribus mē cōnsulem in campō[7] et competītōrēs tuōs interficere

[1] of yours
[2] not
[3] provided that
[4] and especially
[5] too often
[6] at the last consular elections
[7] Campus Martius

[1] A common form of expression, which can be translated by the one word *therefore.*
[2] anaphora and a group of three
[3] Placing the adjective first and separating it from its noun **grātia** gives unusual emphasis, so that **magna** really means **maxima.**
[4] Cicero points to a statue of Jupiter *the Stayer,* who stayed the flight of the Romans when Romulus appealed to him.

voluistī, compressī cōnātūs tuōs nefāriōs amīcōrum praesidiō et cōpiīs, nūllō tumultū pūblicē concitātō; dēnique, quotiēnscumque mē petīstī, per

15 mē tibi obstitī, quamquam vidēbam perniciem meam cum magnā calamitāte reī pūblicae esse coniūnctam. **12.** Nunc iam[8] apertē rem pūblicam ūniversam petis, templa deōrum immortālium, tēcta urbis, vītam₅ omnium cīvium, Italiam tōtam ad exitium et vāstitātem vocās. Quārē, quoniam id₆ quod est prīmum, et quod huius imperī[9] disciplīnaeque maiōrum proprium

20 est, facere nōndum audeō, faciam id quod est ad[10] sevēritātem lēnius, ad commūnem salūtem ūtilius. Nam sī tē interficī iusserō, residēbit in rē pūblicā reliqua coniūrātōrum manus; sīn tū, quod tē iam dūdum hortor, exieris, exhauriētur ex urbe tuōrum comitum magna et perniciōsa sentīna[11] reī pūblicae. **13.** Quid est, Catilīna? Num dubitās id, mē imperante, facere

25 quod iam tuā sponte faciēbās?[12] Exīre ex urbe iubet cōnsul hostem.₇ Interrogās mē, num[13] in exsilium? Nōn iubeō, sed, sī mē cōnsulis, suādeō.

Literary Style: Alliteration

A familiar device in many languages, and especially in poetry, is alliteration, the repetition of the same letter at the beginning of successive words: line 11, **pūblicō mē praesidiō sed prīvātā**; lines 11-13, **comitiīs cōnsulāribus mē cōnsulem in campō et competītōrēs... compressī cōnātūs.**

Find two other examples of alliteration in the preceding reading.

You may recall reading the most striking example in all Latin, used by the poet Ennius: **Ō Tite tūte Tatī, tibi tanta, tyranne, tulistī.** In English there is the familiar: *Peter Piper picked a peck of pickled peppers.* Here is another Latin example: **Sōsia in sōlāriō soleās sarciēbat suās,** *Sosia was sewing his shoes in the solarium.*

How is alliteration like anaphora? Different from anaphora? Find another example of anaphora and a group of three (besides the one in footnote 2).

⟐ TRANSLATION ⟐

1. Depart at once, Catiline, in order to save your life.
2. I have long been urging you to leave the city, Catiline.
3. If you were to remain in Rome, I would not be able to protect you.
4. If Catiline will not leave Rome, his life will be in the greatest danger.

Word Studies

Explain *conjunction, exhaust, exhortation, insidious, intramural, nefarious, purgatory, residue.*

₅ We say *lives* in English; in Latin the plural means *biographies.*
₆ object of **facere**
₇ Calling Catiline a foreign enemy was a deliberate part of Cicero's plan to make it easier to get rid of him. In section 3 he calls him a dangerous citizen, worse than a bitter enemy; in 5, in connection with Manlius' camp at Faesulae he says that the enemy is increasing in number and calls Catiline their commander, as he does again in 10.

Catiline's Criminal Career

Verba Ūtilia: dēdecus, dēvoveō, ēlābor, facinus, ferrum, flāgitium, haereō, necesse, ōdī, omittō, praetermittō, prīdiē, sacer, turpitūdō, vitium

VI. Quid est enim, Catilīna, quod tē iam in hāc urbe dēlectāre possit? In quā nēmō est extrā istam coniūrātiōnem perditōrum hominum quī tē nōn metuat, nēmō quī nōn ōderit. Quae nota domesticae turpitūdinis nōn inusta vītae tuae est? Quod prīvātārum rērum dēdecus nōn haeret in fāmā? Quae libīdō ab oculīs, quod facinus ā manibus tuīs, quod flāgitium ā tōtō corpore 5 āfuit? Cui tū adulēscentulō[1] quem corruptēlārum illecebrīs irrētīssēs nōn aut ad audāciam ferrum aut ad libīdinem facem praetulistī? **14.** Quid vērō? Nūper cum[2] morte speriōris uxōris novīs nūptiīs locum vacuēfēcissēs, nōnne etiam aliō incrēdibilī scelere[3] hoc scelus cumulāvistī? Quod ego praetermittō et facile patior silērī, nē in hāc cīvitāte tantī facinoris immānitās[1] 10 aut exstitisse aut nōn vindicāta esse videātur. Praetermittō ruīnās fortūnārum tuārum quās omnīs proximīs Īdibus[4] tibi impendēre sentiēs. Ad illa veniō quae nōn ad prīvātam ignōminiam vitiōrum tuōrum, nōn ad domesticam tuam difficultātem ac turpitūdinem, sed ad summam rem pūblicam[2] atque ad omnium nostrum vītam salūtemque pertinent. **15.** Potestne tibi haec lūx, 15 Catilīna, aut huius caelī spīritus esse iūcundus, cum sciās esse hōrum nēminem quī nesciat tē prīdiē[3] Kalendās Iānuāriās, Lepidō et Tullō cōnsulibus, stetisse in comitiō cum tēlō, manum[4] cōnsulum et prīncipum cīvitātis interficiendōrum causā parāvisse, scelerī[5] ac furōrī tuō nōn mentem[5] aliquam aut timōrem tuum sed Fortūnam populī Rōmānī obstitisse? Ac iam illa 20 omittō—neque enim sunt aut obscūra aut nōn multa commissa posteā— quotiēns tū mē dēsignātum, quotiēns vērō cōnsulem interficere cōnātus es! Quot ego tuās petītiōnēs[6] ita coniectās ut vītārī posse nōn vidērentur parvā quādam dēclīnātiōne et, ut aiunt, corpore[7] effūgī! Nihil agis, nihil asse- queris, neque tamen cōnārī ac velle dēsistis. **16.** Quotiēns iam tibi[8] extorta 25 est ista sīca dē manibus, quotiēns excidit cāsū aliquō et ēlāpsa est! Quae[6] quidem quibus[9][7] abs tē initiāta sacrīs ac dēvōta sit nesciō, quod[10] eam necesse putās esse in cōnsulis corpore dēfīgere.

1 *this savage crime*
2 *the greatest public interests*
3 *the day before January 1* (the allusion is to Catiline's "first conspiracy," three years earlier)
4 *a band (handful)* (object of **parāvisse**)
5 *(change of) mind*
6 *thrusts* (he is comparing Catiline to a gladiator)
7 *with a kind of little twist of the body*
8 *your* (with **manibus**)
9 *with what rites*
10 *(seeing) that*

---

1 with **praetulistī:** *Before what young man have you not carried the sword for bold deeds or the torch for passion?*
2 conjunction
3 The supposed murder of his only son, done to please his second wife, as the historian Sallust tells us.
4 Debts were payable on the Kalends (first of the month) and Ides (thirteenth or fifteenth of the month). In six days therefore (November 13) Catiline would find himself besieged by creditors.
5 with **obstitisse**
6 i.e., **sīca**
7 The dagger was promised to some god if it performed successfully through the god's aid.

Literary Style: Metaphor

A metaphor is an implied comparison; it identifies one person, object, or idea with another. It is the most common figure of speech and one that is used in many different ways. For example, a metaphor is often used in naming things. The words *car, machine,* and *wagon,* which existed long before the invention of the automobile, were at first metaphorically applied to this vehicle.

The comparison in the literary metaphor usually appeals to the senses, as Cicero's many metaphors indicate. In line 3 of the preceding reading, **nōta... inusta** implies a comparison with the branding of the letter *F* on the forehead of a runaway slave. But Catiline's branding is figurative, not literal. In lines 6-8 Catiline is compared metaphorically with a slave (footnote 1). Near the end of the preceding chapter is another striking metaphor: Catiline's supporters are *sewage,* which *will be drained out* of Rome.

 **TRANSLATION**

1. Who is it that blocked your plans?
2. I can recall no one who does not hate and fear Catiline.
3. Everybody knows that you prepared a band of men for the purpose of killing the senators.

Word Studies

The calendar is so called because its chief function was to indicate the Kalends, the first of the month. In Latin the spelling with a *K* is used only in this and a few other words before *a.* It goes back to the Etruscans, from whom the Romans borrowed the alphabet.

Your Country Begs You to Leave

Verba Ūtilia: abhorreō, caedēs, careō, cōnspiciō, cōnsulāris, ēvertō, inānis, ineō, opīnor, opprimō, plācō, salūtō, socius, tacitus, vītō

VII. Nunc vērō quae tua est ista vīta? Sīc enim iam tēcum loquar, nōn ut odiō permōtus esse videar, quō[1] dēbeō, sed ut[1] misericordiā, quae tibi nūlla[2] dēbētur. Vēnistī paulō ante in senātum. Quis tē ex hāc tantā frequentiā, tot ex tuīs amīcīs ac necessāriīs salūtāvit? Sī hoc post hominum memoriam contigit nēminī, vōcis[2] exspectās contumēliam, cum sīs gravissimō iūdiciō 5 taciturnitātis oppressus? Quid, quod[3] adventū tuō ista[4] subsellia vacuēfacta sunt, quod omnēs cōnsulārēs quī tibi persaepe ad caedem cōnstitūtī fuērunt, simul atque[5] assēdistī, partem istam subselliōrum nūdam atque inānem relīquērunt, quō tandem animō tibi ferendum putās? **17.** Servī mehercule meī sī mē istō pactō metuerent ut tē metuunt omnēs cīvēs tuī, domum 10 meam relinquendam putārem; tū tibi urbem[3] nōn arbitrāris? Et sī mē meīs cīvibus iniūriā[6] suspectum tam graviter atque offēnsum vidērem, carēre mē aspectū[4] cīvium quam[7] īnfestīs omnium oculīs cōnspicī māllem; tū, cum cōnscientiā scelerum tuōrum agnōscās odium omnium iūstum et iam diū tibi dēbitum, dubitās quōrum mentīs sēnsūsque vulnerās, eōrum aspectum 15 praesentiamque vītāre? Sī tē parentēs timērent atque ōdissent tuī neque eōs ratiōne ūllā placāre possēs, ut opīnor, ab eōrum oculīs aliquō[8] concēderēs. Nunc tē patria, quae commūnis est parēns omnium nostrum, ōdit ac metuit et iam diū nihil tē iūdicat nisi dē parricīdiō suō cōgitāre; huius tū neque auctoritātem verēbere nec iūdicium sequēre nec vim pertimēscēs? **18.** Quae[5] 20 tēcum, Catilīna, sīc agit et quōdam modō tacita[9] loquitur: "Nūllum iam aliquot annīs facinus exstitit nisi per tē, nūllum flāgitium sine tē; tibi ūnī multōrum cīvium necēs,[6] tibi vexātiō dīreptiōque sociōrum[7] impūnīta fuit ac lībera; tū nōn sōlum ad neglegendās lēgēs et quaestiōnēs vērum etiam ad ēvertendās perfingendāsque valuistī. Superiōra illa, quamquam ferenda 25 nōn fuērunt, tamen ut[10] potuī, tulī; nunc vērō mē tōtam[11] esse in metū propter ūnum tē, quicquid increpuerit,[12] Catilīnam timērī, nūllum vidērī contrā mē cōnsilium inīrī posse quod ā tuō scelere abhorreat[13] nōn est ferendum.[8] Quam ob rem discēde atque hunc mihi timōrem ēripe; sī est vērus, nē opprimar, sīn falsus, ut tandem aliquandō timēre dēsinam." 30

---

[1] *with which I ought to be*

[2] *spoken (literally, of the voice)*

[3] *What (of the fact) that?*

[4] *those next to you (Cicero perhaps pointed)*

[5] **simul atque,** *as soon as*

[6] *unjustly*

[7] *than*

[8] *somewhere (adverb)*

[9] *though silent*

[10] *as (best as)*

[11] *all of me (Chiasmus, with strong emphasis, in* **mē tōtam... ūnum tē***)*

[12] *at the slightest noise (literally, whatever noise is made)*

[13] *is inconsistent with*

---

[1] Supply **permōtus esse videar.**

[2] more emphatic than **nōn**

[3] Supply **relinquendam esse.**

[4] with **carēre**

[5] i.e., **patria**

[6] Catiline had taken part in the murders of Sulla's day.

[7] Catiline was charged with graft while propraetor in Africa in 67 B.C.

[8] **Esse, timērī, vidērī** are the subjects.

Literary Style: Personification

Personification makes a person out of a thing. In the reading, the long speech of **patria**, "though silent speaking," is a fine example.

Watch for the groups of two's and three's. In the preceding chapter (line 2) we find two **ut** clauses, each containing a relative clause. Then we come to **ex... frequentiā** and **ex... amīcīs**. Note how the second phrase is expanded into a pair: **amīcīs ac necessāriīs**. Next are two **quod** clauses (lines 6-7) and two adjectives, **nūdam** and **inānem**.

Note too the chiastic arrangement of the verbs (lines 10, 12-13, 15-16): **metuerent ut tē metuunt, carēre... mālem** but **dubitās... vītāre.**

Analyze the speech of **patria** in this way.

❧ TRANSLATION ❧

1. If my citizens had feared me so much, I would have left the city at once.
2. The senators left bare that section of seats in which Catiline was sitting.
3. Cicero talks in this manner to Catiline in order that he may seem to be moved by pity.

Word Studies

Explain *contumely, impunity, inane, parricide, placate, vulnerable.*

The suffix **–scō** is added to the stems of verbs and adjectives to form *inceptive* verbs, which have in them the idea of *begin to* (from **incipiō**, *begin*): **pertimēscō**, *begin to fear.* **Hebēscō**, *begin to be dull,* occurred earlier.

On Your Way, Catiline

Verba Ūtilia: carcer, ecquis, fuga, honestus, quiēscō, sodālis, vidēlicet, vīlis, vindicō, voluntās

VIII, 19. Haec sī tēcum, ut dīxī, patria loquātur, nōnne impetrāre dēbeat, etiam sī vim adhibēre nōn possit? Quid, quod tū tē in custōdiam[1] dedistī, quod vītandae suspīciōnis causā ad[1] M'.[2] Lepidum tē habitāre velle dīxistī? Ā quō nōn receptus etiam ad mē venīre ausus es, atque ut domī meae tē
5 asservārem rogāstī. Cum ā mē quoque id respōnsum tulissēs, mē nūllō modō posse īsdem parietibus[3] tūtō esse tēcum, quia magnō in perīculō essem quod īsdem moenibus[4] continērēmur, ad Q. Metellum praetōrem

---

[1] = apud
[2] = Mānium
[3] *within the same walls*
[4] *city walls*, contrasting with **parietibus**, *house walls*

---

1 Catiline asked Lepidus to agree to be responsible for Catiline's appearance in court when and if Catiline was wanted.

One arch and two columns are all that remain of the Basilica Aemilia, which was built by
Emilius Lepidus and Fulvius Nobilior in 179 B.C. Overlooking the central square of the Forum
and facing the Temple of Julius Caesar, it had at least two stories and was especially beautiful.
In front of the building and toward the right in the photo, is a small area marked off with a
low iron fence that marks the spot where the **Cloāca Maxima,** *the major sewer line that*
drained the marshy land of Rome, entered the Forum.

⁵ = iūdicāverit
⁶ *that it votes* (literally, *that it is pleasing to it*)
⁷ *word*
⁸ *at all*
⁹ *violent hands*
¹⁰ *all this* (the temple and the Forum)

vēnistī. Ā quō repudiātus ad sodālem tuum, virum optimum,₂ M. Metellum dēmigrāstī, quem tū vidēlicet et ad custōdiendum tē dīligentissimum et ad
10 suspicandum sagācissimum et ad vindicandum fortissimum fore putāstī. Sed quam longē vidētur ā carcere atque ā vinculīs abesse dēbēre quī sē ipse iam dignum custōdiā iūdicārit?⁵ **20.** Quae cum ita sint, Catilīna, dubitās, sī ēmorī aequō animō nōn potes, abīre in aliquās terrās et vītam istam multīs suppliciīs iūstīs dēbitīsque ēreptam fugae sōlitūdinīque mandāre?

15 "Refer," inquis, "ad senātum;"₃ id enim postulās et, sī hic ōrdō₄ placēre⁶ sibi dēcrēverit tē īre in exsilium, obtemperātūrum tē esse dīcis. Nōn referam, id quod abhorret ā meīs mōribus, et tamen faciam ut intellegās quid hī dē tē sentiant. Ēgredere ex urbe, Catilīna; līberā rem pūblicam metū; in exsilium, sī hanc vōcem⁷ exspectās, proficīscere.₅ Quid est? Ecquid⁸
20 attendis, ecquid animadvertis hōrum silentium? Patiuntur, tacent. Quid exspectās auctōritātem loquentium, quōrum voluntātem tacitōrum perspicis? **21.** At sī hoc idem huic adulēscentī optimō P. Sēstiō, sī fortissimō virō M. Mārcellō dīxissem, iam mihi cōnsulī hōc ipsō in templō senātus iūre optimō vim⁹ et manūs intulisset. Dē tē autem, Catilīna, cum quiēscunt,
25 probant, cum patiuntur, dēcernunt, cum tacent, clāmant,₆ neque hī sōlum quōrum tibi auctōritās est vidēlicet cāra, vīta vīlissima, sed etiam illī equitēs Rōmānī, honestissimī atque optimī virī, cēterīque fortissimī cīvēs quī circumstant senātum, quōrum tū et frequentiam vidēre et studia perspicere et vōcēs paulō ante₇ exaudīre potuistī. Quōrum₈ ego vix abs tē iam diū manūs
30 ac tēla contineō, eōsdem facile addūcam ut tē haec¹⁰ quae vāstāre iam prīdem studēs relinquentem usque ad portās prōsequantur.

Literary Style: Antithesis

Cicero often "sets" words and phrases "against" each other (that is what the Greek word antithesis means). In lines 24–25 **quiēscunt** and **probant** are antithetical, as are **patiuntur** and **dēcernunt, tacent** and **clāmant.** The last pair of verbs illustrates oxymoron, a figure of speech that is nothing more than an antithesis in which the words contradict each other.

Find other antitheses in the preceding reading. Find an instance of alliteration.

₂ **Vidēlicet** shows that this and the following adjectives are ironical.
₃ Presumably Catiline interrupted with this demand.
₄ i.e., the senate
₅ Cicero evidently paused a moment here. The senate could not exile Catiline, but Cicero cleverly maintains that it voted for exile by silence.
₆ another striking oxymoron
₇ Catiline was presumably booed when he entered the senate.
₈ The antecedent, **eōsdem,** follows.

1. If you should flee from Rome the whole world would rejoice.
2. He said that he could not stay in the same city because he was afraid.
3. A man who thinks he can fight against the senate should be sent into exile.
4. Do you believe that Catiline is worthy of the honor of coming into the senate?

Word Studies

Explain *abhorrent, incarcerate, quiescent, sagacious, vile, vindicate.*
Viz. is an abbreviation of **vidēlicet.** The *z* is not really the letter *z* but a sign of abbreviation.

Catiline Wants Civil War

Verba Ūtilia: corrigō, dexter, invidia, iussū, meditor, mōlēs, nex, pertimēscō, poena, quamquam, sēcernō, serviō, sīn, tametsī, utinam

IX, 22. Quamquam[1] quid loquor? Tē ut[2] ūlla rēs frangat, tū ut umquam tē corrigās, tū ut ūllam fugam meditēre, tū ut ūllum exsilium cōgitēs? Utinam tibi istam mentem dī immortālēs duint![1] Tametsī[3] videō, sī meā vōce perterritus īre in exsilium animum indūxeris,[4] quanta tempestās invidiae nōbīs, sī minus[5] in[6] praesēns tempus recentī memoriā scelerum tuōrum, at[7] in posteritātem impendeat. Sed est tantī,[8] dum modo tua ista sit prīvāta calamitās et ā reī pūblicae perīculīs sēiungātur. Sed tū ut vitiīs tuīs commoveāre, ut lēgum poenās pertimēscās, ut temporibus[9] reī pūblicae cēdās nōn est postulandum. Neque enim is[2] es, Catilīna, ut tē aut pudor ā turpitūdine aut metus ā perīculō aut ratiō ā furōre revocārit. **23.** Quam ob rem, ut saepe iam dīxī, proficīscere ac, sī mihi, inimīcō, ut praedicās, tuō, cōnflāre vīs invidiam, rēctā perge in exsilium; vix feram sermōnēs hominum, sī id fēceris, vix mōlem istīus invidiae, sī in exsilium iussū cōnsulis īveris, sustinēbō. Sīn autem servīre meae laudī[3] et glōriae māvīs, ēgredere[4] cum importūnā scelerātōrum manū, cōnfer tē ad Mānlium, concitā perditōs cīvīs, sēcerne tē ā bonīs, īnfer patriae bellum, exsultā impiō latrōciniō, ut ā mē nōn ēiectus ad aliēnōs, sed invītātus ad tuōs īsse

[1] *And yet*
[2] *How could anything crush you?*
[3] *And yet*
[4] *bring yourself* (literally, *bring your mind*)
[5] *if not*
[6] *for*
[7] *at any rate*
[8] *it is worth it*
[9] *critical needs*

---

[1] an early form for **dent**
[2] = **tālis,** followed by a result clause
[3] dative with **servīre**
[4] six imperatives, arranged in three pairs according to the thought

videāris. **24.** Quamquam quid ego tē invītem,[10] ā quō [5] iam sciam esse prae-
missōs quī [6] tibi ad Forum Aurēlium praestōlārentur armātī, cui sciam
20 pactam et cōnstitūtam cum Mānliō diem,[7] ā quō etiam aquilam illam[11] [8]
argenteam, quam tibi ac tuīs omnibus cōnfīdō perniciōsam ac fūnestam
futūram, cui domī tuae sacrārium scelerum cōnstitūtum fuit, sciam esse
praemissam? Tū ut illā carēre diūtius possīs quam venerārī ad caedem
proficīscēns solēbās, ā cuius altāribus saepe istam impiam dexteram ad
25 necem cīvium trānstulistī?

Literary Style: Asyndeton

Asyndeton (a Greek word meaning "not bound together") is the omission
of coordinate conjunctions in a series of words or phrases. This omission
of the connective gives a staccato ("detached") or sharp effect. The six
unconnected imperatives in lines 15–16 are an example of asyndeton.

Find a metaphor in the preceding reading.

 TRANSLATION

1. Oh that the gods would cause Catiline to fear!
2. Do they prefer to stay in Rome or to go to Faesulae?
3. Why should we ask you to stay in this town in which there is so much
   danger?

Word Studies

Explain *aquiline, argentiferous, exultation, fracture, meditation,
molecule.*

Explain the force of the prefix **sē–** in **sēcernō** and **sēiungō**, of **per–** in
pertimēscō, and of **prae–** in **praemittō**.

---

[5] The antecedent is **tē**; causal relative clause.
[6] Supply the antecedent (**virōs**).
[7] October 27
[8] So called because it once had belonged to Marius; the fact that this emblem of a Roman
legion had already been sent from Rome shows that Catiline would soon follow.

Catiline, The Hardened Criminal

Verba Ūtilia: āmentia, cōnsulātus, cupiditās, exerceō, exsultō, famēs, frīgus, iam prīdem, inopia, marītus, obeō, praeclārus, rapiō, somnus, spēs

X, 25. Ībis tandem aliquandō quō tē iam prīdem tua ista cupiditās effrēnāta ac furiōsa rapiēbat; neque enim tibi haec rēs[1] affert dolōrem sed quandam incrēdibilem voluptātem. Ad hanc tē āmentiam nātūra peperit, voluntās exercuit, fortūna servāvit. Numquam tū nōn modo[1] ōtium sed nē bellum quidem nisi nefārium concupīstī. Nactus es ex perditīs atque[2] ab 5 omnī nōn modo Fortūnā[3] vērum etiam spē dērelīctīs cōnflātam[4] improbōrum manum. **26.** Hīc[2] tū quā laetitiā perfruēre, quibus gaudiīs exsultābis, quantā in voluptāte bacchābere, cum in tantō numerō tuōrum neque audiēs virum bonum quemquam neque vidēbis! Ad huius vītae studium meditātī[3] illī sunt quī feruntur[4] labōrēs tuī, iacēre[5] humī nōn 10 sōlum ad obsidendum stuprum[5] vērum etiam ad facinus obeundum, vigilāre nōn sōlum īnsidiantem somnō marītōrum vērum etiam bonīs ōtiōsōrum. Habēs ubi[6] ostentēs tuam illam praeclāram patientiam famis, frīgoris, inopiae rērum omnium quibus tē brevī tempore cōnfectum esse sentiēs. **27.** Tantum prōfēcī, cum tē ā cōnsulātū reppulī,[6] ut exsul potius 15 temptāre quam cōnsul vexāre rem pūblicam possēs, atque ut id quod esset ā tē scelerātē susceptum latrōcinium potius quam bellum nōminārētur.

[1] *not only have you never*
[2] *Here* (i.e., with such followers)
[3] *those hardships were practiced*
[4] *which are told about*
[5] *to practice debauchery*
[6] *(an opportunity) where*

Literary Style: Climax and Word Play

Occasionally Cicero uses climax, a figure of speech in which ideas are arranged in the order of ascending intensity. A good example is in lines 7-8: **perfruēre**, *experience,* **exsultābis**, *exult in,* **bacchābere**, *revel in.* **Bacchābere** is a very stong word, meaning to act like a crazed follower of Bacchus, the god of wine.

Word play to us usually means punning for humorous effect. But Cicero often uses it seriously, even in the most solemn passages. In lines 15-17 the play on **exsul** and **cōnsul** is used very effectively, for Cicero had prevented Catiline from being elected **cōnsul** and now was forcing him to become an **exsul**.

---

[1] i.e., starting a civil war
[2] connects **perditīs** and **dērelīcitīs**
[3] That **Fortūna** is personified is shown by the use of **ab.**
[4] **ex... dērelīctīs** depends on **cōnflātam:** *composed of*
[5] in apposition with and explaining **labōrēs**
[6] Catiline had been a candidate for consul against Cicero.

1. Will you enjoy your exile, Catiline?
2. By preparing a camp in Italy you have produced woe for yourself.
3. In order that Catiline might realize what he had done, Cicero told him very plainly.

Word Studies

Distinguish **parō**, **pāreō**, **pariō**, and **parcō** by giving their principal parts and meanings.

Explain *adjacent, derelict, humus, somnolence.*

Why Don't You Act, Cicero?

Verba Ūtilia: ārdeō, cārus, cūnctus, dēficiō, dēprecor, gradus, inertia, iūs, penitus, quaesō

XI. Nunc, ut ā mē, patrēs cōnscrīptī, quandam prope iūstam patriae querimōniam dētester ac dēprecer,[1] percipite, quaesō, dīligenter quae dīcam,[1] et ea penitus animīs vestrīs mentibusque mandāte. Etenim sī mēcum patria, quae mihi vītā meā multō est cārior, sī cūncta Italia, sī omnis rēs pūblica
5 loquātur:[2] "M. Tullī, quid agis? Tūne[3] eum quem esse hostem comperistī, quem ducem bellī futūrum vidēs, quem exspectārī imperātōrem in castrīs hostium sentīs, auctōrem sceleris, prīncipem coniūrātiōnis, ēvocātōrem servōrum[4] et cīvium perditōrum, exīre patiēre, ut abs tē nōn ēmissus ex urbe, sed immissus in urbem esse videātur? Nōnne hunc in vincula dūcī,
10 nōn ad mortem rapī, nōn summō suppliciō mactārī imperābis?[5] Quid tandem tē impedit? Mōsne maiōrum? **28.** At[6] persaepe etiam prīvātī in hāc rē pūblicā perniciōsōs cīvīs morte multārunt. An lēgēs quae dē cīvium Rōmānōrum suppliciō rogātae sunt? At numquam in hāc urbe quī ā rē pūblicā dēfēcērunt cīvium iūra tenuērunt.[7] An invidiam posteritātis timēs?

[1] turn aside by entreaty and prayer
[2] should say

---

[1] future
[2] The long quotation caused Cicero to forget the conclusion of the condition.
[3] very emphatic, not only because it comes first but because it is so far removed from its verb (**patiēre**)
[4] Catiline was urged to recruit slaves but apparently did not do so. He was clever enough to realize that all Romans were opposed to this.
[5] An **ut** clause is usual with **imperō** but the infinitive may be used in its passive forms.
[6] **At** is often used like quotation marks to indicate a change of speaker.
[7] Here Cicero's strategy becomes clear: Catiline is no longer a citizen but a **hostis;** whether the **senātus cōnsultum ultimum** gave Cicero this right is still unsettled.

Praeclāram₈ vērō populō Rōmānō refers grātiam, quī tē, hominem per tē 15 cognitum, nūllā commendātiōne maiōrum₉ tam mātūrē ad summum imperium₁₀ per omnīs honōrum gradūs extulit, sī propter invidiam aut alicuius perīculī metum salūtem cīvium tuōrum neglegis. **29.** Sed sī quis est invidiae metus, nōn est vehementius sevēritātis[3] ac fortitūdinis invidia quam inertiae ac nequitiae pertimēscenda. An, cum bellō vāstābitur Italia, 20 vexābuntur urbēs, tēcta ārdēbunt, tum tē nōn exīstimās invidiae incendiō cōnflagrātūrum?"

[3] *resulting from severity* (with **invidia**); similarly **inertiae**

Literary Style: Rhythm

Cicero's prose has a definite rhythm, not so pronounced as that of verse but still easily recognizable, especially at the end of sentences. Two of the favorite endings are -˘-|-˘ and -˘˘˘|-˘. An example of the latter rhythm is **esse videātur**, a phrase which occurs very frequently; of the former, **cōnflagrātūrum** at the end of the chapter.

Find six examples of a series of three in the preceding reading.

Note the word play in **ēmissus** and **immissus** (lines 8-9).

Find one metaphor in the preceding reading.

 TRANSLATION

1. The country asked Cicero what he was doing.
2. Cicero says that his country is dearer to him than life.
3. If your country should say such things to you, how would you reply?
4. Do you not think you should seize a man who is making plans for destroying the city?

Word Studies

Explain *defector, deprecate, emissary, gradation, mulct.*

₈ emphatic and ironical

₉ Cicero was a **novus homō** in politics, for no ancestor of his had held a curule office. He became consul at the minimum age of 43.

₁₀ the consulship

Watchful Waiting

Verba Ūtilia: alō, dēleō, dissimulō, exstinguō, fateor, immineō, impendeō, intendō, iūdicō, paulisper, pestis, sanguis, sēmen, stultus, vōx

XII. Hīs ego sānctissimīs reī pūblicae vōcibus et eōrum hominum quī hoc idem sentiunt mentibus[1] pauca respondēbō. Ego, sī hoc optimum factū iūdicārem, patrēs cōnscrīptī, Catilīnam morte multārī, ūnīus ūsūram hōrae gladiātōrī[1] istī ad vīvendum nōn dedissem. Etenim sī summī virī et clāris-
5 simī cīvēs Sāturnīnī et Gracchōrum et Flaccī et superiōrum complūrium[2] sanguine nōn modo sē nōn contāminārunt sed etiam honestārunt, certē verendum mihi nōn erat[3] nē quid,[4] hōc parricīdā[2] cīvium interfectō, invidiae mihi in posteritātem redundāret. Quod sī ea[3] mihi maximē impendēret, tamen hōc animō fuī semper ut invidiam virtūte partam[4] glōriam, nōn
10 invidiam putārem.

30. Quamquam nōn nūllī sunt in hōc ōrdine quī aut ea quae imminent nōn videant aut ea quae vident dissimulent; quī spem Catilīnae mollibus sententiīs aluērunt coniūrātiōnemque nāscentem nōn crēdendō corrōborā-
vērunt; quōrum auctōritāte multī nōn sōlum improbī vērum etiam imperītī,
15 sī in hunc animadvertissem, crūdēliter et rēgiē[5] factum esse dīcerent. Nunc intellegō, sī iste, quō intendit, in Mānliāna castra pervēnerit,[6] nēminem tam stultum fore quī nōn videat coniūrātiōnem esse factam, nēminem tam improbum quī nōn fateātur. Hōc autem ūnō interfectō,[7] intellegō hanc reī pūblicae pestem paulisper reprimī, nōn in perpetuum comprimī posse.
20 Quod sī sēsē ēiecerit sēcumque suōs ēdūxerit et eōdem cēterōs undique collēctōs naufragōs[5] aggregārit, exstinguētur atque dēlēbitur nōn modo haec tam adulta reī pūblicae pestis vērum etiam stirps ac sēmen[6] malōrum omnium.

---

[1] (*unexpressed*) *thoughts*
[2] *of many men of earlier times*
[3] *I did not have to fear*
[4] *any unpopularity* (with **invidiae**)
[5] *wrecks, bums*
[6] *root and seed*

[1] We might say *prizefighter* or *bruiser;* Cicero practically called Catiline a gladiator once before.
[2] The ablative absolute has conditional force.
[3] i.e., **invidia**
[4] from **pariō;** two objects with **putō,** as with verbs of calling
[5] To call a man a king among the Romans was something like calling an American a derogatory name.
[6] Subjunctive in a subordinate clause in indirect discourse, but **intendit** is not subjunctive because the clause is parenthetical.
[7] conditional

The Cūria was the meeting place of the Senate, the most powerful group in Rome for several hundred years. The number of senators varied at times in history, but there were generally about 600 members, chosen from the patrician class. They decided governmental policies and how money should be spent. During the time of the kings, the senators were mainly an advisory group, but during the Republic, they were the main governing body. The Cūria was rebuilt a number of times, but still retained its original shape. Constantine in the early 4th century was the last emperor to refurbish it.

Literary Style: Cicero's Periodic Sentences

Contemporary writers of English, and their readers, generally prefer short sentences. In older English and in Ciceronian oratory, long, complex sentences, with phrases and clauses in groups of two and three, with anaphora, with asyndeton and other rhetorical devices, with the main thought not revealed until the end, were in great favor. The sentence just finished is an example of a period. We have read many such sentences in Cicero, e.g., page 77, line 15, **Potestne**; page 79, line 11, **Et sī mē**; page 86, line 5, **M. Tullī**. In the preceding reading we find **Etenim sī summī**.

Find an example of word play in the preceding reading.

TRANSLATION

1. I fear that he will kill all the citizens.
2. There were men in the senate who did not believe Cicero.
3. I do not know why you wish me to do what I do not want to do.
4. If Cicero had thought it worthwhile, he would have compelled Catiline to flee.

Word Studies

Give the derivation of **corrōborō, redundō, naufragus**.

Explain *imminent, impend, nascent, sanctify, sanguinary, seminal*.

Out with Them All!

Verba Ūtilia: auspicium, bibō, brevis, cūria, dēsinō, ērumpō, fax, foedus *(noun)*, fortasse, frōns (–tis), latrō, morbus, ōmen, patefaciō, societās

XIII, 31. Etenim iam diū, patrēs cōnscrīptī, in hīs perīculīs coniūrātiōnis īnsidiīsque versāmur, sed nesciō quō pactō[1] omnium scelerum ac veteris furōris et audāciae mātūritās in nostrī cōnsulātūs tempus ērūpit. Nunc sī ex tantō latrōciniō[2] iste ūnus tollētur, vidēbimur fortasse ad breve quoddam
5 tempus cūrā et metū esse relevātī, perīculum autem residēbit et erit inclūsum penitus in vēnīs atque in vīsceribus reī pūblicae. Ut saepe hominēs aegrī morbō gravī, cum[1] aestū febrīque[3] iactantur, sī aquam gelidam bibērunt, prīmō relevārī videntur, deinde multō gravius vehementiusque afflīctantur, sīc hic morbus quī est in rē pūblicā relevātus[2] istīus poenā

---

[1] *somehow (literally, I do not know how)*
[2] *(band of) robbers*
[3] *heat of fever*

---

[1] conjunction
[2] conditional, as is the ablative absolute that follows

vehementius, reliquīs vīvīs, ingravēscet. **32.** Quārē sēcēdant improbī,[3] sēcer-   10
nant sē ā bonīs, ūnum in locum congregentur, mūrō dēnique, quod[4] saepe
iam dīxī, sēcernantur ā nōbīs; dēsinant īnsidiārī domī suae cōnsulī,[4] cir-
cumstāre tribūnal praetōris urbānī, obsidēre cum gladiīs cūriam, malleolōs
et facēs[5] ad īnflammandam urbem comparāre; sit dēnique īnscrīptum in
fronte[5] ūnīus cuiusque quid dē rē pūblicā sentiat. Polliceor hoc vōbīs,   15
patrēs cōnscrīptī, tantam in nōbīs cōnsulibus fore dīligentiam, tantam in
vōbīs auctōritātem, tantam in equitibus Rōmānīs virtūtem, tantam in
omnibus bonīs cōnsēnsiōnem ut Catilīnae profectiōne omnia patefacta,
illūstrāta, oppressa, vindicāta esse videātis.[6]

33. Hīsce[7] ōminibus, Catilīna, cum[8] summā reī pūblicae salūte, cum tuā   20
peste ac perniciē cumque eōrum exitiō quī sē tēcum omnī scelere parricī-
diōque iūnxērunt, proficīscere ad impium bellum ac nefārium. Tū,[9]
Iuppiter, quī īsdem quibus haec urbs auspiciīs ā Rōmulō es cōnstitūtus,[6]
quem Statōrem[10] huius urbis atque imperī vērē nōmināmus, hunc et huius
sociōs ā tuīs cēterīsque templīs, ā tēctīs urbis ac moenibus, ā vītā fortūnīsque   25
cīvium omnium arcēbis et hominēs bonōrum inimīcōs, hostīs patriae,
latrōnēs Italiae scelerum foedere inter sē ac nefāriā societāte coniūnctōs
aeternīs suppliciīs vīvōs mortuōsque mactābis.

[4] *as* (literally, *[a thing] which*)
[5] *forehead*
[6] *whose (worship) was established under the same auspices as this city*

Cicero's Style

Cicero ends his speech in a blaze of rhetorical fireworks. In line 19 we
find anaphora, asyndeton, climax, and a periodic sentence ending in the
favored rhythmic phrase **esse videātis.** The four clauses are arranged
in two pairs: consuls and senators, knights and the rest. So are the four
participles: revelation and light, crushing and punishing.

In the long periodic prayer at the end we note a series of pairs: **quī** and
quem clauses, **urbis** and **imperī, hunc** and **sociōs.** Then comes a group
of three phrases introduced by **ā,** each phrase containing a pair: **tuīs
cēterīsque, tēctīs ac moenibus, vītā fortūnīsque.** These are followed
by another group of three: **hominēs, hostīs, latrōnēs,** at the end of which
is the pair **foedere** and **societāte,** each with an adjective. Last comes
another pair, **vīvōs mortuōsque.** The speech ends with one of the favorite
rhythms, **—ōsque mactābis** (‒ ⌣ ⌣ | ‒ ⌣).

---

[3] It becomes clear here that **improbī,** by its contrast with **bonīs,** has a political meaning: *radicals.*

[4] dative with **īnsidiārī**

[5] from **fax**

[6] Because there is no future subjunctive, the present serves in its place.

[7] a stronger form of **Hīs**

[8] We would say *to* rather than *with.*

[9] addressed to the statue of Jupiter in the temple where the senate was meeting

[10] Cicero uses the word here in the sense of *Protector* rather than *Stayer.*

Word Studies

How does the suffix **–scō** affect the meaning of **ingravēscō?**

Explain *bibulous, congregation, febrile, gelid, secession, viscera.*

QUESTIONS

1. Where and when was the senate meeting held?
2. Why did Cicero make this speech?
3. Why did he not have Catiline executed?
4. Why did not the senate vote his execution?
5. What part does the word **hostis** play in Cicero's argument?
6. Who killed Tiberius Gracchus?
7. Who killed Gaius Gracchus?
8. How did Cicero learn of Catiline's plans?
9. Where was Manlius?
10. What happened on November 7?
11. What did Catiline plan for October 28?
12. Did Catiline have any supporters in the senate?

The Government of Rome

Rome developed from a small city-state, founded in the eighth century B.C., into a world empire. At the same time its constitution gradually evolved. Although the Roman constitution was never written down, a body of written legislation grew up, beginning with the Twelve Tables in the fifth century B.C.

Roman citizens came to be divided into three groups: (1) the **nōbilēs,** those who held, or had held, one of the curule offices (namely, consuls, dictators, praetors, and curule aediles) and their descendants; (2) the **equitēs,** the middle class, who were essentially an aristocracy of wealth dominating commerce and banking (the term **equitēs,** *cavalry,* recalls the early times when only the man who could afford a horse had the right of admission to this class); and (3) the **plēbs,** the lowest order of citizens. Slaves were considered property and had no rights.

In the early days of Rome the government was controlled largely by the noble oligarchy. With expansion, the **equitēs** increased their power and often aligned themselves with the aristocracy for effective control of governmental procedures. Meanwhile, there was a continuing struggle on the part of the **plēbs** for greater representation and a more equitable distribution of the functions of state, resulting ultimately (with, of course, other contributing causes) in the Civil War between Pompey and Caesar and the establishment of monarchy (though not so called) under Augustus.

The governing body of the upper classes was the senate, composed of 600 senators, all formally trained in governmental offices. All members were either former magistrates or descendants of nobles. They were called **patrēs cōnscrīptī** (*conscript fathers*), standing for **patrēs et cōnscrīptī**, a term that referred to the time when the first plebeians were admitted to the senate as "enrolled" or "added" members in distinction to the patrician members, the **patrēs.**

The popular assemblies were (1) the **comitia centūriāta**, so called because all the citizens were divided into groups of centuries, or hundreds, which elected the higher magistrates, and (2) the **comitia tribūta**, a grouping by tribes (there were thirty-five) with one vote each. In the **comitia tribūta** the **plēbs** were more influential than the other two orders.

Every Roman official of the senatorial class was well educated and had undergone military and political training. The magistrates were elected annually (and could not immediately succeed themselves) in the cursus honorum. Each official had at least one colleague and thus was prevented from monopolizing power. The officials were not salaried.

The officers in the senatorial **cursus honōrum,** all elected annually were:

OFFICIAL	MINIMUM AGE
1. *Quaestor*	31
Twenty in number. Served in the treasury. Two in Rome, eighteen in the provinces and the army.	
2. *Aedile*	37
Four in number. City officials, in charge of public entertainment and public works.	
3. *Praetor*	40
Eight in number. Judges in civil and criminal courts.	
4. *Consul*	43
Two, with equal powers. Presided over the senate; were the chief executives of the state; brought bills before the assemblies; had charge of elections.	

There were also the censors (two), usually ex-consuls, elected every five years for an eighteen months' term, who were in charge of moral standards and the eligibility of senators. During the remaining three and one-half years the consuls performed the censors' functions. One office, that of the tribune, was in the hands of the **plēbs.** The tribunes of the plebs were ten in number, had the right of veto, and were personally sacrosanct; anyone who attacked a tribune could be put to death without trial. The veto made them very powerful.

After an official served as praetor or consul, he was usually appointed to a post as governor in a province, with the title of proconsul or propraetor.

The dictatorship at Rome was a constitutional office, resorted to in times of emergency. The dictator was appointed by the consuls at the request of the senate for a period of six months at most. Usually he retired as soon as the emergency had been handled.

The Ciceronian Sentence

You have read about Cicero's periodic style. Here are a few other strategies to help you through one of his sentences.

You probably have realized that anaphora, groups of two and three, and other devices actually make it easier to find your way through one of Cicero's formidable periods. You will find it useful to read a sentence aloud, breaking it up into its natural parts. Often these parts are of about equal length. Take the last sentence in the first speech against Catiline:

Tū, Iuppiter, || quī īsdem quibus haec urbs auspiciīs || ā Rōmulō es cōnstitūtus, || quem Statōrem huius urbis atque imperī vērē nōmināmus, || hunc et huius sociōs || ā tuīs cēterīsque templīs, || ā tēctīs urbis ac moenibus, || ā vītā fortūnīsque cīvium omnium arcēbis || et hominēs bonōrum
5 inimīcōs, || hostīs patriae, latrōnēs Italiae || scelerum foedere inter sē ac nefāriā societāte coniūnctōs || aeternīs suppliciīs || vīvōs mortuōsque mactābis.

In translating such a sentence as this, break it up into several short sentences.

Not only does Cicero weld his ideas into a nicely rounded period but, by various devices, he also connects the periods with one another in thought and word. The connecting relative is one such device. But besides the ordinary conjunctions such as **sed** and **et,** there are many other words and phrases used for transitions:

age nunc, *come now*

age vērō, *well then*

at vērō, *but*

autem (never first word), *however, moreover*

dēnique, *in short, in a word*

enim (never first word), *for*

etenim, *for really*

hīc (adv.), *in view of this, under these circumstances*

iam tum, *even then*

iam vērō, *moreover*

igitur, *then, as I was just saying*

itaque, *accordingly*

nam, *for*

nē longum sit, *to be brief*

nunc, *as it is*

nunc vērō, *but as it is*

postrēmō, *finally, at last*

quae cum ita sint, *and since this is so, therefore*

quam ob rem, *and for this reason, and therefore*

quamquam, *and yet, however*

quārē, *and for that reason, therefore*

quid, *tell me, again* (calling attention to a question to follow)

quid est, *listen*

quid igitur, *what then*

quid quod, *what of the fact that*

quid vērō, *look here*

quod sī, *but if;* occasionally, *if then*

sīn autem, *but if on the other hand*

tamen (usually not first word), *nevertheless*

tametsī, *and yet*

vērō (never first word), *in fact, but*

Second Oration Against Catiline

The first speech was made before the senate on November 8, the second before the people on the next day. Catiline left Rome to join Manlius after the senate meeting. In the senate Cicero had a generally sympathetic audience; not so before the people, many of whom sided with Catiline. We can imagine that Cicero had rather a mixed reception. The one new thing in this speech is the detailed description of the six classes of conspirators, most valuable in explaining the background of the plot and therefore the most important part in all four speeches.

Catiline Has Left!

I, 1. Tandem aliquandō, Quirītēs, L. Catilīnam, furentem audāciā, scelus anhēlantem,[1] pestem patriae nefāriē mōlientem, vōbīs₁ atque huic urbī ferrō flammāque minitantem ex urbe vel ēiēcimus vel ēmīsimus[2] vel ipsum ēgredientem verbīs[3]₂ prōsecūtī sumus. Abiit, excessit, ēvāsit, ērūpit.₃

₁ with **minitantem**
₂ **vel,** as distinguished from **aut,** means *or, if you prefer*
₃ Note the rhetorical flavor of this first paragraph. Four participles are arranged in two pairs; in the first pair we have chiasmus. In **pestem patriae** and in **ferrō flammāque** there is alliteration. With the last participle there are two pairs of nouns. Then come the three verbs. The last sentence consists only of four verbs, in two pairs, reaching a climax.

Conspirators: Class I

Verba Ūtilia: aes aliēnum, argentum, certō (–āre), errō, flamma (in reading above), furō (in reading above), locuplēs, sānō, ulcīscor, voveō

VIII, 17. Sed cūr tam diū dē ūnō hoste loquimur, et dē eō hoste quī iam fatētur sē esse hostem,₁ et quem, quia, quod₂ semper voluī, mūrus interest, nōn timeō; dē hīs quī dissimulant, quī Rōmae remanent, quī nōbīscum sunt, nihil dīcimus? Quōs quidem ego, sī ūllō modō fierī possit, nōn tam
5 ulcīscī studeō quam sānāre sibi ipsōs, plācāre reī pūblicae[1] neque id quārē fierī nōn possit, sī iam mē audīre volent, intellegō. Expōnam enim vōbīs, Quirītēs, ex quibus generibus hominum istae cōpiae comparentur; deinde singulīs medicīnam cōnsilī atque ōrātiōnis₃ meae, sī quam[2] poterō, afferam.

18. Ūnum genus est eōrum quī magnō in aere aliēnō[3] maiōrēs etiam
10 possessiōnēs habent, quārum amōre, adductī dissolvī[4] nūllō modō possunt. Hōrum hominum speciēs est honestissima, sunt enim locuplētēs; voluntās vērō et causa impudentissima. Tū₄ agrīs, tū aedificiīs, tū argentō, tū familiā, tū rēbus omnibus ōrnātus et cōpiōsus sīs, et dubitēs dē possessiōne dētrahere, acquīrere ad fidem?[5] Quid enim exspectās? Bellum? Quid ergō?

₁ Note the emphatic repetition of **hostis.**
₂ An excellent example of a common Latin usage that cannot be reproduced in English. The introductory words of three clauses come first, the verbs of each follow in the opposite order: **vōluī** goes with **quod, interest** with **quia, timeō** with **quem.**
₃ hendiadys; the two genitives explain **medicīnam**
₄ He addresses an imaginary member of this class.

In vāstātiōne omnium tuās possessiōnēs sacrōsānctās futūrās putās? An 15
tabulās novās?[6] Errant quī istās ā Catilīnā exspectant; meō beneficiō tabulae
novae prōferuntur, vērum auctiōnāriae;[5] neque enim istī quī possessiōnēs
habent aliā ratiōne ūllā salvī esse possunt. Quod[7] sī mātūrius facere voluis-
sent neque, id quod stultissimum est, certāre cum ūsūrīs frūctibus
praediōrum,[6] et locuplētiōribus hīs et meliōribus cīvibus ūterēmur.[8] Sed 20
hōsce hominēs minimē putō pertimēscendōs, quod aut dēdūcī dē sententiā
possunt aut, sī permanēbunt, magis mihi videntur vōta factūrī contrā rem
pūblicam quam arma lātūrī.

[6] *new accounts* means cancellation of debt, promised by Catiline
[7] *and this* (connecting relative)
[8] *we should find them* (*to be*)

⟨⟩ TRANSLATION ⟨⟩

1. You hesitate to give up your fine houses?
2. I see no one who can compel Catiline to surrender.
3. Although Catiline threatened us, we let him go from Rome.
4. The men who have remained in Rome are to be feared the most.

---

[5] Cicero plans to have mortgaged property sold at auction to pay off the mortgage.
[6] Farm income was insufficient to pay off mortgage interest.

Classes II and III

Verba Ūtilia: adipīscor, agrestis, colōnus, concordia, furor, iactō, īnferī, potior, sūmptus, tenuis

IX, 19. Alterum genus est eōrum quī, quamquam premuntur aere
aliēnō, dominātiōnem tamen exspectant, rērum[1] potīrī volunt, honōrēs[2]
quōs, quiētā rē pūblicā, dēspērant, perturbātā,[1] sē cōnsequī posse arbitrantur. Quibus hoc praecipiendum vidētur, ūnum scīlicet et idem quod reliquīs
omnibus,[2] ut dēspērent id quod cōnantur sē cōnsequī posse: prīmum 5
omnium mē ipsum vigilāre,[3] adesse, prōvidēre reī pūblicae; deinde magnōs
animōs esse in bonīs virīs, magnam concordiam ōrdinum, maximam multitūdinem, magnās praetereā mīlitum cōpiās; deōs dēnique immortālīs huic
invictō populō, clārissimō imperiō, pulcherrimae urbī contrā tantam vim
sceleris praesentīs[3] auxilium esse lātūrōs. Quod sī iam sint id quod summō 10
furōre cupiunt adeptī,[4] num illī in cinere urbis et in sanguine cīvium, quae[5]
mente cōnscelerātā ac nefāriā concupīvērunt, cōnsulēs sē aut dictātōrēs aut
etiam rēgēs spērant futūrōs? Nōn vident id sē cupere quod, sī adeptī sint,
fugitīvō alicui aut gladiātōrī concēdī sit necesse?

[1] *to acquire political control*
[2] *public offices*
[3] *in person* (with **deōs**)
[4] *but supposing they have obtained*
[5] (*things*) *which* (the two preceding nouns are the antecedent)

---

[1] i.e., **rē pūblicā**
[2] Supply **praecipiendum vidētur.**
[3] The infinitives are in apposition with **hoc.**

15 **20.** Tertium genus est aetāte iam affectum, sed tamen exercitātiōne
rōbustum; quō ex genere iste est Mānlius cui nunc Catilīna succēdit. Hī
sunt hominēs ex eīs colōniīs quās Sulla cōnstituit;[4] quās ego ūniversās[6]
cīvium esse optimōrum et fortissimōrum virōrum sentiō, sed tamen eī sunt
colōnī quī sē in īnspērātīs ac repentīnīs pecūniīs sūmptuōsius īnsolen-
20 tiusque iactārunt.[7] Hī dum aedificant tamquam beātī,[8] dum praediīs lēctīs,
familiīs magnīs, convīviīs apparātīs dēlectantur, in tantum aes aliēnum
incidērunt ut, sī salvī esse velint, Sulla sit eīs ab īnferīs excitandus. Quī
etiam nōn nūllōs agrestīs hominēs tenuīs atque egentīs in eandem illam
spem rapīnārum veterum impulērunt. Quōs ego utrōsque in eōdem genere
25 praedātōrum dīreptōrumque pōnō, sed eōs hoc[5] moneō, dēsinant furere ac
prōscrīptiōnēs et dictātūrās cōgitāre. Tantus enim illōrum temporum[6] dolor
inustus est cīvitātī ut iam ista nōn modo hominēs sed nē[9] pecudēs quidem
mihi passūrae esse videantur.

≈≈ **TRANSLATION** ≈≈

1. This is what I urge, that you leave Rome at once.
2. Let them not remain at Rome; let them go to Manlius' camp.
3. They want to get possession of the city and all its wealth.
4. They have fallen into debt because they want to live like rich people.

---

[4] Sulla had confiscated much land in Italy in order to reward 120,000 of his veterans.
[5] **dēsinant** (with **ut** omitted) explains **hoc**
[6] the time of Sulla

Classes IV, V, and VI

Verba Ūtilia: dīlēctus, grex, idcircō, industria, parricīda, pereō, proprius,
quam prīmum, sānē, venēnum

X. 21. Quārtum genus est sānē varium et mixtum et turbulentum; quī
iam prīdem premuntur, quī numquam ēmergunt,[1] quī partim inertiā, partim
male gerendō negōtiō, partim etiam sūmptibus in vetere aere aliēnō vacil-
lant, quī vadimōniīs, iūdiciīs, prōscrīptiōne[2] bonōrum dēfatīgātī permultī
5 et ex urbe et ex agrīs sē in illa castra cōnferre dīcuntur. Hōsce ego nōn tam
mīlitēs ācrīs quam īnfitiātōrēs[3] lentōs esse arbitror. Quī hominēs quam prīmum, sī stāre nōn possunt, corruant, sed ita ut nōn modo cīvitās sed nē
vīcīnī quidem proximī sentiant. Nam illud nōn intellegō quam ob rem, sī
vīvere honestē nōn possunt, perīre turpiter velint, aut cūr minōre dolōre
10 peritūrōs sē cum multīs quam sī sōlī pereant arbitrentur.

[1] never get their heads above water
[2] summons (to court), judgment, forced sale
[3] slow payers

Marginal glosses (top left):

[6] on the whole
[7] made a display of themselves
[8] rich (or blessed)
[9] not only not . . . but not even

Vanni/Art Resource, NY

The Arch of Septimius Severus was built in honor of Septimius, who ruled from 193-211, and his sons, Caracalla and Geta. With its three arched passageways, it is much more elaborate than the Arch of Titus, seen through the main entrance of the arch. Severus was a brilliant general who fought a successful campaign against the Parthians to expand the empire. After a foray into Scotland, he died at Eboracum (modern York, England).

22. Quīntum genus est parricīdārum, sīcāriōrum, dēnique omnium facinorōsōrum. Quōs ego ā Catilīnā nōn revocō; nam neque ab eō dīvellī possunt et pereant sānē in latrōciniō, quoniam sunt ita multī ut eōs carcer capere nōn possit.

⁴ *is* (*last*)
⁵ *Catiline's own*
⁶ *sails* (because they contained so much cloth)
⁷ *herds, gangs*
⁸ *and not only*

15 Postrēmum autem genus est[4] nōn sōlum numerō vērum etiam genere ipsō atque vītā, quod proprium[5] Catilīnae est, dē eius dīlēctū, immō vērō dē complexū eius ac sinū; quōs pexō capillō, nitidōs, aut imberbīs[1] aut bene barbātōs vidētis, manicātīs et tālāribus tunicīs,[2] vēlīs[6] amictōs, nōn togīs; quōrum omnis industria vītae et vigilandī labor in antelūcānīs[3] cēnīs 20 exprōmitur. **23.** In hīs gregibus[7] omnēs āleātōrēs, omnēs adulterī, omnēs impūrī impudīcīque versantur. Hī puerī tam lepidī ac dēlicātī nōn sōlum amāre et amārī neque[8] saltāre et cantāre[4] sed etiam sīcās vibrāre et spargere venēna[5] didicērunt. Quī nisi exeunt, nisi pereunt, etiam sī Catilīna perierit, scītōte[6] hoc in rē pūblicā sēminārium Catilīnārum futūrum. 25 Vērum tamen quid sibi istī miserī volunt? Num suās sēcum mulierculās sunt in castra ductūrī? Quem ad modum autem illīs carēre poterunt, hīs praesertim iam noctibus? Quō autem pactō illī Appennīnum atque illās pruīnās ac nivīs[7] perferent? Nisi idcircō sē facilius hiemem tolerātūrōs putant, quod nūdī in convīviīs saltāre didicērunt.

 **TRANSLATION**

1. By managing business badly they fell into debt.
2. Let them die in the snows of the highest mountains.
3. I do not understand why they want to die in disgrace.
4. I cannot tell whether they are wearing togas or sails.

₁ i.e., teenagers
₂ a sign of effeminacy, for most men wore sleeveless tunics, reaching to the knees
₃ i.e., they don't go home until morning from their all-night banquets
₄ Singing and dancing were not considered proper for "gentlemen."
₅ in wine, presumably
₆ future imperative plural, translated like a present: *I assure you* (literally, *know*)
₇ in contrast to Rome, where it does not snow very often

Third Oration Against Catiline

The third speech against Catiline was made before the people on December 3, more than three weeks after the second speech, as a result of the discovery of sensational and conclusive evidence against Catiline. Before that Cicero had no real proof, and many people no doubt thought that he was just making political speeches, ones not based on fact.

What happened was that, after Catiline left Rome, his representatives began to deal with members of a Gallic tribe, the Allobroges, who were in Rome on an official mission. The Allobroges had complained to the senate about the dishonesty of Romans doing business in their country. The senate paid no attention to their complaints, and naturally the Allobroges were disgruntled. Catiline's men got the idea, clever at first sight, of taking advantage of this indignation. The conspirators proposed that the Allobroges send soldiers to help Catiline fight against his own country. The Allobroges, like other foreign peoples, had a Roman patron, that is, an adviser on legal matters. They consulted him about the conspirators' request, and he reported it to Cicero, who advised the Allobroges to get the request put in writing. This Catiline's representatives were stupid enough to do. Not only that—one of Catiline's men, named Lentulus, wrote Catiline, suggesting that slaves be enrolled as soldiers. His letter was sent by a messenger accompanying the Allobroges, who promised to stop and confer with Catiline at Faesulae.

Cicero arranged to have a force of soldiers intercept the group on the night of December 2. They met them at the Mulvian bridge, now within the city limits, at that time two miles north. The written request for Allobrogian assistance and Lentulus' letter to Catiline were seized and brought to Cicero. The leaders of the conspiracy were arrested and taken to the senate, where they confessed. Later in the day Cicero delivered this third oration in the Forum to tell the people what had happened.

The plan of calling on foreigners for help, of urging the use of slaves— and putting this in writing—appeared incredibly stupid to the Romans. They praised Cicero and, recalling the dangerous slave revolt a few years earlier, rejoiced at being saved by him.

Rome Is Saved

Verba Ūtilia: benevolentia, condō, coniūnx, dēlūbrum, domicilium, ergā, fātum, hodiernus, ignōrō, illūstris, manifēstus, posterus, prīncipium, sēnsus, tollō

I, 1. Rem pūblicam,[1] Quirītēs, vītamque[2] omnium vestrum, bona, fortūnās, coniugēs līberōsque vestrōs atque hoc domicilium clārissimī imperī, fortūnātissimam pulcherrimamque urbem, hodiernō diē deōrum immortālium summō ergā vōs amōre, labōribus, cōnsiliīs, perīculīs meīs ē flammā atque
5 ferrō ac paene ex faucibus fātī ēreptam et vōbīs cōnservātam ac restitūtam vidētis. **2.** Et sī nōn minus nōbīs iūcundī atque illūstrēs sunt eī diēs quibus cōnservāmur quam illī quibus nāscimur, quod salūtis certa laetitia est, nāscendī incerta condiciō,[1] et quod sine sēnsū nāscimur, cum voluptāte servāmur, profectō, quoniam illum quī hanc urbem condidit ad deōs
10 immortālīs benevolentiā fāmāque sustulimus,[2] esse apud vōs posterōsque vestrōs in honōre dēbēbit[3] is quī eandem hanc urbem conditam amplificātamque servāvit. Nam tōtī urbī,[3] templīs, dēlūbrīs, tēctīs ac moenibus subiectōs prope iam ignīs circumdatōsque restīnximus, īdemque[4] gladiōs in rem pūblicam dēstrictōs rettudimus mūcrōnēsque eōrum ā iugulīs
15 vestrīs dēiēcimus.

3. Quae quoniam in senātū illūstrāta, patefacta, comperta sunt per mē, vōbīs iam expōnam breviter ut et quanta et quam manifēsta et quā ratiōne invēstīgāta et comprehēnsa sint vōs quī et ignōrātis et exspectātis scīre possītis. Prīncipiō, ut[5] Catilīna paucīs ante diēbus[4] ērūpit ex urbe, cum
20 sceleris suī sociōs huiusce nefāriī bellī acerrimōs ducēs[6] Rōmae relīquisset, semper vigilāvī et prōvīdī, Quirītēs, quem ad modum in tantīs et tam absconditīs īnsidiīs salvī esse possēmus.

Prepositional Phrases

Unlike English, Latin has few prepositional phrases depending on nouns. For example, the English phrase *a bird in the hand* would be in Latin **avis quae in manū est.** But in Latin a noun expressing feeling or attitude may have a phrase introduced by **ergā** or **in** dependent on it: **ergā vōs amōre** (line 4).

---

[1] *our status at birth*
[2] *we have raised to the gods with our affection and praise*
[3] *he will deserve* (**is** means Cicero)
[4] *(we) too* (literally, *the same we*)
[5] *ever since* (literally, *when*)
[6] *(as) leaders*

---

[1] This periodic sentence is really very simple. Its essential part is **rem pūblicam cōnservātam ac restitūtam vidētis;** the rest is elaboration. **Vītam** goes with **coniugēs līberōsque, bona** and **fortūnās** belong together; **domicilium** and **urbem,** modified by two superlatives, form a pair. **Deōrum amōre** balances in chiastic order **labōribus, cōnsiliīs, perīculīs meīs.**
[2] The plural is used in English.
[3] with **subiectōs**
[4] Time is relative: it was really over three weeks.

1. Don't you see that the city has been saved?
2. Fires were to be applied to the entire city.
3. Cicero explained how he found out what they were planning.

Word Studies

Coniūnx is derived from **con–** and the stem of **iungō:** *joined together.*

Hodiernus diēs is tautological: literally, *today's day.* We have tautologies also in the expressions *long-distance telephone* (for *telephone* means *far speaking*), *symphony concert* ("togetherness" is indicated by both Latin *con–* and its Greek synonym *syn-*), and *head of cabbage* (from **caput**).

Evidence of Treason

Verba Ūtilia: assiduus, comitātus, complūrēs, facultās, hesternus, lēgātus, pōns, restō, sollicitō, vigilia

II. Nam tum cum ex urbe Catilīnam ēiciēbam[1] (nōn enim iam vereor huius verbī [1] invidiam, cum illa[2] magis sit timenda, quod vīvus exierit), sed tum cum illum exterminārī[2] volēbam, aut reliquam coniūrātōrum manum simul exitūram aut eōs quī restitissent[3] īnfirmōs sine illō ac dēbilīs fore putābam. **4.** Atque ego, ut[3] vīdī, quōs maximō furōre et scelere esse īnflam- 5 mātōs sciēbam, eōs nōbīscum esse et Rōmae remānsisse, in eō[4] omnīs diēs noctēsque cōnsūmpsī, ut quid agerent, quid mōlīrentur sentīrem ac vidērem, ut, quoniam auribus vestrīs propter incrēdibilem magnitūdinem sceleris minōrem fidem faceret[5] ōrātiō mea, rem ita comprehenderem ut tum dēmum animīs salūtī vestrae prōvidērētis cum oculīs maleficium ipsum 10 vidērētis. Itaque ut comperī lēgātōs Allobrogum bellī Trānsalpīnī et tumultūs Gallicī excitandī causā ā P. Lentulō esse sollicitātōs, eōsque in Galliam ad suōs cīvīs eōdemque itinere cum litterīs mandātīsque[4] ad Catilīnam esse missōs, comitemque eīs adiūnctum esse T. Volturcium, atque huic esse ad Catilīnam datās litterās, facultātem mihi oblātam putāvī ut (quod[6] erat 15 difficillimum quodque ego semper optābam ab dīs immortālibus) tōta rēs nōn sōlum ā mē sed etiam ā senātū et ā vōbīs manifēstō dēprēnderētur.

[1] *I was trying to drive out*
[2] *exiled* (from **terminus,** *boundary*)
[3] *would remain*
[4] *in this* (*task*) (explained by the following **ut** clause)
[5] *produced too little belief in you* (literally, *in your ears*)
[6] (*a thing*) *which,* referring to the **ut** clause

---

[1] refers to **ēiciēbam**
[2] **invidia**
[3] Watch out for **ut** in this sentence: it occurs four times, all in different uses.
[4] **litterae** were written, **mandāta** were oral

5. Itaque hesternō diē L. Flaccum et C. Pomptīnum praetōrēs, fortissimōs atque amantissimōs reī pūblicae virōs, ad mē vocāvī, rem exposuī, quid

20 fierī placēret ostendī. Illī autem, quī omnia dē rē pūblicā praeclāra atque ēgregia sentīrent,[7] sine recūsātiōne ac sine ūllā morā negōtium suscēpērunt et, cum advesperāsceret, occultē ad pontem Mulvium pervēnērunt atque ibi in proximīs vīllīs ita bipertītō fuērunt ut Tiberis inter eōs et pōns interesset. Eōdem autem et[8] ipsī sine cuiusquam suspīciōne multōs fortīs virōs

25 ēdūxerant, et ego ex praefectūrā Reātīnā complūrīs dēlēctōs adulēscentīs quōrum operā ūtor assiduē in reī pūblicae praesidiō cum gladiīs mīseram. **6.** Interim tertiā ferē vigiliā exāctā,[5] cum iam pontem Mulvium magnō comitātū lēgātī Allobrogēs ingredī inciperent ūnāque Volturcius, fit in eōs impetus; dūcuntur et ab illīs gladiī et ā nostrīs. Rēs praetōribus erat nōta

30 sōlīs, ignōrābātur ā cēterīs.

[7] *since they had all the fine and excellent feelings about the state,* (i.e., they were anti-Catiline)
[8] *both*

◁▶ TRANSLATION ◁▶

1. They proceeded toward the river with many soldiers.
2. In order to see what was happening, he went to the bridge.
3. They were sent with a letter to tell Catiline what he ought to do.
4. They said that they would not fight because they did not believe Cicero.

---

[5] The night was divided into four watches; therefore it was about 3 A.M.

The Conspirators Under Arrest

Verba Ūtilia: aedēs, arcessō, dīlūcēsco, integer, māne, scelus, sēdō

III. Tum interventū Pomptīnī atque Flaccī pugna quae erat commissa sēdātur. Litterae quaecumque erant in eō comitātū, integrīs signīs, praetōribus trāduntur; ipsī[1] comprehēnsī ad mē, cum iam dīlūcēsceret, dēdūcuntur. Atque hōrum omnium scelerum improbissimum māchinātōrem, Cimbrum

5 Gabīnium, statim ad mē nihildum suspicantem vocāvī; deinde item arcessītus est L. Statilius et post eum Cethēgus; tardissimē autem Lentulus vēnit, crēdō quod in litterīs dandīs[2] praeter cōnsuētūdinem proximā nocte vigilārat. **7.** Cum[1] summīs et clārissimīs huius cīvitātis virīs,[3] quī, audītā

[1] *although*

---

[1] the conspirators
[2] ironical, of course: *in writing letters*
[3] with **placēret**

rē, frequentēs ad mē māne convēnerant, litterās ā mē prius aperīrī quam ad
senātum dēferrī [4] placēret, nē, sī nihil esset inventum, temere ā mē tantus 10
tumultus iniectus cīvitātī vidērētur, negāvī [2] mē esse factūrum ut dē perīculō
pūblicō nōn ad cōnsilium pūblicum rem integram dēferrem. Etenim, Quirītēs,
sī ea quae erant ad mē dēlāta reperta nōn essent, tamen ego nōn arbitrābar
in tantīs reī pūblicae perīculīs esse mihi nimiam dīligentiam pertimēscendam. Senātum frequentem[3] celeriter, ut vīdistis, coēgī. **8.** Atque intereā 15
statim admonitū Allobrogum C. Sulpicium praetōrem, fortem virum, mīsī
quī ex aedibus Cethēgī sī quid [4] tēlōrum esset efferret; ex quibus ille maximum sīcārum numerum et gladiōrum extulit.

[2] *I said I would not so act as not to*
[3] *well attended*
[4] *whatever* (with **sī**)

⟨⟩ TRANSLATION ⟨⟩

1. Before he could destroy the letter it was seized.
2. If the letter were not found, what would Cicero do?
3. He sent a brave man to bring back any weapons he found.
4. He said he would not open the letter before the senate saw it.

Word Studies

What two inceptive verbs are in the preceding reading?
Give English derivatives of **gladius, interventus, negō, sēdō, suspicor.**

---

[4] The subjunctive would be more natural, introduced by **prius quam,** but the contrast
with **aperīrī** affects the construction.

Testimony in the Senate

⟨⟩

Verba Ūtilia: fugiō, incendō, indicō, praescrībō, praesidium, praestō,
timor, ūtor, virgō, vix

    IV. Intrōdūxī Volturcium sine Gallīs; fidem pūblicam[1] iussū senātūs
dedī; hortātus sum ut ea quae scīret sine timōre indicāret. Tum ille dīxit,
cum vix sē ex magnō timōre recreāsset, ā P. Lentulō sē habēre ad Catilīnam
mandāta et litterās [2] ut servōrum praesidiō ūterētur, ut ad urbem quam prīmum cum exercitū accēderet; id [1] autem eō cōnsiliō ut, cum urbem ex 5

[1] *official promise* of immunity from prosecution
[2] *a letter*

---

[1] refers to the preceding **ut** clause

omnibus partibus quem ad modum dīscrīptum distribūtumque erat incendissent caedemque īnfīnītam cīvium fēcissent, praestō esset ille₂ quī et fugientīs exciperet₃ et sē cum hīs urbānīs ducibus coniungeret. **9.** Intrōductī autem Gallī iūs iūrandum sibi et litterās ā P. Lentulō, Cethēgō, Statiliō ad
10 suam gentem datās esse dīxērunt, atque ita sibi ab hīs et ā L. Cassiō esse praescrīptum³ ut equitātum in Italiam quam prīmum mitterent; pedestrīs sibi cōpiās nōn dēfutūrās.₄ Lentulum autem sibi cōnfirmāsse ex fātīs Sibyllīnīs haruspicumque respōnsīs sē esse tertium illum Cornēlium₅ ad quem rēgnum₆ huius urbis atque imperium pervenīre esset necesse:
15 Cinnam ante sē et Sullam₇ fuisse. Eundemque dīxisse fātālem⁴ hunc annum esse ad interitum huius urbis atque imperī, quī esset annus decimus post virginum₈ absolūtiōnem, post Capitōlī autem incēnsiōnem vīcēsimus. **10.** Hanc autem Cethēgō⁵ cum cēterīs contrōversiam fuisse dīxērunt quod Lentulō et aliīs Sāturnālibus₉ caedem fierī atque urbem incendī placēret,
20 Cethēgō nimium id longum vidērētur.

 TRANSLATION

1. Did Lentulus warn Catiline not to use slaves?
2. Lentulus asked Catiline to come to Rome in order to burn the city.
3. This day was chosen for the deed since it was the first one after the holiday.

---

³ *they had been directed* (impersonal)
⁴ *fated*
⁵ *Cethegus had had* (with **fuisse**)

₂ Catiline
₃ purpose
₄ Supply *he stated that.*
₅ His whole name was P. Cornelius Lentulus Sura.
₆ Remember how hateful this word was to the Romans, as it was to Americans at the time of the Revolution.
₇ L. Cornelius Cinna and L. Cornelius Sulla
₈ We do not know what the charges against the Vestal Virgins were, but one may guess that they were blamed because the sacred fire went out.
₉ The general license and confusion of the Sāturnālia (beginning December 17) made it a good time for the conspirators to strike.

A view of the Forum Rōmānum, looking across to the Capitoline Hill and the Tabulārium, which was erected in 78 B.C. The Arch of Septimius Severus is on the right and the Rōstra, or speaker's platform, is just to the left of the arch. The Tabulārium, or Record Office, is in the background and shows the foundations and original three arches of the ancient building. The top of the structure is a medieval addition that served as a palace. To the right and behind the Tabulārium is part of the Capitoline square, designed by Michelangelo.

Confession

Verba Ūtilia: argūmentum, cōnfiteor, dēbilitō, dēmēns, imāgō, intueor, recitō, superō, tabella, vultus

V. Ac nē longum sit,[1] Quirītēs, tabellās prōferrī iussimus quae ā quōque dīcēbantur datae.[subscript 1] Prīmō ostendimus Cēthēgō; signum cognōvit.[2] Nōs līnum incīdimus; lēgimus. Erat scrīptum ipsīus manū Allobrogum senātuī et populō sēsē quae eōrum lēgātīs cōnfirmāsset factūrum esse; ōrāre ut
5 item illī facerent quae sibi eōrum lēgātī recēpissent.[3] Tum Cethēgus, quī paulō ante aliquid tamen dē gladiīs ac sīcīs quae apud ipsum[4] erant dēprehēnsa respondisset dīxissetque sē semper bonōrum ferrāmentōrum studiōsum[5] fuisse, recitātīs litterīs, dēbilitātus atque abiectus cōnscientiā repente conticuit. Intrōductus Statilius cognōvit et signum et manum suam. Recitātae
10 sunt tabellae in eandem ferē sententiam;[6] cōnfessus est. Tum ostendī tabellās Lentulō et quaesīvī cognōsceretne[subscript 2] signum. Annuit. "Est vērō," inquam, "nōtum quidem signum, imāgō avī[subscript 3] tuī, clārissimī virī, quī amāvit ūnicē patriam et cīvīs suōs; quae quidem tē ā tantō scelere etiam mūta revocāre dēbuit."[subscript 7][4] **11.** Leguntur eādem ratiōne[8] ad senātum Allobrogum
15 populumque litterae. Sī quid dē hīs rēbus dīcere vellet,[subscript 5] fēcī potestātem. Atque ille prīmō quidem negāvit; post autem aliquantō, tōtō iam indiciō expositō atque ēditō, surrēxit, quaesīvit ā Gallīs quid sibi esset cum eīs[9] quam ob rem[10] domum suam vēnissent, itemque ā Volturciō. Quī cum illī breviter cōnstanterque respondissent per quem ad eum quotiēnsque vēnis-
20 sent, quaesīssentque ab eō nihilne[subscript 2] sēcum esset dē fātīs Sibyllīnīs locūtus, tum ille subitō scelere dēmēns quanta cōnscientiae vīs esset ostendit. Nam, cum id posset īnfitiārī, repente praeter opīniōnem omnium cōnfessus est. Ita eum[subscript 6] nōn modo ingenium illud[11] et dīcendī exercitātiō quā semper valuit sed etiam propter vim sceleris manifēstī atque dēprehēnsī impuden-
25 tia quā superābat omnīs improbitāsque dēfēcit.[subscript 7] **12.** Volturcius vērō subitō litterās prōferrī atque aperīrī iubet quās sibi ā Lentulō ad Catilīnam datās esse dīcēbat. Atque ibi vehementissimē perturbātus Lentulus tamen et

[1] not to be longwinded
[2] he acknowledged (the genuineness of) the seal
[3] had promised (literally, had taken upon themselves)
[4] at his house
[5] interested in fine weapons (meaning that he collected them)
[6] with about the same meaning
[7] ought to have recalled
[8] of the same nature
[9] what he had to do with them
[10] on account of which
[11] well-known

[subscript 1] Supply **esse**.
[subscript 2] **—ne** introduces an indirect question: *whether*
[subscript 3] P. Cornelius Lentulus had been a consul.
[subscript 4] not the oxymoron in **mūta** and **revocāre**
[subscript 5] Indirect discourse is implied and so the subordinate clause is in the subjunctive.
[subscript 6] object of **dēfēcit**
[subscript 7] singular to agree with the nearer subject **improbitās**

signum et manum suam cognōvit. Erant autem sine nōmine,[8] sed ita: "Quis sim sciēs ex eō quem ad tē mīsī. Cūrā [9] ut vir sīs et cōgitā quem in locum[12] sīs prōgressus. Vidē ecquid[13] tibi iam sit necesse et cūrā ut omnium tibi 30 auxilia adiungās, etiam īnfimōrum." [10] Gabīnius deinde intrōductus, cum prīmō impudenter respondēre coepisset, ad extrēmum nihil ex eīs quae Gallī īnsimulābant negāvit. **13.** Ac mihi quidem, Quirītēs, cum[14] illa certissima vīsa sunt argūmenta atque indicia sceleris, tabellae, signa, manūs, dēnique ūnīus cuiusque cōnfessiō, tum multō certiōra illa, color, oculī, 35 vultūs, taciturnitās. Sīc enim obstupuerant, sīc terram intuēbantur, sīc fūrtim nōn numquam inter sēsē aspiciēbant ut nōn iam ab aliīs indicārī sed indicāre sē ipsī vidērentur.

[12] *how far*
[13] *whether anything*
[14] *not only* (balanced by **tum**)

❦ TRANSLATION ❦

1. He begged them to do what they had promised.
2. He asked the Gauls why they had come to his house.
3. Cicero asked Lentulus whether he acknowledged the seal.
4. The seal of Lentulus' grandfather ought to have made him fear.

---

[8] i.e., unsigned
[9] verb
[10] i.e., slaves

The Senate Takes Action

Verba Ūtilia: cōnferō, coniūrātiō, custōdia, domesticus, fidēlis, interest, meritum, particeps, praetūra, togātus

VI. Indiciīs expositīs atque ēditīs, Quirītēs, senātum cōnsuluī dē summā rē pūblicā[1] quid fierī placēret. Dictae sunt ā prīncipibus ācerrimae ac fortissimae sententiae,[1] quās senātus sine ūllā varietāte[2] est secūtus. Et quoniam nōndum est perscrīptum senātūs cōnsultum, ex memoriā vōbīs, Quirītēs, quid senātus cēnsuerit expōnam. **14.** Prīmum mihi grātiae verbīs amplis- 5 simīs aguntur, quod virtūte, cōnsiliō, prōvidentiā meā rēs pūblica maximīs perīculīs sit līberāta.[2] Deinde L. Flaccus et C. Pomptīnus praetōrēs, quod eōrum operā fortī fidēlīque ūsus essem,[3] meritō ac iūre laudantur. Atque etiam virō fortī, collēgae[3] meō, laus impertītur, quod eōs quī huius

[1] *the highest (welfare of the) state*
[2] i.e., *unanimously*
[3] *I had benefited by their services*

---

[1] Cicero, the presiding consul, called on the senators in a fixed order.
[2] quoted reason
[3] Antonius, Cicero's fellow consul

10 coniūrātiōnis participēs fuissent ā suīs et ā reī pūblicae cōnsiliīs remōvis-
set. Atque ita cēnsuērunt ut P. Lentulus, cum sē praetūrā abdicāsset, in
custōdiam trāderētur; itemque utī C. Cethēgus, L. Statilius, P. Gabīnius,
quī omnēs praesentēs[4] erant, in custōdiam trāderentur; atque idem hoc
dēcrētum est in L. Cassium, quī sibi prōcūrātiōnem incendendae urbis
15 dēpoposcerat, in M. Cēpārium, cui ad sollicitandōs pāstōrēs Āpūliam
attribūtam esse erat indicātum, in P. Fūrium, quī est ex eīs colōnīs quōs
Faesulās L. Sulla dēdūxit, in Q. Annium Chīlōnem, quī ūnā cum hōc Fūriō
semper erat in hāc Allobrogum sollicitātiōne versātus, in P. Umbrēnum,
lībertīnum hominem, ā quō prīmum Gallōs ad Gabīnium perductōs esse
20 cōnstābat. Atque eā[4] lēnitāte senātus est ūsus, Quirītēs, ut ex tantā
coniūrātiōne tantāque hāc multitūdine domesticōrum hostium, novem[5]
hominum perditissimōrum poenā rē pūblicā cōnservātā, reliquōrum mentīs
sānārī posse arbitrārētur. **15.** Atque etiam supplicātiō dīs immortālibus prō
singulārī eōrum meritō meō nōmine dēcrēta est, quod mihi prīmum post
25 hanc urbem conditam togātō contigit,[5] et hīs dēcrēta verbīs est: "quod
urbem incendiīs, caede cīvīs, Italiam bellō līberāssem." Quae supplicātiō sī
cum cēterīs supplicātiōnibus cōnferātur,[6] hoc interest, quod cēterae, bene
gestā, haec ūna, cōnservātā rē pūblicā, cōnstitūta est. Atque illud quod
faciendum prīmum fuit factum atque trānsāctum est. Nam P. Lentulus,
30 quamquam patefactīs indiciīs, cōnfessiōnibus suīs, iūdiciō senātūs nōn
modo praetōris iūs vērum etiam cīvis āmīserat, tamen magistrātū sē
abdicāvit, ut quae[7] religiō C. Mariō,[6] clārissimō virō, nōn fuerat quō
minus[7] C. Glauciam, dē quō nihil nōminātim erat dēcrētum, praetōrem
occīderet, eā nōs religiōne[8] in prīvātō[9] P. Lentulō pūniendō līberārēmur.

[4] such
[5] (a thing) which for the first time since this city was founded happened to a civilian (**togātō**) (such as) me
[6] the scruple which Marius did not have
[7] (to keep him) from
[8] from that scruple
[9] private (citizen), in contrast with **praetōrem**

TRANSLATION

1. Nothing can prevent them from leaving the city.
2. If the senate should expel them, where would they go?
3. The task of burning the city had been assigned to Cassius.
4. I say that they should be sent into exile because they are wicked.

Word Studies

What is the meaning of the phrase *particeps criminis,* used in English?
What abbreviation used in English is derived from the Latin word **cōnferō**?
A *pastor* is the "shepherd" of his *congregation* (**con–** and **grex,** *flock*).

---

[4] This word shows that the men mentioned next were not present. Only Ceparius was caught.
[5] but four escaped
[6] The condition is "mixed," i.e., the condition itself is less vivid, the conclusion is one of fact.
[7] The antecedent is **religiōne** below.

If Catiline Had Been in Rome

Verba Ūtilia: callidus, cervīx, dēnūntiō, dum, exīstimō, fūrtum, latrō-cinium, palam, temeritās, testis

VII, 16. Nunc quoniam, Quirītēs, cōnscelerātissimī perīculōsissimīque bellī nefāriōs ducēs captōs iam et comprehēnsōs tenētis, exīstimāre dēbētis omnīs Catilīnae cōpiās, omnīs spēs atque opēs, hīs dēpulsīs urbis perīculīs, concidisse. Quem quidem ego cum ex urbe pellēbam,[1] hoc prōvidēbam animō, Quirītēs, remōtō Catilīnā, nōn mihi esse P. Lentulī somnum nec L. Cassī 5 adipēs nec C. Cethēgī furiōsam temeritātem pertimēscendam. Ille[1] erat ūnus timendus ex istīs[2] omnibus, sed tam diū dum urbis moenibus continē-bātur. Omnia nōrat, omnium aditūs tenēbat;[3] appellāre,[4] temptāre, sollicitāre poterat, audēbat. Erat eī cōnsilium[5] ad facinus aptum, cōnsiliō autem neque lingua neque manus deerat. Iam ad certās rēs cōnficiendās certōs[6] hominēs 10 dēlēctōs ac dēscrīptōs habēbat. Neque vērō, cum aliquid mandārat, cōnfectum putābat: nihil erat quod nōn ipse obīret, occurreret, vigilāret, labōrāret;[3] frīgus, sitim, famem ferre poterat. **17.** Hunc ego hominem tam ācrem, tam audācem, tam parātum, tam callidum, tam in scelere vigilantem, tam[4] in perditīs rēbus dīligentem nisi ex domesticīs īnsidiīs in castrēnse latrō- 15 cinium compulissem—dīcam id quod sentiō, Quirītēs—nōn facile hanc tantam mōlem malī ā cervīcibus vestrīs dēpulissem. Nōn ille nōbīs Sāturnālia cōnstituisset,[5] neque tantō ante[7] exitī ac fātī diem reī pūblicae dēnūntiāvis-set neque commīsisset ut signum, ut litterae suae testēs manifēstī sceleris dēprehenderentur. Quae nunc, illō absente, sīc gesta sunt ut nūllum in 20 prīvātā domō fūrtum umquam sit tam palam inventum quam haec in tōtā rē pūblicā coniūrātiō manifēstō comprehēnsa est. Quod sī Catilīna in urbe ad hanc diem remānsisset, quamquam, quoad fuit, omnibus eius cōnsiliīs occurrī atque obstitī, tamen, ut levissimē dīcam,[8] dīmicandum nōbīs cum illō fuisset, neque nōs umquam, cum ille in urbe hostis esset, tantīs 25 perīculīs rem pūblicam tantā pāce, tantō ōtiō, tantō silentiō līberāssēmus.

[1] *trying to drive*
[2] *of all those fellows* (contemptuous)
[3] *he had (avenues of) approach to everybody*
[4] *call by name*
[5] *judgment*
[6] *particular men for particular things*
[7] *so long beforehand*
[8] *to say the least, we should have had to fight*

TRANSLATION

1. We do not have to fear Catiline any longer.
2. I was trying to force Catiline to leave Rome.
3. But it so happened that we freed the city peacefully.
4. If Catiline had not left Rome, we should have had to fight.

---

[1] Catiline
[2] He knew everybody and knew also which of a man's three names he should use.
[3] The four verbs are in two pairs; then follow three nouns with alliteration and asyndeton.
[4] anaphora with six examples of **tam** arranged in pairs
[5] i.e., so late. That was the fault of Lentulus, objected to by Cethegus.

The Will of the Gods

Verba Ūtilia: caelum, certē, cīvīlis, excelsus, flectō, forum, hūmānus, lūdus, nūmen, nūtus

VIII, 18. Quamquam haec omnia, Quirītēs, ita sunt ā mē administrāta ut deōrum immortālium nūtū atque cōnsiliō et gesta et prōvīsa esse videantur. Idque cum[1] coniectūrā cōnsequī possumus, quod vix vidētur hūmānī cōnsilī[2] tantārum rērum gubernātiō esse potuisse, tum vērō ita praesentēs
5 hīs temporibus opem et auxilium nōbīs tulērunt ut eōs paene oculīs vidēre possīmus. Nam ut illa[3]$_1$ omittam, vīsās nocturnō tempore ab occidente facēs[4] ārdōremque caelī, ut fulminum iactūs, ut terrae mōtūs relinquam, ut omittam cētera quae tam multa, nōbīs cōnsulibus, facta sunt ut haec quae nunc fīunt canere[5] dī immortālēs vidērentur, hoc certē, Quirītēs, quod sum
10 dictūrus neque praetermittendum neque relinquendum est. **19.** Nam profectō memoriā tenētis, Cottā et Torquātō cōnsulibus,$_2$ complūrīs in Capitōliō rēs dē caelō$_3$ esse percussās, cum et simulācra deōrum dēpulsa sunt et statuae veterum hominum dēiectae et lēgum aera[6] liquefacta et tāctus etiam ille quī hanc urbem condidit Rōmulus, quem inaurātum in Capitōliō, parvum atque
15 lactantem, ūberibus lupīnīs inhiantem[7] fuisse meministis. Quō quidem tempore cum haruspicēs ex tōta Etrūriā$_4$ convēnissent, caedīs atque incendia et lēgum interitum et bellum cīvīle ac domesticum et totīus urbis atque imperī occāsum appropinquāre dīxērunt, nisi dī immortālēs omnī ratiōne plācātī suō nūmine prope fāta ipsa flexissent.[8]$_5$ **20.** Itaque illōrum respōnsīs tum
20 et[9] lūdī$_6$ per decem diēs factī sunt neque rēs ūlla quae ad plācandōs deōs pertinēret praetermissa est. Īdemque iussērunt simulācrum Iovis facere maius et in excelsō collocāre et contrā atque[10] anteā fuerat ad orientem convertere; ac sē spērāre dīxērunt, sī illud signum quod vidētis$_7$ sōlis ortum et forum cūriamque cōnspiceret, fore ut[11]$_8$ ea cōnsilia quae clam essent
25 inita contrā salūtem urbis atque imperī illūstrārentur ut ā senātū populōque Rōmānō$_9$ perspicī possent. Atque illud signum collocandum cōnsulēs illī locāvērunt;[12] sed tanta fuit operis tarditās ut neque superiōribus cōnsulibus neque nōbīs ante hodiernum diem collocārētur.

---

[1] *not only . . . but also* (with **tum**)
[2] *could hardly, it seems, have been (a matter) of human wisdom*
[3] *the following*
[4] *meteors in the west* (this and the following phenomena were regarded as signs of bad luck)
[5] *predict*
[6] *bronze tablets* (on which the laws were inscribed)
[7] *whose gilded (statue) as a suckling child, with open mouth* (**inhiantem**) *at the wolf's breast*
[8] *unless the gods should almost bend the fates themselves*
[9] *both . . . and not* (with **neque**)
[10] *opposite to what it was before*
[11] *(the result) would be that*
[12] *contracted to have the statue erected*

---

[1] a fine example of praeteritiō
[2] 65 B.C.
[3] i.e., they were struck by lightning
[4] examination of entrails and other forms of divination originated in Etruria
[5] **Prope** is used because not even the gods could change fate, according to the ancient view.
[6] Chariot races in the Circus Maximus. Supposedly given to appease the gods, they took the minds of the people from the omens. Holy day became holiday.
[7] He points to the statue on the Capitoline Hill, visible from the Forum.
[8] a common substitute for the rare future passive infinitive, **illūstrātum īrī**
[9] The power and glory of Rome is represented by this phrase, usually abbreviated S.P.Q.R. It is still used.

1. I am going to say what I think.
2. They said that they would burn the city.
3. The statue of Jupiter could be seen from the Forum.
4. Everything was so carefully carried out that it seemed a miracle to all.

Jupiter Is Our Savior

Verba Ūtilia: negō, nūtus, odium, pācō, patefaciō, praeceps, praesēns, restō

IX, 21. Hīc[1] quis potest esse tam āversus ā vērō, tam praeceps, tam mente captus[2] quī neget[1] haec omnia quae vidēmus praecipuēque hanc urbem deōrum immortālium nūtū ac potestāte administrārī? Etenim cum esset ita respōnsum, caedīs, incendia, interitum reī pūblicae comparārī, et ea[3] per cīvīs, quae tum propter magnitūdinem scelerum nōn nūllīs incrēdibilia vidēbantur, ea nōn 5 modo cōgitāta ā nefāriīs cīvibus vērum etiam suscepta esse sēnsistis. Illud[2] vērō nōnne ita praesēns est ut nūtū Iovis Optimī Maximī factum esse videātur, ut, cum hodiernō diē māne per forum meō iussū et coniūrātī et eōrum indicēs in aedem Concordiae dūcerentur, eō ipsō tempore signum statuerētur?[3] Quō collocātō atque ad vōs senātumque conversō, omnia et senātus et vōs quae erant 10 contrā salūtem omnium cōgitāta, illūstrāta, et patefacta vīdistis. **22.** Quō[4] etiam maiōre sunt istī odiō supplicīōque dignī quī nōn sōlum vestrīs domiciliīs atque tēctīs sed etiam deōrum templīs atque dēlūbrīs sunt fūnestōs ac nefāriōs ignīs īnferre cōnātī. Quibus ego sī mē restitisse dīcam, nimium mihi sūmam et nōn sim ferendus: ille,[4] ille Iuppiter restitit; ille Capitōlium, ille 15 haec templa, ille cūnctam urbem, ille vōs omnīs salvōs esse voluit. Dīs ego immortālibus ducibus, hanc mentem voluntātemque suscēpī atque ad haec tanta indicia pervēnī. Iam vērō illa Allobrogum sollicitātiō,[5] iam ab Lentulō cēterīsque domesticīs hostibus tam dēmenter tantae rēs crēditae et ignōtīs et barbarīs commissaeque litterae numquam essent profectō, nisi ab dīs 20 immortālibus huic tantae audāciae[5] cōnsilium esset ēreptum. Quid vērō? Ut hominēs Gallī ex cīvitāte male[6] pācātā, quae gēns ūna restat quae bellum populō Rōmānō facere posse et nōn nōlle videātur, spem imperī ac rērum maximārum ultrō sibi ā patriciīs hominibus oblātam neglegerent vestramque salūtem suīs opibus antepōnerent, id[6] nōn dīvīnitus esse factum putātis, prae- 25 sertim quī[7] nōs nōn pugnandō sed tacendō superāre potuērunt?

[1] in view of this (adverb)
[2] insane (literally, seized in mind)
[3] and those (things) by citizens (at that), (things) which
[4] Therefore
[5] unless good sense had been removed from such bold (men)
[6] imperfectly
[7] particularly since they

---

[1] result clause
[2] explained by the **ut** clause
[3] Perhaps Cicero planned it that way.
[4] We can almost see Cicero's gestures as he points to the statue, then to the Capitoline temple, the Forum temples, the city, the people in front of him.
[5] Supply **numquam facta esset** from the following.
[6] in apposition with the preceding **ut** clause

TRANSLATION

1. Who is so wicked that he would not thank Jupiter?
2. They are deserving of punishment who commit such crimes.
3. If they were present it would be difficult to resist them.
4. If I should say that I did this, I would not be telling the truth.

The Greatest of Bloodless Victories

Verba Ūtilia: celebrō, custōs, interimō, lūctus, lūmen, partim, pertineō, quam ob rem, recordor, salvus

X, 23. Quam ob rem, Quirītēs, quoniam ad omnia pulvīnāria supplicātiō dēcrēta est, celebrātōte[1] illōs diēs cum coniugibus ac līberīs vestrīs. Nam multī saepe honōrēs dīs immortālibus iūstī habitī sunt ac dēbitī,[1] sed profectō iūstiōrēs numquam. Ēreptī enim estis ex crūdēlissimō ac miserrimō

5 interitū, ēreptī sine caede, sine sanguine, sine exercitū, sine dīmicātiōne; togātī, mē ūnō togātō duce et imperātōre, vīcistis.[2] **24.** Etenim recordāminī, Quirītēs, omnīs cīvīlīs dissēnsiōnēs, nōn sōlum eās quās audīstis sed eās quās vōsmet ipsī meministis atque vīdistis. L. Sulla P. Sulpicium[3] oppressit: C. Marium,[4] custōdem huius urbis, multōsque fortīs virōs partim ēiēcit

10 ex cīvitāte, partim interēmit. Cn. Octāvius cōnsul armīs expulit ex urbe collēgam:[5] omnis hic locus acervīs corporum et cīvium sanguine redundāvit.[6] Superāvit posteā Cinna cum Mariō: tum vērō, clārissimīs virīs interfectīs, lūmina cīvitātis exstīncta sunt. Ultus est huius victōriae crūdēlitātem posteā Sulla: nē dīcī quidem opus est quantā dēminūtiōne cīvium et quantā

15 calamitāte reī pūblicae. Dissēnsit M. Lepidus ā clārissimō et fortissimō virō Q. Catulō: attulit nōn tam ipsīus interitus reī pūblicae lūctum quam cēterōrum.

[1] *due*

[1] future imperative, used chiefly in legal and religious language
[2] anaphora with **ēreptī**, then with **sine.** The four nouns are grouped in two pairs; **togātō** (the man of peace) joined with **imperātōre** constitutes an oxymoron
[3] He had proposed a bill to take away from Sulla the command of the army against Mithridates and to give it to Marius.
[4] He had saved the city from the Cimbri and Teutons.
[5] Cinna, one of Marius' men.
[6] Note the zeugma, a figure of speech we do not ordinarily tolerate in English. We would not say *overflowed with heaps of bodies and blood.*

25. Atque illae tamen omnēs dissēnsiōnēs erant eius modī quae nōn ad dēlendam sed ad commūtandam rem pūblicam pertinērent. Nōn illī nūllam esse rem pūblicam sed in eā quae esset sē esse prīncipēs, neque hanc 20 urbem cōnflagrāre sed sē in hāc urbe flōrēre voluērunt. Atque illae tamen omnēs dissēnsiōnēs, quārum nūlla exitium reī pūblicae quaesīvit, eius modī fuērunt ut nōn reconciliātiōne concordiae sed internecīōne cīvium diiūdicātae sint. In hōc autem ūnō post hominum memoriam maximō[2] crūdēlissimōque bellō, quāle[3] bellum nūlla umquam barbaria cum suā 25 gente gessit, quō in bellō lēx[4] haec fuit ā Lentulō, Catilīnā, Cethēgō, Cassiō cōnstitūta, ut omnēs quī, salvā urbe, salvī[5] esse possent in hostium numerō dūcerentur, ita mē gessī, Quirītēs, ut salvī omnēs cōnservārēminī, et, cum hostēs vestrī tantum cīvium[6] superfutūrum putāssent quantum īnfīnītae caedī restitisset, tantum autem urbis quantum flamma obīre nōn 30 potuisset, et urbem et cīvīs integrōs incolumīsque servāvī.

[2] *the greatest of all* (with **ūnō**)
[3] *such a war as*
[4] *principle* (explained by the **ut** clause)
[5] here *(financially) safe, solvent*
[6] *(only) so many of the citizens*

❧ TRANSLATION ❧

1. If they had won, you would all be dead.
2. We have won in a war in which no one died.
3. They wanted a state in which they would be the leaders.
4. Go to the games without danger with your wives and children.

Word Studies

Supplicium and **supplicātiō** both are derived from **sub–** and **plicō**, *fold under,* i.e., bend the knee, the former to receive punishment, the latter for prayer.

Explain *extinct, luminary, sanguinary.*

All I Ask Is Gratitude

Verba Ūtilia: assequor, dēlectō, insignis, inveterāscō, postulō

XI, 26. Quibus prō[1] tantīs rēbus, Quirītēs, nūllum ego ā vōbīs praemium virtūtis, nūllum īnsigne honōris, nūllum monumentum laudis postulābō praeterquam huius diēī memoriam sempiternam. In animīs ego vestrīs omnīs triumphōs meōs, omnia ōrnāmenta honōris, monumenta glōriae, laudis īnsignia condī et collocārī volō. Nihil mē mūtum[1] potest dēlectāre, 5 nihil tacitum, nihil dēnique eius modī quod etiam minus dignī assequī

[1] *in return for these great accomplishments*

---

[1] such as a statue

[2] *my achievements will be kept alive*
[3] *literary records*
[4] *time*

possint. Memoriā vestrā, Quirītēs, nostrae rēs alentur,[2] sermōnibus crēscent, litterārum monumentīs[3] inveterāscent et corrōborābuntur; eandemque diem[4] intellegō, quam spērō aeternam fore, propagātam esse et ad salūtem

10 urbis et ad memoriam cōnsulātūs meī, ūnōque tempore in hāc rē pūblicā duōs[2] cīvīs exstitisse, quōrum alter fīnīs vestrī imperī nōn terrae sed caelī regiōnibus termināret, alter huius imperī domicilium sēdīsque servāret.

❧ TRANSLATION ❧

1. I know that you will give what I want.
2. I want none of the things which others can achieve.
3. I realize that the memory of my deeds will remain as long as Rome remains.

---

[2] Pompey, who had conquered Sertorius in the west (Spain) and Mithridates in the east, and Cicero

---

I Need Your Protection

Verba Ūtilia: externus, lacessō, laedō, noceō, ōrnō, prōvideō, rēctē, subigō, violō, vīvō

[1] *the same as* (with **eadem**)
[2] *it is your* (*responsibility*)
[3] *if their deeds are beneficial to others* (*and rightly so*)
[4] *at some time*
[5] *intentions*
[6] *I, at any rate, can no longer be injured by them*
[7] **quam = et hanc:** *and those who disregard this*
[8] = **mihi**

XII, 27. Sed quoniam eārum rērum quās ego gessī nōn eadem est fortūna atque condiciō quae[1] illōrum quī externa bella gessērunt, quod mihi cum eīs vīvendum est quōs vīcī ac subēgī, illī hostīs aut interfectōs aut oppressōs relīquērunt, vestrum est,[2] Quirītēs, sī cēterīs facta sua rēctē

5 prōsunt,[3] mihi mea nē quandō[4] obsint prōvidēre. Mentēs[5] enim hominum audācissimōrum scelerātae ac nefāriae nē vōbīs nocēre possent ego prōvīdī, nē mihi noceant vestrum est prōvidēre. Quamquam, Quirītēs, mihi quidem ipsī nihil ab istīs iam nocērī[6] potest. Magnum enim est in bonīs praesidium quod mihi in perpetuum comparātum est, magna in rē pūblicā

10 dignitās quae mē semper tacita dēfendet, magna vīs cōnscientiae quam[7] quī neglegunt, cum mē violāre volent, sē indicābunt.[1] **28.** Est enim nōbīs[8] is animus, Quirītēs, ut nōn modo nūllīus audāciae cēdāmus sed etiam omnīs improbōs ultrō semper lacessāmus. Quod sī omnis impetus domesticōrum hostium[2] dēpulsus ā vōbīs sē in mē ūnum converterit, vōbīs erit videndum,

---

[1] But only five years later Cicero was banished, partly as a result of the Catiline affair. It almost seems as if Cicero here foresees this possibility.

[2] As **hostis** means *foreign enemy,* **domesticōrum** is a contradiction (oxymoron); but remember that Cicero justified his action against the conspirators on the grounds that they were traitors.

C. M. Dixon

The Capitoline Hill was the lowest and least inhabited of the seven hills of Rome, but for good reason. It was the center of state religion and was actually a fortified citadel and religious sanctuary. Legend has it that the sacred geese of Juno that were kept in a temple on the hill awakened and alerted the Romans to a sneak attack by the Gauls in 390 B.C., saving the city. The equestrian statue of the emperor Marcus Aurelius dates from the 4th century and was selected from the pope's antiquarian holdings by Michelangelo to be the focal point of the Capitoline square on the top of the hill.

[9] *in what situation*
[10] *in the office bestowed by you*
[11] *(acquired by) good character*
[12] *and even make more splendid*
[13] *may redound to my glory*
[14] *just as* (with **aequē**)
[15] *on that previous night*

15 Quirītēs, quā condiciōne[9] posthāc eōs esse velītis quī sē prō salūte vestrā
obtulerint invidiae perīculīsque omnibus: mihi quidem ipsī quid est quod
iam ad vītae frūctum possit acquīrī, cum praesertim neque in honōre
vestrō[10] neque in glōriā virtūtis[11] quicquam videam altius quō mihi libeat
ascendere? **29.** Illud₃ perficiam profectō, Quirītēs, ut ea quae gessī in
20 cōnsulātū prīvātus tuear atque ōrnem,[12] ut, sī qua est invidia in cōnser-
vandā rē pūblicā suscepta, laedat invidōs, mihi valeat[13] ad glōriam.
Dēnique ita mē in rē pūblicā trāctābō ut meminerim semper quae gesserim,
cūremque ut ea virtūte, nōn cāsū, gesta esse videantur. Vōs, Quirītēs, quoniam iam est nox, venerātī Iovem illum, custōdem huius urbis ac vestrum,
25 in vestra tēcta discēdite et ea, quamquam iam est perīculum dēpulsum,
tamen aequē ac[14] priōre[15]₄ nocte custōdiīs vigiliīsque dēfendite. Id nē vōbīs
diūtius faciendum sit atque ut in perpetuā pāce esse possītis prōvidēbō,
Quirītēs.

TRANSLATION

1. Do you believe that Catiline will injure me?
2. He saw to it that they would not destroy the state.
3. I have to remain with the men who were defeated by me.
4. If you should not defend yourselves, you would suffer a great disaster.

QUESTIONS

1. Who were the Allobroges? What were they doing in Rome?
2. What did Lentulus suggest to Catiline? How did Cicero find out about
   this suggestion?
3. What written evidence did Cicero have against the conspirators?
4. How many conspirators were arrested in or near Rome?
5. How many escaped?
6. Where was the evidence seized?
7. Where was Catiline?
8. Where was this speech made?
9. Before whom was it made?
10. What happened earlier in the day?
11. What did seals have to do with the evidence against the conspirators?
12. What did the conspirators plan to do to Rome?
13. How did the people react to Cicero's speech?

₃ explained by the **ut** clause
₄ after the second oration, in which he said to his listeners: **vestra tēcta vigiliīs
custōdiīsque dēfendite**

Fourth Oration Against Catiline

The third oration reported to the people the evidence against the conspirators which had been presented to the senate, sitting as a court of justice. The fourth oration takes us back to the senate two days later (December 5) for the debate to determine the punishment for the five men who were under arrest. The meeting was held in the Temple of Concord, at one end of the Forum, and Cicero again presided. According to regular procedure, the consul-elect, Silanus, was called upon. In his speech he voted for the death penalty. Then Caesar got up and suggested life imprisonment and confiscation of property. After further discussion Cicero summed up the two views in the present speech. In spite of an attempt to take a judicial position, not preferring one view to the other, Cicero made it clear that he favored the death penalty.

Caesar's speech, moderate in tone, had made a strong impression and it looked as if his motion would be carried. Cato then made a stirring speech in favor of the death penalty. As a result, the death penalty was voted by a large majority. Cicero promptly had the men executed in the underground prison called the Tullianum, which is still in existence. It is near one end of the Forum, at the foot of the Capitoline Hill, not far from the Temple of Concord, where the senate met.

Some weeks later Catiline was killed in battle in Etruria.

Don't Worry About Me, Senators

Verba Ūtilia: acerbus, cruciātus, dēlūbrum, exitus, foedus *(adj.)*, fortiter, gēns, perfugium sēdēs vacuus

I, 1. Videō, patrēs cōnscrīptī, in mē omnium vestrum ōra atque oculōs esse conversōs,₁ videō vōs nōn sōlum dē vestrō ac reī pūblicae, vērum etiam, sī id dēpulsum sit, dē meō perīculō esse sollicitōs. Est mihi iūcunda in malīs et grāta in dolōre vestra ergā mē voluntās, sed eam, per deōs immortālēs, dēpōnite atque oblītī salūtis meae, dē vōbīs ac dē vestrīs līberīs cōgitāte. 5

₁ Silanus and Caesar had made their speeches and the discussion seems to have died down. So the senators naturally turned to Cicero.

[1] *if the consulship were given me under these conditions*

[2] *with a certain (amount of) pain for me and fear for you*

Mihi sī haec condiciō cōnsulātūs[1] data est ut omnīs acerbitātēs, omnīs dolōrēs cruciātūsque perferrem, feram[2] nōn sōlum fortiter vērum etiam libenter, dum modo meīs labōribus vōbīs populōque Rōmānō dignitās salūsque pariātur. **2.** Ego sum ille cōnsul, patrēs cōnscrīptī, cui nōn forum,

10 in quō omnis aequitās continētur,[3] nōn campus[4] cōnsulāribus auspiciīs cōnsecrātus, nōn cūria, summum auxilium omnium gentium, nōn domus, commūne perfugium, nōn lectus ad quiētem datus, nōn dēnique haec sēdēs honōris[5] umquam vacua mortis perīculō atque īnsidiīs fuit. Ego multa tacuī, multa pertulī, multa concessī, multa meō quōdam dolōre in vestrō

15 timōre[2] sānāvī. Nunc sī hunc exitum cōnsulātūs meī dī immortālēs esse voluērunt, ut vōs populumque Rōmānum ex caede miserrimā, coniugēs līberōsque vestrōs virginēsque Vestālēs ex acerbissimā vexātiōne, templa atque dēlūbra, hanc pulcherrimam patriam omnium nostrum ex foedissimā flammā, tōtam Ītaliam ex bellō et vāstitāte ēriperem, quaecumque mihi ūnī

20 prōpōnētur fortūna subeātur.

✺ TRANSLATION ✺

1. You will be free from danger as long as I am consul.

2. This he greatly desired, that the safety of the state be preserved.

3. Provided that no harm is done to you, senators, I will endure everything.

---

[2] Note the strong emphasis produced by the chiasmus. When a verb is repeated, as here, the simple form (**feram**) is often used, as the force of the prefix **per–** seems to carry over.

[3] because the law courts were there

[4] The campus Martius, where the elections were held. The auspices were taken to see if the omens were favorable for the election.

[5] The curule chair (**sella curūlis**), which was a symbol of his office.

The Senate Must Decide

Verba Ūtilia: cēnseō, concitō, coniūrātiō, dubitātiō, facinus, poena, praetūra, prīdem, reus

[1] *in unusual language*

   III, 5. Haec omnia indicēs dētulērunt, reī[1] cōnfessī sunt, vōs multīs iam iūdiciīs iūdicāvistis, prīmum quod mihi grātiās ēgistis singulāribus verbīs[1] et meā virtūte atque dīligentiā perditōrum hominum coniūrātiōnem pate-factam esse dēcrēvistis, deinde quod P. Lentulum sē abdicāre praetūrā

5 coēgistis; tum quod eum et cēterōs dē quibus iūdicāstis in custōdiam dandōs

---

[1] from **reus**

cēnsuistis, maximēque quod meō nōmine supplicātiōnem dēcrēvistis, quī
honōs₂ togātō habitus ante mē est nēminī;[2] postrēmō hesternō diē praemia
lēgātīs Allobrogum Titōque Volturciō dedistis amplissima. Quae sunt
omnia eius modī, ut eī quī in custōdiam nōminatim datī sunt sine ūllā
dubitātiōne ā vōbīs damnātī esse videantur. 10

6. Sed ego īnstituī referre ad vōs, patrēs cōnscrīptī, tamquam integrum,[3]
et[4] dē factō quid iūdicētis et dē poenā quid cēnseātis. Illa praedīcam quae
sunt cōnsulis.[5] Ego magnum in rē pūblicā versārī furōrem et nova[6]
quaedam miscērī[7] et concitārī mala iam prīdem vidēbam, sed hanc tantam,
tam exitiōsam habērī coniūrātiōnem ā cīvibus numquam putāvī. Nunc 15
quicquid est, quōcumque vestrae mentēs inclīnant atque sententiae, stat-
uendum vōbīs ante noctem est. Quantum facinus ad vōs dēlātum sit,
vidētis. Huic sī paucōs putātis affīnēs esse, vehementer errātis. Lātius
opīniōne[8] dissēminātum est hoc malum; mānāvit nōn sōlum per Italiam
vērum etiam trānscendit Alpēs et obscūrē serpēns₃ multās iam prōvinciās 20
occupāvit. Id opprimī sustentandō et prōlātandō[9] nūllō pactō potest;
quācumque ratiōne placet, celeriter vōbīs vindicandum est.

[2] *to no one at all*
[3] *I have begun by referring to you as
if (it were) untouched*
[4] *both*
[5] *(the function) of the consul*
[6] *revolution*
[7] *are being stirred up*
[8] *more widely than you think*
[9] *by putting up with it and putting
it off*

 TRANSLATION

1. You must punish these wicked men as soon as possible.
2. He did not want to tell the senators what they should decide.
3. It is (the duty) of the senate to decide what should be done.

₂ an older form of **honor**
₃ participle from **serpō**

Death or Imprisonment?

Verba Ūtilia: adhūc, adimō, formīdō, fruor, inīquitās, mūnicipium, prīvō,
recūsō, spīritus, vinculum

IV, 7. Videō duās adhūc esse sententiās, ūnam D. Sīlānī, quī cēnset eōs
quī haec[1] dēlēre cōnātī sunt morte esse multandōs, alteram C. Caesaris, quī
mortis poenam removet,[2] cēterōrum suppliciōrum omnīs acerbitātēs
amplectitur.[3] Uterque et prō suā dignitāte et prō rērum magnitūdine in
summā sevēritāte versātur.[4] Alter[5] eōs quī nōs omnīs, quī populum 5
Rōmānum vītā prīvāre cōnātī sunt, quī dēlēre imperium, quī populī
Rōmānī nōmen exstinguere, pūnctum temporis[6] fruī vītā et hōc commūnī
spīritū nōn putat oportēre atque hoc genus poenae saepe in improbōs cīvīs
in hāc rē pūblicā esse ūsūrpātum recordātur. Alter[7] intellegit mortem ā dīs

[1] *all this*
[2] *rejects*
[3] *includes*
[4] *is most stern (literally, is engaged
in the greatest severity)*
[5] *the one (Silanus, subject of **putat**)*
[6] *for a moment of time*
[7] *the other (Caesar)*

8 *from troubles*

9 *for life at that* (literally, *and those perpetual*)

10 *involve*

11 *(those) who*

12 *(in accordance with) their position*

13 *be held up to*

14 *men in the old days*

15 *wanted (us to believe)*

16 *what is to my interest*

17 *perhaps* (literally, *I do not know whether*)

18 *more trouble*

19 *consideration*

20 *ancestors*

21 *guarantee* (literally, *hostage*)

10 immortālibus nōn esse supplicī causā cōnstitūtam, sed aut necessitātem nātūrae aut labōrum[8] ac miseriārum quiētem. Itaque eam sapientēs numquam invītī, fortēs saepe etiam libenter oppetīvērunt. Vincula vērō, et ea sempiterna,[9] certē ad singulārem poenam nefāriī sceleris inventa sunt. Mūnicipiīs dispertīrī$_1$ iubet. Habēre[10]$_2$ vidētur ista rēs inīquitātem, sī 15 imperāre velīs, difficultātem, sī rogāre. Dēcernātur tamen, sī placet. **8.** Ego enim suscipiam et, ut spērō, reperiam quī[11] id quod salūtis omnium causā statuerītis nōn putent esse suae dignitātis[12] recūsāre. Adiungit$_3$ gravem poenam mūnicipiīs, sī quis eōrum$_4$ vincula rūperit; horribilīs custōdiās circumdat et dignās scelere hominum perditōrum; sancit nē quis eōrum poe-20 nam quōs condemnat aut per senātum aut per populum levāre possit; ēripit etiam spem, quae sōla hominem in miseriīs cōnsōlārī solet. Bona praetereā pūblicārī iubet, vītam sōlam relinquit nefāriīs hominibus; quam sī ēripuisset, multās ūnō dolōre animī atque corporis miseriās et omnīs scelerum poenās adēmisset. Itaque ut aliqua in vītā formīdō improbīs esset prōposita,[13] apud 25 īnferōs eius modī quaedam illī antīquī[14] supplicia impiīs cōnstitūta esse voluērunt,[15] quod vidēlicet intellegēbant, hīs remōtīs, nōn esse mortem ipsam pertimēscendam.

V, 9. Nunc, patrēs cōnscrīptī, ego meā videō quid intersit.[16] Sī eritis secūtī sententiam C. Caesaris, quoniam hanc is in rē pūblicā viam quae 30 populāris$_5$ habētur secūtus est, fortasse minus erunt, hōc auctōre et cognitōre huiusce sententiae, mihi populārēs impetūs pertimēscendī; sīn illam alteram, nesciō an[17] amplius mihi negōtī[18] contrahātur. Sed tamen meōrum perīculōrum ratiōnēs[19] ūtilitās reī pūblicae vincat. Habēmus enim ā Caesare, sīcut ipsīus dignitās et maiōrum[20] eius amplitūdō postulābat, sententiam 35 tamquam obsidem[21]$_6$ perpetuae in rem pūblicam voluntātis. Intellēctum est,$_7$ quid interesset inter levitātem cōntiōnātōrum et animum vērē populārem salūtī populī cōnsulentem.

***

⟨❦⟩ TRANSLATION ⟨❦⟩

1. A man's love of his country is shown by his actions.
2. If you approve Caesar's opinion I shall not have to fear attack.
3. The one speaker favored the death penalty; the other, prison.
4. Let it be decided thus if that is the action which the senate will decide upon.

***

$_1$ Supply **eōs** as subject.

$_2$ If the senate insisted on the towns being responsible, there would be unfairness if some towns were exempted; if a mere request were made, there would be many refusals.

$_3$ i.e., Caesar

$_4$ with **vincula**

$_5$ Caesar was the leader of the popular, or democratic, group, and was said to have been supporting Catiline.

$_6$ Cicero thus intimates that Caesar had no connection with Catiline's plot.

$_7$ i.e., when Caesar was speaking

What Might Have Happened

Verba Ūtilia: caedēs, cernō, concidō, dēleō, idcircō, perhorrēscō, praebeō, sīcut, trucīdō, vexātiō

VI, 11. Videor enim mihi vidēre hanc urbem, lūcem orbis terrārum atque arcem[1] omnium gentium, subitō ūnō incendiō concidentem. Cernō animō sepultā[2] in patriā miserōs atque īnsepultōs acervōs cīvium, versātur mihi ante oculōs aspectus Cethēgī et furor in vestrā caede bacchantis. **12.** Cum vērō mihi prōposuī rēgnantem Lentulum, sīcut ipse sē ex fātīs 5 spērāsse cōnfessus est, purpurātum[3] esse huic Gabīnium, cum exercitū vēnisse Catilīnam, tum lāmentātiōnem mātrum familiās,[1] tum fugam virginum atque puerōrum ac vexātiōnem virginum Vestālium perhorrēscō et, quia mihi vehementer haec videntur misera atque miseranda, idcircō in eōs quī ea perficere voluērunt mē sevērum vehementemque praebēbō. Etenim 10 quaerō, sī quis pater familiās, līberīs suīs ā servō interfectīs, uxōre occīsā, incēnsā domō, supplicium[4] dē servīs nōn quam acerbissimum sūmpserit,[4] utrum is clēmēns ac misericors an inhūmānissimus et crūdēlissimus esse videātur. Mihi vērō importūnus ac ferreus quī nōn dolōre et cruciātū nocentis suum[2] dolōrem cruciātumque lēnierit. Sīc nōs in[5] hīs hominibus, 15 quī nōs, quī coniugēs, quī līberōs nostrōs trucīdāre voluērunt, quī singulās ūnīus cuiusque nostrum domōs et hoc ūniversum reī pūblicae domicilium dēlēre cōnātī sunt, quī id ēgērunt, ut gentem Allobrogum in vēstīgiīs[6] huius urbis atque in cinere dēflagrātī imperī collocārent, sī vehementissimī fuerimus, misericordēs habēbimur;[3] sīn remissiōrēs esse voluerimus, summae 20 nōbīs crūdēlitātis in patriae cīviumque perniciē fāma[7] subeunda est.

[1] *bulwark*
[2] *devastated* (literally, *buried*)
[3] *dressed in royal purple* (as minister to "King" Lentulus)
[4] *inflict punishment upon*
[5] *in* (*the case of*)
[6] *ruins*
[7] *(bad) reputation*

✦ TRANSLATION ✦

1. Tell me whether Cicero was merciful or severe.
2. Cicero saw very clearly what would have happened.
3. If Catiline had won, the fate of Rome would have been terrible.

---

[1] the old genitive form, used after **pater** and **māter**
[2] chiasmus, with special emphasis on **nocentis** and **suum**
[3] They will be regarded as merciful even if they are very severe.

It Is Up to You, Senators

Verba Ūtilia: anima, āra, benignitās, fānum, fungor, impius, īnsidiae, obsideō, posthāc, supplex

IX, 18. Quae cum ita sint, patrēs cōnscrīptī, vōbīs populī Rōmānī praesidia nōn dēsunt; vōs nē populō Rōmānō deesse videāminī, prōvidēte. Habētis cōnsulem ex plūrimīs perīculīs et īnsidiīs atque ex mediā morte nōn ad vītam suam sed ad salūtem vestram reservātum. Omnēs ōrdinēs ad
5 cōnservandam rem pūblicam mente, voluntāte, studiō, virtūte, vōce cōnsentiunt. Obsessa facibus et tēlīs impiae coniūrātiōnis vōbīs supplex manūs tendit patria commūnis, vōbīs sē, vōbīs vītam[1] omnium cīvium, vōbīs arcem et Capitōlium,[2] vōbīs ārās Penātium,[1] vōbīs illum ignem Vestae sempiternum, vōbīs omnium deōrum templa atque dēlūbra, vōbīs
10 mūrōs atque urbis tēcta commendat. Praetereā dē vestrā vītā, dē coniugum vestrārum atque līberōrum animā, dē fortūnīs omnium, dē sēdibus, dē focīs vestrīs hodiernō diē vōbīs iūdicandum est. **19.** Habētis ducem memorem vestrī,[3] oblītum suī,[3] quae non semper facultās[2] datur; habētis omnīs ōrdinēs, omnīs hominēs, ūniversum populum Rōmānum, id quod in cīvīlī
15 causā[3] hodiernō diē prīmum vidēmus, ūnum atque idem sentientem. Cōgitāte quantīs labōribus fundātum imperium, quantā virtūte stabilītam lībertātem, quantā deōrum benignitāte auctās exaggerātāsque fortūnās ūna nox paene dēlērit.[4] Id nē umquam posthāc nōn modo nōn cōnficī sed nē cōgitārī quidem possit ā cīvibus hodiernō diē prōvidendum est. Atque
20 haec, nōn ut vōs, quī mihi studiō paene praecurritis, excitārem, locūtus sum, sed ut mea vōx, quae dēbet esse in rē pūblicā prīnceps, officiō fūncta cōnsulārī vidērētur.

XI, 24. Quāpropter dē summā salūte vestrā populīque Rōmānī, dē vestrīs coniugibus ac līberīs, dē ārīs ac focīs, dē fānīs atque templīs, dē
25 tōtīus urbis tēctīs ac sēdibus, dē imperiō ac lībertāte, dē salūte Italiae, dē ūniversā rē pūblicā dēcernite dīligenter, ut īnstituistis, ac fortiter. Habētis eum cōnsulem quī et pārēre vestrīs dēcrētīs nōn dubitet et ea quae statuerītis, quoad vīvet, dēfendere et per sē ipsum praestāre[4] possit.

---

[1] the Penates
[2] an advantage which
[3] in a political matter
[4] carry out, perform

[1] Use plural in English.
[2] The Capitoline Hill has two peaks, on one of which the **arx** was placed; on the other, the **Capitōlium,** or Temple of Jupiter.
[3] pronouns, not adjectives
[4] Two ideas are combined in this sentence: *think with what hard work the empire was founded . . . (and how) one night almost destroyed it.*

1. Do not forget my advice, senators.
2. Cicero thought he had performed his duty.
3. Men are not lacking to (who will) defend you.

Word Studies

Sempiternus, from **semper** and **aeternus,** is tautological, for that which is *eternal* lasts *forever.* There is an English derivative, *sempiternal.*

Exaggerō means *to build up a mound* (from **agger**). The higher you build it the more you *exaggerate.*

Unit IV

Sallust's Catiline (Selections)

The 17th century French painter
Claude Lorrain was especially
known for his use of light in his
landscapes and seascapes. From
this angle, you can see the Arch
of Constantine, built in A.D. 313,
and the edge of the Colosseum.
The Arch of Constantine was
made of Carrara marble, much
of which was taken from the
arches of Trajan and Marcus
Aurelius. The inscription reads:
"To the Emperor Caesar Flavius
Constantinus Maximus, the Senate
and the Roman people dedicate
this notable arch in honor of his
triumphs, because, by Divine
inspiration and greatness of mind,
he freed the Republic by just wars
from tyranny and from factions."
This scene is a detail of the larger
painting by Lorrain.

Roman Politics

Cicero was a clever politician as well as a great writer, as you have seen in his speeches against Catiline. You will see his brilliance again in Sallust's account of the conspiracy.

Although Rome had no formal political parties in the modern sense, during the Republic there were generally two groups opposed to each other, conservative and liberal. Originally, it was the patricians against the plebeians, who were not allowed to hold office. But after the plebeians obtained almost all the patrician rights, the distinction between these groups vanished. Then it was the nobles, that is, the officeholders and their descendants, against the new plebeians, who included the general group of poor people and those who were not officeholders. A third group became involved in politics, the well-to-do, called **equitēs.** Cicero had belonged to this group; his family was wealthy but had not held high office. Cicero was proud of the fact that, though a **novus homō,** he had managed to get into the **cursus honōrum** and become a noble. He persuaded the **equitēs** to align themselves with the nobles or senators, and the cornerstone of his politics was the **concordia ōrdinum** between these conservative groups and against the liberal or radical **populārēs.** Cicero calls the former **bonī** or **optimātēs,** the latter, **improbī.**

The method of voting by classes made it possible for the relatively small group of nobles to retain possession of the offices. The classes in which the richer and more conservative men voted were smaller than the others. Thus the vote of a noble might be worth several times as much as that of a **populāris.**

Campaign methods in Rome bear some resemblances to those in the United States today. Our word *candidate* is derived from **candidātus,** "the man in white," because the Roman candidate wore a toga that had just come from the cleaner's. **Ambitiō** literally means "going around" looking for votes. Another word of the same derivation, **ambitus,** took on a bad sense, that of bribery, also used in going around looking for votes. **Prēnsātiō** meant "catching hold of," shaking a voter's hand or buttonholing him.

Political tours, not unlike today's political campaigns, existed even in ancient Rome. When campaigning for the consulship, Cicero wrote that he would go to northern Italy to campaign in September, when the Roman courts were closed most of the month. Ostensibly he was going on a government mission. Such a combination of government business and political campaigning certainly is not unknown today.

Fortunately, a large number of ancient election posters are preserved in Pompeii. They deal with local rather than national elections and they took the form of appeals painted on house fronts. A typical example is: **L. Pop(idium) Secund(um) aed(īlem) d(ignum) r(ē) p(ūblicā) Tiburtīnus rogat:** "Lucius Popidius Secundus for aedile. Deserving of the state. Tiburtinus asks you (to vote for him)." The letters in parentheses represent the parts in abbreviation. Such heavy abbreviation shows that the phrases were frequently used. Often special groups made the appeal, such as barbers, cake bakers, garlic dealers, fishermen, ballplayers. One reads: **Phoebus cum ēmptōribus** (*customers*). Another: **Sāturnīnus cum discentēs rogat.** (Can you show up Saturninus' Latin by pointing out his mistake in grammar?) **Discentēs** probably means *apprentices*. But when we find support being requested by the sneakthieves (**fūrunculī**), the late-drinkers (**sēribibī ūniversī**), and the sleepers (**dormientēs**), we know the opposition candidates or their supporters are at work.

One candidate's platform was: **Commūnem nummum dīvidendum cēnsiō est. Nam noster nummus magna(m) habet pecūniam:** "It is my vote that the public treasury be divided up. For our treasury has much money." The backer of another says: **Hic aerārium cōnservābit,** "He will watch the treasury," apparently running in opposition to the one who favored dividing up the public funds. Of another candidate it is said: **Pānem bonum fert,** "He delivers good bread."

No place seems to have been immune from the attentions of the eager politicians and their friends: a tombstone near Rome has carved on it the prayer that any candidate who puts a poster on it be defeated in the election. This recalls our "Post no bills." On the other hand, an election poster at Pompeii ends with this warning: **Invidiōse quī dēlēs aegrōtēs,** "May the envious person who destroys this notice become sick."

The chief political issue in the hundred years before Cicero was the land problem. Large farm owners worked their lands with cheap slave labor. The small farmers could not survive. They flocked to Rome, where they found it difficult to get work. Thus, every Roman politician had some proposal for solving the land problem. Gaius Gracchus bought wheat at reasonable prices and sold it to the poor at a low price. During his year as consul, Cicero was compelled to make four speeches on agrarian legislation. Eventually, wheat came to be sold by the government at less than cost, and finally was given free to the citizens. The result of all this is summed up in Juvenal's famous remark that all the Roman people cared about was **pānem et circēnsēs.**

Cicero's second oration against Catiline shows that most of Catiline's followers were heavily in debt. Actually, a widespread financial panic had set in, loans were called, and gold flowed out of the country, even as in modern times. Catiline's proposed solution was a simple one: cancel all debts. His proposal was nothing new. In 86 B.C., during a panic, creditors were forced to accept 25 percent of their loans as full payment. During the Civil War in 49 B.C., something similar happened.

Sallust's Life

Gaius Sallustius Crispus was born in 86 and died in 35 B.C. He was of a plebeian family but entered the senatorial career and became quaestor in 59 B.C. The censors expelled him from the senate in 50 B.C. on a charge of improper conduct. In the Civil War he was on the side of Caesar, who reappointed him quaestor in 49 B.C. Later Sallust became praetor in Africa. After the death of Caesar, Sallust retired and lived in great luxury.

Sallust wrote historical works after his retirement from public life. *The Histories,* originally in five books, is preserved only in fragments covering the period of about ten years after the death of Sulla; and two monographs, *The War with Jugurtha* (111-106 B.C.) and *The Conspiracy of Catiline.* Sallust tried to write without partiality. His work is philosophical in concept and vividly written. You may want to compare his account of the conspiracy of Catiline with Cicero's orations.

The Superiority of the Mind

Verba Ūtilia: commūnis, decet, dīvitiae, fingō, nītor, ops, pecus (–oris), sileō, studeō, venter

1. Omnīs hominēs quī sēsē student praestāre cēterīs animālibus summā ope nītī decet, nē vītam silentiō trānseant velutī pecora, quae nātūra prōna[1] atque ventrī oboedientia fīnxit. Sed nostra omnis vīs in animō et corpore sita est: animī imperiō, corporis servitiō magis ūtimur; alterum[2] nōbīs cum
5 dīs, alterum cum bēluīs commūne est. Quō[3] mihi rēctius vidētur ingenī quam vīrium opibus[4] glōriam quaerere, et, quoniam vīta ipsa quā fruimur brevis est, memoriam nostrī quam maximē longam efficere. Nam dīvitiārum et fōrmae glōria fluxa atque fragilis est, virtūs[5] clāra aeternaque habētur.

2. Multī mortālēs, deditī ventrī atque somnō, indoctī incultīque vītam
10 sīcutī peregrīnantēs[6] trānsiēre; quibus profectō contrā nātūram corpus voluptātī, anima onerī fuit. Eōrum ego vītam mortemque iūxtā[7] aestimō, quoniam dē utrāque silētur. Vērum[8] enim vērō[8] is dēmum mihi vīvere atque fruī animā vidētur quī aliquō negōtiō intentus praeclārī facinoris aut artis bonae fāmam quaerit. Sed in magnā cōpiā rērum[1] aliud aliī[9] nātūra
15 iter ostendit. 3. Pulchrum est bene facere reī pūblicae, etiam bene dīcere haud absurdum est; vel pāce[2] vel bellō clārum fierī licet;[10] et quī fēcēre et quī facta aliōrum scrīpsēre, multī[11] laudantur.

---

[1] with heads bent down
[2] the former (**animī imperiō**)
[3] Therefore
[4] with the help of
[5] intellectual excellence
[6] like (men) going abroad
[7] close to (each other), alike
[8] But certainly
[9] one road to one (man), another road to another
[10] (one) may become famous
[11] many of those who (**quī**)

---

1 i.e., those things in which one may succeed, such as those that follow
2 **in pāce** would be more usual

1. Life is short; let us enjoy it while we may.

2. If you desire to surpass others, you must work.

3. We use the body in order to carry out the wishes of the mind.

4. Some prefer to become famous by deeds, others by their writings.

Word Studies

Give Latin words related to **fragilis** and **fluxus**.

Give English derivatives of **decet, fruor, iūxtā, oboediō, onus, prōnus.**

Catiline's Character

Verba Ūtilia: adulēscentia, avāritia, igitur, incitō, in diēs, invādō, libīdō, lūxuria, memorō, suprā

4. Igitur dē Catilīnae coniūrātiōne quam vērissimē poterō paucīs[1] absolvam; nam id facinus in prīmīs ego memorābile exīstimō sceleris atque perīculī novitāte. Dē cuius hominis mōribus pauca prius[2] explānanda sunt quam initium nārrandī faciam.

5. L. Catilīna, nōbilī genere nātus, fuit magnā vī et animī et corporis [5] sed ingeniō malō prāvōque. Huic ab adulēscentiā bella intestīna, caedēs, rapīnae, discordia cīvīlis grāta[3] fuēre, ibique[1] iuventūtem suam exercuit. Corpus[4] patiēns[2] inediae, algōris,[3] vigiliae suprā quam[4] cuiquam crēdibile est. Animus audāx, subdolus,[5] varius, cuius reī libet[5] simulātor ac dissimulātor, aliēnī appetēns, suī profūsus,[6] ārdēns in cupiditātibus; satis ēloquentiae, [10] sapientiae parum. Vāstus[7] animus immoderāta, incrēdibilia, nimis alta semper cupiēbat. Hunc post dominātiōnem L. Sullae libīdō maxima invāserat reī pūblicae capiendae, neque id quibus modīs assequerētur, dum[8] sibi rēgnum parāret, quicquam pēnsī habēbat.[9] Agitābātur magis magisque in diēs[10] animus ferox inopiā reī familiāris et cōnscientiā scelerum, quae [15] utraque[11] eīs artibus auxerat quās suprā memorāvī. Incitābant[6] praetereā corruptī cīvitātis mōrēs, quōs pessima ac dīversa[12] inter sē mala, lūxuria atque avāritia, vexābant.

[1] and in them
[2] able to endure
[3] cold
[4] beyond what (literally, beyond than)
[5] crafty
[6] desirous of the property of another, extravagant with his own
[7] insatiable
[8] provided that
[9] have any scruple at all how (**quibus modīs**)
[10] day by day
[11] both of which things
[12] opposite to each other

---

[1] Supply **verbīs.**
[2] with **quam**
[3] neuter plural because it modifies nouns in varying genders and numbers
[4] Supply **erat.**
[5] for **cuiuslibet reī,** *of everything*
[6] Supply **eum** as object.

1. I shall tell you about him as clearly as I can.
2. I must tell you about the man before I tell you about his deeds.
3. Provided that he got what he wanted he did not care what happened to others.

Rise and Decline of Rome

Verba Ūtilia: arduus, ascendō, cīvitās, cupīdō, fundō, incrēdibilis, initium, nōbilitās, properō, simul ac

6. Urbem Rōmam, sīcutī ego accēpī, condidēre atque habuēre initiō Troiānī, quī, Aenēā duce, profugī, sēdibus incertīs,[1] vagābantur, et cum hīs Aborīginēs,[1] genus hominum agreste, sine lēgibus, sine imperiō, līberum atque solūtum. Hī postquam in ūna moenia[2] convēnēre, disparī genere, dissimilī linguā, 5 aliī aliō mōre vīventēs,[2] incrēdibile memorātū[3] est quam facile coaluerint; ita brevī[3] multitūdō dīversa atqua vaga concordiā cīvitās facta erat. **7.** Sed cīvitās, incrēdibile memorātū est, adeptā lībertāte, quantum brevī crēverit: tanta cupīdō glōriae incesserat. Iam prīmum iuventūs, simul ac[4] bellī patiēns[5] erat, in castrīs per labōrem ūsum mīlitiae discēbat, magisque in 10 decōrīs armīs et mīlitāribus equīs quam in convīviīs libīdinem habēbant.[4] Igitur tālibus virīs nōn labor īnsolitus, nōn locus ūllus asper aut arduus erat, nōn armātus hostis formīdolōsus; virtūs omnia domuerat. Sed glōriae[6] maximum certāmen inter ipsōs erat: sē[5] quisque hostem ferīre, mūrum ascendere, cōnspicī dum tāle facinus faceret properābat; eās[7] dīvitiās, eam 15 bonam fāmam magnamque nōbilitātem putābant. Laudis avidī, pecūniae līberālēs erant; glōriam ingentem, dīvitiās honestās volēbant. Memorāre possum quibus in locīs maximās hostium cōpiās populus Rōmānus parvā manū fūderit, quās urbīs nātūrā mūnītās pugnandō cēperit, nī ea rēs longius nōs ab inceptō traheret. **9.** Igitur domī mīlitiaeque[8] bonī mōrēs colēbantur; 20 concordia maxima, minima avāritia erat; iūs bonumque apud eōs nōn lēgibus magis quam nātūrā valēbat. Iūrgia, discordiās, simultātēs cum hostibus exercēbant, cīvēs cum cīvibus dē virtūte certābant. In suppliciīs[9] deōrum magnificī,[10] domī parcī, in amīcōs fidēlēs erant. Duābus hīs artibus, audāciā in bellō, ubi pāx ēvēnerat, aequitāte, sēque remque pūblicam cūrābant.

[1] *(having) no permanent homes*
[2] *some living in one manner, others in another*
[3] *hard to believe how*
[4] *as soon as* (with **simul**)
[5] *able to endure war* (literally, *enduring (of) war*)
[6] *for glory* (genitive)
[7] *those (things to be) wealth*
[8] *at home and abroad* (locative)
[9] *worship*
[10] *extravagant*

---

[1] *The Aborigines* simply meant the people living at the site of Rome before the Trojans came.
[2] plural in form but singular in meaning, so that the plural **ūna** with singular meaning is used with it: *into one walled* (city)
[3] adverb
[4] Note the shift from singular (**erat, discēbat**) to plural, all with the singular subject **iuventūs.** It looks almost as if Sallust is trying to undermine your faith in the rules of grammar.
[5] subject of **ferīre** but unnecessary

12. Postquam dīvitiae honōrī esse coepēre et eās glōria, imperium, 25
potentia sequēbātur,[6] hebēscere virtūs, paupertās probrō habērī, innocentia
prō malivolentiā dūcī coepit. Igitur ex dīvitiīs iuventūtem lūxuria atque
avāritia cum superbiā invāsēre: rapere,[7] cōnsūmere; sua parvī pendere,[11]
aliēna cupere; pudōrem, pudīcitiam, dīvīna atque hūmāna prōmiscua, nihil
pēnsī neque moderātī habēre.[12] Operae pretium est,[13] cum domōs atque 30
vīllās cognōveris in urbium modum exaedificātās, vīsere templa deōrum,
quae nostrī maiōrēs, religiōsissimī mortālēs, fēcēre, Vērum illī dēlūbra
deōrum pietāte, domōs suās glōriā decorābant,[8] neque victīs quicquam
praeter iniūriae licentiam ēripiēbant. At hī contrā,[9] ignāvissimī hominēs,
per summum scelus omnia ea sociīs adimere[10] quae fortissimī virī victōrēs 35
relīquerant; proinde quasi iniūriam facere id dēmum esset imperiō ūtī.[14]

[11] *considered their own possessions of little value*

[12] *they regarded as all the same* (without distinction) *modesty and chastity, things divine and human, and showed no care for anything nor any moderation*

[13] *it is worthwhile* (literally, *it is the price of the effort*)

[14] *just as if to do wrong was* (the meaning of) *using power* (**id** sums up **iniūriam facere**)

⟋⟍ TRANSLATION ⟋⟍

1. Do you know who founded that city of Rome?
2. Some responded in one way, others in another.
3. It is not permitted to take away property from the conquered.
4. The desire for glory was so great that Rome grew very quickly.

Word Studies

Give English derivatives of **convīvium, crēscō, dissimulō, initium, vagor.**
Give Latin words related by derivation to **aequitās, certāmen, convīvium, cupīdō, incrēdibilis.**

---

[6] The three subjects are thought of together as a single item; **imperium** is military power, **potentia** political power.

[7] Historical infinitives; supply **iuventūs** as subject.

[8] They decorated their temples with piety, not paintings, their homes with glorious deeds, not statues and expensive furnishings.

[9] adverb

[10] Historical infinitive; the governors grab what the victorious generals have left to the provincials.

Catiline Speaks to His Men

Verba Ūtilia: agitō, cōnsīderō, decus, nequeō, pendō, spolia, stīpendium, ūnā, vigeō, vulgus

[1] *you separately*
[2] *But*
[3] *unless we ourselves make our claim to liberty*
[4] *princes*
[5] *tributary*
[6] *dependent on those*
[7] *if the state were strong*
[8] *defeat at the polls*
[9] *trials in court*
[10] *a laughingstock for the insolence of others*
[11] *on the other hand* (adverb)
[12] *events will take care of the rest*
[13] *that wealth be excessive for them*
[14] *leveling*
[15] *build a continuous row of houses*
[16] *embossed ware* (of silver)
[17] *they squander and waste*
[18] *Why don't you wake up then?*
[19] *Look!*
[20] *use me as commander-in-chief or private*

20. "Sed ego quae mente agitāvī, omnēs iam anteā dīversī [1] audīstis. Cēterum[2] mihi in diēs magis animus accenditur, cum cōnsīderō quae condiciō vītae futūra sit, nisi nōsmet[2] ipsī vindicāmus in lībertātem.[3] Nam postquam rēs pūblica in paucōrum potentium iūs atque diciōnem concessit, semper illīs rēgēs, tetrarchae[4] vectīgālēs[5] esse,[3] populī, nātiōnēs stīpendia pendere; cēterī omnēs, strēnuī, bonī, nōbilēs atque ignōbilēs, vulgus fuimus, sine grātiā, sine auctōritāte, eīs obnoxiī[6] quibus, sī rēs pūblica valēret,[7] formīdinī essēmus. Itaque omnis grātia, potentia, honōs,[4] dīvitiae apud illōs sunt aut ubi illī volunt; nōbīs relīquēre perīcula, repulsās,[8] iūdicia,[9] egestātem. Quae quō usque tandem patiēminī, ō fortissimī virī? Nōnne ēmorī per virtūtem praestat quam vītam miseram atque inhonestam, ubi aliēnae superbiae lūdibriō[10] fuerīs, per dēdecus āmittere? Vērum enim vērō, prō[5] deum atque hominum fidem, victōria in manū nōbīs est, viget aetās, animus valet; contrā[11] illīs annīs atque dīvitiīs omnia cōnsenuērunt. Tantum modo inceptō[6] opus est, cētera rēs expediet.[12] Etenim quis mortālium, cui virīle ingenium est, tolerāre potest illīs dīvitiās superāre,[13] quās profundant in exstruendō marī[7] et montibus coaequandīs,[14] nōbīs rem familiārem etiam ad necessāria deesse? Illōs bīnās aut amplius domōs continuāre,[15] nōbīs larem familiārem nusquam ūllum esse? Cum tabulās, signa, toreumata[16] emunt, nova dīruunt, alia aedificant, postrēmō omnibus modīs pecūniam trahunt, vexant,[17] tamen summā libīdine dīvitiās suās vincere nequeunt. At nōbīs est domī inopia, forīs aes aliēnum; mala rēs, spēs multō asperior: dēnique quid reliquī habēmus praeter miseram animam?

"Quīn igitur expergīsciminī?[18] Ēn,[19] illa, illa quam saepe optāstis lībertās, praetereā dīvitiae, decus, glōria in oculīs sita sunt; fortūna omnia ea victōribus praemia posuit. Rēs, tempus, perīcula, egestās, bellī spolia magnifica magis quam ōrātiō mea vōs hortantur. Vel imperātōre vel mīlite mē ūtiminī;[20] neque animus neque corpus ā vōbīs aberit. Haec ipsa, ut spērō, vōbīscum ūnā cōnsul agam, nisi forte mē animus fallit et vōs servīre magis quam imperāre parātī estis."

---

[1] The adjective is used adverbially.
[2] **−met** is an intensive particle: *we ourselves*
[3] historical infinitive, with **rēgēs, tetrarchae** as subject
[4] old form of **honor**
[5] interjection: *Oh!* **deum** is genitive plural
[6] noun, ablative
[7] The Romans built concrete foundations for houses out into the sea.

The Palatine Hill was one of the seven hills of Rome. Tradition has it that Romulus and Remus founded the town that would be Rome on the Palatine. In addition to being the nerve center of the city, it became the hill on which many famous Romans built their personal palaces. It occupied a very important position geographically, too. The Forum was located between the Palatine and the Capitoline and the Colosseum between the Palatine and the Esquiline. In this view, we are looking at the other side of the Palatine, not the one facing the Forum itself.

1. It is a pleasure to me to see you.
2. There is need of help in this matter.
3. Day by day the republic is losing its liberty.
4. Use the opportunity; fight, and I will fight with you.

Word Studies

Give English derivatives of **decus, optō, spolia, stīpendium, vigeō, vulgus**.

To what Latin words are the following related: **agitō, dēdecus, serviō?**

Cherchez La Femme

Verba Ūtilia: cōnfodiō, facinus, flāgitium, introeō, largior, locuplēs, polliceor, probrum, reticeō

21. Catilīna pollicērī[1] tabulās novās, prōscrīptiōnem locuplētium, magistrātūs, sacerdōtia, rapīnās, alia omnia quae bellum atque libīdō victōrum fert. **23.** In eā coniūrātiōne fuit Q. Cūrius, nātus haud obscūrō locō, flāgitiīs atque facinoribus coopertus, quem cēnsōrēs senātū probrī grātiā[1] mōver-

5 ant. Huic hominī nōn minor vānitās inerat quam audācia; neque reticēre quae audierat neque suamet[2] ipse scelera occultāre, prōrsus[3] neque dīcere neque facere quicquam pēnsī habēbat.[4] Erat eī cum Fulviā, muliere nōbilī, vetus cōnsuētūdō.[5] Cui cum minus grātus esset, quia inopiā minus largīrī poterat, repente glōriāns maria montīsque[6] pollicērī coepit, et minārī inter-

10 dum ferrō, nī sibi obnoxia[7] foret; postrēmō ferōcius agitāre quam solitus erat. At Fulvia, īnsolentiae[8] Cūrī causā cognitā, tāle perīculum reī pūblicae haud occultum habuit,[9] sed, sublātō auctōre,[10] dē Catilīnae coniūrātiōne quae quōque[11] modō audierat complūribus nārrāvit.

28. Igitur, perterritīs ac dubitantibus cēterīs, C. Cornēlius, eques Rōmānus,
15 operam suam pollicitus, et cum eō L. Vargunteius senātor cōnstituēre eā nocte paulō post cum armātīs hominibus sīcutī salūtātum[12] introīre ad Cicerōnem, ac dē imprōvīsō[13] domī suae imparātum cōnfodere. Cūrius ubi intellegit quantum perīculum cōnsulī impendeat, properē per Fulviam Cicerōnī dolum quī parābātur ēnūntiat. Ita illī,[2] iānuā prohibitī, tantum facinus frūstrā
20 suscēperant.

---

[1] historical infinitive
[2] Cornelius and Vargunteius

1. The two men tried to enter in order to fight.
2. She told everyone what she knew about the conspiracy.
3. Though he was born of a noble family, he was very stupid.
4. When he realized what would happen he quickly told Cicero.

Word Studies

Explain the derivation of *frustration, occult, sacerdotal.*

Give the Latin words related to **complūrēs, imprōvīsus, rapīna, reticeō, sacerdōtium.**

Catiline and Manlius Speak Up

Verba Ūtilia: certāmen, dēcrētum, egeō, īra, parricīda, pereō, praeceps, supplex, temere, testor

31. Postrēmō dissimulandī causā aut suī expūrgandī, sīcut iūrgiō lacessītus foret,[1] in senātum vēnit. Tum M. Tullius cōnsul, sīve praesentiam eius timēns sīve īrā commōtus, ōrātiōnem habuit lūculentam atque ūtilem reī pūblicae, quam posteā scrīptam ēdidit.[1] Sed ubi ille assēdit, Catilīna, ut erat parātus ad dissimulanda omnia, dēmissō vultū, vōce supplicī postulāre ā patribus coepit nē quid dē sē temere crēderent; eā[2] familiā ortum, ita sē ab adulēscentiā vītam īnstituisse ut omnia bona in spē habēret; nē exīstimārent sibi, patriciō hominī, cuius ipsīus atque maiōrum plūrima beneficia in plēbem Rōmānam essent, perditā rē pūblicā opus esse,[3] cum eam servāret M. Tullius, inquilīnus[2] cīvis urbis Rōmae. Ad hoc 10 maledicta alia cum adderet, obstrepere omnēs,[3] hostem atque parricīdam vocāre. Tum ille furibundus, "Quoniam quidem circumventus," inquit, "ab inimīcīs praeceps agor, incendium meum ruīnā restinguam."[4]

[1] *as if he had been provoked in a (personal) quarrel*
[2] *such*
[3] *that he had need of a ruined state (with **sibi**)*
[4] *foreign-born*

---

[1] the first oration against Catiline
[2] This is a dig at Cicero's being not a native-born Roman but a **novus homō** from Arpinum.
[3] i.e., **senātōrēs**, subject of the historical infinitives
[4] i.e., he will cause general destruction to put out the fire started against him

33. Dum haec Rōmae geruntur, C. Mānlius ex suō numerō lēgātōs ad
15 Mārcium Rēgem[5] mittit cum mandātīs huiusce modī: "Deōs hominēsque
testāmur, imperātor, nōs arma neque contrā patriam cēpisse neque quō[6]
perīculum aliīs facerēmus, sed utī corpora nostra ab iniūriā tūta forent,
quī[7] miserī, egentēs violentiā atque crūdēlitāte faenerātōrum⁵ plērīque
patriā,⁶ sed omnēs fāmā atque fortūnīs expertēs sumus. Saepe maiōrēs
20 vestrum,⁸ miseritī[7] plēbis Rōmānae, dēcrētīs suīs inopiae eius opitulātī[8]
sunt, ac novissimē memoriā nostrā propter magnitūdinem aeris aliēnī,
volentibus omnibus bonīs, argentum aere solūtum est.⁹ Saepe ipsa plēbs,
aut dominandī studiō permōta aut superbiā magistrātuum, armāta ā patribus
sēcessit. At nōs nōn imperium neque dīvitiās petimus, quārum rērum causā
25 bella atque certāmina omnia inter mortālīs sunt, sed lībertātem, quam nēmō
bonus nisi cum animā simul āmittit. Tē atque senātum obtestāmur, cōnsulātis₉
miserīs cīvibus, lēgis praesidium, quod inīquitās praetōris ēripuit, restituātis,
nēve nōbīs eam necessitūdinem impōnātis, ut quaerāmus quōnam modō
maximē ultī sanguinem nostrum pereāmus."[10]

◈ TRANSLATION ◈

1. Cicero was so aroused that he made a fine speech.
2. Was he not a man of noble family, born in Rome?
3. If we should be freed of debt, the state would be safe.
4. Catiline asked the senators not to think that he would destroy the state.

₅ general of the government forces opposing Manlius
₆ for **ut**
₇ Supply **nōs** (implied in **nostra**) as antecedent.
₈ genitive of **vōs**
₉ The clause (with **ut**) is the object of **obtestāmur:** *that you have regard for the citizens.*

The Scum of the Earth

Verba Ūtilia: adeō *(adv.)*, aliēnus, domō, exōrnō, fascis, īnsigne, multitūdō, occāsus, ortus, pāreō

36. Sed ipse paucōs diēs commorātus apud C. Flāminium in agrō
Arrētīnō,¹ dum vīcīnitātem anteā sollicitātam armīs exōrnat, cum fascibus
atque aliīs imperī īnsignibus in castra ad Mānlium contendit. Haec² ubi
Rōmae comperta sunt, senātus Catilīnam et Mānlium hostīs iūdicat.

¹ at Arretium
² these facts

Eā tempestāte[3] mihi imperium populī Rōmānī multō maximē miserābile 5
vīsum est. Cui[1] cum ad occāsum ab ortū sōlis[4] omnia domita armīs pārērent,
domī ōtium atque dīvitiae, quae prīma mortālēs putant, affluerent,[5] fuēre
tamen cīvēs quī sēque remque pūblicam obstinātīs animīs perditum[6] īrent.
Namque duōbus senātī[2] dēcrētīs ex tantā multitūdine neque praemiō
inductus[3] coniūrātiōnem patefēcerat neque ex castrīs Catilīnae quisquam 10
omnium discesserat; tanta vīs morbī, atque utī tābēs,[7] plērōsque[4] cīvium animōs
invāserat.

37. Neque sōlum illīs aliēna[8] mēns erat quī cōnsciī[9] coniūrātiōnis fuerant, sed omnīnō cūncta plēbēs[5] novārum rērum studiō Catilīnae incepta
probābat. Id adeō mōre suō vidēbātur facere.[10] Nam semper in cīvitāte, 15
quibus[6] opēs nūllae sunt bonīs invident, malōs extollunt, vetera ōdēre, nova
exoptant, odiō suārum rērum mūtārī omnia student, turbā atque sēditiōnibus
sine cūrā aluntur, quoniam egestās facile habētur sine damnō.[11] Sed urbāna
plēbēs ea vērō praeceps[12] erat dē multīs causīs. Prīmum omnium quī ubīque
probrō atque petulantiā maximē praestābant, item aliī per dēdecora, pat- 20
rimōniīs āmissīs, postrēmō omnēs quōs flāgitium aut facinus domō expulerat,
eī Rōmam sīcut in sentīnam cōnflūxerant.

3 time
4 from sunrise to sunset, from east to west
5 abounded
6 would go to destroy
7 like a plague
8 alienated
9 aware of
10 The plebs seemed to do this in accordance with their custom.
11 they flourish on rioting and rebellion without worry, since their poverty is easily endured without loss
12 desperate

❧ TRANSLATION ❧

1. He remained a few days at the house of a friend.
2. There were no men who obeyed the decree of the senate.
3. The poor men envy the rich and are eager for revolution.

Word Studies

Explain by derivation: *affluence, extol, fascism, insignia, invidious, mutation.*

What Latin words are related to **cōnfluō, cōnscius, exoptō, inceptum, miserābilis, tempestās, vīcīnitās?**

---

[1] i.e., the **imperium**
[2] old form of genitive for **senātūs**: *in spite of two decrees of the senate* (offering rewards)
[3] modifies **quisquam**, the subject
[4] We might expect the genitive, modifying **cīvium.**
[5] for **plēbs** (singular)
[6] Supply **eī** as antecedent.

Lentulus and the Allobroges

Verba Ūtilia: adeō *(verb)*, doleō, idōneus, magistrātus, miseria, operam dō, remedium, simulō, tālis, vehementer

39. Īsdem temporibus Rōmae Lentulus, sīcutī Catilīna praecēperat, quōscumque mōribus aut fortūnā novīs rēbus idōneōs crēdēbat, aut per sē aut per aliōs sollicitābat, neque sōlum cīvīs, sed cuiusque modī genus hominum,[1] quod modo[2] bellō ūsuī foret.[2] **40.** Igitur P. Umbrēnō cuidam
5 negōtium dat, utī lēgātōs Allobrogum requīrat eōsque, sī possit, impellat ad societātem bellī, exīstimāns pūblicē prīvatimque aere aliēnō oppressōs,[3] praetereā quod nātūrā gēns Gallica bellicōsa esset, facile eōs ad tāle cōnsilium addūcī posse. Umbrēnus quod in Galliā negōtiātus erat, plērīsque prīncipibus cīvitātum nōtus erat atque eōs nōverat. Itaque sine morā, ubi prīmum
10 lēgātōs in forō cōnspexit, percontātus pauca dē statū cīvitātis et quasi dolēns eius[4] cāsum requīrere coepit quem exitum tantīs malīs spērārent. Postquam illōs videt querī dē avāritiā magistrātuum, accūsāre senātum, quod in eō auxilī nihil esset, miseriīs suīs remedium mortem[3] expectāre, "at ego," inquit, "vōbīs, sī modo virī esse vultis, ratiōnem ostendam quā
15 tanta ista mala effugiātis."[4] Haec ubi dīxit, Allobrogēs in maximam spem adductī Umbrēnum ōrāre[5] ut suī[6] miserērētur; nihil tam asperum neque tam difficile esse quod nōn cupidissimē factūrī essent, dum ea rēs cīvitātem aere aliēnō līberāret. Coniūrātiōnem aperit, nōminat sociōs, praetereā multōs cuiusque generis innoxiōs,[5][7] quō lēgātīs animus amplior esset.
20 Deinde eōs pollicitōs operam suam domum dīmittit. **41.** Sed Allobrogēs diū in incertō habuēre[6] quidnam cōnsilī caperent. In alterā parte erat aes aliēnum, studium bellī, magna mercēs in spē victōriae, at in alterā maiōrēs opēs,[8] tūta cōnsilia, prō incertā spē certa praemia. Haec illīs volventibus, tandem vīcit fortūna reī pūblicae. Itaque Q. Fabiō Sangae, cuius patrōciniō[9]
25 cīvitās plūrimum ūtēbātur, rem omnem utī cognōverant aperiunt. Cicerō, per Sangam cōnsiliō cognitō, lēgātīs praecēpit ut studium coniūrātiōnis vehementer simulent, cēterōs adeant, bene polliceantur, dentque operam utī eōs quam maximē manifēstōs habeant.[7]

---

[1] all sorts of men
[2] provided that (literally, which only)
[3] death as a remedy
[4] you may escape
[5] innocent
[6] were uncertain (literally, held (it) in uncertainty)
[7] that they see to it that they catch them (the conspirators) in the act, as far as possible

---

[1] The antecedent of **quod** is **genus**.
[2] = **esset**
[3] modifies **eōs**
[4] refers to **cīvitātis**
[5] historical infinitive
[6] genitive of the reflexive, referring to **Allobrogēs;** it depends on **miserērētur**
[7] perhaps he mentioned members of the popular party, even Caesar
[8] i.e., the resources of the Roman state, which could crush the rebellion
[9] He represented them in legal matters.

1. They begged him to free them from their troubles.
2. See to it that you find out what they are going to do.
3. Provided that you give us help, we will give you rewards.
4. If you will be men you will persuade your friends to do this.

Documents Seized— Caesar Involved?

Verba Ūtilia: aliter, cōnflō, grandis, haud, index, īnfrā, mūnus, praeceptum, prex, suspicor

44. Sed Allobrogēs ex praeceptō Cicerōnis per Gabīnium cēterōs conveniunt. Ab Lentulō, Cethēgō, Statiliō, item Cassiō postulant iūs iūrandum,[1] quod signātum ad cīvīs perferant:[1] aliter haud facile eōs ad tantum negōtium impellī posse. Cēterī nihil suspicantēs dant,[2] Cassius sēmet[3] eō[4] brevī ventūrum pollicētur ac paulō ante lēgātōs ex urbe proficīscitur. Lentulus cum eīs T. Volturcium quendam Crotōniēnsem mittit, ut Allobrogēs, prius quam domum pergerent, cum Catilīnā, datā atque acceptā fidē, societātem cōnfirmārent. Ipse Volturciō litterās ad Catilīnam dat, quārum exemplum īnfrā scrīptum est: "Quī sim, ex eō quem ad tē mīsī cognōscēs. Fac cōgitēs[2] in quantā calamitāte sīs, et meminerīs[5] tē virum esse. Cōnsīderēs 10 quid tuae ratiōnēs postulent. Auxilium petās ab omnibus, etiam ab īnfimīs."[6]

49. Sed īsdem temporibus Q. Catulus et C. Pīsō neque precibus neque grātiā neque pretiō Cicerōnem impellere potuēre utī per Allobrogēs aut alium indicem C. Caesar falsō nōminārētur. Nam uterque cum illō gravīs inimīcitiās exercēbant.[3] Rēs autem opportūna vidēbātur, quod is prīvātim 15 ēgregiā līberālitāte, pūblicē maximīs mūneribus[4] grandem pecūniam dēbēbat. Sed ubi cōnsulem ad tantum facinus impellere nequeunt, ipsī singillātim circumeundō atque ēmentiendō[5] quae sē ex Volturciō aut Allobrogibus audīsse dīcerent, magnam illī invidiam cōnflāverant, usque eō[6] ut nōn nūllī equitēs Rōmānī, quī praesidī causā cum tēlīs erant circum 20 aedem Concordiae, seu perīculī magnitūdine seu animī mōbilitāte impulsī, quō studium suum in rem pūblicam clārius esset, ēgredientī ex senātū Caesarī gladiō minitārentur.

[1] a (written) oath
[2] see that you realize
[3] carried on
[4] games (given at his own expense while aedile)
[5] lying about
[6] to such an extent that

---

[1] relative purpose clause
[2] Supply **iūs iūrandum.**
[3] emphatic for **sē**
[4] i.e., to Gaul
[5] The hortatory subjunctive is sometimes used instead of the imperative; this verb has no present imperative.
[6] He means the slaves.

1. Many asked whether Caesar favored Catiline.
2. They tried to kill Caesar as he came out of the senate.
3. They asked for a letter which they might show to their friends.
4. In order that the matter might be more definite, Lentulus gave them a letter.

Caesar and Cato

Verba Ūtilia: addō, beneficium, cōnstantia, dīves, ignōscō, largior, mānsuētūdō, misericordia, prope, sevēritās

54. Igitur eīs genus, aetās, ēloquentia prope aequālia[1] fuēre, magnitūdō animī pār, item glōria, sed alia aliī.[1] Caesar beneficiīs ac mūnificentiā magnus habēbātur, integritāte vītae Catō. Ille mānsuētūdine et misericordiā clārus factus, huic sevēritās dignitātem addiderat. Caesar dandō, sublevandō,
5 ignōscendō, Catō nihil largiendō[2] glōriam adeptus est. In alterō miserīs perfugium erat, in alterō malīs perniciēs. Illīus facilitās, huius cōnstantia laudābātur. Postrēmō Caesar in animum indūxerat labōrāre, vigilāre; negōtiīs amīcōrum intentus, sua neglegere,[2] nihil dēnegāre quod dōnō dignum esset; sibi magnum imperium, exercitum, bellum novum exoptābat, ubi
10 virtūs ēnitēscere posset. At Catōnī studium modestiae, decoris, sed maximē sevēritātis erat; nōn dīvitiīs cum dīvite neque factiōne cum factiōsō, sed cum strēnuō virtūte, cum modestō pudōre, cum innocente abstinentiā certābat;[3] esse quam vidērī bonus mālēbat: ita, quō minus[3] petēbat glōriam, eō magis illum assequēbātur.[4]

---

[1] neuter because it modifies nouns of different genders
[2] historical infinitives
[3] He did not try to outdo a rich man in wealth, etc., but a vigorous man in courage, etc.
[4] i.e., glory

1. What did Cato prefer to be?
2. They were equal in age and eloquence.
3. He did nothing that was unworthy of him.
4. The former was praised for his kindness, the latter for his sternness.

Word Studies

In the reading find all words with suffixes in **–tās, –tia,** and **–tūdō.**

What Latin words are related to **abstinentia, ēloquentia, innocēns, mūnificentia, perfugium?**

Word Studies

Explain by derivation: *erudition, forensic, sentient, tributary, venial.*

What Latin words are related to **concursus, ērudītus, inūsitātus, lēgitimus, quaestiō, sēgregō?**

Persōna is derived from the Greek word πρόσωπον, *mask* (literally, "face"), worn by actors in plays. The changes in spelling are explained by the fact that the word was first borrowed by the Etruscans, from whom the Romans got it. The masks differed and represented the different *types* or *characters.* Finally **persōna** took on the meaning *individual,* as in English *person.*

Archias Comes to Rome

Verba Ūtilia: adhibeō, antecellō, ars, celeber, cognitiō, hīc, hospitium, nancīscor, plēnus, senectūs

III. Nam, ut prīmum ex puerīs[1] excessit Archiās atque ab eīs artibus quibus aetās puerīlis ad hūmānitātem īnfōrmārī solet, sē ad scrībendī studium contulit, prīmum Antiochīae (nam ibi nātus est locō[2] nōbilī), celebrī[3] quondam urbe[1] et cōpiōsā atque ērudītissimīs hominibus līberālissimīsque studiīs affluentī, celeriter antecellere omnibus ingenī glōriā coepit. Post[2] in cēterīs 5 Asiae partibus cūnctāque Graeciā sīc eius adventūs[4] celebrābantur ut fāmam ingenī expectātiō hominis, expectātiōnem ipsīus adventus admīrātiōque superāret. **5.** Erat Italia tum plēna Graecārum artium ac disciplīnārum,[5] studiaque haec et in Latiō[6] vehementius tum colēbantur quam nunc īsdem in oppidīs et hic Rōmae propter tranquillitātem reī pūblicae nōn neglegēbantur. 10 Itaque hunc et Tarentīnī et Locrēnsēs et Rēgīnī et Neāpolitānī[7] cīvitāte[3] cēterīsque praemiīs dōnārunt, et omnēs quī aliquid dē ingeniīs poterant iūdicāre cognitiōne atque hospitiō dignum[4] exīstimārunt. Hāc tantā celebritāte fāmae cum esset iam absentibus[8] nōtus, Rōmam vēnit, Mariō cōnsule et Catulō. Nactus est prīmum cōnsulēs eōs quōrum alter rēs ad scrībendum maximās, 15 alter cum[9] rēs gestās, tum[9] etiam studium atque aurēs[10] adhibēre posset.

[1] *boyhood*
[2] *rank*
[3] *populous*
[4] *arrival* (at various places)
[5] *sciences*
[6] *Latium*
[7] *the people of Tarentum, Locri, Regium, and Naples*
[8] *to those* (living) *far away*
[9] *not only . . . but also*
[10] *attention* (literally, *ears*)

---

[1] a noun in apposition with a locative (**Antiochīae**) is in the ablative
[2] adverb
[3] i.e., honorary citizenship, as is sometimes done today
[4] Supply **eum.**

[11] *(an indication of his) ability*
[12] *a favorite of* (literally, *agreeable to*)
[13] *was a guest of*
[14] *bound by (ties of) intimacy*

Statim Lūcullī,[5] cum praetextātus[6] etiam tum Archiās esset, eum domum suam recēpērunt. Est iam hoc nōn sōlum ingenī[11] ac litterārum vērum etiam nātūrae atque virtūtis, ut domus quae huius adulēscentiae prīma fāvit eadem esset

20 familiārissima senectūtī. **6.** Erat temporibus illīs iūcundus[12] Q. Metellō illī Numidicō et eius Piō fīliō, audiēbātur ā M. Aemiliō, vīvēbat[13] cum Q. Catulō et patre et fīliō, ā L. Crassō colēbātur, Lūcullōs vērō et Drūsum et Octāviōs et Catōnem et tōtam Hortēnsiōrum domum dēvīnctam cōnsuētūdine[14] cum tenēret, afficiēbātur summō honōre, quod eum nōn sōlum colēbant quī aliquid

25 percipere atque audīre studēbant vērum etiam sī quī forte simulābant.

---

[5] There are two brothers, Lucius and Marcus.
[6] Literally this means *wearing the praetexta,* applied to Roman boys before they put on the **toga cīvīlis** and became citizens.

Archias Enrolled as a Roman Citizen

Verba Ūtilia: corrumpō, dēsīderō, flāgitō, immō, immō vērō, intereō, profiteor, repudiō, satis, testimōnium

[1] *after a rather long interval*
[2] *with very favorable treaty rights* (with Rome)
[3] *although*
[4] *in addition*
[5] *Whoever*
[6] *enroll*
[7] *scrupulous honesty*
[8] *acted (in the matter)*

IV. Interim satis longō intervāllō,[1] cum esset cum M. Lūcullō in Siciliam profectus et cum ex eā prōvinciā cum eōdem Lūcullō dēcēderet, vēnit Hēraclēam. Quae cum esset cīvitās aequissimō iūre ac foedere,[2] ascrībī sē in eam cīvitātem voluit,[1] idque, cum[3] ipse per sē dignus putārētur, tum[4]

5 auctōritāte et grātiā Lūcullī ab Hēracliēnsibus impetrāvit. **7.** Data est cīvitās[2] Silvānī lēge et Carbōnis: *Sī quī[5] foederātīs cīvitātibus ascrīptī fuissent, sī tum cum lēx ferēbātur in Ītaliā domicilium habuissent et sī sexāgintā diēbus apud praetōrem essent professī.*[6][3] Cum hic domicilium Rōmae multōs iam annōs habēret, professus est apud praetōrem Q. Metellum,

10 familiārissimum suum. **8.** Sī nihil aliud nisi dē cīvitāte ac lēge dīcimus, nihil dīcō amplius; causa dicta est. Quid enim hōrum[4] īnfirmārī, Grattī,[5] potest? Hēraclēaene esse tum ascrīptum negābis? Adest vir summā auctōritāte et religiōne[7] et fidē, M. Lūcullus; quī sē nōn opīnārī sed scīre, nōn audīvisse sed vīdisse, nōn interfuisse sed ēgisse[8] dīcit. Adsunt Hēracliēnsēs lēgātī,

---

[1] i.e., Archias
[2] i.e., Roman
[3] Supply *they would become citizens.*
[4] with **quid;** the three conditions mentioned in the law
[5] Grattius, of whom we know nothing, brought the charges against Archias.

nōbilissimī hominēs, huius iūdicī causā cum mandātīs et cum pūblicō tes- 15
timōniō vēnerunt; quī hunc ascrīptum Hēraclēae esse dīcunt. Hīc tū tabulās
dēsīderās Hēracliēnsium pūblicās, quās Italicō bellō,[6] incēnsō tabulāriō,[9]
interīsse scīmus omnēs? Est rīdiculum ad ea quae habēmus nihil dīcere,
quaerere quae habēre nōn possumus, et dē hominum memoriā tacēre, litterārum memoriam[7] flāgitāre et, cum habeās amplissimī virī religiōnem, 20
integerrimī[8] mūnicipī iūs iūrandum fidemque, ea quae dēprāvārī nūllō modō
possunt repudiāre, tabulās quās īdem[10] dīcis solēre corrumpī[9] dēsīderāre.

9. An[10] domicilium Rōmae nōn habuit is quī tot annīs[11] ante cīvitātem
datam sēdem omnium rērum ac fortūnārum suārum Rōmae collocāvit? An
nōn est professus? Immō vērō eīs tabulīs[11] professus quae sōlae ex illā profes- 25
siōne collēgiōque praetōrum[12] obtinent pūblicārum tabulārum auctōritātem.

[9] record office
[10] you yourself [literally, the same (you)]
[11] by means of the records
[12] of the registration books of the board of praetors

Word Studies

From what Latin words are the following derived: *amplification, corruption, desire, federation, incendiary, tabulation?*

What Latin words are related to the following: **ascrībō, corrumpō, domicilium, familiāris, intereō?**

---

[6] the Social War
[7] The *memory* of documents (**litterārum**) means that documents enable us to remember.
[8] Heraclea had a better reputation than some other towns.
[9] Grattius charges that the Roman registration records have been tampered with.
[10] This and the next sentence take up the second and third qualifications required by the law.
[11] thirteen years (102–89 B.C.)

The Census Records

Verba Ūtilia: ascrībō, asservō, dubitō, impertiō, irrēpō, litūra, neglegēns, scaenicus

V. Nam cum Appī tabulae neglegentius asservātae dīcerentur, Gabīnī,[1]
quam diū incolumis[1] fuit, levitās, post damnātiōnem calamitās[2] omnem
tabulārum fidem resignāsset,[3] Metellus, homō sānctissimus modestissimusque
omnium, tantā dīligentiā fuit ut ad L. Lentulum praetōrem et ad iūdicēs
vēnerit[2] et ūnīus nōminis litūrā sē commōtum esse dīxerit. Hīs igitur in 5

[1] before conviction (literally, unharmed)
[2] misfortune
[3] destroyed (literally, unsealed)

---

[1] with **levitās** and **calamitās;** the contrast between **Appī** and **Gabīnī** made unnecessary an **et** before the latter
[2] Metellus, in dealing with another case, said that there was only one erasure in the records, clearly then not that of Archias' name.

4 *why is it that*

5 *the people of Regium, Locri, Naples, Tarentum*

6 *I suppose* (**crēdō** is often used ironically)

7 *takes advantage of*

8 *our* (Roman) *census records*

9 *Of course* (pointing to the irony in **obscūrum**) *it is not known*

10 *in the last censorship*

11 *at that time quaestor* (in apposition with **eōdem**)

12 *had conducted himself as a citizen at that time* (i.e., of the census)

13 *both*

14 *shared in*

15 *rewards* (for special services)

tabulīs nūllam litūram in nōmine A. Licinī vidētis. **10.** Quae cum ita sint, quid est quod[4] dē eius cīvitāte dubitētis, praesertim cum aliīs quoque in cīvitātibus fuerit ascrīptus? Etenim cum mediocribus[3] multīs et aut nūllā aut humilī aliquā arte praeditīs grātuītō cīvitātem in Graeciā[4] hominēs

10 impertiēbant, Rēgīnōs[5] crēdō[6] aut Locrēnsēs aut Neāpolitānōs aut Tarentīnōs, quod[5] scaenicīs[6] artificibus largīrī solēbant, id huic summā ingenī praeditō glōriā nōluisse! Quid? Cum cēterī nōn modo post cīvitātem datam sed etiam post lēgem Pāpiam[7] aliquō modō in eōrum mūnicipiōrum tabulās irrēpsērunt, hic, quī nē ūtitur[7] quidem illīs[8] in quibus est scrīptus, quod

15 semper sē Hēracliēnsem esse voluit, reiciētur? **11.** Cēnsūs[8] nostrōs requīris. Scīlicet,[9] est enim obscūrum proximīs cēnsōribus[10] hunc cum clārissimō imperātōre, L. Lūcullō, apud[9] exercitum fuisse, superiōribus cum eōdem quaestōre[11] fuisse in Asiā, prīmīs, Iūliō et Crassō, nūllam populī partem esse cēnsam. Sed quoniam cēnsus non iūs cīvitātis cōnfirmat ac

20 tantum modo indicat eum quī sit cēnsus ita sē iam tum gessisse prō cīve eīs temporibus,[12] is quem tū[10] crīmināris nē ipsīus[11] quidem iūdiciō in cīvium Rōmānōrum iūre esse versātum, et[13] testāmentum saepe fēcit nostrīs lēgibus et adiit[14] hērēditātēs cīvium Rōmānōrum et in beneficiīs[15] ad aerārium dēlātus est ā L. Lūcullō prō cōnsule.

---

3 dative, with **impertiēbant**

4 He means Magna Graecia, a name for southern Italy.

5 The antecedent is **id** below, referring to citizenship.

6 At this time acting was not highly regarded by the Romans.

7 This law called for the expulsion of all aliens, i.e., those who did not have legal residence. It was under this law that the charges were brought against Archias.

8 Supply **tabulīs,** i.e., those of the Greek cities other than Heraclea that had granted him citizenship.

9 He was *at* the army, not *in* it.

10 Grattius, the plaintiff

11 Grattius argues that Archias himself (**ipsīus**) did not consider himself a citizen because he did nothing to get himself listed.

The Value of Literature

Verba Ūtilia: cotīdiē, doctrīna, fōns, magnō opere, pudet, reprehendō, strepitus, tantō opere, tenebrae, vetustās

VI. Quaere argūmenta, sī quae potes; numquam enim hic neque suō neque amīcōrum iūdiciō revincētur.[1] **12.** Quaerēs ā nōbīs, Grattī, cūr tantō opere hōc homine dēlectēmur.[1] Quia suppeditat nōbīs ubi[2] et animus ex hōc

---

1 Obviously Grattius will ask no such thing; Cicero is simply looking for an excuse to talk about the importance of literature.

The Forum of Julius Caesar was erected in 48 B.C. It is located behind the Forum Romanum and contained both temples and commercial interests. In the background is the monument to Victor Emmanuel II, begun in 1885 and inaugurated in 1911. It houses the Tomb of the Unknown Soldier and honors Italian war dead. The King was highly criticized for building such a Roman "imitation" so near the ancient monuments. Native Romans still call it the "Wedding Cake."

forēnsī strepitū reficiātur et aurēs convīciō dēfessae conquiēscant. An tū
5 exīstimās aut suppetere nōbīs posse[3] quod cotīdiē dīcāmus in tantā varietāte
rērum, nisi animōs nostrōs doctrīnā excolāmus, aut ferre animōs tantam
posse contentiōnem, nisi eōs doctrīnā eādem relaxēmus? Ego vērō fateor
mē hīs studiīs esse dēditum. Cēterōs pudeat,[4] sī quī ita sē litterīs[5] abdidērunt
ut nihil possint ex eīs neque[6] ad commūnem afferre frūctum neque in
10 aspectum lūcemque prōferre;[7] mē autem quid pudeat[8] quī tot annōs ita vīvō,
iūdicēs, ut ā nūllīus umquam mē tempore aut commodō[9] aut ōtium meum
abstrāxerit aut voluptās āvocārit aut dēnique somnus retardārit? **13.** Quārē
quis tandem mē reprehendat,[10] aut quis mihi iūre suscēnseat, sī,[2] quantum
cēterīs[3] ad suās rēs obeundās, quantum ad fēstōs diēs lūdōrum celebrandōs,
15 quantum ad aliās voluptātēs et ad ipsam requiem animī et corporis concēditur
temporum, quantum aliī[11] tribuunt tempestīvīs[12] convīviīs, quantum dēnique
alveolō,[13] quantum pilae, tantum mihi egomet ad haec studia recolenda
sūmpserō? Atque hoc ideō mihi concēdendum est magis, quod ex hīs
studiīs haec quoque crēscit ōrātiō et facultās,[14] quae quantacumque est in
20 mē, numquam amīcōrum perīculīs dēfuit. Quae[4] sī cui levior vidētur, illa[15]
quidem certē quae summa sunt ex quō fonte hauriam sentiō. **14.** Nam nisi
multōrum praeceptīs multīsque litterīs[16] mihi ab adulēscentiā suāsissem
nihil esse in vītā magnō opere expetendum nisi laudem atque honestātem,
in eā autem persequendā omnēs cruciātūs corporis, omnia perīcula mortis
25 atque exilī parvī[17] esse dūcenda, numquam mē prō salūte vestrā in tot ac
tantās dīmicātiōnēs atque in hōs prōflīgātōrum hominum cotīdiānōs
impetūs obiēcissem. Sed plēnī omnēs sunt librī, plēnae sapientium vōcēs,[18]
plēna exemplōrum vetustās; quae iacērent in tenebrīs omnia, nisi litterārum
lūmen accēderet.[19] Quam multās nōbīs imāginēs nōn sōlum ad intuendum
30 vērum etiam ad imitandum fortissimōrum virōrum expressās[20] scrīptōrēs
et Graecī et Latīnī relīquērunt! Quās ego mihi semper in administrandā rē
pūblicā prōpōnēns animum et mentem meam ipsā cōgitātiōne hominum
excellentium cōnfōrmābam.

Word Studies

Explain by derivation: *crescent, festivity, font, impudent, luminosity, reprehensible.*

Give Latin words related to **abdō, abstrahō, doctrīna, retardō, tempestīvus.**

---

[3] *that what we talk about every day could be supplied to us*
[4] *let others be ashamed*
[5] *in literature* (ablative)
[6] *either . . . or*
[7] *bringing nothing to the light (of day),* i.e., *they publish nothing*
[8] *why should I be ashamed*
[9] *from the critical need or advantage of any (client)*
[10] *can criticize*
[11] *some* (in contrast with **cēterīs**, all others)
[12] *early*
[13] *gambling board*
[14] *ability in speaking*
[15] *the following (beliefs)*
[16] *much (reading of) literature*
[17] *are to be considered of little value* (not with **exsilī**)
[18] *the sayings of philosophers*
[19] *if the light of literature did not shine upon them*
[20] *clear-cut portraits* (with **imāginēs**)

[2] introduces the last word, **sūmpserō; quantum** is subject of **concēditur**
[3] dative with **concēditur**
[4] i.e., **facultās**

Natural Ability and Training

Verba Ūtilia: adversus *(adj.)*, efferō, ērudiō, excellēns, eximius, gustō, prōdō, quispiam, secundus, senex

VII, 15. Quaeret quispiam: "Quid? Illī ipsī summī virī quōrum virtūtēs litterīs prōditae sunt, istāne doctrīnā quam tū effers laudibus ērudītī fuērunt?" Difficile est hoc dē omnibus cōnfirmāre, sed tamen est certum quid respondeam.[1] Ego multōs hominēs excellentī animō ac virtūte fuisse sine doctrīnā et nātūrae ipsīus habitū[2] prope dīvīnō per sē ipsōs et 5 moderātōs et gravēs exstitisse[3] fateor; etiam illud adiungō, saepius ad laudem atque virtūtem nātūram sine doctrīnā quam sine nātūrā valuisse[4] doctrīnam. Atque īdem ego hoc contendō, cum ad nātūram eximiam et illūstrem accesserit ratiō quaedam cōnfōrmātiōque doctrīnae,[5] tum illud nesciō quid praeclārum ac singulāre[6] solēre exsistere. **16.** Ex hōc esse hunc 10 numerō quem patrēs nostrī vīdērunt, dīvīnum hominem, Āfricānum,[1] ex hōc C. Laelium, L. Fūrium, moderātissimōs hominēs et continentissimōs, ex hōc fortissimum virum et illīs temporibus doctissimum, M. Catōnem illum senem; quī profectō sī nihil ad percipiendam colendamque virtūtem litterīs adiuvārentur, numquam sē ad eārum studium contulissent. Quod sī[7] 15 nōn hic tantus frūctus ostenderētur, et sī ex hīs studiīs dēlectātiō sōla peterētur, tamen, ut opīnor, hanc animī remissiōnem hūmānissimam ac līberālissimam iūdicārētis. Nam cēterae[2] neque temporum[8] sunt neque aetātum omnium neque locōrum; at haec studia adulēscentiam acuunt, senectūtem oblectant, secundās[9] rēs ōrnant, adversīs perfugium ac 20 sōlācium praebent, dēlectant domī, nōn impediunt forīs, pernoctant nōbīscum, peregrīnantur, rūsticantur. **17.** Quodsī ipsī haec[10] neque attingere neque sēnsū nostrō gustāre possēmus, tamen ea mīrārī dēbērēmus, etiam cum in aliīs vidērēmus.

[1] *what I should say*
[2] *by the quality of their nature*
[3] *stood out as self-controlled and worthy men*
[4] *has succeeded in producing (literally, has had power (with regard) to (with **ad**))*
[5] *a kind of (**quaedam**) systematic training (resulting from) study*
[6] *something ("I don't know what") outstanding and unique*
[7] *But if*
[8] *are not (suitable) for*
[9] *prosperity*
[10] *can neither attain to nor enjoy with our senses these (studies)*

---

[1] Scipio the Younger (185–129 B.C.), who with Laelius and Furius encouraged the development of Greek culture in Rome. Cato (234–149 B.C.), on the other hand, opposed Greek culture and was more of a self-made man.
[2] i.e., **remissiōnēs**

Poets Are Sacred

Verba Ūtilia: admīror, conciliō, dīligō, immānis, īnflō, mōtus, saxum, sōlitūdō, venustās, versus

VIII. Quis nostrum tam animō agrestī ac dūrō fuit ut Rōscī morte nūper nōn commovērētur? Quī cum esset senex mortuus, tamen propter excellentem artem ac venustātem vidēbātur₁ omnīnō morī nōn dēbuisse. Ergō ille corporis mōtū tantum amōrem sibi conciliārat ā nōbīs omnibus; nōs animōrum
5 incrēdibilēs mōtūs celeritātemque ingeniōrum[1] neglegēmus? **18.** Quotiēns ego hunc Archiam vīdī, iūdicēs (ūtar enim vestrā benignitāte,[2] quoniam mē in hōc novō genere dīcendī tam dīligenter attenditis), quotiēns ego hunc vīdī, cum litteram scrīpsisset nūllam,[3] magnum numerum optimōrum versuum dē eīs ipsīs rēbus quae tum agerentur, dīcere ex tempore, quotiēns,
10 revocātum eandem rem dīcere, commūtātīs verbīs atque sententiīs! Quae vērō accūrātē cōgitātēque scrīpsisset, ea sīc vīdī probārī ut ad veterum scrīptōrum laudem pervenīret. Hunc ego nōn dīligam, nōn admīrer, nōn omnī ratiōne dēfendendum putem? Atque sīc ā summīs hominibus ērudītissimīsque accēpimus, cēterārum rērum studia ex doctrīnā et praeceptīs et
15 arte cōnstāre,[4] poētam nātūrā ipsā valēre et mentis vīribus excitārī et quasi dīvīnō quōdam spīritū īnflārī. Quārē suō iūre noster ille Ennius[5] "sānctōs" appellat poētās, quod quasi deōrum aliquō dōnō atque mūnere commendātī nōbīs esse videantur. **19.** Sit igitur, iūdicēs, sānctum apud vōs, hūmānissimōs hominēs, hoc poētae nōmen, quod nūlla umquam barbaria violāvit.
20 Saxa atque sōlitūdinēs vōcī respondent, bēstiae saepe immānēs cantū flectuntur atque cōnsistunt; nōs īnstitūtī rēbus optimīs nōn poētārum vōce moveāmur?[6] Homērum Colophōniī[7]₂ cīvem esse dīcunt suum, Chiī suum vindicant, Salamīniī repetunt, Smyrnaeī vērō suum esse cōnfirmant itaque etiam dēlūbrum eius in oppidō dēdicāvērunt, permultī aliī praetereā pug-
25 nant inter sē atque contendunt.

[1] *activity of mind* (in contrast with **corporis**) *and inborn* (**ingeniōrum**) *alertness*
[2] *I avail myself of your indulgence, I beg your pardon.*
[3] *though he had not written down a single letter*
[4] *are based on*
[5] *that famous poet of ours*
[6] *should we not be moved*
[7] *the people of Colophon, Chios, Salamis, and Smyrna*

Word Studies

Explain *extempore*.
Give English derivatives of **benignitās, bēstia, celeritās, conciliō.**
Name Latin words related to **admīror, cōgitātē, incrēdibilis, mōtus, sōlitūdō.**

₁ The subject is **quī** but in translating it is better to make the verb impersonal: *who, it seemed.*
₂ three other places claimed him: Argos, Athens, and Rhodes

No Fame Without Poets

Verba Ūtilia: aeternus, aiō, attendō, dīmicō, faucēs, impetus, monumentum, ōlim, triumphus, vīvus

IX. Ergō illī aliēnum,[1] quia poēta fuit, post mortem etiam expetunt; nōs hunc vīvum, quī et voluntāte et lēgibus noster est, repudiābimus, praesertim cum omne ōlim studium atque omne ingenium contulerit Archiās ad populī Rōmānī glōriam laudemque celebrandam? Nam et Cimbricās rēs[2] adulēscēns attigit et ipsī illī C. Mariō, quī dūrior[1] ad haec studia vidēbātur, 5 iūcundus fuit. **20.** Neque enim quisquam est tam āversus ā Mūsīs[2] quī nōn mandārī versibus aeternum suōrum labōrum praecōnium facile patiātur. Themistoclem illum,[3] summum Athēnīs virum, dīxisse aiunt, cum ex eō quaererētur quod acroāma[4][3] aut cuius vōcem libentissimē audīret: eius ā quō sua[4] virtūs optimē praedicārētur. Itaque ille Marius item eximiē L. Plōtium 10 dīlēxit, cuius ingeniō putābat ea quae gesserat posse celebrārī. **21.** Mithridāticum vērō bellum, magnum atque difficile et in multā varietāte[5] terrā marīque versātum, tōtum ab hōc[5] expressum est; quī librī nōn modo L. Lūcullum, fortissimum et clārissimum virum, vērum etiam populī Rōmānī nōmen illūstrant. Populus enim Rōmānus aperuit, Lūcullō imperante, Pontum et 15 rēgiīs quondam opibus et ipsā nātūrā et regiōne[6] vāllātum; populī Rōmānī exercitus, eōdem duce, nōn maximā manū innumerābilīs Armeniōrum cōpiās fūdit; populī Rōmānī laus est urbem amīcissimam Cȳzicēnōrum[7] eiusdem cōnsiliō ex omnī impetū rēgiō atque tōtīus bellī ōre ac faucibus ēreptam esse atque servātam; nostra[6] semper ferētur[8] et praedicābitur, L. 20 Lūcullō dīmicante, cum, interfectīs ducibus, dēpressa hostium classis est, incrēdibilis apud Tenedum pugna illa nāvālis; nostra sunt tropaea, nostra monumenta, nostrī triumphī. Quae[9] quōrum ingeniīs efferuntur, ab eīs populī Rōmānī fāma celebrātur. **22.** Cārus fuit Āfricānō superiōrī[7] noster Ennius, itaque etiam in sepulcrō Scīpiōnum putātur is esse cōnstitūtus ex mar- 25 more;[8] at eīs laudibus[9] certē nōn sōlum ipse quī laudātur sed etiam populī Rōmānī nōmen ōrnātur. In caelum huius[10] proavus Catō tollitur; magnus honōs populī Rōmānī rēbus adiungitur. Omnēs dēnique illī[10] Maximī, Mārcellī, Fulviī nōn sine commūnī omnium nostrum laude decorantur.

[1] *rather rough for*
[2] *so unfriendly to literature*
[3] *the famous Themistocles*
[4] *entertainment*
[5] *with many changes of fortune*
[6] *by the nature of the region*
[7] *the people of Cyzicus*
[8] *will be spoken of*
[9] *the fame of the Roman people is made known by those by whose talents these deeds* (**quae**) *are praised*
[10] *famous men such as Maximus,* etc.

---

[1] He would be a *foreigner* to at least six of the seven cities that claimed him.
[2] Marius' defeat of the Cimbri in 101 B.C.
[3] Greek neuter accusative singular, modified by the interrogative adjective **quod**
[4] i.e., of Themistocles
[5] Archias
[6] predicate adjective in agreement with **pugna:** *as ours*
[7] Scipio the Elder
[8] i.e., a bust of marble
[9] The praise was in the *Annales,* a poem by Ennius, of which only fragments have survived.
[10] *the present* Cato, often called Uticensis because he committed suicide at Utica, Africa. His great-grandfather was known as the Censor.

Word Studies

Give English derivatives of **aeternus, attendō, celebrō, impetus, praedicō.**

What Latin words are related to the following: **ēripiō, libenter, impetus, nāvālis, vīvus?**

Poets Give Immortality

Verba Ūtilia: expetō, fīnis, proptereā, quārē, regiō, rūsticus, sānē, sonō, tumulus, vēndō

X. Ergō illum quī haec fēcerat,[1] Rudīnum[2] hominem, maiōrēs nostrī in cīvitātem recēpērunt; nōs hunc Hēracliēnsem multīs cīvitātibus expetītum, in hāc[1] autem lēgibus cōnstitūtum dē nostrā cīvitāte ēiciēmus? **23.** Nam sī quis minōrem glōriae frūctum putat ex Graecīs versibus percipī quam ex Latīnīs, vehementer errat, proptereā quod Graeca[2] leguntur in omnibus ferē gentibus, Latīna suīs fīnibus exiguīs sānē continentur. Quārē sī rēs eae quās gessimus orbis terrae regiōnibus dēfīniuntur, cupere dēbēmus quo[3] manuum nostrārum tēla pervēnerint, eōdem[3] glōriam fāmamque penetrāre, quod cum[4] ipsīs populīs[5] dē quōrum rēbus scrībitur haec ampla sunt,[5] tum[4] eīs certē quī dē[6] vītā glōriae causā dīmicant, hoc maximum et perīculōrum incitāmentum est et labōrum. **24.** Quam multōs scrīptōrēs rērum suārum magnus ille Alexander sēcum habuisse dīcitur! Atque is tamen, cum in Sīgēō[3] ad Achillis tumulum astitisset: "Ō fortūnāte," inquit, "adulēscēns, quī[7] tuae virtūtis Homērum praecōnem invenerīs!" Et vērē. Nam nisi Īlias illa exstitisset, īdem tumulus quī corpus eius contēxerat nōmen etiam obruisset. Quid? Noster hic Magnus[8] quī cum virtūte fortūnam adaequāvit, nōnne Theophanem Mytilēnaeum,[9] scrīptōrem rērum suārum, in cōntiōne mīlitum cīvitāte dōnāvit, et nostrī illī fortēs virī, sed[10] rūsticī ac mīlitēs, dulcēdine quādam glōriae commōtī quasi participēs eiusdem laudis magnō illud clāmōre approbāvērunt? **25.** Itaque, crēdō,[4] sī cīvis Rōmānus Archiās lēgibus nōn esset, ut[5] ab aliquō imperātōre cīvitāte dōnārētur perficere nōn

---

[1] *who composed these (poems)*
[2] *of Rudiae*
[3] *to the same place . . . where*
[4] *not only . . . but also*
[5] *these poems were full of honor for the nations*
[6] *for life*
[7] *since you*
[8] *Our (Pompey) the Great*
[9] *Theŏph´anēs of Mytilē´ne*
[10] *though*

---

[1] i.e., Heraclea
[2] used as a neuter plural noun: *Greek*
[3] *Sigeum* (Sīgē´um), a promontory near Troy
[4] ironical
[5] The clause is object of **perficere.**

potuit. Sulla cum Hispānōs et Gallōs dōnāret,₆ crēdō, hunc petentem repudiāsset; quem₇ nōs in cōntiōne vīdimus, cum eī libellum malus poēta dē populō[11] subiēcisset,[12]₈ quod epigramma₉ in eum fēcisset, tantum modo alternīs versibus longiusculīs,[13] statim ex eīs rēbus quās tum vēndēbat 25 iubēre eī praemium tribuī, sed eā condiciōne, nē quid posteā scrīberet. Quī[14] sēdulitātem malī poētae dūxerit aliquō tamen praemiō dignam, huius ingenium et virtūtem in scrībendō et cōpiam nōn expetīsset? **26.** Quid? Ā Q. Metellō Piō, familiārissimō suō, quī cīvitāte multōs dōnāvit, neque per sē neque per Lūcullōs impetrāvisset? Quī praesertim usque eō[15] dē suīs 30 rēbus scrībī cuperet ut etiam Cordubae[16] nātīs poētīs pingue quiddam sonantibus[17] atque peregrīnum tamen aurēs suās dēderet.

[11] *from among the common people*
[12] *had thrust up*
[13] *every other line being a little bit longer*
[14] *since he* (i.e., Sulla)
[15] *to such an extent*
[16] *Cordova*
[17] *having a sort of dull, foreign sound*

₆ Supply **cīvitāte.**
₇ Sulla
₈ to Sulla, who was sitting on a platform in the Forum while presiding at an auction sale of confiscated property
₉ Greek neuter accusative: *an epigram which;* in apposition with **libellum**

The Statesman's Reward
Is Immortal Fame

Verba Ūtilia: aditus, attingō, bellō, dēspiciō, inchoō, libellus, merx, praeter, stimulus, totiēns

XI. Neque est hoc dissimulandum, quod obscūrārī nōn potest sed prae nōbīs ferendum:[1] trahimur omnēs studiō laudis, et optimus quisque[2] maximē glōriā dūcitur. Ipsī illī philosophī etiam in eīs libellīs quōs dē contemnendā glōriā scrībunt nōmen suum īnscrībunt; in eō ipsō[3] in quō praedicātiōnem nōbilitātemque dēspiciunt praedicārī dē sē ac nōminārī₁ volunt.

27. Decimus quidem Brūtus, summus vir et imperātor, Acciī, amīcissimī suī, carminibus templōrum ac monumentōrum aditūs exōrnāvit suōrum. Iam vērō ille quī cum Aetōlīs, Enniō comite, bellāvit Fulvius nōn dubitāvit Mārtis manubiās[4] Mūsīs cōnsecrāre. Quārē in quā urbe imperātōrēs prope armātī[5] poētārum nōmen et Mūsārum dēlūbra coluērunt, in eā nōn dēbent 10 togātī iūdicēs ā Mūsārum honōre et ā poētārum salūte abhorrēre.

[1] *must be frankly admitted* (literally, *must be carried in front of us*)
[2] *all the best men*
[3] *in the very action*
[4] *spoils of war* (**Mārtis**)
[5] *almost (still) in uniform* (i.e., just after returning from war)

₁ impersonal; we would make **sē** the subject of the infinitives

28. Atque ut id$_2$ libentius faciātis, iam mē vōbīs, iūdicēs, indicābō, et dē meō quōdam amōre glōriae, nimis ācrī fortasse, vērum tamen honestō, vōbīs cōnfitēbor. Nam quās rēs nōs$_3$ in cōnsulātū nostrō vōbīscum simul
15 prō salūte huius urbis atque imperī et prō vītā cīvium prōque ūniversā rē pūblicā gessimus, attigit hic$_4$ versibus atque inchoāvit.$_5$ Quibus audītīs, quod mihi magna rēs et iūcunda vīsa est, hunc ad perficiendum adōrnāvī.[6] Nūllam enim virtūs aliam mercēdem labōrum perīculōrumque dēsīderat praeter hanc laudis et glōriae; quā quidem dētrāctā, iūdicēs, quid est quod[7]
20 in hōc tam exiguō vītae curriculō et tam brevī tantīs nōs$_6$ in labōribus exerceāmus? **29.** Certē, sī nihil animus praesentīret$_7$ in posterum, et sī quibus regiōnibus[8] vītae spatium circumscrīptum est, eīsdem omnēs cōgitātiōnēs termināret suās, nec tantīs sē labōribus frangeret neque tot cūrīs vigiliīsque angerētur nec totiēns dē ipsā vītā dīmicāret. Nunc[9] īnsidet
25 quaedam in optimō quōque virtūs,[10] quae noctēs ac diēs animum glōriae stimulīs concitat atque admonet, nōn cum$_8$ vītae tempore esse dīmittendam commemorātiōnem nōminis nostrī sed cum omnī posteritāte adaequandam.

[6] *I furnished him (with the facts)*
[7] *for which*
[8] *boundaries*
[9] *as it is* (i.e., according to, not contrary to, fact)
[10] *good quality*

$_2$ i.e., see to the welfare of poets
$_3$ plural of modesty, for **ego**
$_4$ Archias
$_5$ The relative clause is the object.
$_6$ object of verb
$_7$ **animus** is subject of all the verbs
$_8$ preposition

Be Kind to the Poet

Verba Ūtilia: auctōritās, cōgitātiō, effigiēs, exprimō, orbis terrae, poliō, simpliciter, spatium, statua, tranquillus

XII, 30. An vērō tam parvī animī[1] videāmur[2] esse omnēs quī in rē pūblicā atque in hīs vītae perīculīs labōribusque versāmur ut, cum usque ad extrēmum spatium$_1$ nūllum tranquillum atque ōtiōsum spīritum dūxerīmus, nōbīscum simul moritūra omnia arbitrēmur? An$_2$ statuās et imāginēs, nōn animōrum
5 simulācra sed corporum, studiōsē multī summī hominēs relīquērunt;

[1] *of such limited outlook* (literally, *so smallminded*)
[2] *are we to seem?*

$_1$ Supply **vītae.**
$_2$ introduces a question, but best translated by *if* or *when*

cōnsiliōrum relinquere ac virtūtum nostrārum effigiem nōnne multō mālle dēbēmus summīs ingeniīs[3] expressam et polītam? Ego vērō omnia quae gerēbam iam tum in gerendō[4] spargere[3] mē ac dissēmināre arbitrābar in orbis terrae memoriam sempiternam. Haec[4] vērō sīve ā meō sēnsū post mortem āfutūra est sīve, ut sapientissimī hominēs putāvērunt, ad aliquam animī meī 10 partem pertinēbit,[5] nunc quidem certē cōgitātiōne quādam spēque dēlector.

31. Quārē cōnservāte, iūdicēs, hominem pudōre eō quem amīcōrum[6] vidētis comprobārī cum dignitāte, tum etiam vetustāte, ingeniō[7] autem tantō quantum id convenit exīstimārī, quod summōrum hominum ingeniīs expetītum esse videātis, causā[8] vērō eius modī quae beneficiō lēgis,[5] 15 auctōritāte mūnicipī, testimōniō Lūcullī, tabulīs Metellī comprobētur. Quae cum ita sint, petimus ā vōbīs, iūdicēs, sī qua nōn modo hūmāna vērum etiam dīvīna in tantīs ingeniīs commendātiō dēbet esse, ut eum[6] quī vōs, quī vestrōs imperātōrēs, quī populī Rōmānī rēs gestās semper ōrnāvit, quī etiam hīs recentibus nostrīs vestrīsque domesticīs perīculīs[7] aeternum sē 20 testimōnium laudis datūrum esse profitētur estque ex eō numerō quī semper apud omnēs sānctī sunt habitī itaque[9] dictī, sīc in vestram accipiātis fidem ut hūmānitāte vestrā levātus potius quam acerbitāte violātus esse vīdeātur.

Quae dē causā prō meā cōnsuētūdine breviter simpliciterque dīxī, 25 iūdicēs, ea cōnfīdō probāta esse omnibus: quae ā forēnsī aliēna iūdiciālīque cōnsuētūdine et dē hominis ingeniō et commūniter dē ipsō studiō locūtus sum, ea, iūdicēs, ā vōbīs spērō esse in bonam partem accepta; ab eō quī iūdicium exercet certō sciō.

Word Studies

What Latin words are related to **dissēminō, domesticus, forēnsis, mūnicipium, ōtiōsus, profiteor?**

In this reading, find five words with the suffix **–tās** and two with the suffix **–tiō.**

---

[3] *by the greatest geniuses,* or *by (men of) the greatest genius*
[4] *even in doing (them)*
[5] *shall belong to,* i.e., *shall be known to*
[6] *proved not only by the high position of but also by the long acquaintance with his friends* (with **dignitāte** and **vetustāte**)
[7] *a man of so much genius as it is fitting to be judged (to be) such as you see has been sought out by men of the greatest genius*
[8] *(a man) with a case*
[9] = **et ita**

---

[3] The next infinitive explains the metaphor.
[4] i.e., **memoria**
[5] the law of 89 B.C.
[6] object of **accipiātis,** which is an indirect command (without **ut**), object of **petimus**
[7] the conspiracy of Catiline, about which Archias had promised to write

Unit VI

Cicero Against Verres and Antony

*In Segesta, Sicily are the remains of a Roman theater. Located in northwest Sicily, ancient Segesta was traditionally a Trojan colony. It became a Carthaginian dependency sometime after 400 B.C. but thrived under later Roman domination. This exceptionally well-preserved theater is well-known for its excellent acoustics. It dates from the 3rd century B.C. and was built on the summit of a hill. From this view, you can see the semi-circular auditorium (**cavea**) around the smaller semi-circular orchestra in front of the stage, typical of many Roman theaters.*

163

Verres and Antony

Cicero's first great success as an orator was achieved with his speeches against Verres; his last success with the speeches against Antony.

In 75 B.C., Cicero was elected quaestor and served in Sicily. His fair treatment of the Sicilians won their respect and friendship, and they asked him to serve as their attorney in the prosecution of their former praetor, Verres, whose plundering of Sicilian towns seems to have broken all records. At the trial of Verres, Cicero made such a devastating attack that Verres went into voluntary exile, thus admitting his guilt. But Cicero had still more evidence against Verres, which he wrote up in five other speeches that were published but not delivered. These speeches against Verres established Cicero's fame, and he became the chief lawyer and orator in Rome.

Toward the end of his life, Cicero had outlived his great triumphs—his consulship and his defeat of Catiline. The murder of Caesar in 44 B.C. temporarily raised Cicero's hopes for a return to the senatorial form of government, but these hopes were dashed by the activities of Antony. Cicero attacked Antony in fourteen speeches, written in 44–43 B.C. These speeches were named *Philippics* because they recalled Demosthenes' well-known speeches against King Philip of Macedon. The most famous *Philippic* (Juvenal called it "divine"), the second, was not delivered but was circulated as a political document. Cicero's reward for these speeches was death—at the hands of agents of Antony.

The Second Action Against Verres

The Importance of Sicily

Verba Ūtilia: antequam, benevolentia, classis, externus, laetor, parcō, ratiō, semel, subsidium, ūtilitās

II, 2. Atque antequam dē incommodīs Siciliae dīcō, pauca mihi videntur esse dē prōvinciae dignitāte, vetustāte, ūtilitāte dīcenda. Nam cum omnium sociōrum prōvinciārumque ratiōnem dīligenter habēre dēbētis, tum praecipuē Siciliae, iūdicēs, plūrimīs iūstissimīsque dē causīs, prīmum quod omnium nātiōnum exterārum prīnceps Sicilia sē ad amīcitiam 5 fidemque populī Rōmānī applicāvit. Prīma omnium, id quod[1] ōrnāmentum imperī est, prōvincia est appellāta; prīma docuit maiōrēs nostrōs quam praeclārum esset exterīs gentibus imperāre; sōla fuit eā fidē benevolentiāque ergā populum Rōmānum ut cīvitātēs eius īnsulae, quae semel[2] in amīcitiam nostram vēnissent, numquam posteā dēficerent, plēraeque autem et 10 maximē illūstrēs in amīcitiā perpetuō manērent. **3.** Itaque maiōribus nos-trīs in Āfricam ex hāc prōvinciā gradus[3] imperī factus est; neque enim tam facile opēs Carthāginis tantae concidissent nisi illud et reī frūmentāriae subsidium et receptāculum classibus nostrīs patēret. Quārē P. Āfricānus, Carthāgine dēlētā,[1] Siculōrum urbīs signīs monumentīsque pulcherrimīs 15 exōrnāvit, ut, quōs[2] victōriā populī Rōmānī maximē laetārī arbitrābātur, apud eōs monumenta victōriae plūrima collocāret. **4.** Dēnique ille ipse M. Mārcellus, cuius in Siciliā virtūtem hostēs, misericordiam victī, fidem cēterī Siculī perspexērunt, nōn sōlum sociīs in eō bellō cōnsuluit,[4] vērum etiam superātīs hostibus temperāvit.[5] Urbem pulcherrimam Syrācūsās 20 (quae cum manū[6] mūnītissima esset, tum locī nātūrā terrā ac marī claud-erētur), cum vī cōnsiliōque cēpisset, nōn sōlum incolumem passus est esse, sed ita relīquit ōrnātam ut esset idem[7] monumentum victōriae, mānsuētūdinis, continentiae, cum hominēs vidērent et quid expugnāsset et quibus peper-cisset et quae relīquisset: tantum ille honōrem habendum Siciliae putāvit ut 25 nē hostium quidem urbem ex sociōrum īnsulā tollendam[8] arbitrārētur. **5.** Itaque ad omnīs rēs sīc illā prōvinciā semper ūsī sumus ut, quicquid[9] ex sēsē pos-set efferre, id nōn apud nōs nāscī, sed domī nostrae conditum iam putārēmus.[9] Quandō illa frūmentum quod dēbēret nōn ad diem[10] dedit? Quandō id quod opus esse putāret nōn ultrō pollicita est? Quandō id quod imperārētur 30 recūsāvit? Itaque ille M. Catō Sapiēns[3] cellam pēnāriam[11] reī pūblicae nos-trae, nūtrīcem plēbis Rōmānae Siciliam nōminābat.

[1] a thing which
[2] once they had (literally, which once)
[3] the step to empire
[4] looked out for (with dative)
[5] spared, (with dative)
[6] by the hand (of man)
[7] at the same time (literally, the same memorial)
[8] destroyed (literally, removed)
[9] whatever she was able to produce from her own (soil) we have come to consider as not grown at home but stored there
[10] on the day (due)
[11] storehouse

---

[1] 146 B.C.
[2] The antecedent is **eōs,** the Sicilians.
[3] Cato the Elder

Verres' "Interest" in Art

1 *interest*
2 *judge the matter by its own*
importance, not that of a name
3 *with so many towns*
4 *pearl*
5 *woven* (*cloth*)
6 *that he did not*
7 i.e., *the straight truth* (in the old
Roman fashion)
8 *Your* (*pets*) *the people of Messina*
9 *to have plundered in a most*
wicked manner

IV, 1. Veniō nunc ad istīus,[1] quem ad modum ipse appellat, studium,[1] ut amīcī eius, morbum et īnsāniam, ut Siculī, latrōcinium; ego quō nōmine appellem nesciō; rem vōbīs prōpōnam, vōs eam suō, nōn nōminis, pondere penditōte.[2] Genus ipsum prius cognōscite, iūdicēs; deinde fortasse nōn
5 magnō opere quaerētis quō id nōmine appellandum putētis. Negō in Siciliā tōtā, tam locuplētī, tam vetere prōvinciā, tot oppidīs,[3] tot familiīs tam cōpiōsīs, ūllum argenteum vās, ūllum Corinthium[2] aut Dēliacum fuisse, ūllam gemmam aut margarītam,[4] quicquam ex aurō aut ebore factum, signum ūllum aēneum, marmoreum, eburneum, negō ūllam pictūram neque
10 in tabulā neque in textilī[5] quīn[6] conquīsierit, īnspexerit, quod placitum sit abstulerit. **2.** Magnum videor dīcere: attendite etiam quem ad modum dīcam. Nōn enim verbī neque crīminis augendī causā complector omnia: cum dīcō nihil istum eius modī rērum in tōtā prōvinciā relīquisse, Latīnē[7] mē scītōte, nōn accūsātōriē loquī. Etiam plānius: nihil in aedibus cuiusquam,
15 nē in hospitis[3] quidem, nihil in locīs commūnibus, nē in fānīs quidem, nihil apud Siculum, nihil apud cīvem Rōmānum, dēnique nihil istum, quod ad oculōs animumque acciderit, neque prīvātī neque pūblicī neque profānī neque sacrī tōtā in Siciliā relīquisse.

3. Unde igitur potius incipiam quam ab eā cīvitāte quae tibi ūna in amōre
20 atque in dēliciīs fuit, aut ex quō potius numerō quam ex ipsīs laudātōribus tuīs? Facilius enim perspiciētur quālis apud eōs fuerīs quī tē ōdērunt, quī accūsant, quī persequuntur, cum apud tuōs Māmertīnōs[8] inveniāre improbissimā ratiōne esse praedātus.[9]

---

1 Verres
2 *Corinthian* was an alloy similar to bronze, the secret of whose manufacture had been lost; hence its value; *Delian* ware was also famous.
3 Supply **aedibus.**

The House of Heius

Verba Ūtilia: aedēs, aes, artifex, fānum, nūdus, pondus, portus, significō, trādō, vīsō

IV, 3. C. Heius est Māmertīnus (omnēs hoc mihi quī Messānam accessērunt facile concēdunt) omnibus rēbus illā in cīvitāte ōrnātissimus. Huius domus est vel[1] optima Messānae, nōtissima quidem certē et nostrīs[1] hominibus apertissima maximēque hospitālis. Ea domus ante istīus adventum ōrnāta sīc fuit ut urbī quoque esset ōrnāmentō; nam ipsa Messāna, quae sitū, moenibus, portūque ōrnāta sit, ab hīs rēbus[2] quibus iste dēlectātur sānē vacua atque nūda est. **4.** Erat apud Heium sacrārium magnā cum dignitāte in aedibus ā maiōribus trāditum perantīquum, in quō signa pulcherrima quattuor summō artificiō, summā nōbilitāte, quae nōn modo istum[3] hominem ingeniōsum et intellegentem, vērum etiam quemvīs nostrum,[4] quōs iste [10] idiōtās[2] appellat, dēlectāre possent, ūnum Cupīdinis marmoreum Praxitelī; nīmīrum didicī etiam, dum in istum inquīrō, artificum nōmina.[5] **5.** Vērum ut ad illud sacrārium redeam, signum erat hoc quod dīcō Cupīdinis ē marmore, ex alterā parte Herculēs ēgregiē factus ex aere. Is dīcēbātur esse Myrōnis, ut opīnor, et certē.[6] Item ante hōs deōs erant ārulae, quae cuivīs religiōnem[3] [15] sacrārī significāre possent. Erant aēnea duo praetereā signa, nōn maxima vērum eximiā venustāte, virginālī habitū[4] atque vestītū, quae, manibus sublātīs, sacra quaedam mōre Athēniēnsium virginum reposita in capitibus sustinēbant; Canēphoroe[7] ipsae vocābantur; sed eārum artificem—quem? Quemnam? Rēctē admonēs—Polyclītum esse dīcēbant. Messānam ut[5] [20] quisque nostrum vēnerat, haec vīsere solēbat; omnibus haec ad vīsendum patēbant cotīdiē; domus erat nōn dominō magis ōrnāmentō quam cīvitātī. **7.** Haec omnia quae dīxī signa, iūdicēs, ab Heiō ē sacrāriō Verrēs abstulit; nūllum, inquam, hōrum relīquit neque aliud ūllum tamen praeter ūnum pervetus ligneum, Bonam Fortūnam, ut opīnor; eam iste habēre domī suae nōluit. [25]

[1] even, quite
[2] ignoramuses
[3] sacred nature
[4] pose
[5] when

[1] i.e., Romans
[2] i.e., works of art
[3] Verres
[4] genitive of **nōs**
[5] Cicero was somewhat of a connoisseur of art and certainly was familiar with the names of the great Greek artists. Here he pretends not to have known anything about them in order to ingratiate himself with the jurors: he wants to make it appear that he is just a rough uncultured Roman like them.
[6] Cicero corrects himself: *yes, it certainly was;* (see footnote 5)
[7] The Greek word means *basket-bearers.*

Prō[8] deum hominumque fidem! Quid hoc est? Quae haec causa est, quae ista impudentia? Quae dīcō signa, antequam abs tē sublāta sunt, Messānam cum imperiō[9] nēmō vēnit quīn[6] vīserit. Tot praetōrēs, tot cōnsulēs in Siciliā cum in pāce tum etiam in bellō fuērunt, tot hominēs cuiusque modī
30 (nōn loquor dē integrīs, innocentibus, religiōsīs) tot cupidī, tot improbī, tot audācēs, quōrum nēmō sibi tam vehemēns, tam potēns, tam nōbilis vīsus est quī ex illō sacrāriō quicquam poscere aut tollere aut attingere audēret; Verrēs quod ubīque erit pulcherrimum auferet? Nihil habēre cuiquam praetereā licēbit? Tot domūs locuplētissimās istīus domus ūna capiet?
35 Idcircō nēmō superiōrum[7] attigit ut hic tolleret?

---

[8] *O!* followed by the accusative of exclamation
[9] Only praetors and consuls had **imperium**, the highest power.

The Temple of Hercules

Verba Ūtilia: attrītus, cōnor, fānum, intempestus, lapidatio, mulcō, ōsculor, percrebrēscō, rictus

IV, 94. Herculis templum est apud Agrigentīnōs nōn longē ā forō, sānē sānctum apud illōs et religiōsum. Ibi est ex aere simulācrum ipsīus Herculis, quō nōn facile dīxerim quicquam mē vīdisse pulchrius (tametsī nōn tam multum in istīs rēbus intellegō quam multa vīdī) usque eō, iūdicēs, ut ric-
5 tum eius ac mentum paulō sit attrītius, quod in precibus et grātulātiōnibus nōn sōlum id venerārī vērum etiam ōsculārī solent.[1] Ad hoc templum, cum esset iste[2] Agrigentī, repente nocte intempestā servōrum armātōrum fit concursus atque impetus. Clāmor ā vigilibus fānīque custōdibus tollitur; quī prīmō cum obsistere ac dēfendere cōnārentur, male mulcātī clāvīs ac
10 fūstibus repelluntur. Intereā ex clāmōre fāma tōtā urbe percrēbruit expugnārī deōs patriōs, nōn hostium adventū necopīnātō neque repentīnō praedōnum impetū, sed ex domō atque ex cohorte praetōriā manum fugitīvōrum īnstrūctam armātamque vēnisse. **95.** Nēmō Agrigentī neque aetāte tam affectā neque vīribus tam īnfirmīs fuit quī nōn illā nocte eō nūntiō excitātus
15 surrēxerit, tēlumque quod cuique fors offerēbat arripuerit. Itaque brevī

---

[1] like the foot of the statue of St. Peter in St. Peter's, Rome
[2] Verres

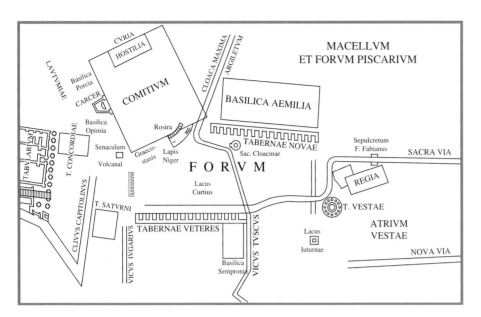

The Forum during the Republic was much simpler than during the Empire, when overcrowding became a problem. The **Tabulārium** is on the far left and from there, you would be looking toward the Palatine Hill and over the Forum itself. The **tabernae** were shops selling everything from food to cloth to lamps. Obviously, the **tabernae novae** were built after the **tabernae veterēs**.

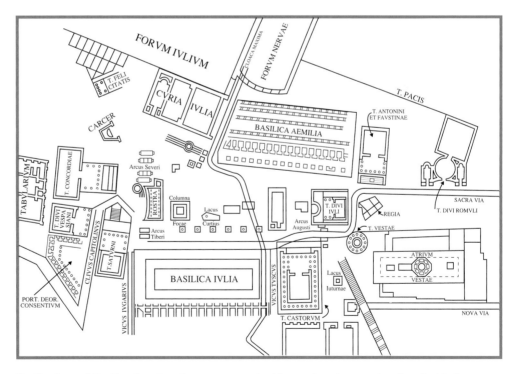

By the time of the Empire, the tabernae veteres had been taken down and replaced with the Basilica Julia. The **Rōstra**, or speaker's stand, was also moved to a more central location, near the Temple of Saturn, to give the speaker a more commanding position. The **Rēgia**, near the Vestal Temple, was the house of Numa, the second king of Rome, according to tradition. The **Lapis Niger**, near the **Comitium**, is supposed to mark the place where Romulus was buried.

1 *people run* (impersonal)
2 *plunderer of sacred places*
3 *that not, to keep them from*

tempore ad fānum ex urbe tōtā concurritur.[1] Ac repente Agrigentīnī concurrunt; fit magna lapidātiō; dant sēsē in fugam istīus praeclārī imperātōris nocturnī mīlitēs. Duo tamen sigilla perparvula tollunt, nē omnīnō inānēs ad istum praedōnem religiōnum[2] revertantur. Numquam tam male est
20 Siculīs quīn[3] aliquid facētē et commodē dīcant, velut in hāc rē aiēbant in labōrēs Herculis nōn minus hunc immānissimum verrem₃ quam illum aprum Erymanthium₄ referrī oportēre.

₃ a pun on Verres' name: **verrēs** means a *boar*
₄ The killing of the Erymanthian boar was one of the twelve labors of Hercules.

Ceres and Proserpina

Verba Ūtilia: altitūdō, celeber, currus, laetus, lūcus, opīniō, perennis, subitō, vertex, vēstīgium

IV, 106. Vetus est haec opīniō, iūdicēs, quae cōnstat ex antīquissimīs Graecōrum litterīs ac monumentīs, īnsulam Siciliam tōtam esse Cererī et Līberae cōnsecrātam. Nam et nātās esse hās in iīs locīs deās et frūgēs[1] in eā terrā prīmum repertās esse arbitrantur, et raptam esse Līberam, quam
5 eandem Prōserpinam vocant, ex Hennēnsium nemore,[2] quī locus, quod in mediā est īnsulā situs, umbilīcus[3] Siciliae nōminātur. Quam₁ cum invēstīgāre et conquīrere Cerēs vellet, dīcitur īnflammāsse taedās[4] iīs ignibus quī ex Aetnae vertice ērumpunt; quās sibi cum ipsa praeferret,[5] orbem omnem peragrāsse terrārum. **107.** Henna autem, ubi ea quae dīcō gesta esse memo-
10 rantur, est locō perexcelsō atque ēditō, quō in summō est aequāta agrī plānitiēs et aquae perennēs, tōta vērō ab omnī aditū circumcīsa atque dīrēcta est;[6] quam circā lacūs lūcīque sunt plūrimī atque laetissimī flōrēs omnī tempore annī, locus ut ipse[7] raptum[8] illum virginis quem iam ā puerīs accēpimus dēclārāre videātur. Etenim prope est spēlunca quaedam con-
15 versa ad aquilōnem īnfīnītā altitūdine, quā Dītem[9] patrem ferunt repente cum currū exstitisse abreptamque ex eō locō virginem sēcum asportāsse et subitō nōn longē ā Syrācūsīs penetrāsse sub terrās, lacumque in eō locō repente exstitisse, ubi usque ad hoc tempus Syrācūsānī fēstōs diēs anniversāriōs agunt celeberrimō virōrum mulierumque conventū. Propter
20 huius opīniōnis vetustātem, quod hōrum₂ in hīs locīs vēstīgia ac prope

1 *grain crops*
2 *the forest of Henna*
3 *navel*
4 *torches*
5 *carrying which before her*
   (literally, *when she carried which before her*)
6 *steep and straight down*
7 *so that the location itself*
8 *carrying off* (noun)
9 *Pluto*

₁ Proserpina
₂ with **deōrum**

incūnābula reperiuntur deōrum, mīra quaedam tōtā Siciliā prīvātim ac pūblicē religiō est Cereris Hennēnsis. **109.** Hoc dīcō, hanc ipsam Cererem antīquissimam, religiōsissimam, prīncipem omnium sacrōrum quae apud omnīs gentīs nātiōnēsque fīunt, ā C. Verre ex suīs templīs ac sēdibus esse sublātam. **111.** Hic dolor erat tantus ut Verrēs alter Orcus vēnisse Hennam 25 et nōn Prōserpinam asportāsse sed ipsam abripuisse Cererem vidērētur. Etenim urbs illa nōn urbs vidētur, sed fānum Cereris esse; habitāre apud sēsē Cererem Hennēnsēs arbitrantur, ut mihi nōn cīvēs illīus cīvitātis, sed omnēs sacerdōtēs, omnēs accolae atque antistiēs Cereris esse videantur. **112.** Hennā[10] tū simulācrum Cereris tollere audēbās, Hennā tū dē manū 30 Cereris Victōriam ēripere et deam deae[11] dētrahere cōnātus es?

[10] *from Henna*
[11] *the goddess* (Victory) *from the goddess* (Ceres)

Word Studies

The ancient grammarians felt that there must be a relationship between **lūcus** and **lūx**—but how did a grove of trees have anything to do with light? They decided that the relationship was by opposites: **lūcus ā nōn lūcendō,** *a grove of trees* (is so called) *from not giving light.* The idea was so far-fetched that the phrase has become the name of a type of absurd reasoning.

Give the Latin word from which the following are derived: *celebrated, excelsior, perennial, rapacious, vestige.*

A Roman Citizen Is Crucified

Verba Ūtilia: anteā, assequor, barbarus, gemitus, ignōtus, impūnē, plēbs, supplicium, ūsūrpō, verber

V, 162. Caedēbātur virgīs[1] in mediō forō Messānae cīvis Rōmānus, iūdicēs, cum intereā nūllus gemitus, nūlla vōx alia illīus miserī inter dolōrem crepitumque plāgārum audiēbātur nisi haec, "Cīvis Rōmānus sum!" Hāc sē commemorātiōne cīvitātis omnia verbera dēpulsūrum, cruciātumque ā corpore dēiectūrum arbitrābātur. Is nōn modo hoc nōn perfēcit, ut virgārum 5 vim dēprecārētur; sed cum implōrāret saepius ūsūrpāretque nōmen cīvitātis, crux −crux, inquam−īnfēlīcī[2] et aerumnōsō, quī numquam istam pestem[1] vīderat, comparābātur.

[1] *was beaten with rods*
[2] *for the unfortunate fellow* (with **comparābātur**)

---

[1] i.e., the cross—or does he mean Verres?

163. Ō nōmen dulce lībertātis! Ō iūs eximium nostrae cīvitātis! Ō lēx
10 Porcia, lēgēsque Semprōniae! Ō graviter dēsīderāta, et aliquandō reddita[2]
plēbī Rōmānae tribūnicia potestās! Hūcine[3] tandem haec omnia recidērunt,
ut cīvis Rōmānus in prōvinciā populī Rōmānī, in oppidō foederātōrum, ab
eō quī beneficiō populī Rōmānī fascīs et secūrīs habēret dēligātus in forō
virgīs caederētur? Quid? Cum ignēs ārdentēsque lāminae[3] cēterīque cru-
15 ciātūs admovēbantur, sī tē[4] illīus acerba implōrātiō et vōx miserābilis nōn
inhibēbat, nē cīvium quidem Rōmānōrum quī tum aderant flētū et gemitū
maximō commovēbāre? In crucem tū agere ausus es quemquam quī sē
cīvem Rōmānum esse dīceret?

166. Sī tū apud Persās aut in extrēmā Indiā dēprehēnsus, Verrēs, ad
20 supplicium dūcerēre, quid aliud clāmitārēs nisi tē cīvem esse Rōmānum?
Et sī tibi ignōtō apud ignōtōs, apud barbarōs, apud hominēs in extrēmīs
atque ultimīs gentibus positōs, nōbile et illūstre apud omnīs nōmen cīvitātis
tuae prōfuisset, ille,[5] quisquis erat, quem tū in crucem rapiēbās, quī tibi
esset ignōtus, cum cīvem sē Rōmānum esse dīceret, apud tē praetōrem, sī
25 nōn effugium, nē moram[4] quidem mortis mentiōne atque ūsūrpātiōne cīvitātis
assequī potuit?

167. Hominēs tenuēs, obscūrō locō[5] nātī, nāvigant, adeunt ad ea loca
quae numquam anteā vīdērunt, ubi neque nōtī esse eīs quō vēnērunt, neque
semper cum cognitōribus[6] esse possunt. Hāc ūnā tamen fīdūciā cīvitātis nōn
30 modo apud nostrōs magistrātūs, quī et lēgum et exīstimātiōnis[7] perīculō
continentur, neque apud cīvīs sōlum Rōmānōs, quī et sermōnis[8] et iūris et
multārum rērum societāte iūnctī sunt, fore sē tūtōs arbitrantur, sed, quōcumque
vēnerint, hanc sibi rem praesidiō spērant futūram. Tolle hanc spem, tolle
hoc praesidium cīvibus Rōmānīs, cōnstitue nihil esse opis in hāc vōce,
35 "Cīvis Rōmānus sum," posse[9] impūne praetōrem aut alium quempiam supplicium quod velit in eum cōnstituere quī sē cīvem Rōmānum esse dīcat,
quod[10] quī sit ignōret: iam omnīs prōvinciās, iam omnia rēgna, iam omnīs
līberās cīvitātēs, iam omnem orbem terrārum, quī semper nostrīs hominibus
maximē patuit, cīvibus Rōmānīs istā dēfēnsiōne praeclūseris.

Word Studies

Define *attenuate, fascicle, impunity, nascent, pestiferous.*

To what Latin words are the following related: **assequor, cruciātus,
fīdūcia, reddō, societās?**

---

[2] with **potestās**; Sulla had reduced the tribune's power to protect a citizen, but that power
had just been restored

[3] = **hūcne**; the original form was **hūcene**, just as **hic** was **hice**, etc.: *have things come to
this point?*

[4] Verres

[5] the man who was beaten in Messina

[3] *hot plates* (of metal)
[4] *delay* (to insure trial before the
people)
[5] *position*
[6] *witnesses* (who could identify
them as Roman citizens)
[7] *public opinion*
[8] *language*
[9] *decide that a praetor can*
(depends, like **esse,** on **cōnstitue**)
[10] *on the ground that he does not
know who* (*the man*) *is*

The Struggles of a *Novus Homō*

Verba Ūtilia: alliciō, crīmen, dēferō, dēiciō, dīiungō, licet, occultus

V, 180. Quaeret aliquis fortasse, "Tantumne igitur labōrem, tantās inimīcitiās tot hominum susceptūrus es?" Nōn studiō[1] quidem hercule[2] ūllō neque voluntāte; sed nōn idem licet mihi quod iīs quī nōbilī genere nātī sunt, quibus omnia populī Rōmānī beneficia dormientibus[3] dēferuntur; longē aliā mihi lēge in hāc cīvitāte et condiciōne vīvendum est. **181.** Vidēmus 5 quantā sit in invidiā quantōque in odiō apud quōsdam nōbilīs hominēs novōrum hominum virtūs et industria; sī tantulum[4] oculōs dēiēcerīmus, praestō[5] esse īnsidiās; sī ūllum locum aperuerīmus suspīciōnī aut crīminī, accipiendum statim vulnus esse; semper nōbīs vigilandum, semper labōrandum vidēmus. **182.** Inimīcitiae sunt,[6]₁ subeantur; labor, suscipiātur; etenim 10 tacitae magis et occultae inimīcitiae timendae sunt quam indictae atque apertae. Hominum nōbilium nōn ferē quisquam nostrae industriae favet; nūllīs nostrīs officiīs benevolentiam illōrum allicere possumus; quasi nātūrā et genere dīiūnctī sint, ita dissident ā nōbīs animō ac voluntāte. Quārē quid habent eōrum inimīcitiae perīculī quōrum animōs iam ante habuerīs inimīcōs 15 et invidōs quam ūllās inimīcitiās suscēperīs?

[1] *on purpose*
[2] *by Hercules*
[3] *while they are asleep* (i.e., with no effort on their part)
[4] *just a little bit*
[5] *at hand, being used*
[6] *if there are enmities, let them be endured*

₁ similarly **labor,** *trouble,* with **est** understood

The Second Speech Against Antony

Cicero, Caesar, and Pompey

Verba Ūtilia: augeō, dīiungō, ēnītor, ops, opus, praetermittō, sērō

23. Quod vērō dīcere ausus es idque multīs verbīs, operā meā Pompeium ā Caesaris amīcitiā esse dīiūnctum ob eamque[1] causam culpā meā bellum cīvīle esse nātum, in eō nōn tū quidem tōtā rē sed, quod maximum est, temporibus errāstī. Ego, M. Bibulō, praestantissimō cīve, cōnsule, nihil[1] 5 praetermīsī, quantum facere ēnītīque potuī, quīn[1] Pompeium ā Caesaris coniūnctiōne āvocārem. In quō Caesar fēlīcior fuit. Ipse enim Pompeium ā meā familiāritāte dīiūnxit. Posteā vērō quam sē tōtum Pompeius Caesarī trādidit, quid ego illum[2] ab eō distrahere cōnārer?[2] Stultī erat[3] spērāre, suādēre impudentis. **24.** Duo tamen tempora incidērunt quibus aliquid con- 10 trā Caesarem Pompeiō suāserim. Ea velim[4] reprehendās, sī potes: ūnum nē quīnquennī[3] imperium Caesarī prōrogāret, alterum nē paterētur ferrī ut absentis eius ratiō habērētur.[5] Quōrum sī utrumvīs persuāsissem, in hās miseriās numquam incidissēmus. Atque īdem ego, cum iam opēs omnīs et suās et populī Rōmānī Pompeius ad Caesarem dētulisset, sērōque ea sen- 15 tīre coepisset quae multō ante prōvīderam, īnferrīque patriae bellum vidērem nefārium, pācis, concordiae, compositiōnis auctor esse non dēstitī, meaque illa vōx est nōta multīs: "Utinam, Cn. Pompeī, cum C. Caesare societātem aut numquam coīssēs aut numquam dirēmissēs! Fuit alterum gravitātis,[6] alterum prūdentiae tuae." Haec mea, M. Antōnī, semper et dē Pompeiō et 20 dē rē pūblicā cōnsilia fuērunt. Quae sī valuissent, rēs pūblica stāret, tū tuīs flāgitiīs, egestāte, īnfamiā concidissēs.

[1] *I have tried everything, as far as I could, to separate Pompey from Caesar (literally, I have omitted nothing (to prevent me) from, etc.)*
[2] *why should I have tried?*
[3] *it was (characteristic) of a foolish person*
[4] *I should like you to find fault*
[5] *that consideration be given to his absence*
[6] *(a matter of) consistency*

---

1 The conjunction **–que** is not usually attached to a monosyllabic preposition.
2 Pompey
3 the five-year prolongation of Caesar's command in Gaul to 49 B.C.

I Am Not Afraid of You, Antony

116. Fuit in illo[1] ingenium, ratiō, memoria, litterae, cūra, cōgitātiō, dīligentia; rēs bellō gesserat, quamvīs reī pūblicae calamitōsās, at tamen magnās; multōs annōs rēgnāre meditātus, magnō labōre, magnīs perīculīs quod cōgitārat effēcerat; mūneribus,[1] monumentīs, congiāriīs,[2] epulīs multitūdinem imperītam dēlēnierat; suōs praemiīs, adversāriōs clēmentiae 5 speciē dēvīnxerat. Quid multa? Attulerat iam līberae cīvitātī partim metū, partim patientiā cōnsuētūdinem serviendī. Cum illō ego tē dominandī cupiditāte cōnferre possum, cēterīs vērō rebus nūllō modō comparandus es. **117.** Sed ex plūrimīs malīs quae ab illō reī pūblicae sunt inusta hoc tamen bonī est,[3] quod didicit iam populus Rōmānus quantum cuique 10 crēderet,[4] quibus sē committeret, ā quibus cavēret. Haec nōn cōgitās, neque intellegis satis esse virīs fortibus didicisse quam sit rē pulchrum,[5][2] beneficiō grātum, fāmā glōriōsum tyrannum occīdere? An, cum illum[3] hominēs nōn tulerint, tē ferent? **118.** Certātim posthāc, mihi crēde, ad hoc opus[4] currētur neque occāsiōnis tarditās exspectābitur.[6] 15

Respice, quaesō, aliquandō rem pūblicam, M. Antōnī, quibus[5] ortus sīs, nōn quibuscum vīvās cōnsiderā; mēcum, ut volēs:[6] redī cum rē pūblicā in grātiam. Sed dē tē tū vīderis;[7] ego dē mē ipse profitēbor. Dēfendī rem pūblicam adulēscēns, nōn dēseram senex; contempsī Catilīnae gladiōs, nōn pertimēscam tuōs. Quīn etiam corpus libenter obtulerim,[8] sī repraesentārī[9] 20 morte meā lībertās cīvitātis potest. **119.** Etenim sī abhinc annōs prope vīgintī hōc ipsō in templō negāvī posse mortem immātūram esse cōnsulārī, quantō vērius nunc negābō senī![7] Mihi vērō, patrēs cōnscrīptī, iam etiam optanda mors est, perfūnctō[8] rebus eīs quās adeptus sum quāsque gessī. Duo modo haec optō, ūnum ut moriēns populum Rōmānum līberum relin- 25 quam (hōc mihi maius ab dīs immortālibus darī nihil potest), alterum ut ita cuique ēveniat ut[10] dē rē pūblicā quisque mereātur.

[1] shows (of gladiators)
[2] gifts
[3] there is this much good
[4] trust every man
[5] how fine it is in fact, how gratifying it is because of its good deed
[6] the slowness of the occasion will not be awaited (i.e., it will happen soon)
[7] you will see to yourself
[8] I would offer
[9] brought about at once
[10] as

[1] Caesar
[2] The subject of **sit** is **occīdere.**
[3] Caesar
[4] killing a tyrant
[5] he was of noble ancestry; his present associates belong to the riffraff
[6] from the following supply **redī in grātiam:** *Return to friendship with me (or not): (at any rate)*
[7] Supply **mortem immātūram esse.**
[8] modifies **mihi** and governs **rēbus**

Unit VII

Cicero's Letters

The Capitoline She-Wolf is the symbol of Rome even today. Though the wolf itself dates from Etruscan times, probably during the early 5th century B.C., the bronzes of Romulus and Remus as babies were added later by Simone del Pollaiuolo (1457-1508). The Etruscans used bronze extensively for household furnishings and military accessories. Freestanding bronze sculpture, like this one, was an Etruscan specialty.

Introducing Cicero's Letters

A number of collections of Cicero's letters were published after his death. About half of the collections have survived, notably the 16 books addressed to his best friend Atticus, who published these letters, and the 16 books published by Tiro, Cicero's secretary. In modern times, the collection published by Tiro has been given the title *Epistulae ad familiārēs,* "Letters to Friends," an inaccurate title because some of the letters are to people who are not, strictly speaking, Cicero's friends and because some of the letters are *to* Cicero, not *from* him.

Remember that Cicero's letters were not intended for publication; many of them were confidential. They are extremely interesting for the light they throw on politics, private life, language, and Cicero's character. Some put Cicero in an unfavorable light, especially some of the confidential letters to Atticus, who did his great friend no service in publishing them. Not many prominent men of the last 2000 years could afford to have *all* their personal letters published.

Nearly 900 of Cicero's letters are extant.

The Campaign for the Consulship

[1] *seeking (for office), candidacy*
[1] *seeking (for office), candidacy*
[2] *as far as*
[3] *is canvassing* (literally, *is grasping hands*)
[4] *He is being turned down in the good old-fashioned way without pretense* (literally, *without pain and pretense*)
[5] *servant*

Petītiōnis[1] nostrae, quam tibi summae cūrae esse sciō, huius modī ratiō est, quod[2] adhūc coniectūrā prōvidērī possit. Prēnsat[3] ūnus P. Galba; sine fūcō ac fallāciīs mōre maiōrum negātur.[4] Ut opīniō est hominum, nōn aliēna ratiōnī nostrae fuit illīus haec praepropera prēnsātiō; nam illī ita negant
5 vulgō ut mihi sē dēbēre dīcant. Ita quiddam spērō nōbīs prōficī, cum hoc percrēbrēscit, plūrimōs nostrōs amīcōs invenīrī. Nōs autem initium prēnsandī facere cōgitārāmus eō ipsō tempore quō tuum puerum[5] cum hīs litterīs proficīscī Cīncius dīcēbat, in campō[1] comitiīs tribūnīciīs a. d. XVI Kal. Sextīlēs.[2] Competītōrēs quī certī esse videantur Galba et Antōnius et Q. Cornificius.
10 Catilīna, sī iūdicātum erit merīdiē nōn lūcēre, certus erit competītor; dē Aufidiō et dē Palicānō nōn putō tē exspectāre dum scrībam. Dē iīs quī

---

[1] the Campus Martius
[2] for **ante diem XVI Kalendās Sextīlēs,** *the sixteenth day before the Kalends of August,* i.e., July 17 (not July 16, for the Romans counted both ends)

nunc₃ petunt, Caesar₄ certus putātur; Thermus cum Silānō contendere exīs-timātur, quī sīc inopēs et ab⁶ amīcīs et exīstimātiōne sunt ut mihi vidētur nōn esse ἀδύνατον₅ Cūrium obdūcere,⁷ sed hoc praeter mē nēminī vidētur. Nostrīs ratiōnibus maximē condūcere vidētur Thermum fierī cum Caesare. 15 Nēmō est enim ex iīs quī nunc petunt quī, sī in nostrum annum reciderit, firmior candidātus fore videātur, proptereā quod cūrātor est viae Flāminiae, quae tum erit absolūta sānē facile; eum libenter nunc Caesarī cōnsulem accūderim.⁸ Petītōrum haec est īnfōrmāta adhūc cōgitātiō. Nōs₆ in omnī mūnere candidātōriō fungendō summam adhibēbimus dīligentiam et fort- 20 asse, quoniam vidētur in suffrāgiīs multum posse⁹ Gallia, cum Rōmae ā iūdiciīs forum refrīxerit,¹⁰₇ excurrēmus mēnse Septembrī lēgātī¹¹ ad Pīsōnem, ut Iānuāriō revertāmur. Cum perspexerō voluntātēs nōbilium, scrībam ad tē. (*A.* I, 1, 1–2)

⁶ *from* (*the standpoint of*)
⁷ *to run Curius* (*for the consulship*)
⁸ *I would gladly add him to Caesar as consul*
⁹ *has much influence*
¹⁰ *has cooled off in regard to trials*
¹¹ *as a commissioner*

₃ i.e., for the consulship of 64
₄ L. (not C.) Caesar
₅ **adynaton,** *impossible.* Cicero uses many Greek words in writing to Atticus, who for many years had been living in Athens.
₆ the plural of modesty, for **ego**
₇ The **lūdī Rōmānī** kept the courts closed during much of September, and there were other interruptions until after the Saturnalia in December.

It's a Boy!

L. Iūliō Caesare, C. Mārciō Figulō cōnsulibus, fīliolō mē auctum¹ scītō,² salvā Terentiā. Abs tē tam diū nihil litterārum! Ego dē meīs ad tē ratiōnibus scrīpsī anteā dīligenter. Hōc tempore Catilīnam, competītōrem nostrum, dēfendere cōgitāmus.₁ Iūdicēs habēmus quōs voluimus, summā accūsātōris voluntāte. Spērō, sī absolūtus erit, coniūnctiōrem illum nōbīs 5 fore in ratiōne petītiōnis; sīn aliter acciderit, hūmāniter ferēmus.

Tuō adventū nōbīs opus est mātūrō; nam prōrsus summa hominum est opīniō tuōs familiārēs, nōbilēs hominēs, adversāriōs honōrī³ nostrō fore. Ad eōrum voluntātem mihi conciliandam maximō tē mihi ūsuī fore videō. Quārē Iānuāriō mēnse, ut cōnstituistī, cūrā ut Rōmae sīs.₂   (*A.* I, 2)   10

¹ *blessed*
² *I should like you to know*
³ *my election*

₁ We say, "Politics makes strange bedfellows," and here we have an example. Nothing came of the plan.
₂ From the fact that Cicero's next letter to Atticus is not until 61 B.C., we may infer that Atticus came to Rome and presumably worked hard and well in his friend's behalf.

The Trial of Clodius[1]

Quaeris ex mē quid acciderit dē iūdiciō, quod tam praeter opīniōnem omnium factum sit, et simul vīs scīre quō modō ego minus quam soleam proeliātus sim. Respondēbō tibi ὕστερον πρότερον Ὁμηρικῶς[2] Ego enim, quam diū senātūs auctōritās mihi dēfendenda fuit, sīc ācriter et vehementer
5 proeliātus sum ut clāmor concursusque maximā cum meā laude fierent. Quod sī tibi umquam sum vīsus in rē pūblicā fortis, certē mē in illā causā admīrātus essēs. Cum enim ille ad cōntiōnēs[1] cōnfūgisset, in iīsque meō nōmine ad invidiam ūterētur, dī immortālēs, quās ego pugnās et quantās strāgēs ēdidī, quōs impetūs in Pīsōnem, in Cūriōnem,[3] in tōtam illam manum
10 fēcī! Quō modō sum īnsectātus levitātem senum, libīdinem iuventūtis!

Itaque, sī causam quaeris absolūtiōnis, ut iam πρὸς τὸ πρότερον[4] revertar, egestās iūdicum fuit et turpitūdō. Summō discessū[2] bonōrum, plēnō forō servōrum,[5] XXV iūdicēs ita fortēs tamen fuērunt ut, summō prōpositō perīculō, vel[3] perīre māluerint quam perdere omnia;[6] XXXI fuērunt quōs
15 famēs magis quam fāma commōverit;[7] quōrum Catulus cum vīdisset quendam, "Quid vōs?" inquit, "praesidium ā nōbīs postulābātis?[8] An nē nummī vōbīs ēriperentur timēbātis?" Habēs, ut[4] brevissimē potuī, genus iūdicī et causam absolūtiōnis.

Ut Īdibus Maiīs in senātum convēnimus, rogātus ego sententiam multa dīxī
20 dē summā rē pūblicā. "Quō usque," inquit,[9] "hunc rēgem ferēmus?" "Rēgem appellās," inquam, "cum Rēx tuī mentiōnem nūllam fēcerit?"[10] Ille autem

---

[1] To Atticus, July, 61 B.C. Cicero had appeared as a witness against Clodius, on trial for sacrilege. Bribery enabled Clodius to go free, but he never forgave Cicero, later bringing about his exile.

[2] **hysteron proteron Homērikōs,** *in the Homeric fashion*

[3] supporters of Clodius

[4] **pros to proteron,** *to the first* (*point*)

[5] Clodius' thugs, whose function it was to overawe decent citizens

[6] They voted for conviction.

[7] They accepted bribes to vote for acquittal, more aware of their empty stomachs than their reputations; majority vote decided cases.

[8] They had asked for police protection, ostensibly against Clodius' slaves (mentioned in footnote 5).

[9] Clodius. The trial is over and Cicero is making a speech. Clodius tries to defend himself.

[10] Clodius had been disappointed in not being left a legacy by a man named Rex ("Mr. King"). This gives Cicero another opportunity to make a pun.

Rēgis hērēditātem spē dēvorārat.— "Domum,"[11] inquit, "ēmistī." "Putēs,"[5] inquam, "dīcere: iūdicēs ēmistī."—"Iūrantī," inquit, "tibi nōn crēdidērunt." "Mihi vērō," inquam, "XXV iūdicēs crēdidērunt, XXXI, quoniam nummōs ante accēpērunt, tibi nihil crēdidērunt."[12] Magnīs clāmōribus afflīctus con- 25 ticuit et concidit.

Nunc est exspectātiō comitiōrum, in quae, omnibus invītīs, trūdit noster Magnus[13] Aulī fīlium,[6] atque in eō neque auctōritāte neque grātiā pugnat, sed quibus[7] Philippus omnia castella expugnārī posse dīcēbat in quae modo[8] asellus onustus aurō posset ascendere.   (A. I, 16, 1–2, 5, 9–10, 12) 30

[11] Cicero had bought a very expensive house on the Palatine Hill; Clodius implies, "Where did you get the money?"
[12] a pun on the two meanings of **crēdō**
[13] Pompey

[5] *one would think you said*
[6] *the son of Aulus* is equivalent to saying *a nobody*
[7] *with those (means) with which*
[8] *provided that into these*

Clodius' Threats

Noster Pūblius[1] mihi minitātur, inimīcus est; impendet negōtium,[1] ad quod tū scīlicet advolābis. Videor mihi nostrum illum cōnsulārem exercitum[2] bonōrum omnium, etiam satis bonōrum[2] habēre firmissimum. Pompeius significat studium ergā mē nōn mediocre. Īdem affirmat verbum dē mē illum[3] nōn esse factūrum, in quō nōn mē ille fallit, sed ipse fallitur. Caesar 5 mē sibi vult esse lēgātum. Honestior[3] haec dēclīnātiō perīculī; sed ego hoc nōn repudiō. Quid ergō est? Pugnāre mālō. Nihil tamen certī. Iterum dīcō: utinam adessēs! Sed tamen, sī erit necesse, arcessēmus. Quid aliud? Quid? Hoc opīnor: certī sumus perīsse omnia. Sed haec scrīpsī properāns et mehercule[4] timidē. Posthāc ad tē aut, sī perfidēlem habēbō cui dem,[5] 10 scrībam plānē omnia, aut, sī obscūrē scrībam, tū tamen intellegēs. In iīs epistulīs mē Laelium, tē Fūrium faciam; cētera erunt ἐν αἰνιγμοῖς.[4] Hīc Caecilium colimus et observāmus dīligenter. Ēdicta Bibulī[5] audiō ad tē missa. Iīs[6] ārdet dolōre et īrā noster Pompeius.   (A. II, 19, 4–5)

[1] *trouble*
[2] *somewhat conservative*
[3] *more honorable*
[4] *by Hercules*
[5] *to whom I can give* (a letter for delivery)
[6] *on account of them*

[1] Clodius
[2] not to be taken literally; he means his conservative supporters
[3] Clodius
[4] **en ainigmois,** *in enigmas,* i.e., obscure to everyone but Atticus should the letters go to the wrong person
[5] Caesar's colleague in the consulship. Ignored by Caesar, he responded by protesting his colleague's actions.

A Tragedy About Britain?

[1] *perhaps* (literally, *I do not know whether*)

[2] **hypothesin,** *story, outline* (for a tragedy)

[3] *owl to Athens* (a proverbial expression)

[4] *to be kept in the dark*

[5] *the first* (*parts*) (of the first book)

[6] **rhathumotera,** *rather easy-going, rather careless*

[7] **charaktēr,** *style*

[8] *not a bit* (literally, *not by even a hair*)

[9] **philalēthōs,** *truthfully*

Veniō nunc ad id quod nesciō an[1] prīmum esse dēbuerit. Ō iūcundās mihi tuās dē Britanniā litterās! Timēbam Ōceanum, timēbam lītus īnsulae. Reliqua nōn equidem contemnō, sed plūs habent tamen speī quam timōris, magisque sum sollicitus exspectātiōne eā quam metū. Tē vērō ὑπόθεσιν[2]
5 scrībendī ēgregiam habēre videō. Quōs tū situs, quās nātūrās rērum et locōrum, quōs mōrēs, quās gentēs, quās pugnās, quem vērō ipsum imperātōrem habēs! Ego tē libenter, ut rogās,[1] quibus rēbus vīs adiuvābō et tibi versūs quōs rogās, hoc est "Athēnās noctuam,"[3] mittam. Sed heus tu, cēlārī[4] videor ā tē. Quōmodōnam, mi frāter, dē nostrīs versibus[2] Caesar? Nam prīmum librum
10 sē lēgisse scrīpsit ad mē ante, et prīma[5] sīc ut neget sē nē Graeca quidem meliōra lēgisse; reliqua ad quendam locum ῥαθυμότερα[6]—hōc enim ūtimur verbō.[3] Dīc mihi vērum: num aut rēs eum aut χαρακτήρ[7] nōn dēlectat? Nihil est quod vereāre; ego enim nē pilō[8] quidem minus mē amābō. Hāc dē rē φιλαλήθως[9] et, ut solēs scrībere, fraternē.   (*Q. Fr.* II, 16, 4–5)

---

[1] Quintus evidently asked his brother to send some verses.
[2] the poem on Cicero's consulship
[3] Cicero means that this is his word, not Caesar's who was not apt to introduce Greek words.

The Best Lawyer In—Samarobriva

[1] *whether*

[2] *let me know for sure*

[3] *well-heeled, with lots of coin*

[4] *there is* (*something for*) *which*

Quid agātis et ecquid[1] in Ītaliam ventūrī sītis hāc hieme fac plānē sciam.[2] Balbus mihi cōnfirmāvit tē dīvitem futūrum. Id utrum Rōmānō mōre[1] locutūs sit, bene nummātum[3] tē futūrum, an quō modō Stoicī dīcunt, omnēs esse dīvitēs quī caelō et terrā fruī possint, posteā vidēbō. Quī istinc
5 veniunt superbiam tuam accūsant, quod negent tē percontantibus respondēre.[2] Sed tamen est quod[4] gaudeās; cōnstat enim inter omnīs nēminem tē ūnō Samarobrīvae[3] iūris perītiōrem esse.   (*F.* VII, 16, 3)

---

[1] i.e., literally, not figuratively
[2] a pun: in the literal and in the legal sense, to give legal advice
[3] a small town, now Amiens in northern France

Te
causa
Igitu
merā
Cum
In Īta
nēmi
simu
Etian

₁ Nov

Li
vitāti
tra er
dubia
quem
quam
adēm
mēcu
aliud
conve
timēt
moles
tuās l

₁ Caes
 an ef
₂ The

PHOTRI/AISA/Vat.

*Since writing surfaces—in this case, treated sheepskin, called **vellum**—were expensive, the writing on older and "unimportant" vellum was scraped off to make way for "more important" works. In this way, materials were recycled. Traces of the older writing always remained faintly behind the new writing. Such manuscripts are called **palimpsests**. Here the larger writing in two columns is from Cicero's* De Republica, *dating from the 4th century, while the smaller writing is from a selection of St. Augustine on the Psalms, dating from the 7th century. The monks probably valued Augustine over Cicero, but in doing so, preserved both! In this way, many Roman writings came down through the ages. You can probably read some of Augustine's words. Notice that there is no attempt to leave spaces between words in sentences. Larger letters are frequently used to begin new thoughts.*

Come Back to Rome[1]

Cum Furnium nostrum tantum vīdissem, neque loquī neque audīre meō
commodō potuissem, properārem[2] atque essem in itinere, praemissīs iam
legiōnibus, praeterīre tamen nōn potuī quīn[1] et scrīberem ad tē et illum mitterem
grātiāsque agerem, etsī hoc et fēcī saepe et saepius mihi factūrus videor:
5 ita dē mē merēris. In prīmīs ā tē petō, quoniam cōnfīdō mē celeriter ad
urbem ventūrum, ut tē ibi videam, ut tuō cōnsiliō, grātiā, dignitāte, ope
omnium rērum ūtī possim. Ad prōpositum revertar: festīnātiōnī meae brevitātīque litterārum ignōscēs;[3] reliqua ex Furniō cognōscēs.   (*A.* IX, 6A)

[1] without

[1] a very friendly letter *from* Caesar *to* Cicero, March, 49 B.C.
[2] still with **cum**
[3] with dative

Cicero the Peacemaker

Ut lēgī tuās litterās, quās ā Furniō nostrō accēperam, quibus mēcum
agēbās ut ad urbem essem, tē velle ūtī cōnsiliō et dignitāte meā minus sum
admīrātus; dē grātiā et dē ope quid significārēs, mēcum ipse quaerēbam, spē
tamen dēdūcēbar ad eam cōgitātiōnem, ut tē pro tuā admīrābilī ac singulārī
5 sapientiā dē ōtiō, dē pāce, dē concordiā cīvium agī velle arbitrārer, et ad eam
ratiōnem exīstimābam satis aptam esse et nātūram et persōnam meam. Quod sī
ita est et sī qua[1] dē Pompeiō nostrō tuendō et tibi ac reī pūblicae reconciliandō
cūra tē attingit, magis idōneum quam ego sum ad eam causam profectō reperiēs
nēminem, quī et illī semper et senātuī, cum prīmum potuī, pācis auctor fuī, nec,
10 sūmptīs armīs, bellī[2] ūllam partem attigī, iūdicāvīque eō bellō tē violārī, contrā
cuius honōrem populī Rōmānī beneficiō[3] concessum inimīcī atque invidī
nīterentur. Sed, ut eō tempore nōn modo ipse fautor dignitātis tuae fuī, vērum
etiam cēterīs auctor ad tē adiuvandum, sīc mē nunc Pompeī dignitās vehementer
movet; aliquot enim sunt annī cum vōs duo dēlēgī quōs praecipuē colerem et
15 quibus essem, sīcut sum, amīcissimus. Quam ob rem ā tē petō vel potius
omnibus tē precibus ōrō et obtestor ut in tuīs maximīs cūrīs aliquid impertiās
temporis huic quoque cōgitātiōnī, ut tuō beneficiō[4] bonus[5] vir, grātus, pius[1]
dēnique esse in maximī beneficī memoriā possim.   (*A.* IX, 11A)

[1] *loyal* (to Pompey)

[1] with **cūra**
[2] Cicero had not yet joined Pompey.
[3] A law had been passed permitting Caesar to run for the consulship while still in Gaul.
[4] by not forcing Cicero to choose sides between Caesar and Pompey
[5] a conservative politically, siding with the senate

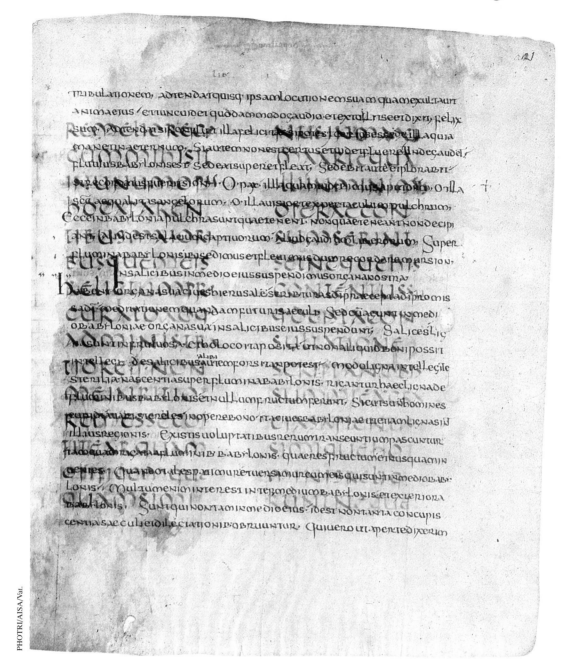

PHOTRI/AISA/Vat.

*Since writing surfaces—in this case, treated sheepskin, called **vellum**—were expensive, the writing on older and "unimportant" vellum was scraped off to make way for "more important" works. In this way, materials were recycled. Traces of the older writing always remained faintly behind the new writing. Such manuscripts are called **palimpsests**. Here the larger writing in two columns is from Cicero's De Republica, dating from the 4th century, while the smaller writing is from a selection of St. Augustine on the Psalms, dating from the 7th century. The monks probably valued Augustine over Cicero, but in doing so, preserved both! In this way, many Roman writings came down through the ages. You can probably read some of Augustine's words. Notice that there is no attempt to leave spaces between words in sentences. Larger letters are frequently used to begin new thoughts.*

Trebatius Is No Channel Swimmer

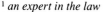

Lēgī tuās litterās, ex quibus intellēxī tē Caesarī nostrō valdē iūre cōnsultum[1] vidērī. Est quod gaudeās tē in ista loca vēnisse ubi aliquid sapere vidērēre.[2] Quod sī in Britanniam quoque profectus essēs,[1] profectō nēmō in illā tantā īnsulā perītior tē fuisset. Vērum tamen (rīdeāmus licet;

5 sum enim ā tē invītātus) subinvideō[2] tibi, ultrō etiam accersītum ab eō ad quem cēterī nōn propter superbiam eius sed propter occupātiōnem aspīrāre nōn possunt. Sed tū in istā epistulā nihil mihi scrīpsistī dē tuīs rēbus, quae mercule[3] mihi nōn minōrī cūrae sunt quam meae. Valdē metuō nē frīgeās in hībernīs. Quamquam vōs nunc istīc satis calēre[3] audiō; quō quidem nūntiō

10 valdē mercule dē tē timueram. Sed tū in rē mīlitārī multō es cautior quam in advocātiōnibus, quī neque in Ōceanō natāre voluerīs, studiōsissimus homō natandī, neque spectāre essedāriōs,[4] quem anteā nē andābatā[5] quidem dēfraudāre poterāmus. Sed iam satis iocātī sumus. Ego dē tē ad Caesarem quam dīligenter scrīpserim, tūte scīs, quam saepe, ego; sed mer-

15 cule iam intermīseram, nē vidērer līberālissimī hominis meīque amantissimī voluntātī ergā mē diffīdere.[4]   (*F.* VII, 10, 1–3)

[1] The contrary-to-fact condition shows that Trebatius had refused Caesar's invitation to go to Britain.
[2] The prefix means *just a little bit.*
[3] The Gauls are making it "hot" for the Romans.
[4] with dative

The Panthers Protest

Dē pantherīs, per eōs quī vēnārī solent agitur mandātū meō dīligenter; sed mīra paucitās est, et eās quae sunt valdē aiunt querī quod nihil cuiquam īnsidiārum in meā prōvinciā nisi sibi fīat; itaque cōnstituisse dīcuntur in Cāriam ex nostrā prōvinciā dēcēdere. Sed tamen sēdulō fit. Quicquid erit,

5 tibi erit, sed quid esset plānē nesciēbāmus. Mihi mercule magnae cūrae est aedīlitās tua; ipse diēs mē admonēbat, scrīpsī enim haec ipsīs Megalēnsibus.[1] Tū velim ad mē dē omnī reī pūblicae statū quam dīligentissimē perscrībās; ea enim certissima putābō quae ex tē cognōrō.   (*F.* II, 11, 2)

[1] The festival of the goddess Cybele, or Magna Mater, at which time important games were held.

Get Well!

[1] *plan* (of writing)
[2] *to whom I could give* (*a letter*)
[3] *that, because*
[4] *Patrae*
[5] *there is no* (*reason*) *that*

Tertiam ad tē hanc epistulam scrīpsī eōdem diē, magis īnstitūtī[1] meī tenendī causā, quia nactus eram cui darem,[2] quam quō[3] habērem quid scrīberem. Igitur illa: quantum mē dīligis, tantum adhibē in tē dīligentiae; ad tua innumerābilia in mē officia adde hoc, quod mihi erit grātissimum omnium. Cum valētūdinis ratiōnem, ut spērō, habueris, habētō etiam nāvigātiōnis. 5 In Ītaliam euntibus omnibus ad mē litterās dabis, ut ego euntem Patrās[4] nēminem praetermittō. Cūrā, cūrā tē, mī Tīrō. Quoniam nōn contigit ut simul nāvigārēs, nihil est[5] quod festīnēs, nec quicquam cūrēs nisi ut valeās. Etiam atque etiam valē. VII Īdūs Nov.[1] Actiō vesperī.   (*F.* XVI, 6)

---

[1] November 7

Peace or War

[1] *sore eyes*
[2] *handwriting* (subject)
[3] *reports from Brundisium*
[4] Caesar
[5] Pompey
[6] Caesar
[7] *from anyone*

Lippitūdinis[1] meae signum tibi sit librārī manus[2] et eadem causa brevitātis, etsī nunc quidem quod scrīberem nihil erat. Omnis exspectātiō nostra erat in nūntiīs Brundisīnīs.[3] Sī nactus hic[4] esset Gnaeum nostrum, spēs dubia pācis; sīn ille[5] ante trāmīsisset, exitiōsī bellī metus. Sed vidēsne in quem hominem[6] inciderit rēs pūblica, quam acūtum, quam vigilantem, 5 quam parātum? Sī mehercule nēminem occīderit nec cuiquam[7][1] quicquam adēmerit, ab iīs quī eum maximē timuerant maximē dīligētur. Multum mēcum mūnicipālēs hominēs loquuntur, multum rūsticānī. Nihil prōrsus aliud cūrant nisi agrōs, nisi vīllulās, nisi nummulōs[2] suōs. Et vidē quam conversa rēs est: illum quō anteā cōnfīdēbant metuunt, hunc amant quem 10 timēbant. Id quantīs nostrīs peccātīs vitiīsque ēvēnerit nōn possum sine molestiā cōgitāre. Quae autem impendēre putārem, scrīpseram ad tē et iam tuās litterās exspectābam.   (*A.* VIII, 13)

---

[1] Caesar's **clēmentia**, known from the war in Gaul, was being continued and was having an effect.

[2] The diminutives show contempt: *their precious farm houses and their filthy money.*

Come Back to Rome[1]

[1] without

Cum Furnium nostrum tantum vīdissem, neque loquī neque audīre meō commodō potuissem, properārem[2] atque essem in itinere, praemissīs iam legiōnibus, praeterīre tamen nōn potuī quīn[1] et scrīberem ad tē et illum mitterem grātiāsque agerem, etsī hoc et fēcī saepe et saepius mihi factūrus videor: 5 ita dē mē merēris. In prīmīs ā tē petō, quoniam cōnfīdō mē celeriter ad urbem ventūrum, ut tē ibi videam, ut tuō cōnsiliō, grātiā, dignitāte, ope omnium rērum ūtī possim. Ad prōpositum revertar: festīnātiōnī meae brevitātīque litterārum ignōscēs;[3] reliqua ex Furniō cognōscēs.   (A. IX, 6A)

---

[1] a very friendly letter *from* Caesar *to* Cicero, March, 49 B.C.
[2] still with **cum**
[3] with dative

Cicero the Peacemaker

Ut lēgī tuās litterās, quās ā Furniō nostrō accēperam, quibus mēcum agēbās ut ad urbem essem, tē velle ūtī cōnsiliō et dignitāte meā minus sum admīrātus; dē grātiā et dē ope quid significārēs, mēcum ipse quaerēbam, spē tamen dēdūcēbar ad eam cōgitātiōnem, ut tē pro tuā admīrābilī ac singulārī 5 sapientiā dē ōtiō, dē pāce, dē concordiā cīvium agī velle arbitrārer, et ad eam ratiōnem exīstimābam satis aptam esse et nātūram et persōnam meam. Quod sī ita est et sī qua[1] dē Pompeiō nostrō tuendō et tibi ac reī pūblicae reconciliandō cūra tē attingit, magis idōneum quam ego sum ad eam causam profectō reperiēs nēminem, quī et illī semper et senātuī, cum prīmum potuī, pācis auctor fuī, nec, 10 sūmptīs armīs, bellī[2] ūllam partem attigī, iūdicāvīque eō bellō tē violārī, contrā cuius honōrem populī Rōmānī beneficiō[3] concessum inimīcī atque invidī nīterentur. Sed, ut eō tempore nōn modo ipse fautor dignitātis tuae fuī, vērum etiam cēterīs auctor ad tē adiuvandum, sīc mē nunc Pompeī dignitās vehementer movet; aliquot enim sunt annī cum vōs duo dēlēgī quōs praecipuē colerem et 15 quibus essem, sīcut sum, amīcissimus. Quam ob rem ā tē petō vel potius omnibus tē precibus ōrō et obtestor ut in tuīs maximīs cūrīs aliquid impertiās temporis huic quoque cōgitātiōnī, ut tuō beneficiō[4] bonus[5] vir, grātus, pius[1] dēnique esse in maximī beneficī memoriā possim.   (A. IX, 11A)

[1] *loyal* (to Pompey)

---

[1] with **cūra**
[2] Cicero had not yet joined Pompey.
[3] A law had been passed permitting Caesar to run for the consulship while still in Gaul.
[4] by not forcing Cicero to choose sides between Caesar and Pompey
[5] a conservative politically, siding with the senate

Tullia's Illness

In maximīs meīs dolōribus excruciat[1] mē valētūdō Tulliae nostrae, dē
quā nihil est quod ad tē plūra scrībam; tibi enim aequē magnae cūrae esse
certō sciō. Quod[2] mē propius vultis accēdere, videō ita esse faciendum;
etiam ante fēcissem, sed mē multa impedīvērunt, quae nē nunc quidem
expedīta sunt. Sed ā Pompōniō₁ exspectō litterās, quās ad mē quam prī- 5
mum perferendās cūrēs velim. Dā operam ut valeās.   (*F.* XIV, 19)

[1] *tortures*
[2] *as to the fact that*

₁ Atticus, who would send his letters to Cicero at Rome, where Terentia was

Tullia Has Arrived

S. v. b. E. v.₁ Tullia nostra vēnit ad mē pr.[1] Īdūs Iūn. Cuius summā
virtūte et singulārī hūmānitāte graviōre etiam sum dolōre affectus nostrā
factum esse neglegentiā, ut longē aliā[2] in fortūnā esset atque[2] eius pietās[3]
ac dignitās postulābat. Nōbīs erat in animō Cicerōnem₂ ad Caesarem mittere, et cum eō Cn. Sallustium.₃ Sī profectus erit, faciam tē certiōrem. 5
Valētūdinem tuam cūrā dīligenter. Valē. XVII Kal. Quīnctīlīs.   (*F.* XIV, 11)

[1] *= **prīdiē***
[2] *different than*
[3] *devotion* (to her family)

₁ **Sī valēs benest** (for **bene est**). **Ego valeō.** A very formal old-fashioned formula, which
confirms that he and Terentia were not getting along well. They were divorced soon
after.
₂ Cicero's son
₃ not the historian Sallust

Have Everything Ready

In Tusculānum[1] nōs ventūrōs putāmus aut Nōnīs aut postrīdiē. Ibi ut₁
sint omnia parāta. Plūrēs enim fortasse nōbīscum erunt et, ut arbitror,
diūtius ibi commorābimur.₂ Lābrum[2] sī in balineō nōn est, ut₁ sit; item
cētera quae sunt ad vīctum et ad valētūdinem necessāria. Valē. Kal. Oct. dē
Venusīnō.[3]   (*F.* XIV, 20).

[1] *country home at Tusculum* (not far from Rome)
[2] *tub*
[3] *country home at Venusia*

5

₁ The **ut** clause depends on a verb such as **cūrā** to be supplied.
₂ This is rather casual, perhaps intended to infuriate Terentia: How many guests? How
long will they stay? When will they arrive?

My Day

Haec igitur est nunc vīta nostra: māne salūtāmus[1] domī et bonōs[2] virōs multōs, sed trīstīs, et hōs laetōs victōrēs, quī mē quidem perofficiōsē et peramanter observant. Ubi salūtātiō dēflūxit,[3] litterīs mē involvō: aut scrībō aut legō. Veniunt etiam quī mē audiunt quasi doctum hominem, quia
5 paulō sum quam ipsī doctior. Inde corporī omne tempus datur. Patriam ēlūxī[2] iam et gravius et diūtius quam ūlla māter ūnicum fīlium. Sed cūrā, sī mē amās, ut valeās, nē ego, tē iacente,[3] bona tua comedim;[4] statuī enim tibi nē aegrōtō quidem parcere.   (*F.* IX, 20, 3)

[1] *is ended*
[2] *I have mourned for* (from **ēlūgeō**)
[3] *while you lie ill*

---

[1] at the morning **salūtātiō** (reception)
[2] in the usual sense of *conservatives*
[3] The metaphor is a good one, for the visitors seem to *flow away.*
[4] an old form for **comedam:** *eat up*

Only Solitude Brings Comfort

Tē, tuīs negōtiīs relīctīs, nōlō ad mē venīre. Ego potius accēdam, sī diūtius impediēre; etsī nē discessissem quidem ē cōnspectū tuō, nisi mē plānē nihil ūlla rēs adiuvāret. Quod sī esset aliquod levāmen, id esset in tē ūnō, et cum prīmum ab aliquō poterit esse, ā tē erit. Nunc tamen ipsum[1]
5 sine tē esse nōn possum. Sed nec tuae domī probābātur[2] nec meae poteram,[1] nec, sī propius essem uspiam, tēcum tamen essem; idem enim tē impedīret quō minus mēcum essēs quod nunc etiam impedit. Mihi adhūc nihil prius[3] fuit hāc sōlitūdine, quam vereor nē Philippus[2] tollat; herī enim vesperī vēnerat.[3] Mē scrīptiō[4] et litterae[4] nōn lēniunt, sed obturbant.   (*A.* XII, 16)

[1] *at this very time* (literally, *now itself*)
[2] *I did not like it* (literally, *it was not approved* [*by me*])
[3] *preferable, better*
[4] *literary writing*

---

[1] Supply **esse.**
[2] a neighbor
[3] i.e., he arrived at his own villa from Rome

Mother-in-Law Trouble
and a Boy in College

Haec ad tē meā manū.[1] Vidē, quaesō, quid agendum sit. Pūblilia ad mē scrīpsit mātrem suam—ut cum Pūbliliō loquerer[2]—ad mē cum illō ventūram et sē ūnā,[1] sī ego paterer. Ōrat multīs et supplicibus verbīs ut liceat et ut sibi rescrībam. Rēs quam molesta sit vidēs. Rescrīpsī mihi etiam gravius esse quam tum cum illī dīxissem mē sōlum esse velle; quārē nōlle mē hōc 5 tempore eam ad mē venīre. Putābam, sī nihil rescrīpsissem, illam cum mātre ventūram, nunc nōn putō; appārēbat enim illās litterās nōn illīus esse.[3] Illud autem quod fore videō ipsum volō vītāre, nē illae ad mē veniant. Et ūna est vītātiō, ut aliō:[2] nōllem,[3] sed necesse est. Tē hoc nunc rogō ut explōrēs ad quam diem hīc ita possim esse ut nē opprimar. Agēs, ut 10 scrībis, temperātē.

Cicerōnī[4] velim hoc prōpōnās, ita[4] tamen sī[4] tibi nōn inīquum vidēbitur, ut sūmptūs[5] huius peregrīnātiōnis, quibus,[6] sī Rōmae esset domumque condūceret, quod facere cōgitābat, facile contentus futūrus erat, accommodet ad mercēdēs Argilētī et Aventīnī et, cum eī prōposueris, ipse velim 15 reliqua moderēre, quemadmodum ex iīs mercēdibus suppeditēmus eī quod opus sit. Praestābō nec Bibulum nec Acidīnum nec Messallam,[7] quōs Athēnīs futūrōs audiō, maiōrēs sūmptūs factūrōs quam quod ex iīs mercēdibus recipiētur. Itaque velim videās, prīmum, conductōrēs[5] quī sint et quantī,[6] deinde, ut sint quī ad diem[7] solvant, et quid viāticī, quid īnstrūmentī satis 20 sit. Iūmentō[8] certē Athēnīs nihil opus erit; quibus autem in viā ūtātur, domī sunt plūra quam opus erit, quod etiam tū animadvertis.   (A. XII, 32)

[1] along (with them)
[2] that I go elsewhere (Supply **discēdam.**)
[3] I could wish not
[4] only if
[5] renters (of Cicero's apartments)
[6] at what price
[7] on the day (due)
[8] horses (for carrying baggage)

---

1 This implies that many of his letters were dictated to a secretary. This one was confidential.
2 Cicero is so excited that he is incoherent; he should have said that the mother *and brother* were coming.
3 i.e., the letter was written by the mother in Publilia's name
4 young Cicero
5 object of **accommodet**
6 The antecedent is **mercēdēs.**
7 rich fellow students, of the best families in Rome

What a Father Likes to Hear[1]

[1] *and with the highest reputation for proper behavior*
[2] *how highly I value you*
[3] *on account of*
[4] *such a blessing* (as having such a son)
[5] *that I am flattering you* (literally, *(just) giving this to your ears*)
[6] *in fact*
[7] *to those*
[8] *brought into the conversation* (i.e., *hinted*)
[9] *perform your function* (as a father)
[10] *on vacation from* (with **illum**)
[11] *at a run* (literally, *with full step*)
[12] = **ut**

Athēnās vēnī a. d. XI Kal. Iūn. atque ibi, quod maximē optābam, vīdī fīlium tuum dēditum optimīs studiīs summāque modestiae fāmā.[1] Quā ex rē quantam voluptātem cēperim scīre poteris, etiam mē tacente; nōn enim nescīs quantī[2] tē faciam et quam prō[3] nostrō veterrimō vērissimōque amōre 5 omnibus tuīs etiam minimīs commodīs, nōn modo tantō bonō[4] gaudeam. Nōlī putāre, mī Cicerō, mē hoc auribus tuīs dare;[5] nihil adulēscente[2] tuō atque adeō[6] nostrō (nihil enim mihi ā tē potest esse sēiūnctum) aut amābilius omnibus iīs[7] quī Athēnīs sunt est aut studiōsius eārum artium quās tū maximē amās, hoc est optimārum. Itaque tibi, quod vērē facere possum, 10 libenter quoque grātulor nec minus etiam nōbīs, quod eum, quem necesse erat dīligere quāliscumque esset, tālem habēmus ut libenter quoque dīligāmus.

Quī cum mihi in sermōne iniēcisset[8] sē velle Asiam vīsere, nōn modo invītātus, sed etiam rogātus est ā mē ut id, potissimum nōbīs obtinentibus prōvinciam,[3] faceret; cui nōs et cāritāte et amōre tuum officium praestātūrōs[9] 15 nōn dēbēs dubitāre. Illud quoque erit nōbīs cūrae, ut Cratippus[4] ūnā cum eō sit, nē putēs in Asiā fēriātum[10] illum ab iīs studiīs in quae tuā cohortātiōne incitātur futūrum; nam illum parātum, ut videō, et ingressum plēnō gradū[11] cohortārī nōn intermittēmus, quō[12] in diēs longius discendō exercendōque sē prōcēdat.   (*F.* XII, 16, 1–2)

[1] written *by* Trebonius *to* Cicero, May, 55 B.C.
[2] with **amābilius**
[3] Trebonius stopped in Athens on his way to his province in Asia Minor.
[4] The young man's philosophy teacher. Of course it was the young Cicero's suggestion that Cratippus come along.

Young Cicero Puts on the Charm[1]

Verba Ūtilia: amplector, cōnspectus, cotīdiānus, cumulus, dulcis, ēnītor, in diēs, praedium, rūmor, suspīciō

Cum vehementer tabellāriōs exspectārem cotīdiē, aliquandō vēnērunt post diem quadrāgēsimum et sextum quam[2] ā vōbīs discesserant. Quōrum mihi fuit adventus exoptātissimus; nam cum maximam cēpissem laetitiam ex hūmānissimī et cārissimī patris epistulā, tum vērō iūcundissimae tuae 5 litterae cumulum mihi gaudī attulērunt.

[1] young Cicero to Tiro, July-October, 44 B.C.
[2] with **post**

Grātōs tibi optātōsque esse quī dē mē rūmōrēs afferuntur nōn dubitō, mī dulcissime Tīrō, praestābōque et ēnītar ut in diēs magis magisque haec nāscēns dē mē duplicētur opīniō. Quārē, quod pollicēris tē būcinātōrem[1] fore exīstimātiōnis meae, firmō id cōnstantīque animō faciās licet; tantum enim mihi dolōrem cruciātumque attulērunt errāta aetātis meae ut nōn sōlum 10 animus ā factīs, sed aurēs quoque ā commemorātiōne abhorreant. Quoniam igitur tum ex mē doluistī, nunc ut duplicētur tuum ex mē gaudium praestābō. Cratippō mē scītō[2] nōn ut discipulum sed ut fīlium esse coniūnctissimum; nam cum audiō illum libenter, tum etiam propriam eius suāvitātem vehementer amplector. Sum tōtōs diēs cum eō noctisque saepenumerō[3] partem; 15 exōrō enim ut mēcum quam saepissimē cēnet. Hāc intrōductā cōnsuētūdine, saepe īnscientibus nōbīs et cēnantibus obrēpit, sublātāque sevēritāte philosophiae, hūmānissimē nōbīscum iocātur. Quārē dā operam ut hunc tālem, tam iūcundum, tam excellentem virum videās quam prīmum. Nam quid ego dē Bruttiō dīcam? Huic ego locum in proximō[4] condūxī et, ut pos- 20 sum, ex meīs angustiīs[5] illīus sustentō tenuitātem. Praetereā dēclāmitāre Graecē apud Cassium īnstituī; Latīnē autem apud Bruttium exercērī volō.

Dē Gorgiā autem quod mihi scrībis, erat quidem ille in cotīdiānā dēclāmātiōne ūtilis, sed omnia postposuī dum modo praeceptīs patris pārērem;[3] διαρρήδην[6] enim scrīpserat ut eum dīmitterem statim. Tergiversārī[7] nōluī, 25 nē mea nimia σπουδή[8] suspīciōnem eī[4] aliquam importāret; deinde illud etiam mihi succurrēbat, grave esse mē dē iūdiciō patris iūdicāre. Tuum tamen studium et cōnsilium grātum acceptumque est mihi. Excūsātiōnem angustiārum[9] tuī temporis accipiō; sciō enim quam soleās esse occupātus.

Ēmisse tē praedium vehementer gaudeō, fēlīciterque tibi rem istam 30 ēvenīre cupiō. Rūsticus Rōmānus factus es. Quō modō ego mihi nunc ante oculōs tuum iūcundissimum cōnspectum prōpōnō? Videor enim vidēre ementem tē rūsticās rēs, cum vīlicō loquentem, in laciniā[10] servantem ex mēnsā secundā[11] sēmina.

De mandātīs, quod tibi cūrae fuit, est mihi grātum; sed petō ā tē ut quam 35 celerrimē mihi librārius[12][5] mittātur, maximē quidem Graecus; multum mihi enim ēripitur operae in exscrībendīs hypomnēmatīs.[13]   (F. XVI, 21, 1–4, 6–8)

---

[1] *trumpeter* (Tiro will blow Cicero's horn for him.)
[2] *know, I assure you*
[3] = **saepe**
[4] *nearby*
[5] *slender means* (anything but true)
[6] **diarrēdēn,** *definitely*
[7] *be evasive*
[8] **spoudē,** *zeal* (for Gorgias)
[9] *lack*
[10] *in a fold* (of your tunic)
[11] *dessert*
[12] *secretary* (to copy his notes)
[13] *notes*

[3] Cicero had ordered his son to dismiss Gorgias for his bad influence.
[4] the father, who might get the idea that his son really liked Gorgias
[5] "The poor boy," Tiro may have said, "has to copy his own notes."

Scala/Art Resource, NY

Unit VIII

Cicero's Philosophical Works

The Acropolis of Athens sits atop the highest point in the city. Its beauty and majesty probably provided much inspiration to the early Greek philosophers. The Romans borrowed much of their philosophy from the Greeks. There were several schools of Greek philosophy, the best known of which were Stoicism and Epicureanism. Western philosophy actually began in Greece with Thales of Miletus. His two best-known students were Anaximander and Anaximenes. They sought an element or force behind things that would explain everything. Thales believed this element was water, Anaximander thought it was the infinite, and Anaximenes said it was air. Socrates of Athens was more concerned with values, morals, and how a person should act—the right way of life. Plato was a disciple of Socrates and founder of the Academy. He developed the first comprehensive philosophical system. Aristotle was a pupil of Plato but broke with him. He stressed the importance of explaining the changing world that people live in.

Introducing Cicero's Philosophical Works

Perhaps the word philosophy suggests to you something obscure and formidable. Sometimes it is just that; for example, the philosophy of the ancient Greek Zeno. But it is not frightening in the form in which Cicero offered it. He presented Greek philosophy in a popular way to his Latin-speaking audience.

It is difficult to describe the nature and boundaries of the study of philosophy, especially since philosophers themselves have not always agreed on this point. However, we can say that over the centuries many philosophers have wrestled with some of the same questions, among them: What is truth? What is beauty? How should we act to achieve happiness?

Ethics, the branch of philosophy dealing with this last type of question, was particularly attractive to the practical Romans, who were interested in such considerations as the relationship of conduct to the good life, or happiness. And so Cicero's *Dē officiīs,* "On Duties," written for his son, a student in Athens, had great appeal (but probably not for its chief target). As is apparent from letters of this period, young Cicero needed something of this sort, though there is no indication that he profited by it.

The *Dē senectūte,* "On Old Age," is put in the form of a dialogue between Cato the Elder and two young men. Cato is chosen because he is a good example of a man who remained vigorous in old age. The essay denies that old age is something undesirable and stresses its positive advantages.

The *Dē amīcitiā,* "On Friendship," is also in dialogue form. Both treatises are dedicated to Cicero's old friend Atticus; you have already read some of Cicero's letters to him.

We are indebted to Cicero the philosopher chiefly because he made the glories of Greek thought available and palatable to his fellow Romans and to later ages, and since Latin in Cicero's time had few words for Greek philosophical concepts, he had to and did create them. The influence of Cicero's Latin philosophical vocabulary is felt even in modern times.

Justice

Sed cum statuissem scrībere ad tē[1] aliquid hōc tempore, multa posthāc, ab eō ōrdīrī maximē voluī quod et aetātī tuae esset[1] aptissimum et auctōritātī meae. Nam cum[2] multa sint in philosophiā et gravia et ūtilia accūrātē cōpiōsēque ā philosophīs disputāta, lātissimē patēre[3] videntur ea quae dē officiīs trādita ab illīs et praecepta sunt. Nūlla enim vītae pars neque 5 pūblicīs neque prīvātīs, neque forēnsibus neque domesticīs in rēbus, neque sī tēcum agās quid[4] neque sī cum alterō contrahās, vacāre officiō[5] potest, in eōque[2] et colendō sita vītae est honestās[6] omnis et neglegendō turpitūdō.

Sed iūstitiae prīmum mūnus est ut nē cui quis noceat nisi lacessītus iniūriā, deinde ut commūnibus prō[7] commūnibus ūtātur, prīvātīs ut suīs. 10 Sunt autem prīvāta nūlla nātūrā, sed aut vetere occupātiōne, ut quī quondam in vacuā[8] vēnērunt, aut victōriā, ut quī bellō potītī sunt, aut lēge,[3] pactiōne,[9] condiciōne,[9] sorte;[9] ex quō fit ut ager Arpīnās Arpīnātium[10] dīcātur, Tusculānus Tusculānōrum, similisque est prīvātārum possessiōnum discrīptiō.[11] Ex quō, quia suum[12] cuiusque fit eōrum quae nātūrā fuerant 15 commūnia,[12] quod cuique obtigit, id quisque teneat; eō plūs[13] sī quis sibi appetet, violābit iūs hūmānae societātis.

Fundāmentum autem est iūstitiae fidēs, id est dictōrum[14] conventōrumque cōnstantia et vēritās.[14]

Meminerīmus autem etiam adversus[15] īnfimōs iūstitiam esse servandam. 20 Est autem īnfima condiciō et fortūna servōrum, quibus[16] nōn male praecipiunt quī ita iubent ūtī ut mercennāriīs:[17] operam exigendam, iūsta praebenda.[18] Cum autem duōbus modīs, id est aut vī aut fraude, fīat iniūria, fraus quasi vulpēculae,[19] vīs leōnis vidētur: utrumque homine aliēnissimum,[4] sed fraus odiō digna maiōre. Tōtīus autem iniūstitiae nūlla capitālior[20] est quam 25 eōrum[5] quī tum cum maximē fallunt id agunt ut virī bonī esse videantur. Dē iūstitiā satis dictum.   (*Off.* I, 4, 20, 23, 41)

[1] *would be*
[2] *although*
[3] *to have the widest practical application* (literally, *to spread most widely*)
[4] *if you are dealing with something by yourself*
[5] *be free from duty*
[6] *all that is honorable*
[7] *as*
[8] *unoccupied* (*lands*)
[9] *agreement, terms* (*of purchase*), *or allotment*
[10] *to belong to the people of Arpinum*
[11] *assignment*
[12] *of those things which had been common* (*property*) (*part*) *becomes the property of an individual*
[13] *more than that*
[14] *truthfully abiding by things promised and agreed upon*
[15] *toward* (preposition)
[16] *to use whom* (with **ūtī**)
[17] *hired men*
[18] *necessities to be furnished*
[19] *fox*
[20] *more deserving of capital punishment*

---

[1] Cicero's son
[2] for **inque eō,** but **–que** is not attached to monosyllabic prepositions
[3] such as laws giving public land to veterans
[4] We say *alien to* rather than *from.*
[5] i.e., hypocrites

Sense of Duty

[1] *services*
[2] *looks to us* (for help)
[3] *friendly*

Sed sī contentiō quaedam et comparātiō fīat quibus plūrimum tribuendum sit officī, prīncipēs sint patria et parentēs, quōrum beneficiīs[1] maximīs obligātī sumus, proximī līberī tōtaque domus, quae spectat[2] in nōs sōlōs neque aliud ūllum potest habēre perfugium, deinceps bene convenientēs[3] propinquī, quibuscum commūnis etiam fortūna plērumque est. (*Off.* I, 58)

Civic Courage

[1] *attack is made*
[2] *Let arms yield to the toga* (worn by civilians); *let the laurel wreath* (of the general) *yield to* (civilian) *glory.*
[3] *to omit*
[4] *peace*
[5] *he would have gained*
[6] (*a place*) *where*
[7] *civic courage*

Illud autem optimum est, in quod invādī[1] solēre ab improbīs et invidīs audiō:

Cēdant arma togae, concēdat laurea laudī.[2]

Ut enim aliōs omittam,[3] nōbīs rem pūblicam gubernantibus, nōnne togae arma cessērunt? Neque enim perīculum in rē pūblicā fuit gravius umquam nec maius ōtium.[4] Ita cōnsiliīs dīligentiāque nostrā celeriter dē manibus audācissimōrum cīvium dēlāpsa arma ipsa cecidērunt. Quae rēs igitur gesta umquam in bellō tanta? Quī triumphus cōnferendus?

Licet enim mihi, M. fīlī, apud tē glōriārī, ad quem et hērēditās huius glōriae et factōrum imitātiō pertinet. Mihi quidem certē vir abundāns bellicīs laudibus, Cn. Pompeius, multīs audientibus, hoc tribuit, ut dīceret frūstrā sē triumphum tertium dēportātūrum fuisse[5] nisi meō in rem pūblicam beneficiō ubi[6] triumphāret esset habitūrus. Sunt igitur domesticae fortitūdinēs[7] nōn īnferiōrēs mīlitāribus; in quibus plūs etiam quam in hīs operae studīque pōnendum est.   (*Off.* I, 77–78)

Choice of a Career

Cōnstituendum est quōs nōs et quālēs esse velīmus et in quō genere[1] vītae; quae dēlīberātiō est omnium difficillima. Ineunte enim adulēscentiā,[2] cum est maxima imbecillitās cōnsilī,[3] tum id sibi quisque genus aetātis dēgendae cōnstituit quod maximē adamāvit. Itaque ante₁ implicātur aliquō certō genere cursūque vīvendī quam potuit quod optimum esset iūdicāre. Plērumque autem parentium praeceptīs imbūtī ad eōrum cōnsuētūdinem mōremque[4] dēdūcimur. Aliī multitūdinis iūdiciō feruntur,[5] quaeque maiōrī partī pulcherrima videntur, ea maximē exoptant; nōn nūllī tamen sīve fēlīcitāte quādam[6] sīve bonitāte nātūrae sine parentium disciplīnā rēctam vītae secūtī sunt viam. Illud autem maximē rārum genus est eōrum quī aut 10 excellentī ingenī magnitūdine aut praeclārā ērudītiōne atque doctrīnā aut utrāque rē ōrnātī spatium etiam dēlīberandī habuērunt quem potissimum vītae cursum sequī vellent; in quā dēlīberātiōne ad suam cuiusque nātūram cōnsilium est omne revocandum.[7]   (*Off.* I, 117–119)

Marginal notes:
[1] *career*
[2] *at the beginning of youth*
[3] *judgment*
[4] *their* (the parents') *customs and manners*
[5] *are carried away*
[6] *by a sort of good luck*
[7] *the judgment must be based on each person's nature* (literally, *must be called back to*)

Personal Appearance

Cum autem pulchritūdinis duo genera sint, quōrum in alterō venustās[1] sit, in alterō dignitās, venustātem muliebrem dūcere[2] dēbēmus, dignitātem virīlem. Ergō et ā fōrmā removeātur omnis virō nōn dignus ōrnātus[3] et huic simile vitium in gestū mōtūque caveātur. Nam et palaestricī mōtūs[4] sunt saepe odiōsiōrēs et histriōnum nōn nūllī gestūs[5] ineptiīs[6] nōn vacant et in 5 utrōque genere quae sunt rēcta et simplicia laudantur. Fōrmae autem dignitās colōris[7] bonitāte tuenda est, color exercitātiōnibus corporis. Adhibenda praetereā munditia est nōn odiōsa neque exquīsīta nimis, tantum[8] quae fugiat agrestem et inhūmānam neglegentiam. Eadem ratiō est habenda vestītūs, in quō, sīcut in plērīsque rēbus, mediocritās optima est.   (*Off.* I, 130)   10

Marginal notes:
[1] *loveliness*
[2] *consider*
[3] *every adornment not becoming to a man*
[4] *the movements* (taught in the) *gymnasium*
[5] *some gestures of actors*
[6] *affectation*
[7] *complexion*
[8] *only enough to avoid*

Honorable Careers
for Gentlemen

[1] trades and gainful occupations
[2] tax collectors and usurers
[3] manual labor
[4] contract
[5] fraud
[6] fishsellers, butchers, cooks, sausage makers, fishermen
[7] burlesque show
[8] the teaching of worthy subjects
[9] these are honorable for those whose social status they suit
[10] importing
[11] distributing to many without fraud
[12] as they often made their way from the high seas to the harbor, so they made their way from the harbor to the country

Iam dē artificiīs et quaestibus,[1] quī līberālēs habendī, quī sordidī sint, haec ferē accēpimus. Prīmum improbantur iī quaestūs quī in odia hominum incurrunt, ut portītōrum,[2] ut faenerātōrum. Illīberālēs autem et sordidī quaestūs mercennāriōrum omnium, quōrum operae,[3] nōn quōrum artēs emuntur; est enim in illīs ipsa mercēs auctōrāmentum[4] servitūtis. Sordidī etiam putandī quī mercentur ā mercātōribus quod statim vēndant;[1] nihil enim prōficiant nisi admodum mentiantur, nec vērō est quicquam turpius vānitāte.[5] Opificēsque omnēs in sordidā arte versantur; nec enim quicquam ingenuum potest habēre officīna. Minimēque artēs eae probandae quae ministrae sunt voluptātum:

Cētāriī, laniī, coquī, fartōrēs, piscātōrēs,[6][2]

ut ait Terentius. Adde hūc, sī placet, unguentāriōs, saltātōrēs, tōtumque lūdum tālārium.[7] In quibus autem artibus aut prūdentia maior inest aut nōn mediocris ūtilitās quaeritur, ut medicīna, ut architectūra, ut doctrīna[8] rērum honestārum, hae[9] sunt eīs quōrum ōrdinī conveniunt honestae.[9] Mercātūra autem, sī tenuis est, sordida putanda est; sīn magna et cōpiōsa, multa undique apportāns[10] multīsque sine vānitāte impertiēns,[11] nōn est admodum vituperanda, atque etiam sī satiāta[3] quaestū vel contenta potius, ut saepe ex altō in portum,[12] ex ipsō portū sē in agrōs possessiōnēsque contulit, vidētur iūre optimō posse laudārī. Omnium autem rērum ex quibus aliquid acquīritur, nihil est agrī cultūrā melius, nihil dulcius, nihil ūberius, nihil homine līberō dignius; dē quā quoniam in Catōne maiōre satis multa dīximus, illinc assūmēs quae ad hunc locum pertinēbunt. (*Off.* I, 150–151)

---

[1] i.e., retailers
[2] quoted from Terence, writer of comedy
[3] modifies **mercātūra** but actually refers to those engaged in business

Knowledge and Courage and Their Value in Society

Atque ut apium exāmina[1] nōn fingendōrum favōrum[2] causā congregantur, sed, cum congregābilia nātūrā sint, fingunt favōs, sīc hominēs (ac multō etiam magis nātūrā congregātī) adhibent agendī cōgitandīque[1] sollertiam. Itaque nisi ea virtūs[2] quae cōnstat ex hominibus tuendīs, id est ex societāte generis hūmānī, attingat[3] cognitiōnem rērum, sōlivaga[4] cognitiō et iēiūna videātur, itemque magnitūdō animī,[5] remōtā commūnitāte coniūnctiōneque hūmānā,[6] feritās sit quaedam et immānitās. Ita fit ut vincat cognitiōnis studium cōnsociātiō hominum atque commūnitās.[7] Nec vērum est quod dīcitur ā quibusdam, propter necessitātem vītae,[3] quod ea quae nātūra dēsīderāret cōnsequī sine aliīs atque efficere nōn possēmus, idcircō initam esse cum hominibus commūnitātem et societātem; quod sī omnia nōbīs quae ad vīctum cultumque pertinent, quasi virgulā[8] dīvīnā, ut aiunt, suppeditārentur, tum optimō quisque ingeniō, negōtiīs omnibus omissīs, tōtum sē in cognitiōne et scientiā collocāret. Nōn est ita. Nam et sōlitūdinem fugeret et socium studī quaereret, tum docēre, tum discere vellet, tum audīre, tum dīcere. Ergō omne officium quod ad coniūnctiōnem hominum et ad societātem tuendam valet antepōnendum est illī officiō quod cognitiōne et scientiā continētur.   (*Off.* I, 157–158)

[1] *swarms of bees*
[2] *honeycombs*
[3] *is attached to*
[4] *solitary*
[5] *courage*
[6] *if a social attitude is left out* (literally, *is removed*)
[7] *social needs take precedence over the pursuit of knowledge (by an individual)*
[8] *wand*

[1] i.e., together with others
[2] i.e., justice
[3] In translating, put the last part of the sentence (from **idcircō**) next, then the **quod** clause: *it is not true that social life began on account of the need of obtaining food because,* etc.

Honor Among Thieves

Atque eīs etiam quī vēndunt, emunt, condūcunt, locant, contrahendīsque negōtiīs implicantur, iūstitia ad rem gerendam necessāria est, cuius tanta vīs est ut nē illī quidem quī maleficiō et scelere pāscuntur[1] possint sine ūllā particulā iūstitiae vīvere. Nam quī eōrum cuipiam[2] quī ūnā[3] latrōcinantur

[1] *live by crime*
[2] *from any of those who*
[3] *with him*

5 fūrātur aliquid aut ēripit, is sibi nē in latrōciniō quidem relinquit locum;[1] ille autem quī archipīrāta dīcitur, nisi aequābiliter praedam dispertiat, aut interficiātur ā sociīs aut relinquātur. Quīn etiam lēgēs latrōnum esse dīcuntur, quibus pāreant, quās observent. Itaque propter aequābilem praedae partītiōnem et Bardūlis Illyrius latrō, dē quō est apud Theopompum,
10 magnās opēs habuit et multō maiōrēs Viriāthus Lūsitānus, cui quidem etiam exercitūs nostrī imperātōrēsque cessērunt, quem C. Laelius, is quī Sapiēns ūsūrpātur,[4] praetor frēgit et comminuit ferōcitātemque eius ita repressit ut facile bellum reliquīs trāderet. Cum igitur tanta vīs iūstitiae sit ut ea etiam latrōnum opēs firmet atque augeat, quantam eius vim inter
15 lēgēs et iūdicia et in cōnstitūtā rē pūblicā fore putāmus? (*Off.* 11, 40)

---

[1] i.e., he loses his place in the gang of robbers (**latrōciniō**)

The Responsibility of Wealth

Id quidem nōn dubium est, quīn[1] illa benignitās quae cōnstet ex operā[2] et industriā et honestior sit et lātius pateat[3] et possit prōdesse plūribus; nōn numquam tamen est largiendum,[4] nec hoc benignitātis genus omnīnō repudiandum est et saepe idōneīs hominibus indigentibus dē rē familiārī[5]
5 impertiendum, sed dīligenter atque moderātē. Multī enim patrimōnia effūdērunt incōnsultē largiendō.

Atque etiam illae impēnsae meliōrēs, mūrī, nāvālia,[6] portūs, aquārum ductūs omniaque quae ad ūsum reī pūblicae pertinent. Quamquam quod praesēns tamquam in manum[7] datur iūcundius est; tamen haec in posterum
10 grātiōra. Theātra, porticūs, nova templa verēcundius[8] reprehendō propter Pompeium. Tōta igitur ratiō tālium[1] largītiōnum genere[9] vitiōsa est, temporibus[10] necessāria, et tum ipsum[11] et ad facultātēs accommodanda et mediocritāte moderanda est. In illō autem alterō genere largiendī,[2] quod ā līberālitāte proficīscitur, nōn ūnō modō in disparibus causīs affectī esse
15 dēbēmus. Alia causa est eius quī calamitāte premitur et eius quī rēs meliōrēs quaerit, nūllīs suīs rēbus adversīs.[12] Prōpēnsior benignitās esse dēbēbit in calamitōsōs, nisi forte erunt dignī calamitāte. (*Off.* II, 54, 60, 61)

---

[1] i.e., of such large amounts
[2] i.e., to individuals

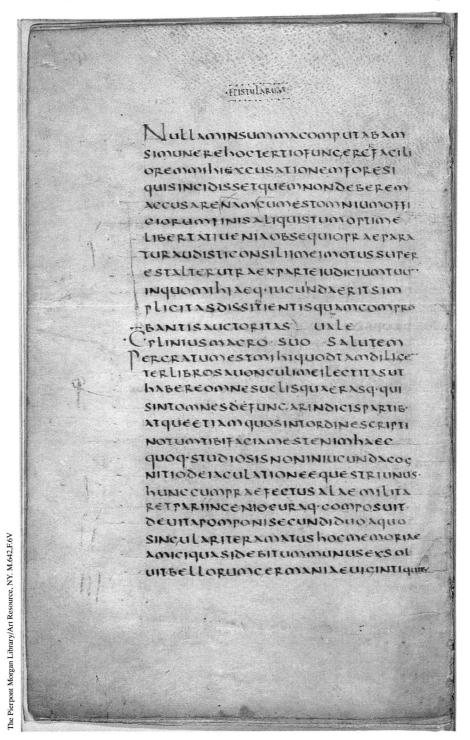

*This manuscript from the early 6th century is the oldest known copy of Pliny's letters. You can see the word **Epistulārum** at the very top. The first line reads **Nūllam in summā computābam**. What other words can you pick out? Notice that, like other ancient manuscripts, no spaces are left between words, and hyphens are not used at the end of a line. Pliny's name appears in red near the center. How can you tell—what words give you a clue—that the red line is the beginning of something new?*

Cancellation of Debts

Tabulae vērō novae[1] quid habent argumentī,[2] nisi ut emās meā$_1$ pecūniā fundum, eum tū habeās, ego nōn habeam pecūniam? Quam ob rem nē sit aes aliēnum quod[3] reī pūblicae noceat, prōvidendum est; quod multīs ratiōnibus cavērī potest; nōn,[4] sī fuerit, ut locuplētēs suum perdant,
5 dēbitōrēs lucrentur aliēnum.[5] Nec enim ūlla rēs vehementius rem pūblicam continet[6] quam fidēs, quae esse nūlla potest nisi erit necessāria solūtiō rērum crēditārum.[7] Numquam vehementius āctum est quam, mē cōnsule, nē solverētur.[8] Armīs et castrīs temptāta rēs est ab omnī genere hominum et ōrdine; quibus ita restitī ut hoc tōtum malum dē rē pūblicā tollerētur.
10 Numquam nec maius aes aliēnum fuit nec melius nec$_2$ facilius dissolūtum est; fraudandī enim spē sublātā, solvendī necessitās cōnsecūta est. At vērō hic nunc victor, tum quidem victus, quae cōgitārat ea perfēcit, cum eius iam nihil interesset.[9] Tanta in eō peccandī libīdō fuit ut hoc ipsum eum dēlectāret, peccāre, etiam sī causa nōn esset.   (*Off.* II, 84)

$_1$ i.e., that of the lender
$_2$ We would say *or.*

The Activities of Old Age

Ā rēbus gerendīs senectūs abstrahit.$_1$ Quibus? An eīs quae iuventūte geruntur et vīribus? Nūllaene igitur rēs sunt senīlēs, quae, vel īnfirmīs corporibus, animō tamen administrentur?

Nihil igitur afferunt quī in rē gerendā versārī senectūtem negant, sim-
5 ilēsque[1] sunt ut sī quī gubernātōrem in nāvigandō nihil agere dīcant, cum aliī mālōs scandant, aliī per forōs cursent, aliī sentīnam exhauriant, ille autem clāvum tenēns quiētus sedeat in puppī. Nōn facit ea quae iuvenēs, at vērō multō maiōra et meliōra facit. Nōn vīribus aut vēlōcitāte aut celeritāte corpōrum rēs magnae geruntur, sed cōnsiliō, auctōritāte, sententiā; quibus
10 nōn modo nōn orbārī, sed etiam augērī senectūs solet. Nisi forte ego vōbīs, quī et mīles et tribūnus et lēgātus et cōnsul versātus sum in variō genere bellōrum, cessāre nunc videor cum bella nōn gerō. At senātuī quae sint gerenda praescrībō et quō modō; Carthāginī male iam diū cōgitantī[2] bellum multō ante dēnūntiō; dē quā verērī nōn ante dēsinam quam illam
15 excīsam esse cognōverō.   (*Sen.* 15, 17–18)

$_1$ This is the charge made by some people.

A Busy Old Age

Cedo,[1] quī[2] vestram rem pūblicam tantam āmīsistis tam citō?

Sīc enim percontantur in Naevī poētae Lūdō; respondentur et alia et hoc in prīmīs:

Prōveniēbant ōrātōrēs novī, stultī adulēscentulī.

Temeritās est vidēlicet flōrentis aetātis, prūdentia senēscentis. 5

Possum nōmināre ex agrō Sabīnō rūsticōs Rōmānōs, vīcīnōs et familiārēs meōs, quibus absentibus, numquam ferē ūlla in agrō maiōra opera fīunt, nōn serendīs,[3] nōn percipiendīs, nōn condendīs frūctibus. Quamquam in aliīs[4] minus hoc mīrum est; nēmō enim est tam senex quī sē annum[5] nōn putet posse vīvere; sed īdem in eīs ēlabōrant quae sciunt nihil ad sē omnīnō 10 pertinēre:

Serit arborēs quae alterī saeculō prōsint,

ut ait Stātius noster in Synephēbīs.[6]

Vidētis ut[7] senectūs nōn modo languida atque iners nōn sit, vērum etiam sit operōsa et semper agēns aliquid et mōliēns, tāle scīlicet quāle cuiusque 15 studium in superiōre vītā fuit. Quid quī[8] etiam addiscunt aliquid? Ut et [9] Solōnem versibus glōriantem vidēmus, quī sē cotīdiē aliquid addiscentem dīcit senem fierī, et ego fēcī, quī litterās Graecās senex didicī; quās quidem sīc avidē arripuī (quasi diūturnam sitim explēre cupiēns) ut ea ipsa mihi nōta essent quibus mē nunc exemplīs[10] ūtī vidētis. Quod cum fēcisse 20 Sōcratem in fidibus audīrem,[11] vellem[12] equidem etiam illud (discēbant enim fidibus[1] antīquī), sed in litterīs certē ēlabōrāvī.   (Sen. 20, 24, 26)

[1] *Tell me*
[2] *how* (adverb)
[3] *at* (*the time of*) *sowing*
[4] *other things* (than the one which follows, about planting trees)
[5] *another year*
[6] *The Young Companions* (a play)
[7] *how*
[8] *What of those who?*
[9] *not only . . . but also* (with the next **et**)
[10] *as examples*
[11] *when I heard that Socrates had done this* (i.e., learned in old age) *on the lyre*
[12] *I could have wished*

---

[1] Supply **canere**, *to play.*

Occupations in Old Age

Quid in leviōribus studiīs, sed tamen acūtīs?[1] Quam gaudēbat bellō suō
Pūnicō Naevius! Quam Truculentō Plautus, quam Pseudolō! Vīdī etiam
senem Līvium; quī cum sex annīs ante quam ego nātus sum, fābulam
docuisset,[1] Centōne Tuditānōque cōnsulibus,[2] usque ad adulēscentiam
5 meam prōcessit aetāte.[2]

Veniō nunc ad voluptātēs agricolārum, quibus ego incrēdibiliter dēlector; quae nec ūllā impediuntur senectūte et mihi ad sapientis vītam proximē
videntur accēdere. Habent enim ratiōnem[3] cum terrā, quae numquam
recūsat imperium[4] nec umquam sine ūsūrā reddit quod accēpit, sed aliās[5]
10 minōre, plērumque maiōre cum faenore. Quamquam mē quidem nōn
frūctus modo, sed etiam ipsīus terrae vīs ac nātūra[6] dēlectat.

Sed veniō ad agricolās, nē ā mē ipsō recēdam. In agrīs erant[3] tum senātōrēs,
id est senēs,[4] siquidem arantī L. Quīnctiō Cincinnātō nūntiātum est eum dictātōrem esse factum; cuius dictātōris iussū magister equitum,[5] C. Servīlius Ahāla,
15 Sp. Maelium rēgnum appetentem occupātum interēmit.[7]   (*Sen.* 50, 51, 56)

[1] *had produced a play* (literally, *he, as author,* taught *it to the actors*)
[2] *continued to live* (literally, *went on in life*)
[3] *account*
[4] *draft* (a demand for payment)
[5] *at times*
[6] *the natural forces of the earth*
[7] *took by surprise and put to death*

---

[1] i.e., that demand keenness
[2] 240 B.C.
[3] i.e., they lived on farms
[4] **Senātor** is derived from **senex.**
[5] The *master of the horse* was the dictator's assistant.

Authority, The Reward of Old Age

Sed in omnī ōrātiōne[1] mementōte eam mē senectūtem laudāre quae
fundāmentīs adulēscentiae cōnstitūta sit.[1] Ex quō efficitur, id quod ego
magnō quondam cum assēnsū omnium dīxī, miseram esse senectūtem quae
sē ōrātiōne dēfenderet. Nōn cānī[2] nec rūgae repente auctōritātem arripere
5 possunt, sed honestē ācta superior aetās frūctūs capit auctōritātis extrēmōs.[3]
Haec enim ipsa sunt honōrābilia, quae videntur levia atque commūnia,

[1] *that kind of old age which*
[2] *white hair* (Supply **capillī**.)
[3] *at the end* (literally, *last,* with **frūctūs**)

---

[1] Supply **meā.**

salūtārī,[2] appetī, dēcēdī, assurgī, dēdūcī,[4] redūcī,[4] cōnsulī; quae et apud nōs et in aliīs cīvitātibus, ut quaeque optimē mōrāta est,[5] ita dīligentissimē observantur. Lysandrum Lacedaemonium dīcere aiunt solitum Lacedaemonem esse honestissimum domicilium senectūtis; nusquam enim tantum tribuitur[6] aetātī, nusquam est senectūs honōrātior. Quīn etiam memoriae prōditum est, cum Athēnīs lūdīs[7] quīdam in theātrum grandis nātū[8] vēnisset, magnō cōnsessū,[9] locum nusquam eī datum ā suīs cīvibus; cum autem ad Lacedaemoniōs accessisset, quī lēgātī cum essent,[10] certō[11] in locō cōnsēderant, cōnsurrēxisse omnēs illī dīcuntur et senem sessum[12] recēpisse. Quibus cum ā cūnctō cōnsessū plausus esset multiplex datus, dīxisse ex eīs quendam Athēniēnsēs scīre quae rēcta essent, sed facere nōlle.   (*Sen.* 62–64)

4 *that they escort us* (to the Forum) *and back* (home)
5 *to the degree that each state has a high code of morals*
6 *so much respect shown*
7 *at the games*
8 *old man* (literally, *great as to birth* [or *age*])
9 *in the great crowd*
10 *being ambassadors* (literally, *who, since they were ambassadors*)
11 *fixed, reserved*
12 *to sit down*

---

2 In translating, it would be a good idea to use the active voice, since two of the infinitives, **dēcēdī** and **assurgī**, are impersonal: *that people greet us,* etc.

The Meaning of Friendship

Est enim amīcitia nihil aliud nisi omnium dīvīnārum hūmānārumque rērum cum benevolentiā et cāritāte cōnsēnsiō; quā quidem haud sciō an,[1] exceptā sapientiā, nihil melius hominī sit ā dīs immortālibus datum. Dīvitiās aliī praepōnunt, bonam aliī valētūdinem, aliī potentiam, aliī honōrēs,[2] multī etiam voluptātēs. Bēluārum hoc quidem extrēmum,[3] illa autem superiōra cadūca et incerta, posita[4] nōn tam in cōnsiliīs nostrīs quam in fortūnae temeritāte. Quī autem in virtūte summum bonum[5] pōnunt, praeclārē illī quidem,[1] sed haec ipsa virtūs amīcitiam et gignit et continet,[6] nec sine virtūte amīcitia esse ūllō pactō potest.

Quid dulcius quam habēre quīcum[7] omnia audeās sīc loquī ut tēcum? Quī[8] esset tantus frūctus in prōsperīs rēbus, nisi habērēs quī illīs aequē ac[9] tū ipse gaudēret? Adversās[2] vērō ferre difficile esset sine eō quī illās gravius etiam quam tū ferret.   (*Am.* 20, 22)

1 **haud sciō an = nesciō an,** *perhaps* (literally, *I do not know whether*)
2 *political offices*
3 *this last* (i.e., **voluptātēs**) *is* (*characteristic*) *of wild beasts*
4 *dependent on*
5 *the highest good*
6 *preserves*
7 = **quōcum, cum quō**
8 *how*
9 *equally as*

---

1 Supply **faciunt.**
2 Supply **rēs;** in contrast with **prōsperīs.**

The Ultimate in Friendship

Quī clāmōrēs tōtā caveā¹ nūper in hospitis et amīcī meī M. Pācuvī novā fābulā, cum, ignōrante rēge uter Orestēs esset, Pyladēs Orestem sē esse dīceret, ut prō illō necārētur, Orestēs autem, ita ut erat, Orestem sē esse persevērāret. Stantēs₁ plaudēbant in rē fictā; quid arbitrāmur in vērā 5 factūrōs fuisse? Facile indicābat ipsa nātūra vim suam, cum hominēs, quod₂ facere ipsī nōn possent, id rēctē fierī in alterō iūdicārent.   (*Am.* 24)

₁ i.e., the audience in the theater
₂ i.e., die for someone else

The Friendship of Laelius and Scīpiō

Sed quoniam rēs hūmānae fragilēs cadūcaeque sunt, semper aliquī anquīrendī sunt quōs dīligāmus et ā quibus dīligāmur; cāritāte enim benevolentiāque sublātā, omnis est ē vītā sublāta iūcunditās. Mihi¹ quidem Scīpiō, quamquam est subitō ēreptus, vīvit tamen semperque vīvet; virtūtem² 5 enim amāvī illīus virī, quae exstīncta nōn est; nec mihi sōlī versātur ante oculōs, quī illam semper in manibus habuī,³ sed etiam posterīs erit clāra et īnsignis. Nēmō umquam animō aut spē maiōra⁴ suscipiet quī sibi nōn illīus memoriam atque imāginem prōpōnendam putet.⁵ Equidem ex omnibus rēbus quās mihi aut fortūna aut nātūra tribuit nihil habeō quod cum amīci-10 tiā Scīpiōnis possim comparāre. In hāc mihi dē rē pūblicā cōnsēnsus, in hāc rērum prīvātārum cōnsilium, in eādem requiēs plēna oblectātiōnis fuit. Numquam illum nē minimā quidem rē offendī, quod⁶ quidem sēnserim, nihil audīvī ex eō ipse quod nōllem; ūna domus erat, īdem vīctus isque

commūnis, neque sōlum mīlitia₁ sed etiam peregrīnātiōnēs rūsticātiōnēsque
commūnēs. Nam quid ego dē studiīs dīcam cognōscendī semper aliquid 15
atque discendī? In quibus remōtī ab oculīs populī omne ōtiōsum tempus
contrīvimus. Quārum rērum recordātiō et memoria sī ūnā cum illō occidis-
set, dēsīderium coniūnctissimī atque amantissimī virī ferre nūllō modō
possem. Sed nec₂ illa₃ exstīncta sunt alunturque potius et augentur
cōgitātiōne et memoriā meā, et, sī illīs plānē orbātus essem, magnum 20
tamen affert mihi aetās⁷ ipsa sōlācium. Diūtius enim iam in hōc dēsīderiō   ⁷ *age*
esse nōn possum. Omnia autem brevia tolerābilia esse dēbent, etiam sī
magna sunt.   (*Am.* 102–104).

₁ one of the subjects of **erant,** to be supplied; **commūnēs** is predicate adjective
₂ = **et nōn,** correlative with the following **et**
₃ i.e., **recordātiō et memoria**

Unit IX

Two Thousand Years of Latin

*The nine Muses were daughters of Zeus and Mnemosyne (Memory). **Apollo**, god of music and poetry, is in the center. As the principal god of culture, he presides with the Muses over the various arts and sciences. Each Muse (from left to right) had a different realm of responsibility: **Cliō** was the Muse of history, **Euterpē** of music, **Thalia** of comedy, **Melpomenē** of tragedy, **Terpsichorē** of dance, **Eratō** of love poetry, **Polyhymnia** of poetry, **Ourania** of astronomy, and **Calliopē** of eloquence. You can see their names in Greek along the bottom of this painting, entitled* Apollo and the Muses, *by Baldassarre Peruzzi (1481-1536).*

Plautus

The third and second centuries B.C. were the great centuries of Roman comedy, which was an adaptation and imitation of the Greek comedy of Menander and others. The plays of two Roman comedy writers, Plautus (ca. 254–184 B.C.) and Terence (ca. 190–159 B.C.), have survived. The *Menaechmī* of Plautus is named after twin brothers who look so much alike that they are constantly confused with each other—and by the confusion hangs the humor. The Menaechmi were separated in boyhood. After Menaechmus II grows up, he travels around looking for his brother. Unaware that he has arrived at the town where his brother lives, he meets a girl who takes him for Menaechmus I and gives him an expensive dress to be altered. The dress is one that Menaechmus I had taken from his wife's wardrobe and given to the girl. The scene below shows Menaechmus II and the wife *(matrōna)* of Menaechmus I. The *matrōna* mistakes Menaechmus II for her husband and recognizes the dress.

As in other Roman comedies, the characters in the *Menaechmī* are Greek, and the scenes are laid in Greece.

Who Is Who?

MA. Adībo atque hominem accipiam quibus dictīs meret.
Nōn tē pudet prōdīre in cōnspectum meum,
flāgitium hominis,[1] cum istōc ōrnātū? ME. Quid est?
710   Quae tē rēs agitat, mulier? MA. Etiamne, impudēns,
muttīre verbum ūnum audēs aut mēcum loquī?
ME. Quid tandem admīsī in mē[2] ut loquī nōn audeam?
MA. Rogās mē? Hominis impudentem audāciam!
ME. Nōn tū scīs, mulier, Hecubam quāpropter canem
715   Grāiī esse praedicābant? Ma. Nōn equidem sciō.
ME. Quia idem faciēbat Hecuba quod tū nunc facis.
Omnia mala[3] ingerēbat quemquem aspexerat.
Itaque adeō iūre coepta appellārī est canēs.₁
MA. Nōn ego istaec flāgitia possum perpetī.
720   Nam mēd₂ aetātem[4] viduam esse māvelim₃
quam istaec flāgitia tua patī quae tū facis.
ME. Quid id ad mē, tū tē nuptam possīs₄ perpetī,

[1] *disgrace of a man*
[2] *What have I brought on myself;* i.e., *what have I done?*
[3] *curses on*
[4] *(all my) life*

₁ nominative for **canis**
₂ old form of **mē**
₃ old form of **mālim**
₄ Supply *whether* in translation.

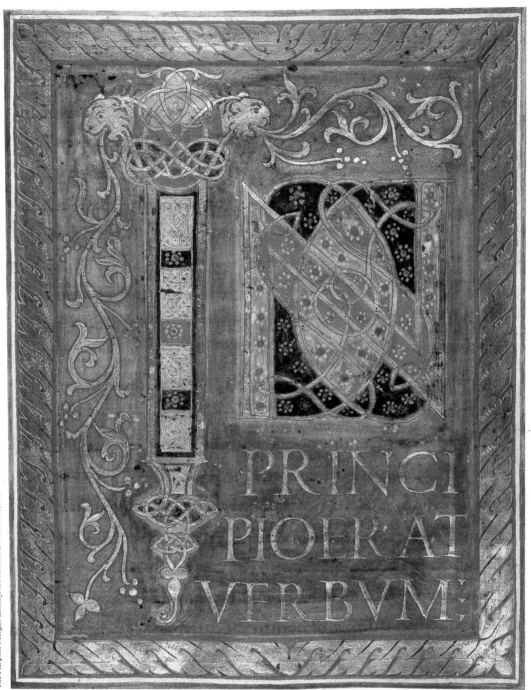

*Many ancient and medieval manuscripts are beautifully scripted and decorated. This page comes from the beginning of the Gospel according to John. It begins, **In prīncipiō erat verbum**. (In English, the next words are: "And the word was with God and the Word was God." Can you translate this part into Latin?) Notice that the **In** is so integrated into the design that it is hardly visible. If you compare this manuscript to the ones in Units VII and VIII, you can clearly see the increased sophistication and beauty that was added to manuscripts. Dating from the 9th century, the script used in this piece is Carolingian (French).*

Phaedrus

Fables, which are part of folklore, were passed on by word of mouth. The Greek writer Aesop wrote some of them down; his fables are still famous and have been translated into many languages. The Roman Phaedrus translated them into Latin verse during the Age of Augustus. For a long time fables of Phaedrus, and versions of them, were the ones generally known, until in modern times Aesop was again translated.

Mūlī Duo et Raptōrēs (Two Mules and Thieves)

[1] *money bags*
[2] *barley*
[3] *poverty*
[4] **= perīculō**
[5] *subject to*

Mūlī gravātī sarcinīs ībant duo:
ūnus ferēbat fiscōs[1] cum pecūniā,
alter tumentēs multō saccōs hordeō.[2]
Ille onere dīves celsā cervīce ēminet
5   clārumque collō iactat tintinnābulum;
comes quiētō sequitur et placidō gradū.
Subitō latrōnēs ex īnsidiīs advolant
interque caedem ferrō mūlum sauciant,
dīripiunt nummōs, neglegunt vīle hordeum.
10   Spoliātus igitur cāsūs cum flēret suōs:
"Equidem," inquit alter, "mē contemptum gaudeō,
nam nīl āmīsī nec sum laesus vulnere."
Hōc argumentō tūta est hominum tenuitās;[3]
Magnae perīclō[4] sunt opēs obnoxiae.[5]
(II, 7)

Lupus ad Canem (The Wolf to the Dog)

[1] *well fed*
[2] *to greet each other*
[3] *when*

Quam dulcis sit lībertās breviter prōloquar.
Canī perpāstō[1] maciē cōnfectus lupus
forte occucurrit. Dein salūtātum[2] invicem
ut[3] restitērunt: "Unde sīc, quaesō, nitēs?
5   Aut quō cibō fēcistī tantum corporis?
Ego, quī sum longē fortior, pereō fame."
Canis simpliciter: "Eadem est condiciō tibi,
Praestāre dominō sī pār officium potes."
"Quod?" inquit ille. "Custōs ut sīs līminis,
10   ā fūribus tueāris et noctū domum."
"Ego vērō sum parātus; nunc patior nivēs
imbrēsque in silvīs asperam vītam trahēns.
Quantō est facilius mihi sub tēctō vīvere,

et ōtiōsum largō satiārī cibō!"
"Venī ergō mēcum." Dum prōcēdunt, aspicit 15
lupus ā catēnā collum dētrītum canī.[4]
"Unde hoc, amīce?" "Nihil est." "Dīc, quaesō, tamen."
"Quia videor ācer, alligant mē interdiū,
lūce ut quiēscam, et vigilem nox cum vēnerit;
crepusculō[5] solūtus, quā vīsum est[6] vagor. 20
Affertur ultrō pānis; dē mēnsā suā
dat ossa dominus; frūsta iactant familia
et quod fastīdit quisque pulmentārium.[7]
Sīc sine labōre venter implētur meus."
"Age, abīre sī quō est animus, est licentia?" 25
"Nōn plānē est," inquit. "Fruere quae laudās, canis;
rēgnāre nōlō, līber ut[8] nōn sim mihi."
(III, 7)

[4] for the dog (we would say of)
[5] at twilight
[6] wherever I like
[7] whatever food anyone doesn't like
[8] on condition that

Soror et Frāter (Sister and Brother)

Praeceptō monitus saepe tē cōnsīderā.[1]
Habēbat quīdam fīliam turpissimam
īdemque īnsignem pulchrā faciē fīlium.
Hī, speculum in cathedrā mātris ut positum fuit,
puerīliter lūdentēs forte īnspexērunt. 5
Hic sē formōsum iactat; illa īrāscitur
nec glōriantis[2] sustinet frātris iocōs,
accipiēns quippe cūncta in contumēliam.[3]
Ergō ad patrem dēcurrit laesūra[4] invicem
magnāque invidiā crīminātur fīlium, 10
vir nātus quod rem fēminārum tetigerit.[5]
Amplexus ille utrumque et carpēns ōscula
dulcemque in ambōs cāritātem partiēns;
"cotīdiē," inquit, "speculō vōs ūtī volō;
tū fōrmam nē corrumpās nēquitiae malīs; 15
tū faciem ut istam mōribus vincās bonīs."
(III, 8)

[1] look at yourself
[2] boasting brother
[3] as an insult (to herself)
[4] to hurt (her brother)
[5] because, though born a man, he touched women's things
   (i.e., mirrors)

Dē Vitiīs Hominum (The Imperfections of Men)

Pērās[1] imposuit Iuppiter nōbīs duās:
propriīs replētam vitiīs post tergum dedit,
aliēnīs₁ ante pectus suspendit gravem.
Hāc rē vidēre nostra mala nōn possumus;
aliī simul[2] dēlinquunt, cēnsōrēs sumus. 5
(IV, 10)

[1] sacks
[2] as soon as

₁ Supply vitiīs.

Seneca

Seneca the Younger wrote verse tragedies that had a great influence on Shakespeare and other Elizabethan writers, and philosophical works in prose, in which he preached Stoic doctrines. These too had a wide influence.

Seneca was Nero's tutor and later became his adviser, in effect his prime minister during the first five "golden years," as they were called, of Nero's reign. Then Nero forced Seneca to commit suicide and started on his mad course.

The following selections are from Seneca's letters to his friend Lucilius. They are not really letters, but essays.

Read Intensively, Not Extensively

Illud autem vidē, nē ista lēctiō auctōrum multōrum et omnis generis volūminum habeat aliquid vagum et īnstabile. Certīs ingeniīs₁ immorārī et innūtrīrī oportet, sī velīs aliquid trahere quod in animō fidēliter sedeat. Nusquam est quī ubīque est. Vītam in peregrīnātiōne exigentibus hoc

5 ēvenit, ut multa hospitia habeant, nūllās amīcitiās. Idem accidat necesse est hīs quī nūllīus sē ingeniō familiāriter applicant, sed omnia cursim et properantēs trānsmittunt. Nōn prōdest cibus nec corporī accēdit quī statim sūmptus ēmittitur. Nihil aequē sānitātem impedit quam remediōrum crēbra mūtātiō. Nōn venit vulnus ad cicātrīcem in quō medicāmenta temptantur.

10 Nōn convalēscit planta quae saepe trānsfertur. Nihil tam ūtile est ut in trānsitū¹ prōsit: distringit librōrum multitūdō. Itaque cum legere nōn possīs quantum habuerīs, satis est habēre quantum legās. "Sed modo," inquis, "hunc librum ēvolvere volō, modo illum." Fastīdientis stomachī est multa dēgustāre, quae ubi varia sunt et dīversa, inquinant, nōn alunt. Probātōs itaque

15 semper lege, et sī quandō ad aliōs dīvertī libuerit, ad priōrēs redī; aliquid cotīdiē adversus paupertātem, aliquid adversus mortem auxiliī comparā, nec minus adversus cēterās pestēs. Et cum multa percurrerīs, ūnum excerpe quod illō diē concoquās.² Hoc ipse quoque faciō: ex plūribus quae lēgī aliquid apprehendō. Hodiernum hoc est quod apud Epicūrum nānctus

20 sum (soleō enim et in aliēna castra trānsīre, nōn tamquam trānsfuga, sed tamquam explōrātor): "Honesta," inquit, "rēs est laeta paupertās." Illa vērō nōn est paupertās, sī laeta est; cui cum paupertāte bene convenit,³ dīves est. Nōn quī parum habet, sed quī plūs cupit, pauper est.   *(Epist. 2, 2–6)*

¹ *in transit,* i.e., when used only in passing
² *can digest*
³ *he who is on good terms with poverty*

₁ i.e., books written by geniuses

The Proper Treatment of Slaves

Libenter ex hīs quī ā tē veniunt cognōvī familiāriter tē cum servīs tuīs
vīvere. Hoc prūdentiam tuam, hoc ērudītiōnem decet. "Servī sunt." Immō
hominēs. "Servī sunt." Immō contubernālēs. "Servī sunt." Immō humilēs
amīcī. "Servī sunt." Immō cōnservī. Itaque rīdeō istōs quī turpe exīstimant
cum servō suō cēnāre. Quārē? Nisi quia superbissima cōnsuētūdō cēnantī 5
dominō stantium servōrum turbam circumdedit. Deinde eiusdem arrogan-
tiae prōverbium iactātur: *totidem hostēs esse quot servōs.* Nōn habēmus
illōs hostēs sed facimus. Alius pretiōsās avēs scindit:[1] per pectus et clūnēs
certīs ductibus circumferēns ērudītam manum frūsta excutit. Īnfēlīx quī
huic ūnī reī vīvit, ut altilia decenter secet; nisi quod miserior est quī hoc 10
voluptātis causā docet quam quī necessitātis[2] discit. Adice obsōnātōrēs,[1]
quibus dominicī palātī nōtitia subtilis est, quī sciunt cuius illum reī sapor
excitet,[2] cuius dēlectet aspectus, cuius novitāte nausiābundus ērigī possit,
quid iam ipsā satietāte fastīdiat, quid illō diē ēsuriat.[3] Cum hīs cēnāre nōn
sustinet et maiestātis suae dīminūtiōnem putat ad eandem mēnsam cum 15
servō suō accēdere. Vīs tū[4] cōgitāre istum quem servum tuum vocās, ex
iīsdem sēminibus ortum, eōdem fruī caelō, aequē spīrāre, aequē vīvere,
aequē morī? Nōlō in ingentem mē locum immittere et dē ūsū servōrum
disputāre, in quōs superbissimī, crūdēlissimī, contumēliōsissimī sumus.
Haec tamen praeceptī meī summa est: sīc cum īnferiōre vīvās quemad- 20
modum tēcum superiōrem[5] velīs vīvere. Quotiēns in mentem venerit quantum tibi in servum liceat, veniat in mentem tantundem in tē dominō tuō
licēre. Vīve cum servō clēmenter, comiter quoque, et in sermōnem illum
admitte et in cōnsilium et in convīctum. Nē illud quidem vidētis quam[6]
omnem invidiam maiōrēs nostrī dominīs, omnem contumēliam servīs 25
dētrāxerint? Dominum patrem familiae appellāvērunt, servōs, familiārēs.
Īnstituērunt diem fēstum, nōn quō sōlō cum servīs dominī vēscerentur, sed
quō utique honōrēs illīs in domō gerere, iūs dīcere permīsērunt et domum
pusillam rem pūblicam esse iūdicāvērunt. Quid ergō? Omnēs servōs
admovēbō mēnsae meae? Nōn magis quam omnēs līberōs. Errās sī exīs- 30
timās mē quōsdam quasi sordidiōris operae reiectūrum, ut putā[7] illum
mūliōnem et illum bubulcum: nōn ministeriīs illōs aestimābō, sed mōribus.
Sibi quisque dat mōrēs: ministeria cāsus[8] assignat. Nōn est, mī Lūcilī,
quod amīcum tantum in forō et in cūriā quaerās; sī dīligenter attenderis, et
domī inveniēs. "Servus est." Sed fortasse līber animō. "Servus est." Hoc 35
illī nocēbit? Ostende quis nōn sit: alius libīdinī servit, alius avāritiae, alius
ambitiōnī, omnēs timōrī.   (*Epist.* 47, 1–2, 5–6, 8, 10–11, 13–17)

[1] *The ones who go to market*
[2] *the taste of what thing will tempt
   the master*
[3] *what he is hungry for*
[4] *Won't you*
[5] *your master*
[6] *how*
[7] *for example*
[8] *chance assigns their jobs*

---

[1] the expert carver
[2] Supply **causā.**

Petronius

Petronius, who lived in the age of Nero, wrote a novel telling of the adventures of three rascals as they wandered about southern Italy, constantly getting into difficulties through cheating, stealing, and similar activities. Unfortunately much of the novel has been lost, but we do have the description of a dinner party given by an extremely rich self-made man, whose education left much to be desired. In the following selection the host, Trimalchio, boasts of his collection of antiques.

Trimalchio's Dinner

Quam cum Agamemnōn[1] propius cōnsīderāret, ait Trimalchiō: "Sōlus sum quī vēra Corinthia habeam." Exspectābam ut prō[1] reliquā īnsolentiā dīceret sibi vāsa Corinthō[2] afferrī. Sed ille melius et "forsitan," inquit, "quaeris quārē sōlus Corinthia vēra possideam. Quia scīlicet aerārius[3] ā
5 quō emō Corinthus vocātur. Quid est autem Corinthium nisi quis Corinthum[4] habeat? Et nē mē putētis nesapium[5] esse, valdē bene sciō unde prīmum Corinthia nāta sint. Cum Īlium captum est, Hannibal, homō vafer et magnus stēliō,[6] omnēs statuās aēneās et aureās et argenteās in ūnum rogum congessit et eās incendit. Factae sunt in ūnum aera miscellānea.[7] Ita ex hāc
10 māssā fabrī sustulērunt et fēcērunt catilla[8] et parapsidēs[8] et statuncula. Sīc Corinthia nāta sunt, ex omnibus in ūnum, nec hoc nec illud."   (50, 2–6)

[1] in accordance with
[2] from Corinth
[3] worker in bronze
[4] has a Corinthus (to make it)
[5] nit-wit
[6] rascal
[7] into one miscellaneous mass
[8] dishes

---

[1] one of the guests

Quintilian

The school teacher M. Fabius Quintilianus (ca. 35–96 A.D.) has left us a famous textbook on teaching, called *Institutio Oratoria, Introduction to Public Speaking*. How could a textbook on public speaking be a textbook on teaching? Because most teaching, especially at the higher levels, prepared for law and a public career, and therefore involved public speaking. This passage deals with the education of the young.

Mihi ille dētur puer quem laus excitet, quem glōria iuvet, quī victus fleat. Hic erit alendus ambitū, hunc mordēbit obiūrgātiō, hunc honor excitābit, in hōc dēsidiam numquam verēbor. Danda est tamen omnibus aliqua remissiō,[1] nōn sōlum quia nūlla rēs est quae perferre possit continuum labōrem, atque ea quoque quae sēnsū et animā carent, ut servāre vim 5 suam possint, velut quiēte alternā retenduntur,[2] sed quod studium discendī voluntāte, quae cōgī nōn potest, cōnstat.[3] Itaque et vīrium plūs afferunt ad discendum renovātī ac recentēs et ācriōrem animum, quī ferē necessitātibus[4] repugnat. Nec me offenderit lūsus in puerīs (est et hoc signum alacritātis). Modus tamen sit remissiōnibus, nē aut odium studiōrum faciant negātae[5] 10 aut ōtiī cōnsuētūdinem nimiae.[5] Sunt etiam nōnnūllī acuendīs puerōrum ingeniīs nōn inūtilēs lūsūs, cum positīs invicem cuiusque generis quaestiunculīs aemulantur. Mōrēs quoque sē inter lūdendum simplicius dētegunt.
(I, 3, 7–12)

[1] *relaxation*
[2] *are relaxed by alternating rest periods, so to speak*
[3] *is based on willingness*
[4] *fights against requirements*
[5] *if denied . . . if excessive*

Martial

The first century A.D. was the Spanish century of Latin literature. As at an earlier date Catullus, Vergil, Livy, and others had come from Cisalpine Gaul (northern Italy), so now we have the two Senecas, Lucan, Martial, and Quintilian from Spain. Martial is famous for his epigrams; in fact, it was he who gave the word epigram its present meaning—a short poem with a clever point, sometimes not revealed until the last word.

1. Petit Gemellus nūptiās Marōnillae
   et cupit et īnstat et precātur et dōnat.
Adeōne pulchra est? Immō foedius nīl est.
   Quid ergō in illā petitur et placet? Tussit.
(I, 10)

2. Nōn amo tē, Sabidī, nec possum dīcere quārē;
   hoc tantum possum dīcere, nōn amo tē.
(I, 32)

3. Nūper erat medicus, nunc est vispillo[1] Diaulus;
   quod vispillo facit, fēcerat et medicus.
(I, 47)

[1] *undertaker*

4. Vērōna doctī syllabās amat vātis,[1]
Marōne[2] fēlīx Mantua est,
cēnsētur Aponī[3] Līviō suō tellus
Stēllaque[4] nec Flaccō[4] minus,

5   Apollodōrō[5] plaudit imbrifer Nīlus,
Nāsōne Paelignī[6] sonant,
duōs Senecās ūnicumque Lūcānum
fācunda loquitur[2] Corduba,
gaudent iocōsae Caniō suō Gādēs,

10   Ēmerita[7] Deciānō meō:
tē, Liciniāne, glōriābitur nostra
nec mē tacēbit Bilbilis.
(I, 61)

[2] *speaks of*

5. "Rīdē, sī sapis, Ō puella, rīdē,"
Paelignus, putō, dīxerat poēta;[8]
sed nōn dīxerat omnibus puellīs.
Vērum ut[3] dīxerit omnibus puellīs,

5   nōn dīxit tibi; tū puella nōn es,
et trēs[4] sunt tibi, Maximīna, dentēs,
sed plānē piceīque buxeīque.[5]
Quārē sī speculō mihīque crēdis,
dēbēs nōn aliter timēre rīsum

10   quam ventum Spanius manumque Prīscus,[9]
quam crētāta[6] timet Fabulla nimbum,
cērussāta[7] timet Sabella sōlem.
Vultūs indue tū magis sevērōs
quam coniūnx Priamī nurusque maior.

15   Mīmōs rīdiculī Philistiōnis
et convīvia nequiōra vītā[10]
et quicquid lepidā procācitāte
laxat perspicuō labella rīsū.

[3] *grant that*
[4] *(only) three*
[5] *black and brown* (literally, *like fir and boxwood*)
[6] *powdered* (literally, *chalked*)
[7] *painted with white lead*

---

[1] Catullus
[2] Vergil
[3] Aponus was a spring near Padua, Livy's birthplace.
[4] unknown contemporary writer from Padua
[5] another unknown
[6] Ovid's birthplace was Sulmo, in the country of the Paeligni.
[7] Merida
[8] Ovid
[9] Spanius fears that the wind might disarrange his carefully combed hair; Priscus did not want to have his toga disturbed.
[10] verb

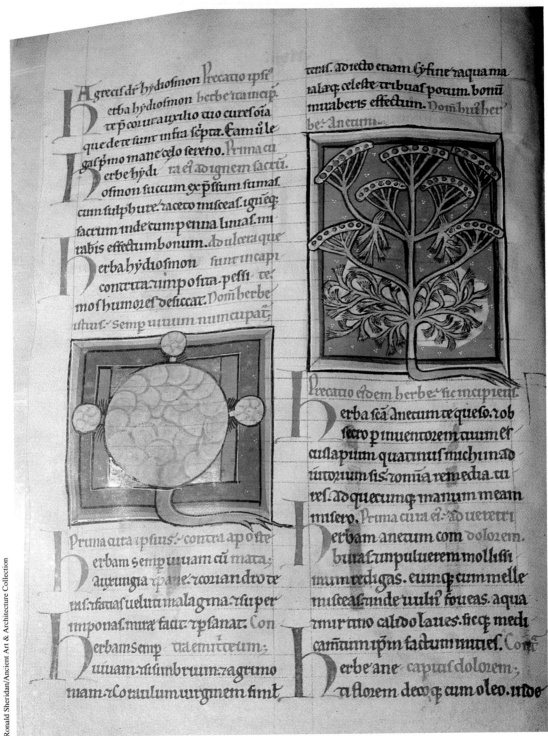

From the 12th century, we have a fine example of a page from a medical text describing the uses of herbs. The illustrations not only make the text more beautiful to look at but also more informative to the reader. Many monasteries grew herbs for both culinary and medicinal purposes. Hildegard von Bingen (see page 235) was especially well known for her knowledge of the uses of herbs and medicines.

te maestae decet assidēre mātrī
20 lūgentīque virum piumve frātrem,
et tantum tragicīs vacāre Mūsīs.
at tū iūdicium secūta nostrum
plōrā, sī sapis, Ō puella, plōrā.
(II, 41)

6. Hanc tibi, Fronto pater, genetrīx Flācilla, puellam[11]
ōscula[12] commendō dēliciāsque meās,
parvula nē nigrās horrēscat Erōtion umbrās
ōraque Tartareī[8] prōdigiōsa canis.
5 Implētūra fuit sextae modo frīgora brūmae,
vīxisset totidem[13] nī minus illa diēs.
Inter tam veterēs lūdat lascīva patrōnōs
et nōmen blaesō garriat ōre meum.
Mollia nōn rigidus caespes tegat ossa nec illī,
10 terra, gravis fuerīs:[14] nōn fuit illa tibi.
(V, 34)

7. Vītam quae faciant beātiōrem,
iūcundissime Martiālis,[15] haec sunt:
rēs[9] nōn parta labōre sed relīcta,
nōn ingrātus ager, focus perennis,
5 līs numquam, toga rāra, mēns quiēta,
vīrēs ingenuae,[16] salūbre corpus,
prūdēns simplicitās, parēs amīcī,
convīctus facilis, sine arte[10] mēnsa,
nox nōn ēbria sed solūta cūrīs,
10 nōn trīstis torus et tamen pudīcus,
somnus quī faciat brevēs tenebrās,
quod sīs esse velīs[11] nihilque mālīs,
summum nec metuās diem nec optēs.
(X, 47)

[8] of Tartarus
[9] property
[10] plain, not fancy
[11] wish to be what you are and prefer nothing else

---

[11] Unlike most of the epigrams of Martial, this one accords with the early Greek sense of an epitaph; it is about a little girl named Erotion, *Lovey,* similar to *Mabel,* from *Amabilis.* He asks his father and mother, now in the Lower World, to take care of the girl.
[12] in apposition with **puellam:** *sweetheart*
[13] i.e., six
[14] a variant of the formula found on hundreds of Roman tombstones: **sit tibi terra levis**
[15] not the poet but a friend by the same name
[16] suitable for a "gentleman," not an athlete or a working man

Apuleius

Apuleius was born in northern Africa about A.D. 125. His greatest work was the *Metamorphoses,* in which he tells, among others, the charming story of Cupid and Psyche. Psyche was so beautiful that, human though she was, she made the goddess Venus jealous. So Venus told her son Cupid to marry her off to some impossible man. But Cupid fell in love with her and married her, though remaining invisible. With the aid of a lamp, Psyche discovered that her husband was very handsome. But then her troubles began, for she was punished by Venus. Finally Cupid appealed to Jupiter, and everything ended happily with a marriage in heaven.

Nec mora,[1] cum cēna nūptiālis affluēns exhibētur. Accumbēbat summum torum marītus, Psȳchēn gremiō suō complexus. Sīc et cum suā Iūnōne Iuppiter ac deinde per ōrdinem tōtī[2] deī. Tunc, dum pōculum nectaris, quod vīnum deōrum est, Iovī quidem suus pōcillātor,[3] ille rūsticus puer, cēterīs vērō Līber ministrābat, Vulcānus cēnam coquēbat, Hōrae rosīs et cēterīs 5
flōribus purpurābant omnia, Grātiae spargēbant balsama, Apollō cantābat ad citharam, Mūsae quoque canōra personābant, Venus suāvī mūsicae superingressa[4] fōrmōsa saltāvit, scaenā sibi sīc concinnātā ut Mūsae quidem chorum canerent et tībiās īnflārent, Satyrus et Pāniscus ad fistulam dīcerent. Sīc rītē Psȳchē convenit in manum Cupīdinis et nāscitur illīs 10
mātūrō partū fīlia, quam Voluptātem nōmināmus.   (*Met.* VI, 23)

[1] *without delay* (literally, (*there is*) *no delay when*)
[2] = **omnēs**
[3] *cupbearer*
[4] *coming in to the music*

Hadrian

The historian Spartianus, in the collection of biographies of emperors called *Scriptores Historiae Augustae,* tells us that on his deathbed the emperor Hadrian, who died in A.D. 138, composed these verses about his soul:

> Animula[1] vagula, blandula,
> hospes comesque corporis,
> quae nunc abībis in loca[2]
> pallidula, rigida, nūdula,
> nec, ut solēs, dabis iocōs.   5
> (25)

---

[1] **Anima** is not merely *soul* in our sense, but *life, the breath of life.*
[2] The Lower World is pictured as dark, cold, and bare.

Macrobius

About the year A.D. 400 Macrobius wrote a book called *Saturnalia,* somewhat similar to the *Attic Nights* of Aulus Gellius. A group of cultured men meet on the Saturnalia and discuss literary and historical subjects. They get to talking about Cicero's jokes. Macrobius found these in a Cicero jokebook prepared by Cicero's secretary Tiro. The purpose of the book was to supply material for public speakers.

[1] *have kept silent about the jokes*
[2] *It doesn't show its age*
[3] *miracle*
[4] *Cicero had been reluctant*
[5] *those saying* (dative)

Sed mīror omnēs vōs ioca tacuisse[1] Cicerōnis, in quibus fācundissimus, ut in omnibus, fuit. Cicerō, cum apud Damasippum cēnāret, et ille, mediocrī vīnō positō, dīceret: "Bibite Falernum[1] hoc; annōrum quadrāgintā est," "Bene," inquit, "aetātem fert."[2]

5 Īdem cum Lentulum, generum suum, exiguae statūrae hominem, longō gladiō accīnctum vīdisset, "Quis," inquit, "generum meum ad gladium alligāvit?"

Nec Q. Cicerōnī frātrī pepercit. Nam cum in eā prōvinciā quam ille[2] rēxerat vīdisset imāginem eius[3] ingentibus līneāmentīs usque ad pectus ex 10 mōre pictam (erat autem Quīntus ipse statūrae parvae), ait: "Frāter meus dīmidius[4] maior est quam tōtus."

In cōnsulātū Vatīniī, quem paucīs diēbus gessit, notābilis Cicerōnis urbānitās circumferēbātur. "Magnum ostentum,"[3] inquit, "annō Vatīniī factum est, quod, illō cōnsule, nec brūma nec vēr nec aestās nec autumnus fuit."

15 Querentī deinde Vatīniō, quod gravātus esset[4] ad sē īnfirmum venīre, respondit: "Voluī in cōnsulātū tuō venīre, sed nox mē comprehendit."

Pompeius Cicerōnis facētiārum impatiēns fuit. Cum Cicerō ad Pompeium vēnisset, dīcentibus[5] sērō eum vēnisse respondit: "Minimē sērō vēnī: nam nihil hīc parātum videō." Deinde interrogantī Pompeiō ubi gener eius 20 Dolābella[5] esset, Cicerō respondit: "Cum socerō tuō." (II, 3)

---

[1] an excellent brand of wine
[2] Marcus Cicero
[3] Quintus
[4] The painting showed the bust but was larger than the whole of the real Quintus.
[5] Pompey, knowing that Dolabella had joined Caesar, reproaches Cicero for having a relative on the other side. Cicero neatly reminds Pompey that he (Pompey) was the son-in-law of Caesar.

The Vulgate

The Vulgate is the Latin translation of the Bible made by Jerome (Hieronymus) before and after the year 400. He translated the Old Testament from the Hebrew and the New Testament from the Greek. Jerome's translation is still an accepted version used in the Catholic Church. The following selection is from the first chapter of Genesis.

In prīncipiō creāvit Deus caelum et terram.

Terra autem erat inānis et vacua, et tenebrae erant super faciem abyssī; et Spīritus Deī ferēbātur super aquās.

Dīxitque Deus: "Fīat lūx." Et facta est lūx.

Et vīdit Deus lūcem quod[1] esset bona, et dīvīsit lūcem ā tenebrīs.

Appellāvitque lūcem diem, et tenebrās noctem; factumque est vespere et māne, diēs ūnus.

Dīxit quoque Deus: "Fīat firmāmentum in mediō aquārum; et dīvidat aquās ab aquīs."

Et fēcit Deus firmāmentum dīvīsitque aquās quae erant sub firmāmentō 10 ab hīs quae erant super firmāmentum. Et factum est ita.

Vocāvitque Deus firmāmentum caelum; et factum est vespere et māne, diēs secundus.

Dīxit vērō Deus: "Congregentur aquae quae sub caelō sunt in locum ūnum, et appāreat ārida." Et factum est ita.   15

Et vocāvit Deus āridam terram, congregātiōnēsque aquārum appellāvit maria. Et vīdit Deus quod esset bonum.

Et ait: "Germinet terra herbam virentem et facientem sēmen, et lignum pōmiferum faciēns frūctum iūxtā genus suum, cuius sēmen in sēmetipsō[2] sit super terram." Et factum est ita.   20

Et prōtulit terra herbam virentem et facientem sēmen iūxtā genus suum, lignumque faciēns frūctum et habēns ūnumquodque[3] sēmentem secundum speciem suam. Et vīdit Deus quod esset bonum.

Et factum est vespere et māne, diēs tertius.

Dīxit autem Deus: "Fīant lūmināria in firmāmentō caelī, et dīvidant 25 diem ac noctem, et sint in[4] signa et tempora et diēs et annōs.

Ut lūceant in firmāmentō caelī et illūminent terram." Et factum est ita.

Fēcitque Deus duo lūmināria magna: lūmināre maius ut praeesset[5] diēī, et lūmināre minus ut praeesset noctī, et stēllās.

Et posuit eās in firmāmentō caelī ut lūcērent super terram.   30

(I, 1–17)

5 [1] *that*
[2] *in itself*
[3] *each one*
[4] *for*
[5] *rule*

Bede

Bede was an Englishman who lived in the seventh century. The best of his writings is the *Historia ecclēsiastica gentis Anglōrum,* for which he has been called the father of English history. The selection that follows tells about the conversion of Britain to Christianity.

[1] *story*
[2] *placed* there for sale as slaves
[3] *O grief*
[4] *the author of darkness*
[5] *such beauty of an exterior*
[6] *the word* (*of God*)

Nec silentiō praetereunda opīniō[1] quae dē beātō Gregoriō trāditiōne maiōrum ad nōs usque perlāta est; quā vidēlicet ex causā admonitus tam sēdulam ergā salūtem nostrae gentis cūram gesserit. Dīcunt quia diē quādam cum, advenientibus nūper mercātōribus, multa vēnālia in forum
5 fuissent collāta, multī ad emendum cōnflūxissent, et ipsum Gregorium inter aliōs advēnisse ac vīdisse inter alia puerōs vēnālēs positōs[2] candidī corporis ac venustī vultūs, capillōrum quoque fōrmā ēgregiā. Quōs cum aspiceret, interrogāvit, ut aiunt, dē quā regiōne vel terrā essent allātī. Dictumque est quia dē Britanniā īnsulā, cuius incolae tālis essent aspectūs.
10 Rūrsus interrogāvit utrum īdem īnsulānī Chrīstiānī an pāgānīs adhūc errōribus essent implicātī. Dictum est quod essent pāgānī. At ille, intimō ex corde longa trahēns suspīria: "Heu, prō dolor!"[3] inquit, "quod tam lūcidī vultūs hominēs tenebrārum auctor[4] possidet, tantaque grātia frontispiciī[5] mentem ab internā grātiā[1] vacuam gestat!" Rūrsus ergō interrogāvit
15 quod esset vocābulum gentis illīus. Respōnsum est quod Anglī vocārentur. At ille: "Bene," inquit; "nam et angelicam habent faciem, et tālēs angelōrum in caelīs decet esse cohērēdēs. Quod habet nōmen ipsa prōvincia dē quā istī sunt allātī?" Respōnsum est quod Deīrī vocārentur īdem prōvinciālēs. At ille: "Bene," inquit, "Deīrī; dē īrā ērutī, et ad misericordiam Chrīstī
20 vocātī. Rēx prōvinciae illīus quōmodo appellātur?" Respōnsum est quod Aellī dīcerētur. At ille allūdēns ad nōmen ait: "Allēlūia, laudem Deī Creātōris, illīs in partibus oportet cantārī."

Accēdēnsque ad pontificem Rōmānae et apostolicae sēdis (nōndum enim erat ipse pontifex factus), rogāvit ut gentī Anglōrum in Britanniam
25 aliquōs verbī[6] ministrōs per quōs ad Chrīstum converterētur mitteret; sē ipsum parātum esse in hoc opus, Dominō cooperante, perficiendum, sī tamen apostolicō papae hoc ut fieret placēret. Quod dum perficere nōn posset, quia, etsī pontifex concēdere illī quod petierat voluit, nōn tamen cīvēs Rōmānī ut tam longē ab urbe sēcēderet potuēre permittere; mox ut ipse
30 pontificātūs officiō[2] fūnctus est, perfēcit opus diū dēsīderātum.   (II, 1)

[1] in the Christian sense of *grace*
[2] A.D. 590–604

Paulus Diaconus

Paul the Deacon was a Lombard from northern Italy who lived in the eighth century. He was a Benedictine monk of the famous monastery of Monte Cassino. The following selection is from his history of the Lombards.

Haud ab rē esse arbitror paulisper nārrandī ōrdinem postpōnere, et quia adhūc stilus[1] in Germāniā vertitur, mīrāculum quod illīc apud omnēs celebre habētur, seu[1] et quaedam alia breviter intimāre. In extrēmīs circium versus[2] Germāniae fīnibus, in ipsō ōceanī lītore, antrum sub ēminentī rūpe cōnspicitur, ubi septem virī, incertum ex quō tempore, longō sōpitī sopōre quiēscunt, ita illaesīs nōn sōlum corporibus sed etiam vestīmentīs, ut ex hōc ipsō, quod sine ūllā per tot annōrum curricula corruptiōne perdūrant, apud indocilēs eāsdem et barbarās nātiōnēs venerātiōne habeantur. Hī dēnique, quantum ad habitum spectat, Rōmānī esse cernuntur. Ē quibus dum ūnum quīdam cupiditāte stimulātus vellet exuere,[3] mox eius, ut dīcitur, bracchia āruērunt,[4] poenaque sua[5] cēterōs perterruit nē quis eōs ulterius contingere audēret.   (I, 4)

5

10

[1] *and also* (with **et**)
[2] *toward the northwest*
[3] *strip, take off his clothes*
[4] *dried up, withered*
[5] = **eius**

---

[1] **stilus vertitur** literally means *my stilus is turned* (for erasure) but here means *my pen is engaged*

Hildegard von Bingen

Hildegard von Bingen (1098-1179) was the first German female physician, the mother of German botany, and one of the most accomplished abbesses of the Middle Ages. She also wrote numerous songs and at least one play, all embracing good virtues and showing the constant battle between good and evil. The following are excerpts from her play, *The Virtues*.

Ecce quadrāgēsimō tertiō temporālis cursus meī annō,
cum cēlestī magnō timōre,
tremulā intentiōne inhērerem,[1]
vīdī maximum splendōrem,
in quō facta est vōx dē cēlō[2] ad mē dicēns:
ō homō fragilis,
et cinis cineris
et pūtrēdō pūtrēdinis
dīc et scrībe quē vidēs et audīs.
***

[1] *I dwelt*
[2] = **caelō**

5

[3] all creation was verdant
[4] greenness
[5] champion
[6] to grow dry
[7] are exposed to mockery
[8] reach

In principiō omnēs creāturē viruērunt[3]

in mediō flōrēs flōruērunt;

posteā viriditās[4] dēscendit.

Et istud vir prēliātor[5] vīdit et dīxit:

5 Hoc sciō, sed aureus numerus nōndum est plēnus.

Tū ergō, paternum speculum aspice:

in corpore meō fatīgātiōnem sustineō,

parvulī etiam meī dēficiunt.

Nunc memor estō, quod plēnitūdō quē in prīmō facta est

10 ārēscere[6] nōn dēbuit,

et tunc in tē habuistī

quod oculus tuus numquam cēderet

usque dum corpus meum vidērēs plēnum gemmārum.

Nam mē fatīgat quod omnia membra mea in irrisiōnem vādunt.[7]

15 Pater, vidē, vulnera mea tibi ostendō.

Ergō nunc, omnēs hominēs,

genua vestra ad patrem vestrum flectite,

ut vōbīs manum suam porrigat.[8]

Caesar of Heisterbach

Caesar was a monk in the monastery of Heisterbach, near Bonn, in the thirteenth century. He wrote a book of miracles, of which the following is one.

[1] of Treves
[2] subject, theme
[3] homage
[4] yes

In ecclēsiā sānctī Simeōnis diōcēsis Trēverēnsis[1] scholāris parvulus erat. Hic cum diē quādam, datā eī māteriā[2] ā magistrō suō, versūs ex eā compōnere nequīret trīstisque sedēret, sōlī sīc sedentī diabolus in speciē hominis appāruit. Cui cum dīceret: "Quid dolēs, puer, quid sīc trīstis 5 sedēs?" respondit puer: "Magistrum meum timeō, quia de themate[2] quod ab eō recēpī versūs compōnere nequeō." Et ille: "Vīs mihi facere hominium[3] et ego versūs tibi compōnam?" Puerō vērō nōn intelligente quod inimīcus omnium diabolus tenderet ad malum suum, respondit: "Etiam,[4] domine, parātus sum facere quicquid iusseris, dum modo versūs habeam et nōn 10 vāpulem." Nesciēbat enim quis esset. Porrēxit eī manum, hominium eī faciēns. Ā quō continuō versūs dictātōs in tabulīs accipiēns, dictātōrem amplius nōn vīdit.

Quōs₁ cum tempore congruō magistrō suō redderet, ille versuum excellentiam mīrātus expāvit, dīvīnam, nōn hominis, in illīs cōnsīderāns scien- 15 tiam. Quī ait: "Dīc mihi, quis tibi dictāvit hōs versūs?" Dīcente puerō, "Ego,

---

₁ i.e., the verses

Cicero's rhetorical work, **Dē Ōrātōre,** *dealt with the history and theory of oratory, as well as the education and characteristics of the ideal orator. This manuscript page from the late 13th century is a translation into French of Cicero's work. Richly decorated, it even includes a drawing, complete with a caption, of a professor lecturing to six students and two adults. The upheld book represents the work he is lecturing on. Notice that, at least in the French version, small spaces are left between the words.*

magister," et ille omnīnō, dum nōn crēderet, immō puerum dīligentius īnstāret interrogātiōnis verbum saepius repetēns, cōnfessus est puer omnia secundum ōrdinem quae gesserat. Tunc ait magister: "Fīlī, malus ille versificātor fuit, scīlicet diabolus," et adiēcit: "Cārissime, paeniteat tē sēductōrī
20 illī hominium fēcisse?" Respondente puerō: "Etiam, magister," ait ille: "Modo abrenūntiā diabolō et hominiō eius et omnibus pompīs eius et omnibus eius operibus." Et fēcit sīc. Magister autem superpellicī eius manicās abscīdēns[5] diabolō iactāvit dīcēns: "Hae manicae tuae sunt, hominum sēductor, nīl aliud in hāc deī creātūrā possidēbis." Statimque raptae sunt manicae cōram[6]
25 omnibus et fulminātae[7] sunt, corpore tamen puerī incorruptō. Haec mihi dicta sunt ā quōdam priōre Trēverēnsis ecclēsiae.   (II, 14)

[5] cutting off the sleeves from the surplice (an outer garment)
[6] in the presence of
[7] were struck by lightning

Petrarch

Petrarch (1304–1374) was born at Arezzo, Italy, but early in life he moved to southern France. He is most famous for his Italian poems but he wrote far more in Latin, including his letters. He had a great enthusiasm for the ancient classics and awakened other people's interest in them. Cicero was one of his favorite authors.

Petrarch searched far and wide for copies of the classics. He played a very important part in starting the movement called the Renaissance, a revival of interest in the classics.

The Craving for Books

[1] I flatter myself
[2] other things of this sort
[3] to the heart, deep within (adverb)

Ūna inexplēbilis cupiditās mē tenet, quam frēnāre hāctenus nec potuī certē nec voluī; mihi enim interblandior[1] honestārum rērum nōn inhonestam esse cupīdinem. Exspectās audīre morbī genus? Librīs satiārī nequeō. Et habeō plūrēs forte quam oportet; sed sīcut in cēterīs rēbus, sīc et in
5 librīs accidit: quaerendī successus avāritiae calcar est. Quīn immō, singulāre quiddam in librīs est: aurum, argentum, gemmae, purpurea vestis, marmorea domus, cultus ager, pictae tabulae, cēteraque id genus,[2] mūtam habent et superficiāriam voluptātem; librī medullitus[3] dēlectant, colloquuntur, cōnsulunt et vīvā quādam nōbīs atque argūtā familiāritāte iunguntur, neque sōlum
10 sēsē lēctōribus quisque suīs īnsinuat, sed et aliōrum nōmen ingerit et alter alterius dēsīderium facit. Ac nē rēs egeat exemplō, Mārcum mihi Varrōnem

cārum et amābilem Cicerōnis *Academicus*[1] fēcit; Enniī nōmen in *Officiōrum* librīs audīvī; prīmum Terentiī amōrem ex *Tusculānārum quaestiōnum* lēctiōne concēpī.

Sunt quī librōs, ut cētera, nōn ūtendī studiō cumulent, sed habendī libī- 15 dine, neque tam ut ingeniī praesidium, quam ut thalamī ōrnāmentum. Ammōnicus Serēnus bibliothēcam habuisse memorātur sexāgintā duo librōrum mīlia continentem, quōs omnēs Gordiānō minōrī, quī tunc erat imperātor, amantissimō discipulō suō, moriēns relīquit; quae rēs nōn minus illum quōdam modō quam imperium honestāvit. Haec prō excūsātiōne vitiī 20 meī prōque sōlāciō tantōrum comitum dicta sint. Tū vērō, sī tibi cārus sum, aliquibus fīdīs et litterātīs virīs hanc cūram impōnitō: Etrūriam perquīrant, religiōsōrum[4] armāria[5] ēvolvant cēterōrumque studiōsōrum hominum, sī quid usquam ēmergeret lēniendae dīcam an[6] irrītandae sitī meae idōneum. Quōque vigilantior fīās, scītō mē eāsdem precēs amīcīs 25 aliīs in Britanniam Galliāsque et Hispāniās dēstināsse.   (*Fam.* III, 18)

[4] *monks*
[5] *shelves*
[6] *or shall I say*

---

[1] title of a book by Cicero

To Marcus Tullius Cicero

Ō Rōmānī ēloquiī summe parēns, nec sōlus ego sed omnēs tibi grātiās agimus, quīcumque Latīnae linguae flōribus ōrnāmur; tuīs enim prāta dē fontibus irrigāmus, tuō ducātū dīrēctōs,[1] tuīs suffrāgiīs adiūtōs,[1] tuō nōs lūmine illūstrātōs ingenuē profitēmur; tuīs dēnique, ut ita dīcam, auspiciīs ad hanc, quantulacumque est, scrībendī facultātem ac prōpositum pervēnisse. 5

Quid dē vītā, quid dē ingeniō tuō sentiam, audīstī. Exspectās audīre dē librīs tuīs, quaenam illōs excēperit fortūna, quam seu vulgō seu doctiōribus probentur?[1] Exstant equidem praeclāra volūmina, quae nē dīcam[2] perlegere, sed nec[3] ēnumerāre sufficimus. Fāma rērum tuārum celeberrima atque ingēns et sonōrum nōmen; perrārī autem studiōsī,[2] seu temporum adver- 10 sitās seu ingeniōrum hebetūdō ac sēgnitiēs seu, quod magis arbitror, aliō[4] cōgēns animōs cupiditās causa est. Itaque librōrum aliquī, nesciō quidem an irreparābiliter, nōbīs tamen quī nunc vīvimus, nisi fallor, periēre; magnus dolor meus, magnus saeculī nostrī pudor, magna posteritātis iniūria.

Reliquum est ut urbis Rōmae ac Rōmānae reī pūblicae statum audīre 15 velīs, quae patriae faciēs, quae cīvium concordia, ad quōs rērum summa pervēnerit, quibus manibus quantōque cōnsiliō frēna trāctentur imperiī; Histerne[5] et Gangēs, Hibērus, Nīlus et Tanais līmitēs nostrī sint, an vērō quisquam surrēxerit "Imperium Ōceanō, fāmam quī terminet astrīs." Vērum enimvērō tacēre melius fuerit; crēde enim mihi, Cicerō, sī quō in 20 statū rēs nostrae sint audieris, excident tibi lacrimae, quamlibet[6] vel caelī vel Erebī partem tenēs. Aeternum valē.   (*Fam.* XXIV, 4)

[1] *how they are regarded by the common people and the more learned*
[2] *not to say*
[3] *not even*
[4] *in other directions*
[5] *whether the Danube*
[6] *whatever*

---

[1] with **nōs**
[2] Supply **sunt.**

Coluccio Salutati

Coluccio Salutati (1331–1406) was a busy man as chancellor of Florence for more than thirty years, but he still had time to follow in Petrarch's footsteps, becoming an eager reader of the ancient classics and interesting a large number of young men in them. Thus he founded the group of humanists who made Florence the center of the new learning and developed the great movement called the Renaissance. He was chiefly responsible for bringing the Greek teacher Manuel Chrysoloras to Florence in 1396, thus starting the study of Greek, largely unknown in the West before that time.

To Manuel Chrysoloras

. . . Nunc autem scītō mē tibi quod[1] in hāc urbe rēgiā Graecās doceās litterās salāriō pūblicō prōcūrāsse;[1] nec pigēbit, ut arbitror, mūtāsse caelum,[1] cum hīc et honorābilem vītam et plūrimōs quī tē colent invēneris. Quid tē deceat quī tam ā longē[2] vocāris, Graecus in Ītaliam, Thrācius in
5 Tusciam et Byzantius Flōrentiam, tū vidēbis.

---

[1] i.e., changed your home

The Defense of Poetry

Vīdī nūper et rīsī, venerābilis in Chrīstō pater, litterās tuās quās mittis ad ēgregium virum Angelum Corbinellum, dīlēctissimum fīlium[1] meum, quibus eum mōre tuō cōnāris ā poēticīs et saeculāribus studiīs revocāre, vel, quō rēctius dīxerim,[1] dēterrēre. Quod an rēctē faciās tū vīderīs.[2] Vērum

5 tē videō nōndum quaestiōnis terminōs intellegere versārīque in illō tuae simplicitātis errōre, quō reputās ista nostra poētica grave et inexpiābile nefās esse et perniciōsa mendācia. Quod sī vērum est, nec potest sub verbōrum cortice mendācium latēre pūritās et integritās vēritātis, dīc, obsecrō, quō modō vērum est: "spīritus Dominī ferēbātur super aquās"; et
10 illud: "dīxit Deus: 'fīat lūx'";[2] et sescenta[3] tālia? Quō modō fertur enim, quod corporālium est, "spīritus Dominī super aquās," quī prōrsus incorporeus est? Quō modō: "dīxit Deus: 'fīat lūx'"; cum Deus nec ōs habeat nec linguam,

---

[1] not literally
[2] Coluccio's point is that these two passages from the Bible cannot be understood literally, that therefore poetry need not be so understood.
[3] we would say *thousand*

quae sunt necessāria membra īnstrūmentaque dīcentis? Vērum haec aliās. Nunc autem, quō vidēre possīs liquidius vēritātem, ostendam prius quid per poēticam intellegere dēbeāmus; cōnsequenter clārum efficiam sacrās 15 litterās dīvīnamque Scrīptūram nēdum[3] habēre cum istā[4] commercium, sed vērē nihil esse nisi poēticam; tertiō vērō quantum oportet annītar ostendere etiam fidēlibus Chrīstiānīs nōn esse prohibendam gentīlium poētarum lēctiōnem; tandemque cōnābor ad illa quae dīxerīs respondēre.

Quid inter istōs est cūr dēbeant prohibērī? Sciō legōque cotīdiē apud 20 Hieronymum, Ambrosium, et Augustīnum ēgregia philosophōrum et ōrātōrum dicta carmināque poētarum, quae velut sīdus aliquod inter trāctātūs illōs sānctissimōs ēminent et resplendent; quae quidem tē nōn arbitror quasi crīmen aliquod condemnāre. Sī vēra, sī sāncta, sī decōra pulchraque sunt apud istōs doctōrēs inventa et ibi sine peccātō leguntur, cūr apud auctōrēs 25 suōs dīcī dēbent nefāria vel profāna? Cūr nōbīs prohibita, sī sacrīs doctōribus concessa sunt?

[3] *not only*

<hr>

[4] i.e., poetry

<hr>

Leonardo Bruni

Leonardo Bruni was a disciple of Coluccio. In this letter he writes to Poggio, another of Coluccio's disciples, about Poggio's discoveries of manuscripts of previously unknown authors and better manuscripts of other authors.

Sī valēs, bene est; ego quidem valeō. Lēgī apud Nīcolāum[1] nostrum litterās quās dē hāc ultimā profectiōne ac dē inventiōne quōrundam librōrum scrīpsistī. Nec tantum dē iīs sed dē optimā spē quam prō cēterōrum adeptiōne suscēpisse tē videō laetandum exīstimō. Erit profectō haec tua glōria, ut āmissa iam ac perdita excellentium virōrum scrīpta tuō labōre ac dīli- 5 gentiā saeculō nostrō restituās. Nec ea rēs sōlum nōbīs grāta erit sed et posterīs nostrīs, id est studiōrum nostrōrum successōribus. Neque enim silēbuntur ista nec oblitterābuntur sed exstābit memoriā haec[2] dūdum longō intervāllō perdita et iam plānē dēplōrāta per tuam industriam recuperāta ac restitūta nōbīs fuisse. Utque Camillus secundus ā Rōmulō conditor[1] 10 dictus est, quod ille[3] statuit urbem, hic āmissam restituit, sīc tū omnium quae iam āmissa tuā virtūte ac dīligentiā nōbīs restitūta fuerint secundus auctor meritō nuncupābere.

[1] *second founder (of Rome) after Romulus*

<hr>

[1] Niccolò Niccoli was another disciple of Coluccio.
[2] i.e., **scrīpta**
[3] Romulus

Quārē tē hortātum ōrātumque maximē velim, nē in hōc praeclārō opere
15 dēsideās, sed ērigās tē atque īnsistās. Nam reī pecūniāriae tenuitās nē tibi
impedīmentō sit, nostra iam hīc prōvidentia erit, atque in hāc inventiōne
tuā scītō maius lucrum factum esse quam tū sentīre videāris. Quīntiliānus
enim prius lacer atque discerptus cūncta membra sua per tē recuperābit.
Vīdī enim capita librōrum; tōtus est, cum vix nōbīs media pars et ea ipsa
20 lacera superesset. Ō lucrum ingēns! Ō īnspērātum gaudium! Ego tē, Ō
Mārce Fabī,[4] tōtum integrumque aspiciam? Ōrō tē, Poggī, fac mē quam
cito huius dēsīderiī compotem, ut hunc prius vīderim quam ē vītā dēcēdam.
Nam dē Ascōniō quidem et Flaccō, licet uterque placeat, tamen nōn usque
adeō labōrandum exīstimō; quōrum sī neuter umquam fuisset, nihilō ferē
25 minus Latīnitās habēret. At Quīntiliānus, rhētoricae pater et ōrātōriae magister, eius modī est, ut, cum tū illum diūturnō ac ferreō barbarōrum carcere
līberātum hūc mīseris, omnēs Etrūriae populī grātulātum[2] concurrere
dēbeant; mīrorque tē et illōs quī tēcum erant nōn statim in hunc[5] manūs
avidās iniēcisse, sed leviōribus perscrībendīs hunc posthabuisse,[3] quem
30 ego post Cicerōnis *Dē rē pūblicā* librōs plūrimum ā Latīnīs dēsīderātum et
prae cūnctīs dēplōrātum affirmāre ausim.

Proximum est, ut tē moneam, nē in iīs quae hīc habēmus tempus terās,
sed quae nōn habēmus conquīrās, quōrum maximē Varrōnis et Cicerōnis
opera tibi prōposita sint. Valē et mē amā. Flōrentiae, Īdibus Septembr.
35 MCCCCXVI.

Poggio Bracciolini

Poggio was Coluccio's most important disciple, particularly famous
for discovering manuscripts, especially at the monastery of St. Gall in
Switzerland, which he visited while attending a church council at Constance,
Germany. He spent several years in England and helped spread the new
gospel of humanism (the reading of the classics) there. He was a papal
secretary and, like Bruni, chancellor of Florence.

Great Discoveries

Sed quam temere persaepe ēveniunt quae nōn audeās optāre! ut inquit
Terentius noster. Fortūna quaedam fuit cum sua tum maximē nostra[1] ut,
cum essēmus Cōnstantiae ōtiōsī, cupīdō incesseret videndī eius locī quō
ille[1] reclūsus tenēbātur. Est autem monastērium Sānctī Gallī prope urbem
hanc. Itaque nōnnūllī[2] animī[2] laxandī et simul perquīrendōrum librōrum, 5
quōrum magnus numerus esse dīcēbātur, grātiā eō perrēximus. Ibi inter
cōnfertissimam librōrum cōpiam, quōs longum esset recēnsēre, Quīntiliānum
comperimus adhūc salvum et incolumem, plēnum tamen sitū et pulvere
squālentem. Erant enim nōn in bibliothēcā librī illī, ut eōrum dignitās postulābat, sed in taeterrimō quōdam et obscūrō carcere, fundō scīlicet ūnīus 10
turris, quō nē capitālis quidem reī damnātī[3] retrūderentur. Atquī ego prō
certō exīstimō, sī essent quī haec barbarōrum ergastula, quibus hōs dētinent
virōs,[3] rīmārentur ac recognōscerent mōre maiōrum, similem fortūnam
expertūrōs in multīs.

[1] *not only his* (Quintilian's) *but
especially mine,* with **fortūna**
[2] *several* (*of us*)
[3] *not even those convicted of a
capital crime*

[1] Quintilian
[2] with **grātiā**
[3] i.e., their writings

The Ruins of Rome

Nūper, cum pontifex Martīnus, paulō antequam diem suum obīret,[1] ab
urbe in agrum Tusculānum[1] sēcessisset valētūdinis grātiā, nōs autem
essēmus negōtiīs cūrīsque pūblicīs vacuī, vīsēbāmus saepe dēserta urbis,
Antōnius Luscus,[2] vir clārissimus, egoque, admīrantēs animō tum ob vet-
erem collāpsōrum aedificiōrum magnitūdinem et vāstās urbis antīquae 5
ruīnās, tum ob tantī imperiī ingentem strāgem stupendam profectō ac
dēplōrandam fortūnae varietātem. Cum autem cōnscendissēmus aliquandō
Capitōlīnum collem, Antōnius obequitandō paulum fessus cum quiētem
appeteret, dēscendentēs ex equīs cōnsēdimus in ipsīs Tarpeiae arcis[3] ruīnīs
pōne[2] ingēns portae cuiusdam, ut putō, templī marmoreum līmen plūrimāsque 10
passim cōnfrāctās columnās, unde magnā ex parte prōspectus urbis patet.

Hīc Antōnius, cum aliquantum hūc illūc oculōs circumtulisset, suspīrāns
stupentīque similis,[3] "Ō quantum," inquit, "Poggī, haec Capitōlia ab illīs
distant quae noster Marō cecinit,

Aurea nunc, ōlim silvestribus horrida dūmīs! 15

[1] *met his day,* i.e., *died*
[2] *behind* (preposition)
[3] *like one who was stupefied*

[1] Tusculum was in the hills southeast of Rome.
[2] Antonio Loschi was still another of Coluccio's disciples.
[3] the Capitoline Hill, where the Tarpeian rock was

Ēvolvās licet[4] historiās omnēs, omnia scrīptōrum monumenta pertrāctēs, omnēs gestārum rērum annālēs scrūtēris, nūlla umquam exempla mūtātiōnis suae maiōra fortūna prōtulit quam urbem Rōmam, pulcherrimam ōlim ac magnificentissimam omnium quae aut fuēre aut futūrae sunt.

20 Id vērō gravissimum et haud parvā cum admīrātiōne recēnsendum, hunc Capitōliī collem, caput quondam Rōmānī imperiī atque orbis terrārum arcem, quem omnēs rēgēs ac prīncipēs tremēbant, in quem triumphantēs tot imperātōrēs ascendērunt, dōnīs ac spoliīs tot tantārumque gentium ōrnātum flōrentemque ac ūniversō orbī spectandum, adeō dēsōlātum atque

25 ēversum et ā priōre illō statū immūtātum ut vīneae in senātōrum subsellia successerint.

Lorenzo Valla

Lorenzo Valla (1407–1457) wrote a book on the Latin language and was one of the most prominent humanists in the Italy of his time.

Magnum Latīnī sermōnis sacrāmentum[1] est, magnum profectō nūmen, quod apud peregrīnōs, apud barbarōs, apud hostēs sānctē ac religiōsē per tot saecula custōdītur, ut nōn tam dolendum nōbīs Rōmānīs[2] quam gaudendum sit atque, ipsō etiam terrārum orbe exaudiente, glōriandum. Āmīsimus

5 Rōmam, āmīsimus rēgnum, āmīsimus dominātum, tametsī nōn nostrā sed temporum culpā, vērum tamen per hunc splendidiōrem dominātum[1] in magnā adhūc orbis parte rēgnāmus. Nostra est Ītalia, nostra Gallia, nostra Hispānia, Germānia, Pannonia, Dalmatia, Illyricum, multaeque aliae nātiōnēs. Ibi namque Rōmānum imperium est ubicumque Rōmāna lingua dominātur.

---

[1] i.e., of the Latin language

Pius II
(Enea Silvio Piccolomini)

Pope Pius II (1405–1464), a Sienese poet in his youth, and a famous pope in his later years (1458–1464), was a great supporter of the Roman classics. Here he gives advice to his nephew.

Rettulit mihi Nannēs, pater tuus, tē, dum puer adhūc forēs, mīrō litterārum amōre fuisse incēnsum, postquam vērō ex ephēbīs[1] excessistī, nēminem esse quī tibi amplius ut studeās queat persuādēre; quae rēs nōn mīra tantum mihi sed stupenda fuit. Cēterī enim pueritiam simul et stultitiam dēpōnunt, virīlem togam et prūdentiam induentēs. Tū contrā sapiēns 5 puer, stultus vir cupis vidērī et barbam quasi umbrāculum[2] virtūtis recipis. Doleō certē tuī causā nec quid dē tē futūrum sit sciō. Iubet Cicerō ut quīlibet in adulēscentiā viam ēligat et genus vītae honestum quō ūtī dēbeat. Idem Herculēs factitāvit. Nam cum per quiētem[3] duae sibi mulierēs suprā hūmānam fōrmam venustae appārērent et altera sibi voluptātem, labōrem altera 10 prōmitteret, hanc secūtus est sciēns quod post labōrem praemium certāminis datur. Nec corōnātur, ut inquit apostolus, nisi quī lēgitimē certāverit. Tū vērō, ut audiō, vagārī vīs semper nec aliquod genus vītae honestum amplectī studēs. Litterās, quās puer amāstī, iam vir odiō habēs. Pudet mē tuī causā. Nesciō enim quid esse possīs absque[4] litterīs, nisi asinus bipēs. Quid enim 15 homō est absque doctrīnā quantumvīs[5] dīves, quantumvīs potēns? Quid inter hominem illitterātum et marmoream statuam interest? Nōn dux, nōn rēx, nōn imperātor alicuius pretiī est litterārum ignārus.

[1] *from boyhood*
[2] *umbrella*
[3] *in sleep*
[4] *without*
[5] *no matter how*

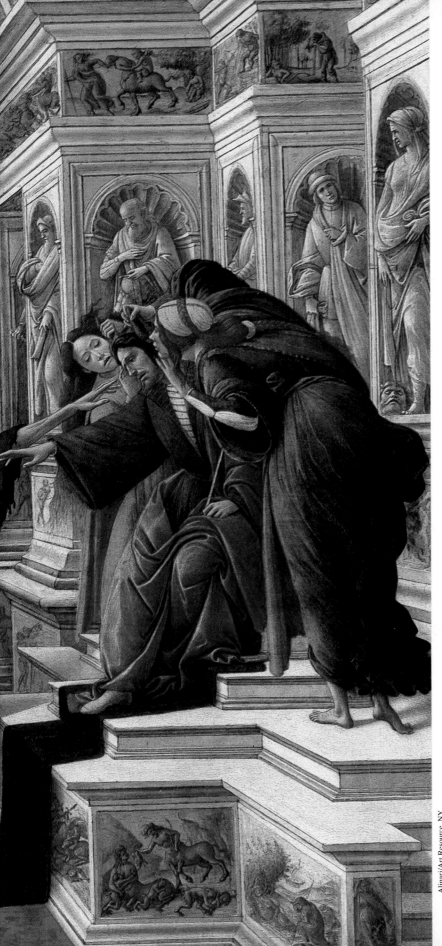

Alinari/Art Resource, NY

Unit X

Ovid

Apelles was a very famous Greek
artist who lived in the 4th century
B.C. Pliny the Elder thought him
the greatest painter who ever lived.
He was a friend of Alexander the
Great and was court painter to
Philip of Macedon. His style was
characterized by graceful figures,
spatial depth, fine line quality,
and attention to detail. He was
conscious of showing realism and
only used four colors, which he
considered basic earth colors:
black, white, red, and yellow.
Unfortunately, all of his works
are lost, but in the 15th century,
Sandro Botticelli, the great Italian
Renaissance painter tried to
recreate two of them based on
descriptions in Pliny and Lucan.
This one is called The Calumny
of Apelles, and shows King
Midas, with donkey's ears, sitting
in judgment on "Ignorance" and
"Suspicion," as "Calumny" is
brought in as a witness.

247

Ovid's Life

Pūblius Ovidius Nāsō was born on March 20, 43 B.C. in Sulmo, about 90 miles southeast of Rome. After studying law, Ovid began a career in public life, but soon turned away to give his full attention to the writing of poetry. He said of himself that he was unable to write prose, that every statement came out as poetry. He became the most cherished poet of the smart set, brilliant and witty and popular. At the age of 50 he was removed from his position as a poet of pleasure in cosmopolitan Rome by exile to Tomis on the Black Sea, where he died in A.D. 17. The reasons for his exile, resulting from the displeasure of the emperor Augustus, are still a mystery; the allusions Ovid makes to those reasons are couched in veiled terms.

In his earlier years Ovid was acclaimed for his love poems (*Amōrēs, Ars Amatōria, Heroidēs*), but his greatest work was the *Metamorphōsēs,* 15 books of stories of transformation of animals, human beings, and inanimate objects into other forms. A work on the calendar, the *Fastī,* was left unfinished (six books, one for each month of the first half of the year), interrupted by exile. At Tomis, Ovid wrote the *Trīstia* and *Epistulae ex Pontō,* elegies with some pleas for recall.

The *Metamorphōsēs,* comprising 250 stories of changes, from the creation of the world out of chaos down to the transformation of Julius Caesar into a star, constitutes our main storehouse of Greek and Roman mythology. Ovid was an excellent poet technically, writing with grace, humor, and charm. He is one of the great poets of Rome.

Poetic Word Order

The order of words in Latin poetry is even freer than in prose. Words that belong together are often widely separated. This is especially true of adjectives and their nouns. Note particularly the following points, illustrated by references to lines in the first selection, "Pyramus and Thisbe":

1. The order adjective—preposition—noun is common. Often a number of other words come between the adjective and the preposition. In such cases preposition and noun are likely to be at the end of the line. Cf. lines 100, 166.
2. An interlocking order, in which two or more phrases are involved, occurs frequently. A particular favorite is the use of two nouns and two adjectives in all possible combinations. Cf. lines 57–58, 69–70, 81, 100, 104.

3. A verb or participle is particularly likely to come between adjective and noun. Cf. lines 57, 62, 81, 82, 83, 87.

4. Subjects and other words often precede the introductory word of the subordinate clauses to which they belong. Cf. lines 111, 147.

5. Coordinate conjunctions (**et, sed,** etc.) sometimes come second instead of first in their clauses.

6. Other remarkable characteristics are illustrated in the following lines: 64 (**magis tegitur, tēctus magis**); 71 (**hinc Thisbē, Pȳramus illinc**); 91–92 (**lūx... praecipitātur aquīs et aquīs nox exit**); 117 (**dedit nōtae lacrimās, dedit ōscula vestī**).

Reading Latin Verse

The rhythm of Latin verse does not depend on word accent as does that of English but on the length of syllables. The rules for determining the length of syllables are:

1. A syllable is long *by nature* if it contains a long vowel or a diphthong.

2. A syllable is long *by position* if it contains a short vowel followed by two or more consonants or the consonant **x (= cs).**

In poetry a long syllable is treated as twice the length of a short syllable. Since a line of poetry is considered one long word, in a case like **is facit** the first word is a long syllable because the (short) vowel is followed by two consonants (**s, f**).

Several syllables are combined to form a foot. The *dactyl* is a foot consisting of a long syllable followed by two short syllables, written – ˘ ˘.

The *spondee* consists of two long syllables, – –. When a line contains six feet, it is called a hexameter. The *Metamorphoses* is written in the dactylic hexameter. A spondee may be substituted for a dactyl in every foot except the fifth, though occasionally a spondee is used even here. The sixth foot is always a spondee.[1] The beat is on the first syllable of each foot.

---

[1] The last syllable is often short, but the "rest" at the end of the line fills out the foot.

Elision

If a word ends in a vowel or a vowel plus **m** and the next word begins with a vowel or **h**, the first vowel disappears entirely. This is called *elision;* the vowel is said to be "elided."

> **foribusqu(e) excēdere** is pronounced **foribusquexcēdere.**

Before **es** or **est,** *prodelision* occurs—that is, the first vowel of the following word disappears.

> **nimium est** is pronounced **nimiumst.**

Scansion

The first five lines of *Pyramus and Thisbe* are scanned (marked) to show the meter, as follows:

$$\bar{\text{P}}\bar{\text{y}}\text{ramus} \mid \text{et This}\mid\text{bē, iuve}\mid\text{num pul}\mid\text{cherrimus} \mid \text{alter,} \mid$$
$$\text{altera,} \mid \text{quās Ori}\mid\text{ēns habu}\mid\text{it, prae}\mid\text{lāta pu}\mid\text{ellīs,} \mid$$
$$\text{contigu}\mid\text{ās tenu}\mid\text{ēre do}\mid\text{mōs, ubi} \mid \text{dīcitur} \mid \text{altam} \mid$$
$$\text{coctili}\mid\text{bus mū}\mid\text{rīs cīn}\mid\text{xisse Se}\mid\text{mīramis} \mid \text{urbem.} \mid$$
$$\text{Nōtiti}\mid\text{am prī}\mid\text{mōsque gra}\mid\text{dūs vī}\mid\text{cīnia} \mid \text{fēcit} \mid$$

Pyramus and Thisbe

This is the famous story of two lovers living in adjacent homes in ancient Babylonia who were forbidden by their parents to see each other. Conversing through a crack in the common wall between the two houses, they arranged a secret meeting at night outside the city. Their trysting place was under a mulberry tree. The metamorphosis in this story is the change in the color of the fruit of the mulberry from white to red, from the blood of the young people.

55   Pyramus et Thisbē, iuvenum pulcherrimus alter,
altera, quās[1] Oriēns habuit, praelāta puellīs,
contiguās tenuēre domōs, ubi dīcitur altam
coctilibus[1] mūrīs cīnxisse Semīramis urbem.
Nōtitiam prīmōsque gradūs[2] vīcīnia fēcit,
60   tempore crēvit amor; taedae quoque iūre[3] coīssent,

[1] *of brick* (literally, *baked*)
[2] i.e., *of love*
[3] *in lawful wedlock* (literally, *by the law of the torch*)

---

[1] The relative clause precedes the antecedent, **puellīs.**

sed vetuēre patrēs. Quod nōn potuēre vetāre,
ex aequō captīs ārdēbant mentibus ambō.
Cōnscius omnis abest; nūtū signīsque loquuntur,
quōque[4] magis tegitur, tēctus magis aestuat ignis.
Fissus erat[2] tenuī rīmā, quam dūxerat[5] ōlim
cum fieret, pariēs domuī commūnis utrīque.
Id vitium nūllī per saecula longa notātum
(quid nōn sentit amor?) prīmī vīdistis amantēs
et vōcis fēcistis iter;[6] tūtaeque per illud
murmure blanditiae minimō trānsīre solēbant.
Saepe, ubi cōnstiterant, hinc Thisbē, Pȳramus illinc,
inque vicēs fuerat captātus anhēlitus ōris,[7]
"Invide," dīcēbant, "pariēs, quid amantibus obstās?
Quantum erat[8] ut sinerēs tōtō nōs corpore iungī,
aut, hoc sī nimium est, vel ad ōscula danda patērēs!"[3]
Nec sumus ingrātī; tibi nōs dēbēre fatēmur
quod[9] datus est verbīs ad amīcās trānsitus aurēs."
Tālia dīversā nēquīquam sēde locūtī
sub noctem[10] dīxēre, "Valē," partīque dedēre
ōscula quisque[11] suae nōn pervenientia contrā.
Postera nocturnōs Aurōra remōverat ignēs,
sōlque pruīnōsās radiīs siccāverat herbās;
ad solitum coiēre locum. Tum murmure parvō
multa prius questī,[4] statuunt ut nocte silentī
fallere custōdēs foribusque excēdere temptent,[5]
cumque domō exierint, urbis quoque tēcta relinquant,[5]
nēve sit errandum lātō spatiantibus[6] arvō,
conveniant[5] ad busta Ninī[7] lateantque[5] sub umbrā
arboris: arbor ibī niveīs ūberrima pōmīs,
ardua mōrus,[12] erat gelidō contermina fontī.
Pācta placent; et lūx[13] tardē discēdere vīsa
praecipitātur aquīs et aquīs nox exit ab īsdem.
Callida per tenebrās, versātō cardine,[14] Thisbē
ēgreditur fallitque suōs adopertaque vultum
pervenit ad tumulum distāque sub arbore sēdit.
Audācem[8] faciēbat amor. Venit ecce recentī
caede leaena boum[9] spūmantēs oblita[15] rictūs[16]

65

70

75

80

85

90

95

[4] *the more*
[5] *it had acquired*
[6] *a passage for the voice*
[7] *and each had heard the other's breathing*
[8] *how small a thing it would be*
[9] *the fact that*
[10] *at nightfall*
[11] *each*
[12] *mulberry tree* (feminine)
[13] *daylight*
[14] *opening the door* (literally, *turning the hinge*)
[15] *smeared* (from **oblinō**)
[16] *jaws*

---

[2] The subject is **pariēs**.
[3] i.e., wide enough (from **pateō**)
[4] from **queror**
[5] volitive clause, object of **statuunt**
[6] modifies **eīs** understood, dative of agent: *that they need not wander at random*
[7] Semiramis' husband
[8] Supply **eam**.
[9] from **bōs**; genitive with **caede**

[17] *to quench*
[18] *from her back* (with **lāpsa**)
[19] *it is* (*the part of*) *a coward*
[20] *just as when a faulty lead water pipe splits and sends long (streams of) water through the small, hissing hole and bursts through the air with its jets*
[21] *spray*
[22] *is anxious*
[23] *and although . . . yet*
[24] *seen* (*before*) (with **arbore**)

dēpositūra[17] sitim vīcīnī fontis in undā.

Quam procul ad lūnae radiōs Babylōnia Thisbē

vīdit et obscūrum timidō pede fūgit in antrum;   100

dumque fugit tergō [18] vēlāmina lāpsa relīquit.

Ut lea saeva sitim multā compescuit undā,

dum redit in silvās, inventōs forte sine ipsā [10]

ōre cruentātō tenuēs laniāvit amictūs.

Sērius ēgressus vēstīgia vīdit in altō   105

pulvere certa ferae tōtōque expalluit ōre

Pȳramus. Ut vērō vestem quoque sanguine tīnctam

repperit, "Ūna duōs," inquit, "nox perdet amantēs,

ē quibus illa fuit longā dignissima vītā;

nostra nocēns anima est. Ego tē, miseranda, perēmī,   110

in loca plēna metūs quī iussī nocte venīrēs

nec prior hūc vēnī. Nostrum dīvellite corpus

et scelerāta ferō cōnsūmite vīscera morsū,

Ō quīcumque sub hāc habitātis rūpe, leōnēs!

Sed timidī [19] est optāre necem!" Vēlāmina Thisbēs[11]   115

tollit et ad pāctae sēcum fert arboris umbram.

Utque dedit nōtae[12] lacrimās, dedit ōscula vestī,

"Accipe nunc," inquit, "nostrī quoque sanguinis haustūs."

Quōque[13] erat accīnctus dēmīsit in īlia ferrum,

nec mora,[14] ferventī moriēns ē vulnere trāxit[15]   120

et iacuit resupīnus humō.[16] Cruor ēmicat altē,

nōn aliter[20] quam cum vitiātō fistula plumbō

scinditur et tenuī strīdente forāmine longās

ēiaculātur aquās atque ictibus āera rumpit.[20]

Arboreī fētūs aspergine[21] caedis in ātram   125

vertuntur faciem, madefactaque sanguine rādīx

purpureō tingit pendentia mōra colōre.

Ecce metū nōndum positō, nē fallat amantem,

illa redit iuvenemque oculīs animōque requīrit,

quantaque vītārit nārrare perīcula gestit.[22]   130

Utque[23] locum et vīsā [24] cognōscit in arbore fōrmam,

sīc[23] facit incertam pōmī color: haeret an haec sit.

---

[10] i.e., Thisbe
[11] genitive
[12] modifies **vestī**
[13] = **quō** and –**que**; **ferrum** is the antecedent
[14] Supply **est.**
[15] Supply **ferrum.**
[16] ablative (instead of locative **humī**): *on the ground*

Dum dubitat, tremebunda videt pulsāre cruentum
membra solum[25] retrōque pedem tulit ōraque buxō [26]
pallidiōra gerēns exhorruit aequoris īnstar[27]
quod tremit exiguā cum summum[28] stringitur aurā.
Sed postquam remorāta suōs cognōvit amōrēs,[29]
percutit indignōs[17] clārō plangōre lacertōs
et laniāta comās amplexaque corpus amātum
vulnera supplēvit lacrimīs flētumque cruōrī
miscuit et gelidīs in vultibus ōscula fīgēns
"Pȳrame," clāmāvit,"quis tē mihi cāsus adēmit?
Pȳrame, respondē! Tua tē cārissima Thisbē
nōminat; exaudī vultūsque attolle iacentēs!"
Ad nōmen Thisbēs oculōs ā morte gravātōs
Pȳramus ērēxit vīsāque recondidit illā.
Quae postquam vestemque suam cognōvit et ēnse[18]
vīdit ebur [30] vacuum, "Tua tē manus," inquit, "amorque
perdidit, īnfēlīx. Est et mihi fortis in ūnum
hoc[31] manus; est et amor; dabit hic in vulnera vīrēs.
Persequar exstīnctum[19] lētīque miserrima dīcar
causa comesque tuī; quīque ā mē morte revellī
heu sōlā poterās, poteris nec[32] morte revellī.
Hoc[20] tamen ambōrum verbīs estōte[33] rogātī,
Ō multum miserī meus illīusque parentēs,
ut quōs certus amor, quōs hōra novissima iūnxit,
compōnī tumulō nōn invideātis eōdem.
At tū quae rāmīs arbor[21] miserābile corpus
nunc tegis ūnīus, mox es tēctūra duōrum,
signa tenē caedis pullōsque et lūctibus aptōs
semper habē fētūs, geminī monumenta cruōris."
Dīxit et aptātō pectus mūcrōne sub īmum
incubuit ferrō, quod adhūc ā caede tepēbat.
Vōta tamen tetigēre deōs, tetigēre parentēs;
nam color in pōmō est, ubi permātūruit, āter,
quodque rogīs[34] superest, ūnā requiēscit in urnā.
(IV, 55–166)

135
140
145
150
155
160
165

[25] ground
[26] paler than boxwood
[27] like the sea
[28] surface
[29] lover
[30] sheath (literally, ivory)
[31] for this one act
[32] not even
[33] let me make this request (literally, be asked)
[34] and what remains from the pyres (i.e., the ashes)

---

[17] i.e., they did not deserve a beating
[18] ablative of separation with **vacuum**
[19] Supply **tē.**
[20] object of **rogātī**
[21] prose order: **tū, arbor, quae**

Midas

Midas, king of Phrygia, helped restore to Bacchus his companion and attendant, the Satyr (half goat, half man) Silenus. In return for this service Bacchus offered Midas anything he desired.

[1] *day*
[2] *foster son, i.e., Bacchus*
[3] *free choice*
[4] *foster father*
[5] *of Ceres (grain)*
[6] *you would think*
[7] *grasps*
[8] *and not without bread* (literally, *not lacking baked grain*)

	Quem[1] simul agnōvit[2] socium comitemque sacrōrum,[3]
95	hospitis adventū fēstum geniāliter ēgit
	per bis quīnque diēs et iūnctās ōrdine noctēs.
	Et iam stellārum sublīme coēgerat agmen
	Lūcifer [1] ūndecimus, Lȳdōs cum laetus in agrōs
	rēx venit et iuvenī Sīlēnum reddit alumnō.[2]
100	Huic deus optandī grātum sed inūtile fēcit
	mūneris arbitrium,[3] gaudēns altōre[4] receptō.
	Ille[4] male ūsūrus dōnīs ait, "Effice quicquid
	corpore contigerō fulvum vertātur[5] in aurum."
	Annuit optātis[6] nocitūraque mūnera solvit
105	Līber[7] et indoluit quod nōn meliōra petīsset.
	Laetus abit gaudetque malō Berecyntius hērōs[8]
	pollicitīque fidem tangendō singula temptat.
	Vixque sibī crēdēns, nōn altā[9] fronde virentem
	īlice dētrāxit virgam: virga aurea facta est.
110	Tollit humō saxum: saxum quoque palluit aurō.
	Contigit et glaebam: contāctū glaeba potentī
	māssa fit. Ārentēs Cereris[5] dēcerpsit aristās:
	aurea messis erat. Dēmptum tenet arbore pōmum:
	Hesperidās dōnāsse putēs.[6] Sī postibus altīs
115	admōvit digitōs, postēs radiāre videntur.
118	Vix spēs ipse suās animō capit,[7] aurea fingēns
	omnia. Gaudentī [10] mēnsās posuēre ministrī
120	exstrūctās dapibus nec tostae frūgis egentēs.[8]

---

[1] Bacchus
[2] The subject is Midas.
[3] Midas was celebrating a festival.
[4] Midas
[5] Supply **ut.**
[6] Supply **rēbus:** *his choice of gift.*
[7] Bacchus
[8] Midas
[9] modifies **īlice**
[10] Supply **eī.**

Ovid's mythological subject matter was obviously a joy to illustrate (see the small pictures). This 14th century manuscript is from an early part of the Metamorphoses. *You can just read the words **Liber prīmus** at the top. The rest of the manuscript is in French. Annotations made are in the margins among the birds and vines. The really popular works of Latin authors were translated into many languages. This work of Ovid was among the most popular. The manuscript itself was written and illustrated for a French nobleman.*

Tum vērō, sīve ille suā Cereālia dextrā
mūnera contigerat, Cereālia dōna rigēbant;
sīve dapēs avidō convellere dente parābat,
lāmina[9] fulva dapēs, admōtō dente, premēbat;[9]

miscuerat pūrīs auctōrem[10] mūneris undīs:
fūsile[11] per rictūs aurum fluitāre vidērēs.[11]
Attonitus novitāte malī dīvēsque miserque
effugere optat opēs et quae modo vōverat ōdit.
Cōpia nūlla famem relevat; sitis ārida guttur

ūrit, et invīsō meritus torquētur ab aurō,
ad caelumque manūs et splendida bracchia tollēns,
"Dā veniam, Lēnaee[12] pater! Peccāvimus," inquit,
"sed miserēre, precor, speciōsōque ēripe[11] damnō."
Mīte deum[13] nūmen: Bacchus peccāsse fatentem

restituit factīque fidē[14] data mūnera solvit.[15]
"Nēve male optātō maneās circumlitus[16] aurō,
vāde," ait, "ad magnīs vīcīnum Sardibus amnem
perque iugum Lȳdum lābentibus obvius undīs[17]
carpe viam, dōnec veniās ad flūminis ortūs.

Spūmigerōque tuum fontī, quā plūrimus exit,
subde caput corpusque simul, simul ēlue crīmen."
Rēx iussae succēdit aquae: vīs aurea tīnxit
flūmen et hūmānō dē corpore cessit in amnem.
Nunc quoque, iam veteris perceptō sēmine vēnae,[18]

arva rigent aurō[12] madidīs pallentia glaebīs.
Ille perōsus opēs silvās et rūra colēbat
Pānaque[13] montānīs habitantem semper in antrīs.
Pingue[19] sed ingenium mānsit, nocitūraque, ut ante,
rūrsus erant dominō stultae praecordia mentis.[14]

Nam freta prōspiciēns lātē riget arduus altō
Tmōlus in ascēnsū clīvōque extēnsus utrōque
Sardibus hinc, illinc parvīs fīnītur Hypaepīs.
Pān ibi dum tenerīs iactat sua carmina nymphīs
et leve cērātā modulātur[20] harundine carmen,[20]

ausus Apollineōs prae[21] sē contemnere cantūs,
iūdice sub Tmōlō[15] certāmen vēnit ad impār.

125

130

135

140

145

150

155

[9] a golden layer covered the food
[10] the author (giver) of the gift (Bacchus), i.e., wine
[11] You might have seen liquid gold flowing over his jaws.
[12] Bacchus
[13] = deōrum
[14] a proof
[15] removed the gift
[16] smeared
[17] meeting the waters, i.e., going upstream
[18] having received the seed of ancient vein
[19] fat, i.e., stupid
[20] plays a song
[21] compared to himself

[11] Supply mē as object.
[12] with madidīs
[13] accusative singular
[14] stultae praecordia mentis = stulta mēns
[15] here the god of the mountain

Monte suō senior iūdex cōnsēdit et aurēs
līberat arboribus. Quercū coma caerula tantum
cingitur, et pendent circum cava tempora glandēs.
Isque deum[16] pecoris spectāns, "In iūdice," dīxit,   160
"nūlla mora est." Calamīs agrestibus īnsonat ille
barbaricōque Midān (aderat nam forte canentī)
carmine dēlēnit. Post hunc sacer ōra retorsit
Tmōlus ad ōs Phoebī; vultum sua silva secūta est.
Ille caput flāvum laurō Parnāside vīnctus   165
verrit humum Tyriō saturātā mūrice pallā,
īnstrictamque fidem[22] gemmīs et dentibus Indīs
sustinet ā laevā,[23] tenuit manus altera plēctrum;
artificis status ipse fuit. Tum stāmina[24] doctō
pollice sollicitat, quōrum dulcēdine captus   170
Pāna iubet Tmōlus citharae[17] summittere cannās.
Iūdicium sānctīque placet sententia montis
omnibus; arguitur[25] tamen atque iniūsta vocātur
ūnīus sermōne Midae. Nec Dēlius[18] aurēs
hūmānam stolidās patitur retinēre figūram,   175
sed trahit in spatium[26] vīllīsque albentibus implet
īnstabilēsque īmās[27] facit et dat[28] posse movērī.
Cētera sunt hominis; partem damnātur in ūnam[29]
induiturque aurēs lentē gradientis asellī.
Ille quidem cēlāre cupit turpīque pudōre   180
tempora purpureīs temptat vēlāre tiārīs;
sed solitus longōs ferrō resecāre capillōs
vīderat hoc famulus;[19] quī cum nec prōdere vīsum
dēdecus audēret, cupiēns efferre sub aurās,[30]
nec posset reticēre tamen, sēcēdit humumque   185
effodit et, dominī quālēs aspexerit aurēs,
vōce refert parvā terraeque immurmurat haustae[31]
indiciumque suae vōcis, tellūre regestā,
obruit et scrobibus[32] tacitus discēdit opertīs.
Crēber harundinibus tremulīs ibi surgere lūcus   190
coepit et, ut prīmum plēnō mātūruit annō
prōdidit agricolam:[20] lēnī nam mōtus ab austrō
obruta verba refert dominīque coarguit aurēs.
(XI, 94–193)

[22] *lyre*
[23] *on the left (side)*
[24] *strings*
[25] *(the judgment) is challenged*
[26] *lengthens them* (literally, *draws them into space*)
[27] *loose at the bottom*
[28] *causes them*
[29] *in respect to one part*
[30] *in the open*
[31] *dug out*
[32] *hole*

---

[16] Pan
[17] dative
[18] Apollo
[19] i.e., his servant saw it while cutting his hair
[20] i.e., the **famulus** (barber)

[1] *surrounded by a throng*

[2] *tossing, along with her head, her hair flowing down on*

[3] *tall, standing erect*

[4] *to prefer gods (merely) heard of to those (you have) seen*

[5] *incense (used in worship)*

[6] *father*

[7] *royal palace*

[8] *put together by the lyre*

[9] *there is in addition*

[10] *some Coeus or other*

[11] *a Titan's daughter, born of Coeus*

[12] *to whom about to give birth* (with **cui**)

[13] *offspring* (literally, *womb*)

[14] *I am too great for Fortune to harm*

[15] *grant that*

[16] *my wealth* (i.e., my children) *has gone beyond fear*

[17] *even if I am robbed*

[18] *Latona's crowd* (in apposition with **duōrum**)

Ecce venit comitum Niobē crēberrima[1] turbā,

vestibus intextō Phrygiīs spectābilis aurō

et, quantum īra sinit, fōrmōsa movēnsque decōrō

cum capite immissōs umerum per utrumque capillōs.[2]

Cōnstitit, utque oculōs circumtulit alta[3] superbōs,

"Quis furor$_1$ audītōs," [4] inquit, "praepōnere vīsīs

caelestēs? Aut cūr colitur Lātōna per ārās,

nūmen adhūc sine tūre[5] meum est? Mihi Tantalus auctor,[6]

cui licuit sōlī superōrum tangere mēnsās;

Plēiadum soror est genetrīx mea; maximus Atlās

est avus, aetherium quī fert cervīcibus axem;

Iuppiter alter avus; socerō quoque glōrior illō.

Mē gentēs metuunt Phrygiae, mē rēgia[7] Cadmī

sub dominā$_2$ est, fidibusque meī commissa[8] marītī

moenia cum populīs ā mēque virōque reguntur.

In quamcumque domūs advertī lūmina partem

immēnsae spectantur opēs. Accēdit eōdem[9]

digna deā faciēs; hūc nātās adice septem

et totidem iuvenēs et mox generōsque nurūsque.

Quaerite nunc, habeat quam nostra superbia causam;

nesciō quōque[10]$_3$ audēte satam[11] Tītānida[11] Cōeō

Lātōnam praeferre mihī, cui maxima quondam

exiguam sēdem paritūrae[12] terra negāvit.

Nec caelō nec humō nec aquīs dea vestra recepta est;

exsul erat mundī, dōnec miserāta$_4$ vagantem,

'Hospita tū terrīs errās, ego,' dīxit, 'in undīs,'

īnstabilemque$_5$ locum Dēlos dedit. Illa duōrum

facta parēns; uterī[13] pars haec est septima nostrī.

Sum fēlīx (quis enim neget hoc?) fēlīxque manēbō

(hoc quoque quis dubitet?) tūtam mē cōpia fēcit.

Maior sum quam cui possit Fortūna nocēre,[14]

multaque ut[15] ēripiat, multō mihi plūra relinquet.

Excessēre[16] metum mea iam bona.[16] Fingite$_6$ dēmī

huic aliquid populō nātōrum posse meōrum,$_6$

nōn tamen ad numerum redigar spoliāta[17] duōrum,

Lātōnae turbae:[18] quae quantum distat ab orbā?

$_1$ Supply **est**.

$_2$ with **mē**

$_3$ **nesciō** here = two long syllables

$_4$ modifies **Dēlos**

$_5$ Delos was then a floating island.

$_6$ *suppose that something could be taken from this nation (that) my children constitute,* i.e., her children are so numerous that they form a nation

Īte satis properē sacrīs[19] laurumque capillīs
pōnite."[20] Dēpōnunt et sacra īnfecta[21] relinquunt,
quodque[7] licet, tacitō venerantur murmure nūmen.
Indignāta dea est summōque in vertice Cynthī
tālibus est dictīs geminā cum prōle locūta:
"Ēn ego vestra parēns, vōbīs animōsa creātīs,[22]
et nisi Iūnōnī nūllī cessūra deārum,
an dea sim dubitor,[23] perque omnia saecula cultīs[8]
arceor, Ō nātī, nisi vōs succurritis, ārīs.
Nec dolor hic sōlus: dīrō convīcia factō
Tantalis[24] adiēcit vōsque est postpōnere nātīs
ausa suīs et mē (quod in ipsam reccidat)[25] orbam
dīxit et exhibuit linguam scelerāta paternam."
Adiectūra precēs erat hīs Lātōna relātīs:
"Dēsine," Phoebus ait, "poenae mora longa querēla est."   215
Dīxit idem Phoebē celerīque per āera lāpsū
contigerant tēctī Cadmēida[26] nūbibus arcem.
Plānus erat lātēque patēns prope moenia campus,
assiduīs pulsātus equīs, ubi turba rotārum
dūraque mollierat subiectās ungula glaebās.   220
Pars ibi dē septem genitīs Amphīone fortēs
cōnscendunt in equōs Tyriōque rubentia sūcō[27]
terga premunt aurōque gravēs moderantur habēnās.
Ē quibus Ismēnus, quī mātrī sarcina[28] quondam
prīma suae fuerat, dum certum flectit in orbem   225
quadrupedis cursūs spūmantiaque ōra coercet,
"Ei[29] mihi!" conclāmat mediōque in pectore fīxa
tēla gerit, frēnīsque manū moriente remissīs,
in latus[9] ā dextrō paulātim dēfluit armō.[30]
Proximus, audītō sonitū per ināne[10] pharetrae,   230
frēna dabat Sipylus, velutī cum praescius imbris
nūbe fugit vīsā, pendentiaque undique rēctor[31]
carbasa dēdūcit,[32] nē quā[33] levis effluat aura;
frēna tamen dantem nōn ēvītābile tēlum
cōnsequitur, summāque tremēns cervīce sagitta   235
haesit, et exstābat nūdum dē gutture ferrum.
Ille, ut erat prōnus, per colla admissa iubāsque[34]
volvitur et calidō tellūrem sanguine foedat.

[19] *go away from the rites quickly*
[20] = **dēpōnite**
[21] *unfinished*
[22] *proud of you (whom I have) borne*
[23] *my divinity is being questioned*
[24] *daughter of Tantalus,* i.e., Niobe
205 [25] *may this fall to her lot*
[26] *of Cadmus* (with **arcem**)
[27] *dye* (used on the saddlecloth)
[28] *burden,* i.e., *child*
[29] *Oh!* **mihi** is dative of reference
[30] *shoulder* (of the horse)
[31] *pilot* (of a ship)
210 [32] *unfurls the sails*
[33] *anywhere*
[34] *the swift neck and the mane* (of the horse)

---

[7] The antecedent is the clause that follows.
[8] with **ārīs**
[9] accusative of the noun **latus,** *side*
[10] noun

Phaedimus īnfēlīx et avītī nōminis hērēs,

Tantalus, ut solitō fīnem imposuēre labōrī,

trānsierant ad opus nitidae iuvenāle palaestrae,[35]

et iam contulerant artō luctantia nexū

pectora pectoribus: contentō concita[36] nervō,

sīcut erant iūnctī, trāiēcit utrumque sagitta.

Ingemuēre simul, simul incurvāta[37] dolōre

membra solō[38] posuēre, simul suprēma[39] iacentēs

lūmina versārunt, animam simul exhālārunt.[40]

Aspicit Alphēnor laniātaque pectora plangēns[41]

ēvolat, ut gelidōs complexibus allevet artūs,

inque piō cadit officiō; nam Dēlius illī

intima fātiferō rūpit praecordia ferrō.

Quod simul[42] ēductum est, pars[43] et pulmōnis in hāmīs

ēruta[43] cumque animā cruor est effūsus in aurās.

At nōn[11] intōnsum simplex Damasichthona[12] vulnus

afficit: ictus erat quā crūs esse incipit et quā

mollia nervōsus facit internōdia poples.

Dumque manū temptat trahere exitiābile tēlum,

altera per iugulum pennīs tenus[44] ācta sagitta est.

Expulit hanc sanguis sēque ēiaculātus in altum

ēmicat et longē terebrāta prōsilit aurā.

Ultimus Īlioneus nōn prōfectūra[45] precandō

bracchia sustulerat "dī" que "Ō commūniter omnēs,"

dīxerat, ignārus nōn omnēs[13] esse rogandōs,

"parcite!" Mōtus erat, cum iam revocābile tēlum

nōn fuit, Arcitenēns. Minimō tamen occidit ille

vulnere, nōn altē percussō corde sagittā.

Fāma malī populīque dolor lacrimaeque suōrum

tam subitae mātrem certam fēcēre ruīnae,[46]

mīrantem potuisse,[47] īrāscentemque quod ausī

hōc essent superī, quod tantum iūris habērent.

Nam[14] pater Amphīōn, ferrō per pectus adāctō,

fīnierat moriēns pariter cum lūce dolōrem.

Heu quantum haec Niobē Niobē distābat ab illā

quae modo Lātōīs populum summōverat ārīs

et mediam tulerat[48] gressūs resupīna per urbem,[48]

invidiōsa suīs, at nunc miseranda vel hostī!

240

[35] *of the glistening (with oil) wrestling places*
[36] *an arrow sent from the taut string (of the bow)* (with **sagitta**)
[37] *writhing*
[38] *on the ground*
245
[39] *they moved their eyes (for the) last (time)* (with **lūmina**)
[40] *expired*
[41] *beating his torn breast (but of course it was not torn until he beat it)*
[42] = **simul ac**
[43] *part of his lungs was torn out (and stuck to) the barbs (of the arrow)*
250
[44] *up to the feathers*
[45] i.e., *in vain*
[46] *informed the mother of the sudden disaster*
[47] *wondering (that the gods) could (do this)*
255
[48] *had walked proudly through the city*

260

265

270

275

---

[11] with **simplex**
[12] accusative (Greek form)
[13] a prayer to Apollo would have been preferable
[14] This line and the next explain why Niobe was not joined in grief by her husband.

Erich Lessing/Art Resource, NY

This magnificent French manuscript from the 15th century is richly illustrated throughout in true Renaissance style, including detailed scenes, a fancy initial capital letter, and marginal flora and fauna. The text tells the story of the landing in England by Julius Caesar. It was written by the historian, Jean Mansel. You can read Caesar's name in French (Cesar) in the second line of column 1 and the fifth line of column 2. By the 15th century, the making of manuscripts was a fairly large industry and not all confined to monasteries. Soon printing on paper (1450 onward) would supplant manuscripts and provide many copies of the same work to an increasingly expanded reading public. From then on, the Roman and Greek classics were safely preserved!

Corporibus gelidīs incumbit et ōrdine nūllō
ōscula dispēnsat nātōs suprēma per omnēs.
Ā quibus ad caelum līventia[15] bracchia tollēns,
     280   "pāscere, crūdēlis, nostrō, Lātōna, dolōre;
pāscere," ait, "satiāque meō tua pectora lūctū
corque ferum satiā," dīxit. "Per fūnera septem
efferor.[49] Exsultā victrīxque inimīca triumphā!
Cūr autem victrīx? Miserae mihi plūra supersunt
     285   quam tibi fēlīcī; post tot quoque fūnera vincō."
Dīxerat, et sonuit contentō nervus ab arcū,[16]
quī praeter Niobēn ūnam conterruit omnēs;
illa malō[50] est audāx. Stābant cum vestibus ātrīs
ante torōs[51] frātrum, dēmissō crīne, sorōrēs.
     290   Ē quibus ūna trahēns haerentia vīscere tēla[52]
impositō[53] frātrī moribunda relanguit ōre.
Altera sōlārī miserum cōnāta parentem
conticuit subitō duplicātaque[54] vulnere caecō est,
ōraque compressit, nisi postquam spīritus ībat.[55]
     295   Haec frūstrā fugiēns collābitur; illa sorōrī
immoritur; latet haec; illam trepidāre vidērēs.
Sexque datīs lētō dīversaque vulnera passīs,
ultima restābat. Quam tōtō corpore māter,
tōtā veste tegēns, "Ūnam minimamque[56] relinque!
     300   Dē multīs minimam poscō," clāmāvit, "et ūnam."
Dumque rogat, prō quā [17] rogat occidit. Orba resēdit
exanimēs inter nātōs nātāsque virumque
dēriguitque malīs; nūllōs movet aura capillōs,
in vultū color est sine sanguine, lūmina maestīs
     305   stant immōta genīs, nihil est in imāgine vīvum.
Ipsa quoque interius cum dūrō lingua palātō
congelat, et vēnae dēsistunt posse movērī;
nec flectī cervīx nec bracchia reddere mōtūs
nec pēs īre potest; intrā quoque vīscera saxum est.
     310   Flet tamen et validī circumdata turbine ventī [57]
in patriam[18] rapta est. Ibi fīxa cacūmine montis
līquitur, et lacrimās etiam nunc marmora mānant.[19]
(VI, 165–312)

[49] *I am carried out* (i.e., *to the grave*)
[50] *because of her misfortune*
[51] *biers*
[52] *the weapon fixed in (her brother's) heart*
[53] *her face placed upon her brother*
[54] *was bent double*
[55] *after her breath left her,* i.e., when she died, her mouth opened
[56] *the youngest*
[57] *a strong gust of wind*

---

[15] as a result of beating herself in grief
[16] of Diana, who will kill the daughters
[17] Supply **ea** as antecedent of **quā** and subject of **occidit.**
[18] Phrygia
[19] The rock on Mt. Sipylus was called Niobe and resembled a female form. The tears are explained by the spring trickling down the face of the figure.

Philemon and Baucis

A kind aged couple of Phrygia entertain to the best of their resources Jupiter and Mercury who, disguised as wanderers, have been refused hospitality in other homes. The gods reward Philemon and Baucis for their purity with many blessings in life and in death.

Iuppiter hūc[1] speciē mortālī, cumque parente
vēnit Atlantiadēs positīs cādūcifer[1] ālīs.
Mīlle domōs adiēre locum requiemque petentēs,
mīlle domōs clausēre serae.[2] Tamen ūna recēpit,
parva quidem stipulīs[3] et cannā tēcta palūstrī,[3]   630
sed pia Baucis anus[4] parilīque aetāte Philēmōn
illā[2] sunt annīs iūnctī iuvenālibus, illā[2]
cōnsenuēre casā paupertātemque fatendō
effēcēre levem nec inīquā mente ferendō.
Nec rēfert[5] dominōs illīc famulōsne requīrās;   635
tōta domus duo sunt, īdem pārentque iubentque.
Ergō ubi caelicolae parvōs tetigēre Penātēs[6]
submissōque humilēs intrārunt vertice[7] postēs,
membra senex positō iussit relevāre sedīlī,
quō superiniēcit textum rude sēdula Baucis;   640
inque focō tepidum cinerem dīmōvit et ignēs
suscitat hesternōs foliīsque et cortice siccō
nūtrit et ad flammās animā prōdūcit anīlī,
multifidāsque[8] facēs[8] rāmāliaque[9] ārida tēctō[10]
dētulit et minuit[11] parvōque admōvit aēnō.[12]   645
Quodque suus coniūnx riguō collēgerat hortō,
truncat holus foliīs. Furcā levat ille bicornī
sordida terga suis[3] nigrō pendentia tignō
servātōque diū resecat dē tergore partem
exiguam sectamque domat[13] ferventibus undīs.   650
Intereā mediās fallunt[14] sermōnibus hōrās,   651
concutiuntque torum[15] dē mollī flūminis ulvā[16]   655
impositum lectō spondā[17] pedibusque salignīs.[17]

[1] the bearer of the caduceus (a wand), i.e., Mercury
[2] locks
[3] covered with straw and marsh reeds
[4] old woman
[5] It does not matter whether . . . or (**–ne**)
[6] household gods, i.e., house
[7] head(s)
[8] fine-split kindling
[9] branches
[10] from (under the) roof
[11] broke into pieces
[12] kettle
[13] makes tender
[14] they pass the time
[15] mattress
[16] sedge-grass
[17] with willow frame and feet

---

[1] the home of Philemon and Baucis
[2] with **casā**
[3] **suis** from **sūs**, *pork blackened* (by smoke)

[18] = **etiam**
[19] *reclined at the table*
[20] *with tucked up skirts* (literally, *girded up*)
[21] *green mint wiped the balanced (table)*
[22] *cornel berries preserved in the lees of wine*
[23] *endive*
[24] *cheese*
[25] *earthenware dishes*
[26] *the same silver*
[27] *coated on the inside* (literally, *where they are hollow) with yellow wax* (to prevent leaks)
[28] *the second course, i.e., dessert*
[29] *figs*
[30] *you will be exempt from this misfortune*

Vestibus hunc vēlant quās nōn nisi tempore fēstō
sternere cōnsuerant, sed et [18] haec vīlisque vetusque
vestis erat lectō nōn indignanda salignō.
Accubuēre[19] deī. Mēnsam succīncta[20] tremēnsque   660
pōnit anus, mēnsae sed erat pēs tertius impār:[4]
testa parem fēcit; quae postquam subdita clīvum
sustulit, aequātam mentae[21] tersēre virentēs.[21]
Pōnitur hīc bicolor[5] sincērae bāca Minervae,[5]
conditaque in liquidā corna[22] autumnālia faece[22]   665
intibaque[23] et rādīx et lactis[24] māssa coāctī,[24]
ōvaque nōn ācrī leviter versāta favīllā,
omnia fictilibus,[25] Post haec caelātus eōdem
sistitur argentō [26][6] crāter fabricātaque fāgō
pōcula, quā [27] cava sunt, flāventibus illita cērīs.[27]   670
Parva mora est, epulāsque focī mīsēre calentēs,
nec longae rūrsus referuntur vīna senectae,
dantque locum mēnsīs paulum sēducta secundīs.[28]
Hīc nux, hīc mixta est rūgōsīs cārica[29] palmīs
prūnaque et in patulīs redolentia māla canistrīs   675
et dē purpureīs collēctae vītibus ūvae.
Candidus in mediō favus est; super omnia vultūs
accessēre bonī nec iners pauperque voluntās.
Intereā totiēns haustum crātēra[7] replērī
sponte suā per sēque vident succrēscere vīna.   680
Attonitī novitāte pavent manibusque supīnīs
concipiunt Baucisque precēs timidusque Philēmōn
et veniam dapibus nūllīsque parātibus[8] ōrant.
Ūnicus ānser erat, minimae custōdia vīllae,
quem dīs hospitibus dominī mactāre parābant.   685
Ille celer pennā tardōs aetāte fatīgat
ēlūditque diū, tandemque est vīsus ad ipsōs
cōnfūgisse deōs; superī vetuēre necārī
"di" que "sumus, meritāsque luet vīcīnia poenās
impia," dīxērunt; "vōbīs[30] immūnibus huius   690
esse malī dabitur.[30] Modo vestra relinquite tēcta
ac nostrōs comitāte gradūs et in ardua montis
īte simul." Pārent ambō baculīsque levātī
nītuntur longō vēstīgia pōnere clīvō.

---

[4] The table had three legs.
[5] i.e., green and black (ripe) olives
[6] a humorous reference to **fictilibus**
[7] accusative singular (Greek form)
[8] i.e., poor entertainment; literally, *for no preparation*

Tantum aberant summō [31] quantum semel īre sagitta
missa potest; flexēre oculōs et mersa palūdē
cētera prōspiciunt, tantum sua tēcta manēre.
Dumque ea mīrantur, dum dēflent fāta suōrum,
illa vetus dominīs etiam casa parva duōbus
vertitur in templum. Furcās subiēre columnae,[32]
strāmina flāvēscunt, adopertaque marmore tellūs
caelātaeque forēs aurātaque tēcta videntur.
Tālia tum placidō Sāturnius[9] ēdidit ōre:
"Dīcite, iūste senex et fēmina coniuge iūstō
digna, quid optētis." Cum Baucide pauca locūtus
iūdicium superīs aperit commūne Philēmōn:
"Esse sacerdōtēs dēlūbraque vestra tuērī
poscimus, et quoniam concordēs ēgimus annōs,
auferat hōra duōs eadem, nec coniugis umquam
busta meae videam neu sim tumulandus[33] ab illā."
Vōta fidēs sequitur;[10] templī tutēla fuēre,
dōnec vīta data est. Annīs aevōque solūtī [34]
ante gradūs sacrōs cum stārent forte locīque
nārrārent cāsūs, frondēre Philēmona Baucis,
Baucida cōnspexit senior frondēre Philēmōn.
Iamque super geminōs crēscente cacūmine vultūs,
mūtua, dum licuit, reddēbant dicta "Valē" que
"Ō coniūnx" [35] dīxēre simul, simul abdita tēxit
ōra frutex.[36] Ostendit adhūc Thynēius[37] illīc
incola dē geminō vīcīnōs corpore truncōs.
Haec mihi nōn vānī (neque erat cūr fallere vellent)
nārrāvēre senēs. Equidem pendentia vīdī
serta super rāmōs pōnēnsque recentia dīxī
"Cūra deum dī sint, et quī coluēre colantur."
(VIII, 626–724)

695 [31] *the top*
[32] *columns took the place of the (wooden) supports (forks)*
[33] *buried*
[34] *weakened*
[35] *dear mate*
[36] *foliage*
700 [37] *Bithynian*

705

710

715

720

[9] Jupiter
[10] i.e., their prayer was answered

Daphne and Apollo

Apollo, the god of archery, falls in love with Daphne, the daughter of the river god Peneus. Cupid, out of envy and revenge, inspired Apollo with his passion for Daphne, a passion made hopeless by her resistance, also caused by Cupid. She turned into a laurel tree.

[1] *bow*   455
[2] *equipment*
[3] *some love or other* (with **amōrēs**)
[4] *do not lay claim to my honors*
[5] *as much as all living things yield to (you), a god*
[6] *striking the air by beating his wings*   460
[7] *of opposite effects*
[8] *the (arrow) which*
[9] *is tipped with lead* (literally, *has lead under the shaft*)
[10] *struck the heart of Apollo, piercing the bones*
[11] *the rival of the maiden Diana*   465

Prīmus amor Phoebī Daphnē Pēnēia, quem nōn
fors ignāra dedit sed saeva Cupīdinis īra.
Dēlius[1] hunc, nūper victō serpente superbus,
vīderat adductō flectentem[2] cornua[1] nervō
"quid" que[3] "tibī,[4] lascīve puer, cum fortibus armīs?"
dīxerat; "ista decent umerōs gestāmina[2] nostrōs,
quī dare certa ferae, dare vulnera possumus hostī,
quī modo pestiferō tot iūgera ventre prementem
strāvimus innumerīs tumidum Pȳthōna[5] sagittīs.
Tū face nesciō quōs[3] estō contentus amōrēs
irrītāre tuā,[6] nec laudēs assere nostrās."[4]
Fīlius huic Veneris, "Fīgat tuus omnia, Phoebe,
tē meus arcus," ait, "quantōque[5] animālia cēdunt
cūncta deō,[5] tantō minor est tua glōria nostrā."
Dīxit et, ēlīsō[6] percussīs āere pennīs,[6]
impiger umbrōsā Parnāsī cōnstitit arce
ēque[7] sagittiferā prōmpsit duo tēla pharetrā
dīversōrum operum:[7] fugat hoc,[8] facit illud[8] amōrem.
Quod[8] facit, aurātum est et cuspide fulget acūtā;
quod fugat, obtūsum est et habet sub harundine plumbum.[9]
Hoc deus in nymphā Pēnēide[9] fīxit; at illō
laesit[10] Apollineās trāiecta per ossa medullās.[10]
Prōtinus alter amat, fugit altera nōmen amantis
silvārum latebrīs captīvārumque ferārum
exuviīs gaudēns innuptaeque aemula Phoebēs.[11]

470
475

---

[1] Apollo
[2] Supply **eum**, Cupid.
[3] connects the two verbs **vīderat** and **dīxerat**
[4] Originally the second *i* of **tibi** was long; supply **est**.
[5] accusative (Greek form)
[6] modifies **face**
[7] = **ē** and **-que**
[8] Supply **tēlum.**
[9] ablative of **Pēnēis**, daughter of Peneus, i.e., Daphne

Vitta coercēbat positōs sine lēge capillōs.

Multī illam petiēre, illa āversāta petentēs[12]

impatiēns expersque virī nemora āvia lūstrat,

nec quid Hymēn, quid Amor, quid sint cōnūbia cūrat.

Saepe pater dīxit, "generum mihi, fīlia, dēbēs";

saepe pater dīxit, "dēbēs mihi, nāta, nepōtēs."

Illa, velut crīmen taedās exōsa iugālēs

pulchra verēcundō suffūderat ōra rubōre

inque patris blandīs haerēns cervīce lacertīs,

"Dā[13] mihi perpetuā, genitor cārissime," dīxit,

"virginitāte fruī.[13] Dedit hoc pater ante[10] Diānae."

Ille quidem obsequitur. Sed tē decor iste quod[14] optās

esse vetat,[14] vōtōque tuō tua fōrma repugnat.

Phoebus amat vīsaeque[11] cupit cōnūbia Daphnēs,

quodque cupit, spērat, suaque illum ōrācula[12] fallunt.

Utque levēs stipulae dēmptīs[15] adolentur aristīs,[15]

ut facibus saepēs ārdent quās forte viātor

vel nimis admōvit vel iam sub lūce relīquit,

sīc deus in flammās abiit,[16] sīc pectore tōtō

ūritur et sterilem spērandō nūtrit amōrem.

Spectat inōrnātōs collō pendēre capillōs,

et "quid sī cōmantur?" ait; videt igne micantēs

sīderibus similēs oculōs, videt ōscula,[17] quae nōn

est vīdisse satis; laudat digitōsque manūsque

bracchiaque et nūdōs[18] mediā plūs parte lacertōs;[18]

sī qua latent meliōra putat.[19] Fugit ōcior aurā

illa levī neque ad haec revocantis verba resistit:

"Nympha, precor, Pēnēi, manē! Nōn īnsequor hostis;[20]

nympha, manē! Sīc agna lupum, sīc cerva leōnem,

sīc aquilam pennā fugiunt trepidante columbae,

hostēs quaeque suōs: amor est mihi causa sequendī.

Mē miserum![21] Nē[22] prōna cadās, indignave[23] laedī

crūra notent sentēs,[24] et sim tibi causa dolōris.

Aspera quā properās loca sunt. Moderātius, ōrō,

curre fugamque inhibē, moderātius īnsequar ipse.

[12] *rejecting* (object of **āversāta**)
[13] *grant me to enjoy*
[14] *forbids you to be what you desire*
480 (i.e., remain unmarried)
[15] *when the grain has been harvested*
[16] *went up in flames* (of love)
[17] *mouth,* which then came to mean *kiss*
[18] *arms more than half bare*
485 [19] *he believes her hidden features lovelier*
[20] *as an enemy* (nominative)
[21] *How wretched I am!*
[22] *for fear that*
[23] *that do not deserve it* (with **crūra**)
[24] *thorns*

490

495

500

505

510

---

[10] adverb
[11] with **Daphnēs,** genitive (Greek form): *at first sight*
[12] i.e., gifts of prophecy

Appendix

Important Dates, Events, and People

B.C.

753	Rome founded (traditional date)
753–509	Legendary kings
509	Republic established
494	Secession of the plebs
451–450	Laws of the Twelve Tables
390	Gauls capture Rome
280–275	War with Pyrrhus
264–241	First Punic War
254–184	Plautus, comic writer
218–201	Second Punic War
149–146	Third Punic War
146	Capture of Corinth
111–106	War with Jugurtha
106–48	Pompey, general
106–43	Cicero, orator, statesman
100–44	Caesar, general, statesman
99?–24?	Cornelius Nepos
96?–55	Lucretius, poet
90–88	Social War
87?–54?	Catullus, poet
86–34	Sallust, historian
70	Cicero against Verres
70–19	Vergil, poet
65–8	Horace, poet
63–A.D. 14	Augustus
62	Cicero defends Archias
60	First triumvirate (Caesar, Crassus, Pompey)
59–A.D. 17	Livy, historian
58–50	Caesar in Gaul
51	Cicero governor of Cilicia
49	Caesar crosses the Rubicon, precipitating the Civil War
48	Battle of Pharsalus, Pompey defeated
46	Caesar reforms calendar
44	Caesar assassinated, March 15; Cicero against Antony
43	Cicero's death
43–A.D. 17	Ovid, poet
31–A.D. 14	Reign of Augustus
15?–A.D. 50?	Phaedrus, fabulist
4?–A.D. 65	Seneca, philosopher
?–A.D. 66?	Petronius

A.D.

8	Ovid banished
14–37	Reign of Tiberius
35–96?	Quintilian, teacher
37–41	Reign of Caligula
40?–104	Martial, epigrammatist
41–54	Reign of Claudius
54–68	Reign of Nero
62–114?	Pliny the Younger
68–69	Reigns of Galba, Otho, Vitellius
69–79	Reign of Vespasian
79–81	Reign of Titus
81–96	Reign of Domitian
96–98	Reign of Nerva
98–117	Reign of Trajan
117–138	Reign of Hadrian
125?–?	Apuleius, philosopher
138–161	Reign of Antonius Pius
161–180	Reign of Marcus Aurelius

Basic Forms

Nouns

	First Declension		**Second Declension**	
	SINGULAR	PLURAL	SINGULAR	PLURAL
NOM.	via	viae	serv**us**	serv**ī**
GEN.	viae	vi**ārum**	serv**ī**	serv**ōrum**
DAT.	viae	vi**īs**	serv**ō**	serv**īs**
ACC.	vi**am**	vi**ās**	serv**um**	serv**ōs**
ABL.	vi**ā**	vi**īs**	serv**ō**	serv**īs**
VOC.			serv**e**	

Nouns in **–ius** often have **–ī** in the genitive and vocative singular: **fīlī, Cornēlī**. The accent does not change.[1]

Second Declension

	SING.	PLUR.	SING.	PLUR.	SING.	PLUR.
NOM.	ager	agr**ī**	puer	puer**ī**	sign**um**	sign**a**
GEN.	agr**ī**	agr**ōrum**	puer**ī**	puer**ōrum**	sign**ī**	sign**ōrum**
DAT.	agr**ō**	agr**īs**	puer**ō**	puer**īs**	sign**ō**	sign**īs**
ACC.	agr**um**	agr**ōs**	puer**um**	puer**ōs**	sign**um**	sign**a**
ABL.	agr**ō**	agr**īs**	puer**ō**	puer**īs**	sign**ō**	sign**īs**

Nouns in **–ium** often have **–ī** in the genitive singular: **cōnsilī**. The accent does not change.[1]

Third Declension

	SING.	PLUR.	SING.	PLUR.	SING.	PLUR.
NOM.	mīles	mīlit**ēs**	lēx	lēg**ēs**	corpus	corpor**a**
GEN.	mīlit**is**	mīlit**um**	lēg**is**	lēg**um**	corpor**is**	corpor**um**
DAT.	mīlit**ī**	mīlit**ibus**	lēg**ī**	lēg**ibus**	corpor**ī**	corpor**ibus**
ACC.	mīlit**em**	mīlit**ēs**	lēg**em**	lēg**ēs**	corpus	corpor**a**
ABL.	mīlit**e**	mīlit**ibus**	lēg**e**	lēg**ibus**	corpor**e**	corpor**ibus**

Third Declension I–Stems

	SINGULAR	PLURAL	SINGULAR	PLURAL
NOM.	cīv**is**	cīv**ēs**	mare	mar**ia**
GEN.	cīv**is**	cīv**ium**	maris	mar**ium**
DAT.	cīv**ī**	cīv**ibus**	mar**ī**	mar**ibus**
ACC.	cīv**em**	cīv**ēs** (**–īs**)	mare	mar**ia**
ABL.	cīv**e**	cīv**ibus**	mar**ī**	mar**ibus**

Turris and a few proper nouns have **–im** in the accusative singular. **Turris, ignis, nāvis, securis,** and a few proper nouns sometimes have **–ī** in the ablative singular.

The rules for determining whether or not a noun is an ī–stem are:

(a) The class of masculine and feminine ī–stem nouns are:

1. Nouns ending in **–is** and **–ēs** in the nominative with the same numbers of syllables in the genitive: **cīvis, nūbēs.**
2. Nouns of one syllable whose base ends in two consonants: **pars** (gen. **part–is**), **nox** (gen. **noct–is**).
3. Nouns whose nominative ends in **–ns** or **–rs: cliēns, adulēscēns.**

(b) Neuter nouns whose nominative ends in **–e, –al,** or **–ar: mare, animal, calcar.**

---

[1] From the time of Augustus, the form in **–iī** becomes common.

Fourth Declension

	SINGULAR	PLURAL		SINGULAR	PLURAL
NOM.	cāsus	cāsūs		cornū	cornua
GEN.	cāsūs	cāsuum		cornūs	cornuum
DAT.	cāsuī	cāsibus		cornū	cornibus
ACC.	cāsum	cāsūs		cornū	cornua
ABL.	cāsū	cāsibus		cornū	cornibus

Fifth Declension

	SINGULAR	PLURAL		SINGULAR	PLURAL
NOM.	diēs	diēs		rēs	rēs
GEN.	diēī	diērum		reī	rērum
DAT.	diēī	diēbus		reī	rēbus
ACC.	diem	diēs		rem	rēs
ABL.	diē	diēbus		rē	rēbus

Irregular Nouns

	SING.	PLUR.	SING.	SING.	PLUR.
NOM.	vīs	vīrēs	nēmō	domus	domūs
GEN.	———	vīrium	(nūllīus)	domūs (–ī)	domuum (–ōrum)
DAT.	———	vīribus	nēminī	domuī (–ō)	domibus
ACC.	vim	vīrēs (–īs)	nēminem	domum	domōs (–ūs)
ABL.	vī	vīribus	(nūllō)	domō (–ū)	domibus
LOC.				domī	

Adjectives and Adverbs

First and Second Declensions

	SINGULAR			PLURAL		
	M	F	N	M	F	N
NOM.	magnus	magna	magnum	magnī	magnae	magna
GEN.	magnī	magnae	magnī	magnōrum	magnārum	magnōrum
DAT.	magnō	magnae	magnō	magnīs	magnīs	magnīs
ACC.	magnum	magnam	magnum	magnōs	magnās	magna
ABL.	magnō	magnā	magnō	magnīs	magnīs	magnīs
VOC.	magne					

	SINGULAR			SINGULAR		
	M	F	N	M	F	N
NOM.	līber	lībera	līberum	noster	nostra	nostrum
GEN.	līberī	līberae	līberī	nostrī	nostrae	nostrī
DAT.	līberō	līberae	līberō	nostrō	nostrae	nostrō
ACC.	līberum	līberam	līberum	nostrum	nostram	nostrum
ABL.	līberō	līberā	līberō	nostrō	nostrā	nostrō

Plural, **līberī, līberae, lībera**, etc.   Plural, **nostrī, –ae, –a**, etc.

Third Declension

(a) THREE ENDINGS

	SINGULAR M	F	N	PLURAL M	F	N
NOM.	ācer	ācris	ācre	ācrēs	ācrēs	ācria
GEN.	ācris	ācris	ācris	ācrium	ācrium	ācrium
DAT.	ācrī	ācrī	ācrī	ācribus	ācribus	ācribus
ACC.	ācrem	ācrem	ācre	ācrēs (–īs)	ācrēs (–īs)	ācria
ABL.	ācrī	ācrī	ācrī	ācribus	ācribus	ācribus

(b) TWO ENDINGS

	SINGULAR M F	N	PLURAL M F	N
NOM.	fortis	forte	fortēs	fortia
GEN.	fortis	fortis	fortium	fortium
DAT.	fortī	fortī	fortibus	fortibus
ACC.	fortem	forte	fortēs (–īs)	fortia
ABL.	fortī	fortī	fortibus	fortibus

(c) ONE ENDING[1]

	SINGULAR M F	N	PLURAL M F	N
NOM.	pār	pār	parēs	paria
GEN.	paris	paris	parium	parium
DAT.	parī	parī	paribus	paribus
ACC.	parem	pār	parēs (–īs)	paria
ABL.	parī	parī	paribus	paribus

PRESENT PARTICIPLE

	SINGULAR M F	N	PLURAL M F	N
NOM.	portāns	portāns	portantēs	portantia
GEN.	portantis	portantis	portantium	portanium
DAT.	portantī	portantī	portantibus	portantibus
ACC.	portantem	portāns	portantēs (–īs)	portantia
ABL.	portante (–ī)	portante (–ī)	portantibus	portantibus

The ablative singular regularly ends in **–e**, but **–ī** is used wherever the participle is used simply as an adjective.

IRREGULAR ADJECTIVES AND NUMERALS

	M	F	N	M F	N
NOM.	ūnus	ūna	ūnum	trēs	tria
GEN.	ūnīus	ūnīus	ūnīus	trium	trium
DAT.	ūnī	ūnī	ūnī	tribus	tribus
ACC.	ūnum	ūnam	ūnum	trēs	tria
ABL.	ūnō	ūnā	ūnō	tribus	tribus

	M	F	N	M F N (*adj.*)	N (*noun*)
NOM.	duo	duae	duo	mīlle	mīlia
GEN.	duōrum	duārum	duōrum	mīlle	mīlium
DAT.	duōbus	duābus	duōbus	mīlle	mīlibus
ACC.	duōs	duās	duo	mīlle	mīlia
ABL.	duōbus	duābus	duōbus	mīlle	mīlibus

---

[1] **Vetus** has **vetere** in the ablative singular and **veterum** in the genitive plural.

Declined like **ūnus** are **alius, alter, ūllus, nūllus, sōlus, tōtus, uter, neuter, uterque;** the plurals are regular. The nominative and accusative singular neuter of **alius** is **aliud;** for the genitive singular, **alterius** is generally used. **Ambō** is declined like **duo.**

Comparison of Regular Adjectives and Adverbs

POSITIVE		COMPARATIVE		SUPERLATIVE	
ADJ.	ADV.	ADJ.	ADV.	ADJ.	ADV.
altus	altē	altior	altius	altissimus	altissimē
fortis	fortiter	fortior	fortius	fortissimus	fortissimē
līber	līberē	līberior	līberius	līberrimus	līberrimē
ācer	ācriter	ācrior	ācrius	ācerrimus	ācerrimē
facilis	facile	facilior	facilius	facillimus	facillimē

Like **facilis** are **difficilis, similis, dissimilis, gracilis, humilis,** but their adverbs (not used in this book) vary in the positive degree. Adjectives in **–er** are like **līber** or **ācer.**

Comparison of Irregular Adjectives

POSITIVE	COMPARATIVE	SUPERLATIVE
bonus	melior	optimus
malus	peior	pessimus
magnus	maior	maximus
parvus	minor	minimus
multus	——, plūs	plūrimus
īnferus	īnferior	īnfimus *or* īmus
superus	superior	suprēmus *or* summus
——	prior	prīmus
——	propior	proximus
——	ulterior	ultimus

Comparison of Irregular Adverbs

bene	melius	optimē
male	peius	pessimē
(magnopere)	magis	maximē
——	minus	minimē
multum	plūs	plūrimum
diū	diūtius	diūtissimē
prope	propius	proximē

Declension of Comparatives

	SINGULAR		PLURAL		SINGULAR	PLURAL	
	M F	N	M F	N	N	M F	N
NOM.	altior	altius	altiōres	altiōra	plūs[1]	plūrēs	plūra
GEN.	altiōris	altiōris	altiōrum	altiōrum	plūris	plūrium	plūrium
DAT.	altiōrī	altiōrī	altiōribus	altiōribus	——	plūribus	plūribus
ACC.	altiōrem	altius	altiōrēs	altiōra	plūs	plūrēs	plūra
ABL.	altiōre	altiōre	altiōribus	altiōribus	plūre	plūribus	plūribus

[1] Masculine and feminine lacking in the singular.

Numerals

	ROMAN	CARDINAL	ORDINAL
1.	I	ūnus, –a, –um	prīmus, –a, –um
2.	II	duo, duae, duo	secundus (alter)
3.	III	trēs, tria	tertius
4.	IIII *or* IV	quattuor	quārtus
5.	V	quīnque	quīntus
6.	VI	sex	sextus
7.	VII	septem	septimus
8.	VIII	octō	octāvus
9.	VIIII *or* IX	novem	nōnus
10.	X	decem	decimus
11.	XI	ūndecim	ūndecimus
12.	XII	duodecim	duodecimus
13.	XIII	tredecim	tertius decimus
14.	XIIII *or* XIV	quattuordecim	quārtus decimus
15.	XV	quīndecim	quīntus decimus
16.	XVI	sēdecim	sextus decimus
17.	XVII	septendecim	septimus decimus
18.	XVIII	duodēvīgintī	duodēvīcēsimus[1]
19.	XVIIII *or* XIX	ūndēvīgintī	ūndēvīcēsimus
20.	XX	vīgintī	vīcēsimus
21.	XXI	vīgintī ūnus *or* ūnus et vīgintī	vīcēsimus prīmus *or* ūnus et vīcēsimus
30.	XXX	trīgintā	trīcēsimus
40.	XXXX *or* XL	quadrāgintā	quadrāgēsimus
50.	L	quīnquāgintā	quīnquāgēsimus
60.	LX	sexāgintā	sexāgēsimus
70.	LXX	septuāgintā	septuāgēsimus
80.	LXXX	octōgintā	octōgēsimus
90.	LXXXX *or* XC	nōnāgintā	nōnāgēsimus
100.	C	centum	centēsimus
101.	CI	centum (et) ūnus	centēsimus (et) prīmus
200.	CC	ducentī, –ae, –a	ducentēsimus
300.	CCC	trecentī, –ae, –a	trecentēsimus
400.	CCCC	quadringentī, –ae, –a	quadringentēsimus
500.	D	quīngentī, –ae, –a	quīngentēsimus
600.	DC	sescentī, –ae, –a	sescentēsimus
700.	DCC	septingentī, –ae, –a	septingentēsimus
800.	DCCC	octingentī, –ae, –a	octingentēsimus
900.	DCCCC	nōngentī, –ae, –a	nōngentēsimus
1000.	M	mīlle	mīllēsimus
2000.	MM	duo mīlia	bis mīllēsimus

---

[1] The forms in **–ēsimus** are sometimes spelled **–ēnsimus**.

	SINGULAR		SINGULAR	
	M F	N	M F	N
NOM.	quisquam	quicquam (quidquam)	quisque	quidque
GEN.	cuiusquam	cuiusquam	cuiusque	cuiusque
DAT.	cuiquam	cuiquam	cuique	cuique
ACC.	quemquam	quicquam (quidquam)	quemque	quidque
ABL.	quōquam	quōquam	quōque	quōque
	(The plural is lacking.)		(The plural is rare.)	

The adjective form of **quisque** is **quisque, quaeque, quodque,** etc.

The indefinite pronoun **quis** (declined like the interrogative) and adjective **quī** (declined like the relative, but in the nominative feminime singular and the nominative and accusative neuter plural **qua** may be used for **quae**) are used chiefly after **sī, nisi, num,** and **nē.**

Verbs

First Conjugation

PRINCIPAL PARTS: **portō, portāre, portāvī, portātus**

	ACTIVE		PASSIVE	

INDICATIVE

PRESENT	*I carry,* etc.		*I am carried,* etc.	
	portō	portāmus	portor	portāmur
	portās	portātis	portāris (–re)	portāminī
	portat	portant	portātur	portantur

IMPERFECT	*I was carrying,* etc.		*I was (being) carried,* etc.	
	portābam	portābāmus	portābar	portābāmur
	portābās	portābātis	portābāris (–re)	portābāminī
	portābat	portābant	portābātur	portābantur

FUTURE	*I shall carry,* etc.		*I shall be carried,* etc.	
	portābō	portābimus	portābor	portābimur
	portābis	portābitis	portāberis (–re)	portābiminī
	portābit	portābunt	portābitur	portabuntur

PERFECT	*I carried, have carried,* etc.		*I was carried, have been carried,* etc.	
	portāvī	portāvimus	portātus { sum	portātī { sumus
	portāvistī	portāvistis	(–a, –um) { es	(–ae, –a) { estis
	portāvit	portāvērunt (–ēre)	{ est	{ sunt

PLUPERFECT	*I had carried,* etc.		*I had been carried,* etc.	
	portāveram	portāverāmus	portātus { eram	portātī { erāmus
	portāverās	portāverātis	(–a, –um) { erās	(–ae, –a) { erātis
	portāverat	portāverant	{ erat	{ erant

	ACTIVE		PASSIVE	

	ACTIVE	PASSIVE
FUTURE PERFECT	*I shall have carried*, etc.	*I shall have been carried*, etc.

	ACTIVE		PASSIVE	
FUTURE PERFECT	portāverō	portāverimus	portātus (–a, –um) { erō / eris / erit	portātī (–ae, –a) { erimus / eritis / erunt
	portāveris	portāveritis		
	portāverit	portāverint		

SUBJUNCTIVE

	ACTIVE		PASSIVE	
PRESENT	portem	portēmus	porter	portēmur
	portēs	portētis	portēris (–re)	portēminī
	portet	portent	portētur	portentur
IMPERFECT	portārem	portārēmus	portārer	portārēmur
	portārēs	portārētis	portārēris (–re)	portārēminī
	portāret	portārent	portārētur	portārentur
PERFECT	portāverim	portāverīmus	portātus (–a, –um) { sim / sīs / sit	portātī (–ae, –a) { sīmus / sītis / sint
	portāverīs	portāverītis		
	portāverit	portāverint		
PLUPERFECT	portāvissem	portāvissēmus	portātus (–a, –um) { essem / essēs / esset	portātī (–ae, –a) { essēmus / essētis / essent
	portāvissēs	portāvissētis		
	portāvisset	portāvissent		

PRESENT IMPERATIVE

2D SING.	portā, *carry*	portāre, *be carried*
2D PLUR.	portāte, *carry*	portāminī, *be carried*

FUTURE IMPERATIVE

2D SING.	portātō, *carry*	portātor, *be carried*
3D SING.	portātō, *he shall carry*	portātor, *he shall be carried*
2D PLUR.	portātōte, *carry*	
3D PLUR.	portantō, *they shall carry*	portantor, *they shall be carried*

INFINITIVE

PRESENT	portāre, *to carry*	portārī, *to be carried*
PERFECT	portāvisse, *to have carried*	portātus esse, *to have been carried*
FUTURE	portātūrus esse, *to be going to carry*	(portātum īrī, *to be going to be carried*)

PARTICIPLE

PRESENT	portāns, *carrying*	
PERFECT		portātus *(having been) carried*
FUTURE	portātūrus, *going to carry*	portandus, *(necessary) to be carried*

GERUND

GEN. portandī, *of carrying*, etc.   DAT. portandō   ACC. portandum   ABL. portandō

SUPINE

ACC. portātum, *in order to carry*   ABL. portātū, *in carrying*

	2d Conj.	3d Conj.	4th Conj.	3d Conj. (–iō)
		FUTURE IMPERATIVE ACTIVE		
2D SING.	docētō	pōnitō	mūnītō	capitō
3D SING.	docētō	pōnitō	mūnītō	capitō
2D PLUR.	docētōte	pōnitōte	mūnītōte	capitōte
3D PLUR.	docentō	pōnuntō	mūniuntō	capiuntō
		INFINITIVE ACTIVE		
PRESENT	docēre	pōnere	mūnīre	capere
PERFECT	docuisse	posuisse	mūnīvisse	cēpisse
FUTURE	doctūrus esse	positūrus esse	mūnītūrus esse	captūrus esse
		PARTICIPLE ACTIVE		
PRESENT	docēns	pōnēns	mūniēns	capiēns
FUTURE	doctūrus	positūrus	mūnītūrus	captūrus
		GERUND		
GEN.	docendī	pōnendī	mūniendī	capiendī
DAT.	docendō	pōnendō	mūniendō	capiendō
ACC.	docendum	pōnendum	mūniendum	capiendum
ABL.	docendō	pōnendō	mūniendō	capiendō
		SUPINE		
ACC.	doctum	positum	mūnītum	captum
ABL.	doctū	positū	mūnītū	captū
		INDICATIVE PASSIVE		
PRESENT	doceor	pōnor	mūnior	capior
	docēris (–re)	pōneris (–re)	mūnīris (–re)	caperis (–re)
	docētur	pōnitur	mūnītur	capitur
	docēmur	pōnimur	mūnīmur	capimur
	docēminī	pōniminī	mūnīminī	capiminī
	docentur	pōnuntur	mūniuntur	capiuntur
IMPERFECT	docēbar	pōnēbar	mūniēbar	capiēbar
	docēbāris (–re)	pōnēbāris (–re)	mūniēbāris (–re)	capiēbāris (–re)
	docēbātur	pōnēbātur	mūniēbātur	capiēbātur
	docēbāmur	pōnēbāmur	mūniēbāmur	capiēbāmur
	docēbāminī	pōnēbāminī	mūniēbāminī	capiēbāminī
	docēbantur	pōnēbantur	mūniēbantur	capiēbantur

		2d Conj.	3d Conj.	4th Conj.	3d Conj. (–iō)
	FUTURE	docēbor	pōnar	mūniar	capiar
PR		docēberis (–re)	pōnēris (–re)	mūniēris (–re)	capiēris (–re)
		docēbitur	pōnētur	mūniētur	capiētur
IM		docēbimur	pōnēmur	mūniēmur	capiēmur
		docēbiminī	pōnēminī	mūniēminī	capiēminī
FU		docēbuntur	pōnentur	mūnientur	capientur
PE	PERFECT	doctus sum	positus sum	mūnītus sum	captus sum
		doctus es	positus es	mūnītus es	captus es
PL		doctus est	positus est	mūnītus est	captus est
		doctī sumus	positī sumus	mūnītī sumus	captī sumus
FU		doctī estis	positī estis	mūnītī estis	captī estis
		doctī sunt	positī sunt	mūnītī sunt	captī sunt
	PLUPERFECT	doctus eram	positus eram	mūnītus eram	captus eram
PR		doctus erās	positus erās	mūnītus erās	captus erās
		doctus erat	positus erat	mūnītus erat	captus erat
IM		doctī erāmus	positī erāmus	mūnītī erāmus	captī erāmus
PE		doctī erātis	positī erātis	mūnitī erātis	captī erātis
		doctī erant	positī erant	mūnītī erant	captī erant
PL	FUTURE PERFECT	doctus erō	positus erō	mūnītus erō	captus erō
		doctus eris	positus eris	mūnītus eris	captus eris
		doctus erit	positus erit	mūnītus erit	captus erit
PF		doctī erimus	positī erimus	mūnītī erimus	captī erimus
FU		doctī eritis	positī eritis	mūnītī eritis	captī eritis
		doctī erunt	positī erunt	mūnītī erunt	captī erunt

SUBJUNCTIVE PASSIVE

		2d Conj.	3d Conj.	4th Conj.	3d Conj. (–iō)
PF	PRESENT	docear	pōnar	mūniar	capiar
PE		doceāris (–re)	pōnāris (–re)	mūniāris (–re)	capiāris (–re)
		doceātur	pōnātur	mūniātur	capiātur
FU		doceāmur	pōnāmur	mūniāmur	capiāmur
		doceāminī	pōnāminī	mūniāminī	capiāminī
		doceantur	pōnantur	mūniantur	capiantur
PF	IMPERFECT	docērer	pōnerer	mūnīrer	caperer
		docērēris (–re)	pōnerēris (–re)	mūnīrēris (–re)	caperēris (–re)
PF		docērētur	pōnerētur	mūnīrētur	caperētur
FU		docērēmur	pōnerēmur	mūnīrēmur	caperēmur
FU		docērēminī	pōnerēminī	mūnīrēminī	caperēminī
		docērentur	pōnerentur	mūnīrentur	caperentur

	1st Conj.	2d Conj.	3d Conj.	4th Conj.	3d Conj. (–iō)
			GERUND		
GEN.	arbitra**ndī**, etc.	vere**ndī**, etc.	loque**ndī**, etc.	ori**endī**, etc.	gradi**endī**, etc.
			SUPINE		
ACC.	arbitrā**tum**	veri**tum**	locū**tum**	or**tum**	gress**um**
ABL.	arbitrā**tū**	veri**tū**	locū**tū**	or**tū**	gress**ū**

A few verbs (called "semideponent") are active in the present system and deponent in the perfect system, as **audeō, audēre, ausus**.

Irregular Verbs
PRINCIPAL PARTS: **sum, esse, fuī, futūrus**

<table>
<tr><td colspan="3">INDICATIVE</td><td colspan="3">SUBJUNCTIVE</td></tr>
<tr><td>PRESENT</td><td>su**m**, I am</td><td>su**mus**, we are</td><td>PRESENT</td><td>si**m**</td><td>sī**mus**</td></tr>
<tr><td></td><td>e**s**, you are</td><td>es**tis**, you are</td><td></td><td>sī**s**</td><td>sī**tis**</td></tr>
<tr><td></td><td>es**t**, he is</td><td>su**nt**, they are</td><td></td><td>si**t**</td><td>si**nt**</td></tr>
<tr><td>IMPERFECT</td><td colspan="2">I was, etc.</td><td></td><td></td><td></td></tr>
<tr><td></td><td>era**m**</td><td>erā**mus**</td><td>IMPERFECT</td><td>esse**m**
(fore**m**)</td><td>essē**mus**</td></tr>
<tr><td></td><td>erā**s**</td><td>erā**tis**</td><td></td><td>essē**s**
(forē**s**)</td><td>essē**tis**</td></tr>
<tr><td></td><td>era**t**</td><td>era**nt**</td><td></td><td>esse**t**
(fore**t**)</td><td>esse**nt**
(fore**nt**)</td></tr>
<tr><td>FUTURE</td><td colspan="2">I shall be, etc.</td><td></td><td></td><td></td></tr>
<tr><td></td><td>er**ō**</td><td>er**imus**</td><td></td><td></td><td></td></tr>
<tr><td></td><td>er**is**</td><td>er**itis**</td><td></td><td></td><td></td></tr>
<tr><td></td><td>er**it**</td><td>er**unt**</td><td></td><td></td><td></td></tr>
<tr><td>PERFECT</td><td colspan="2">I was, etc.</td><td></td><td></td><td></td></tr>
<tr><td></td><td>fu**ī**</td><td>fu**imus**</td><td>PERFECT</td><td>fue**rim**</td><td>fue**rīmus**</td></tr>
<tr><td></td><td>fu**istī**</td><td>fu**istis**</td><td></td><td>fue**rīs**</td><td>fue**rītis**</td></tr>
<tr><td></td><td>fu**it**</td><td>fu**ērunt (–ēre)**</td><td></td><td>fue**rit**</td><td>fue**rint**</td></tr>
<tr><td>PLUPERFECT</td><td colspan="2">I had been, etc.</td><td></td><td></td><td></td></tr>
<tr><td></td><td>fue**ram**</td><td>fue**rāmus**</td><td>PLUPERFECT</td><td>fuisse**m**</td><td>fuissē**mus**</td></tr>
<tr><td></td><td>fue**rās**</td><td>fue**rātis**</td><td></td><td>fuissē**s**</td><td>fuissē**tis**</td></tr>
<tr><td></td><td>fue**rat**</td><td>fue**rant**</td><td></td><td>fuisse**t**</td><td>fuisse**nt**</td></tr>
<tr><td>FUTURE PERFECT</td><td colspan="2">I shall have been, etc.</td><td></td><td></td><td></td></tr>
<tr><td></td><td>fue**rō**</td><td>fue**rimus**</td><td></td><td></td><td></td></tr>
<tr><td></td><td>fue**ris**</td><td>fue**ritis**</td><td></td><td></td><td></td></tr>
<tr><td></td><td>fue**rit**</td><td>fue**rint**</td><td></td><td></td><td></td></tr>
</table>

	INFINITIVE		PRESENT IMPERATIVE			
PRESENT	esse, *to be*		2D SING.	es, *be*	2D PLUR.	este, *be*
PERFECT	fuisse, *to have been*					
FUTURE	futūrus esse (fore), *to be going to be*		FUTURE IMPERATIVE			
			2D SING.	estō	2D PLUR.	estōte
			3D SING.	estō	3D PLUR.	suntō

	PARTICIPLE
FUTURE	futūrus, *going to be*

PRINCIPAL PARTS: **possum, posse, potuī, ——**

	INDICATIVE			SUBJUNCTIVE	
PRESENT	*I am able, I can,* etc.				
	possum	possumus	PRESENT	possim	possīmus
	potes	potestis		possīs	possītis
	potest	possunt		possit	possint
IMPERFECT	*I was able, I could,* etc.				
	poteram, etc.		IMPERFECT	possem, etc.	
FUTURE	*I shall be able,* etc.				
	poterō, etc.				
PERFECT	*I was able, I could,* etc.				
	potuī, etc.		PERFECT	potuerim, etc.	
PLUPERFECT	*I had been able,* etc.				
	potueram, etc.		PLUPERFECT	potuissem, etc.	
FUTURE PERFECT	*I shall have been able,* etc.				
	potuerō, etc.				

	INFINITIVE		PARTICIPLE	
PRESENT	posse, *to be able*	PRESENT	potēns (*adj.*), *powerful*	
PERFECT	potuisse, *to have been able*			

PRINCIPAL PARTS: **ferō, ferre, tulī, lātus**

	ACTIVE		PASSIVE	
		INDICATIVE		
PRESENT	**ferō**	**ferimus**	**feror**	**ferimur**
	fers	**fertis**	**ferris (–re)**	**feriminī**
	fert	**ferunt**	**fertur**	**feruntur**
IMPERFECT	**ferēbam**, etc.		**ferēbar**, etc.	
FUTURE	**feram, ferēs**, etc.		**ferar, ferēris**, etc.	
PERFECT	**tulī**, etc.		**lātus sum**, etc.	
PLUPERFECT	**tuleram**, etc.		**lātus eram**, etc.	
FUTURE PERFECT	**tulerō**, etc.		**lātus erō**, etc.	

ACTIVE		PASSIVE	
	SUBJUNCTIVE		
PRESENT	**feram, ferās,** etc.	**ferar, ferāris,** etc.	
IMPERFECT	**ferrem,** etc.	**ferrer,** etc.	
PERFECT	**tulerim,** etc.	**lātus sim,** etc.	
PLUPERFECT	**tulissem,** etc.	**lātus essem,** etc.	

PRESENT IMPERATIVE

2D PERS.	**fer**	**ferte**	**ferre**	**feriminī**

FUTURE IMPERATIVE

2D PERS.	**fertō**	**fertōte**	**fertor**	
3D PERS.	**fertō**	**feruntō**	**fertor**	**feruntor**

INFINITIVE

PRESENT	**ferre**	**ferrī**
PERFECT	**tulisse**	**lātus esse**
FUTURE	**lātūrus esse**	**(lātum īrī)**

PARTICIPLE

PRESENT	**ferēns**	
PERFECT		**lātus**
FUTURE	**lātūrus**	**ferendus**

GERUND

GEN. **ferendī**	DAT. **ferendō**	ACC. **ferendum**	ABL. **ferendō**

SUPINE

ACC. **lātum**	ABL. **lātū**

PRINCIPAL PARTS: **eō, īre, iī, itūrus**

	INDICATIVE		SUBJUNCTIVE	INFINITIVE
PRESENT	**eō**	**īmus**	**eam,** etc.	**īre**
	īs	**ītis**		
	it	**eunt**		
IMPERFECT	**ībam,** etc.		**īrem,** etc.	
FUTURE	**ībō**	**ībimus**		**itūrus esse**
	ībis	**ībitis**		
	ībit	**ībunt**		
PERFECT	**iī**	**iimus**	**ierim,** etc.	**īsse**
	īstī	**īstis**		
	iit	**iērunt (–ēre)**		
PLUPERFECT	**ieram,** etc.		**īssem,** etc.	
FUTURE PERFECT	**ierō,** etc.			

	PARTICIPLE		IMPERATIVE	
PRESENT	iēns, GEN. euntis		ī	īte
FUTURE	itūrus (PASSIVE eundus)		ītō	ītōte
			ītō	euntō

	GERUND	SUPINE
GEN.	eundī	
DAT.	eundō	
ACC.	eundum	itum
ABL.	eundō	itū

PRINCIPAL PARTS

volō	nōlō	mālō
velle	nōlle	mālle
voluī	nōluī	māluī

INDICATIVE

PRESENT	volō	volumus	nōlō	nōlumus	mālō	mālumus
	vīs	vultis	nōn vīs	nōn vultis	māvīs	māvultis
	vult	volunt	nōn vult	nōlunt	māvult	mālunt
IMPERFECT	volēbam, etc.		nōlēbam, etc.		mālēbam, etc.	
FUTURE	volam, volēs, etc.		nōlam, nōlēs, etc.		mālam, mālēs, etc.	
PERFECT	voluī, etc.		nōluī, etc.		māluī, etc.	
PLUPERFECT	volueram, etc.		nōlueram, etc.		mālueram, etc.	
FUTURE PERFECT	voluerō, etc.		nōluerō, etc.		māluerō, etc.	

SUBJUNCTIVE

PRESENT	velim	velīmus	nōlim	nōlīmus	mālim	mālīmus
	velīs	velītis	nōlīs	nōlītis	mālīs	mālītis
	velit	velint	nōlit	nōlint	mālit	mālint
IMPERFECT	vellem, etc.		nōllem, etc.		māllem, etc.	
PERFECT	voluerim, etc.		nōluerim, etc.		māluerim, etc.	
PLUPERFECT	voluissem, etc.		nōluissem, etc.		māluissem, etc.	

PRESENT AND FUTURE IMPERATIVE

2D PERS.	——	——	nōlī	nōlīte	——	——
2D PERS.	——	——	nōlītō	nōlītōte	——	——

INFINITIVE

PRESENT	velle	nōlle	mālle
PERFECT	voluisse	nōluisse	māluisse

PRESENT	**volēns**	**nōlēns**	——

PRINCIPAL PARTS: **fīō, fierī, (factus)**

	INDICATIVE		SUBJUNCTIVE	IMPERATIVE		INFINITIVE
PRESENT	**fīō**	**fīmus**	**fīam,** etc.			**fierī**
	fīs	**fītīs**		**fī**	**fīte**	
	fit	**fīunt**				
IMPERFECT	**fīēbam,** etc.		**fierem,** etc.			
FUTURE	**fīam, fīēs,** etc.					

Defective Verbs

Coepī is used only in the perfect system. For the present system **incipiō** is used. With a passive infinitive the passive of **coepī** is used: **Lapidēs iacī coeptī sunt,** *Stones began to be thrown.* **Meminī** and **ōdī** likewise are used only in the perfect system, but with present meaning. The former has an imperative **mementō, mementōte.**

The only forms of **inquam** in common use are in the present indicative: **inquam, inquis, inquit, inquiunt.** Similarly **aiō, ais, ait, aiunt,** and the imperfect: **aiēbam,** etc.

Impersonal verbs are used only in the third personal singular and the infinitive: **decet, libet, licet, miseret, oportet, piget, pudet, taedet.**

Contracted Forms

Verbs having perfect stems ending in **–āv–** or **–ēv–** are sometimes contracted by dropping **–ve–** before **–r–** and **–vi–** before **–s–: amārunt, cōnsuēsse.** Verbs having perfect stems ending in **–īv–** drop **–vi–** before **–s–** but only **–v–** before **–r–: audīsset, audierat.**

Syntax[1]

Questions

Information questions are introduced by interrogative pronouns or adverbs (**quis, ubi,** etc.) Other questions are introduced as follows:

1. In questions the answer to which might be either *yes* or *no* the particle **–ne** is attached to the first word.

   Frāterne venit?   *Is your brother coming?*

2. In questions that expect a *yes* answer, the introductory word is **nōnne** (i.e., **nōn + ne;** cf. English).

   Nōnne frāter venit?   *Isn't your brother coming?*
   Your brother is coming, isn't he?

3. In questions that expect a *no* answer the introductory word is **num.**

   Num frāter venit?   *Your brother is not coming, is he?*

   Double questions are introduced by **utrum, –ne,** or nothing at all and are connected by **an.**

   Frāterne bonus an malus est?   *Is your brother good or bad?*

Reflexive Pronouns and Adjectives

The personal pronouns of the first and second persons and the possessive adjectives derived from them may be used reflexively. It is only in the third person that the Latin uses a distinct reflexive pronoun, **suī** (adjective **suus**).

   a. Both **suī** and **suus** commonly refer to the subject of the clause in which they stand (direct reflexive).

   Sē suaque omnia dēdidērunt.   *They surrendered themselves and all their possessions.*

   b. Sometimes **suī** or **suus,** occurring in a subordinate clause, refers not to the subject of its own clause, but to the subject of the main verb (indirect reflexive).

   Petēbant utī Caesar sibi potestātem faceret.   *They begged that Caesar give them a chance.*

Agreement

1. *Adjectives.* Adjectives and participles agree in number, gender, and case with the nouns they modify. When an adjective modifies several nouns of different numbers or genders, it either agrees with the last or is put in the neuter plural.

2. *Adjectives as Nouns (substantives).* Sometimes adjectives are used as nouns: **nostrī,** *our (men);* **malum,** *evil.*

---

[1] In this summary only those constructions that are relatively more important and that recur repeatedly in the text or are referred to in the book are included.

3. *Verbs*. Verbs agree in person and number with their subjects. When two subjects are connected by **aut, aut... aut, neque... neque,** the verb agrees with the nearer subject.

4. *Relative Pronoun*. The relative pronoun agrees in gender and number with its antecedent but its case depends upon its use in its own clause.

   a. The antecedent of the relative pronoun is sometimes omitted.

   b. Sometimes the antecedent is represented by an entire clause, in which case the pronoun is best translated *a thing which.*

   c. In Latin a relative pronoun is often used at the beginning of a sentence to refer to the entire thought of the preceding sentence. The English idiom calls for a demonstrative or personal pronoun.

   quā dē cāusā　　　　　　*for this reason*

5. *Appositives*. Appositives agree in case. It is often best to supply *as* in translating the appositive.

   eōdem homine magistrō ūtī　　*to use the same man as teacher*

Noun Syntax
Nominative

1. *Subject*. The subject of a finite verb is in the nominative case.
2. *Predicate*.

   a. A noun or adjective used in the predicate with a linking verb (*is, are, seem,* etc.) is in the nominative.

   Īnsula est magna.　　　　*The island is large.*
   Sicilia est īnsula.　　　　*Sicily is an island.*

   b. Predicate nouns and adjectives are used not only with **sum** but also with **fīō** and the passive voice of verbs meaning *call, choose, appoint, elect,* and the like.

   Caesar dux factus est.　　*Caesar was made leader.*
   Cicerō Pater Patriae　　　*Cicero was called the Father*
   appellātus est.　　　　　*of his Country.*

Genitive

1. *Of Possession*. Possession is expressed by the genitive.

   viae īnsulae　　　　　*the roads of the island*

2. *Predicate*. The possessive genitive may be used in the predicate with **sum** (or **faciō**), often translated *it is the part of, the duty of,* etc.

   Sapientiae est vidēre.　　*It is the part of wisdom to see.*

3. *Of Description*. The genitive, if modified by an adjective, may be used to describe a person or thing.

   virī magnae virtūtis　　　*men of great courage*
   spatium decem pedum　　　*a space of ten feet*

4. *Of the Whole.* The genitive of the whole (also called partitive genitive) represents the whole to which the part belongs.

hōrum omnium fortissimī	*the bravest of all these*
nihil praesidī	*no guard*

    a. This is similar to the English idiom except when the genitive is used with such words as **nihil, satis, quid.**

    b. Instead of the genitive of the whole, the ablative with **ex** or **dē** is regularly used with cardinal numerals (except **mīlia**) and **quīdam,** often also with other words, such as **paucī** and **complūrēs.**

quīnque ex nostrīs	*five of our men*
quīdam ex mīlitibus	*certain of the soldiers*

5. *Subjective.* The subjective genitive expresses the subject of the verbal idea of the noun on which it depends. If this noun is turned into a verb, the genitive becomes subject.

timor populī	*the fear of the people*
	(i.e., *the people feared*)

6. *Objective.* The objective genitive expresses the object of the verbal idea of the noun or adjective on which it depends. If this noun or adjective is turned into a verb, the genitive becomes object.

amantissimōs reī pūblicae virōs	*patriotic men* (i.e., *they loved the state*)

7. *Of the Charge and Penalty.* With verbs of *accusing, condemning,* or *acquitting* the genitive is used to indicate either the charge or the penalty.

capitis damnātum	*condemned to death* (lit., *of the head*)
Accūsō tē inertiae.	*I accuse you of inaction.*

8. *Of Indefinite Value.* The genitive is used with **sum** and other verbs to express indefinite value.

Est tantī.	*It is worth that much.*
parvī esse dūcenda	*to be considered of little value*

9. *With Special Verbs.* With **oblīvīscor** (*forget*), **meminī, reminīscor** (*remember*), **misereor** (*pity*), and occasionally **potior** (*get possession of*), the genitive is used.

Oblīvīscere caedis atque incendiōrum.	*Forget bloodshed and burning.*

10. *With Adjectives.* The genitive is used with certain adjectives. In many cases the English idiom is the same; in others, it is not.

bellandī cupidus	*desirous of waging war*
reī mīlitāris perītus	*skilled in warfare*
tuī similis	*like you*

NOTĀ·BENE

Sometimes the accusative is used with **meminī** and **reminīscor**; regularly so with **recordor** (*remember*).

11. *Of Plenty and Want.* With certain adjectives and verbs having the idea of plenty or want the genitive is regularly used: **plēnus** and **refertus**, *full of;* **inānis, inops,** and **expers,** *empty, without, devoid of.*

Dative

1. *Of Indirect Object.* The indirect object of a verb is in the dative. It is used with verbs of *giving, reporting, telling,* etc.

   Nautae pecūniam dōnō.   *I give money to the sailor.*

2. *Of Purpose.* The dative is sometimes used to express purpose.

   Locum castrīs dēlēgit.   *He chose a place for a camp.*

3. *Of Reference.* The dative of reference shows the person concerned or referred to.

   sī mihi dignī esse vultis   *if you wish to be worthy in my sight* (literally, *for me*)

   Haec castra erunt praesidiō oppidō.   *This camp will be (for) a protection to the town.*

4. *Of Separation.* The dative of separation (really reference) is usually confined to persons and occurs chiefly with verbs compounded with **ab, dē,** and **ex.**

   scūtō ūnī mīlitī dētrāctō   *having seized a shield from a soldier*

5. *With Adjectives.* The dative is used with certain adjectives, as **amīcus, idōneus, pār, proximus, similis, ūtilis,** and their opposites. In many cases the English idiom is the same.

   Hic liber est similis illī.   *This book is similar to that.*

6. *With Special Verbs.* The dative is used with a few intransitive verbs, such as **cōnfīdō, crēdō, dēsum, faveō, ignōscō, imperō, invideō, minitor, noceō, parcō, pāreō, persuādeō, placeō, praestō, resistō, serviō,** and **studeō.**

   Tibi pāret sed mihi resistit.   *He obeys you but resists me.*

   a. Some of these verbs become impersonal in the passive and the dative is retained. The perfect passive participle of such verbs is used only in the neuter.

   Eī persuāsum est.   *He was persuaded.*

   b. A neuter pronoun or adjective or an **ut** clause may be used as a direct object with **imperō** and **persuādeō.**

   Hoc mihi persuāsit.   *He persuaded me of this.*

7. *With Compounds.* The dative is often used with certain compound verbs, especially when the noun goes closely with the prefix of the verb. No general rule can be given. Sometimes both an accusative and a dative are used when the main part of the verb is transitive.

Gallīs bellum intulit.   *He made war against the Gauls.*

8. *Possession.* The possessor may be expressed by the dative with **sum.**

Liber mihi est.   *I have a book.*

9. *Agent.* The dative of agent is used with the gerundive (future passive participle) to indicate the person upon whom the obligation rests. Occasionally it is used with the perfect participle.

Hoc opus vōbīs faciendum est.   *This work is to be done by you, i.e., This work must be done by you.*

Accusative

1. *Of Direct Object.* The direct object of a transitive verb is in the accusative.

Viam parāmus.   *We are preparing a way.*

2. *Of Extent of Space* and *Duration of Time.* Extent of time or space is expressed by the accusative without a preposition.

Duōs annōs remānsit.   *He remained two years.*
Flūmen decem pedēs altum est.   *The river is ten feet deep.*

3. *Of Place to Which.* The accusative with **ad** (*to*) or **in** (*into*) expresses *place to which.* These prepositions, however, are omitted before **domum** and names of towns and cities.

Lēgātōs ad eum mittunt.   *They send envoys to him.*
Rōmam eunt.   *They go to Rome.*

4. *Subject of Infinitive.* The subject of an infinitive is in the accusative.

Puerōs esse bonōs volumus.   *We want the boys to be good.*

5. *Two Accusatives.* With **trādūcō** and **trānsportō** two accusatives are used. In the passive the word closely connected with the prefix remains to the accusative.

Cōpiās *Rhēnum* trādūcit.   *He leads his forces across the Rhine.*

Cōpiae *Rhēnum* trādūcuntur.   *The forces are led across the Rhine.*

6. *With Prepositions.* The accusative is used with prepositions (except those listed in **Ablative,** 19). When **in** and **sub** show the direction toward which a thing moves, the accusative is used.

NOTA·BENE

When the preposition **ad** is used with names of towns it means *to the vicinity of.*

The infinitive is often used with **prohibeō** (*prevent*) and with **dubitō** when it means *hesitate*.

Caesar prohibuit eōs trānsīre.
Caesar prevented them from crossing.

a. With **iubeō** (*order*), unlike **imperō**, the infinitive is generally used. The subject of the infinitive is in the accusative.

Iussit eōs venīre.	*He ordered them to come.*
Imperāvit eīs ut venīrent.	*He ordered them to come.*

b. **Vetō** (*forbid*) and **cupiō** (*desire*) are used like **iubeō**.

6. *Clauses with Verbs of Hindering.* With verbs of hindering, preventing, and doubting, as **impediō, dēterreō,** and **dubitō**, the subjunctive introduced by **nē** or **quō minus** is used if the main clause is affirmative, by **quīn** if negative.

Tū dēterrēre potes nē maior multitūdō trādūcātur.	*You can prevent a greater number from being brought over.*

7. *Clauses of Fear.* With verbs of fearing, clauses in the subjunctive introduced by **nē** (*that*) and **ut** (*that not*) are used.

Verēbātur nē tū aeger essēs.	*He feared that you were sick.*
Timuī ut venīrent.	*I was afraid that they would not come.*

8. *Result Clauses.* The result of the action or state of the principal verb is expressed by a subordinate clause with **ut (utī),** negative **ut nōn (utī nōn),** and the subjunctive.

Tantum est perīculum ut paucī veniant.	*So great is the danger that few are coming.*
Ita bene erant castra mūnīta ut nōn capī possent.	*So well had the camp been fortified that it could not be taken.*

9. *Noun Clauses of Result.* Verbs meaning *to happen* (**accidō**) or *to cause* or *effect* (**efficiō**) require clauses of result in the subjunctive with **ut (utī)** or **ut (utī) nōn,** used as subject or object of the main verb:

Accidit ut mē nōn vidēret.	*It happened that he did not see me.*
Efficiam ut veniat.	*I shall cause him to come.*

10. *Descriptive Relative Clauses.* A relative clause with the subjunctive may be used to describe an indefinite antecedent. Such clauses are called relative clauses of description (characteristic) and are especially common after such expressions as **ūnus** and **sōlus, sunt quī** (*there are those who*), and **nēmō est quī** (*there is no one who*).

11. *Cum Clauses.* In secondary sequence **cum** (*when*) is used with the imperfect or the past pluperfect subjunctive to describe the circumstances under which the action of the main verb occurred.

Cum mīlitēs redīssent, Caesar ōrātiōnem habuit.	*When the soldiers had returned, Caesar made a speech.*

a. In some clauses **cum** with the subjunctive is best translated *since.*

Cum ita sint, nōn ībō.

Since this is so, I shall not go (literally, *When this is so*).

b. In some clauses **cum** with the subjunctive is best translated *although.*

Cum ea ita sint, tamen nōn ībō.

Although this is so, yet I shall not go (literally, *When,* etc.).

When **ut** means *although, granted that,* its clause is in the subjunctive.

12. *Anticipatory Clauses.* **Dum** (*until*), **antequam,** and **priusquam** (*before*) introduce clauses (*a*) in the indicative to indicate *an actual fact,* (*b*) in the subjunctive to indicate an act as *anticipated.*

Silentium fuit dum tū vēnistī.

There was silence until you came.

Caesar exspectāvit dum nāvēs convenīrent.

Caesar waited until the ships should assemble.

Priusquam tēlum adigī posset, omnēs fūgērunt.

Before a weapon could be thrown, all fled.

13. *Indirect Questions.* In a question indirectly quoted or expressed after some introductory verb such as *ask, doubt, learn, know, tell, hear,* etc., the verb is in the subjunctive.

Rogant quis sit.

They ask who he is.

14. *Subordinate Clauses in Indirect Discourse.* An indicative in a subordinate clause becomes subjunctive in indirect discourse. If the clause is not regarded as an essential part of the quotation but is merely explanatory or parenthetical, its verb may be in the indicative.

Dīxit sē pecūniam invēnisse quam āmīsisset.

He said that he found the money which he had lost.

15. *By Attraction.* A verb in a clause dependent upon a subjunctive or an infinitive, is frequently "attracted" to the subjunctive, especially if its clause is an essential part of the statement.

Dat negōtium hīs utī ea quae apud Belgās gerantur cognōscant.

He directs them to learn what is going on among the Belgians.

16. *Quod Causal Clauses.* Causal clauses introduced by **quod** (or **proptereā quod**) and **quoniam** (*since, because*) are in the indicative when they give the writer's or speaker's reason, the subjunctive when the reason is presented as that of another person.

Amīcō grātiās ēgī quod mihi pecūniam dederat.

I thanked my friend because he had given me money.

Rōmānīs bellum intulit quod agrōs suōs vāstāvissent.

He made war against the Romans because (as he alleged) they had laid waste his lands.

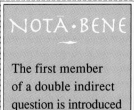

NOTĀ·BENE

The first member of a double indirect question is introduced by **utrum** or **–ne,** the second by **an.**

Quaerō utrum vērum an falsum sit.

I ask whether it is true or false.

17. *Proviso Clauses.* The subjunctive with **dum, dum modo, modo,** meaning *provided that,* is used to express a proviso (negative **nē**).

modo inter mē atque tē mūrus intersit	*provided that a wall is between you and me*

18. *Deliberative.* In questions of doubt and perplexity where the speaker asks himself or someone else for advice, or in questions or exclamations expressing surprise or indignation, the subjunctive is used, sometimes with **ut.** The negative is **nōn.** The deliberative subjunctive is commonly used in questions that expect a *no* answer, and is therefore purely rhetorical.

Quid fīat?	*What shall be done?*
Cūr ego nōn laeter?	*Why should I not rejoice?*
Tū ut umquam tē corrigās?	*You ever reform?*

19. *Optative.* The optative (**optō**) subjunctive represents a wish. It frequently is preceded by **utinam** (*would that*). The negative is **nē.**

a. The present (rarely the perfect) is used when the wish can come true:

Vīvās fēlīciter!	*May you live happily!*

b. The imperfect expresses a wish contrary to fact in present time:

Utinam venīret!	*Oh, that he were coming (but he is not)!*

c. The pluperfect expresses a wish contrary to fact in past time:

Utinam nē vēnisset!	*Would that he had not come (but he did)!*

20. *Potential.* The potential subjunctive expresses the possibility or capability of something being done. The negative is **nōn.** The present and perfect refer to present or future time, the imperfect to past time. It is variously translated by *may, might, can, could.*

Aliquis mihi dīcat.	*Someone may say to me.*
Aurum fluitāre vidērēs.	*You might have seen the gold flowing.*

21. *Of Obligation.* The negative is **nōn.** It is translated by *should* or *ought.*

Quid ego cōnārer?	*Why should I have tried?*

22. *Of Comparison.* With words meaning *as if* (**quasi, velut,** etc.) the subjunctive is used.

quasi nātūrā dīiūnctī sint	*as if they were naturally separated*

23. *Second Singular Indefinite.* When the second person singular is not applied to an individual but generally (where we use *one* in English), the subjunctive may be used.

Putēs dīcere.	*One might think you are saying.*

Conditions

    a. Subordinate clause (condition) introduced by **sī**, **nisi**, or **sī nōn**.

    b. Principal clause (conclusion).

1. *Simple* (nothing implied as to truth). Any possible combination of tenses of the indicative, as in English.

    Sī mē laudat, laetus sum.   *If he praises me, I am glad.*

2. *Contrary-to-Fact.*

    a. Present: imperfect subjunctive in both clauses.

    Sī mē laudāret, laetus essem.   *If he were praising me* (but he isn't), *I should be glad* (now).

    b. Past: past perfect subjunctive in both clauses.

    Sī mē laudāvisset, laetus fuissem.   *If he had praised me* (but he didn't) *I should have been glad* (then).

    c. Mixed: past condition and present conclusion.

    Sī mē laudāvisset, laetus essem.   *If he had praised me* (but he didn't) *I should be glad* (now).

3. *Future Less Vivid* (should/would). Present subjunctive in both clauses.

    Sī mē laudet, laetus sim.   *If he should praise me, I would be glad.*

NOTĀ·BENE

Sometimes the indicative is used in the conclusion for greater vividness or to emphasize the certainty of the result if the condition were or had been true.

Imperative Mood

    Affirmative commands are expressed by the imperative; negative commands by the present imperative of **nōlō (nōlī, nōlīte)** and the infinitive. The imperative with **nē** is used in poetry.

    Amā inimīcōs tuōs.   *Love your enemies.*

    Nōlīte īre.   *Do not go* (literally, *Be unwilling to go*).

    a. The future imperative is rare, being found chiefly in religious and legal language.

    b. Exhortations (volitive subjunctive) and commands, though main clauses, become subjunctive in indirect discourse.

    (Direct) **Īte!**   *Go!*

    (Indirect) **Dīxit īrent.**   *He said that they should go.*

    c. Occasionally the subjunctive is used instead of the imperative.

    Mihi hās lēgēs.   *Will these to me.*

Impersonal Verbs

    a. Some verbs are used only impersonally and therefore have no forms in the first and second persons.

    b. The various constructions with **licet** are as follows:

Licet $\left\{ \begin{array}{c} \textbf{tibi} \\ \textbf{tē} \end{array} \right\}$ **īre.** *You may go.*

Licet (ut) eās.   *You may go.*

    c. Other verbs may at times be used impersonally, i.e., without a personal subject.

    d. Intransitive verbs are used only impersonally in the passive.

Ventum erat.   *He* (or *they*) *had come.*

                                See also **Dative,** 6, *a.*

Reflexive Use of the Passive

    Occasionally the passive form of a verb or participle is used in a "middle" or reflexive sense.

armārī   *to arm themselves*

Participle

1. The tenses of the participles (present, perfect, future) indicate time *present, past,* or *future* from the standpoint of the main verb.

2. *a.* Perfect participles are often used simply as adjectives: **nōtus,** *known.*

    b. Participles, like adjectives, may be used as nouns: **factum,** "having been done," *deed.*

3. The Latin participle is often a *one-word substitute* for a subordinate clause in English introduced by *who* or *which, when* or *after, since* or *because, although,* and *if.*

Gerundive (Future Passive Participle)

    The gerundive (future passive participle) is a verbal adjective, having thirty forms. It has two distinct uses:

1. As a predicate adjective with forms of **sum,**[1] when it natually indicates, as in English, *what must be done.* The person upon whom the obligation rests is in the dative.

Caesarī omnia erant agenda.   *Caesar had to do all things* (literally, *all things were to be done by Caesar*).

2. As modifier of a noun or pronoun in various constructions, with no idea of obligation:

dē Rōmā cōnstituendā   *about founding Rome* (literally, *about Rome to be founded*)

---

[1] The so-called passive periphrastic, a term not used in this book. The term should be avoided because it is not only useless but troublesome.

3. With phrases introduced by **ad** and the accusative or by **causā** (or **grātiā**) and the genitive it expresses purpose. **Causā** and **grātiā** are always placed after the participle.

Ad eās rēs cōnficiendās Mārcus dēligitur.	*Marcus is chosen to accomplish these things* (literally, *for these things to be accomplished*).
Caesaris videndī causā (or grātiā) vēnit.	*He came for the sake of seeing Caesar* (literally, *for the sake of Caesar to be seen*).

4. It is used in agreement with the object of **cūrō, locō, dō,** etc.

Pontem faciendum cūrat.	*He attends to having a bridge built.*

Gerund

The gerund is a verbal noun of the second declension with only four forms—genitive, dative, accusative, and ablative singular.

The uses of the gerund are similar to some of those of the gerundive.

cupidus bellandī	*desirous of waging war*
Ad discendum vēnī.	*I came for learning* (i.e., *to learn*).
Discendī causā (or **grātiā**) **vēnī.**	*I came for the sake of learning.*

Infinitive

1. The infinitive is an indeclinable neuter verbal noun, and as such it may be used as the subject of a verb.

Errāre hūmānum est.	*Too err is human.*
Vidēre est crēdere.	*To see is to believe.*

2. With many verbs the infinitive, like other nouns, may be used as a direct object.

Cōpiās movēre parat.	*He prepares to move the troops.*

3. The infinitive object of some verbs, such as **iubeō, volō, nōlō,** and **doceō,** often has a noun or pronoun subject in the accusative.

4. Statements that give indirectly the thoughts or words of another, used as the objects of verbs of *saying, thinking, knowing, hearing, perceiving,* etc., have verbs in the infinitive with their subjects in the accusative.

(Direct) **Dīcit, "Puerī veniunt."**	*He says, "The boys are coming."*
(Indirect) **Dīcit puerōs venīre.**	*He says that the boys are coming.*

āles, *gen.* **–itis**, winged; *as noun, m. and f.*, bird

Alexander, –drī, *m.*, Alexander, *king of Macedonia*

Alexandrīnus, –a, –um, Alexandrian

algor, –ōris, *m.*, coldness

aliēnus, –a, –um, of another, another's, foreign; unfavorable; *as noun, m.*, stranger

aliōquī, *adv.*, besides, moreover

aliquamdiū, *adv.*, a while, for some time

aliquandō, *adv.*, some time, at last

aliquantō, *adv.*, a little

aliquantum, –ī, *n.*, for some time

aliquis, aliquid, someone, anyone; some, any; something, anything

aliquot, *indecl. adj.*, some, several, few

aliter, *adv.*, otherwise

alius, alia, aliud, other, another; different, else; **alius... alius**, one . . . another; **aliī... aliī**, some . . . others

Allēlūia, *interj.*, praise ye Jehovah

allevō, 1, raise

alliciō, –ere, allexī, allectus, attract

alligō, 1, tie (to), fasten

Allobrogēs, –um, *m. pl.*, the Allobroges, *a Gallic tribe*

allocūtiō, –ōnis, *f.*, address, comforting

alloquor, alloquī, allocūtus, speak to, address

allūdō, –ere, allūsī, allūsūrus, play, joke, pun

alō, –ere, aluī, altus (alitus), feed, nourish, sustain

Alpēs, –ium, *f. pl.*, the Alps

Alphēnōr, –oris, *m.*, Alphē´nor, *one of Niobe's sons*

altāria, –ium, *n. pl.*, altar

altē, *adv.*, high, deeply, far

alter, altera, alterum, the other (*of two*), another, second; **alter... alter**, the one . . . the other

alternus, –a, –um, alternating

alteruter, –utra, –utrum, one or the other, either this or that, one of two

altilis, –is, fattened, fat; *as noun, f.*, a fattened bird

altitūdō, –dinis, *f.*, height, depth

altus, –a, –um, high, tall, deep

amābilis, –e, lovely, attractive

amāns, *gen.* **amantis**, fond, loving; *as noun, m.*, lover

ambiguum, ī, *n.*, doubt

ambiguus, –a, –um, uncertain, wavering; obscure

ambiō, ambīre, ambiī, ambitūrus, go round, encircle, canvass for votes, solicit

ambitiō, –ōnis, *f.*, courting, flattery; desire for honor

ambitus, –ūs, *m.*, circuit; suing for office

ambō, -ae, -o, both

Ambrosius, –sī, *m.*, Ambrose

ambulō, 1, walk

āmentia, –ae, *f.*, madness, folly

Americānus, –a, –um, American; **Americānus, –ī**, *m.*, an American

amīca, –ae, *f.*, friend

amīcitia, –ae, *f.*, friendship

amictus, –a, –um, clothed

amictus, –ūs, *m.*, mantle

amīcus, –a, –um, friendly; **amīcus, –ī**, *m.*, friend **amīca, –ae**, *f.*, friend

āmittō, –ere, āmīsī, āmissus, lose, let go, send away

Ammōnicus, Ammonicus Serenus

amnis, –is, *m.*, stream, river

amō, 1, love, like

amoenitās, –tātis, *f.*, delightfulness, charm

amoenus, –a, –um, pleasant

amor, –ōris, *m.*, love, affection

Amphīōn, –ōnis, *m.*, Amphī´on, *husband of Niobe*

amphitheātrum, –ī, *n.*, amphitheater

amplector, –ī, amplexus, embrace

amplificō, 1, enlarge, increase

amplitūdō, –dinis, *f.*, greatness

amplius, *adv.*, more, further

amplus, –a, –um, great, ample, generous, distinguished

an, *conj.*, or, *introducing the second part of a double question;* **utrum... an**, (whether) . . . or; *w. indir. question,* whether; *w.* **vērō**, or indeed

anceps, ancipitis, double, two-headed; doubtful; dangerous

angelicus, –a, –um, like an angel, angelic

angelus, –ī, *m.*, angel

Angelus, Angelo (Corbinelli)

Anglī, –ōrum, *m. pl.*, the Angles

Anglicus, –a, –um, English

angō, –ere, —, —, trouble

angulus, –ī, *m.,* angle, corner

anhēlitus, –ūs, *m.,* panting

anīlis, –e, old woman's, feeble

anima, –ae, *f.,* breath, soul; existence

animadvertō, –ere, –vertī, –versus, give attention to, notice, punish

animal, –ālis, *n.,* animal

animālis, –e, of life, living

animula, –ae, *f.,* little soul

animus, –ī, *m.,* soul, spirit, heart, mind, feeling, courage, desire

annālis, –e, relating to a year; *as noun, m.,* a record of events, annals

annectō, –ere, annexuī, annexus, tie to, fasten on, annex

annītor, ī, annixus, lean upon; strive

anniversārius, –a, –um, annual, yearly

annuō, –ere, annuī, —, nod (to), assent to

annus, –ī, *m.,* year

anquīrō, –ere, –sīvī, –sītus, look about, search after; inquire diligently

ānser, –eris, *m.,* goose

ante, *adv. and prep. w. acc.,* before (*of time or place*), beforehand, ago

anteā, *adv.,* before

antecēdō, –ere, –cessī, –cessūrus, go before, take the lead

antecellō, –ere, —, —, excel

anteeō, –īre, –iī, –itūrus, precede; surpass; anticipate

antelūcānus, –a, –um, before dawn

antepōnō, –ere, –posuī, –positus, place before, prefer

antequam (ante quam), *conj.,* before

Antiochia, –ae, *f.,* Antioch, *chief city of Syria*

Antiochus, –ī, *m.,* Antiochus, *king of Syria*

antīquitās, –tātis, *f.,* antiquity

antīquus, –a, –um, old, ancient

antistes, –itis, *m., and f.,* priest

Antōnius, –nī, *m.,* Antonius, Antony

antrum, –ī, *n.,* cave

anus, –ūs, *f.,* old woman

ānxius, –a, –um, troubled, causing anxiety; cautious

aper, aprī, *m.,* wild boar

aperiō, –īre, aperuī, apertus, open, uncover

apertē, *adv.,* openly, frankly

apertus, –a, –um, open, unprotected

Apollineus, –a, –um, of Apollo

Apollō, –inis, *m.,* Apollo, *god of prophecy*

Apollodorus, –ī, *m.,* Apollodorus

Aponius, –nī, *m.,* Aponius

apostolicus, –a, –um, apostolic

apostolus, –ī, *m.,* apostle

apparātus, –a, –um, well prepared

apparātus, –ūs, *m.,* preparation, splendor

appāreō, –ēre, –uī, –itūrus, appear

appellō, 1, call, speak to, name, address

Appennīnus, –ī, *m.,* Appennines, *mountain range in Italy*

appetō, –ere, appetīvī, appetītus, seek for

Appius, –a, –um, *adj.,* of Appius, Appian; **Appius, –pī,** *m.,* Appius

applicō, 1, apply, direct (to); drive to

apprehendō, –ere, –dī, –sus, seize

approbō, 1, approve

appropinquō, 1, draw near

Aprīlis, –e, (of) April

aptō, 1, fit, place carefully

aptus, –a, –um, fit, suited, suitable (*w. dat.*)

apud, *prep. w. acc.,* at, among, near, with, before, in the presence of, at the house of

aqua, –ae, *f.,* water

aquaeductus, –ūs, *m.,* aqueduct

aquila, –ae, *f.,* eagle; legionary standard

aquilō, –ōnis, *m.,* north wind, north

Aquītānus, –ī, *m.,* an Aquitanian

āra, –ae, *f.,* altar

arātor, –ōris, *m.,* ploughman

arbiter, –trī, *m.,* witness, judge

arbitrium, –rī, *n.,* judgment, opinion, choice

arbitror, 1, think

arbor, –oris, *f.,* tree

arboreus, –a, –um, of a tree

arbuscula, –ae, *f.,* small tree

arcānus, –a, –um, secret

arceō, –ēre, –uī, —, keep away, ward off, prevent

arcessō, –ere, arcessīvī, arcessītus, summon, invite, accuse

Archiās, –ae, *m.*, Archias, *a Greek poet*

archipīrāta, –ae, *m.*, pirate captain

architectūra, –ae, *f.*, architecture

architectus, –ī, *m.*, architect

Arcitenēns, –entis, *m.*, (bowbearing), Apollo

arcus, –ūs, *m.*, bow, arch

ārdeō, –ēre, ārsī, ārsus, be on fire, burn; be aroused

arduus, –a, –um, steep, lofty; *as noun, n. pl.*, heights

ārea, –ae, *f.*, flat surface; threshing-floor

arēna, –ae, *f.*, arena, sand, desert, seashore

arēnōsus, –a, –um, full of sand

āreō, –ēre, –uī, —, be parched

argenteus, –a, –um, of silver, silvery

argentum, –ī, *n.*, silver, money

argumentum, –ī, *n.*, proof, argument, subject

arguō, –ere, –uī, –ūtus, make known, accuse

argūtus, –a, –um, bright

āridus, –a, –um, dry, arid

arista, –ae, *f.*, head of grain

arma, –ōrum, *n. pl.*, arms, weapons

armārium, –rī, *n.*, closet, chest, safe

armātūra, –ae, *f.*, equipment

armātus, –a, –um, armed

armentum, –ī, *n.*, cattle, herd

arō, 1, plow

Arpīnās, *gen.*, –ātis, of Arpinum

arripiō, –ere, arripuī, arreptus, grasp

arrogantia, –ae, *f.*, arrogance, insolence

arrogō, 1, associate with, claim

ars, artis, *f.*, skill, art, profession, practice

artifex, –ficis, *m.*, artist; *w.* **scaenicus**, actor

artificium, –cī, *n.*, profession, trade; theory; art, craft

artus, –a, –um, tight

artus, –ūs, *m.*, joint, limb

ārula, –ae, *f.*, small altar

arundō, –inis, *f.*, reed, fishing-rod, shepherd's pipe, flute

arvum, –ī, *n.*, field

arx, arcis, *f.*, citadel

as, assis, *m.*, whole; penny

ascendō, –ere, ascendī, ascēnsus, climb (up), mount, ascend

ascēnsus, –ūs, *m.*, ascent

ascīscō, –ere, ascīvī, ascītus, admit

Ascōnius, –nī, *m.*, Asconius

ascrībō, –ere, ascrīpsī, ascrīptus, enroll

asellus, –ī, *m.*, donkey

Asia, –ae, *f.*, Asia

asinus, –ī, *m.*, ass, fool

aspectus, –ūs, *m.*, appearance, sight

asper, –era, –erum, rough, harsh, cruel

aspiciō, –ere, aspexī, aspectus, look at, behold, see

aspīrō, 1, aspire, reach

asportō, 1, carry off

assēnsus, –ūs, *m.*, agreement, approval

assentiō, –īre, assēnsī, assēnsus, agree with, approve

assequor, assequī, assecūtus, accomplish, obtain

asserō, –ere, asseruī, assertus, claim, appropriate

asservō, 1, watch over, keep

assevērō, 1, assert

assīdō, –ere, assēdī, assessus, sit near, sit at the side of, be seated

assiduus, –a, –um, continual, incessant

assignō, 1, allot, assign; entrust; ascribe

assuēscō, –ere, assuēvī, assuētus, become accustomed

assūmō, –ere, assūmpsī, assūmptus, take

assurgō, –ere, assurrēxī, assurrēctus, rise up, stand up

astrum, –ī, *n.*, star, constellation

at, *conj.*, but, on the other hand

Ateius, –eī, *m.*, Ateius

āter, ātra, ātrum, black, dark

Athēna, *f.*, *a Greek goddess* = Minerva

Athēnae, –ārum, *f. pl.*, Athens

Athēniēnsēs, –ium, *m., pl.*, the Athenians

Atlantiadēs, –ae, *m.*, Mercury

Atlās, –antis, *m.*, Atlas, *a giant*

atque (ac), *conj.*, and, and especially; than

ātrium, ātrī, *n.*, atrium, entry hall, house

atrōx, *gen.* **–ōcis**, cruel, inhuman

attendō, –ere, attendī, attentus, (stretch toward), direct, give heed (to), listen

attentus, –a, –um, attentive

atterō, –ere, attrīvī, attrītus, rub or wear away

attineō, –ēre, attinuī, —, detain, delay; reach; concern

attingō, –ere, attigī, attāctus, assign

attollō, –ere, —, —, lift

attonitus, –a, –um, astounded

attribuō, –ere, attribuī, attribūtus, assign

attrītus, –a, –um, worn

auctor, –ōris, *m.,* maker, author, authority, writer, voucher

auctōritās, –tātis, *f.,* authority, influence, opinion

audācia, –ae, *f.,* boldness

audāx, *gen.* **audācis,** bold, daring, courageous

audeō, –ēre, ausus, *semideponent,* dare

audiō, –īre, –īvī, (–iī), –ītus, hear, hear of, listen (to)

audītiō, –ōnis, *f.,* lecture

audītor, –ōris, *m.,* hearer, auditor

auferō, auferre, abstulī, ablātus, take away, remove

Aufidius, –dī, *m.,* Aufidius

augeō, –ēre, auxī, auctus, increase

Augustīnus, –ī, *m.,* Augustine

Augustus, –a, –um, of Augustus; *as noun, m.,* Augustus, *the emperor*

aura, –ae, *f.,* breeze, air

aurātus, –a, –um, covered with gold

Aurēlia, –ae, *f.,* Aurelia

aureus, –a, –um, golden, made of gold; *as noun, m.,* gold piece

aurīga, –ae, *m.,* charioteer

auris, –is, *f.,* ear

Aurōra, –ae, *f.,* morning, dawn

aurum, –ī, *n.,* gold

auspicātus, –a, –um, auspicious

auspicia, –ōrum, *n. pl.,* auspices

auspicor, 1, take the auspices

auster, –trī, *m.,* south wind

aut, or; **aut... aut,** either . . . or

autem, *conj.* (*never first word*), however, but, moreover

autumnālis, –e, of autumn

autumus, –ī, *m.* autumn, fall

auxiliārius, –a, –um, auxiliary

auxilium, –lī, *n.,* aid, help, assistance; *pl.* reinforcements

avārē, *adv.,* greedily

avāritia, –ae, *f.,* greed, avarice

avēna, –ae, *f.,* reed

aveō, –ēre, —, —, long for, crave

aversor, 1, repulse, avoid

avertō, –ere, avertī, aversus, turn from, turn away, turn off, remove

āvia, –ōrum, *n. pl.,* pathless regions

avidus, –a, –um, eager

avis, avis, *f.,* bird

avītus, –a, –um, of a grandfather

āvocō, 1, call away *or* aside

avus, –ī, *m.,* grandfather, ancestor

axis, –is, *f.,* axle, chariot; globe

B

Babylōnius, –a, –um, Babylonian

bāca, –ae, *f.,* fruit, berry

bacchor, 1, revel

Bacchus, –ī, *m.,* Bacchus, *god of wine*

baculum, –ī, *n.,* staff

Bagrada, –ae, *m.,* Bagrada

Balbus, –ī, *m.,* Balbus

balineum (balneum), –ī, *n.,* bath

ballista, –ae, *f.,* ballista

balsamum, –ī, *n.,* fragrant gum, balsam

barba, –ae, *f.,* beard

barbaria, –ae, *f.,* savage people

barbaricus, –a, –um, barbaric

barbarus, –a, –um, foreign; savage, uncivilized, barbarous; *as noun, m.,* foreigner, barbarian

barbātus, –a, –um, bearded

Bardulis, –is, *m.,* Bardulis, *king of Illyria*

basilica, –ae, *f.,* basilica

Baucis, –idis (*acc.* **–ida**), *f.,* Baucis (Bausis), *wife of Philemon*

beātus, –a, –um, happy, blessed, rich

Belgae, –ārum, *m. pl.,* the Belgians; the Belgian people

bellicōsus, –a, –um, warlike

bellō, 1, wage war

bellum, –ī, *n.,* war

bellus, –a, –um, nice

bēlua, –ae, *f.,* (wild) beast

bene, *adv.,* well, well done, successfully; *comp.*
   melius, better; *superl.* **optimē,** best, very good

beneficium, –cī, *n.,* kindness, favor; honor, benefit

benevolentia, –ae, *f.,* good will, kindness

benignē, thank you

benignitās, –tātis, *f.,* kindness

benignus, –a, –um, kind

Berecyntius, –a, –um, Berecyntian

bēstia, –ae, *f.,* beast

bibliothēca, –ae, *f.,* library

bibō, –ere, bibī, —, drink

Bibulus, –ī, *m.,* Bibulus

bicolor, –ōris, two-colored

bicornis, –e, two-pronged

Bilbilis, –is, *f.,* Bilbilis, *a town in Spain*

bīnī, –ae, –a, two each, two

bipertītō, *adv.,* in two divisions

bipēs, bipedis, two-footed

bis, *adv.,* twice

Bithynia, –ae, *f.,* Bithynia, *a province in Asia Minor*

blaesus, –a, –um, lisping

blanditiae, –ārum, *f.,* fond words

blandulus, –a, –um, pleasing, charming

blandus, –a, –um, coaxing, caressing

bonitās, –tātis, *f.,* goodness

bonus, –a, –um, good; *comp.* **melior, melius,**
   better; *superl.* **optimus, –a, –um,** best; **bona,**
   –ōrum, *n.,* goods, property

Boōtes, –ae, *m.,* Bo-o´tes, *a constellation*

bōs, bovis, *m. and f.,* ox, cow; *pl.* cattle (*gen. pl.,*
   boum *or* **bovum**)

bracchium, –chī, *n.,* arm

brevī, *adv.,* in a short time, soon

brevis, –e, short

brevitās, –tātis, *f.,* brevity

breviter, *adv.,* briefly

Britannia, –ae, *f.,* Britain

Britannus, –ī, *m.,* a Briton

brūma, –ae, *f.,* winter

Brūtus, –ī, *m.,* Brutus

bubulcus, –ī, *m.,* ploughman

bustum, –ī, *n.,* pyre; tomb

Byzantius, –a, –um, Byzantine, of Byzantium
   (*Constantinople*)

C

C., *abbreviation for* **Gāius**

cacūmen, –minis, *n.,* peak; tree top

Cadmus, –ī, *m.,* Cadmus, *founder of Thebes*

cadō, –ere, cecidī, cāsūrus, fall, die, be slain

cadūcus, –a, –um, falling, frail, perishable

Caecilius, –lī, *m.,* Caecilius

caedēs, –is, *f.,* slaughter, murder, bloodshed

caedō, –ere, cecīdī, caesus, cut, beat

caelestis, –is, *m. and f.,* heavenly being

caelicola, –ae, *m.,* god

Caelius, –lī, m., Caelius

caelō, 1, carve, emboss

caelum, –ī, *n.,* sky; weather

caerulus (-eus), –a, –um, blue

Caesar, –aris, *m.,* Caesar; emperor

caespes, –itis, *m.,* sod, earth

calamitās, –tātis, *f.,* loss, misfortune, defeat, ruin

calamitōsus, –a, –um, unfortunate, disastrous

calamus, –ī, *m.,* reed, reed-pipe

calcar, –āris, *n.,* stimulus, goad

Calchas, –antis, *m.,* Calchas, *a mythological seer*

calcō, 1, tread

caleō, –ēre, –uī, –itūrus, be warm *or* hot

calidus, –a, –um, warm

calliditās, –tātis, *f.,* shrewdness, cunning

callidus, –a, –um, cunning

calor, –ōris, *m.,* heat

Calymnē, –ēs, *f.,* Calym´ne, *an island in the Aegean*

Camillus, –ī, *m.,* Camillus

campus, –ī, *m.,* field, plain; the Campus Martius, *a*
   park and place of assembly at Rome

candeō, –ēre, –uī, —, shine, be brilliant, glitter

candidātōrius, –a, –um, of a candidate

candidātus, –ī, *m.,* candidate

candidus, –a, –um, white, clear

Canīnius, –nī, *m.,* Caninius

canis, –is, *m. and f.,* dog

canistrum, –ī, *n.,* reed basket

Canius, –nī, *m.,* Canius

canna, –ae, *f.,* reed

Cannēnsis, –e, of Cannae

canō, –ere, cecinī, cantus, sing, predict, play

canōrus, –a, –um, melodious, harmonious

cantō, 1, sing

cantus, –ūs, *m.,* song

cānus, –a, –um, white, hoary

capāx, *gen.* **capācis,** spacious; capable of

caper, caprī, *m.,* goat

capessō, –ere, –īvī, –ītus, strive to reach, undertake

capillus, –ī, *m.,* hair; *pl.,* locks, hair

capiō, –ere, cēpī, captus, take, seize, hold, captivate, capture; **cōnsilium capiō,** adopt a plan

Capitō, –ōnis, *m.,* Capito

Capitōlium, –lī, *n.,* the Capitol, *temple of Jupiter at Rome;* the Capitoline Hill

captiō, –ōnis, *f.,* deception; sophism; injury, loss

captīvus, –a, –um, captive; captured; *as noun, m.,* prisoner

captīvus, –ī, *m.;* **captīva, –ae,** *f.,* prisoner

captō, 1, capture, grasp, seize

caput, capitis, *n.,* head

Carbō, –ōnis, *m.,* Carbo

carcer, –eris, *m.,* prison

cardō, –dinis, *m.,* hinge

careō, –ēre, caruī, caritūrus, be without, lack, be deprived of

Cāria, –ae, *f.,* Caria, *a province in Asia Minor*

cāritās, –tātis, *f.,* high price; affection

carmen, –minis, *n.,* song, poem

carpō, –ere, carpsī, carptus, pick, seize; *of a road,* pursue, traverse

carrus, –ī, *m.,* cart, wagon

Carthāginiēnsēs, –ium, *m. pl.,* the Carthaginians

Carthāgō, –ginis, *f.,* Carthage, *a city in Africa;* **Carthāgō Nova,** New Carthage, *in Spain*

cārus, –a, –um, dear

casa, –ae, *f.,* house, cottage

Cassius, –sī, *m.,* Cassius

castellum, –ī, *n.,* fort

Castor, –oris, *m.,* Castor, *one of the twins, with* Pollux

castra, –ōrum, *n. pl.,* camp

castrēnsis, –e, of the camp, open

cāsus, –ūs, *m.,* fall, chance, event, misfortune, accident; case

catapulta, –ae, *f.,* catapult

catēna, –ae, *f.,* chain; constraint

cathedra, –ae, *f.,* chair, litter; professor's chair

Catilīna, –ae, *m.,* Catiline, *the conspirator of 63 B.C.*

Catō, –ōnis, *m.,* Cato, *a Roman senator*

Catulus, –ī, *m.,* Catulus

Caucasus, –ī, *m.,* Caucasus, *a chain of mountains in Asia*

causa, –ae, *f.,* cause, reason; case, pretext; position; **causā,** for the sake of, for the purpose of

cautus, –a, –um, cautious

cavea, –ae, *f.,* cage, den; *(in a theater)* auditorium, spectators' seats

caveō, –ēre, cāvī, cautūrus, beware (of), take care

cavus, –a, –um, hollow

–ce, *(enclitic),* here, this, that

cēdō, –ere, cessī, cessūrus, go away, retreat, retire, yield

celeber, –bris, –bre, populous, crowded

celebritās, –tātis, *f.,* throng; renown

celebrō, 1, throng, celebrate, attend, honor

celer, celeris, celere, swift

celeritās, –tātis, *f.,* speed, swiftness, quickness

celeriter, *adv.,* quickly, swiftly

cella, –ae, *f.,* storeroom; closet

cēlō, 1, hide, keep secret

celsus, –a, –um, high

Celtae, –ārum, *m. pl.,* Celts, *a people of Gaul*

cēna, –ae, *f.,* dinner

cēnō, 1, dine

cēnseō, –ēre, cēnsuī, cēnsus, enroll; think; decree

cēnsiō, –ōnis, *f.,* census

cēnsor, –ōris, *m.,* censor

cēnsūra, –ae, *f.,* censorship

cēnsus, –ūs, *m.,* census

centum, hundred

centumvirī, –ōrum, *m. pl.,* the hundred men, *a special jury for important civil suits*

cēnula, –ae, *f.,* little dinner

Cēpārius, –rī, *m.,* Ceparius

cēra, –ae, *f.,* wax

cērātus, –a, –um, waxed

Cereālis, –e, of Ceres; **Cereālia, –ium,** *n. pl.,* the festival of Ceres

Cerēs, Cereris, *f.,* Ceres, *goddess of agriculture*

cernō, –ere, crēvī, crētus, separate, discern, see

certāmen, –minis, *n.,* contest

certātim, *adv.* earnestly, eagerly

certātiō, –ōnis, *f.,* strife, dispute

certē, *adv.,* certainly

certō, 1, struggle

certus, –a, –um, fixed, certain, sure; **certiōrem facere,** inform (him); **certior fierī,** be informed

cerva, –ae, *f.,* deer

cervīx, –īcis, *f.,* neck; *pl.,* shoulders

cessō, 1, delay, stop, be idle

cēterī, –ae, –a, the other(s), the rest; everything else

Cethēgus, –ī, *m.,* Cethegus

chorus, –ī, *m.,* choral dance; choir

Chrīstiānus, –a, –um, *adj. and n.,* Christian

Chrīstus, –ī, *m.,* Christ

cibus, –ī, *m.,* food

cicātrīx, –īcis, *m.,* scar

cicer, –eris, *n.,* chickpea

Cicerō, –ōnis, *m.,* Cicero (Marcus Tullius, *the orator;* Quintus, *his brother;* Marcus, *his son*)

cingō, –ere, cīnxī, cīnctus, surround; crown

cinis, cineris, *m.,* ashes

circā, *adv. and prep. w. acc.,* around, about

Circē, –ae, *f.,* Circe, *a sorceress*

circum, *prep. w. acc.,* about, around

circumagō, –ere, –ēgī, –āctus, drive *or* turn around

circumcīsus, –a, –um, cut off, steep, inaccessible

circumclūdō, –ere, –clūsī, –clūsus, surround

circumdō, –dare, –dedī, –datus, put around, surround (with)

circumeō, –īre, –iī, –itus, go around

circumferō, –ferre, –tulī, –lātus, bear *or* spread around, cast about

circumscrībō, –ere, –scrīpsī, –scrīptus, bound, circumscribe

circumspiciō, –ere, –spexī, –spectus, look around

circumstō, –āre, –stetī, —, stand around

circumveniō, –īre, –vēnī, –ventus, surround

circus, –ī, *m.,* circle, circus, *esp. the Circus Maximus at Rome*

cithara, –ae, *f.,* cithara, lyre

citus, –a, –um, swift; **citō,** quickly, speedily

cīvīlis, –e, civil

cīvis, cīvis, *m. and f.,* citizen

cīvitās, –tātis, *f.,* citizenship, state; city

clam, *adv.,* secretly

clāmitō, 1, keep shouting

clāmō, 1, noise, shout, cry out

clāmor, –ōris, *m.,* shout(ing), noise, uproar; applause

clandestīnus, –a, –um, secret

clārē, *adv.,* clearly

clāritās, –tātis, *f.,* fame

Claros, –ī, *f.,* Claros

clārus, –a, –um, clear, brilliant, illustrious, loud, famous

classis, –is, *f.,* class, fleet

Claudius, –dī, *m.,* Claudius, *Roman emperor*

claudō, –ere, clausī, clausus, close, shut, cut off, bar

clāva, –ae, *f.,* rough stick, club

clāvus, –ī, *m.,* nail; rudder, helm

clēmēns, *gen.* **–entis,** mild, gentle, merciful

clēmenter, *adv.,* gently, with forbearance

clēmentia, –ae, *f.,* mercy

clīvus, –ī, *m.,* slope, hillside

clūnis, –is, *m. and f.,* buttock, haunch

Cn., *abbreviation for* **Gnaeus, –ī,** *m.,* Roman **praenōmen**

coalēscō, –ere, –aluī, –alitus, grow together

coarguō, –ere, –uī, —, make known, betray

coartō, 1, compress, confine; abridge, shorten

coccum, –ī, n., berry *(yielding a scarlet dye)*

codicillī, –ōrum, *m. pl.,* writing tablet, petition, will

coeō, –īre, –iī, –itūrus, come together, assemble, unite

coepī, coepisse, coeptus *(used only in perfect tenses),* have begun, began

coerceō, –ēre, –uī, –itus, check, repress

coetus, –ūs, *m.,* meeting

cōgitātē, *adv.,* thoughtfully

cōgitātiō, –ōnis, *f.,* thought, meditation

cōgitō, 1, think (of), consider, plan

cognātiō, –ōnis, *f.,* kinship

cognātus, –ī, *m.,* kinsman

cognitiō, –ōnis, *f.,* (learning to know), trial, acquaintance

cognitor, –ōris, *m.,* supporter

cognōmen, –minis, *n.,* nickname, surname

cognōscō, –ere, cognōvī, cognitus, become acquainted with, learn; recognize, note; *perf.,* have learned, know, understand

cōgō, –ere, coēgī, coāctus, (drive together), assemble; force, compel, collect

cohaereō, –ēre, cohaesī, cohaesus, cling together, be connected with

cohērēs, –ēdis, *m. and f.,* fellow heir

cohors, cohortis, *f.,* cohort

cohortātiō, –ōnis, *f.,* encouragement

cohortor, 1, urge

collābor, –lābī, –lāpsus, fall in ruin, sink down

collēga, –ae, *m.,* colleague

collēgium, –gī, *n.,* company

colligō, –ere, –lēgī, –lēctus, collect, infer

collis, –is, *m.,* hill

collocō, 1, put, establish, set up

colloquor, –loquī, –locūtus, talk (with), hold a conference

collum, –ī, *n.,* neck

colō, –ere, coluī, cultus, worship, cultivate, till, inhabit, attend, cherish, honor

colōnia, –ae, *f.,* colony

colōnus, –ī, *m.,* settler, colonist

color, –ōris, *m.,* color

Colossēum, –ī, *n.,* the Colosseum, *an amphitheater at Rome*

columba, –ae, *f.,* dove, pigeon

columna, –ae, *f.,* pillar, column

coma, –ae, *f.,* hair

comes, –itis, *m.,* companion

cōmitās, –tātis, *f.,* courtesy, kindness, friendliness

comitātus, –ūs, *m.,* escort, company

cōmiter, *adv.,* affably

comitium, –tī, *n.,* comitium, *an assembly place in Rome; pl.,* election, assembly

comitō, comitor, 1, accompany

commeminī, –isse, remember

commemorātiō, –ōnis, *f.,* remembrance, mention

commendātiō, –ōnis, *f.,* recommendation

commendō, 1, entrust, commend, approve

commercium, –cī, *n.,* trade, commerce; fellowship

comminuō, –ere, –uī, –ūtus, weaken

committō, –ere, –mīsī, –missus, join together, commit, start, entrust; **proelium committō,** begin battle

commodē, *adv.,* suitably

commodus, –a, –um, fit, suitable, favorable, convenient; *as noun, n.,* advantage

commoror, 1, linger, remain

commoveō, –ēre, –mōvī, –mōtus, disturb, move

commūnis, –e, common

commūnitās, –tātis, *f.,* fellowship

commūniter, *adv.,* in general

commūtō, 1, change, alter

cōmō, –ere, cōmpsī, cōmptus, comb, adorn

comoedus, –ī, *m.,* comedian, comic actor

comparātiō, –ōnis, *f.,* comparison

comparō, 1, get ready, prepare; collect, provide; constitute; compare

comperiō, –īre, –perī, –pertus, find out, discover

compescō, –ere, –pescuī, —, check

competītor, –ōris, *m.,* rival, competitor

complector, –plectī, –plexus, embrace, include

complexus, –ūs, *m.,* embrace

complūrēs, –a (–ia), several, many

compōnō, –ere, –posuī, –positus, (put together), compose, settle, arrange; bury

compos, –potis, master of, possessing

compositiō, –ōnis, *f.,* agreement

comprehendō, (comprēndō), –ere, –hendī, –hēnsus, seize, catch, detect, understand; arrest

comprimō, –ere, –pressī, –pressus, press together, restrain, repress

comprobō, 1, approve

compugnō, 1, fight together

computō, 1, sum up, compute; count

cōnātus, –ūs, *m.,* attempt

concēdō, –ere, –cessī, –cessūrus, give way, retire, grant

concidō, –ere, –cidī, —, fall (together), collapse

conciliō, 1, win (over)

concilium, –lī, *n.,* meeting, council

concinnō, 1, cause, produce, make fit

concipiō, –ere, cēpī, –ceptus, take up, receive, utter

concitō, 1, arouse

conclāmō, 1, cry out, exclaim, shout

conclāve, –is, *n.,* room, chamber

concordia, –ae, *f.,* harmony, concord

concordō, 1, agree, be consistent

concors, *gen.* **–cordis**, in harmony

concupīscō, –ere, –cupīvī, –ītus, long (for), desire, covet

concurrō, –ere, –currī, –cursūrus, run, gather

concursus, –ūs, *m.,* running together, gathering, throng

concutiō, –ere, –cussī, –cussus, strike together, shake (up)

condemnō, 1, condemn

condiciō, –ōnis, *f.,* condition, terms

condītus, –a, –um, seasoned; ornamented

condō, –ere, –didī, –ditus, found, establish; bring to an end; bury

condūco, –ere, –duxī, –ductus, hire, rent, be of help

conexus, –a, –um, adjoining

cōnfābulor, 1, talk

cōnferō, cōnferre, contulī, collātus, bring together, join, compare, collect; postpone; **mē conferō**, go, proceed

cōnfertus, –a, –um, crowded, compact, full

cōnfessiō, –ōnis, *f.,* confession

cōnfestim, *adv.,* at once

cōnficiō, –ere, –fēcī, –fectus, do up, complete, exhaust, destroy

cōnfīdō, –ere, cōnfīsus, *semideponent,* trust, be confident, rely on, have confidence (in)

cōnfirmō, 1, strengthen, assure, establish, declare, encourage, make firm

cōnfiteor, –ērī, cōnfessus, confess, admit

cōnflagrō, 1, be consumed *(by fire)*

cōnflīctiō, –ōnis, *f.,* combat

cōnflīctor, 1, struggle, conflict, contend

cōnflō, 1, blow up, kindle, excite; compose

cōnfluō, –ere, –flūxī, –flūxus, flock (together)

cōnfodiō, –ere, –fōdī, –fossus, stab

cōnfōrmō, 1, mold, train

cōnfringō, –ere, –frēgī, –frāctus, shatter, destroy

cōnfugiō, –ere, –fūgī, –fugitūrus, flee for refuge

congelō, 1, freeze; stiffen

congerō, –ere, –gessī, –gestus, bring together, collect

congredior, –ī, –gressus, meet

congregābilis, –e, easily brought together, social

congregātiō, –ōnis, *f.,* union, society, association

congregō, 1, collect; *pass.,* assemble

congruō, –ere, –uī, —, coincide, agree, suit, accord

congruus, –a, –um, suitable

coniciō, –ere, –iēcī, –iectus, throw, aim

coniectūra, –ae, *f.,* guess

coniūnctiō, –ōnis, *f.,* association

coniungō, –ere, –iūnxī, –iūnctus, join with, connect

coniūnx, –iugis, *m. and f.,* husband, wife

coniūrātī, –ōrum, *m. pl.,* conspirators

coniūrātiō, –ōnis, *f.,* conspiracy

cōnor, 1, attempt, try, endeavor

conquiēscō, –ere, –quiēvī, –quiētus, find rest

conquīrō, –ere, –quīsīvī, –quīsītus, seek out, hunt up, collect

cōnscelerātus, –a, –um, wicked

cōnscendō, –ere, –scendī, –scēnsus, climb, mount, scale, embark

cōnscientia, –ae, *f.,* consciousness, conscience

cōnscius, –cī, *m.,* witness

cōnscrīptī, patrēs cōnscrīptī, senators

cōnsecrō, 1, dedicate

cōnsenēscō, –ere, –senuī, —, grow old together

cōnsēnsiō, –ōnis, *f.,* agreement

cōnsēnsus, –ūs, *m.,* agreement

cōnsentiō, –īre, –sēnsī, –sēnsus, agree

cōnsequenter, *adv.,* then

cōnsequor, –ī, cōnsecūtus, follow (up), pursue; result; obtain, accomplish

cōnserō, –ere, –sēvī, –situs, plant

cōnserō, –ere, –seruī, –sertus, bind, join, connect

cōnservō, 1, keep, save, maintain, preserve

cōnservus, –ī, *m.,* fellow slave

cōnsīderō, 1, consider

cōnsīdō, –ere, –sēdī, –sessūrus, sit down, encamp, sink

cōnsilium, –lī, *n.,* plan, purpose, prudence, advice, wisdom; council, counsel

cōnsistō, –ere, cōnstitī, cōnstitūrus, stop, stand still

cōnsociātiō, –ōnis, *f.,* union, association

cōnsōlātiō, –ōnis, *f.,* consolation, comfort

cōnsōlor, 1, comfort

cōnspectus, –ūs, *m.,* sight

cōnspiciō, –ere, –spexī, –spectus, catch sight of, look upon, see

cōnspicor, 1, catch sight of

cōnstāns, *gen.* **–antis,** firm

cōnstanter, *adv.,* firmly, consistently

cōnstantia, –ae, *f.,* firmness

Cōnstantia, –ae, *f.,* Constance

cōnstituō, –ere, –stituī, –stitūtus, put, establish, settle; appoint, create; determine, decide, agree upon

cōnstō, –stāre, –stitī, –stātūrus, stand together, agree; **cōnstat,** it is evident, it is agreed

cōnstringō, –ere, –strīnxī, –strictus, bind, hold in check

cōnstrūctiō, –ōnis, *f.,* construction

cōnstruō, –ere, –strūxī, –strūctus, heap together; pile up; erect

cōnsuēscō, –ere, –suēvī, –suētus, become accustomed; *perfect,* be accustomed

cōnsuētūdō, –dinis, *f.,* custom, habit, practice; intimacy

cōnsul, –ulis, *m.,* consul, *the highest Roman official*

cōnsulāris, –e, consular, of consular rank; *as noun, m.,* ex-consul, man of consular rank

cōnsulātus, –ūs, *m.,* consulship

cōnsulō, –ere, –suluī, –sultus, consider, consult, put the question; look out for

cōnsultātiō, –ōnis, *f.,* consultation

cōnsultum, –ī, *n.,* decree

cōnsummō, 1, complete

cōnsūmō, –ere, –sūmpsī, –sūmptus, take (wholly), spend; destroy, consume

cōnsurgō, –ere, –surrēxī, –surrēctūrus, rise together

contāctus, –ūs, *m.,* touch

contāgiō, –ōnis, *f.,* touch, infection

contāminō, 1, stain, defile

contegō, –ere, –tēxī, –tēctus, cover

contemnō, –ere, –tempsī, –temptus, despise, disregard

contemptus, –ūs, *m.,* contempt, scorn, disgrace

contendō, –ere, –tendī, –tentus, contend, struggle, hasten, stretch

contineō, –ēre, –uī, –tentus, hold (together), contain

contentiō, –ōnis, *f.,* struggle, dispute

contentus, –a, –um, satisfied, content

conterminus, –a, –um, adjoining, neighboring

conterō, –ere, –trīvī, –trītus, waste

conterreō, –ēre, –uī, –itus, terrify

conticēscō, –ere, –uī, —, be silent, be still

contiguus, –a, –um, adjoining

continēns, *gen.* **–entis,** temperate, self-restrained; *as noun, f.,* the mainland

continentia, –ae, *f.,* self-control

contineō, –ēre, –tinuī, –tentus, bound; hold fast; restrain; comprise

contingō, –ere, –tigī, –tāctus, touch, reach; happen

continuō, 1, prolong

continuō, *adv.,* continuously

continuus, –a, –um, successive

contiō, –ōnis, *f.,* assembly, meeting

cōntiōnātor, –ōris, *m.,* demagogue

contrā, *adv. and prep. w. acc.,* against, contrary to, opposite; to the other side

contrahō, –ere, –trāxī, –trāctus, draw together; contract

contrārius, –a, –um, opposite, opposed

contrōversia, –ae, *f.,* dispute

contubernālis, –is, *m. and f.,* companion, mate

contubernium, –nī, *n.,* dwelling together; household

contumēlia, –ae, *f.,* insult, abuse

contumēliōsus, –a, –um, abusive, insulting

cōnūbium, –bī, *n.,* marriage

convalēscō, –ere, –valuī, —, recover from an illness, regain health

convellō, –ere, –vellī, –vulsus, tear away

conveniō, –īre, –vēnī, –ventūrus, come together, assemble, meet; be suited to; *impers.,* it is fitting or agreed

conventum, –ī, *n.,* agreement

conventus, –ūs, *m.,* assembly

convertō, –ere, –vertī, –versus, turn, change

convīcium, –cī, *n.,* violent reproach, wrangling

convīctus, –ūs, *m.,* (living together), intimacy

convīva, –ae, *m. and f.,* table companion, guest

convīvium, –vī, *n.,* feast, banquet

convocō, –āre, –āvī, –ātus, 1, call together

cooperiō, –īre, cooperuī, coopertus, overwhelm

cooperor, 1, work with or together, unite

cōpia, –ae, *f.,* supply, abundance; fluency; *pl.,* resources, troops, forces

cōpiōsus, –a, –um, well-supplied, plentiful, rich

coquō, –ere, coxī, coctus, cook, burn

cor, cordis, *n.,* heart

Corduba, –ae, *f.,* Cor´dova, *a city in Spain*

Corinthius, –a, –um, Corinthian

Corinthus, –ī, *f.,* Corinth, *a city in Greece*

Cornēlius, –lī, *m.,* Cornelius

cornū, –ūs, *n.,* horn; wing *(of an army),* flank, tip *(of the moon)*

corōna, –ae, *f.,* wreath, crown

corōnō, 1, crown

corporālis, –e, corporeal

corpus, –poris, *n.,* body

corpusculum, –ī, *n.,* a little body, dear person

corrigō, –ere, –rēxī, –rēctus, correct

corrōborō, 1, strengthen

corrumpō, –ere, –rūpī, –ruptus, corrupt, falsify; waste

corruō, –ere, –ruī, —, fall together

corruptēla, –ae, *f.,* corruption

corruptiō, –ōnis, *f.,* bribery, illness

cortex, –ticis, *m. and f.,* bark, shell, hull

Corvīnus, –ī, *m.,* Corvinus

cotīdiānus, –a, –um, daily

cotīdiē, *adv.,* daily

crās, tomorrow

Crassus, –ī, *m.,* Crassus

crātēr, –is, *m.,* large bowl

Cratippus, –ī, *m.,* Cratippus

Creātor, –oris, *m.,* the Creator

creātūra, –ae, *f.,* creation, act of creation

crēber, –bra, –brum, thick, frequent, numerous

crēdibilis, –e, credible

crēditor, –ōris, *m.,* creditor

crēdō, –ere, –didī, –ditus, believe, suppose; entrust *(w. dat.)*

crēdulus, –a, –um, credulous, unsuspecting, trustful

creō, 1, make, create

crepitus, –ūs, *m.,* sound

crēscō, –ere, crēvī, crētus, grow, increase

Crēta, –ae, *f.,* (acc. **Crētan**), Crete, *an island south of Greece*

crīmen, –minis, *n.,* accusation, charge, crime

crīminor, 1, charge

crīnis, –is, *m.,* hair

Crotōniēnsis, –e, Crotonian, of Croton *(a city in southern Italy)*

cruciātus, –ūs, *m.,* torture

cruciō, 1, torture; afflict

crūdēlis, –e, cruel

crūdēliter, *adv.,* cruelly

crūdēlitās, –tātis, *f.,* cruelty

cruentus, –a, –um, bloody

cruentātus, –a, –um, bloody

cruor, cruōris, *m.,* blood

crūs, crūris, *n.,* leg

crux, crucis, *f.,* cross

cubiculum, –ī, *n.,* bedroom, lounging room

cubō, –āre, –uī, –itūrus, lie down; sleep

culpa, –ae, *f.,* fault, guilt

cultūra, –ae, *f.,* cultivation; **agrī cultūra,** agriculture

cultus, –ūs, *m.,* culture

cum, *prep. w. abl.,* with

cum, *conj.,* when, while, since, although; **cum... tum,** not only . . . but also

cumulō, 1, heap up, crown

cumulus, –ī, *m.,* heap, increase

cūnctanter, *adv.,* reluctantly

cūnctātiō, –ōnis, *f.,* hesitancy, uncertainty

cūnctus, –a, –um, all together, all

cupiditās, –tātis, *f.,* desire, greed

cupīdō, –dinis, *f.,* desire, longing; love

cupidus, –a, –um, eager

cupiō, –ere, cupīvī, cupītus, desire, be eager, wish, want

cūr, *adv.,* why

cūra, –ae, *f.*, care, concern, anxiety; **(cum) magnā cūrā,** very carefully

cūrātiō, –ōnis, *f.*, care; cure

cūrātor, –ōris, *m.*, manager, commissioner, guardian

cūria, –ae, *f.*, curia, senate house

cūriōsē, *adv.*, carefully

Curius, –rī, *m.*, Curius

cūrō, 1, care for, look after; take care, arrange, cause *(to be done)*, cure

curriculum, –ī, *n.*, course

currō, –ere, cucurrī, cursūrus, run; fly

currus, –ūs, *m.*, chariot

cursim, *adv.*, quickly, speedily

cursitō, –āre, —, —, run constantly

cursō, 1, run around

cursus, -ūs, *m.* running; race, way, voyage, course, career

curvāmen, –minis, *n.*, curve

curvō, 1, curve

cuspis, –idis, *f.*, point; sting

custōdia, –ae, *f.*, guard, custody, protection, prison

custōdiō, –īre, –īvī, –ītus, guard, watch

custōs, –ōdis, *m.*, guard, custodian, parent

Cynthus, –ī, *m.*, Cynthus, *a mountain on Delos*

D

Dalmatia, –ae, f., Dalmatia, *a region on the eastern shore of the Adriatic*

Damasichthōn, –onis, *m.*, Damasich´thon, *one of Niobe's sons*

Damasippus, –ī, *m.*, Damasip´pus

damnātiō, –ōnis, *f.*, conviction

damnō, 1, condemn

damnōsus, –a, –um, harmful

damnum, –ī, *n.*, loss; fine, penalty; curse

Daphnē, – ēs, *f.*, Daphne, *daughter of the river-god Peneus*

daps, dapis, *f.*, meal, feast; food

Daunius, –a, –um, Daunian, Apulian

dē, *prep. w. abl.*, from, down from, concerning, about, for, during

dea, –ae, *f.*, goddess

deambulō, –āre, —, —, take a walk

dēbeō, –ēre, dēbuī, dēbitus, ought, owe, should, must; *pass.*, be due

dēbilis, –e, weak, helpless

dēbilitō, 1, weaken

dēbitor, –ōris, *m.* debtor

dēcēdō, –ere, –cessī, –cessūrus, depart

decem, ten

decenter, *adv.*, becomingly, properly

dēcernō, –ere, –crēvī, –crētus, decide, decree, vote (for)

dēcerpō, –ere, –cerpsī, –cerptus, pluck

decet, –ēre, decuit, *impers.*, becomes, befits

Deciānus, –ī, *m.*, Decianus

decimus, –a, –um, tenth; **Decimus, –ī,** *m.*, Decimus

Decius, –ci, *m.*, Decius

dēclamatiō, –ōnis, *f.*, oratorical exercise, declamation

dēclāmitō, 1, declaim

dēclārō, 1, show, declare

dēclīnatiō, –ōnis, *f.*, bending aside, avoidance

decor, –ōris, *m.*, charm, beauty

decorō, 1, adorn, honor, embellish

decōrus, –a, –um, handsome, proper

dēcrētum, –ī, *n.*, decree

decurrō, –ere, –cucurrī (–currī), –cursūrus, run (down), hasten

decus, decoris, *n.*, honor

dēdecus, –coris, *n.*, disgrace, vice

dēdicō, 1, dedicate

dēdō, –ere, dēdidī, dēditus, hand over, surrender, devote

dēdūcō, –ere, –dūxī, –ductus, lead (away)

dēfatīgō, 1, wear out

dēfendō, –ere, dēfendī, dēfēnsus, defend

dēfēnsiō, –ōnis, *f.*, defense

dēferō, dēferre, dētulī, dēlātus, bring, report

dēfessus, –a, –um, wearied

dēficiō, –ere, dēfēcī, dēfectus, fail, revolt

dēfīgō, –ere, dēfīxī, dēfīxus, fix, plunge

dēfīniō, –īre, dēfīnīvī, dēfīnītus, limit, fix, appoint, define

dēfīnītiō, –ōnis, *f.*, definition

dēflagrō, 1, burn down

dēfleō, –ēre, dēflēvī, dēflētus, weep over

dēfluō, –ere, dēflūxī, dēflūxus, flow *or* sink down

dēfraudō, 1, cheat out of

dēgerō, –ere, —, —, carry off

dēgō, –ere, dēgī, —, spend, pass

dēgustō, 1, taste

dēiciō, –ere, dēiēcī, dēiectus, throw *or* cast down, push aside

dēierō, dēiūrō, 1, swear

dein, deinde, *adv.,* then, next

deinceps, *adv.,* next

Deīrī, –ōrum, *a tribe of the Angles*

dēlabor, –ī, dēlāpsus, fall, sink

dēlectātiō, –ōnis, *f.,* delight

dēlecto, 1, please, charm, delight in

dēlēniō, –īre, dēlēnīvī, dēlēnītus, allay, charm

dēleō, –ēre, dēlēvī, dēlētus, blot out, destroy

dēlīberātiō, –ōnis, *f.,* deliberation, question

dēlīberō, 1, think about, consider

dēlicātus, –a, –um, effeminate

dēliciae, –ārum, *f. pl.,* delight, pleasure

dēligō, 1, tie up

dēligō, –ere, dēlēgī, dēlēctus, select, choose

dēlinquō, –ere, dēlīquī, dēlictus, fail, do wrong

dēlīrō, 1, be crazy, rave

Dēlius, –a, –um, Delian, of Delos

Dēlos, –ī, *f.,* Delos, *an island in the Aegean*

Delphicus, –a, –um, Delphic, of Delphi, *a famous Greek oracle*

dēlūbrum, –ī, *n.,* shrine

dēmēns, *gen.* **–entis,** mad

dēmenter, *adv.,* foolishly

dēmigro, 1, go off, depart

dēminūtiō, –ōnis, *f.,* sacrifice, loss

dēmissus, –a, –um, downcast; *w.* **crīne,** disheveled

dēmittō, –ere, dēmīsī, dēmissus, let down

dēmō, –ere, dēmpsī, dēmptus, take away

dēmōnstrō, 1, point out, show

dēmum, *adv.,* at length, at last

dēnegō, 1, deny

dēnique, *adv.,* finally, after all, in short

dēns, dentis, *m.,* tooth

dēnūntiō, 1, threaten

dēnuō, *adv.,* once more, again

dēpellō, –ere, dēpulī, depulsus, drive from, avert, remove, overthrow

dēplōrō, 1, lament, deplore

dēpōnō, –ere, dēposuī, dēpositus, put down, lay aside, put aside; quench

dēpositum, –ī, *n.,* deposit, loan

dēprāvō, 1, corrupt, tamper with

dēprecor, 1, avert by prayer

dēprendō, –ere, dēprendī, dēprēnsus, seize, catch; perceive

dēprimō, –ere, dēpressī, dēpressus, press down, sink

dērādō, –ere, dērāsī, dērāsus, scrape off

dērelinquō, –ere, dērelīquī, dērelictus, abandon, forsake

dērīdeō, –ēre, dērīsī, dērīsus, laugh at, mock

dērigēscō, –ere, dēriguī, —, become rigid

dēscendō, –ere, dēscendī, dēscēnsus, descend, resort

dēserō, –ere, dēseruī, dēsertus, desert

dēsertus, –a, –um, lonely

dēsideō, –ēre, dēsēdī, dēsessūrus, be idle

dēsīderium, –rī, *n.,* longing, desire

dēsīderō, 1, desire, miss

dēsidia, –ae, *f.,* idleness

dēsignō, 1, mark out, elect, choose

dēsiliō, –īre, dēsiluī, dēsultūrus, jump down, dismount

dēsinō, –ere, dēsiī, dēsitus, cease

dēsipiō, –ere, dēsipuī, —, be silly *or* foolish

dēsistō, –ere, dēstitī, dēstitus, stand away, cease

dēsōlō, 1, leave alone, desert

dēspērātiō, –ōnis, *f.,* hopelessness, despair

dēspērō, 1, despair (of)

dēspiciō, –ere, dēspexī, dēspectus, look down on, despise

dēspondeō, –ēre, dēspondī, dēspōnsus, promise, betroth

dēstinō, 1, bind; intend, determine

dēstringō, –ere, dēstrīnxī, dēstrictus, unsheath

dēstruō, –ere, destrūxī, destrūctus, tear down, destroy

dēsum, dēesse, dēfuī, dēfutūrus, fail, be lacking

dētegō, –ere, dētēxī, dētēctus, uncover

dēterō, –ere, dētrīvī, dētrītus, wear away, weaken

dēterreō, –ēre, dēterruī, dēterritus, deter

dētestor, 1, curse, denounce, deprecate

dētineō, –ēre, dētinuī, dētentus, hold

dētrahō, –ere, dētrāxī, dētrāctus, draw *or* take from, pull off, remove, withdraw

dētrimentum, –ī, *n.,* loss, defeat

deūrō, –ere, deussī, deustus, burn up

deus, –ī, *m.,* god; *nom. pl.,* diī *or* dī

dēvinciō, –īre, dēvinxī, dēvinctus, bind, unite

dēvorō, 1, devour, swallow

dēvoveō, –ēre, dēvōvī, dēvōtus, vow, dedicate; curse

dexter, –tra (–tera), –trum (–terum), right; *comp.* dexterior, –ius, right; *as noun, f.,* right hand

diabolus, –ī, *m.,* devil

dialecticus, –a, –um, dialectic; *as noun, m.,* logician

Diāna, –ae, *f.,* Diana, *goddess of hunting*

Diaulus, –ī, Diaulus

diciō, –ōnis, *f.,* power

dīcō, –ere, dīxī, dictus, say, speak, tell, call

dictātor, –ōris, *m.,* dictator

dictātūra, –ae, *f.,* dictatorship

dictō, 1, dictate

dictum, –ī, *n.,* word

diēs, diēī, *m. and f.,* day

differō, diferre, distulī, dīlātus, postpone; differ

difficilis, –e, difficult, hard

difficultās, –tātis, *f.,* difficulty, trouble

diffīdō, –ere, –fīsus, *semideponent,* mistrust

diffundō, –ere, –fūdī, –fūsus, spread out

dīgerō, –ere, dīgessī, dīgestus, force apart, separate

digitus, –ī, *m.,* finger

dignitās, –tātis, *f.,* dignity

dignus, –a, –um, worthy

dīiūdicō, 1, decide, settle

dīiungō, –ere, dīiūnxī, dīiūnctus, separate

dīlēctus, –ūs, *m.,* choice

dīligēns, *gen.* –entis, careful, scrupulous

dīligenter, *adv.,* carefully

dīligentia, –ae, *f.,* care, diligence

dīligō, –ere, dīlexī, dīlectus, single out, esteem, love

dīlūcēscō, –ere, dīlūxī, —, grow light

dīmētior, –īrī, dīmēnsus, measure, lay out

dīmicātiō, –ōnis, *f.,* struggle

dīmicō, 1, fight, contend, struggle

dīmidius, –a, –um, half

dīminūtiō, –ōnis, *f.,* decrease

dīmittō, –ere, dīmīsī, dīmissus, let go, lose, abandon, send away, dismiss

dīmoveō, –ēre, dīmōvī, dīmōtus, move apart, stir

diocēsis, –is, *f.,* diocese *(district ruled by a bishop)*

dīrēctus, –a, –um, straight

dīreptiō, –ōnis, *f.,* plundering, loot

dīreptor, –ōris, *m.,* plunderer

dirimō, –ere, dirēmī, dirēmptus, break off

dīripiō, –ere, dīripuī, dīrēptus, plunder

dīruō, –ere, dīruī, dīrutus, tear down

dīrus, –a, –um, awful

discēdō, –ere, –cessī, –cessūrus, go away, depart

discernō, –ere, –crēvī, crētus, set apart, distinguish, discern

discerpō, –ere, –cerpsī, –cerptus, tear in pieces

discessus, –ūs, *m.,* departure

disciplīna, –ae, *f.,* training, instruction, discipline

discipulus, –ī, *m.,* discipula, –ae, *f.,* student learner, pupil, disciple, follower

discō, –ere, didicī, —, learn

discordia, –ae, *f.,* discord

discrībō, –ere, discrīpsī, discrīptus, assign

discrīmen, –minis, *n.,* difference, decision, danger, crisis

discrīminō, 1, divide, separate

dispār, *gen.* –paris, unequal

dispēnso, 1, distribute

dispertiō, –īre, –īvī, –ītus, distribute

dispiciō, –ere, dispexī, dispectus, consider

dispōnō, –ere, –posuī, –positus, place here and there, arrange, dispose

disputō, 1, discuss, argue

dissēminō, 1, spread abroad

dissēnsiō, –ōnis, *f.,* quarrel

dissentiō, –īre, –sēnsī, –sēnsus, disagree, differ

disserō, –ēre, disseruī, disertus, examine, discuss, discourse

dissideō, –ēre, –sēdī, –sessus, disagree

dissimilis, –e, unlike

errō, 1, wander, be mistaken

error, –ōris, *m.*, error

ērudiō, –īre, –īvī, –ītus, teach

ērudītiō, –ōnis, *f.*, instruction

ērudītus, –a, –um, educated, learned

ērumpō, –ere, ērūpī, ēruptus, break out, burst forth

ēruō, ēruere, ēruī, ērutus, tear out

ervum, –ī, *n.*, bitter vetch *(a plant)*

et, *conj.*, and, even, also, too; **et... et**, both . . . and

etenim, *conj.*, for truly, and indeed

etiam, *adv.*, even, also, too, still; **nōn sōlum... sed etiam**, not only . . . but also; **etiam atque etiam**, again and again

Etrūria, –ae, *f.*, Etruria, *a district of Italy*

Etrūscī, –ōrum, *m. pl.*, the Etruscans

Eumaeus, –ī, *m.*, Eumaeus (Ūmē´us)

Eurōpa, –ae, *f.*, Europe

ēvādō, –ere, ēvāsī, ēvāsūrus, go out, escape

ēveniō, –īre, ēvēnī, ēventūrus, (come out), turn out, happen

ēventus, –ūs, *m.*, occurrence; fate

ēvertō, –ere, ēvertī, ēversus, overthrow, destroy, ruin

ēvigilō, 1, awake

ēvītābilis, –e, avoidable

ēvocātor, –ōris, *m.*, a caller to arms

ēvocō, 1, summon, call out

ēvolō, 1, fly *or* rush forth

ēvolvō, –ere, ēvolvī, evolūtus, unroll (and read)

ex, *see* **ē**

exaedificō, 1, finish building, erect

exaggerō, 1, increase

exanimis, –e, lifeless, dead

exaudiō, –īre, –īvī, –ītus, hear (plainly)

excēdō, –ere, –cessī, –cessūrus, go forth, withdraw, depart

excellēns, *gen.* **–entis**, superior, remarkable

excellentia, –ae, *f.*, superiority, excellence

excelsus, –a, –um, elevated, high

excerpō, –ere, –cerpsī, –cerptus, choose, select

excīdō, –ere, –cidī, —, fall (out), disappear

excīdō, –ere, –cīdī, –cīsus, destroy

excipiō, –ere, –cēpī, –ceptus, take out *or* up, receive, catch, intercept; follow; except

excitō, 1, arouse; raise

exclamō, 1, shout

exclūdō, –ere, –clūsī, –clūsus, shut out

excolō, –ere, –uī, excultus, cultivate

excruciō, 1, torment, torture, harass

excurrō, –ere, –cucurrī, –curūrsus, run out *or* up

excūsātiō, –ōnis, *f.*, excuse

excutiō, –ere, –cussī, –cussus, shake off, force away; search, examine

exemplum, –ī, *n.*, example, copy, precedent

exeō, –īre, –iī, –itūrus, go *or* come forth, depart

exerceō, –ēre, exercuī, exercitus, train, exercise; keep busy; conduct

exercitātiō, –ōnis, *f.*, training, exercise

exercitus, –ūs, *m.*, (trained) army

exhauriō, –īre, exhausī, exhaustus, drain

exhibeō, –ēre, –uī, –itus, show

exhorreō, –ēre, uī, —, shudder at, dread

exigō, –ere, exēgī, exāctus, drive out, demand; *of time*, spend, pass

exiguus, –a, –um, small, slight, narrow

exilis, –e, thin, meager, poor; worthless

eximiē, *adv.*, exceedingly

eximius, –a, –um, extraordinary

eximō, –ere, exēmī, exēmptus, take away, consume

exīstimātiō, –ōnis, *f.*, reputation

exīstimō, 1, think, suppose, consider

exit, he goes out

exitiābilis, –e, fatal

exitiōsus, –a, –um, deadly

exitium, –tī, *n.*, ruin, destruction, death

exitus, –ūs, *m.*, end

exoptātus, –a, –um, earnestly desired, longed for

exoptō, 1, desire

exōrnō, 1, adorn

exōrō, 1, beg

exōsus, –a, –um, hating, detesting

espallēscō, –ere, expalluī, —, turn pale

expavēscō, –ere, expāvī, —, be terrified, dread

expectātiō, –ōnis, *f.*, awaiting, expectation, longing

expediō, –īre, –iī, –ītus, set free, procure

expellō, –ere, expulī, expulsus, drive out, expel; deprive of

experior, –īrī, expertus, try, test; find

expers, expertis, having no share in

expertus, –a, –um, tried, proved; experienced in

expetō, –ere, –īvī, –ītus, seek

explānō, 1, explain

expleō, –ēre, explēvī, explētus, fill, satisfy

explicō, 1, unfold, explain

explōrātor, –ōris, *m.,* spy, scout

explōrō, 1, investigate, explore

expoliō, –īre, –īvī, ītus, smooth, polish, adorn, refine

expōnō, –ere, exposuī, expositus, put out, expose, explain

exprimō, –ere, expressī, espressus, press out, portray, describe

exprobrō, 1, accuse of, charge

exprōmō, –ere, exprōmpsī, exprōmptus, display; disclose

expugnō, 1, take by storm, capture, capture by assault

expūrgō, 1, clear

exquīsītus, –a, –um, exquisite, excessive

exscrībō, –ere, exscrīpsī, exscrīptus, copy

exsiliō, –īre, exsiluī, —, leap up

exsilium, –lī, *n.,* exile, banishment

exsistō, –ere, exstitī, —, stand forth, appear

exspectātiō, –ōnis, *f.,* waiting, anticipation

exspectō, 1, look out for, expect, await, wait (for)

exstinguō, –ere, exstīnxī, exstīnctus, extinguish, destroy

exstō, –āre, —, —, stand out, protrude; exist

exstruō, –ere, exstrūxī, exstrūctus, heap up, build

exsul, –ulis, *m. and f.,* exile

exsultō, 1, (leap up), exult

exsuperantia, –ae, *f.,* superiority

extemplō, *adv.,* immediately

extendō, –ere, –tendī, –tentus (–tēnsus), stretch out, prolong

externus, –a, –um, foreign

exterus, –a, –um, outside, foreign

extollō, –ere, —, —, raise up

extorqueō, –ēre, extorsī, extortus, wrest

extrā, *(prep. w. acc.),* outside (of), beyond

extrēmus, –a, –um, farthest, last, end of

exūrō, –ere, exussī, exustus, burn (up)

exuviae, –ārum, *f.,* spoils

F

faber, –brī, *m.,* mechanic, fireman

fabricō, 1, build, construct

fābula, –ae, *f.,* story, play

Fabulla, –ae, *f.,* Fabulla

Fabullus, –ī, *m.,* Fabullus

fābulor, 1, speak, say, utter

fābulōsus, –a, –um, storied, fabulous

facētē, *adv.,* wittily

facētiae, –ārum, *f. pl.,* jest, wit

faciēs, –ēī, *f.,* appearance, face

facile, *adv.,* easily, readily

facilis, –e, easy

facilitās, –tātis, *f.,* friendliness

facinorōsus, –ī, *m.,* criminal

facinus, –noris, *n.,* deed, crime

faciō, –ere, fēcī, factus, do, make, form, cause; **proelium faciō,** fight a battle; **verba faciō,** speak, make a speech

factiō, –ōnis, *f.,* faction

factiōsus, –a, –um, seditious

factitō, 1, make *or* do frequently

factum, –ī, *n.,* deed

facultās, –tātis, *f.,* ability, means, opportunity

fācundus, –a, –um, eloquent

faenerātor, –ōris, *m.,* moneylender

faenus, faenoris, *n.,* interest

Faesulae, –ārum, *f.,* Faesulae, Fiesole, *a town in Etruria*

fāgus, –ī, *f.,* beech tree, beechwood

Falernum, –ī, *n.,* Falernian wine

fallō, –ere, fefellī, falsus, deceive, elude, escape the notice of; disappoint; *w.* **fidem,** break one's word

falsus, –a, –um, false

fāma, –ae, *f.,* report, story; fame, reputation; *w.* **est,** it is said

famēs, –is, *f.,* hunger

familia, –ae, *f.,* household, family; slaves

familiāris, –e, belonging to the family, friendly, private, intimate; *as noun, m.,* intimate friend

familiāritās, –tātis, *f.,* friendship

familiāriter, *adv.,* intimately

famulus, –ī, *m.,* servant

fāmōsus, –a, –um, famous, notorious

Fannius, –nī, *m.,* Fannius

fānum, –ī, *n.,* shrine

fās, *indeclinable, n.,* right

fascis, –is, *m.,* bundle; *pl.,* **fascēs**

fastīdiō, –īre, fastīdīvī, fastīdītus, feel disgust, disdain

fastīdium, –dī, *n.,* loathing, aversion

fatālis, –e, fated, deadly

fateor, –ērī, fassus, confess, admit

fātifer, –era, –erum, deathbringing, fatal

fatīgō, 1, weary

fātum, –ī, *n.,* fate; *often personified,* the Fates

faucēs, –ium, *f. pl.,* throat, jaws; pass

fautor, –ōris, *m.,* promoter

faveō, –ēre, fāvī, fautus, be favorable to, favor

favilla, –ae, *f.,* embers

favor, –ōris, *m.,* favor; cheering

favus, –ī, *m.,* honeycomb

fax, facis, *f.,* torch

febricula, –ae, *f.,* fever, slight fever

fēcundus, –a, –um, fruitful, rich

fēlīx, *gen.* **fēlīcis,** happy, fortunate, productive

fēmina, –ae, *f.,* woman, wife

fenestra, –ae, *f.,* window

fera, –ae, *f.,* wild beast

ferē, fermē, *adv.,* almost, about; *w. neg.,* hardly

fēriae, –ārum, *f. pl.,* holidays

ferio, –īre, –īvī, –ītus, hit, strike, knock

feritās, –tātis, *f.,* wildness

fermē, *see* **ferē**

ferō, ferre, tulī, lātus, bear, carry, bring, direct, produce, obtain; say; *w.* **lēgem,** propose, pass; *w.* **pedem retrō,** start back

ferōcitās, –tātis, *f.,* fierceness

ferōciter, *adv.,* fiercely

ferōx, –ōcis, fierce

ferrāmentum, –ī, *n.,* sword, dagger

ferreus, –a, –um, of iron, hard

ferrum, –ī, *n.,* iron; sword, point

ferus, –a, –um, savage, cruel

fervēns, *gen.* **–entis,** hot, burning

fessus, –a, –um, wearied, worn out

festīnātiō, –ōnis, *f.,* haste, despatch, speed

festīnō, 1, hasten, hurry

fēstīvus, –a, –um, gay, pleasant, kind

fēstum, –ī, *n.,* holiday

fēstus, –a, –um, festive

fētus, –ūs, *m.,* offspring, fruit

fidēlis, –e, faithful

fidēliter, *adv.,* faithfully, loyally

fidēs, –eī, *f.,* trust, belief; credit, honor, loyalty, pledge

fīdūcia, –ae, *f.,* trust, confidence

fīdus, –a, –um, trusty, faithful, reliable, loyal

fīgō, –ere, fīxī, fīxus, fix, set

Figulus, –ī, *m.,* Figulus

figūra, –ae, *f.,* shape, figure

fīlia, –ae, *f.,* daughter

fīliolus, –ī, *m.,* little son

fīlius, –lī, *m.,* son

fingō, ere, fīnxī, fictus, form, imagine, suppose

fīniō, –īre, –īvī, –ītus, end, finish, bound

fīnis, –is, *m.,* end, limit; *pl.,* borders, territory

fīnitimus, –a, –um, neighboring, near; *as noun,* neighbor

fiō, fierī, —, factus, become, be made, be done, happen

firmāmentum, –ī, *n.,* foundation, firmament

firmiter, *adv.,* firmly

firmō, 1, strengthen

firmus, –a, –um, strong, firm

fissus, –a, –um, split

fistula, –ae, *f.,* (shepherd's) pipe

fīxus, *see* **fīgō**

Flaccus, –ī, *m.,* Flaccus

Flacilla, –ae, *f.,* Flacilla

flagellum, –ī, *n.,* whip

flāgitium, –tī, *n.,* disgraceful act, crime

flāgitō, 1, demand, insist upon

flāmen, –inis, *n.,* breeze

Flāminius, –nī, Flaminius

Flāminius, –a, –um, Flaminian

flamma, –ae, *f.,* flame, fire

flāvēscō, –ere, —, —, become golden

flāvus, –a, –um, yellow, golden

flectō, –ere, flexī, flexus, turn, bend, influence

fleō, flēre, flēvī, flētus, weep

flētus, –ūs, *m.,* weeping

Flōrentia, –ae, *f.,* Florence, *a city in Italy*

flōreō, –ēre, –uī, —, bloom, flourish

flōs, flōris, *m.,* flower

fluctus, -ūs, *m.,* wave

flūmen, flūminis, *n.,* river

fluō, –ere, flūxī, flūxus, flow

flūxus, –a, –um, fleeting

focus, –ī, *m.,* hearth

foederātus, –a, –um, allied

foedō, 1, stain

foedus, –a, –um, vile, shameful

foedus, –deris, *n.,* league, alliance, compact

folium, –lī, *n.,* leaf

fōns, fontis, *m.,* spring, fountain, source

forēnsis, –e, of the Forum, public

foris, –is, *f.,* door

forīs, *adv.,* out of doors, abroad

fōrma, –ae, *f.,* shape, image, form, beauty, plan

formīdō, –dinis, *f.,* fear, dread

formīdolōsus, –a, –um, alarming, formidable

fōrmō, 1, form, compose

fōrmōsus, –a, –um, handsome, beautiful

fors, fortis, *f.,* chance

forsitan, *adv.,* perhaps

fortasse, *adv.,* perhaps

forte, *adv.,* by chance

fortis, –e, strong, brave

fortiter, *adv.,* bravely

fortitūdō, –dinis, *f.,* strength

fortuitus, –a, –um, accidental

fortūna, –ae, *f.,* fortune, luck

fortūnātus, –a, –um, happy, fortunate

forum, –ī, *n.,* forum, market place; **Forum Aurēlium,** *n., a town in Etruria,* Forum (*at Rome*)

forus, –ī, *m.,* gangway

foveō, –ēre, fōvī, fōtus, warm, cherish, support

fragilis, –e, fragile, weak

frangō, –ere, frēgī, frāctus, break, shatter, crush, overcome

frāter, frātris, *m.,* brother

frāternus, –a, –um, of one's brother

fraudulentus, –a, –um, deceitful

fraus, fraudis, *f.,* fraud, deceit

frēna (–ī), –ōrum, *n. or m. pl.,* bridle, rein

frēnō, 1, bridle, curb

frequēns, *gen.* **–entis,** in crowds

frequenter, *adv.,* often, in great numbers

frequentia, –ae, *f.,* throng, large number

fretum, –ī, *n.,* strait, sea, water

frētus, –a, –um, relying on

frīgeō, –ēre, —, —, be cold, freeze

frīgidārius, –a, –um, cooling

frīgidus, –a, –um, cold

frīgus, –goris, *n.,* cold, coolness

frondeō, –ēre, —, —, put forth leaves

frōns, frondis, *f.,* leaf

frōns, frontis, *f.,* front, forehead

Frontō, –ōnis, *m.,* Fronto, *a Roman writer*

frūctus, –ūs, *m.,* enjoyment, fruit, income, benefit, products

frugālitās, –tātis, *f.,* thrift

frūmentārius, –a, –um, of grain; *w.* **auxilium,** granary; *w.* **rēs,** grain supply

frūmentum, –ī, *n.,* grain

fruor, fruī, frūctus, (+ *abl.*), enjoy

frūstrā, *adv.,* in vain

frūstum, –ī, *n.,* bit

fūcus, –ī, *m.,* red dye; pretense

fuga, –ae, *f.,* flight; **in fugam dō,** put to flight

fugāx, *gen.* **–ācis,** fleeing

fugiō, –ere, fūgī, fugitūrus, run away, flee, avoid, escape

fugitīvus, –ī, *m.,* runaway slave

fugō, 1, put to flight, repel

fulgeō, –ēre, fulsī, —, gleam

fulmen, –minis, *n.,* lightning, thunderbolt

Fulvia, –ae, *f.,* Fulvia

Fulvius, –vī, *m.,* Fulvius

fulvus, –a, um, yellow

fundāmentum, –ī, *n.,* foundation, basis, beginning

fundō, 1, found

fundō, –ere, fūdī, fūsus, pour; rout

fundus, –ī, *m.,* estate, bottom

funestus, –a, –um, fatal

fungor, –ī, functus, perform

fūnus, fūneris, *n.,* funeral, death; ruin

fūr, fūris, *m. and f.,* thief, robber

furca, –ae, *f.,* forked pole
furibundus, –a, –um, full of rage
furiōsus, –a, –um, insane, furious
Fūrius, –rī, *m.,* Furius
Furnius, –nī, *m.,* Furnius
furō, –ere, –uī, —, rage, be mad
furor, –ōris, *m.,* madness, fury
fūrtim, *adv.,* secretly
fūrtum, –ī, *n.,* theft
Fuscus, –ī, *m.,* Fuscus
fūstis, –is, *m.,* staff, club
futūrus, *see* **sum**

G

Gadēs, –ium, *f. pl.,* Cadiz, *a city in Spain*
Gāius, –ī, *m.,* Gaius
Galba, –ae, *m.,* Galba, *a Roman emperor*
galea, –ae, *f.,* helmet
Gallia, –ae, *f.,* Gaul, *ancient France*
Gallicus, –a, –um, Gallic, of Gaul
Gallus, –a, -um, Gallic *(from Gaul); as noun, m.,*
     a Gaul
Gangēs, –is, *m.,* Ganges, *a river in India*
garriō, īre, –īvī, –ītūrus, chatter
gaudeō, –ēre, gāvīsus, *semideponent,* rejoice
gaudium, –dī, *n.,* joy, gladness, delight
gelidus, –a, –um, cold
Gemellus, –ī, *m.,* Gemellus
geminus, –a, –um, twin, two, both
gemitus, –ūs, *m.,* groan, lamentation
gemma, –ae, *f.,* precious stone
gena, –ae, *f.,* cheek
gener, –erī, *m.,* son-in-law
genetrīx, –īcis, *f.,* mother
geniāliter, *adv.,* merrily
genitor, –ōris, *m.,* father
gēns, gentis, *f.,* tribe, people, nation, family, class
gentīlis, –e, belonging to the same clan *or* race;
     pagan
genus, generis, *n.,* birth, race; kind, class,
     family, sort
Germānia, –ae, *f.,* Germany
Germānus, –ī, *m.,* a German
germinō, 1, bud, germinate, sprout

gerō, –ere, gessī, gestus, bear, carry on, manage,
     do, accomplish, wear; hold; **mē gerō,** act
gestāmen, –inis, *n.,* load; *pl.,* arms
gestō, 1, carry, bear; *pass.,* ride
gestus, –ūs, *m.,* gesture
gignō, –ere, genuī, genitus, bring forth, produce;
     pass., be born
gladiātor, –ōris, *m.,* gladiator
gladius, –dī, *m.,* sword
glaeba, –ae, *f.,* clod
glāns, glandis, *f.,* acorn
glōria, –ae, *f.,* glory, fame
glorior, 1, boast
glōriōsus, –a, –um, glorious
Gnaeus, –ī, *m.,* Gnaeus
Gordiānus, –ī, *m.,* Gordianus
Gorgiās, –ae, *m.,* Gorgias
Gracchus, –ī, *m.,* Gracchus
gracilis, –e, thin, slender
gradior, –ī, gressus, step, walk
gradus, –ūs, *m.,* step, grade
Graecia, –ae, *f.,* Greece
Graecus, –a, –um, Greek; **Graecus, –ī,** *m.,* a
     Greek; *as noun, m. pl.,* the Greeks
Graiī, –ōrum, *m.,* the Greeks
grammaticus, –ī, *m.,* school teacher, grammarian
grandis, –e, large; **grandis nātū,** old man
grātē, *adv.,* gratefully
grātia, –ae, *f.,* gratitude, favor, influence; **grātiās
     agō,** thank; **grātiam referō,** show one's
     gratitude; **grātiam habeō,** feel grateful; **grātiā,**
     for the sake of; **Grātiae, –ārum,** *f. pl.,* the Graces
grātiōsus, –a, –um, popular, acceptable, agreeable
Grattius, –tī, *m.,* Grattius
grātuītō, *adv.,* without pay, freely
grātulātiō, –ōnis, *f.,* congratulation
grātulor, 1, congratulate
grātus, –a, –um, pleasing, grateful; **grātum faciō,**
     do a favor
gravidus, –a, –um, heavy
gravis, –e, heavy, difficult, important, severe
gravitās, –tātis, *f.,* weight, dignity, seriousness
graviter, *adv.,* heavily, seriously, strongly
gravō, 1, make heavy, weigh down; *pass.,* be reluctant

Gregorius, –rī, *m.,* Gregory

gremium, –mī, *n.,* bosom

grex, gregis, *m.,* herd

gubernāculum, –ī, *n.,* rudder; guidance, government

gubernātiō, –ōnis, *f.,* control

gubernātor, –ōris, *m.,* pilot

gubernō, 1, steer, navigate

gustō, 1, taste, enjoy

guttur, –uris, *n.,* throat

gymnasium, –sī, *n.,* gymnasium; lecture room

H

habēna, –ae, *f.,* rein

habeō, –ēre, habuī, habitus, have, hold, regard, consider; **grātiam habeō,** feel grateful (*w. dat.*); **ōrātiōnem habeō,** deliver an oration

habitō, 1, live, dwell

habitus, –ūs, *m.,* nature

hāctenus, *adv.,* so far

haereō, –ēre, haesī, haesus, stick, cling; be in doubt

haesitō, 1, stick fast, be undecided, be at a loss

Hamilcar, –aris, *m.,* Hamilcar, *the father of Hannibal*

Hannibal, –alis, *m.,* Hannibal, *a Carthaginian general*

haruspex, –picis, *m.,* soothsayer, fortune teller

Hasdrubal, –alis, *m.,* Hasdrubal, *a brother and an uncle of Hannibal*

haud, *adv.,* not, by no means

hauriō, –īre, hausī, haustus, draw; empty

haustus, –ūs, *m.,* drawing, shedding

hebēscō, –ere, —, —, grow dull

hebetūdō, –inis, *f.,* bluntness, dullness

Hecuba, –ae, *f.,* Hecuba, *wife of Priam, king of Troy*

Heius, –ī, *m.,* Heius

Helicē, –ēs, *f.,* Helice (Hel′isē), *a constellation*

Hēraclēa, –ae, *f.,* Heraclea, *a Greek city in southern Italy*

Hēraclīēnsis, –e, of Heraclea; *as noun, m.,* a Heraclean

herba, –ae, *f.,* herb, plant; *pl.* grass

hercle! by Hercules! (*used by men*)

Herculāneum, –eī, *n.,* Herculaneum, *a town of Campania*

Herculēs, –is, *m.,* Hercules, *a Greek hero*

hērēditās, –tātis, *f.,* inheritance

hērēs, –ēdis, *m. and f.,* heir, heiress

herī, *adv.,* yesterday

hērōs, –ōis, *m.,* hero

Hesperidēs, –um, *f. pl.,* Hesperides, *daughters of Atlas*

hesternus, –a, –um, of yesterday; *w.* **diēs,** yesterday

heu! *interj.,* alas!

hīberna, –ōrum, *n.,* winter quarters

Hibernia, –ae, *f.,* Ireland

Hibērus, –ī, *m.,* the Ebro, *a river in Spain*

hic, haec, hoc, *dem. pron.,* this, the latter; he, she, it (*enclitic* **–ce** *added for emphasis*)

hīc, *adv.,* here, hereupon, in view of this

hiems, hiemis, *f.,* winter

Hieronymus, –ī, *m.,* Jerome, *a Father of the Church*

hilaris, –e, cheerful, glad

hilaritās, –tātis, *f.,* gaiety

hilum, –ī, *n.,* shred, trifle

hinc, *adv.,* from this place; **hinc... illinc,** on this side . . . on that

hiō, 1, gape; be amazed; long for

Hispānia, –ae, *f.,* Spain

Hispānus, –ī, *m.,* Spaniard

Hister, –trī, *m.,* Danube River

historia, –ae, *f.,* history, account

hodiē, *adv.,* today

hodiernus diēs, this day, today

holus, –leris, *n.,* vegetables

Homērus, –i, *m.,* Homer

hominium, –nī, *m.,* homage

homō, hominis, *m.,* man, person, human being; *pl.,* people

honestās, –tātis, *f.,* honor, honesty

honestō, 1, honor, distinguish

honestus, –a, –um, honorable

honor, –ōris, *m.,* honor, office

honōrābilis, –e, honorable

honōrātus, –a, –um, honored

hōra, –ae, *f.,* hour

hordeum, –ī, *n.,* barley

hornus, –a, –um, of this year

horrēscō, –ere, horruī, —, grow rough; tremble

horribilis, –e, dreadful

horridus, –a, –um, rough, crude, wild

hortātus, –ūs, m., urging

Hortēnsius, –sī, m., Hortensius

hortor, 1, urge, encourage

hortus, –ī, m., garden

hospes, –pitis, m. and f., stranger, guest; host

hospita, –ae, f., guest, stranger

hospitālis, –e, of a guest, of a host, hospitable

hospitium, –tī, n., (tie of) hospitality

hostis, –is, m., enemy (usually pl.)

hūc, adv., to this place, here

hūmānitās, –tātis, f., kindness, sympathy, culture

hūmānus, –a, –um, human, cultured, refining

humilis, –e, low, humble

humus, –ī, f., ground, earth

Hydaspēs, –is, m., a river in India

Hymēn, –enis, m., Hymen, the god of marriage

Hypaepa, –ōrum, n. pl., Hypaepa (Hype´pa), a town at the base of Mt. Tmolus

I

iaceō, –ēre, iacuī, —, lie, be prostrate

iaciō, –ere, iēcī, iactus, throw, hurl

iactō, 1, throw, toss; boast of; w. mē, display myself

iactus, –ūs, m., throwing; stroke

iaculum, –ī, n., dart, javelin

iam, adv., already, now; w. neg., no longer; of future time, soon, presently; w. diū dūdum, or prīdem, long ago; w. vērō, furthermore

iānua, –ae, f., door

Iānuārius, –a, –um, January

ibi, adv., there, then

ibīdem, adv., in the same place

Īcarus, –ī, m., Icarus, son of Daedalus

īcō, (–ere), īcī, ictus, strike

idcircō, adv., for this (that) reason, therefore

īdem, eadem, idem, dem. pron., same; also, likewise

identidem, adv., again and again

ideō, adv., for this reason, therefore

idōneus, –a, –um, suitable

Īdūs, –uum, f. pl., the Ides (15th of March, May, July, and October; 13th of the other months)

iēiūnus, –a, –um, poor

igitur, adv., therefore

ignārus, –a, –um, not knowing, ignorant

ignāvus, –a, –um, lazy; cowardly

ignis, –is, m., fire

ignōbilis, –e, not noble

ignōminia, –ae, f., disgrace

ignōrantia, –ae, f., want of knowledge, ignorance

ignōrō, 1, be ignorant of, not know

ignōscō, –ere, ignōvī, ignōtus, overlook; forgive

ignōtus, –a, –um, unknown

īlex, īlicis, f., oak

īlia, –ōrum, n. pl., abdomen, groin

Ilias, Iliadis, f., the Iliad

Ilioneus, –ī, m., Ilí´oneus, one of Niobe's sons

Ilium, –lī, n., Troy, a city in Asia Minor

illāc, adv., that way

illaesus, –a, –um, unharmed, unhurt

ille, illa, illud, dem. pron., that, the former; he, she, it

illecebra, –ae, f. enticement

illīberālis, –e, ignoble, sordid, mean

illīc, adv., in that place, there

illinc, adv., from that side

illinō, –ere, illēvī, illitus, smear, cover

illitterātus, –a, –um, unlettered, illiterate

illūc, adv., there

illūminō, 1, illuminate, make conspicuous

illūstris, –e, brilliant, noble, glorious

illūstrō, 1, bring to light, reveal, glorify

Īllyricus, –a, –um; Illyrius, –a, –um, Illyrian, of Illyria, a country on the Adriatic Sea

imāgō, –ginis, f., likeness, image, statue; appearance

imbecillitās, –tātis, f., weakness

imbecillus, –a, –um, weak

imber, imbris, m., rain, storm

imberbis, –e, beardless

imbrifer, –era, –erum, rain-bringing

imbuō, –ere, –uī, –ūtus, wet, soak

imitābilis, –e, imitable

imitātiō, –ōnis, f., imitation

imitor, 1, imitate

immānis, –e, vast; savage

immānitās, –tātis, f., enormity; fierceness, barbarism

immātūrus, –a, –um, untimely

immēnsus, –a, –um, immeasurable, boundless

immineō, –ēre, —, —, threaten

immittō, –ere, immīsī, immissus, let loose, send in *or* against

immō, *adv.,* on the contrary; *w.* **vērō,** rather

immōbilis, –e, immovable

immoderātus, –a, –um, immoderate

immodicus, –a, –um, beyond measure, excessive

immorior, –morī, –mortuus, die upon

immoror, 1, remain in, linger near

immortālis, –e, immortal

immōtus, –a, –um, unmoved; fixed

immurmurō, 1, murmur into

immūtātus, –a, –um, changed

impār, *gen.* **imparis,** unequal; short

imparātus, –a, –um, unprepared

impatiēns, *gen.* **–entis,** not bearing, impatient

impedīmentum, –ī, *n.,* hindrance, impediment; *pl.,* baggage

impediō, –īre, –īvī, –ītus, hinder, prevent

impellō, –ere, impulī, impulsus, urge on, prevail upon, induce

impendeō, –ēre, —, —, overhang, threaten

impendium, –dī, *n.,* outlay, expense

impēnsa, –ae, *f.,* expense

imperātor, –ōris, *m.,* commander-in-chief, general; emperor

imperfectus, –a, –um, unfinished

imperītus, –a, –um, inexperienced, ignorant

imperium, –rī, *n.,* command, control, military power, government, empire

imperō, 1, command, govern, command (*w. dat.*)

impertiō, –īre, –īvī, –ītus, share with, bestow

impetrō, 1, gain (a request), obtain

impetus, –ūs, *m.,* attack, fury, force; **impetum faciō in** (*w. acc.*), make an attack against

impiger, –gra, –grum, diligent, quick

impius, –a, –um, undutiful, wicked

impleō, –ēre, implēvī, implētus, fill, fulfill

implicō, –āre, implicuī, implicitus, enfold, involve, unite

implōrātiō, –ōnis, *f.,* entreaty

implōrō, 1, implore

impōnō, –ere, imposuī, impositus, place upon, put

importō, 1, bring

importūnus, –a, –um, cruel

improbitās, –tātis, *f.,* wickedness, dishonesty

improbō, 1, disapprove

improbus, –a, –um, wicked

imprōvīsus, –a, –um, unexpected

impudēns, *gen.* **–entis,** shameless, presumptuous

impudenter, *adv.,* impudently

impudentia, –ae, *f.,* shamelessness, effrontery

impudīcus, –a, –um, shameless

impūnē, *adv.,* without punishment

impūnītus, –a, –um, unpunished

impūrus, –a, –um, vile, impure

īmus, –a, –um, *see* **īnferus**

in, *prep. w. acc.,* into, to, toward, against, for; *w. abl.,* in, on, upon

inānis, –e, empty

inaurō, 1, overlay with gold

incēdo, –ere, incessī, incessūrus, advance, proceed

incēnātus, –a, –um, without dinner

incendium, –dī, *n.,* fire, burning, conflagration

incendō, –ere, incendī, incēnsus, set on fire, burn

incēnsiō, –ōnis, *f.,* burning

inceptum, –ī, *n.,* beginning, undertaking

incertus, –a, –um, uncertain

inchoō, 1, begin

incidō, –ere, incidī, —, fall, happen

incīdō, –ere, incīdī, incīsus, cut into

incipiō, –ere, incēpī, inceptus, take to, begin

incitāmentum, –ī, *n.,* incentive, stimulus

incitō, 1, urge on, arouse

inclinō, 1, lean, sink

inclūdō, –ere, inclūsī, inclūsus, shut up, confine

inclutus, –a, –um, famous

incognitus, –a, –um, unknown

incola, –ae, *m. and f.,* inhabitant

incolō, –ere, incoluī, incultus, live, inhabit

incolumis, –e, unharmed, safe; undefeated

incommodum, –ī, *n.,* inconvenience; loss, defeat

inconditē, *adv.,* without order

incōnsultē, *adv.,* thoughtlessly

incorporeus, –a, –um, incorporeal, without body

incorruptus, –a, –um, unspoiled, uninjured

incrēdibilis, –e, extraordinary, incredible

incrēdibiliter, *adv.,* incredibly

incultus, –a, –um, untilled; rude

incumbō, –ere, incubuī, incubitūrus, bend to, devote oneself, press on

incūnābula, –ōrum, *n. pl.,* cradle, birthplace, beginnings

incurrō, –ere, –currī, –cursūrus, run into *or* up against

inde, *adv.,* then, from there

index, –dicis, *m.,* informer, witness

indicium, –cī, *n.,* testimony, proof

indicō, 1, point out, prove

indictus, –a, –um, declared

indigēns, *gen.* **–entis,** in need of, wanting

indignātiō, –ōnis, *f.,* indignation

indignē, *adv.,* unworthily

indignor, 1, regard as unworthy; be angry

indignus, –a, –um, unworthy

indocilis, –e, unteachable, ignorant

indoctus, –a, –um, ignorant; unskilled

indolēs, –is, *f.,* native quality, nature

indolēscō, –ere, indoluī, —, be grieved

indūcō, –ere, indūxī, inductus, bring in, influence

indulgentia, –ae, *f.,* kindness

indulgeō, –ēre, indulsi, indultus, yield to, favor

induō, –ere, induī, indūtus, put on, assume

Indus, –a, –um, Indian

industria, –ae, *f.,* diligence, care

industrius, –a, –um, enterprising

inedia, –ae, *f.,* fasting

ineō, inīre, iniī, initūrus, enter upon

inermis, –e, unarmed

inerrō, 1, wander, roam upon

iners, *gen.* **inertis,** unskilled; sluggish

inertia, –ae, *f.,* lack of skill, inactivity, laziness

inexpiābilis, –e, irreconcilable, implacable

inexplēbilis, –e, insatiable

infāmia, –ae, *f.,* disgrace

īnfēlīx, *gen.* **īnfēlīcis,** unhappy, unfortunate

īnferī, –ōrum, *m.,* inhabitants of the Underworld

īnferō, īnferre, intulī, illātus, apply, bring

īnferus, –a, –um, below; *as noun, m. pl.,* the dead; *comp.* **īnferior, -ius,** lower; *superl.,* **īnfimus, īmus,** lowest

īnfēstus, –a, –um, hostile, dangerous

īnfimus, *see* **īnferus**

īnfīnītus, –a, –um, endless

īnfirmitās, –tātis, *f.,* sickness, weakness

īnfirmō, 1, weaken, refute

īnfirmus, –a, –um, weak, sick

īnfitior, 1, deny

īnflammō, 1, set on fire, burn; inflame

inflexibilis, –e, unbending, inflexible

īnflō, 1, blow into; inspire

īnfōrmō, 1, mold, train

īnfrā, *adv.,* below

ingemēscō, –ere, –uī, —, groan, sigh (over)

ingeniōsus, –a, –um, clever

ingenium, –nī, *n.,* ability, nature, spirit, genius

ingēns, *gen.* **ingentis,** huge

ingenuē, *adv.,* nobly

ingenuus, –a, –um, noble

ingerō, –ere, ingessī, ingestus, press upon

ingrātus, –a, –um, ungrateful

ingravēscō, –ere, —, —, become heavier, grow worse

ingredior, ingredī, ingressus, step into, enter (upon)

ingressus, –ūs, *m.,* entrance

inhabitō, 1, dwell in

inhaereō, –ēre, inhaesī, inhaesus, cling, stick to

inhibeō, –ēre, –uī, –itus, restrain

inhiō, 1, gape

inhonestus, –a, –um, dishonorable

inhospitālis, –e, inhospitable

inhūmānus, –a, –um, inhuman; rude

iniciō, –ere, iniēcī, iniectus, throw into, cause, inspire

inimīcitia, –ae, *f.,* enmity

inimīcus, –a, –um, unfriendly, hostile; *as noun, m.,* enemy

inīquitās, –tātis, *f.,* unfairness, injustice

inīquus, –a, –um, unequal, sloping; unfavorable, discontented

initiō, 1, initiate, consecrate

initium, –tī, *n.,* beginning

iniūrātus, –a, –um, not having sworn

iniūria, –ae, *f.,* injustice, wrong, injury

iniūriōsus, –a, –um, harmful

iniūrus, –a, –um, unjust

iniūstus, –a, –um, unjust

innītor, innītī, innīxus, lean upon

innocēns, *gen.* **–entis,** harmless

innocentia, –ae, *f.,* innocence

innumerābilis, –e, countless

innumerus, –a, –um, countless

innuptus, –a, –um, unmarried; *as noun, f.,* virgin

innūtriō, –īre, –īvī, –ītus, nourish

inopia, –ae, *f.,* lack (of funds), poverty, need

inops, *gen.* **inopis,** poor

inōrnātus, –a, –um, unadorned

inprīmīs, *adv.,* especially

inquam, inquis, inquit, *defective,* say; **inquit,** he/ she says

inquinō, 1, stain, defile

inquīrō, –ere, inquīsīvī, inquīsītus, inquire (into)

īnsānia, –ae, *f.,* madness

insānus, –a, –um, insane

īnsciēns, *gen.* **–entis,** not knowing

īnscitia, –ae, *f.,* ignorance

īnscius, –a, –um, not knowing; ignorant

īnscrībō, –ere, īnscrīpsī, īnscrīptus, inscribe, entitle

īnscrīptiō, –ōnis, *f.,* inscription

īnsecō, –āre, īnsecuī, īnsectus, cut into

īnsector, 1, attack

īnsepultus, –a, –um, unburied

īnsequor, īnsequī, īnsecūtus, follow up, pursue

īnserō, –ere, īnseruī, īnsertus, thrust into

īnsideō, –ēre, īnsēdī, īnsessūrus, (sit upon), take possession of; dwell, be fixed

īnsidiae, –ārum, *f. pl.,* plot, danger

īnsidior, 1, plot against

īnsigne, –is, *n.,* mark

īnsignis, –e, remarkable, notable

īnsiliō, –īre, –uī, —, leap upon

īnsinuō, 1, ingratiate oneself

īnsistō, –ere, īnstitī, —, pursue

īnsolēns, *gen.* **–entis,** unaccustomed; haughty

īnsolentia, –ae, *f.,* insolence

īnsolitus, –a, –um, unusual

īnsonō, –āre, –uī, —, play on

īnspērātus, –a, –um, unexpected

īnspiciō, –ere, īnspexī, īnspectus, look at, inspect, examine

īnstabilis, –e, unstable

īnstanter, *adv.,* earnestly

īnstituō, –ere, īnstituī, īnstitūtus, establish, decide (upon), begin; train

īnstō, –āre, īnstitī, —, threaten, press on, pursue

īnstringō, –ere, īnstrīnxī, īnstrictus, fasten; set

īnstruō, –ere, īnstrūxī, īnstrūctus, arrange, provide, draw up, instruct

īnsula, –ae, *f.,* island

īnsulānus, –ī, *m.,* islander

īnsum, inesse, īnfuī —, be in

integer, –gra, –grum, untouched, fresh

intellegō, –ere, –lexī, –lectus, understand

intempestus, –a, –um, timeless; unhealthy

intendō, –ere, intendī, intentus, stretch, intend

inter, *prep. w. acc.,* between, among

intereā, *adv.,* meanwhile

intercipiō, –ere, –cēpī, –ceptus, intercept, cut off, steal

interclūdō, –ere, –clūsī, –clūsus, cut off

interficiō, –ere, –fēcī, –fectus, kill

interiaceō, –ēre, –uī, —, lie between

interim, *adv.,* meanwhile

interimō –ere, –ēmī, ēmptus, kill

interitus, –ūs, *m.,* destruction, death

interius, *adv.,* within

intermittō, –ere, –mīsī, –missus, let go, stop, interrupt, neglect

interneciō, –ōnis, *f.,* massacre

internōdium, –dī, *n.,* space between two joints

internus, –a, –um, inward, internal

interpellātiō, –ōnis, *f.,* interruption

interpres, –pretis, *m.,* interpreter

interrogātiō, –ōnis, *f.,* inquiry, examination

interrogō, 1, ask

intersum, –esse, –fuī, –futūrus, be between, be present, be different

intervāllum, –ī, *n.,* interval, distance

interveniō, –īre, –vēnī, –ventūrus, come in (between), interrupt

interventus, –ūs, *m.,* intervention

intestīnus, –a, –um, internal, civil

intexō, –ere, –texuī, –textus, interweave, envelop

intimō, 1, intimate

intimus, –a, –um, inmost

intōnsus, –a, –um, unshorn, long-haired

intrā, *prep. w. acc.,* within

intrepidus, –a, –um, unshaken, undaunted

intrō, 1, enter

intrōdūcō, –ere, –dūxī, –ductus, bring in, introduce

introeō, –īre, –iī, –itūrus, enter

intueor, –ērī, –itus, look at *or* upon

inūrō, –ere, inussī, inustus, burn in, brand

inūsitātus, –a, –um, unusual

inūtilis, –e, useless

invādō, –ere, invāsī, invāsus, rush upon, seize

inveniō, –īre, invēnī, inventus, find, come upon, invent

inventiō, –ōnis, *f.,* invention

invēstīgō, 1, track, discover

inveterāscō, –ere, –āvī, —, become established

invicem, *adv.,* in turn, alternately

invictus, –a, –um, unconquered, invincible

invideō, –ēre, invīdī, invīsus, envy

invidia, –ae, *f.,* envy, unpopularity

invidiōsus, –a, –um, hateful

invidus, –a, –um, envious

inviolātē, *adv.,* inviolably

invīsitātus, –a, –um, uncommon

invīsus, –a, –um, hated, displeasing

invītō, 1, invite

invītus, –a, –um, unwilling

involvō, –ere, involvī, involūtus, wrap up in, bury

iō, *interj.,* hurrah!

iocor, 1, joke

iocōsus, –a, –um, humorous

iocus, –ī, *m.* (pl. **ioca,** *n.*), joke

Iovis, Iovī, see **Iuppiter**

ipse, ipsa, ipsum, –self, the very

īra, –ae, *f.,* anger

īrāscor, –ī, īrātus, be angry at

irreparābiliter, *adv.,* irreparably

irrēpō, –ere, irrēpsī, —, creep in

irrētiō, –īre, –īvī, –ītus, ensnare

irrigō, 1, water, irrigate

irritō, 1, excite, stir up

is, ea, id, *dem. pron.,* this, that; *as pron.,* he, she, it

Ismēnus, –ī, *m.,* Ismenus, *one of Niobe's sons*

iste, ista, istud, *dem. pron.,* that (of yours), such this; that fellow

istīc, *adv.,* there

istōc, *adv.,* that way

ita, *adv.,* so, in this way, thus; as follows; *w.* **ut,** just as

Ītalia, –ae, *f.,* Italy

Ītalicus, –a, –um, Italian

itaque, *adv.,* and so, therefore, accordingly, and as a result

item, *adv.,* also

iter, itineris, *n.,* journey, road, march, route

iterum, *adv.,* again, a second time

itō, itāre, —, —, go

iubeō, –ēre, iussī, iussus, order, command

iūcunditās, –tātis, *f.,* pleasantness, delight

iūcundus, –a, –um, pleasant, agreeable

iūdex, iūdicis, *m.,* judge, juror

iūdiciālis, –e, judicial

iūdicium, –cī, *n.,* judgment, opinion, trial; court

iūdicō, 1, judge

iugālis, –e, yoked, together

iūgerum, –ī, *n.,* acre

iugulum, –ī, *n.,* throat

iugum, –ī, *n.,* yoke; ridge

Iūlius, –lī, *m.,* Julius; **Iūlia, –ae,** *f.,* Julia

iūnctim, *adv.,* jointly, together

iungō, –ere, iūnxī, iūnctus, join (to), harness

iūnior, –ius, younger, junior

Iūnius, –a, –um, of June

Iūnō, –ōnis, *f.,* Juno, *a goddess, sister and wife of Jupiter*

Iūnōnius, –a, –um, sacred to Juno

Iuppiter, Iovis, *m.,* Jupiter, *king of the gods*

iūrgium, –gī, *n.,* quarrel

iūrō, 1, take an oath, swear

iūs, iūris, *n.,* right, justice, law, authority; **iūs iūrandum, iūris, –ī,** *n.,* oath

iussū, *abl.,* by order

iussum, –ī, *n.,* order

iūstē, *adv.*, justly

iūstitia, **–ae**, *f.*, justice

iūstus, **–a**, **–um**, just, proper

iuvenālis, **–e**, youthful

iuvenis, **–is**, *m. and f.*, youth

iuventa, **–ae**, *f.*, **iuventūs**, **–tūtis**, *f.*, youth

iuvō, **–āre**, **iūvī**, **iūtus**, help, aid; please

iūxtā, *adv. and prep. w. acc.*, near, close to

L

L., *abbreviation for* **Lūcius**

labefactō, 1, cause to fall, weaken, destroy

labellum, **–ī**, *n.*, little lip

labor, **–ōris**, *m.*, work, trouble, effort, hardship

lābor, **–ī**, **lāpsus**, slip, glide; err

labōrō, 1, work

labrum, **–ī**, *n.*, lip; edge, tub

lac, **lactis**, *n.*, milk

Lacedaemonius, **–a**, **–um**, Spartan

lacer, **–era**, **–erum**, shattered

lacertus, **–ī**, *m.*, arm

lacessō, **–ere**, **lacessīvī**, **lacessītus**, provoke, attack

lacrima, **–ae**, *f.*, tear

lacrimō, 1, weep

lactō, 1, suck milk

lacus, **–ūs**, *m.*, lake

Laeca, **–ae**, *m.*, Laeca

laedō, **–ere**, **laesī**, **laesus**, hurt

Laelius, **–lī**, *m.*, Laelius

laetitia, **–ae**, *f.*, joy

laetor, 1, be glad, rejoice

laetus, **–a**, **–um**, joyous, glad

laevus, **–a**, **–um**, left

Lalagē, **–ēs**, *f.*, Lalage, *a girl's name*

lambō, **–ere**, **lambī**, **lambitus**, lick

lāmentātiō, **–ōnis**, *f.*, lamentation

lancea, **–ae**, *f.*, lance

languidus, **–a**, **–um**, weak

laniō, 1, tear (in pieces)

lanterna, **–ae**, *f.*, lantern

lapidātiō, **–ōnis**, *f.*, stoning

lapis, **lapidis**, *m.*, stone

lāpsus, **–ūs**, *m.*, gliding, flight

Lār, **Laris**, *m.*, Lar, hearth; *a household god; w.* **familiāris**, home

lardum, **–ī**, *n.*, lard

largior, **–īrī**, **ītus**, be lavish, bestow

largītiō, **–ōnis**, *f.*, gift

largus, **–a**, **–um**, plentiful, large

lascīvē, *adv.*, wantonly, licentiously

lascīvus, **–a**, **–um**, wanton, playful

lassitūdō, **–tūdinis**, *f.*, weariness

lassus, **–a**, **–um**, tired

lātē, *adv.*, widely, far and wide

latebra, **–ae**, *f.*, secret code; *pl.*, hiding place

lateō, **–ēre**, **latuī**, **—**, lie hidden, hide, escape notice

Latīnē, *adv.*, in Latin

Latīnus, **–a**, **–um**, Latin, belonging to Latium; **Latīni**, **–ōrum**, *m.*, the Latins

Latīnus, **–ī**, *m.*, Latinus

Latium, **–tī**, *n.*, Latium, (Lā´shium), *a district of central Italy*

Latius, **–a**, **–um**, of Latium

Lātōna, **–ae**, *f.*, Latona, *mother of Apollo and Diana*

Lātōus, **–a**, **–um**, of Latona

latrō, **–ōnis**, *m.*, bandit, robber

latrōcinium, **–nī**, *n.*, robbery, brigandage

latrōcinor, 1, plunder

latus, **lateris**, *n.*, side, flank

lātus, **–a**, **–um**, wide, broad

laudātor, **–ōris**, *m.*, praiser

laudō, 1, praise

Laurentīnus, **–a**, **–um**, of Laurentum

laurus, **–ī**, *f.*, laurel

laus, **laudis**, *f.*, praise

lavō, **–āre**, **lāvī**, **lautus**, wash, bathe

laxō, 1, relax

laxus, **–a**, **–um**, open, relaxed

lea, **–ae**; **leaena**, **–ae**, *f.*, lioness

Lebinthus, **–ī**, *f.*, Lebinthus, *an island in the Aegean*

lēctiō, **–ōnis**, *f.*, reading

lēctitō, 1, read eagerly

lēctor, **–ōris**, *m.*, reader

lēctus, **–a**, **–um**, choice, excellent

lectus, **–ī**, *m.*, couch, bed

lēgātus, **–ī**, *m.*, envoy; legate, lieutenant general

legiō, –ōnis, *f.,* legion

lēgitimē, *adv.,* lawfully

lēgitimus, –a, –um, lawful

lēgō, 1, appoint, bequeath

legō, –ere, lēgī, lectus, collect, gather, choose, pick; read

lēniō, –īre, –īvī, –ītus, soften, conciliate

lēnis, –e, gentle, mild

lēnitās, –tātis, *f.,* leniency

lentē, *adv.,* slowly

Lentulus, –ī, *m.,* Lentulus

lentus, –a, –um, flexible; slow, lazy

leō, –ōnis, *m.,* lion

lepidus, –a, –um, charming

Lepidus, –ī, *m.,* Lepidus

lepōs, –ōris, *m.,* charm

lētum, –ī, *n.,* death

levāmen, –minis, *n.,* relief

levis, –e, light (*in weight*); trivial

levitās, –tātis, *f.,* lack of principle

leviter, *adv.,* lightly, gently

levō, 1, lift, lighten, relieve

lēx, lēgis, *f.,* law, condition, bill

libellus, –ī, *m.,* (little) book, manuscript; indictment

libenter, *adv.,* gladly, with pleasure

līber, –era, –erum, free, unrestricted

Līber, –erī, *m.,* Bacchus

liber, librī, *m.,* book

Lībera, –ae, *f.,* Proserpina

līberālis, –e, liberal

līberē, *adv.,* freely; boldly

līberī, –ōrum, *m. pl.,* children

līberō, 1, free, set free

lībertās, –tātis, *f.,* freedom, liberty

lībertīnus, –ī, *m.,* freedman

lībertus, –ī, *m.,* freedman

libet, –ēre, libuit *or* **libitum,** it pleases

libīdo, –dinis, *f.,* longing, pleasure, lust

lībō, 1, sip, offer; skim

lībrārius, –rī, *m.,* secretary

lībrō, 1, balance

licentia, –ae, *f.,* liberty, freedom

licet, –ēre, licuit *or* **licitum,** it is permitted, one may

Liciniānus, –ī, *m.,* Licinianus

Licinius, –nī, *m.,* Licinius (Lisin´ius)

ligneus, –a, –um, wooden

lignum, –ī, *n.,* piece of wood; *n. pl.,* firewood

ligō, 1, bind, tie

līmen, līminis, *n.,* threshold, door

līmes, līmitis, *m.,* path

līneāmentum, –ī, *n.,* line, feature

lingua, –ae, *f.,* tongue, language

līnum, –ī, *n.,* string, thread

liquefaciō, –ere, –fēcī, –factus, melt

liquidus, –a, –um, flowing, clear

līquor, –ī, —, —, flow, melt

līs, lītis, *f.,* lawsuit

littera, –ae, *f.,* letter (*of the alphabet*), *pl.,* a letter (*epistle*), letters (*if modified by an adjective such as* **multae**), literature; learning

litterātus, –a, –um, lettered, well-educated

litūra, –ae, *f.,* erasure

lītus, –ōris, *n.,* shore

līvēns, *gen.* **–entis,** black and blue, bruised

Līvius, –vī, *m.,* Livy, *a Roman historian*

locō, 1, place

locuplēs, *gen.* **–ētis,** rich

locuplētō, 1, enrich

locus, –ī, *m.,* (*pl.* **loca, –ōrum,** *n.*), place, room, rank, occasion

longē, *adv.,* far, far away, by far; long

longus, –a, –um, long; distant

loquāx, *gen.* **–ācis,** talkative, chattering

loquor, loquī, locūtus, speak, talk

Lūcānus, –ī, *m.,* Lucan, *a Roman poet*

lūceō, –ēre, lūxī, —, be light, shine

lūcidus, –a, –um, bright, shining

Lūcilius, –lī, *m.,* Lucilius

Lūcius, –cī, *m.,* Lucius

lucrum, –ī, *n.,* gain, profit

luctāns, *gen.* **–antis,** struggling, reluctant

lūctus, –ūs, *m.,* sorrow, affliction

lūculentus, –a, –um, brilliant

Lūcullus, –ī, *m.,* Lucullus

lūcus, –ī, *m.,* grove

lūdō, –ere, lūsī, lūsus, play

lūdus, ī, *m.,* game, sport; school; *pl.,* public games

lūgeō, –ēre, lūxī, lūctus, mourn

lūmen, lūminis, *n.,* light; eye

lūmināre, –āris, *n.,* lamp

lūna, –ae, *f.,* moon

luō, –ere, luī, —, loose; suffer

lupus, –ī, *m.,* wolf

Lūsitānia, –ae, *f.,* Portugal

Lūsitānus, –a, –um, Lusitanian, Portuguese

lūstrō, 1, light up, survey

lūsus, –ūs, *m.,* playing

lūx, lūcis, *f.,* light, daylight; life

lūxuria, –ae, *f.,* extravagance

Lydus, –a, –um, Lydian

M

M., *abbreviation for* **Mārcus, –ī,** *m.,* Marcus; **M'**
 for **Mānius, –nī,** *m.,* Manius

māchinātor, –ōris, *m.,* plotter

māchinor, 1, devise, plot

maciēs, –ēī, *f.,* thinness

mactē, *interj.,* well done!

mactō, 1, sacrifice, put to death, afflict

madefaciō, –ere, –fēcī, –factus, soak

mādēscō, –ere, maduī, —, become moist

madidus, –a, –um, drenched, dripping

maestus, –a, –um, sad

magis, *adv.,* more, rather; *superl.* **maximē,** most,
 especially

magister, –trī, *m.,* teacher

magistrātus, –ūs, *m.,* (public) office; magistrate

magnificēns, *gen.* **–entis,** magnifying, glorifying

magnificus, –a, –um, splendid

magnitūdō, –dinis, *f.,* greatness, size, importance

magnus, –a, –um, large, great; *comp.* **maior,**
 maius, greater; **maiōrēs (nātū),** older men,
 ancestors, forefathers; *superl.* **maximus, –a,**
 –um, greatest, very great; **magnō opere**
 or **magnopere,** greatly

maiestās, –tātis, *f.,* majesty

maior, *see* **magnus**

Maius, –a, –um, of May

male, *adv.,* badly, unsuccessfully; *comp.,* **peius,**
 worse; *superl.* **pessimē,** worst

maledīcō, –ere, –dīxī, –dictus, curse

maledictum, –ī, *n.,* insult

maleficium, –cī, *n.,* evil deed, wrong

malivolentia, –ae, *f.,* hatred, envy

malleolus, –ī, *m.,* firebrand

mālō, mālle, māluī, —, prefer

malum, –ī, *n.,* evil, trouble

mālum, –ī, *n.,* apple

malus, –a, –um, bad; *comp.* **peior, peius,** worse;
 superl. **pessimus, –a, –um,** very bad, worst

Mamertīnus, –a, –um, of Messina

mandātum, –ī, *n.,* order, instruction, command

mandātū, by order

mandō, 1, commit, instruct, entrust

māne, *adv.,* early in the morning

maneō, –ēre, mānsī, mānsūrus, remain, last

manicae, –ārum, *f. pl.,* handcuffs

manifēstus, –a, –um, clear, plain

Mānius, –nī, *m.,* Manius

Mānliānus, –a, –um, of Manlius

Mānlius, –lī, *m.,* Manlius

mānō, 1, flow, drip

mānsuētūdō, –dinis, *f.,* gentleness

Mantua, –ae, *f.,* Mantua, *a town of northern Italy*

manus, –ūs, *f.,* hand, handwriting; force, band

Mārcius, –cī, *m.,* Marcius (Mar´shus)

Mārcus, –ī, *m.,* Marcus

mare, maris, *n.,* sea

marītus, –ī, *m.,* husband

Marius, –rī, *m.,* Marius, *a Roman general*

marmor, –oris, *n.,* marble

marmoreus, –a, –um, made of marble, marble

Marō, –ōnis, *m.,* Maro (Vergil)

Maronilla, –ae, *f.,* Maronilla

Mārs, Mārtis, *m.,* Mars, *god of war*

Martiālis, –is, *m.,* Martial

Martīnus, –ī, *m.,* Martin

massa, –ae, *f.,* mass; mound, lump (of gold)

māter, mātris, *f.,* mother

māteria, –ae, *f.,* matter, timber

mātrimōnium, –nī, *n.,* marriage

mātūrēscō, –ere, mātūruī, —, come to maturity

mātūritās, –tātis, *f.,* ripeness, maturity

mātūrō, 1, hasten

mātūrus, –a, –um, ripe, mature; early

Maurī, –ōrum, *m. pl.,* the Moors, Mauritanians

maximē, *adv.,* very greatly, especially; *see* **magis**

Maximīna, –ae, *f.,* Maximina

maximus, *see* **magnus**

Maximus, –ī, *m.,* Maximus

mēcastor! *interj.,* by Castor!

medicāmentum, –ī, *n.,* medicine

medicīna, –ae, *f.,* medicine

medicus, –ī, *m.,* doctor, physician

mediocris, –cre, moderate, ordinary

mediocritās, –tātis, *f.,* mean, moderation; mediocrity

mediocriter, *adv.,* slightly, moderately

Mediterrāneum (Mare), Mediterranean Sea

meditor, 1, plan, compose

medius, –a, –um, middle; midst (of); intervening; *as noun,* n., middle

medulla, –ae, *f.,* marrow

mehercule, meherculēs! *interj.,* by Hercules!

mel, mellis, *n.,* honey

melior, *see* **bonus**

membrum, –ī, *n.,* limb, member

meminī, meminisse, *(perf. translated as pres.),* remember

memor, –oris, mindful of

memorābilis, –e, memorable

memoria, –ae, *f.,* memory; **memoriā teneō,** remember

memorō, 1, call to mind, relate

mendācium, –cī, *n.,* lie

mendāx, *gen.* **–ācis,** lying

mēns, mentis, *f.,* mind, intention, feeling, heart

mēnsa, –ae, *f.,* table, banquet

mēnsis, –is, *m.,* month

mēnsūra, –ae, *f.,* measurement, extent

mentiō, –ōnis, *f.,* mention

mentior, –īrī, –ītus, lie, deceive; invent

mentum, –ī, *n.,* chin

mercātor, –ōris, *m.,* merchant

mercātūra, –ae, *f.,* trade

mercennārius, –rī, *m.,* hired man

mercēs, –ēdis, *f.,* pay, reward

mercor, 1, trade

Mercurius, –rī, *m.,* Mercury

mereō, –ēre, meruī, meritus, deserve, earn

mergō, –ere, mersī, mersus, sink

merīdiēs, –ēī, *m.,* noon

Messāla, –ae, *m.,* Messala

–met, *enclitic,* -self

mēta, –ae, *f.,* goal, turning post (*in the Circus*)

metuō, –ere, –uī, —, fear

metus, –ūs, *m.,* fear

meus, –a, –um, my, mine

micō, 1, flash

migrō, 1, depart

mīles, mīlitis, *m.,* soldier

mīlitia, –ae, *f.,* warfare

mīlle, *pl.,* **mīlia,** thousand

Minerva, –ae, *f.,* Minerva, *a goddess*

minister, –trī, *m.,* **ministra, –ae,** *f.,* servant

minimē, *adv.,* not at all; *interj.,* no

minimus, minor, *see* **parvus**

minor, 1, jut out, threaten

Mīnōs, –ōis, *m.,* Minos

mīrābilis, –e, remarkable

mīrāculum, –ī, *n.,* miracle

mīrē, *adv.,* wonderfully, strangely

mīrificus, –a, –um, singular, extraordinary

mīror, 1, wonder, admire

mīrus, –a, –um, strange, wonderful

misceō, –ēre, –uī, mixtus, mix, mingle

miser, –era, –erum, unhappy, poor, wretched

miserābilis, –e, pitiable, wretched

miserātiō, –ōnis, *f.,* pity

miserē, *adv.,* wretchedness, miserably

misereor, –ērī, misertus, pity

miseria, –ae, *f.,* wretchedness, trouble

misericordia, –ae, *f.,* pity

misericors, –cordis, compassionate

miseror, 1, pity

Mithridātēs, –is, *m.,* Mithridá´tes, *king of Pontus*

Mithridāticus –a, –um, Mithridatic

mītis, –e, mild, kind

mittō, –ere, mīsī, missus, let go, send

mōbilitas, –tātis, *f.,* fickleness

moderātus, –a, –um, self-controlled, restrained

moderor, 1, guide

modestia, –ae, *f.,* restraint

modestus, –a, –um, moderate, scrupulous

modicus, –a, –um, moderate, small

modius, –dī, *m.,* bushel

modo, *adv.,* only, merely; just now; **nōn modo... sed** (*or* **vērum**) **etiam,** not only . . . but also; **modo... modo,** now . . . now; *conj.,* provided (that)

modus, –ī, *m.,* measure; moderation; manner, method, way; **quem ad modum,** how, as; **eius** (*or* **huius**) **modī,** of this kind, such

moenia, –ium, *n. pl.,* (city) walls

mōlēs, –is, *f.,* mass, burden

molestia, –ae, *f.,* annoyance

molestus, –a, –um, troublesome, annoying, disagreeable

mōlior, –īrī, –ītus, strive, plan, undertake; plot

molliō, –īre, –īvī, –ītus, soften

mollis, –e, soft; easy, mild

molliter, *adv.,* softly, gently

molō, –ere, –uī, itus, grind

Molossī, –ōrum, *m. pl.,* the Molossians, *people of Epirus*

monastērium, –rī, *n.,* monastery

moneō, –ēre, -uī, -itus, remind, warn, advise; suggest

monitus, –ūs, *m.,* warning

mōns, montis, *m.,* mountain, hill

mōnstrō, 1, point out, show, indicate

montānus, –a, –um, of the mountains

monumentum, –ī, *n.,* memorial, monument, remembrance

mora, –ae, *f.,* delay

morbus, –ī, *m.,* disease

mordeō, –ēre, momordī, morsus, bite

moribundus, –a, –um, dying

morior, morī, mortuus, die

moror, 1, delay, linger

mors, mortis, *f.,* death

morsus, –ūs, *m.,* biting, teeth

mortālis, –e, mortal, human; *as noun, m.,* a mortal

mortuus, –a, –um, dead

mōs, mōris, *m.,* custom, manner; *pl.,* customs, character

mōtus, –ūs, *m.,* movement, activity

moveō, –ēre, mōvī, mōtus, move; influence, disturb

mox, *adv.,* soon

mūcrō, –ōnis, *m.,* point, edge

mulcō, 1, beat, injure

muliebris, –e, womanly, feminine

mulier, mulieris, *f.,* woman

mūliō, –ōnis, *m.,* mule driver

multiplex, –icis, manifold, many

multitūdo, –dinis, *f.,* multitude, great number

multō, 1, punish

multō, *adv.,* much, by far

multum, *adv.,* much; *comp.,* **plūs,** more; *superl.,* **plūrimum,** most

multus, –a, –um, much; *pl.,* many; *comp.* **plūrēs, plūra,** more, several; *superl.* **plūrimus, –a, –um,** most, very many

mūlus, –ī, *m.,* mule

Mulvius, –a, –um, Mulvian

munditia, –ae, *f.,* neatness

mundus, –ī, *m.,* world

mūniceps, –cipis, *m.,* fellow citizen

municipālis, –e, of the towns

mūnicipium, –pī, *n.,* town

mūnificentia, –ae, *f.,* generosity

mūniō, –īre, –īvī, –ītus, fortify, defend; **viam mūniō,** build a road

mūnus, mūneris, *n.,* duty, office, service; gift

mūrex, –ricis, *m.,* (shellfish), purple

murmur, –uris, *n.,* whisper

mūrus, –ī, *m.,* wall

mūs, mūris, *m.,* mouse

Mūsa, –ae, *f.,* Muse, *one of the nine goddesses of the fine arts*

mūsica, –ae, *f.,* music

mūtātiō, –ōnis, *f.,* change

mutātus, –a, –um, changed

mūtō, 1, change

muttiō, –īre, –īvī, —, mutter

mūtus, –a, –um, mute

mūtuus, –a, –um, mutual

N

nactus, *part of* **nancīscor**

Naevius, –vī, *m.,* Naevius

nam, namque, *conj.,* for

nancīscor, nancīscī, nactus, (nānctus), get, gain, obtain, find, meet with

Nannēs, –is, *m.*, Nannes, *brother of Pope Pius II*

nārrō, 1, tell, relate

nāscor, nāscī, nātus, be born, be found; **duōs annōs nātus**, two years old; **nātus, –ī**, *m.*, son

Nāsō, –ōnis, *m.*, P. Ovidius Naso, *the poet Ovid*

nāsus, –ī, *m.*, nose

nātālis, –e, of one's birth; *as noun, m.*, birthday, natural

nātiō, –ōnis, *f.*, nation, tribe

natō, 1, swim, float

nātūra, –ae, *f.*, nature, character

nātūrālis, –e, natural

nātus, –a, –um, born; *as noun, m. and f.*, son, daughter; *pl.*, children

nausiābundus, –a, –um, seasick

nauta, –ae, *m.*, sailor

nāvālis, –e, naval

nāvicula, –ae, *f.*, small vessel, boat

nāvigātiō, –ōnis, *f.*, sailing

nāvigō, 1, sail

nāvis, –is, *f.*, ship

nē, *adv.*, no, not; **nē... quidem** (*emphatic word between*), not even; *conj.*, that . . . not, not to, lest, for fear that

–ne, (*enclitic*), *introduces question;* whether

nebula, –ae, *f.*, mist, cloud

nec, *see* **neque**

necdum, *adv.*, not yet

necessārius, –a, –um, necessary; *as noun, m.*, relative, friend

necesse, *indecl. adj.*, necessary

necessitās, –tātis, *f.*, necessity

necessitūdō, –dinis, *f.*, necessity; relationship

necō, 1, kill, put to death, murder

necopīnātus, –a, –um, unexpected

nectar, –aris, *n.*, nectar, *the drink of the gods*

nefārius, –a, –um, impious, base

nefās, *indeclinable, n.*, sin

neglegēns, *gen.* **–entis**, careless

neglegenter, *adv.*, carelessly

neglegentia, –ae, *f.*, negligence

neglegō, –ere, –lēxī, –lēctus, disregard, neglect

negō, 1, say no, deny, say . . . not

negōtior, 1, carry on business, be a trader

negōtium, –tī, *n.*, business, affair, trouble; undertaking

nēmō, *dat.* **nēminī**, *acc.* **nēminem** (*no other forms*), no one

nemus, –oris, *n.*, grove, forest

nepōs, –ōtis, *m.*, grandson

Neptūnus, –ī, *m.*, Neptune, *god of the sea*

nēquam, *indecl. adj.*, worthless, wretched; *compar.* **nēquior**

neque (*or* **nec**), and not, nor; **neque... neque**, neither . . . nor

nequeō, –īre, –īvī, —, be unable

nēquīquam, *adv.*, in vain

nēquitia, –ae, *f.*, worthlessness, neglect

nervōsus, –a, –um, sinewy

nervus, –ī, *m.*, sinew, nerve; string

nesciō, –īre, –īvī, –ītus, —, not know, be ignorant; *w.* **an**, I know not whether, very likely

neuter, –tra, –trum, neither (*of two*)

nēve (**neu**), *conj.*, and not, nor, and that . . . not

nex, necis, *f.*, murder, (violent) death

nexus, –ūs, *m.*, (binding together), embrace

nī, *see* **nisi**

Nicaeēnsis, –e, Nicene

Nīcānor, –oris, *m.*, Nicanor

Nīcomēdensis, –e, of the Nicomedians; *as noun, m. pl.*, Nicomedians

Nīcomēdia, –ae, *f.*, Nicomedia, *capital of Bithynia*

Nīcopolis, –is, *f.*, Nicopolis

nīdus, –ī, *m.*, nest

niger, –gra, –grum, black

nihil, *adv.*, nothing; not at all; **nihildum**, nothing as yet

nihil, *indeclinable, n.*, nothing

nihilō minus, *adv.*, none the less, nevertheless

Nīlus, –ī, *m.*, the Nile, *a river in Egypt*

nimbus, –ī, *m.*, cloud; rain cloud

nīmīrum, *adv.*, of course

nimis, *adv.*, too much, too

nimium, *adv.*, too, too much

Ninus, –ī *m.*, Ninus, *an Assyrian king*

nisi, nī, *conj.*, unless, except, if not

niteō, –ēre, —, —, shine, be well fed

nitēscō, –ere, nituī, —, grow sleek (*of animals*)

nītor, nītī, nīxus (nīsus), strive, struggle

niveus, –a, –um, snow-white

nix, nivis, *f.,* snow

nōbilis, –e, noble

nōbilitās, –tātis, *f.,* fame; nobility

nōbīscum = cum nōbīs

nocēns, *gen.* **–entis,** harmful; guilty

noceō, –ēre, nocuī, nocitūrus, do harm to, injure (*w. dat.*)

noctū, *adv.,* at night

nocturnus, –a, –um, of *or* by night

nōlō, nōlle, nōluī, —, be unwilling, not wish

nōmen, nōminis, *n.,* name

nōminātim, *adv.,* by name, expressly

nōminō, 1, name, call

nōn, *adv.,* not; **nōn iam,** no longer

Nōnae, –ārum, *f. pl.,* Nones

nōndum, *adv.,* not yet

Nōniānus, –ī, *m.,* Nonianus

nōnne, *interrog. adv.* (*in a direct question*), not; (*in an indirect question*), if not, whether not

nōnnullus, –a, –um, some, several

nōs, nostrum, we, *pl. of* **ego**

nōscitō, –āre, —, —, know, recognize

nōscō, –ere, nōvī, nōtus, learn; *in perf. tenses,* have learned, know

noster, –tra, –trum, our

nota, –ae, *f.,* mark

notābilis, –e, noteworthy, remarkable

notārius, –rī, *m.,* secretary

nōtitiā, –ae, *f.,* knowledge, acquaintance

notō, 1, note, mark, observe

nōtus, –a, –um, known, familiar

novem, nine

novitās, –tātis, *f.,* newness, strangeness

novus, –a, –um, new, strange; last

nox, noctis, *f.,* night

nūbēs, –is, *f.,* cloud

nūbō, –ere, nūpsī, nūptus, veil oneself, wed

nūdō, 1, strip, expose

nūdulus, –a, –um, bare, exposed

nūdus, –a, –um, bare, naked, vacant

nūgae, –ārum, *f. pl.,* nonsense

nūllus, –a, –um, no, none; *as noun, m.,* no one; **nōn nūllī,** some

num, *adv., introduces questions expecting negative answer; conj.,* whether

nūmen, nūminis, *n.,* nod; divine will *or* power; divinity

numerōsus, –a, –um, numerous; manifold; full of rhythm

numerus, –ī, *m.,* number

Numidae, –ārum, *m. pl.,* the Numidians

Numidicus, –ī, *m.,* Numidicus

nummus, –ī, *m.,* coin, money

numquam, *adv.,* never

nunc, *adv.,* now

nuncupō, 1, call by name, name

nūntiō, 1, report, announce

nūntius, –tī, *m.,* messenger; message, news, report

nūper, *adv.,* recently

nūptiae, –ārum, *f. pl.,* wedding

nūptiālis, –e, nuptial

nūrus, –ī, *f.,* daughter-in-law

nusquam, *adv.,* nowhere

nūtriō, –īre, –īvī, –ītus, nourish, keep alive, foster

nūtrīx, –īcis, *f.,* nurse

nūtus, –ūs, *m.,* nod, will

nux, nucis, *f.,* nut

nympha, –ae, *f.,* nymph

O

ō! *interj.,* O! oh!

ob, *prep. w. acc.,* because of, on account of, for

obeō, –īre, obīvī, obitūrus, go to meet, attend to, engage in; reach

obequitō, 1, ride toward

obiciō, –ere, obiēcī, obiectus, throw to *or* against, put in the way, oppose

obiurgātiō, –ōnis, *f.,* rebuke

oblectātiō, –ōnis, *f.,* delight

oblectō, 1, delight

obligō, 1, bind

oblinō, –ere, oblēvī, oblitus, smear, stain

oblitterō, 1, erase

oblīviō, –ōnis, *f.,* forgetting, forgetfulness

oblīvīscor, –ī, oblītus, forget

obnoxius, –a, –um, obliged, servile, weak

oboediō, –īre, oboedīvī, oboedītus, give heed to

obrēpō, –ere, obrepsī, obreptus, steal in

obruō, –ere, obruī, obrutus, overwhelm, bury

obscūrō, 1, darken, hide

obscūrus, –a, –um, dark, secret, obscure

obsecrō, 1, implore

obsequor, –ī, obsecūtus, yield, comply

observō, 1, observe, watch, heed

obses, obsidis, m., hostage

obsideō, –ēre, obsēdī, obsessus, beset, besiege, blockade, hem in

obsidiō, –ōnis, f., siege

obsistō, –ere, obstitī, obstitūrus, resist

obstinātiō, –ōnis, f., stubbornness

obstinātus, –a, –um, stubborn

obstō, –āre, obstitī, obstātūrus, prevent, withstand, stand in the way

obstrepō, –ere, obstrepuī, —, drown out (*with noise*)

obstringō, –ere, obstrīnxī, obstrictus, bind

obstruō, –ere, obstrūxī, obstrūctus, block

obstupēscō, –ere, obstupuī, —, be astounded

obsum, obesse, obfuī, —, injure

obtemperō, 1, submit to, obey, consult

obtestor, 1, entreat, pray

obtineō, –ēre, obtinuī, obtentus, hold, obtain

obtingō, –ere, obtigī, —, happen

obturbō, 1, confuse, disturb

obtūsus, –a, –um, blunt, dull; weak

obviam, adv., in the way; *w.* **veniō,** come to meet

obvius, –a, –um, meeting, encountering

occāsiō, –ōnis, f., opportunity

occāsus, –ūs, m., going down, downfall, setting; **occāsus sōlis,** sunset, west

occidō, –ere, occidī, occāsūrus, set, fall down; die

occīdo, –ere, occīdi, occīsus, kill

occultē, adv., secretly

occultō, 1, conceal, hide

occultus, –a, –um, secret, hidden

occupātiō, –ōnis, f., occupation, business

occupō, 1, seize, occupy

occupātus, –a, –um, busy

occurrō, –ere, occurrī, occursūrus, run against, meet, occur

ōceanus, –ī, m., ocean (*esp. the Atlantic Ocean*)

ōcior, ōcius, comp. adj., swifter

Octāviānus, –ī, m., Octavian, *the emperor Augustus*

Octāvius, –vī, m., Octavius

octāvus, –a, –um, eighth

octō, eight

oculus, –ī, m., eye

ōdī, ōdisse, ōsūrus (*perf. translated as pres.*), hate

odiōsus, –a, –um, hateful, offensive

odium, odī, n., hatred

odōrātus, –a, –um, fragrant

offendō, –ere, offendī, offēnsus, (strike against); come upon, find

offerō, offerre, obtulī, oblātus, bear to, offer, present, expose; **mē offerō,** rush against

officīna, –ae, f., factory

officiōsus, –a, –um, obliging, dutiful

officium, –cī, n., duty, service, allegiance, function

ōh! interj., oh!

olfaciō, –ere, olfēcī, olfactus, smell

ōlim, adv., once, formerly; hereafter, sometime

Olympia, –ae, f., Olympia, *a Greek city*

Olympicus, –a, –um, Olympic

Olympiēum, –ī, n., Olympieum, *temple of the Olympian Jupiter*

ōmen, ōminis, n., omen, sign

ōminor, 1, augur, prophesy

omittō, –ere, omīsī, omissus, let go, pass over, drop, disregard

omnīnō, adv., altogether, in all, entirely, at all, to be sure

omnis, omne, all, every, whole

onerārius, –a, –um, for freight; **nāvis onerāria,** transport

onerōsus, –a, –um, heavy

onus, oneris, n., weight, load, burden, cargo

onustus, –a, –um, loaded

opācus, –a, –um, gloomy

opera, –ae, f., work, service, assistance, aid, effort; *w.* **dare,** see to it

operiō, –īre, operuī, opertus, cover

operōsus, –a, –um, painstaking, industrious; troublesome

opifer, –era, –erum, helping

opifex, –ficis, *m.,* workman

opīniō, –ōnis, *f.,* belief, opinion, expectation; reputation

opīnor, 1, imagine, judge, think

opitulor, 1, bring aid, help

oportet, –ēre, oportuit, it is fitting *or* necessary, ought

oppetō, –ere, –īvī, –ītus, seek

oppidum, –ī, *n.,* town

opportūnitās, –tātis, *f.,* suitableness

opportūnus, –a, –um, fit, timely, opportune, convenient, advantageous

opprimō, –ere, oppressī, oppressus; overcome, surprise, crush, oppress

oppugnātiō, –ōnis, *f.,* siege, method of attack

oppugnō, 1, attack, besiege

ops, opis, *f.,* aid, might; *pl.,* wealth, resources, influence

optimē, *see* **bene**

optimus, *see* **bonus**

optō, 1, desire, wish

opus, operis, *n.,* work, labor, task, exercise; **magnō opere** *or* **magnopere,** greatly; **tantō opere,** so greatly

opus, *n., indeclinable,* need; necessary, necessity; **opus est,** it is necessary, there is need

ōra, –ae, *f.,* coast, edge

ōrāculum, –ī, *n.,* oracle, prophesy

ōrārius, –a, –um, of the coast, coastal

ōrātiō, –ōnis, *f.,* speech, words, eloquence; argument

ōrātor, –ōris, *m.,* speaker, orator

ōrātōria, –ae, *f.,* oratory

orbis, –is, *m.,* circle; *esp. w. or without* **terrae** *or* **terrārum,** the world (*i.e., the circle of lands around the Mediterranean*)

orbō, 1, deprive, rob; bereave

orbus, –a, –um, childless

Orcus, –ī, *m.,* Orcus, *god of Hades;* Hades; the Lower World; Pluto

ōrdior, –īrī, ōrsus, begin

ōrdō, ōrdinis, *m.,* row, order, turn, rank, company, body; class

oriēns, –entis, *m.,* rising sun, east

orīgo, originis, *f.,* origin

Ōrīōn, –ōnis, *m.,* Orion, *a constellation*

orior, orīrī, ortus, rise, arise, begin, descend, be descended from

ōrnāmentum, –ī, *n.,* (mark of) distinction, decoration, ornament

ōrnātus, –ūs, *m.,* adornment, decoration

ōrnō, 1, adorn, furnish, equip; honor, **ōrnātus,** fitted out

ōrō, 1, beg, ask, pray (for), plead, implore

Orpheus, –ī, *m.,* Orpheus (Or'fūs), *a famous musician*

ortus, –ūs., *m.,* rising; east

ōs, ōris, *m.,* mouth, face, expression; lips

os, ossis, (*gen. pl.,* **ossium**) *n.,* bone

Oscē, *adv.,* in Oscan

ōsculor, 1, kiss, embrace

ōsculum, –ī, *n.,* kiss

ostendō, –ere, ostendī, ostentus, (stretch out), point out, show, display; declare

ostentō, 1, hold up, display

Ōstiēnsis, –e, to Ostia

ōtiōsus, –a, –um, idle, unemployed; peaceful

ōtium, ōtī, *n.,* leisure, quiet, peace

Ovidius, –dī, *m.,* Ovid

ovis, –is, *f.,* sheep

ōvum, –ī, *n.,* egg

P

P., *abbreviation for* **Pūblius**

pābulos, 1, forage

pābulum, –ī, *n.,* food (for cattle), fodder

pacīscor, –ī, pactus, agree, appoint

pācō, 1, pacify, subdue

pactum, –ī, *n.,* agreement; manner

Paelignus, –a, –um, Pelignian, *of a people of central Italy*

paene, *adv.,* almost

paenitentia, –ae, *f.,* repentence

paenitet, –ēre, –uit, *impers.,* it makes regret, it grieves

Paestum, –ī, *n.,* Paestum, *a town in southern Italy*

pāgānus, –a, –um, rustic, pagan

pāgus, –ī, *m.,* district, canton

palam, *adv.,* openly, publicly

Palātīnus (mōns), –ī, *m.,* **Palātium, –tī,** *n.,* the Palatine Hill; palace

Palātium, –tī, *n.,* the Palatine, *one of the seven hills of Rome*

palātum, –ī *n.,* palate

palea, –ae, *f.,* chaff, straw

Palicānus, –ī, *m.,* Palicanus

palla, –ae, *f.,* robe

pallēscō, –ere, palluī, —, become pale, turn yellow

pallidus, –a, –um, pale

palma, –ae, *f.,* hand, palm; date

palūs, palūdis, *f.,* marsh, swamp

Pān, Pānis, *m.,* Pan, *god of shepherds*

pānis, –is, *m.,* bread

Pāniscus, –ī, *m.,* Paniscus, *a rural deity*

Pannonia, –ae, *f.,* Hungary

panthēra, –ae, *f.,* panther

Papa, –ae, *m.,* the pope

papae! *interj.,* indeed!

pār, *gen.* **paris,** equal, like, fair; *as noun, n.,* pair

parātus, –a, –um, ready, prepared

parcē, *adv.,* sparingly

parcō, –ere, pepercī, parsūrus, spare, save

parcus, –a, –um, sparing, economical, frugal, saving

parēns, –entis, *m. and f.,* parent

pāreō, –ēre, pāruī, pāritūrus, (appear), obey

pariēs, –ētis, *m.,* wall

parilis, –e, equal

pariō, –ere, peperī, partus, give birth, produce; gain

pariter, *adv.,* equally, in like manner, likewise

Parnāsis, –idis, of Parnassus

Parnassius, –a, –um, Parnassian

Parnassus, –ī, *m.,* Parnassus, *a mountain range in central Greece*

parō, 1, get, get ready (for), prepare; **parātus, –a, –um,** prepared, ready

Paros, –ī, *f.,* Paros, *an island in the Aegean*

parricīda, –ae, *m.,* murderer

parricīdium, –dī, *n.,* parricide, murder

pars, partis, *f.,* part, role, side; direction; duty

particeps, participis, *m.,* participant, sharer

particula, –ae, *f.,* small part, particle

partim, *adv.,* partly

partiō, –īre, –īvī, –ītus, divide

partītiō, –ōnis, *f.,* division

partus, –ūs, *m.,* birth

parum, *adv.,* little, too little

parvulus, –a, –um, very small, little, petty

parvus, –a, –um, small, little, slight, low; *comp.* **minor, minus,** smaller, less, lesser, younger; *superl.* **minimus, –a, –um,** smallest, least, very little, youngest

pāscō, –ere, pāvī, pāstus, feed, feast

passim, *adv.,* everywhere

passus, –ūs, *m.,* step, pace (*about five feet*); **mīlle passūs,** mile

passus, *part. of* **patior**

pāstor, –ōris, *m.,* shepherd

Patareus, –a, –um, of Patara, *a seaport of Lycia*

patefaciō, –ere, –fēcī, –factus, open (up), lay open, expose

patēns, *gen.* **patentis,** open, extending

pateō, –ēre, patuī, —, stand *or* be open, be exposed; extend

pater, patris, *m.,* father, senator; *pl.,* **patrēs cōnscrīptī,** senators, patricians

paternus, –a, –um, of the father

patienter, *adv.,* patiently

patientia, –ae, *f.,* patience

patior, patī, passus, suffer, endure, allow, permit

patria, –ae, *f.,* fatherland, native land, country

patricius, –a, –um, patrician

patrīmonium, –nī, *n.,* paternal estate; inheritance

patrius, –a, –um, of a father, father's, ancestral

patrōcinium, –nī, *n.,* patronage

patrōnus, –ī, *m.,* patron

patruus, –ī, *m.,* uncle

patulus, –a, –um, spreading, wide

paucī, –ae, –a, few, only a few

paucitās, –tātis, *f.,* small number, scarcity

pauculus, –a, –um, very few, very little

paucus, –a, –um, little; *pl.,* few, only a few

paulātim, *adv.,* gradually, little by little; a few at a time

paulisper, *adv.,* for a little while; for a short time

paulō and **paulum,** *adv.,* shortly, a little

paulum, –ī, *n.,* a little

pauper, *gen.* **pauperis,** poor

paupertās, –tātis, *f.,* poverty

paveō, –ēre, pāvī, —, be afraid, tremble with fear

pavidus, –a, –um, trembling, scared

pāx, pācis, *f.,* peace, truce

peccātum, –ī, *n.,* mistake

peccō, 1, sin

pectus, pectoris, *n.,* breast, heart

pecūnia, –ae, *f.,* money; *pl.,* riches

pecūniārius, –a, –um, pecuniary

pecus, pecoris, *n.,* cattle, flock

pecus, –udis, *f.,* beast; *pl.,* herds

pedes, peditis, *m.,* foot soldier; *pl.,* infantry

pedester, –tris, –tre, (of) infantry; on foot

peditātus, –ūs, *m.,* infantry

peierō, 1, commit perjury

pelagus, –ī, *n.,* sea

pellis, –is, *f.,* skin

pellō, –ere, pepulī, pulsus, beat, drive, put to flight; banish, defeat

pendeō, –ēre, pependī, —, hang, hover

pendō, –ere, pependī, pēnsus, hang, weigh, pay

penetrō, 1, penetrate

Pēnēius, –a, –um, Penē´an (*of a river in Thessaly*)

penetrō, 1, penetrate, enter

penitus, –a, –um, remote

penitus, *adv.,* deeply, within

penna, –ae, *f.,* feather, wing

per, *prep. w. acc.,* through, by, over, among, during, along, by means of, during; in the name of

peragō, –ere, –ēgī, –āctus, complete; obey

peragrō, 1, traverse

peramanter, *adv.,* very lovingly

perantīquus, –a, –um, very ancient

percipiō, –ere, –cēpī, –ceptus, seize; hear, feel, learn, appreciate, obtain

percontor, 1, inquire

percrebrēscō, –ere, –crēbruī, —, grow prevalent, be spread abroad

percurrō, –ere, –cucurrī, –cursūrus, hasten through, run over

percutiō, –ere, –cussī –cussus, strike, pierce, beat

perdiscō, –ere, –didicī, —, learn thoroughly

perditus, –a, –um, lost; desperate, corrupt

perdō, –ere, –didī, –ditus, lose, destroy, waste

perdūcō, –ere, –dūxī, –ductus, lead *or* bring through, extend, win over

perdūrō, 1, harden, endure

peregrīnātiō, –ōnis, *f.,* foreign travel

peregrīnor, 1, go abroad

peregrīnus, –a, –um, strange, foreign; *as noun m.,* foreigner

perennis, –e, through the year, unceasing, perpetual

pereō, –īre, –iī (–īvī), –itūrus, perish, pass away, be lost, disappear

perexcelsus, –a, –um, exalted

perfero, –ferre, –tulī, –lātus, carry (through), report, bring; endure

perficiō, –ere, –fēcī, –fectus, do thoroughly, accomplish, make of, bring about, finish, carry out; cause

perfidēlis, –e, very faithful

perfidia, –ae, *f.,* faithlessness, treachery

perfidus, –a, –um, treacherous, dishonest, faithless

perfringō, –ere, –frēgī, –frāctus, break through *or* down, violate

perfruor, –fruī, –frūctus, enjoy fully

perfuga, –ae, *m.,* deserter

perfugiō, –ere, –fūgī, —, flee

perfugium, –gī, *n.,* refuge

perfungor, –ī, –fūnctus, perform

Pergamum, –ī, *n.,* Troy

pergō, –ere, perrēxī, perrēctus, proceed, continue, hasten

perhorrēscō, –ere, –horruī, shudder at

perīclitor, 1, try, risk, endanger

perīculōsus, –a, –um, dangerous

perīculum, –ī, *n.,* trial, danger

perimō, –ere, –ēmī, –ēmptus, destroy

perior, *see* **malus**

perītus, –a, –um, skilled, experienced, acquainted with

periūrus, –a, –um, oath-breaking, perjured

perlegō, –ere, –lēgī, –lēctus, read through, examine thoroughly

permaneō, –ēre, –mānsī, –mānsūrus, remain

permātūrēscō, –ere, –mātūrui, —, ripen fully

permittō, –ere, –mīsī, –missus, let go through, leave, allow, grant, entrust, permit

permoveō, –ēre, –mōvī, –mōtus, move deeply, induce, alarm

permultus, –a, –um, very much, very many

permūtātiō, –ōnis, *f.,* exchange

permūtō, 1, exchange

perniciēs, –ēī, *f.,* destruction, ruin

perniciōsus, –a, –um, destructive, dangerous

pernoctō, 1, spend the night

perofficiōsē, *adv.,* very attentively

peropportūnus, –a, –um, very seasonable *or* opportune

perōsus, –a, –um, loathing

perparvulus, –a, –um, very little, very small

perpaucī, –ae, –a, very few

perpetior, –ī, perpessus, bear steadfastly, suffer firmly, endure

perpetuō, *adv.,* permanently

perpetuus, –a, –um, constant, lasting; **in perpetuum,** forever

perquīrō, –ere, –quīsīvī, –quīsītus, make a diligent search for

perrārus, –a, –um, very rare

perrumpō, –ere, –rūpī, –ruptus, break through

Persae, –ārum, *m. pl.,* the Persians

persaepe, *adv.,* very often

perscrībō, –ere, perscrīpsī, perscrīptus, write out

persequor, –sequī, –secūtus, follow up, pursue, punish, avenge

persevērō, 1, persist, continue

persōna, –ae, *f.,* part, character, personage

personō, –āre, personuī, personitus, resound

perspiciō, –ere, –spexī, –spectus, see (through, clearly), perceive, examine

perspicuus, –a, –um, clear, manifest

perstō, –āre, –stitī, –stātūrus, persist, continue standing

persuādeo, –ēre, –suāsī, –suāsūrus, persuade

perterreō, –ēre, –terruī, –territus, frighten thoroughly, scare thoroughly, alarm

pertimēscō –ere, pertimuī, —, become thoroughly alarmed; fear, dread

pertinācia, –ae, *f.,* obstinacy

pertināciter, *adv.,* persistently

pertineō, –ēre, –tinuī, –tentūrus, extend (to), pertain to, belong to, concern

pertrāctō, 1, touch, investigate

pertrānseō, –īre, –īvī, –itūrus, pass through

perturbō, 1, disturb, alarm, throw into confusion

perturbātiō, –ōnis, *f.,* confusion

pervagor, 1, wander through, spread through, pervade

perveniō, –īre, –vēnī, –ventūrus, come (through), arrive (at), reach, attain

pervetus, *gen.* **–eris,** very old, most ancient

pēs, pedis, *m.,* foot; **pedibus,** on foot

pessimus, *see* **malus**

pestifer, –era, –erum, destructive

pestis, –is, *f.,* plague, destruction, curse, ruin

petītiō, –ōnis, *f.,* candidacy

petītor, –ōris, *m.,* candidate

petō, –ere, petīvī, petītus, seek, ask, beg; attack

petulantia, –ae, *f.,* wantonness

pexus, –a, –um, combed

Phaedimus, –ī, *m.,* Phaedimus, *one of Niobe's sons*

pharetra, –ae, *f.,* quiver

Pharsālus, –ī, *f.,* Pharsalus, *a town in Thessaly*

Philēmōn, –onis, *m.,* Philemon, *husband of Baucis*

Philippī, –ōrum, *m. pl.,* Philippi, *a city in Macedonia*

Philippus, –ī, *m.,* Philip

Philistiōn, –ōnis, *m.,* Philistion

philosophia, –ae, *f.,* philosophy

philosophus, –ī, *m.,* philosopher

Phoebus, –ī, *m.,* Phoebus, Apollo

Phrygius, –a, –um, Phrygian

pictūra, –ae, *f.,* picture, painting

pictus, –a, –um, painted

pietās, –tātis, *f.,* dutiful conduct, devotion, piety

piger, –gra, –grum, reluctant, slow, lazy, dull

piget, –ēre, piguit, it grieves

pigrē, *adv.,* slowly, reluctantly

pila, –ae, *f.,* ball, ballplaying

pilula, –ae, *f.,* pill

pīlum, –ī, *n.,* spear (*for throwing*), javelin

piscis, –is, *m.,* fish

piscor, 1, fish

Pīsistratus, –ī, *m.,* Pisistratus, *a tyrant of Athens*

Pīsō, –ōnis, *m.,* Piso

pius, –a, –um, dutiful, righteous, pious, devoted, loyal, loving

Pius, –ī, *m.,* Pius

placeō, –ēre, placuī, placitus, be pleasing to, please; *impers.,* it seems best, (he) decides, it is decided by, **placet,** it pleases (him), *i.e.,* (he) decides, be decided

placidus, –a, –um, gentle, calm

plācō, 1, appease

plāga, –ae, *f.,* blow; disaster

plānē, *adv.,* plainly

plangor, –ōris, *m.,* beating (*of the breast*); shrieking

plānitiēs, –iēī, *f.,* level ground, plain

planta, –ae, *f.,* sprout, twig

plānus, –a, –um, level, plane

Platō, –ōnis, *m.,* Plato, *a Greek philosopher*

plaudō, –ere, plausī, plausus, applaud

plausus, –ūs, *m.,* clapping of hands, applause

plēbs, plēbis, *f.,* people, common people

plēctrum, –ī, *n.,* pick (*for striking the lyre*)

Plēiades, –um, *f.,* Pleiades, *the seven daughters of Atlas*

plēnus, –a, –um, full, abounding in

plērīque, –aeque, –aque, most, the majority

plērumque, *adv.,* usually

plexus, –a, –um, woven

plōrō, 1, cry out, wail, lament

Plōtius, –tī, *m.,* Plotius

plūma, –ae, *f.,* feather

plumbum, –ī, *n.,* lead

plūrēs, *see* **multus**

plūrimum, adv., very much, most, especially, *see* **multum**

plūrimus, *see* **multus**

plūs, *see* **multum, multus**

pōcillātor, –ōris, *m.,* cupbearer

pōculum, –ī, *n.,* cup

poena, –ae, *f.,* penalty, punishment; **poenam dō,** pay the penalty

Poenī, –ōrum, *m. pl.,* the Carthaginians

Poenicus, *see* **Pūnicus**

Poenus, –a, –um, Punic; *as noun, m. pl.,* the Carthaginians

poēta, –ae, *m.,* poet

poēticus, –a, –um, poetic

Poggius, –ī, *m.,* Poggio

pol! *interj.,* by Pollux!

poliō, –īre, polīvī, polītus, polish

pollex, –icis, *m.,* thumb

polliceor, pollicērī, pollicitus, promise

pollicitātiō, –ōnis, *f.,* promise

Pollux, –cis, *m.,* Pollux

pōmārium, –rī, *n.,* orchard

pōmifer, –era, –erum, fruit-bearing

pompa, –ae, *f.,* parade, procession

Pompeiānus, –a, –um, of Pompeii

Pompeius, –peī, *m.,* Pompey

Pompōnius, –nī, *m.,* Pomponius

Pomptīnae palūdēs, Pontine Marshes, *south of Rome*

Pomptīnus, –a, –um, Pontine

pōmum, –ī, *n.,* fruit, apple, berry

pondus, ponderis, *n.,* weight

pōnō, –ere, posuī, positus, put, place, set, pitch, lay aside, serve, lay down; *pass.,* be situated, depend upon; *w.* **castra,** pitch

pōns, pontis, *m.,* bridge

pontifex, pontificis, *m.,* priest

pontificātus, –ūs, *m.,* pontificate

pontus, –ī, *m.,* sea

Pontus, –ī, *m.,* Pontus, *the region south of the Black Sea*

poples, –litis, *m.,* knee

poposcī, *see* **poscō**

populāris, –e, popular

populor, 1, destroy

populus, –ī, *m.,* people; *pl.,* peoples

Porcius, –a, –um, Porcian

porrigō, –ere, porrēxī, porrēctus, stretch out, extend

porrō, *adv.,* then

porta, –ae, *f.,* gate, door

portentum, –ī, *n.,* portent

Porthaōn, –ōnis, *m., a mythological character*

porticus, –ūs, *f.,* colonnade, gallery, porch

portō, 1, carry

portus, –ūs, *m.,* harbor, port

poscō, –ere, poposcī, —, demand, call for, ask

possessiō, –ōnis, *f.,* possession

possideō, –ēre, possēdī, possessus, own, possess

possum, posse, potuī, —, can, can do, be able; **multum (plūs, plūrimum) possum,** be very powerful

post, *adv. and prep. w. acc.,* behind; after, later, since; **paulō post,** a little later

posteā, *adv.,* afterwards, later

posteāquam, *conj.,* after

posteritās, –tātis, *f.,* the future, posterity

posterus, –a, –um, following, next; **in posterum,** for the future; *as noun, m. pl.,* posterity, descendants

posthāc, *adv.,* hereafter

postis, –is, *m.,* doorpost; *pl.,* door

postpōnō, –ere, –posuī, –positus, put after, esteem less

postquam, *conj.,* after

postrēmō, *adv.,* at last, finally; in short

postrēmus, –a, –um, last

postrīdiē, *adv.,* on the next day

postulō, 1, demand

potēns, *gen.* **potentis,** strong, powerful

potentia, –ae, *f.,* power

potestās, –tātis, *f.,* power, opportunity

pōtiō, –ōnis, *f.,* drink

potior, potīrī, potītus, get possession of, gain possession of (*w. gen. or abl.*)

potissimum, *adv.,* especially, above all, in preference to all others

potius, *adv.,* rather

prae, *prep. w. abl.,* before; in comparison with

praeacūtus, –a, –um, pointed

praebeō, –ēre, –uī, –itus, offer, hold forth, furnish, present, show

praecēdō, –ere, –cessī, –cessūrus, go before, precede

praeceps, *gen.* **praecipitis,** headlong, rash; rushing, steep; **in praeceps,** headfirst

praeceptum, –ī, *n.,* precept, rule; instructions

praecipiō, –ere, –cēpī, –ceptus, instruct, direct, lay down a rule

praecipitō, 1, rush headlong, sink

praecipuē, *adv.,* especially

praeclārus, –a, –um, brilliant, remarkable

praeclūdō, –ere, –clūsī, –clūsus, shut, close, hinder, impede

praecō, praecōnis, *m.,* announcer, crier, herald

praecōnium, –nī, *n.,* public praise

praecordia, –ōrum, *n.,* breast, heart

praecurrō, –ere, –cucurrī (–currī), –cursūrus, run before, precede, excel

praeda, –ae, *f.,* loot, prey

praedātor, –ōris, *m.,* robber

praedicātiō, –ōnis, *f.,* proclamation

praedicō, 1, announce, declare, say, proclaim

praedīcō, –ere, –dīxī, –dictus, predict, foretell

praediolum, –ī, *n.,* small estate

praeditus, –a, –um, endowed, possessing

praedium, –dī, *n.,* farm, estate

praedō, –ōnis, *m.,* pirate

praedor, 1, loot

praedūcō, –ere, –dūxī, –ductus, extend

praefātiō, –ōnis, *f.,* preface, prologue

praefectūra, –ae, *f.,* prefecture

praefectus, –ī, *m.,* commander, prefect

praeferō, –ferre, –tulī, –lātus, carry before, prefer

praeficiō, –ere, –fēcī, –fectus, put *or* place in charge of, set over, put in command of

praefor, 1, say, beforehand, preface

praefulgeō, –ēre, —, —, beam forth, shine greatly

praelambō, –ere, —, —, wash lightly

praemittō, –ere, –mīsī, –missus, send ahead

praemium, –mī, *n.,* reward, prize

praemūniō = mūniō

praenōscō, –ere, –nōvī, –nōtus, learn beforehand

praeparō, 1, prepare

praepōnō, –ere, –posuī, –positus, prefer

praeproperus, –a, –um, too hasty, sudden

praerumpō, –ere, –rūpī, –ruptus, break off

praescius, –a, –um, foreknowing, foreseeing

praescrībō, –ere, –scrīpsī, –scrīptus, direct, require of

praescrīptum, –ī, *n.,* order

praesēns, *gen.* **praesentis,** present, in person, evident; providential

praesentia, –ae, *f.,* presence; **in praesentiā,** for the present

praesentiō, –īre, –sēnsī, –sēnsus, foresee, look forward to

praesertim, *adv.,* especially

praesidium, –dī, *n.,* garrison, guard, fortification; protection, aid, help

praestāns, *gen.* **praestantis,** outstanding, preeminent

praestō, –āre, –stitī, –stitūrus, stand before, excel; guarantee; offer, perform, show; **praestat,** *impers.,* it is better

praestō, *adv.,* at hand, ready

praestōlor, 1, wait for

praesum, –esse, –fuī, –futūrus, be in charge of, be in command of

praesūmō, –ere, –sūmpsī, –sūmptus, undertake

praeter, *prep. w. acc.,* besides, contrary to, beyond; except

praetereā, *adv.,* besides, furthermore, moreover

praetereō, –īre, –iī, –itus, go by, pass by, omit; outstrip

praeterhāc, adv., besides, moreover

praeteritus, –a, –um, past; *as noun, n. pl.,* the past

praetermittō, –ere, –mīsī, –missus, let go, omit, pass over

praeterquam, *adv.,* other than, *conj.,* except

praetor, –ōris, *m.,* praetor (*an official*), judge, *a Roman judicial magistrate*

praetōrium, –rī, *n.,* headquarters

praetōrius, –a, –um, praetorian; *as noun, m.,* ex-praetor

praetūra, –ae, *f.,* the praetorship

praevaleō, –ēre, –valuī, –valitūrus, prevail

prandium, –dī, *n.,* lunch

prātum, –ī, *n.,* meadow

prāvus, –a, –um, crooked, vicious, depraved

precor, 1, entreat, pray

prehendō, –ere, –hendī, –hēnsus, grasp, seize, catch

premō, –ere, pressī, pressus, press, press hard, oppress, crowd; cover

prēndō = prehendō

prēndō, –ere, prēndī, prēnsus, seize

prēnsātiō, –ōnis, *f.,* soliciting, canvassing

pretiōsus, –a, –um, costly

pretium, –tī, *n.,* price; reward

prex, precis, *f.,* prayer, entreaty

prīdem, *adv.,* long ago; *w.* **iam,** now for a long time

prīdiē, *adv.,* on the day before

prīmō, *adv.,* at first

prīmum, *adv.,* first, in the first place, at first, for the first time; *w.* **quam,** as soon as possible; *w.* **ut** *or* **cum,** as soon as

prīmus, –a, –um, first, foremost; **in prīmīs,** especially

prīnceps, prīncipis, *adj. and noun, m.,* chief, first (man), leader, emperor; **prīnceps,** under the direction of

prīncipātus, –ūs, *m.,* first place, leadership

prīncipiō, *adv.,* in the first place

prīncipium, –pī, *n.,* beginning

prior, prius, former, first; **prior, –ōris,** *m.,* prior

prīscus, –a, –um, ancient, primitive

Prīscus, –ī, *m.,* Priscus

prīstinus, –a, –um, former

prius, *compar. adv.,* before, first

priusquam (prius... quam), *conj.,* before

prīvātim, *adv.,* privately

prīvātus, –a, –um, private; *as noun, m.,* private citizen

prīvō, 1, deprive

prō, *prep. w. abl.,* in front of, before, for, instead of, as, in accordance with, in proportion to, in behalf of, in return for, on account of, instead of, according to

proavus, –ī, *m.,* great-grandfather

probitās, –tātis, *f.,* honesty

probō, 1, prove; approve

probrum, –ī, *n.,* disgraceful conduct

probus, –a, –um, upright

procācitās, –tātis, *f.,* boldness, impudence

prōcēdō, –ere, –cessī, –cessūrus, go forward, advance, proceed

prōcēritās, –tātis, *f.,* height, tallness

procul, *adv.,* at a distance, far off

prōcumbō, –ere, –cubuī, –cubitūrus, lie down, sink down

prōcūrō, 1, take care of

prōcurrō, –ere, –currī, –cursūrus, run forward

prōdeō, –īre, prōdiī, prōditus, go *or* come forth

prōdigiōsus, –a, –um, unnatural, strange

prōdō, –ere, –didī, –ditus, give (forth), hand down, betray, transmit

prōdūcō, –ere, –dūxī, –ductus, lead forth *or* bring out, induce, prolong, coax (*of a fire*)

proelior, 1, battle

proelium, –lī, *n.,* battle

profānus, –a, –um, unholy, profane

profectiō, –ōnis, *f.,* departure

profectō, *adv.,* for a fact, certainly, doubtless

prōferō, –ferre, –tulī, –lātus, bring out, bring forth, produce, extend

professor, –ōris, *m.,* professor

prōficiō, –ere, –fēcī, –fectus, accomplish

proficīscor, proficīscī, profectus, set out, start, march, depart

profiteor, –ērī, professus, confess; offer, promise; register

prōflīgātus, –a, –um, corrupt, unprincipled

profugiō, –ere, –fūgī, –fugitūrus, flee, escape

profugus, –ī, *m.,* fugitive

profundō, –ere, –fūdī, –fūsus, waste

prōgeniēs, –iēī, *f.,* descendants

prōgredior, –gredī, –gressus, proceed, step forward, advance

prōgnātus, –a, –um, descended

prohibeō, –ēre, –hibuī, –hibitus, prevent, keep from, cut off, protect

prōiciō, –ere, –iēcī, –iectus, throw, thrust (forward), abandon

proinde, *adv.,* therefore

prōlabor, –ī, prōlāpsus, slip

prōlēs, –is, *f.,* offspring, young son

prōloquor, –loquī, –locūtus, say

prōmiscuus, –a, –um, mixed

prōmittō, –ere, –mīsī, –missus, let go; promise; **prōmissus, –a, –um,** long

prōmō, –ere, prōmpsī, prōmptus, give out, bring forth

prōmoveō, –ēre, –mōvī, –mōtus, move forward

prōmptus, –a, –um, ready

prōnūntiō, 1, announce, recite

prōnus, –a, –um, flat, headlong, steep

prōpāgō, 1, extend

prope, *adv.,* almost; *prep. w. acc.,* near

prōpellō, –ere, –pulī, –pulsus, drive away, dislodge

propemodum, *adv.,* nearly, almost

prōpēnsus, –a, –um, coming near; inclined, ready

properē, *adv.,* quickly

properō, 1, hasten, hurry (on)

propinquitās, –tātis, *f.,* nearness

propinquus, –a, –um, near; *as noun, m.,* relative

propitius, –a, –um, favorable, kind

prōpōnō, –ere, –posuī, –positus, explain, present, offer, raise, propose

prōpositum, –ī, *n.,* subject

proprius, –a, –um, (one's) own, characteristic of, belonging to, proper

propter, *prep. w. acc.,* because of, on account of, for the sake of; *adv.,* near

proptereā, *adv.,* on this account; **proptereā quod,** because

prōpugnātiō, –ōnis, *f.,* defense, vindication

prōpugnō, 1, fight on the offensive, fight for, defend

prōra, –ae, *f.,* prow

prōrogō, 1, prolong, continue

prōrsum, prōrsus, *adv.,* forward; certainly

prōscrīptiō, –ōnis, *f.,* prescription, list of condemned

prōsequor, –sequī, –secūtus, pursue, address, accompany, follow (after)

Prōserpina, –ae, *f.,* Proser´pina, *wife of Pluto*

prōsiliō, –īre, prōsiluī, —, leap forth

prōspectō, 1, look at, look for

prōspectus, –ūs, *m.,* view

prosperus, –a, –um, favorable

prōspiciō, –ere, –spexī, –spectus, look out for *or* over, foresee, look forward to prōsternō, –ere, –strāvī, –strātus, overthrow

prōsum, prōdesse, prōfuī, —, benefit, help, profit

prōtegō, –ere, –tēxī, –tēctus, cover

prōtinus, *adv.*, immediately, at once

prōvehō, –ere, –vexī, –vectus, carry forward

prōverbium, –bī, *n.*, saying, proverb

prōvidentia, –ae, *f.*, foresight

prōvideō, –ēre, –vīdī, –vīsus, foresee, provide, look out for

prōvincia, –ae, *f.*, province

prōvinciālis, –e, provincial

proximē, *adv.*, recently

proximus, –a, –um, nearest, last, next, very near; *as noun, n.*, neighborhood

prūdēns, *gen.* prūdentis, sensible, wise

prūdentia, –ae, *f.*, foresight, good sense, discretion

pruīna, –ae, *f.*, frost

pruīnōsus, –a, –um, frosty

prūnum, –i, *n.*, plum

Prūsēnsis, –e, of Prusa, *a Bithynian town*

Psychē, –ēs, *f.*, Psyche

Ptolemaeus, –a, –um, public; Ptolemaic, Egyptian; *as noun, m.*, Ptolemy, *general name for the Egyptian kings*

pūblicē, *adv.*, publicly

pūblicō, 1, confiscate

pūblicus, –a, –um, public

Pūblilia, –ae, *f.*, Publilia

Pūblius, –lī, *m.*, Publius

pudet, –ēre, puduit, *impers.*, it makes ashamed

pudicitia, –ae, *f.*, virtue

pudicus, –a, –um, modest, chaste

pudor, –ōris, *m.*, (sense of) shame, modesty, sense of honor

puella, –ae, *f.*, girl

puer, puerī, *m.*, boy, child

puerīlis, –e, boyish, childish, youthful

puerīliter, *adv.*, childishly, foolishly

pueritia, –ae, *f.*, childhood, boyhood

pugillārēs, –ium, *m. pl.*, writing tablets

pugna, –ae, *f.*, fight, battle

pugnō, 1, fight

pulcher, –chra, –chrum, beautiful; honorable, fine

pulchritūdō, –dinis, *f.*, beauty

pullus, –a, –um, dark-colored

pulsō, 1, dash against, beat

pulsus, *part. of* pellō

pulvīnārius, –a, –um, of *or* belonging to the couches of the gods

pulvis, –eris, *m.*, dust

Pūnicus, –a, –um, Punic, Carthaginian

pūniō, –īre, –īvī, –ītus, punish

puppis, –is, *f., acc.* –im, *abl.* –ī, stern; ship

pūrgō, 1, cleanse

pūritās, –tātis, *f.*, cleanness, purity

purpurātus, –a, –um, purple

purpureus, –a, –um, purple

purpurō, 1, beautify, adorn

pūrus, –a, –um, clean, pure

pusillus, –a, –um, very little, petty

putō, 1, think, consider

Pyramus, –ī, *m.*, Pyramus

Pȳthōn, –ōnis, Python, *a mythological serpent*

Pȳrēnaeī montēs, Pyrenees Mountains

Q

Q., *abbreviation for* Quīntus

quā, *adv.*, where; *w.* nē, in any way

quadrāgēsimus, –a, –um, the fortieth; *as noun, f.*, a tax of one fortieth

quadrāgintā, forty

quadringentī, –ae, –a, four hundred

quadrupēs, –pedis, *m.*, horse, steed

quaerō, –ere, quaesīvī, quaesītus, seek, inquire, ask, examine

quaesō, –ere, —, —, beg

quaestiō, –ōnis, *f.*, investigation, trial; question

quaestiuncula, –ae, *f.*, a little question

quaestor, –ōris, *m.*, quaestor (*a Roman official*), treasury official

quaestus, –ūs, *m.*, gain, profit; business

quālis, –e, what kind of, what, such as, of what sort, of such a kind as; *w.* tālis, as

quāliscumque, quālecumque, of whatever sort

quam, *adv. and conj.*, how, as; *w. comp.*, than; *w. superl.*, as . . . possible; quam prīmum, as soon as possible; quam diū, as long as, how long

quamlibet, *adv.*, according to inclination; however much, to any extent

quamobrem (quam ob rem), *interrog. adv.*, for what reason, why

quamquam, *conj.*, although; however; and yet

quamvīs, *adv.*, however

quandō, *adv. and conj.*, when; at any time, ever

quandōquidem, *adv.*, since

quantuluscumque, –lacumque, –lumcumque, however small

quantum, *adv.*, how much

quantus, –a, –um, how great, how much, what, as (great *or* much as); **quantō... tantō**, the . . . the

quantuscumque, –tacumque, –tumcumque, however great, however small

quāpropter, *adv.*, why, for what reason

quārē, *adv.*, why, wherefore; therefore

quartus, –a, –um, fourth; **quārtus decimus**, fourteenth

quasi, *adv. and conj.*, as if, like, as it were

quatiō, –ere, —, quassus, shake, flutter

quattuor, four

–que, *conj.* (*added to second word*), (*enclitic*), and

quemadmodum, *adv.*, in what manner

queō, quīre, quīvī, —, be able, can

quercus, –ūs, *f.*, oak; garland

querēla, –ae, *f.*, complaint

querimōnia, –ae, *f.*, complaint

queror, querī, questus, complain

quī, quae, quod, *rel. pron.*, who, which, what, that; *interrog. adj.*, what; **quī, qua, quod**, *indef. adj.*, any

quia, *conj.*, because

quīcumque, quaecumque, quodcumque, *rel. pron.*, whoever, whatever

quid, *adv.*, why

quīdam, quaedam, quiddam (*adj.* **quoddam**), *indef. pron.*, a certain one *or* thing; *adj.*, certain, some, a, one

quidem, *adv.* (*follows emphasized word*), at least, to be sure; **nē... quidem**, not even

quidnam, what in the world

quiēs, quiētis, *f.*, rest, sleep, quiet, repose

quiēscō, –ere, quiēvī, quiētūrus, be quiet, rest

quiētus, –a, –um, quiet, undisturbed; **quiētē**, *adv.*, quietly

quīn, *conj.*, (but) that; *adv.*, why not; *w.* **etiam**, in fact, moreover

Quīnctīlis, –e, (of) July

quīngentī, –ae, –a, five hundred

quīnquāgintā, fifty

quīnque, five

quīnquennium, –nī, *n.*, five-year period

Quīntiliānus, –ī, *m.*, Quintilian

quīntus, –a, –um, fifth

Quīntus, –ī, *m.*, Quintus

quippe, *adv. and conj.*, surely, indeed

Quirīnālis (mōns), –is, *m.*, Quirinal Hill

Quirītēs, –ium, *m. pl.*, fellow citizens

quis, quid, *interrog, pron.*, who, what; **quid**, again; **quid quod**, what of the fact that

quis, quid, *indef. pron.*, **quī, qua, quod**, *indef. adj.*, any, anyone, anything (*usually after* **sī**, **nisi**, **nē** *or* **num**)

quisnam, quaenam, quidnam, *interrog. pron.*, who *or* what in the world

quispiam, quaepiam, quidpiam (quodpiam), *indef. pron.*, anyone, any; someone, something

quisquam, quicquam, *indef. pron.*, anyone, anything, any; **neque quisquam**, not a single one

quisque, quidque, *indef. pron.*, each one, each thing, each, every

quisquis, quicquid, *rel. pron.*, whoever, whatever

quīvīs, quaevīs, quidvīs, *indef. pron.*, any

quō, *adv.*, where, wherefore, to which; **quō usque**, how long; **quō modō**, how

quō, *conj.*, in order that, that; **quō minus (quōminus)**, that not

quoad, *conj.*, as long as

quōcumque, *adv.*, wherever

quod, *conj.*, because, that, since; **quod sī**, but if

quōmodō, *adv.*, how

quōmodōnam, *adv.*, how then

quondam, *adv.*, once (upon a time)

quoniam, *conj.*, since, because

quoque, *adv.*, also, even, too (*follows the word it emphasizes*)

quot, *indeclinable adj.*, how many; as (many as), as

quotannīs, *adv.*, every year

quotiēns, *adv.*, as often as; how often

quotiēnscumque, *adv.*, as often as

R

radiō, 1, shine, gleam

radius, **–dī**, *m.*, rod; ray, beam; spoke

rādīx, **–dīcis**, *f.*, root, radish

raeda, **–ae**, *f.*, carriage, bus

rāmulus, **–ī**, *m.*, branch

rāmus, **–ī**, *m.*, branch

rana, **–ae**, *f.*, frog

rapiditās, **–tātis**, *f.*, swiftness

rapidus, **–a**, **–um**, fierce, swift

rapīna, **–ae**, *f.*, plunder, robbery

rapiō, **–ere**, **rapuī**, **raptus**, seize, carry off, hurry along

raptor, **–ōris**, *m.*, thief

rārō, *adv.*, rarely

rārus, **–a**, **–um**, rare

ratiō, **–ōnis**, *f.*, reckoning, account, plan, manner, reason, consideration, method, theory, system, judgment, means, nature

ratis, **–is**, *f.*, raft

rebelliō, **–ōnis**, *f.*, rebellion

Rebilus, **–ī**, *m.*, Rebilus

recēdō, **–ere**, **recessī**, **recessūrus**, withdraw, go back

recēns, *gen.* **recentis**, new, recent, fresh

recēnseō, **–ēre**, **recēnsuī**, **recēnsus**, count again, review

receptāculum, **–ī**, *n.*, receptacle, shelter

receptus, **–ūs**, *m.*, retreat, place of refuge

recidō, **–ere**, **recīdī**, **recāsūrus**, fall

recingō, **–ere**, **recīnxī**, **recīnctus**, loosen

recipiō, **–ere**, **recēpī**, **receptus**, take (back), receive, recover; **mē recipiō**, withdraw, recover, retire, retreat

recitātiō, **–ōnis**, *f.*, reading, recitation

recitātor, **–ōris**, *m.*, reader, reciter

recitō, 1, recite, read aloud

reclīnō, 1, bend back; *pass.*, lean

reclūdō, **–ere**, **reclūsī**, **reclūsus**, disclose, reveal; shut off *or* up

recognōscō, **–ere**, **recognōvī**, **recognitus**, recognize; review

recolō, **–ere**, **recoluī**, **recultus**, renew

reconciliātiō, **–ōnis**, *f.*, reconciliation

reconciliō, 1, reconcile

recondō, **–ere**, **recondidī**, **reconditus**, hide; close

recordātiō, **–ōnis**, *f.*, recollection

recordor, 1, call to mind

recreō, 1, recreate, restore; *w.* **mē**, recover

rēctē, *adv.*, rightly, correctly

rēctus, **–a**, **–um**, right; **rēctā**, *adv.*, straight; *see* **regō**

recumbō, **–ere**, **recubuī**, **—**, lie down; fall

recuperō, 1, get back, recover

recursō, 1, run back and forth

recūsātiō, **–ōnis**, *f.*, declining

recūsō, 1, refuse, reluctant to do

reddō, **–ere**, **reddidī**, **redditus**, give (back), render, return, restore, make, deliver; reflect; vomit

redeō, **–īre**, **rediī**, **reditūrus**, go back, return

redigō, **–ere**, **redēgī**, **redāctus**, bring (back), drive back, reduce

redimō, **–ere**, **redēmī**, **redēmptus**, buy back, ransom

redintegrō, 1, renew

reditus, **–ūs**, *m.*, return, revenue

redolēns, *gen.*, **–entis**, fragrant

redormiō, **–īre**, **redormīvī**, **redormītus**, sleep again

redūcō, **–ere**, **redūxī**, **reductus**, lead back, bring back, restore

redundō, 1, overflow, rodound

referō, **referre**, **rettulī**, **relātus**, bring *or* carry (back), lay *or* bring before, report, reply, reproduce; **pedem referō**, withdraw; **grātiam referō**, show gratitude

reficiō, **–ere**, **refēcī**, **refectus**, repair, renew, refresh, restore, recruit, reinforce

refugiō, **–ere**, **refūgī**, **refugitūrus**, flee back, flee for safety, escape

regerō, **–ere**, **regessī**, **regestus**, throw back

rēgia, –ae, *f.,* palace

rēgīna, –ae, *f.,* queen

regiō, –ōnis, *f.,* district, region

rēgius, –a, –um, royal

rēgnō, 1, reign, rule

rēgnum, –ī, *n.,* royal power, kingdom, rule

regō, –ere, rēxī, rēctus, guide, rule, direct, control; **rēctus,** straight

regredior, –ī, regressus, return

Rēgulus, –ī, *m.,* Regulus

reiciō, –ere, reiēcī, reiectus, throw, drive back, reject; vomit

relābor, relābī, relāpsus, slip back

relanguēscō, –ere, –languī, —, become weak, sink down

relaxō, 1, relax

relevō, 1, lighten, relieve, rest

religiō, –ōnis, *f.,* religion, superstition, scrupulousness, sacredness

religiōsē, *adv.,* religiously

religiōsus, –a, –um, sacred

relinquō, –ere, relīquī, relictus, leave (behind), abandon; leave unmentioned

reliquiae, –ārum, *f. pl.,* remains, relics

reliquus, –a, –um, remaining, rest (of), left, future; *w.* **tempus,** the future; **reliquum est,** it remains

remaneō, –ēre, remānsī, remānsūrus, remain (behind)

remedium, –dī, *n.,* remedy

rēmigō, –āre, —, —, row

remigrō, 1, go back

remissiō, –ōnis, *f.,* forgiveness, relaxation, recreation

remissus, –a, –um, gentle, mild

remittō, –ere, remīsī, remissus, send *or* throw back, remit, relax; drop

remoror, 1, hold back, delay

removeō, –ēre, remōvī, remōtus, move back, remove; **remōtus, –a, –um,** remote

rēmus, –ī, *m.,* oar

Rēmus, –ī, *m.,* a Rē´man

renīdeō, –ere, —, —, shine; smile

renovō, 1, renew

renūntiō, 1, report, declare elected

reparō, 1, restore

repellō, –ere, reppulī, repulsus, drive back, repulse

repente, *adv.,* suddenly

repentīnus, –a, –um, sudden

reperiō, –īre, repperī, repertus, find, discover

repetō, –ere, –īvī, –ītus, seek back, seek again, demand; repeat

repleō, –ēre, replēvī, replētus, fill again

repōnō, –ere, reposuī, repositus, place

reportō, 1, carry *or* bring back

reposcō, –ere, repoposcī, —, demand in return

repraesentō, 1, show, represent

reprehendō, –ere, reprehendī, reprehēnsus, (hold back), censure, criticize

reprimō, –ere, repressī, repressus, stop, press back, check, thwart

rēptō, –āre, —, —, creep, crawl

repudiō, 1, divorce, reject, scorn

repugnō, 1, oppose, fight against, resist

reputō, 1, compute, ponder

requiēs, –ētis, *f.,* rest

requiēscō, –ere, –ēvī, –ētus, rest, repose

requīrō, –ere, requīsīvī, requīsītus, hunt up, search for, inquire; demand; miss

rēs, reī, *f.,* thing, fact, matter, affair, object, circumstance; **novae rēs, novārum rerum,** *f. pl.,* revolution; **rēs frūmentāria, reī frūmentāriae,** *f.,* grain supply, supplies; **rēs mīlitāris,** military affairs, art of war, warfare; **rēs pūblica,** republic, state, public interest, public affairs, government, state; **rēs gestae,** deeds

rescindō, –ere, rescidī, rescissus, cut down

rescrībō, –ere, rescrīpsī, rescrīptus, write back

resecō, –āre, resecuī, resectus, cut off

reservō, 1, reserve

resideō, –ēre, resēdī, —, remain, be left, sit down

resistō, –ere, restitī, —, stand against; resist, stop

resolūtiō, –ōnis, *f.,* relaxing, looseness; solution

resolvō, –ere, resolvī, resolūtus, loosen, solve

respiciō, –ere, respexī, respectus, look back (at), look at, consider

resplendeō, –ēre, —, —, shine brightly, gleam

respondeō, –ēre, respondī, respōnsus, reply, answer

respōnsum, –ī, *n.,* answer, reply

respuō, –ere, respui, —, reject

restinguō, –ere, restīnxī, restīnctus, extinguish

restituō, –ere, restituī, restitūtus, restore

restō, –āre, restitī, —, remain, withstand, be left

restringō, –ere, restrīnxī, restrictus, bind back, restrict

resupīnus, –a, –um, on one's back

resūmō, –ere, resūmpsī, resūmptus, take up again, resume

resurgō = surgō

retardō, 1, check, hinder

reticeō, –ēre, reticuī, —, be *or* keep silent

retineō, –ēre, retinuī, retentus, hold back, restrain, keep, hold to

retorqueō, –ēre, retorsī, retortus, turn back

retrahō, –ere, retrāxī, retrāctus, drag back

retrō, *adv.,* back, backward

retrūdō, –ere, —, retrūsus, thrust back

retundō, –ere, rettudī, retūsus, beat back

rettulī, *see* **referō**

reus, –ī, *m.,* defendant

revellō, –ere, revellī, revulsus, tear away

revereor, reverērī, reveritus, respect

revertō, –ere, revertī, reversus, (*sometimes deponent*), turn back, return

revīsō, –ere, —, —, revisit

revocābilis, –e, revocable

revocō, 1, recall, call back

revolō, 1, fly back

rēx, rēgis, *m.,* king

Rhēnus, –ī, *m.,* Rhine river

rhētor, –ōris, *m.,* rhetorician, orator

rhētorica, –ae, *f.,* rhetoric

rhētoricus, –a, –um, rhetorical

Rhodanus, –ī, *m.,* Rhone river

rictus, –ūs, *m.,* jaws

rīdeō, –ēre, rīsī, rīsus, laugh (at)

rīdiculus, –a, –um, absurd

rigeō, –ēre, —, —, be stiff

rigidus, a, um, stiff (with cold)

rigor, –ōris, *m.,* stiffness

riguus, –a, –um, well-watered

rīma, –ae, *f.,* crack

rīmor, 1, tear up; examine

rīpa, –ae, *f.,* bank (*of a river*)

rīte, *adv.,* duly, rightly

rōborō, 1, strengthen

rōbur, rōboris, *n.,* oak; strength

rōbustus, –a, –um, (of oak), hardy, robust

rogātus, –ūs, *m.,* request

rogitō, 1, keep on asking

rogō, 1, ask, beg; propose, pass

rogus, –ī, *m.,* funeral pile, grave

Rōma, –ae, *f.,* Rome

Rōmānus, –a, –um, Roman; *as noun,* a Roman, *m. pl.,* the Romans

rosa, –ae, *f.,* rose

rostrum, –ī, *n.,* prow (of a ship); beak, mouth, bill

rota, –ae, *f.,* wheel; *pl.,* chariot

rotundus, –a, –um, round

rubēns, *gen.* **–entis,** red

ruber, rubra, rubrum, red

rubor, –ōris, *m.,* redness, blush; modesty

rudis, –e, untrained, ignorant, rough

Rūfus, –ī, *m.,* Rufus

rūgōsus, –a, –um, wrinkled

ruīna, –ae, *f.,* ruin, destruction

rūmor, –ōris, *m.,* rumor

rumpō, –ere, rūpī, ruptus, break, pierce

rūpēs, –is, *f.,* cliff, rock

rūrsus, *adv.,* again

rūs, rūris, *n.,* country; farm; pl., fields

rūsticānus, –a, –um, rural

rūsticatiō, –ōnis, *f.,* living in the country

rūsticor, 1, go into the country

rūsticus, –a, –um, rustic

S

Sabella, –ae, *f.,* Sabella

Sabellus, –a, –um, Sabellian, Sabine

Sabidus, –ī, *m.,* Sabidus

Sabīna, –ae, *f.,* Sabine woman

Sabīnus, –a, –um, Sabine: *as noun, pl.,* the Sabines, *a people of Italy*

sacculus, –ī, *m.,* little sack

saccus, –ī, *m.,* sack, bag

sacer, sacra, sacrum, sacred; *n. pl.,* sacred rites, ceremonies

sacerdōs, –dōtis, *m. and f.,* priest, priestess

sacerdōtium, –tī, *n.,* priesthood

sacramentum, –ī, *n.,* oath

sacrārium, –rī, *n.,* shrine

sacrificium, –cī, *n.,* sacrifice

sacrificō, 1, sacrifice

sacrōsānctus, –a, –um, sacred, inviolable

saeculāris, –e, secular

saeculum (saeclum), –ī, *n.,* age, generation

saepe, *adv.,* often

saepēs, –is, *f.,* hedge, fence; enclosure

saeviō, –īre, saevīvī, saevītus, rage, rant

saevitia, –ae, *f.,* fierceness

saevus, –a, –um, cruel, fierce

sagāx, *gen.* **–ācis,** keen

sagitta, –ae, *f.,* arrow

sagittārius, –rī, *m.,* bowman

sagittifer, –fera, –ferum, arrow-bearing

sagulum, –ī, *n.,* small military cloak

sāl, salis, *m.,* salt

salārium, –rī, *n.,* pension, stipend

salignus, –a, –um, of willow

Saliī, –ōrum, *m. pl.,* the Salii *or* "Jumpers" (*priests of Mars*)

saliō, –īre, saluī, saltūrus, jump, beat

saltātor, –ōris, *m.,* dancer

saltō, 1, dance

salūbris, –e, wholesome, healthy, healthful

salūbritās, –tātis, *f.,* health

salūs, –ūtis, *f.,* health, safety, greeting

salūtātor, –ōris, *m.,* greeter, visitor

salūtō, 1, greet, pay one's respects

salvē, salvēte, be well, greetings, hail

salvus, –a, –um, safe, well, solvent

Samos, –ī, *f.,* Samos, *an island in the Aegean Sea*

sānābilis, –e, curable

sānciō, –īre, sānxī, sānctus, decree

sānctē, *adv.,* religiously, scrupulously

sānctus, –a, –um, sacred, holy, venerable, upright

sānē, *adv.,* indeed, truly, of course

Sanga, –ae, *m.,* Sanga

sanguis, sanguinis, *m.,* blood

sānitās, –tātis, *f.,* sanity, soundness of mind

sānō, 1, make sound, cure

sānus, –a, –um, sound, in one's right mind, sane

sapiēns, *gen.* **sapientis,** wise; *as noun, m.,* philosopher

sapienter, *adv.,* wisely

sapientia, –ae, *f.,* wisdom

sapiō, –ere, sapīvī, —, taste, savor

sarcina, –ae, *f.,* burden, load

Sardēs, –ium, *f. pl.,* Sardis, *capital of Lydia, in Asia Minor*

Sardinia, –ae, *f.,* Sardinia

satelles, –litis, *m. and f.,* attendant; accomplice

satietās, –tātis, *f.,* abundance, satiety

satiō, 1, satisfy, sate

satira, –ae, *f.,* miscellany, satire

satis, *adv. and indeclinable adj.,* enough, rather; quite, sufficiently; *comp.,* **satius,** better

satisfaciō, –ere, –fēcī, –factus, satisfy

Sāturnālia, –ium, *n. pl.,* the Saturnalia, *a festival in honor of Saturn*

Sāturnius, –a, –um, of Saturn, Saturnian

Sāturnus, –ī, *m.,* Saturn

saturō, 1, fill, saturate

Satyrus, –ī, *m.,* Satyr, wood-deity

sauciō, 1, wound

saxum, –ī, *n.,* rock, stone

scaena, –ae, *f.,* stage, theater

scaenicus, –a, –um, of the theater, of the stage; *w.* **lūdī,** stage plays

scandō, –ere, —, —, rise, climb

scelerātē, *adv.,* wickedly, impiously

scelerātus, –a, –um, wicked, accursed, criminal

scelus, sceleris, *n.,* crime, wickedness

scēptrum, –ī, *n.,* scepter

schola, –ae, *f.,* school

scholāris, –e, of *or* belonging to a school

scholasticus, –a, –um, scholastic; *as noun, m.,* student

scientia, –ae, *f.,* knowledge

scīlicet, *adv.,* of course, doubtless

scindō, –ere, scidī, scissus, cut, split

sciō, scīre, scīvī, scītus, know, know how

Scīpiō, –ōnis, *m.,* Scipio

scītē, *adv.,* skillfully, well

scitor, 1, inquire

scrība, –ae, *m.,* secretary

scrībō, –ere, scrīpsī, scrīptus, write

scrīptor, –ōris, *m.,* writer

scrīptum, –ī, *n.,* writing

scrīptūra, –ae, *f.,* writing, Scripture

scrūtor, 1, examine thoroughly

sculpō, –ere, sculpsī, sculptus, carve

scūtum, –ī, *n.,* shield

Scythae, –ārum, *m. pl.,* the Scythians, *people beyond the Black Sea*

sē, *acc. and abl. of* **suī**

sēcēdō, –ere, sēcessī, sēcessūrus, secede, withdraw, go away, retire

sēcernō, –ere, sēcrēvī, sēcrētus, separate

sēcessus, –ūs, *m.,* departure, retirement

secō, secāre, secuī, sectus, cut

sēcrētō, *adv.,* in private, secretly

sectus, –a, –um, cut off

sēcum = cum sē

secundum, *prep. w. acc.,* following, according to, behind, next to

secundus, –a, –um, second, favorable; successful; *w.* **rēs,** prosperity

Secundus, –ī, *m.,* Secundus

secūris, –is, *f.,* ax

sed, *conj.,* but

sedeō, –ēre, sēdī, sessūrus, sit, sit down, lie idle

sēdēs, –is, *f.,* abode, place; seat

sedīle, –is, *n.,* seat

sēditiō, –ōnis, *f.,* rebellion, sedition

sēdō, 1, quiet, bring to an end, stop

sēdūcō, –ere, sēdūxī, sēductus, set aside

sēductor, –ōris, *m.,* misleader, seducer

sēductus, –a, –um, separated

sēdulitās, –tātis, *f.,* diligence

sēdulō, *adv.,* busily, carefully, eagerly

sēdulus, –a, –um, diligent

segnitiēs, –eī, *f.,* slowness, inactivity

sēgregō, 1, exclude

sēiungō, –ere, sēiūnxī, sēiūnctus, disjoint, separate, sever

Seleucus, –ī, *m.,* Seleucus, *king of Syria*

sella, –ae, *f.,* chair, seat, stool

semel, *adv.,* once

sēmen, –minis, *n.,* seed

sēmēsus, –a, –um, half-eaten

sēmibarbarus, –a, –um, half-barbarian

sēminārium, –rī, *n.,* nursery

semita, –ae, *f.,* path, footpath

semper, *adv.,* always

sempiternus, –a, –um, everlasting, perpetual

Semprōnius, –a, –um, Sempronian

senātor, –ōris, *m.,* senator

senātōrius, –a, –um, senatorial

senātus, –ūs, *m.,* senate

Seneca, –ae, *m.,* Seneca

senecta, –ae, *f.,* old age

senectūs, –tūtis, *f.,* old age

senēscō, –ere, senuī, —, grow old

senex, senis, *m.,* old man; *adj.,* old; *comp.* **senior**

senīlis, –e, of an old man

senior, –ius, older; aged

sēnsus, –ūs, *m.,* feeling; consciousness

sententia, –ae, *f.,* feeling, opinion; proposal; meaning, sentiment

sentīna, –ae, *f.,* sewage, sewer

sentiō, –īre, sēnsī, sēnsus, feel, think, realize, vote, perceive, know

sentis, –is, *m.,* thorn, briar

sepeliō, –īre, –īvī, sepultus, bury

sēpōnō, –ere, sēposuī, sēpositus, separate, assign

septem, seven

September, –bris, –bre, (of) September

septentriōnēs, –um, *m. pl.,* seven plow-oxen (*the seven stars of the constellation Great Bear or Big Dipper*), north

septimus, –a, –um, seventh

septingentī, –ae, –a, seven hundred

sepulchrum, –ī, *n.,* tomb

sepultūra, –ae, *f.,* burial

Sēquana, –ae, *m.,* the Seine river

Sēquanus, –a, –um, Sequanian; *as noun, m. pl.,* the Sequanians

sequor, sequī, secūtus, follow, pursue, seek

serēnō, 1, clear up

serēnus, –a, –um, quiet, clear, serene

Serēnus, –ī, *m.,* Serenus

Sergius, –gī, *m.,* Sergius

sērius, –a, –um, grave, serious; *comp. adv.,* later

sermō, –ōnis, *m.,* conversation, talk, speech, report

serō, –ere, sēvī, satus, plant, sow, produce; **satus, –a, –um,** sprung from

sērō, *adv.,* late

serpēns, *gen.* **–entis,** *m. and f.,* snake

serpō, –ere, serpsī, serptus, crawl

sertum, –ī, *n.,* wreath of flowers, garland

sērus, –a, –um, late

serva, –ae, *f.,* slave

servīlis, –e, of a slave

serviō, –īre, servīvī, servītus, be a slave (to), serve, have regard for, court

servitium, –tī, *n.,* slavery

servitūs, –tūtis, *f.,* slavery

Servius Tullius, *m.,* Servius Tullius, *a Roman king*

servō, 1, save, preserve, guard, keep

servus, –ī, *m.,* slave

sescentī, –ae, –a, six hundred

sēsē, *acc. and abl. of* **suī**

seu, *see* **sīve**

sevērē, *adv.,* severely

sevēritās, –tātis, *f.,* severity

sevērus, –a, –um, stern, severe

sex, six

sexāgintā, sixty

Sextīlis, –e, August

sextus, –a, –um, sixth

sexus, –ūs, *m.,* sex

sī, *conj.,* if

Sibylla, –ae, *f.,* the Sibyl, *a prophetess*

Sibyllīnus, –a, –um, Sibylline

sīc, *adv.,* so, thus, in this way

sīca, –ae, *f.,* dagger

sīcārius, –rī, *m.,* assassin

siccō, 1, dry up

siccus, –a, –um, dry

Sicilia, –ae, *f.,* Sicily

Siculī, –ōrum, *m.,* Sicilians

sīcutī (sīcut), *adv.,* just as, as if

sīdus, sīderis, *n.,* star, constellation

sigilla, –ōrum, *n. pl.,* small statues

signifer, –ferī, *m.,* standard bearer

significātiō, –ōnis, *f.,* signal, meaning

significō, 1, indicate, mean, show

signō, 1, seal, mark

signum, –ī, *n.,* sign, token, signal; standard; seal, mark

Silānus, –ī, *m.,* Silanus

silentium, –tī, *n.,* silence

silva, –ae, *f.,* forest, woods

Sīlēnus, –ī, *m.,* Silenus

sileō, –ēre, siluī, —, be silent, leave unmentioned

silva, –ae, *f.,* forest, woods

Silvānus, –ī, *m.,* Silvanus

silvestris, –e, wild

Simeōn, –ōnis, *m.,* Simeon

similis, –e, like, similar

similitūdō, –dinis, *f.,* likeness, resemblance

simplex, –plicis, simple, single

simplicitās, –tātis, *f.,* simplicity, frankness, naturalness

simpliciter, *adv.,* plainly, openly

simul, *adv.,* at the same time, at once, together; **simul atque (ac),** as soon as

simulācrum, –ī, *n.,* figure, image, likeness

simulātor, –ōris, *m.,* pretender

simulō, 1, pretend

simultās, –tatis, *f.,* rivalry, enmity

sīn, *conj.,* but if

sincērus, –a, –um, pure, chaste

sine, *prep. w. abl.,* without

singillātim, *adv.,* one by one, individually, singly

singulāris, –e, one by one, remarkable, unique, separate

singulārius, –a, –um, single, separate; singular

singulī, –ae, –a, *pl.* only, separate, each, one after another, one at a time; one each, single

sinister, –tra, –trum, left; *comp.,* **sinisterior,** the left

sinō, –ere, sīvī, situs, allow

Sinōpēnsis, –e, of Sinope, *a Greek colony; as noun, m. pl.,* the people of Sinope

sinus, –ūs, *m.,* fold; bosom; bay

Sipylus, –ī, *m.,* Sipylus, *a son of Niobe*

sistō, –ere, stitī, status, place; stop, check

sitiō, –īre, sitīvī, —, be thirsty

sitis, –is, *f.,* thirst

situs, –a, –um, placed; **situm est,** it lies

situs, –ūs, *m.,* position

sīve (seu), *conj.,* or if, or; **sīve (seu)... sīve (seu),** whether . . . or, either . . . or

sōbrius, –a, –um, sober

socer, –erī, *m.,* father-in-law

societās, –tātis, *f.,* fellowship, alliance

socius, –cī, *m.,* comrade, companion, associate, ally, accomplice; *pl.,* allies, provincials

Sōcratēs, –is, *m.,* Socrates

sodālis, –is, *m.,* companion

sōl, sōlis, *m.,* sun

sōlācium, –cī, *n.,* comfort

solea, –ae, *f.,* sandal, shoe

soleō, –ēre, solitus, *semideponent,* be used to, be accustomed

solidus, –a, –um, solid

sōlitūdō, –dinis, *f.,* wilderness, solitude

solitus, –a, –um, customary

sollemnis, –e, (annual), customary, appointed, solemn

sollertia, –ae, *f.,* skill, ingenuity, adroitness

sollicitātiō, –ōnis, *f.,* inciting

sollicitō, 1, stir up, disturb, incite to revolt, tamper with

sollicitūdō, –dinis, *f.,* uneasiness, anxiety

sollicitus, –a, –um, anxious, worried

Solōn, –ōnis, *m.,* Solon

sōlor, 1, comfort

solum, –ī, *n.,* soil

sōlum, *adv.,* only, alone; **nōn sōlum... sed (vērum) etiam,** not only . . . but also

sōlus, –a, –um, alone, only, lonely

solūtiō, –ōnis, *f.,* payment

solvō, –ere, solvī, solūtus, loose, break, free, release, solve; set sail; *w.* **poenam,** pay

somnium, –nī, *n.,* dream

somnus, –ī, *m.,* sleep

sonitus, –ūs, *m.,* sound

sonō, –āre, sonuī, sonitus, resound; **sonāns,** *gen.* **–antis,** clanking

sonōrus, –a, –um, sonorous

sonus, –ī, *m.,* sound, noise

Sophia, –ae, *f.,* Wisdom

sophisma, –atis, *n.,* false conclusion, sophism

sōpiō, –īre, sōpīvī, sōpītus, lull to sleep, stun

sopor, –ōris, *m.,* deep sleep, stupor; laziness

sordidus, –a, –um, dirty, stained, mean

soror, –ōris, *f.,* sister

sors, sortis, *f.,* lot, prophecy

sortior, –īrī, sortītus, cast lots, ballot

sortītō, *adv.,* by lot

Spanius, –ī, *m.,* Spanius

spargō, –ere, sparsī, sparsus, scatter, sprinkle, spread

Sparta, –ae, *f.,* Sparta, *a Greek city*

Spartacus, –ī, *m.,* Spartacus, *leader in a revolt of gladiators*

Spartānus, –ī, *m.,* a Spartan

spatior, 1, take a walk, walk

spatiōsus, –a, –um, roomy, large

spatium, –tī, *n.,* space, distance; time, period

speciēs, speciēī, *f.,* appearance, sight

speciōsus, –a, –um, showy, glittering

spectābilis, –e, conspicuous, beautiful

spectāculum, –ī, *n.,* spectacle, show

spectātiō, –ōnis, *f.,* viewing

spectātor, –ōris, *m.,* spectator

spectō, 1, look at *or* on, face, see

speculāria, –ōrum, *n. pl.,* windows

speculātor, –ōris, *m.,* spy

speculor, 1, watch

speculum, –ī, *n.,* mirror; copy

spēlunca, –ae, *f.,* cave, cavern, den

spērō, 1, hope (for)

spēs, speī, *f.,* hope

spīna, –ae, *f.,* thorn

spīritus, –ūs, *m.,* breath, spirit, air; pride

spīrō, 1, breathe

splendidus, –a, –um, shining, brilliant, distinguished

spolia, –ōrum, *n., pl.,* spoils, booty

spoliō, 1, rob, deprive

spondeo, –ēre, spopondi, sponsus, promise, engage

sponsa, –ae, *f.,* a betrothed woman

sponsus, –ī, *m.,* a betrothed man

sponte, *w.* **suā,** of his/her/their own accord, by his/her/their own influence, voluntarily

spūmāns, *gen.* **–antis,** foaming

spūmiger, –gera, –gerum, foaming

squālēns, *gen.* **squālentis,** foul

squāleō, –ēre, squāluī, —, be stiff, be filthy

st! *interj.,* hush!

stabilitās, –tātis, *f.,* steadfastness, firmness

stabulum, –ī, *n.,* stable

Statilius, –lī, *m.,* Statilius

statim, *adv.,* at once, immediately

statiō, –ōnis, *f.,* outpost, guard, picket, station

statua, –ae, *f.,* statue

statunculum, –ī, *n.,* a little statue

statuō, –ere, statuī, statūtus, decide, determine, set up, place

statūra, –ae, *f.,* stature

status, –a, –um, fixed, appointed

status, –ūs, *m.,* state, position, condition, status

stēlla, –ae, *f.,* star

sterilis, –e, barren, unproductive, unfruitful

sternō, –ere, strāvī, strātus, strew, scatter; level, cover; overthrow, raze

stetī, *see* **stō**

stilus, –ī, *m.,* stylus (*instrument used in writing on wax tablets*)

stimulō, 1, urge on; disturb

stimulus, –ī, *m.,* incentive

stīpendiārius, –a, –um, tributary

stīpendium, –dī, *n.,* pay, tribute; campaign

stīpes, –itis, *m.,* log, post, trunk, stake

stipula, –ae, *f.,* stem, straw

stō, stāre, stetī, statūrus, stand, stop

stolidus, –a, –um, dull, stupid

stomachus, –ī, *m.,* stomach

Strabō, –ōnis, *m.,* Strabo

stragēs, –is, *f.,* overthrowing, confusion; destruction

strāmen, –minis, *n.,* straw; *pl.,* thatch

strātum, –ī, *n.,* cover, horse blanket

strēnuē, *adv.,* briskly, actively

strēnuus, –a, –um, energetic

strepitus, –ūs, *m.,* noise

stringō, –ere, strīnxī, strictus, draw (tight); ruffle

studeō, –ēre, studuī, —, be eager (for), study, desire

studiōsē, *adv.,* eagerly

studiōsus, –a, –um, fond of

studium, –dī, *n.,* eagerness, desire, interest, zeal, enthusiasm; study, pursuit

stultitia, –ae, *f.,* stupidity, folly, foolishness, silliness

stultus, –a, –um, foolish, stupid

stupendus, –a, –um, stupendous

stupeō, –ēre, –uī, —, be amazed, stand aghast

suādeō, –ēre, suāsī, suāsūrus, urge, advise, persuade

suāvis, –e, sweet, pleasant, agreeable

suāvitās, –tātis, *f.,* sweetness, pleasantness, agreeableness

sub, *prep.,* under, close to, at the foot of, just before (*w. acc. after verbs of motion; w. abl. after verbs of rest or position*)

subdō, –ere, subdidī, subditus, put *or* plunge under

subdūcō, –ere, –dūxī, –ductus, lead up; draw up

subeō, –īre, –iī, –itūrus, go under, enter, come up, undergo

subiciō, –ere, –iēcī, –iectus, throw under, spread beneath, throw from below, subject, conquer; **subiectus,** lying beneath

subigō, –ere, –ēgī, –āctus, force, subdue

subinde, *adv.,* suddenly

subinvideō, –ēre, —, —, be envious of

subitō, *adv.,* suddenly

subitus, –a, –um, sudden

sublātus, *part. of* **tollō**

sublevō, 1, lighten, help, raise; *w. reflex.,* rise

sublīmē, *adv.,* aloft, on high

submergō, –ere, –mersī, –mersus, plunge

subministrō, 1, furnish

submittō, –ere, –mīsī, –missus, send, *see* **summittō**

submoveō, –ēre, –mōvī, –mōtus, drive back, send away, remove

subrēpō, –ere, –rēpsī, —, creep *or* steal along

subruō, –ere, –ruī, –rutus, undermine

subsellium, –lī, *n.,* bench, seat

subsequor, –sequī, –secūtus, follow (closely)

subsidium, –dī, *n.,* aid, reserve

substō, –āre, —, —, stand firm

subterrāneus, –a, –um, subterranean

subtilis, –e, fine, slender

subveniō, –īre, –vēnī, –ventūrus, come to help

succēdō, –ere, –cessī, –cessūrus, come up, enter, follow, succeed (*w. dat.*)

successor, –ōris, *m,* follower, successor

successus, –ūs, *m.,* success

succrēscō, –ere, –crēvī, –crētus, grow

succurrō, –ere, –currī, –cursūrus, run to help, run to one's aid

Suēbī, –ōrum, *m. pl.,* the Suebans *or* Suebi

sufferō, –ere, sustulī, sublātus, hold up, sustain; undergo

sufficiō, –ere, –fēcī, –fectus, suffice

suffrāgium, –gī, *n.,* vote, ballot

suffundō, –ere, suffūdī, suffūsus, pour into, overspread, infuse

suī, *reflexive pron.,* of himself, herself, itself, themselves

Sulla, –ae, *m.,* Sulla

sum, esse, fuī, futūrus, be, exist

summa, –ae, *f.,* sum, total, chief part, substance; leadership; **summa rērum,** general interest; **summa imperī,** supreme command; **ad summam,** in short

summittō, –ere, –mīsī, –missus, lower

summus, –a, –um, highest, most important, greatest; top of, surface of

summum, –ī, *n.,* top, greatest

sūmō, –ere, sūmpsī, sūmptus, take, assume

sūmptuōsē, *adv.,* extravagantly

sūmptuōsus, –a, –um, extravagant; very expensive; lavish

sūmptus, –ūs, *m.,* expense, extravagance

super, *prep. w. acc.,* over, upon, above

superbē, *adv.,* arrogantly

superbia, –ae, *f.,* pride, arrogance

superbus, –a, –um, haughty, proud

superficiārius, –a, –um, situated on another man's land

superiniciō, –ere, –iniēcī, –iniectus, cast over, scatter upon

superior, –ius, higher, elder, upper, superior; previous, former

superō, 1, overcome, conquer; surpass; beat; defeat; pass over

superstitiō, –ōnis, *f.,* superstition

supersum, –esse, –fuī, –futūrus, be left (over), remain, survive

superus, –a, –um, upper; *as noun, m. pl.,* gods (above)

supīnus, –a, –um, thrown backwards, on the back, supine; sloping

suppeditō, 1, supply

suppetō, –ere, suppetīvī, suppetītus, be at hand, be present; be sufficient for

suppīlō, 1, pilfer, rob

suppleō, –ere, supplēvī, supplētus, fill

supplex, *gen.* **supplicis,** begging, suppliant

supplicātiō, –ōnis, *f.,* thanksgiving, public prayer

supplicium, –cī, *n.,* punishment, torture

supplicō, 1, kneel down (to), pray, worship

suprā, *adv. and prep. w. acc.,* above, beyond, before, previously

suprēmus, –a, –um, highest, last, dying

surgō, –ere, surrēxī, surrēctūrus, rise, arise

surripiō, –ere, –ripuī, –reptus, seize (secretly), steal

suscēnseō, –ēre, –cēnsuī, —, be angry with

suscipiō, –ere, –cēpī, –ceptus, undertake, incur, suffer

suscitō, 1, rekindle

suspendō, –ere, –pendī, hang, suspend; **suspēnsus, –a, –um,** in suspense

suspīciō, –ōnis, *f.,* suspicion

suspiciō, –ere, suspexī, suspectus, esteem, admire; suspect

suspicor, 1, suspect

suspīro, 1, sigh

suspīrium, –rī, *n.,* sigh

sustentō, 1, maintain

sustineō, –ēre, –tinuī, –tentus, hold up, keep up *or* back; bear, endure, withstand, hold out, check

sustulī, *see* **tollō**

suus, –a, –um, *reflexive adj.,* his, her, its, their; his own, her own, etc.; *as noun,* **suī,** his (her, their) men, friends; **sua,** *n.,* his (her, their) possessions

syllaba, –ae, *f.,* syllable

Syrācūsae, –ārum, *f. pl.,* Syracuse, *a city in Sicily*

Syrtis, –is, *f.,* Syrtis

T

T., *abbreviation for* **Titus**

tabella, –ae, *f.,* tablet; *pl.,* letter, ballot, record

tabellārius, –rī, *m.,* letter carrier

taberna, –ae, *f.,* shop, tavern

tābēscō, –ere, tābuī, —, melt

tabula, –ae, *f.,* board, painting; table, tablet (of the law); writing tablet; *pl.,* records, accounts

taceō, –ēre, tacuī, be silent, leave unmentioned

taciturnitās, –tātis, *f.,* silence

tacitus, –a, –um, silent, secret

taeda, –ae, *f.,* torch; wedding

taeter, –tra, –trum, foul, revolting

tālāris, –e, reaching the ankles

tālis, –e, such

tam, *adv.,* so, so much (*w. adj. and adv.*)

tamen, *adv.,* yet, still, nevertheless; however

tametsī, *conj.,* although

tamquam, *adv.,* as if, as, as it were

Tanais, –is, *m.,* Tanais, *a river*

tandem, *adv.,* at last, finally; *in questions,* I ask

tangō, –ere, tetigī, tāctus, touch, move, reach; partake of

Tantalus, –ī, *m.,* Tantalus, (1) *Niobe's father,* (2) *son of Niobe*

tantō, *adv.,* so much

tantulus, –a, –um, so small

tantum, *adv.,* so much, so greatly; only, merely; *w.* **modo,** only, merely

tantus, –a, –um, so great, so much, so large, such

tantusdem, tantadem, tantundem, as great *or* large

tardē, *adv.,* slowly, late, tardily

tarditās, –tātis, *f.,* slowness

tardō, 1, slow up, delay, check

tardus, –a, –um, slow, late

Tarentīnī, –ōrum, *m. pl.,* the people of Tarentum

Tarpeius, –a, –um, Tarpeian

Tarquinius, –nī, *m.,* Tarquinius, Tarquin

Tarquinius Superbus, –ī, *m.,* Tarquin the Proud, *king of Rome*

Tartarus, –ī, *m.,* Hades

taurus, –ī, *m.,* bull

tēctum, –ī, *n.,* roof, house, dwelling, home

tegimentum, –ī, *n.,* cover

tegō, –ere, tēxī, tēctus, cover, conceal; protect

tellūs, –ūris, *f.,* earth; land

tēlum, –ī, *n.,* weapon, missile, shaft

temerārius, –a, –um, rash

temere, *adv.,* rashly, without reason

temeritās, –tātis, *f.,* rashness

temperāmentum, –ī, *n.,* right proportion; moderation

temperātē, *adv.,* moderately

temperātus, –a, –um, temperate

tempestās, –tātis, *f.,* weather, storm; season

templum, –ī, *n.,* temple

temptō, 1, test, try, attempt, tempt; attack

tempus, temporis, *n.,* time, period, temple (*of the head*); *w.* **ex,** offhand

tenāx, *gen.* **tenācis,** tenacious

tendō, –ere, tetendī, tentus, stretch, extend, go

tenebrae, –ārum, *f. pl.,* darkness

Tenedos, –ī, *f.,* Tenedos, *an island*

teneō, –ēre, tenuī, tentus, hold, keep, possess; **memoriā teneō,** remember

tener, –era, –erum, tender; young

tenuis, –e, thin, little; humble

tenuitās, –tātis, thinness, slenderness; poverty

tenuō, 1, make thin *or* slender

tenus, *postpositive prep. w. abl.,* up to

tepeō, –ēre, —, —, be warm

tepidus, –a, –um, warm

tepor, –ōris, gentle warmth

ter, *adv.,* three times

terebrō, 1, pierce

Terentius, –tī, *m.,* Terence

tergum, –ī, *n.,* **tergus, –goris,** *n.,* back; side (of pork); **ā tergō,** in the rear

terminō, 1, bound, limit; end, close

terminus, –ī, *m.,* boundary

ternī, –ae, –a, three at a time

terō, –ere, trīvī, trītus, wear away, grind; exhaust

terra, –ae, *f.,* land, earth, ground

terreō, –ēre, terruī, territus, scare, frighten, terrify

terrestris, –e, terrestrial

terribilis, –e, frightful

terror, –ōris, *m.,* terror

tertius, –a, –um, third

testa, –ae, *f.,* brick

testāmentum, –ī, *n.,* will

testimōnium, –nī, *n.,* testimony, proof

testis, –is, *m.,* witness

testor, 1, call to witness

testūdō, –dinis, *f.,* shed, turtle, testudo

Teutonī, –ōrum, *m. pl.,* the Teutons

thalamus, –ī, *m.,* bedchamber; marriage bed, marriage

theātrum, –ī, *n.,* theater

Thēbae, –ārum, *f. pl.,* Thebes, *a Greek city*

thema, –atis, *n.,* theme

Thermus, –ī, *m.,* Thermus

Thessalia, –ae, *f.,* Thessaly, *part of Greece*

Thisbē, –ēs, *f.,* Thisbe

Thrācia, –ae, *f.,* Thrace, *a country north of Greece*

Thrācius, –a, –um, Thracian; of Thrace, *a country north of Greece*

Thrāx, –ācis, *m.,* a Thracian

thronus, –ī *m.,* throne

Thynēius, –a, –um, of Thynaeum

tiāra, –ae, *f.,* turban, tiara

Tiberis, –is, *m.,* Tiber River, the Tiber, *a river in Italy*

Tiberius, –rī, *m.,* Tiberius

tībia, –ae, *f.,* pipe, flute

tignum, –ī, *n.,* beam

Tigurīnus, –ī, *m.,* Tigurinus, *a Helvetian canton; pl.,* the Tigurini

timeō, –ēre, timuī, —, fear, be afraid

timidus, –a, –um, timid, cowardly; **timidē,** *adv.,* timidly

timor, –ōris, *m.,* fear

tingō, –ere, tīnxī, tīnctus, wet; color, stain

tintinnābulum, –ī, *n.,* bell

Tīrō, –ōnis, *m.,* Tiro

Titius, –tī, *m.,* Titius

titulus, –ī, *m.,* title, sign

Tmōlus, –ī, *m.,* Tmolus, *a mountain in Lydia*

toga, –ae, *f.,* toga (*cloak*)

togātus, –a, –um, in civilian garb, toga-clad

tolerābilis, –e, endurable, tolerable

tolerō, 1, bear

tollō, –ere, sustulī, sublātus, raise, take *or* pick up, carry, remove, destroy

tormentum, –ī, *n.,* torture; artillery, hurling machine

torpor, –ōris, *m.,* numbness, sluggishness

torqueō, –ēre, torsī, tortus, twist, whirl, turn; torture

torus, –ī, *m.,* cushion, couch

torreō, –ēre, torruī, tostus, roast, scorch

tot, *indecl. adj.,* so many

totidem, *indecl. adj.,* just as many, the same number

totiēns, *adv.,* so often

tōtus, –a, –um, whole, entire, all

trabs, trabis, *f.,* beam

trāctātus, –ūs, m., handling, treatment

trāctō, 1, handle, treat, conduct; draw into

trāditiō, –ōnis, *f.,* surrender

trādō, –ere, –didī, –ditus, give *or* hand over, transmit, relate, surrender; deliver

trādūcō, –ere, –dūxī, –ductus, lead across, win over

tragicus, –a, –um, of tragedy, tragic

trāgula, –ae, *f.,* javelin

trahō, –ere, trāxī, trāctus, draw, influence, derive, drag; take on; *w.* **ad mē,** claim

trāiciō, –ere, –iēcī, –iectus, strike through, hurl through, pierce

trāmittō, –ere, –mīsī, –missus, transmit, hand over; cross

trānō, 1, swim across

tranquillitās, –tātis, *f.,* calm, tranquility

tranquillus, –a, –um, peaceful, quiet

trāns, *prep. w. acc.,* across

Trānsalpīnus, –a, –um, beyond the Alps, Transalpine

trānscendō, –ere, –cendī, —, board, climb over

trānscurrō, –ere, –currī, –cursūrus, traverse

trānseō, –īre, –iī, –itūrus, cross, pass, go over

trānsferō, –ferre, –tulī, –lātus, carry over, transfer

trānsfīgō, –ere, –fīxī, –fīxus, pierce through

trānsfodiō, –ere, –fōdī, –fossus, pierce through

trānsfuga, –ae, *m.,* deserter

trānsigō, –ere, –ēgī, –āctus, carry out

trānsiliō, –īre, –siluī, —, jump across

trānsitus, –ūs, *m.*, passage

trānsmittō, –ere, –mīsī, –missus, pass on

trānsportō, 1, carry over, transport

trānsverberō, –āre, —, —, strike through, pierce through

trānsversus, –a, –um, cross

trecentī, –ae, –a, three hundred

tremebundus, –a, –um, shake, trembling

tremō, –ere, tremuī, —, shake, tremble

tremor, –ōris, *m.*, shaking

tremulus, –a, –um, trembling

trepidō, 1, tremble; rush about

trepidus, –a, –um, trembling

trēs, tria, three

tribūnicius, –a, –um, tribunician

tribūnus, –ī, *m.*, tribune

tribuō, –ere, tribuī, tribūtus, bestow, grant, assign

tribūtum, –ī, *n.*, tax, tribute

trīclinium, –nī, *n.*, dining room, dining couch

trīduum, –ī, *n.*, three days

triennium, –nī, *n.*, (a period of) three years

trīgintā, thirty

Trimalchiō, –ōnis, *m.*, Trimalchio

triplex, *gen.* **triplicis**, threefold, triple

trīstis, –e, sad, severe

trīstitia, –ae, *f.*, sadness

triumphō, 1, triumph, celebrate a triumph

triumphus, –ī, *m.*, triumph, triumphal procession

Troia, –ae, *f.*, Troy, *a city in Asia Minor*

Troiānus, –a, –um, Trojan; *as noun, m. pl.*, the Trojans

tropaeum, –ī, *n.*, trophy

trucīdō, 1, butcher, murder

trūdō, –ere, trūsī, trūsus, thrust, shove forward

truncō, 1, strip

truncus, –ī, *m.*, trunk (*of a tree*)

tū, tuī, *pers. pron.* you, yourself

tuba, –ae, *f.*, trumpet

Tuberō, –ōnis, *m.*, Tubero

tubulātus, –a, –um, formed like a pipe, tubular

tueor, tuērī, tūtus, watch, look, guard, defend, maintain

tulī, *see* **ferō**

Tullia, Tulliola, –ae, *f.*, Tullia

Tullius, –lī, *m.*, Tullius

tum, *adv.*, then

tumeō, –ēre, —, —, swell

tumidus, –a, –um, swollen; enraged; haughty

tumultus, –ūs, *m.*, uproar, disturbance

tumulus, –ī, *m.*, hill, tomb

tunc, *adv.*, then; accordingly

tunica, –ae, *f.*, tunic

turba, –ae, *f.*, turmoil, throng

turbō, 1, roughen

turbulentus, –a, –um, muddy, disorderly, violent

turma, –ae, *f.*, troop (*of cavalry*)

turpis, –e, disgraceful, ugly

turpiter, *adv.*, basely

turpitūdō, –dinis, *f.*, disgrace, baseness

turris, –is, *f.*, tower

tūs, tūris, *n.*, incense

Tuscia, –ae, *f.*, Tuscany

Tusculānī, –ōrum, *m. pl.*, the Tusculans, people of Tusculum, *a town in Italy*

Tusculānum, –ī, *n.*, Tuscan estate

Tusculānus, –a, –um, Tusculan; *as noun, m.*, a citizen of Tusculum

tussiō, –īre, —, —, cough

tutēla, –ae, *f.*, charge, guardian

tūtō, *adv.*, safely

tūtus, –a, –um, safe

tuus, –a, –um, your, yours (*referring to one person*)

tyrannus, –ī, *m.*, tyrant

Tyrius, –a, –um, Tyrian

U

ūber, –eris, abounding, full

ubi, *adv.*, where; when; **ubi prīmum**, as soon as

ubicumque, *adv.*, wherever

ubinam, *adv.*, where

ubīque, *adv.*, everywhere

ulcīscor, ulcīscī, ultus, avenge, punish

ūllus, –a, –um, any, anyone

ulterior, –ius, farther; **ultimus, –a, –um**, farthest, last

ultimus, –a, –um, last, farthest

ultrā, *adv. and prep. w. acc.,* beyond, more

ultrīx, *gen.* **ultrīcis,** avenging

ultrō, *adv.,* voluntarily; actually

ultus, *part. of* **ulcīscor**

umbra, –ae, *f.,* shade, shadow

Umbrēnus, –ī, *m.,* Umbrenus

umbrōsus, –a, –um, shady, shading

umerus, –ī, *m.,* shoulder

umidus, –a, –um, moist, dewy

umquam, *adv.,* ever, at any time

ūnā, *adv.,* at the same time, along with, together

ūnanimus, –a, –um, of one mind, sympathetic

unda, –ae, *f.,* wave; water

unde, *adv.,* from which (place), by which, from where

undecimus, –a, –um, eleventh

undique, *adv.,* from *or* on all sides, everywhere

ungō, –ere, ūnxī, ūnctus, anoint

unguentārius, –ī, *m.,* ointment, perfume

unguentum, –ī, *n.,* ointment, perfume, salve

unguis, –is, *m.,* nail (*of finger or toe*); claw

ungula, –ae, *f.,* hoof, claw

ūnicē, *adv.,* singularly, devotedly

ūnicus, –a, –um, only

ūniversus, –a, –um, all (together), whole, in a body

ūnus, –a, –um, one, alone, single, sole

urbānitās, –tātis, *f.,* wit

urbānus, –a, –um, of *or* in the city; polished; facetious

urbs, urbis, *f.,* city

urgeō, urgēre, ursī, ursus, press hard

urna, –ae, *f.,* urn

ūrō, –ere, ussī, ustus, burn, parch

uspiam, *adv.,* anywhere

usque, *adv.,* even (to), all the time, as far as, up to, continuously, still; *w.* **adeō,** to such an extent

usquequāque, *adv.,* in everything, on every occasion

ūsūra, –ae, *f.,* use, enjoyment

ūsūrpātiō, –ōnis, *f.,* use

ūsūrpō, 1, use, employ

ūsus, –ūs, *m.,* use, need, advantage; practice, experience

ut, utī, *conj.,* (in order) that, to, so that; as (to), when; *adv.,* how as; **ut... non,** that . . . not

uter, utra, utrum, which (of two); whichever

uterque, utraque, utrumque, each (of two), either, both

utervīs, utravīs, utrumvīs, either

utī = ut

ūtilis, –e, useful, helpful

ūtilitās, –tātis, *f.,* usefulness, advantage

utinam! *adv.,* o that! would that!

utique, *adv.,* certainly

ūtor, ūtī, ūsus, use, employ, make use of (*w. abl.*), enjoy

utrimque, *adv.,* on both sides

utrum, *conj.,* whether; **utrum... an,** whether . . . or; *in dir. quest. it cannot be translated*

ūva, –ae, *f.,* grapes

uxor, –ōris, *f.,* wife

V

vacillō, 1, stagger

vacō, 1, be uninhabited, have leisure, empty

vacuēfaciō, –ere, –fēcī, –factus, make empty, free

vacuus, –a, –um, empty, free, without

vadimōnium, –nī, *n.,* bail bond

vādō, –ere, —, —; go

vadum, –ī, *n.,* ford, shallow place

vafer, vafra, vafrum, sly, crafty

vāgīna, –ae, *f.,* sheath

vagor, 1, wander

vagulus, –a, –um, wandering

vagus, –a, –um, wandering, uncertain, vague

valdē, *adv.,* strongly, very (much)

valeō, –ēre, valuī, valitūrus, be strong, be well, be able, be powerful, prevail; have influence, excel; *imper.,* **valē, valēte,** farewell

Valerius, –rī, *m.,* Valerius

valētūdō, –dinis, *f.,* health; illness, sickness

validus, –a, –um, strong

vallēs, –is, *f.,* valley

vāllō, 1, defend

vāllum, –ī, *n.,* rampart, wall, barricade

valvae, –ārum, *f. pl.,* doors

vānitās, –tātis, *f.,* folly, vanity

vānum, –ī, *n.,* emptiness

vānus, –a, –um, empty, false, vain

vapor, –ōris, *m.,* steam, heat

vāpulō, 1, be flogged

Vargunteius, –ī, *m.,* Vargunteius

varietās, –tātis, *f.,* variety, variation

varius, –a, –um, changing, varying, various

Varrō, –ōnis, *m.,* Varro

vas, vadis, *m.,* bail, security

vās, vāsis, *n.,* kettle, pot, vessel, dish, utensil; baggage

vāstitās, –tātis, *f.,* devastation

vāstō, 1, destroy, ruin

vāstus, –a, –um, huge, vast, immense

Vatīnius, –nī, *m.,* Vatinius

vātēs, –is, *m.,* prophet; poet

–ve, *enclitic,* or

vehemēns, *gen.* **vehementis,** vigorous, rigorous, strong

vehementer, *adv.,* violently, greatly, earnestly

vehiculum, –ī, *n.,* carriage

vehō, –ere, vexī, vectus, carry, bear; *pass.,* sail, ride

Veiī, –ōrum, *m. pl.,* Veii, *a town in Italy*

vel, *conj.,* or; **vel... vel,** either . . . or; *adv.,* even, at least; very; *w. superl.,* the most . . . possible

vēlāmen, –minis, *n.,* veil, cloak

Velleius Blaesus, –ī, *m.,* Velleius Blaesus

vellus, –eris, *n.,* fleece, wool

vēlō, 1, cover, veil

vēlōcitās, –tātis, *f.,* swiftness

vēlōx, –ōcis, swift

vēlum, –ī, *n.,* sail; awning

velut, velutī, *adv.,* just as, as, like

vēna, –ae, *f.,* vein

vēnābulum, –ī, *n.,* hunting spear

vēnālis, –e, for sale

vēnātiō, –ōnis, *f.,* hunting, hunt

vēnditō, 1, try to sell, sell

vendō, –ere, –didī, –ditus, sell

venēnō, 1, poison

venēnum, –ī, *n.,* poison

venerābilis, –e, reverend

venerātiō, –ōnis, *f.,* reverence, veneration

veneror, 1, worship

venia, –ae, *f.,* favor, pardon

Venetī, –ōrum, *m. pl.,* the Veneti

veniō, –īre, vēnī, ventūrus, come

vēnor, 1, hunt

venter, –tris, *m.,* belly, stomach

ventus, –ī, *m.,* wind

Venus, –eris, *f.,* Venus, *goddess of love and beauty*

venustās, –tātis, *f.,* charm

venustē, *adv.,* gracefully, beautifully

venustus, –a, –um, lovely, charming

vēr, vēris, *n.,* spring

Verānia, –ae, *f.,* Verania

verber, –eris, *n.,* blow

verberō, 1, beat, strike

verbum, –ī, *n.,* word; **verba faciō,** speak, make a speech

Vercingetorīx, –īgis, *m.,* Vercingetorix

vērē, *adv.,* truly

verēcundia, –ae, *f.,* modesty

verēcundus, –a, –um, ashamed, shy, modest

vereor, verērī, veritus, fear, respect

Vergilius, –lī, *m.,* Vergil

Verginius, –nī, *m.,* Verginius

vergo, –ere, —, —, slope, lie

vēritās, –tātis, *f.,* truth

vernīliter, *adv.,* servilely

vernus, –a, –um, of spring, spring

vērō, *adv.,* in truth, in fact; but, however

Vērōna, –ae, *f.,* Verona

verrēs, –is, *m.,* boar

Verrēs, –is, *m.,* Verres

verrō, –ere, verrī, versus, sweep

versicolor, *gen.* **–ōris,** of various colors

versificātor, –ōris, *m.,* versifier, poet

versō, 1, turn over, turn (often); *pass.,* live, be engaged in, be employed; remain, exist; be skilled; depend on

versor, 1, move about, be engaged, live, be

versus, –ūs, *m.,* line, verse

vertex, –ticis, *m.,* (whirl), head, peak

vertō, –ere, vertī, versus, turn; *pass.,* turn (oneself); *sometimes deponent;* **vertō,** wheel about

vērum, *adv.,* but

vērus, –a, –um, true; *as noun, n.,* truth; **rē vērā,** really

vēscor, vēscī, —, —, feed, eat

Vespasiānus, –ī, *m.,* Vespasian, *the emperor*

vesper, –erī, *m.,* evening; **vesperī,** in the evening

vespera, –ae, *f.,* the evening star, evening

Vesta, –ae, *f.,* Vesta, *goddess of the hearth*

Vestālis, –e, Vestal, of Vesta

vester, –tra, –trum, your, yours (*referring to two or more persons*)

vēstibulum, –ī, *n.,* entrance

vēstīgium, –gī, *n.,* footprint, foot, footstep, track, sole (*of the foot*); *pl.,* fragments

vestīmentum, –ī, *n.,* clothing

vestiō, –īre, –īvī, –ītus, clothe, dress

vestis, –is, *f.,* clothing, garment, robe

vestītus, –ūs, *m.,* clothing

veterānus, –a, –um, veteran, experienced

vetō, –āre, vetuī, vetitus, forbid

vetus, *gen.* veteris, old, former, ancient

vetustās, –tātis, *f.,* old age, age

vetustus, –a, –um, old, ancient

vexātiō, –ōnis, *f.,* harassment

vexō, 1, disturb, trouble, harass

via, –ae, *f.,* way, road, street; journey; **viam mūniō,** build a road

viāticum, –ī, *n.,* traveling money

viātor, –ōris, *m.,* traveler; court officer

Vibō, –ōnis, *f.,* Vibo

vibrō, 1, brandish

vīcēnī, –ae, –a, twenty (each)

vīcēsimus, –a, –um, twentieth

vīciēs, *adv.,* twenty times

vīcīnia, –ae, *f.,* neighborhood, nearness

vīcīnitās, –tātis, *f.,* neighborhood, vicinity

vīcīnus, –a, –um, neighboring; *as noun, m.,* neighbor

(vicis), –is, *f.,* change; **in vicem** *or* **vicēs,** in turn

victima, –ae, *f.,* victim

victor, –ōris, *m.,* victor; *adj.,* victorious

victōria, –ae, *f.,* victory

victrīx, –īcis, *f.,* victor

vīctus, –ūs, *m.,* living, food

vīcus, –ī, *m.,* village, street

vidēlicet, *adv.,* evidently; of course, doubtless

videō, –ēre, vīdī, vīsus, see; *pass.,* be seen, seem, seem best

viduus, –a, –um, widowed

vigeō, –ēre, viguī, —, be vigorous, thrive

vigil, *gen.* vigilis, wakeful, watchful

vigilāns, *gen.* –antis, watchful, active

vigilia, –ae, *f.,* loss of sleep, guarding; watchman, watch; sentinel (*a fourth part of the night*)

vigilō, 1, keep awake, watch

vīgintī, twenty

vigor, –ōris, *m.,* force, vigor

vīlicus, –ī, *m.,* farm manager

vīlis, –e, cheap, worthless

vīlla, –ae, *f.,* farmhouse, country home, villa

vīllula, –ae, *f.,* small villa

vīllus, –ī, *m.,* shaggy hair

Vīminālis (mōns), –is, *m.,* the Viminal Hill

vinciō, –īre, vinxī, vinctus, bind

vincō, –ere, vīcī, victus, conquer, defeat, overcome, win; exhaust

vinculum, –ī, *n.,* bond, chain, fastening

Vindex, –dicis, *n.,* Vindex

vindicō, 1, avenge, punish; claim, assert one's claim to, appropriate

vīnea, –ae, *f.,* grape arbor, shed, vineyard

vīnētum, –ī, *n.,* vineyard

vīnum, –ī, *n.,* wine

violō, 1, wrong, dishonor, injure

vir, virī, *m.,* man, husband

virēns, *gen.* –entis, green

virga, –ae, *f.,* twig, rod

virginālis, –e, maidenly, virgin

virginitās, –tātis, *f.,* virginity

virgō, –ginis, *f.,* virgin, maiden

Viriāthus, –ī, *m.,* Viriathus

virīlis, –e, manly

virtūs, –tūtis, *f.,* manliness, courage, virtue, character, ability

vīs, —, *f.,* force, power, violence, energy; *pl.,* **vīrēs, vīrium,** strength

vīscera, –um, *n. pl.,* vitals

vīsō, –ere, vīsī, vīsus, go to see, view

vīta, –ae, *f.,* life

vītātiō, –ōnis, *f.,* shunning, avoidance

vīticula, –ae, *f.,* little vine

vitiōsus, –a, –um, full of faults, wrong

vītis, –is, *f.,* vine

vitium, –tī, *n.,* fault, defect, vice

vītō, 1, avoid, escape

vitta, –ae, *f.,* headband

vituperō, 1, blame, censure

vīvo, –ere, vīxī, victus, live

vīvus, –a, –um, alive, living

vix, *adv.,* hardly, scarcely, with difficulty, hardly

vōbīscum = cum vōbīs

vocābulum, –ī, *n.,* word

vocātīvus, –a, –um, vocative

vocō, 1, call, summon, invite, invoke

volātus, –ūs, *m.,* flying, flight

volō, 1, fly

volō, velle, voluī, —, want, wish, intend, be willing

Volscī, –ōrum, *m. pl.,* the Volscians

Volturcius, –cī, *m.,* Volturcius

volucris, –ris, *f.,* bird

volūmen, –minis, *n.,* roll, volume

voluntās, –tātis, *f.,* will, good will, wish, purpose; consent

voluptās, –tātis, *f.,* pleasure

volvō, –ere, volvī, volūtus, roll (up); turn over, ponder; *pass.,* roll, be hurled, toss about

vōs, you, *pl. of* **tū**

vōsmet, you yourselves

vōtum, –ī, *n.,* vow, wish, prayer

voveō, –ēre, vōvī, vōtus, vow, wish for, promise

vōx, vōcis, *f.,* voice, cry; word, remark, talk

Vulcānus, –ī, *m.,* Vulcan, *god of fire*

vulgus, –ī, *n.,* common people, crowd

vulnerō, 1, wound

vulnus, vulneris, *n.,* wound

vultus, –ūs, *m.,* expression, face, features; presence

X

Xerxēs, –is, *m.,* Xerxes, *king of Persia*

English–Latin

For proper nouns and proper adjectives not given in this vocabulary, see the Latin–English Vocabulary or the text.

Verbs of the first conjugation whose parts are regular are indicated by the figure 1.

A

able (be), possum, posse, potuī, —
about, dē, *w. abl.*
accomplice, socius, –cī, *m.*
accomplish, cōnficiō, –ere, –fēcī, –fectus
account, ratiō, –ōnis, *f.;* **on account of,** *see* **on,** ob, propter
accustomed (be), cōnsuēscō, –ere, –suēvī, –suētus
achieve, cōnsequor, cōnsequī, cōnsecūtus; efficiō, –ere, effēcī, effectus
acknowledge, cognōscō, –ere, cognōvī, cognitus
across, trāns, *w. acc.*
action, factum, –ī, *n.*
add, adiciō, –ere, adiēcī, adiectus
admire, admīror, 1
adopt, adoptō, 1
adorn, ōrnō, 1
advice, cōnsilium, –lī, *n.*
affairs (public), rēs pūblica, reī pūblicae, *f.*
afraid (be), timeō, –ēre, timuī, —
after, post (*conj.*), postquam; *use abl. abs.*
again, rūrsus, iterum
against, contrā, *w. acc.*
age, aetās, –tātis, *f.*
agree, cōnsentiō, –īre, –sēnsī, –sēnsus
aid, auxilium, –lī, *n.*
all, omnis, –e; tōtus, –a, –um; **all other,** cēterī, –ae, –a
allow, licet, –ēre, licuit *or* licitum est
almost, paene
alone, sōlus, –a, –um
already, iam
also, etiam
although, etsī, cum; quamquam; *use participle or abl. abs.*
always, semper
among, inter, *w. acc.*

and, et; –que
another, alius, alia, aliud
answer, solūtio, –ōnis, *f.*
any, ūllus, –a, –um; **any longer (not),** nōn iam
anyone, quisquam, quicquam; quis, quid (*after* sī)
appear, appāreō, –ēre, appāruī, appāritūrus
Appian, Appius, –a, –um
apply, subiciō, –ere, subiēcī, subiectus
approach (*noun*), adventus, –ūs, *m.;* (*verb*), accēdō, –ere, accessī, accessūrus (*w.* ad); adeō, adīre, adiī, aditūrus; appropinquō, 1 (*w. dat.*)
approve, probō, 1
arena, arēna, –ae, *f.*
arise, orior, orīrī, ortus
arouse, commoveō, –ēre, commōvī, commōtus
arm, armō, 1
arms, arma, –ōrum, *n. pl.*
army, exercitus, –ūs, *m.*
arrival, adventus, –ūs, *m.*
arrive, perveniō, –īre, –vēnī, –ventūrus
art, ars, artis, *f.*
as, quantum; **as... as,** quam; **as long as,** dum; **as much,** tantum; **as... as possible,** quam, *w. superl.;* **as soon as possible,** quam prīmum; **as to,** ut
ask, rogō, 1; **ask for,** petō, –ere, petīvī, petītus
assign, attribuō, –ere, –uī, –ūtus
at (near), ad, *w. acc.; abl. of time or place*
at once, statim
Athens, Athēnae, –ārum, *f. pl.*
attack, impetus, –ūs, *m.;* oppugnō, 1; aggredior, aggredī, aggressus
author, auctor, –ōris, *m.*
await, exspectō, 1
away (be), absum, –esse, āfuī, āfutūrus
away (go), discēdō, –ere, cessī, –cessūrus

B

bad, malus, –a, –um

badly, male

baggage, impedīmenta, –ōrum, *n. pl.*

band, manus, –ūs, *f.*

bandit, latrō, –ōnis, *m.*

banish, expellō, –ere, expulī, expulsus

battle line, aciēs, aciēī, *f.*

be, sum, esse, fuī, futūrus

bear, ferō, ferre, tulī, lātus

beat, superō, 1

beautiful, pulcher, –chra, –chrum

because, *use participle or abl. abs.;* quod, quoniam

become, fīō, fierī, (factus)

before, priusquam, (*adv. and prep.*), ante, *w. acc.*

beg, ōrō, 1; petō, –ere, petīvī, petītus

begin, incipiō, –ere, incēpī, inceptus; **began**, coepī, coeptus

believe, crēdō, –ere, crēdidī, crēditus (*w. dat.*)

besiege, obsideō, –ēre, obsēdī, obsessus

best, optimus, –a, –um

betroth, dēspondeō, –ēre, dēspondī, dēspōnsus

better, melior, melius

between, inter, *w. acc.*

blame, accūsō, 1

block, comprimō, –ere, compressī, compressus

body, corpus, –oris, *n.*

book, liber, librī, *m.*

born (be), nāscor, nāscī, nātus

boy, puer, puerī, *m.*

brave, fortis, –e; **bravely**, fortiter

bridge, pōns, pontis, *m.*

bring, ferō, ferre, tulī, lātus; afferō, afferre, attulī, allātus; īnferō, īnferre, intulī, illātus; **bring together**, condūcō, –ere, –dūxī, –ductus; **bring back**, reportō, 1

Britons, Britannī, –ōrum, *m. pl.*

build, exstruō, –ere, exstrūxī, exstrūctus; aedificō, 1

building, aedificium, –cī, *n.*

burn, incendō, –ere, incendī, incēnsus

business, negōtium, –tī, *n.*

but, sed; **but also**, sed etiam

buy, emō, –ere, –ēmī, ēmptus

by, ā, ab, *w. abl.; sometimes abl. alone*

C

Caesar, Caesar, –aris, *m.*

call, appellō, 1

camp, castra, –ōrum, *n. pl.*

can, possum, posse, potuī, —

capture, expugnō, 1; capiō, –ere, cēpī, captus

care, eī cūra est

careful, dīligēns, *gen.* dīligentis; **carefully**, dīligenter

carry, portō, 1; ferō, ferre, tulī, lātus; **carry on war**, bellum gerō; **carry back**, referō, referre, rettulī, relātus

carry out, administrō, 1

Carthage, Carthāgō, –ginis, *f.*

Catiline, Catilīna, –ae, *m.*

Cato, Catō, –ōnis, *m.*

cause, efficiō, –ere, effēcī, effectus (*w. ut and subjunct.*)

cavalry, equitātus, –ūs, *m.;* equitēs, –um, *m. pl.*

censor, cēnsor, –ōris, *m.*

certain, a certain (one), quīdam, quaedam, quiddam; **certainly**, certē

chain, vinculum, –ī, *n.*

chance, occāsiō, –ōnis, *f.*

charge, crīmen, –minis, *n.*

check, sustineō, –ēre, –tinuī, –tentus

children, līberī, –ōrum, *m. pl.*

choose, dēligō, –ere, dēlēgī, dēlēctus

Cicero, Cicerō, –ōnis, *m.*

circumstance, rēs, reī, *f.*

citadel, arx, arcis, *f.*

citizen, cīvis, –is, *m. and f.*

city, urbs, urbis, *f.*

civil, cīvīlis, –e

clearly, clārē

client, cliēns, –entis, *m.*

close, claudō, –ere, clausī, clausus

collect, conferō, conferre, contulī, collātus

come, veniō, –īre, vēnī, ventūrus; **come out**, ēgredior, ēgredī, ēgressus

command (be in), praesum, –esse, –fuī, –futūrus (*w. dat.*)

commit, faciō, –ere, fēcī, factus

common people, plēbs, plēbis, *f.*

compel, cōgō, –ere, coēgī, coāctus

complain, queror, querī, questus

complete, cōnficiō, –ere, –fēcī, –fectus

conceal, cēlō, 1

concern, cūra, –ae, *f.*

condemn, damnō, 1

condition, condiciō, –ōnis, *f.*

conference, colloquium, –quī, *n.*

conquer, vincō, –ere, vīcī, victus; superō, 1

conspiracy, coniūrātiō, –ōnis, *f.*

conspire, coniūrō, 1

consul, cōnsul, –sulis, *m.*

consult (for), cōnsulō, –ere, –suluī, –sultus

correct, vērus, –a, –um

country, patria, –ae, *f.*

courage, virtūs, –tūtis, *f.*

cover, tegō, –ere, tēxī, tēctus

creditor, crēditor, –ōris, *m.*

crime, scelus, sceleris, *n.*

criticize, accūsō, 1

cross, trānseō, –īre, –iī, –itūrus

crow, corvus, –ī, *m.*

crowded together, cōnfertus, –a, –um

cruel, crūdēlis, –e

cruelty, crūdēlitās, –tātis, *f.*

custom, mōs, mōris, *m.*

cut off, interclūdō, –ere, –clūsī, –clūsus

D

danger, perīculum, –ī, *n.*

dare, audeō, –ēre, ausus

daughter, fīlia, –ae, *f.*

day, diēs, diēī, *m. and f.;* **day by day,** in diēs

dead, mortuus, –a, –um

dear, cārus, –a, –um

debt, aes aliēnum, aeris aliēnī, *n.*

decide, cōnstituō, –ere, –stituī, –stitūtus

decided (be), placet, –ēre, placuit

decorated, adōrnātus, –a, –um

decree *(noun),* dēcrētum, –ī, *n.; (verb),* dēcernō, –ere, dēcrēvī, dēcrētus

deed, factum, –ī, *n.*

defeat, superō, 1

defeat *(noun),* calamitās, –tātis, *f.; (verb),* superō, 1; pellō, –ere, pepulī, pulsus; vincō, –ere, vīcī, victus

defend, dēfendō, –ere, dēfendī, dēfēnsus

defenses, mūnītiō, –ōnis, *f.*

definite, certus, –a, –um

delay, mora, –ae, *f.*

demand, postulō, 1

depart, dēcēdō, –ere, dēcessī, dēcessūrus; proficīscor, proficīscī, profectus; excēdō, –ere, excessī, excessūrus

departure, exitus, –ūs, *m.;* profectiō, –ōnis, *f.*

deserve, mereō, –ēre, meruī, meritus

desire, *(noun),* cupiditās, –tātis, *f.; (verb),* cupiō, –īre, –īvī, –ītus

despair (of), dēspērō, 1

destroy, dēleō, –ēre, –ēvī, –ētus; ēvertō, –ere, –ēvertī, ēversus

determine, cōnstituō, –ere, –stituī, –stitūtus

dictate, dictō, 1

die, morior, –īrī, mortuus

differ, differō, differre, distulī, dīlātus

difficult, difficilis, –e

dinner, cēna, –ae, *f.;* convīvium, –vī, *n.*

divide, dīvidō, –ere, dīvīsī, dīvīsus

disagree, dissentiō, –īre, dissēnsī, dissēnsus

disaster, calamitās, –tātis, *f.*

disgrace (in), turpiter

do, faciō, –ere, fēcī, factus; agō, –ere, ēgī, āctus

Domitian, Domitiānus, –ī, *m.*

draw up, īnstruō, –ere, īnstrūxī, īnstrūctus

drive out, ēiciō, –ere, ēiēcī, ēiectus; expellō, –ere, expulī, expulsus

during, per, *w. acc.*

dutiful, pius, –a, –um

duty, officium, –cī, *n.*

E

each one, quisque, quidque

eager, cupidus, –a, –um

eager for (be), studeō, –ēre, studuī, — *(w. dat.)*

eagerness, studium, –dī, *n.*

earn, mereō, –ēre, meruī, meritus

earth, terra, –ae, *f.*

easy, facilis, –e; **easily,** facile

eat, edō, –ere, –ēdī, ēsus

elect, creō, 1

elevated, ēditus, –a, –um

eloquence, ēloquentia, –ae, *f.*

embassy, lēgātiō, –ōnis, *f.*

empire, imperium, –rī, *n.*

encourage, cōnfirmō, 1

endure, ferō, ferre, tulī, lātus

enemy (*personal*), inimīcus, –ī, *m.;* (*national*), hostis, –is, *m.*

enjoy, fruor, fruī, frūctus; ūtor, ūtī, ūsus (*w. abl.*)

enmity, inimīcitia, –ae, *f.*

enter, introeō, –īre, –iī, –itūrus; ingredior, ingredī, ingressus

entire, tōtus, –a, –um

entrust, mandō, 1

envoy, lēgātus, –ī, *m.*

envy, invideō, –ēre, invīdī, invīsus (*w. dat.*)

equal, aequālis, –e

erect, exstruō, –ere, exstrūxī, exstrūctus

escape, fugiō, –ere, fūgī, fugitūrus

establish, cōnstituō, –ere, –stituī, –stitūtus

ever, umquam

everybody, omnēs

everyone, omnis, –is, *m. and f.*

everything, omne *or* omnia, omnium, *n. pl.*

examine, excutiō, –ere, excussī, excussus

example, exemplum, –ī, *n.*

excel, praestō, –āre, –stitī, –stitūrus (*w. dat.*)

excellent, bonus, –a, –um; optimus, –a, –um

exclaim, (ex)clāmō, 1

exile, exsilium, –lī, *n.*

expel, expellō, –ere, expulī, expulsus

explain, expōnō, –ere, –posuī, –positus

F

facility, facultās, –tātis, *f.*

fact that, quod

Faesulae, Faesulae, –ārum, *f. pl.*

fall, incidō, –ere, incidī, —

fame, fāma, –ae, *f.,*

family, familia, –ae, *f.*

famous, clārus, –a, –um

farm, ager, agrī, *m.,*

farmer, agricola, –ae, *m.*

farthest, extrēmus, –a, –um; ultimus, –a, –um

fate, fātum, –ī, *n.*

father, pater, patris, *m.*

fault, culpa, –ae, *f.*

favor, faveō, –ēre, fāvī, fautūrus

fear, timeō, –ēre, timuī, —; vereor, verērī, veritus

feel, sentiō, –īre, sēnsī, sēnsus

few, paucī, –ae, –a

fierce, ferus, –a, –um

fiercely, ferōciter

fight, pugnō, 1

find, find out, inveniō, –īre, invēnī, inventus

fine, pulcher, pulchra, pulchrum

finish, cōnficiō, –ere, –fēcī, –fectus

fire, incendium, –dī, *n.*

firm, firmus, –a, –um

first, prīmus, –a, –um; (*adv.*), prīmum; **at first,** prīmō

flame, flamma, –ae, *f.*

flee, fugiō, –ere, fūgī, fugitūrus

food, cibus, –ī, *m.*

foot, pēs, pedis, *m.*

for (*conj.*), nam; (*prep.*), ad, ob, *w. acc.;* prō, *w. abl.;* **for the purpose** *or* **sake of,** causā *or* grātiā (*preceded by gen.*); *sometimes not expressed*

force, cōgō, –ere, coēgī, coāctus

forest, silva, –ae, *f.*

forget, oblivīscor, –ī, oblītus

former, ille, illa, illud; **the former . . . the latter,** ille... hic

fortify, mūniō, –īre, –īvī, –ītus

fortune, fortūna, –ae, *f.*

Forum, Forum, –ī, *n.*

found, condō, –ere, condidī, conditus

four, quattuor

free (*adj.*), līber, –era, –erum; (*verb*), līberō, 1; **be free,** careō, –ēre, caruī, caritūrus

freedom, lībertās, –tātis, *f.*

fresh, integer, –gra, –grum

friend, amīcus, –ī; *m.;* **(girl) friend,** amīca, –ae, *f.*

friendly, amīcus, –a, –um

frighten, terreō, –ēre, terruī, territus

frog, rāna, –ae, *f.*

from, ē, ex, ā, ab, dē, *w. abl.;* **from one another,** inter sē

furnish, praebeō, –ēre, –uī, –itus

G

game, lūdus, –ī, *m.*

garden, hortus, –ī, *m.*

gate, porta, –ae, *f.*

Gaul, Gallus, –ī, *m.; * Gallia, –ae, *f.; * **Gauls,** Gallī, –ōrum, *m. pl.*

general, dux, ducis, *m.; * lēgātus, –ī, *m.*

get, accipiō, –ere, accēpī, acceptus; parō, 1; **get (possession of),** potior, potīrī, potītus (*w. abl.*)

girl, puella, –ae, *f.*

give, dō, dare, dedī, datus; **give up,** dēdō, –ere, dēdidī, dēditus

gladiator, gladiātor, –ōris, *m.; * **gladiatorial,** gladiātōrius, –a, –um

glory, glōria, –ae, *f.*

go, eō, īre, iī, itūrus; **go out,** ēgredior, ēgredī, ēgressus; exeō, exīre, exiī, exitūrus; **go away,** discēdō, –ere, discessī, discessūrus; **go from,** abeō, abīre, abiī, abitūrus

god, deus, –ī, *m.*

goddess, dea, –ae, *f.*

gold, aurum, –ī, *n.*

good, bonus, –a, –um

government, rēs pūblica, reī pūblicae, *f.*

grain, frūmentum, –ī, *n.*

grammarian, grammaticus, –ī, *m.*

grandfather, avus, –ī, *m.*

great, magnus, –a, –um; **greater,** maior, maius; **greatest,** maximus, –a, –um; summus, –a, –um; **great deal,** plūrimum; **so great,** tantus, –a, –um

Greece, Graecia, –ae, *f.*

Greek, Graecus, –a, –um

grow, crēscō, –ere, crēvī, crētus

guard, praesidium, –dī, *n.*

guest-friend, hospes, –itis, *m.*

H

happen, ēveniō, –īre, ēvēnī, ēventūrus; accidō, –ere, accidī, —

harbor, portus, –ūs, *m.*

hardly, vix

harm, damnum, –ī, *n.; * dētrīmentum, –ī, *n.*

harsh, dūrus, –a, –um

hasten, properō, 1; contendō, –ere, –tendī, –tentūrus

hate, ōdī, ōsūrus

have, habeō, –ēre, habuī, habitus; **have to,** *use fut. pass. part.*

he, is; hic; ille; *often not expressed*

head, caput, capitis, *n.*

hear, audiō, –īre, –īvī, –ītus

heat, aestus, –ūs, *m.*

height, altitūdō, –dinis, *f.*

heir, hērēs, –ēdis, *m.*

help, auxilium, –lī, *n.*

her (*poss.*), eius; (*reflex.*), suus, –a, –um; **herself** (*reflex.*), suī

hesitate, dubitō, 1

high, altus, –a, –um

hill, mōns, montis, *m.; * collis, –is, *m.*

himself (*reflex.*), suī; (*intens.*), ipse

hinder, impediō, –īre, –īvī, –ītus

his (*poss.*), eius; **his own** (*reflex.*), suus, –a, –um

history, historia, –ae, *f.*

holiday, fēriae, –ārum, *f. pl.*

home, domus, –ūs, *f.*

honor, honor, –ōris, *m.*

Horace, Horātius, –tī, *m.*

horse, equus, –ī, *m.*

horseman, eques, equitis, *m.*

host, dominus, –ī, *m.*

hostage, obses, obsidis, *m.*

hour, hōra, –ae, *f.*

house, domus, –ūs, *f.*

how, quōmodō; **how much,** quantus, –a, –um

however, autem (*never first word*)

humble, humilis, –e

hurry (on), properō, 1

I

I, ego, meī; *often not expressed*

if, sī

ill, aeger, aegra, aegrum

immediately, statim

impel, impellō, –ere, impulī, impulsus

in, in, *w. abl.; * **in order to** *or* **that,** ut (*w. subjunctive*); **in order not to,** nē

inferior, īnferior, –ius

influence (*verb*) addūcō, –ere, addūxī, adductus; (*noun*), auctōritās, –tātis, *f.*

inform, (eum) certiōrem faciō, –ere, fēcī, factus; *pass.,* certior fīō, fierī

inhabit, incolō, –ere, incoluī, —

injure, noceō, –ēre, nocuī, nocitūrus

inspire, iniciō, –ere, iniēcī, iniectus

into, in, *w. acc.*

investigate, explōrō, 1

invite, vocō, 1

it, is, ea, id; hic, haec, hoc; ille, illa, illud; *often not expressed*

Italy, Italia, –ae, *f.*

J

journey, iter, itineris, *n.*

Jupiter, Iuppiter, Iovis, *m.*

K

keep, retineō, –ēre, retinuī, retentus; **keep from,** prohibeō, –ēre, –hibuī, –hibitus

kill, interficiō, –ere, –fēcī, –fectus; caedō, –ere, cecīdī, caesus; occīdo, –ere, occīdi, occīsus

kind, genus, generis, *n.*

kindness, beneficium, –cī, *n.*

king, rēx, rēgis, *m.*

knight, eques, equitis, *m.*

know, sciō, scīre, scīvī, scītus; *perf. of* nōscō, –ere, nōvī, nōtus, *or of* cognōscō, –ere, –nōvī, –nitus; **not know,** nesciō, –īre, nescīvī, —

L

lack, careō, –ēre, caruī, caritūrus; **be lacking,** dēsum, deesse, dēfuī, dēfutūrus

large, magnus, –a, –um; **so large,** tantus, –a, –um

last (*adj.*), proximus, –a, –um; (*verb*), maneō, –ēre, mānsī, mānsūrus

later, posteā, post

latter, hic, haec, hoc

law, lēx, lēgis, *f.*

lay aside, dēpōnō, –ere, dēposuī, dēpositus

lead, dūċō, –ere, dūxī, ductus; **lead a life,** vītam agō

leader, dux, ducis, *m.;* prīnceps, prīncipis, *m.*

learn, discō, –ere, didicī, —; cognōscō, –ere, –nōvī, –nitus

leave (behind), relinquō, –ere, relīquī, relīctus; **leave bare,** vacuēfaciō, –ere, –fēcī, –factus

legion, legiō, –ōnis, *f.*

let, permittō, –ere, –mīsī, –missus

let go, mittō, –ere, –mīsī, –missus

letter (*epistle*), litterae, –ārum, *f. pl.*

liberty, lībertās, –tātis, *f.*

life, vīta, –ae, *f.*

like, (*adj,*), similis, –e; (*verb*), amō, 1; (*adv.*), tamquam

little, paulum, –ī, *n.*

little later, paulō post

live (a life), agō, –ere, ēgī, āctus; (*dwell*), habitō, 1; vīvō, –ere, vīxī, vīctus

long, longus, –a, –um; **long** (*adv.*), **(for) a long time,** diū; **as long as,** dum; **not any longer,** nōn iam

look at *or* **on,** spectō, 1

lose, āmittō, –ere, āmīsī, āmissus; perdō, –ere, –didī, –ditus

loss, dētrīmentum, –ī, *n.*

love, (*noun*) amor, amōris, *m.;* (*verb*), amō, 1

luxurious, lautus, –a, –um

luxury, lūxuria, –ae, *f.*

M

make, faciō, –ere, fēcī, factus; **make war upon,** bellum īnferō (*w. dat.*)

man, vir, virī, *m.;* homō, hominis, *m.*

manage, gerō, –ere, gessī, gestus

manner, modus, –ī, *m.*

many, multī, –ae, –a; **so many,** tot; **very many,** plūrimī, –ae, –a

march, iter, itineris, *n.*

master, dominus, –ī, *m.*

matter, rēs, reī, *f.*

may, licet, –ēre, licuit *or* licitum est

meanwhile, intereā, interim

meet (in battle), congredior, congredī, congressus

memory, memoria, –ae, *f.*

merciful, misericors, *gen.* –cordis

mercy, clēmentia, –ae, *f.*

messenger, nūntius, –tī, *m.*

method, modus, –ī, *m.*

mile, mīlle passūs; *pl.* mīlia passuum

mind, animus, –ī, *m.*

miracle, mīrāculum, –ī, *n.*

molest, noceō, –ēre, nocuī, nocitūrus (*w. dat.*)

money, pecūnia, –ae, *f.*

month, mēnsis, –is *m.*

monument, monumentum, –ī, *n.*

more, magis, plūs, amplius; *use comparative*

most, maximē

mother, māter, mātris, *f.*

mountain, mōns, montis, *m.*

move, moveō, –ēre, mōvī, mōtus; afficiō, –ere, affēcī, affectus

much, multus, –a, –um

murder, caedēs, –is, *f.*

must, *use fut. pass. part.*

my, meus, –a, –um

N

name, nōmen, nōminis, *n.*

narrow, angustus, –a, –um

nature, nātūra, –ae, *f.*

near, ad *w. acc.; (adj.)*, propinquus, –a, –um

necessary (it is), oportet, –ēre, oportuit; necesse est

need (is), opus est

neglect, neglegō, –ere, –lēxī, –lectus

neighbors, fīnitimī, –ōrum, *m.*

never, numquam

nevertheless, tamen

new, novus, –a, –um

next, proximus, –a, –um

night, nox, noctis, *f.*

no, nōn, nūllus, –a, –um; **no longer,** nōn iam

noble, nōbilis, –e

no one, nēmō, *dat.* nēminī, *acc.* nēminem

none, nūllus, –a, –um

not, nōn, nē (*w. negative volitive and purpose clauses*); **not only,** nōn sōlum

noted, īnsignis, –e; nōtus, –a, –um

nothing, nihil

now, nunc

notice, animadvertō, –ere, –vertī, –versus

number, numerus, –ī, *m.*

numerous, multus, –a, –um

O

obey, pāreō, –ēre, pāruī, pāritūrus (*w. dat.*)

obstruct, impediō, –īre, –īvī, –ītus

obtain (one's request), impetrō, 1

occupy, occupō, 1

occur, intercēdō, –ere, –cessī, –cessus

often, saepe

Oh! utinam!

old man, senex, senis, *m.*

omen, ōmen, ōminis, *n.*

on, in, *w. abl.;* **on account of,** ob *or* propter, *w. acc.*

once (at), statim

one, ūnus, –a, –um; **one (the) . . . the other,** alius... alius

only, sōlum

open, aperiō, –īre, aperuī, apertus

opinion, sententia, –ae, *f.*

opportunity, occāsiō, –ōnis, *f.*

oppress, opprimō, –ere, oppressī, oppressus

or, vel, aut; an

oracle, ōrāculum, –ī, *n.*

oratory, ēloquentia, –ae, *f.*

order (*noun***),** imperium, –rī, *n.;* (*verb*), iubeō, –ēre, iussī, iussus; imperō, 1, (*w. dat.*); **in order to** *or* **that,** ut; **in order not to** *or* **that,** nē

other, alius, alia, alium; **the other,** alter, –a, –um; **others,** *see* **some; all other,** *see* **all**

ought, dēbeō, –ēre, dēbuī, dēbitus; oportet, –ēre, oportuit; *use fut. pass. part.*

our, noster, –tra, –trum

ourselves, nōs, nostrī

overcome, superō, 1; vincō, –ere, vīcī, victus

P

part, pars, partis, *f.*

pass over, praetereō, –īre, –iī, –itus

pay, solvō, –ere, solvī, solūtus; pendō, –ere, pependī, pēnsus; **pay the penalty,** poenam dō

peace, pāx, pācis, *f.*

peacefully, tranquillē

people, populus, –ī, *m.;* hominēs, –um, *m. pl.*

perform, fungor, fungī, functus

Pergamum, Pergamum, –ī, *n.*

permit, licet, –ēre, licuit *or* licitum est; permittō, –ere, –mīsī, –missus

persuade, persuādeō, –ēre, –suāsī, –suāsūrus (*w. dat.*)

philosopher, philosophus, –ī, *m.*

pity, misericordia, –ae, *f.*

place (*noun*), locus, –ī, *m.; pl.* loca, –ōrum, *n.;* (*verb*), pōnō, –ere, posuī, positus; **place in charge,** praeficiō, –ere, –fēcī, –fectus

plainly, simpliciter

plan (*noun*), cōnsilium, –lī, *n.;* (*verb*), in animō habeō; cōgitō, 1

please, be pleasing to, placeō, –ēre, placuī, placitus (*w. dat.*)

pleasure to me, mihi placet

Pliny, Plīnius, –nī, *m.*

plot, coniūrō, 1

poem, carmen, carminis, *n.*

poet, poēta, –ae, *m.*

Pompey, Pompeius, –peī, *m.*

poor, pauper, *gen.* –eris

possession of (get), potior, potīrī, potītus (*w. gen. or abl.*)

possible (as soon as), quam prīmum

power, potestās, –tātis, *f.;* imperium, –rī, *n.*

praetor, praetor, –ōris, *m.*

praise, laudō, 1

prefer, mālō, mālle, māluī, —

prepare, parō, 1

present (be), adsum, adesse, adfuī, adfutūrus

preserve, cōnservō, 1

prevent, prohibeō, –ēre, –hibuī, –hibitus

prison, carcer, –eris, *m.*

prisoner, captīvus, –ī, *m.*

prize, praemium, –mī, *n.*

proceed, prōcēdō, –ere, –cessī, –cessūrus

procession, pompa, –ae, *f.*

produce, pariō, –ere, peperī, partus

promise, polliceor, pollicērī, pollicitus

property, bona, –ōrum, *n. pl.*

protect, tegō, –ere, tēxī, tēctus

protection, praesidium, –dī, *n.*

provided that, dum

public affairs, rēs pūblica, reī pūblicae, *f.*

punish, pūniō, –īre, –īvī, –ītus

punishment, supplicium, –cī, *n.*

purpose (for the), causā, grātiā

pursue, īnsequor, īnsequī, īnsecūtus

put in charge of, praeficiō, –ere, –fēcī, –fectus

Q

queen, rēgīna, –ae, *f.*

question, quaestiō, –ōnis, *f.*

quickly, celeriter

R

reach, perveniō, –īre, –vēnī, –ventūrus

read, legō, –ere, lēgī, lēctus

ready, parātus, –a, –um

realize, intellegō, –ere, –lēxī, –lēctus

reason, causa, –ae, *f.*

recall, recordor, 1; revocō, 1

receive, accipiō, –ere, accēpī, acceptus; excipiō, –ere, excēpī, exceptus

recitation, recitātiō, –ōnis, *f.*

recite, recitō, 1

recognize, cognōscō, –ere, –nōvī, –nitus

reconnoiter, explōrō, 1

refrain, abstineō, –ēre, –tinuī, –tentus

region, regiō, –ōnis, *f.*

rejoice, gaudeō, –ēre, gāvīsus

remain, maneō, –ēre, mānsī, mānsūrus

remember, memoriā teneō

repair, reficiō, –ere, refēcī, refectus

reply, respondeō, –ēre, respondī, respōnsus

report (*noun*), nūntius, –tī, *m.;* (*verb*), nūntiō, 1

republic, rēs pūblica, reī pūblicae, *f.*

reputation, fāma, –ae, *f.*

reserve, reservō, 1

resist, resistō, –ere, restitī, — (*w. dat.*)

resources, opēs, –um, *f. pl.*

respond, respondeō, –ēre, respondī, respōnsus

rest (of), reliquus, –a, –um; cēterī, –ae, –a

retire, mē recipiō

return (*verb*), redeō, –īre, rediī, reditūrus; (*noun*), reditus, –ūs, *m.*

revolution, novae rēs, novārum rērum, *f. pl.*

reward, praemium dō, dare, dedī, datus

rich, beātus, –a, –um; dīves, *gen.* dīvitis

right, rēctus, –a, –um

river, flūmen, flūminis, *n.*

road, via, –ae, *f.;* iter, itineris, *n.*

Roman, Rōmānus, –a, –um

Rome, Rōma, –ae, *f.*

rule, regō, –ere, rēxī, rēctus; imperō, 1 (*w. dat.*)

S

sacrifice, sacrificium, –cī, *n.*

safe, tūtus, –a, –um

safety, salūs, –ūtis, *f.*

sail, vēlum, –ī, *n.;* nāvigō, 1

sailor, nauta, –ae, *m.*

sake of (for the), causā *or* grātiā (*w. gen. preceding*)

sally, ēruptiō, –ōnis, *f.*

same, īdem, eadem, idem

save, servō, 1

say, dīcō, –ere, dīxī, dictus; inquit (*w. direct quotations*)

scare, terreō, –ēre, terruī, territus

school, lūdus, –ī, *m.*

Scipio, Scīpiō, –ōnis, *m.*

scout, explōrātor, –ōris, *m.*

sea, mare, maris, *n.*

seal, signum, –ī, *n.*

seats, subsellia, –ōrum, *n. pl.*

section, pars, partis, *f.*

see, videō, –ēre, vīdī, vīsus; **see to it,** prōvideō, –ēre, –vīdī, –vīsus

seek, petō, –ere, petīvī, petītus

seem, seem best, videor, vidērī, vīsus

seize, capiō, –ere, cēpī, captus; occupō, 1; comprehendō, –ere, –hendī, –hēnsus

select, legō, –ere, lēgī, lēctus; dēligō, 1

senate, senātus, –ūs, *m.*

senator, senātor, –ōris, *m.*

send, mittō, –ere, mīsī, missus; **send out,** dīmittō, –ere, –mīsī, –missus; **send ahead,** praemittō, –ere, –mīsī, –missus; **send for,** arcessō, –ere, –īvī, –ītus

set out, proficīscor, proficīscī, profectus; **set on fire,** incendō, –ere, incendī, incensus

severe, acerbus, –a, –um

she, ea; haec; illa; *often not expressed*

shield, scūtum, –ī, *n.*

ship, nāvis, –is, *f.*

short, brevis, –e

show (*noun*), mūnus, –eris, *n.; (verb),* ostendō, –ere, ostendī, ostentus; dēmōnstrō, 1; monstro, 1

sign, signal, signum, –ī, *n.*

sight, cōnspectus, –ūs, *m.*

since, quod, cum, quoniam; *use abl. abs.*

sing, cantō, 1

singing teacher, cantandī magister, –trī, *m.*

single one (not a), neque quisquam

sister, soror, –ōris, *f.*

sit, sedeō, –ēre, sēdī, sessūrus

six, sex; **sixty,** sexāgintā

size, magnitūdō, –dinis, *f.*

slave, servus, –ī, *m.*

slavery, servitūs, servitūtis, *f.*

small, parvus, –a, –um

snow, nix, nivis, *f.*

so, ita, tam; **so great, so much** *or* **so large,** tantus, –a, –um; (*adv.*), tantopere; **so that,** ut; **so as not to, so that not,** nē

soldier, mīles, mīlitis, *m.*

some, nōn nūllī, –ae, –a; quīdam, quaedam, quiddam; **some . . . others,** aliī... aliī; **some (one),** aliquis

son, fīlius, –lī, *m.*

soon as possible (as), quam prīmum

speak, dīcō, –ere, dīxī, dictus; loquor, loquī, locūtus; verba faciō

speaker, ōrātor, –ōris, *m.*

spear, pīlum, –ī, *n.*

spectacle, spectāculum, –ī, *n.*

speech, ōrātiō, –ōnis, *f.*

spend, cōnsūmō, –ere, –sūmpsī, –sūmptus; (*of time*), agō, –ere, ēgī, āctus; **spend the winter,** hiemō, 1

stand, stō, stāre, stetī, stātūrus

start, proficīscor, proficīscī, profectus

state, rēs pūblica, reī pūblicae, *f.; (noun),* cīvitās, –tātis, *f.; (verb),* dīcō, –ere, dīxī, dictus

station, collocō, 1

statue, statua, –ae, *f.*

stay, maneō, –ēre, mānsī, mānsūrus

sternness, sevēritās, –tātis, *f.*

stop, subsistō, –ere, substitī, —; cōnsistō, –ere, –stitī, –stitūrus

storm, tempestās, –tātis, *f.*

story, fābula, –ae, *f.*

strange, novus, –a, –um

strive, contendō, –ere, –tendī, –tentūrus

struggle, labōrō, 1

stupid, stultus, –a, um

succeed, succēdō, –ere, –cessī, –cessus

such, tālis, –e; tantus, –a, –um

suffer, patior, patī, passus

suffice, sufficiō, –ere, fēcī, –fectus

summer, aestās, –tātis, *f.*

summon, vocō, 1; convocō, 1

supplies, commeātus, –ūs, *m.*

surpass, superō, 1

surrender, mē dēdō, dēdere, dēdidī; trādō, –ere, –didī, –ditus

surround, circumsistō, –ere, –stetī, —

survive, supersum, –esse, –fuī, –futūrus

suspect, suspicor, 1

swear, iūrō, 1

swiftly, celeriter

swim, natō, 1

T

tablet (of the law), tabula, –ae, *f.*

take away, adimō, –ere, adēmī, adēmptus

talk, loquor, loquī, locūtus

tall, altus, –a, –um

task, opus, operis, *n.*

teach, doceō, –ēre, docuī, doctus

teacher, magister, –trī, *m.*

tell, dīcō, –ere, dīxī, dictus

temple, templum, –ī, *n.*

tempt, temptō, 1

tenant, colōnus, –ī, *m.*

terrible, terribilis, –e

terrify, terreō, –ēre, terruī, territus

territory, fīnēs, –ium, *m. pl.*

terror, terror, –ōris, *m.*

than, quam

thank, grātiās agō, agere, ēgī, āctus

that (*dem. pron.*), ille, illa, illud; is, ea, id; (*conj.*), quod, ut; **so that,** ut; **that not,** nē;

that, in order that, so that (*conj.*), ut(ī); **that . . . not** (*purpose*), nē; (*result*), ut... nōn

their (*poss.*), eōrum, eārum, eōrum; (*reflex.*), suus, –a, –um

themselves (*reflex.*), suī; (*intens.*), ipsī, –ae, –a

then, tum

they, eī, eae, ea; illī, illae, illa; *often not expressed*

thing, rēs, reī, *f.; often not expressed*

think, putō, 1; existimō, 1; arbitror, 1

third, tertius, –a, –um

this, hic, haec, hoc; is, ea, id

thousand, mīlle; *pl.* mīlia

threaten, minitor, 1

throw, iaciō, –ere, iēcī, iactus; coniciō, –ere, –iēcī, –iectus; **throw down,** dēiciō, –ere, dēiēcī, deiectus; proiciō, –ere, –iēcī, –iectus

thus, ita

time, tempus, temporis, *n.*

to, ad, in, *w. acc.; (purpose),* ut

toga, toga, –ae, *f.*

too, quoque; *use comparative*

too much, nimius, –a, –um

top (of), summus, –a, –um

torture, cruciātus, –ūs, *m.*

toward, ad, *w. acc.*

tower, turris, –is, *f.*

town, oppidum, –ī, *n.*

train, instituō, –ere, instituī, institūtus

Trajan, Traiānus, –ī, *m.*

travel, iter faciō

traveler, viātor, –ōris, *m.*

tribe, gēns, gentis, *f.*

troops, cōpiae, –ārum, *f. pl.*

trouble, labor, –ōris, *m.*

trust, crēdō, –ere, crēdidī, crēditus

truth, vērum, –ī, *n.*

try, cōnor, 1

tunic, tunica, –ae, *f.*

twenty, vīgintī

two, duo, duae, duo

U

under, sub, *w. abl.;* **under the direction of,** dux *or* prīnceps *in abl. abs.*

understand, intellegō, –ere, –lēxī, –lēctus

unfriendly, inimīcus, –a, –um

unharmed, incolumis, –e

unless, nisi

unlike, dissimilis, –e

until, dum

unwilling (be), nōlō, nōlle, nōluī, —

unworthy, indignus, –a, –um

urge, hortor, 1; impellō, –ere, impulī, impulsus

use, ūtor, ūtī, ūsus (*w. abl.*)

V

various, varius, –a, –um

verse, versus, –ūs, *m.*

very, *use superlative;* **very many,** plūrimī, –ae, –a

victory, victōria, –ae, *f.*

villa, vīlla, –ae, *f.*

village, vīcus, –ī, *m.*

Vergil, Vergilius, –lī, *m.*

W

wage war, bellum gerō, –ere, gessī, gestus

wait, exspectō, 1

walk, ambulō, 1

want, volō, velle, voluī, —

war, bellum, –ī, *n.*

warn, moneō, –ēre, monuī, monitus

waste, cōnsūmō, –ere, –sūmpsī, –sūmptus

water, aqua, –ae, *f.*

wave, unda, –ae, *f.*

way, via, –ae, *f.*

we, nōs, nostrī; *often not expressed*

wealth, opēs, opum, *f. pl.*

weapon, tēlum, –ī, *n.;* **weapons,** tēlā, –ōrum, *n. pl.*

wear, gerō, –ere, gessī, gestus

wearied, dēfessus, –a, –um

wedding, nūptiae, –ārum, *f. pl.*

weep, fleō, flēre, flēvī, flētus

well, bene

well (be), valeō –ēre, valuī, valitūrus

what (*pron*), quis, quid; (*adj.*), quī, quae, quod

when, ubi; cum; *expressed by participle or abl. abs.*

where in the world, ubinam gentium

whether, utrum

which (*rel. pron.*), quī, quae, quod; **which (of two),** uter, utra, utrum

while, dum

who (*rel. pron.*), quī, quae, quod; (*interrog. pron.*), quis, quid

whole, tōtus, –a, –um

wholesome, salūbris, –e

why, cūr

wicked, nefārius, –a, –um

wife, uxor, –ōris, *f.*

will, testāmentum, –ī, *n.*

willing (be), volō, velle, voluī, —; **be unwilling,** nōlō, nōlle, nōluī, —

win, capiō, –ere, cēpī, captus; vincō, –ere, vīcī, victus; mereō, –ēre, meruī, meritus

window, fenestra, –ae, *f.*

winter, hiems, hiemis, *f.*

wisely, sapienter

wish, (*noun*), voluntās, –tātis, *f.,* cupiō, –ere, –īvī, –ītus; (*verb*), volō, velle, voluī, —; **wish not,** nōlō, nōlle, nōluī, —

with, cum, *w. abl.; sometimes abl. alone*

withdraw, concēdō, –ere, –cessī, –cessūrus; discēdō, –ere, –cessī, –cessūrus

without, sine, *w. abl.*

woe, dolor, –ōris, *m.*

woman, mulier, –eris, *f.;* fēmina, –ae, *f.*

wonder, mīror, 1

word, verbum, –ī, *n.*

work (*noun*), labor, –ōris, *m.;* opus, operis, *n.;* (*verb*), labōrō, 1; **worship,** colō, –ere, coluī, cultus

world, mundus, –ī, *m.;* **where in the world,** ubinam gentium

worthwhile, operae pretium

worthy, dignus, –a, –um

write, scrībō, –ere, scrīpsī, scrīptus

writing, scrīptum, –ī, *n.*

Y

year, annus, –ī, *m.*

yield, cēdō, –ere, cessī, cessūrus; concēdō, –ere, –cessī, –cessūrus

you, tū (*sing.*); tuī, vōs (*pl.*); *often not expressed*

young man, adulēscēns, –entis; iuvenis, –is, *m.*

your, tuus, –a, –um; **yourself** (*reflex.*), tuī

youth, adulēscēns, –entis, *m.*

Subject Index

C

Caesar
    Forum of Julius, *153*
    Julius, 38, 39, 54, 64, 65, 69, 92, 119, 122, 130,
        141, 142, 164, 174, 175, 181, 184, 186, 187,
        188, 232, 248, *263*
    of Heisterbach, 236
    Temple of Julius, *71, 81*
Calliopē, *211*
Calpurnia, 5
Calumny of Apelles, The, *247*
Campus Martius, 120, 178
candidātus, 128
Capitoline
    Hill, *iv, 107,* 112, *117,* 119, 124, *135,* 243
    She-Wolf, *177*
    Square, *107, 117*
Caracalla, *99*
Carolingian script, *221*
Carrara marble, *127*
Carthage, 41, 42
Carthaginians, *37*
Castor and Pollus, Temple of, *9*
Catilīna, Lucius Sergius, Units III & IV, 161, 164
Catiline, see **Catilīna**
Cato, 38, 39, 119, 142, 143, 155
    the Elder, 146, 165, 196
Catullus, C. Valerius, 214, 227, 228
cavea, 163
Censor, the, 157
Ceparius, 110
Ceres, 170-171
Cerinthus, 220
Cethegus, 111
Christianity, *29*
Christians, 34, 35
Chrysoloras, Manuel, 240
Church of
    Saints Cosmas and Damian, *29*
    St. Mary, *1*
Cicero, Marcus Tullius, Units III-VIII, 232,
    237, 239
Cilicia, 65
Cimbri, 114, 157

Cinna, 114
Circus Maximus, 112
Cisalpine Gaul, 227
Claudia, *49*
Claudius, Emperor, 2
Cliō, *211*
Cloāca Maxima, *1, 81*
Clodius, 65, 180-181, 182
College of Augurs, 65
Colosseum, *127, 135*
Coluccio Salutati, 240, 241, 242
Column of Phocas, *9*
comitia centūriāta, 93
comitia tribūta, 93
Comitium, 169
Como, Italy, 2
Concord, Temple of, 119
concordia ōrdinum, 128
Conspiracy of Catiline, The, 130
Constance, Germany, 242
Constantine, *23, 89*
    Arch of, *127*
    Basilica of, *23*
consul, 93
Corvinus, 44, 45
Cosmedin, *1*
Crassus, 38, 39, 65
Cratippus, 192
Crete, 258
Cupid, 231, 268
Cūria, *71, 89*
Curius, 74
cursus honōrum, 64, 128
cūriōsa fēlīcitās, 218
Cybele, 186

D

Daedalus, 258
Daphne, 268
Dē amīcitiā, 196
Dē officiīs, 196
Dē Ōrātōre, 237
Dē senectūte, 196
Delos, 260

L

Laelius, 155, 208
Lalage, 218
Lapis Niger, 169
Latona, 259
Laurentum, 19
Lentulus (P. Cornelius Lentulus Sura), 101, 106,
      108-111, 140
Lepidus, 65
   Aemilius, 46, 47
   Emilius, 80, *81*
Lesbia, 214
Licinius, 146
Livy, Titus, 215, 218, 227, 228
Lombards, 235
Lorrain, Claude, *127*
Loschi, Antonio, 243
Lucan, 227, *247*
Lucilius, 224
Lucullus, 146, 147

M

Macaulay, 66
Macrobius, 232
Maelius, 69
Magna
   Graecia, 152
   Mater, 186
Manlius, 76, 95, 98, 137
Mansel, Jean, *263*
Marcus Aurelius, *43, 117*
   Arch of, *127*
Marius, 67, 84, 114, 157
Martial, 227, 230
Maxentius, *23*
   Basilica of, *23*
Maximus, Fabius, *37,* 45
Maximus, Flavius Constantinus, *127*
Melpomenē, *211*
Menaechmī, 212
Menander, 212
Menippus, 48
Mercury, 265
Merida, 228

Messalla, 220
Messina, 172
Metamorphōsēs, 231, 248, 249, *255*
Metellus, 151
Michelangelo, *107, 117*
Midas, King, *247,* 254
Milan, Italy, 2
Minerva, *57*
Minos, King, 258
Minotaur, 258
Mithridates, 64, 114, 116, 146
Mnemosyne, *211*
Monte Cassino, 235
Mouth of Truth, *1*
Mt. Vesuvius, 2
Mulvian bridge, 101
Muses, *211*

N

Naevius, 40
Nero, 224, 226
Nerva, 2
Nicaea, 26
Niccoli, Niccolo, 241
Niobe, 259, 264
Nobilior, Fulvius, *81*
novus homō, 87, 128, 173
nōbilēs, 67, 92
Numa, *57, 169*

O

Octavian, 65, *71*
Odyssey, 146
optimātēs, 128
Oscan, 61
Ourania, *211*
Ovid (Pūblius Ovidius Nāsō), 218, 228, Unit X

P

Padua, Italy, 215, 228
Paeligni, 228
Palatine Hill, *9,* 69, *135, 169,* 181
Pales, 69
palimpsests, *185*
Parthians, *99*

Silanus, 119
Silenus, 254
Social War, 64, 146, 151
sociī, 146
Socrates, *195*
Spartianus, 231
S.P.Q.R., 112
St. Gall, Switzerland, 242
St. Peter's
    Basilica, *23*
    statue, 168
Stoicism, *195*
Sulla, 67, 79, 98, 114, 130, 159, 172
Sulmo, 228, 248
Sulpicia, 220

T

tabernae, 169
Tabulārium, 9, 107, 169
Tacitus, 7, 8, 12, 13
Tarpeian rock, 243
Temple of
    Antoninus and Faustina, *iv, 43*
    Castor and Pollus, *9*
    Concord, 119
    Hercules, 168
    Jerusalem, *15*
    Julius Caesar, *71, 81*
    Jupiter, *iv,* 124
    Jupiter Stator, 67
    Romulus, *29*
    Saturn, *169*
    Vesta, *9, 49, 57, 169*
Terence, 212
Terentia, 64, 65, 189
Terpsichorē, *211*
tetrachs, *145*
Teutons, 114
Thales of Miletus, *195*
Thalia, *211*
Thebes, 259
Thisbe, 250
Tiber River, 146
Tibullus, 218, 200

Tiro, 178, 232
Titus, Arch of, *iv, 9, 15, 99*
Tomb of the Unknown Soldier, *153*
Tomis, 248
Trajan, Emperor, 2, 22, 26, *145*
    Arch of, *127*
Trebatius, 186
Trebonius, 192
Trimalchio, 226
Trio, 192-193
triumvirate
    first, 65
    second, 65
Troy, *57*
Tullia, 65, 189
Tullianum, 119
Tusculum, 243

V

Valerius, 44, 45
Valla, Lorenzo, 244
Varro, 48
vellum, 185
Venus, 231
Vergil, 218, 227, 228
Verona, Italy, 215
Verres, 64, Unit VI
Vesta, Temple of, *9, 49, 57, 169*
Vestal Virgins, *iv, 57,* 106
    House of the, *49*
Via Sacra, iv, 9
Victor Emmanuel II, *153*
Virtues, The, 235
Vulgate, 233

W

War with Jugurtha, The, 130
"Wedding Cake," *153*

Z

Zama, *37*
Zeno, 196
Zeus, *211*
Zosimus, 14

Grammar/Vocabulary Index

gerund, 3, 309
gerundive, 3, 308-309

H

hortatory subjunctive, 40, 141

I

impersonal verbs, 3, 13, 308
inceptive verbs, 80
indefinite
    antecedent, 3
    pronouns, 24
indirect
    commands, 18, 39
    discourse, 88
    questions, 3, 39
    statement, 39
infinitives, 27, 309
irony, 72
irregular adjectives, 16

J

jussive subjunctive, 40

L

locative case, 24, 149, 301

M

metaphor, 78

N

noun clauses of result, 13
numerals, 16, 275, 277

O

origin, ablative of, 45
oxymoron, 82, 114, 116

P

palace, 69
partitive genetive, 11
periodic sentences/style, Cicero's, 90, 91, 94, 102
persōna, 149
personal pronouns, 18
personification, 80

place
    from which, ablative of, 53
    where, ablative of, 24
poetic word order, 248-249
praeteritiō, 69
prepositional phrases, 102
pronouns, 278-280
    demonstrative, 11
    indefinite, 24
    personal, 18
    reflexive, 18
purpose
    clauses, 6, 16
    dative of, 6

Q

questions, indirect, 3, 39, 305

R

reference, dative of, 6
reflexive pronouns, 18
relative
    descriptive clauses, 3
    purpose clauses, 6, 303
respect, ablative of, 8
result, noun clauses of, 13
rhythm, 87

S

scansion, 250
separation, ablative of, 53
simple condition, 24, 48, 307
spondee, 249
statement, indirect, 39, 309-310
subjunctive, 303-307
    after verbs of fearing, 13
    by attraction, 39
    hortatory, 40, 141
    jussive, 40
    with anticipatory clauses, 42
    with indirect discourse, 88
superlatives, 8
syllable length, 249

V

verse, Latin, 249-250

W

whole, genitive of the, 11

word
order, poetic, 248-249
play, 85

Z

zeugma, 114